G000161135

SALISBURY. The southern end of High Street and the gateway to the Close.

ROYAL COMMISSION ON HISTORICAL MONUMENTS
(ENGLAND)

Ancient and Historical Monuments
in the
CITY OF
SALISBURY

Volume One

LONDON · HER MAJESTY'S STATIONERY OFFICE

© Crown copyright 1980
First published 1980

ISBN 0 11 700849 4* (Red Binding)
ISBN 0 11 700850 8* (Grey Binding)

TABLE OF CONTENTS

PAGE

LIST OF ILLUSTRATIONS v
COMMISSIONERS in Office at completion of the
    Survey (1976) xiv
CHAIRMAN'S FOREWORD xv
THE ROYAL WARRANT xvii
REPORT, with a List of Monuments selected by the
    Commissioners as Most Worthy of Preservation . . . xx
PREFACE
    Documentary Sources xxv
    Historical Summary xxviii
    Architecture. 1
INVENTORY
    Old Sarum 1
    Ecclesiastical Monuments 24
    Secular Monuments 46
APPENDIX. Repairs at Old Sarum 1366 173
ABBREVIATIONS and Shortened Titles of Works Consulted . 175
GLOSSARY 177
HERALDIC INDEX. 182
PLATES . . . . between pages 184 & 185
ANALYTICAL INDEX 185

LIST OF ILLUSTRATIONS

PLATE OR
(p) PAGE

GENERAL

Area map, scale 6 ins. to 1 mile, showing position of outlying monuments   End-pocket
Map of the city . . . .   End-pocket
Roads, settlements etc. before 1220 . . . . . .   p.   xxx
Settlements etc. after 1220 . . . . . .   p.   xxxiii
Water channels . . . .   p.   xxxv
Wards and parishes . . . .   p.   xxxix
Classified examples of house-plans . . . . .   p.   lxiv
View of Salisbury from S., 1588   1
     Do.   from N.E., before 1771 . . .   9
Perspective map by John Speed, 1611   1
Map of Salisbury by William Naish, 1716   16
Air view of central part of city   17
Elizabethan Council House, Bishop's Guildhall and adjoining houses
     before 1785   2
Demolition of Bishop's Guildhall, c. 1790   8
Plan of Bishop's Guildhall by J. Buckler   12
Demolition of mediaeval building adjoining Trinity Hospital . .   14
     Do.   do.   do.   in Mitre Chequer . .   15

Street Elevations
Southern part of High Street, looking S.E. . . . .   Frontispiece
Maidenhead Inn and No. 1 Castle Street before 1857 . . .   14
Winchester Street, looking W., c. 1860   15
Minister Street and Silver Street, looking N.W.   100
Queen Street. W. elevation of Cross Keys Chequer . . .   101
High Street, looking N., c. 1860   104
High Street, looking S.E., 1966   102
Crane Street, south side   103

OLD SARUM

General plan, scale 1:2,500, with N.–S. and E.–W. cross-sections .   End-pocket
Comparative plans . . . .   p.   2
General view from N.   24
Air views   26
     (1) Old Sarum Castle.   Dated plan of inner bailey etc.   opp. p.   5
     Do.   E. gate of inner bailey and S.E. sector of
            curtain wall   25
     Do.   Courtyard House from S.E. . . .   27
     Do.   do.   Kitchen . . .   28
     Do.   Great Tower. Plinth   28
     Do.   Outer curtain wall. W. gateway as seen in 1912   27
     (2) Cathedral at Old Sarum.   Dated plan of church and adjacent
            buildings . . . . .   opp. p.   15
     Do.   Plan of Bishop Osmund's church .   p.   17
     Do.   Plan of Bishop Roger's church .   p.   18
     Do.   E. end of Bishop Roger's church.
            Conjectural restoration . .   p.   19
     Do.   Bishop Roger's treasury . .   28
     Do.   Carved stonework . . .   29
     Do.   Tombs of Bishops Osmund and Jocelyn   30

ECCLESIASTICAL MONUMENTS

PLATE OR
(p) PAGE

(3) St. Thomas's Church.	Dated plan	p. 25
Do.	Antecedent plans (conjectural) . .	p. lii
Do.	Exterior from S.E.	32
Do.	do. from N.W. . . .	33
Do.	Interior of nave, looking E. . .	34
Do.	Brasses of John Webbe . . .	48
Do.	Capitals, N. and S. sides of chancel . .	35
Do.	do. N. side of chancel . .	42
Do.	Merchant marks	pp. 26, 27, 30
Do.	Chest	53
Do.	Misericord	46
Do.	Monument (1) of William Wroughton, 1770	50
Do.	do. (6) of John Gough, 1709/10	52
Do.	do. (8) of Sir Alexander Powell, 1748 . .	50
Do.	do. (9) of Christopher Eyre, 1624	49
Do.	do. (10) of Thomas Eyre, 1628	49
Do.	do. (11) of Sir Robert Eyre, 1724	45
Do.	do. (15) of Humphrey Beckham, 1671 . . .	47
Do.	Roof of S. chapel	47
Do.	Royal Arms of Elizabeth I . . .	56
Do.	Table tomb, 15th century . . .	p. lvii
Do.	Textile, embroidered, 15th century .	53
Do.	Wall-paintings. Adoration, Annunciation and Visitation . . .	43
Do.	do. Last Judgement . .	35
(4) St. Martin's Church.	Dated plan	p. 32
Do.	Exterior from N.W. . . .	36
Do.	do. of chancel from S.E. . .	31
Do.	Interior, looking S.E. . . .	39
Do.	do. W. end of S. aisle . . .	36
Do.	Stone brackets in N. aisle . . .	42
Do.	Almsdish, 1662	54
Do.	Cup and cover-paten, 1595 . . .	54
Do.	Flagon, 1669	55
Do.	Font	41
Do.	Lectern, 15th century	53
Do.	Monument (2) of William Ludlow, 1749	51
Do.	do. (3) of Bennet and Thomas Swayne, 1747—8	50
Do.	do. (6) of Mary Thomas, 1781 .	51
Do.	do. (7) of Joseph Willis, 1772 .	51
Do.	do. (11) of James Bartlett, 1768 .	52
Do.	do. (12) of Edward Baker, 1796 .	51
Do.	do. (13) of Thomas Snow, 1776 .	51
Do.	do. (14) of Mary Edgar, 1770 .	51
Do.	Floorslab of Catherine Egerton and Elizabeth Grevile, 1743—5 . . .	50
Do.	Niche in S. aisle	40
Do.	Piscina in chancel	40
Do.	do. in S. chapel . . .	40
Do.	Pulpit now in St. Mark's Church . .	46
Do.	Royal Arms of Elizabeth I . . .	56
Do.	Wall-shaft and cornice in N. aisle . .	44
Do.	Rear-arch corbel	42
(5) St. Edmund's Church.	Dated plan	p. 36
Do.	Exterior from W.	33
Do.	do. from N.W. . . .	33
Do.	Stone corbel	42

			PLATE OR (p) PAGE
ECCLESIASTICAL MONUMENTS (*cont.*)			
(5) St. Edmund's Church	15th-century floorslab in S. aisle	.	48
Do.	Monument (8) of Marshall Hill, 1707		52
Do.	Almsdish, 1743		55
Do.	Paten, 1533		55
Do.	Royal Arms of George III on mace-stand		56
Do.	Inscription over W. door, 1653 . .		20
(6) St. Lawrence's Church.	Dated plan		p. 39
Do.	Exterior from S.W.		38
Do.	Monument (6) of James Townsend, 1679		p. 41
Do.	Pulpit		46
Do.	Stuart Royal Arms		56
Do.	Screen between nave and chancel	.	44
Do.	Wooden corbels and bosses	. .	47
(7) St. Clement's Church.	Font now in St. Paul's Church	. .	41
(8) St. Andrew's Church.	Dated plan		p. 42
Do.	Door		46
(9) St. George's Church.	Dated plan		p. 43
Do.	Exterior from N.E. Drawing by J. Buckler, 1803		11
Do.	Interior, looking E.		37
Do.	N. doorway		38
Do.	Piscina in chancel		40
Do.	do. in S. chapel		40
Do.	Screen in S. Chapel		44
(10) St. Osmund's Church.	Dated plan		p. 45
Do.	Exterior from W.		38
(11) St. John's Chapel.	Dated plan		p. 45
Do.	Head-corbel		42
MAJOR SECULAR BUILDINGS			
(13) The Guildhall. Plan .	. . . . . .		p. 47
Do. N. front	. . . . . .		18
Do. Demolition of former Guildhall, *c.* 1790 .		.	8
Do. Civic insignia etc. .	. . . .		21
(14) St. Edmund's College.	Plan		p. 48
Do.	Plan by S.P. Cockerell, 1788 . .		3
Do.	S. front, 1690		3
Do.	Exterior from S.E.		18
Do.	Staircase		89
Do.	Porch formerly at Salisbury Cathedral. Plan		p. 49
Do.	do. do. Exterior		59
(15) The Poultry Cross.	Plan		p. 50
Do.	From E. Drawing by J. Buckler, 1810	.	2
Do.	From S.E.		57
(16) City Defences. Castle Street Gate. Plan	. . . .		p. 51
Do.	do. Royal Arms . .		20
Do.	Remains of Rampart . . .		17
Do.	Remains of Wynman Gate (?), *c.* 1860 .		15
(17) Ayleswade Bridge	. . . . . .		19
(18) Crane Bridge .	. . . . .		19
(19) Milford Bridge	. . . . . .		19
(22) General Infirmary.	Plans, 1819		p. 53
Do.	S. elevation		23
Do.	N. front, *c.* 1860		15
(24) County Gaol. Plan, *c.* 1854	. . . . .		p. 54
ALMSHOUSES Etc.			
(26) St. Nicholas's Hospital.	Dated plan		p. 55
Do.	From N.W. Drawing by J. Buckler, 1803		11
Do.	Central arcade, from N. . . .		58

ALMSHOUSES Etc. (*cont.*)

PLATE OR
(p) PAGE

(26) St. Nicholas's Hospital Piscina in former N. chapel . . . 40
(27) Trinity Hospital. Ground and first-floor plans . . . p. 57
    Do.   S. front 22
    Do.   Courtyard, looking N. . . . 22
    Do.   do.   looking S. . . . 22
(29) Culver Street Almshouses. Plan and elevation . . . p. 58
(30) Hayter's Almshouses. Plan . . . . . p. 58
(31) Thomas Brown's Almshouses. Plan . . . . p. 58
(33) Frowd's Almshouses. Plan . . . . . p. 59
    Do.   N. doorway 23
    Do.   From S.W. 23

OTHER SECULAR BUILDINGS

Market Place
General plan of Market Place and adjacent streets . . . p. 60
(36) No. 29 Cheesemarket. First-floor plan . . . p. 60
    Do.   Staircase . . . 87
(42–3) Nos. 16 and 17 Oatmeal Row. Second-floor plan . . p. 62

Minster Street
(55–6) Nos. 3 and 5, and Haunch of Vension Inn. Plans . . p. 63
    Do.   do.   E. front . . 100
(55) Nos. 3 and 5. Chimneypiece 90
    Do.   Merchant mark . . . . p. 64

Silver Street
(57) Corner House. Exterior from S.E. 100
(63) No. 50. 15th-century window . . . . p. 65
    Do.   From S.W. Drawing by W.H. Charlton, 1813 . . 10

Butcher and Fish Rows
(71) Wheatsheaf Inn. First-floor plan . . . . p. 65
    Do.   N. front 64
    Do.   Chimneypiece 90

High Street
General plan . . . . p. 66
(77) Nos. 32–4. Pynnok's Inn. Former boundaries . . . p. 67
    No. 32. Staircase 88
    No. 34. First-floor plan and detail of staircase . . . p. 67
(81) No. 50. Reset head-corbel 84
(82) Nos. 52–4. Perspective drawing of timber framework . . p. 69
    Do.   Exterior from N.E. . . . 60
(83–4) Nos. 56–8. Plan, 1849 . . . . p. 70
    (84) No. 58. Ornamental framework in E. front. Elevation and section p. 70
(87) No. 47. Plans of ground and first floors . . . p. 71
    Do. Hall, looking E. 97
    Do. First-floor drawing room 96
(92) No. 35. Window . . . . . . p. 72

Crane Street
General plan . . . . p. 66
(94) Nos. 82–4. Second-floor plan . . . . . p. 72
    Do.   Timber framework of roof . . . p. 73
(95) No. 86. Painted frieze 43
(97) Church House. Dated plan . . . . p. 74
    Do.   Plan, 1742 12
    Do.   N. front. Drawing by W. Twopeny, 1833 . 9
    Do.   Courtyard, looking W. Drawing by J. Buckler, 1805 11
    Do.   Gateway, from N. . . . 59
    Do.   Oriel window and stair tower . . 59

			PLATE OR (p) PAGE

Crane Street (cont.)

(97) Church House	Stone corbels in hall	85
Do.	Hall roof	83
Do.	Chimneypieces	90—91
Do.	Merchant mark	p. 76
(99) Audley House. N. front		74
(100) No. 95. Plan		p. 76
Do. N. front		103
(101) No. 93 N. front		73
Do. Vestibule and staircase		96
Do. Chimneypiece		92
(101—2) Nos. 91—3 Dated plan and cross-section		p. 77
(102) No. 91. N. front		71
Do. 14th-century doorway		91

New Street

General plan	p. 95
(106—7) No. 47 and New Inn. Dated plan and cross-sections . .	p. 79
(107) New Inn. N. front	62
(111) No. 31. Chimneypieces	94

Mitre Chequer

General plan	p. 95
Demolition of mediaeval building	15

Cross Keys Chequer

General plan	p. 81
(128) No. 8 Queen Street. First-floor plan	p. 82
Do. W. front	63
Do. Chimneypiece	92
(129) No. 9 Queen Street. Plan, cross-sections etc.	p. 83
Do. Interior of hall, looking N.E. . . .	82
(131) No. 14 Queen Street. First-floor plan	p. 85
(132) Plume of Feathers Inn. Nos. 15—18 Queen Street. First-floor plan	p. 85
Do. do. Plans, sections and elevations opp. p. 87	
Do. do. Part reconstruction	86
Do. do. 17th-century staircase . .	86
Do. do. Door-head .	p. 87
Do. do. Roof-truss .	p. 87
(133) No. 20 Queen Street. Plan	p. 88
Do. W. front	101
Do. Staircase	88
Do. Carving on chimneypiece . . .	95
(139) Cathedral Hotel. Staircase	89

Black Horse Chequer

General plan	p. 89
(140) Nos. 21 Milford Street and 13 Brown Street. 19th-century plan	p. 90
Do. do. Detail of roof truss	p. 90
(151) Catherine Wheel Inn. Framework of hall roof. . .	p. 91
Site plan	p. 92
(153) Milford Arms Inn. Timber framework	p. 92

Swayne's Chequer

General plan	p. 93
(155) No. 41 Milford Street. S. front, 1969	66
Do. First-floor plan	p. 93
(156) No. 62—4 Winchester Street. First-floor plan . . .	p. 93
(165) Tailors' Guild Hall. First-floor plan	p. 94
Do. Exterior from N.W.	67

                                                                    PLATE OR
                                                                    (p) PAGE

Chequer on E. of Guilder Lane
  General plan .   .   .   .   p. 94

New Street Chequer
  General plan .   .   .   .   p. 95
  (173) George Inn.   Ground, first and second-floor plans . .   p. 96
    Do.   Cross-sections .   .   .   .   .   pp. 98, 99
    Do.   Plan by F.R. Fisher, *c.* 1850 .   .   .   13
    Do.   W. front. Drawing by J. Buckler, 1805 .   .   4
    Do.   do.   do.   W. Twopeny, 1833 .   .   5
    Do.   do.   Photograph, *c* 1860 .   .   .   104
    Do.   do.   do.   before 1967   .   .   .   61
    Do.   Courtyard, looking W. Drawing by W.H. Charlton, 1813 6
    Do.   do.   do. E.   do.   W. Twopeny, 1833   7
    Do.   do.   do. N.W. Painting by E.A. Goodall and
                         J.B. Surgey, *c.* 1850 .   .   4
    Do.   do.   do. E. Drawing by Sir H. Dryden, 1859   6
    Do.   Carved oak post flanking gateway .   .   .   84
    Do.   do.   do.   Drawing (Parker)   4
    Do.   Crown-post rafter roof   83
    Do.   Carved hammer-beams   84
    Do.   Plaster casing of beam   93
    Do.   Staircase, before 1967   87
  (174) Nos. 11–13 High Street. First-floor plan .   .   .   p. 99
    Do.   W. front   102
    Do.   Chimneypiece   92
  (177) Nos. 47–9 New Canal. Site plan .   .   .   .   p. 100
    Do.   Ground plan and cross-sections .   .   p. 101
    Do.   Windows .   .   .   .   p. 102
    Do.   N. front.   Drawing by W. Twopeny, 1833   7
    Do.   do.   As seen in 1961 .   .   60
  (180) No. 35 New Canal. Ground-floor plan .   .   .   p. 102
  (181) No. 33   do.   Staircase   89
  (185) Hall of John Hall. Dated plan .   .   .   .   p. 103
    Do.   E. front   59
    Do.   Roof   83
    Do.   Chimneypiece   90
    Do.   Merchant mark .   .   .   .   p. 104
  (199) No. 4 New Street. Ground and first-floor plans .   .   p. 106
    Do.   S. front   76
    Do.   Chimneypieces   94

Antelope Chequer
  General plan .   .   .   .   p. 107
  (203) Bell and Crown Inn. First-floor plan .   .   .   .   p. 107
  (219) Red Lion Hotel (formerly White Bear). N. front .   .   80
    Do.   do.   Ground and first-floor plans,
              cross-sections and detail of jetty .   .   p. 110

Trinity Chequer
  General plan .   .   .   .   p. 111
  Demolition of mediaeval building   14
  (230) Nos. 37–9 Brown Street. Dated plan .   .   .   p. 112
      Do.   W. front   73
  (234) No. 34 Milford Street. 17th-century plasterwork .   .   93

Rolfe's Chequer
  General plan .   .   .   .   p. 114

Barnard's Cross Chequer
  General plan .   .   .   .   p. 114
  (247) No. 53 Payne's Hill. Plan .   .   .   .   .   p. 115
      Do.   S. front   74

		PLATE OR (p) PAGE

Barnard's Cross Chequer (cont.)

(250) No. 88 Milford Street.	Ground and first-floor plans	p.115
Do.	Cross-section	p.116
Do.	N. front	65

White Hart Chequer

General plan		p.116
(252) King's Arms Hotel.	Plan	p.117
Do.	W. front	66
Do.	Chimneypiece	92
Do.	Merchant marks	p.117
(254) White Hart Hotel.	W. front	81
(258) 'The Barracks'.	Site plan, 1854	p.118
Do.	E. front. Drawing by W. Twopeny, 1833	9

Marsh Chequer

General plan		p.119
(266) No. 89 Brown Street.	W. front	79
Do.	Niche head	95

Pound Chequer and Chequer on E. of Dolphin Street

General plan		p.120
(273) Barnard's Cross House.	Dated plan	p.121
Do.	N. front	72
Do.	Staircase	89

St. Martin's Church Street

| General plan | | p.120 |

St. Ann's Street

General plan (see also Marsh and White Hart Chequers)		p.120
(286) Moorland House. Dated plan		p.122
Do. Staircase		88
(287) No. 82. Dated plan		p.122
Do. N. front		75
(289) No. 68. N. front		78
Do. Doorway		98
(290–1) Nos. 60–66. N. front		62
(293) Joiners' Hall. First-floor plan		p.123
Do. N. front		67
Do. do. Drawing by W. Twopeny, 1833		10
(297) Vale House. N. front		76
Do. Doorway		98
(299) No. 40. Rotunda, now in Salisbury Museum. Plasterwork		95
(300) Nos. 36–8. Plan		p.125
Do. N. front		78
(302) Windover House. Dated plan. Details of roof		p.125
Do. Plaster casing of beam		93
Do. Staircase		87
(304) Houses in Friary Lane. Dated plan		p.127
Do. E. front		70
(305) No. 18 St. Ann's Street. Plans		p.128
Do. Exterior from N.E.		60
(307) 'St. Ann's Manor'. Plan		p.128
Do. Staircase		87
Do. Drawing-room window		96

Exeter Street and St. Nicholas' Road

| (323) No. 114 Exeter Street. Plan | | p.130 |
| (327) De Vaux House. Dated plan | | p.130 |

Blue Boar Chequer

| General plan | | p.132 |
| (338) No. 47 Blue Boar Row. Photograph, *c.* 1840 | | 14 |

PLATE OR
(p) PAGE

Blue Boar Chequer (cont.)

(342) No. 13 Endless Street. Doorway 99
(344) Former Blue Boar Inn. Dated plans and cross-sections . . p.134

Three Swans Chequer
General plan p.134
(350) Old George Inn. Exterior, from S.E. 79
Do. Staircase 87

Three Cups Chequer
General plan p.135
(351) Balle's Place. Plan, 1851−5 . . . . . . p.136
Do. Hall roof before demolition 83
Do. do. cross-section p.137
Do. Nos. 25−9 Winchester Street. Roofs . . p.137
(354) Nos. 10−12 Rolleston Street. Dated plan . . . p.138
Do. do. W. front, 1963 . . . 15
(355) No. 14 Rolleston Street. Dated plan . . . p.138
Do. Pilaster capital 95
(359) No. 47 Winchester Street. Plan p.139
Do. Exterior, from S.E. . . . 70

Griffin Chequer
General plan p.140
(368) No. 24 St. Edmund's Church Street. Plan . . . p.141
Do. W. front . . . 72
(376) Nos. 53−5 Winchester Street. Cruck roof truss . . p.141

White Horse Chequer
General plan p.142
(381) No. 26 Castle Street. Plan p.142
Do. Doorway 99
(383) Toone's Court. Plan with detail of framework p.143
Do. Exterior from S. 65

Gore's Chequer
General plan p.144
(391) Loder House. Dated plan p.144
Do. Chimneypiece in dining-room . . . 94
Do. Wall mirror in first-floor room . . . 95
(397) No. 24 Bedwin Street. Doorway 99
(399) Pheasant Inn (Shoemaker's Hall). First-floor plan . . . p.145
Do. Exterior, from S.E. 64

Parsons Chequer
General plan p.146

Vanner's Chequer
General plan p.147

Castle Street
General plan (see also Blue Boar and White Horse Chequers) . . p.149
(419) No. 1. Dated first-floor plan p.148
Do. E. front 77
Do. do. before 1857 14
(422) Nos. 19−25. E. front 80
(427) Nos. 43−5. Dated plan p.150
Do. E. front 75
Do. do. c. 1850 14
Do. Staircase 88
(438) George and Dragon Inn. Plan p.152
(442) No. 93. Doorway 98
(443) Warehouse. Plan and cross-sections p.152

		PLATE OR (p) PAGE
Castle Street (cont.)		
(446) No. 206. Plan	. . . .	p. lxiv
Do. Doorway	. . . .	99
Endless Street		
General plan	. . . .	p. 154
(462) Bellvue House. Plan	. . . .	p. 154
(467) No. 56. Plan	. . . .	p. 155
(468) No. 54. Plan	. . . .	p. 155
Do. W. front	. . . .	77
Do. Doorway	. . . .	98
Fisherton		
General plan (Tithe Map, 1843)	. . . . . .	p. 156
(476) Former Gaol. Carved gyves	. . . . .	20
(492) Nos. 89—93 Fisherton Street. Cross-section	. . .	p. 158
(497) Fisherton Rectory. Dated plan	. . . . .	p. 159
(506) Crane Lodge. Plan	. . . .	p. 160
Do. Chimneypiece	. . . . .	94
Bemerton		
(521) Manor House. Plan	. . . .	p. 161
(526) Cottage. Plan and cross-section	. . . . .	p. 162
(528) Rectory. Dated plan	. . . . . .	p. 163
Do. N. wing, from N.E.	. . . . .	68
(533) Nos. 81—3 Devizes Road. Plan	. . . .	p. 164
Stratford-sub-Castle		
(549) Parsonage Farm House. Dated plan	. . . .	p. 165
(556) Vicarage. Dated plan	. . . . . .	p. 166
Do. N. front	. . . .	70
(557) Mawarden Court. Dated plan	. . . . .	p. 167
Do. E. and W. fronts	. . . .	69
Do. Drawing room	. . . .	97
(559) Dean's Farm House. Plan	. . . . . .	p. 167
Harnham		
(576) Rose and Crown Hotel. Plan	. . . . .	p. 169
(581) Old Parsonage Farm. Dated first-floor plan	. . .	p. 170
Do. Plaster ceiling	. . . .	93
(588) Harnham Mill. Dated ground and first-floor plans, with cross-sections	. . . .	p. 171
Do. Exterior, from N.E.	. . . .	58
Do. do. Drawing by J. Buckler, 1808		11

The Plates include a number of drawings and photographs reproduced here by permission of the owners or holders. William Smith's view of Salisbury is the property of the British Library. William Twopeny's drawings are in the Print Room of the British Museum. John Buckler's drawings are in Devizes Museum and belong to the Wilts Archaeological and Natural History Society. Other drawings are reproduced by permission of the Trustees of Salisbury Museum. A drawing on Plate 6 belongs to Northampton Public Library. The air view of Salisbury on Plate 17 is reproduced by permission of Wilts County Council and a number of early photographs in the Lovibond Collection are published here by permission of Salisbury District Council.

COMMISSIONERS

The Right Honourable the Lord Adeane, P.C., G.C.B., G.C.V.O. *(Chairman)*

Her Majesty's Lieutenant in the County of Wilts *(ex officio)*

Henry Clifford Darby, Esq., O.B.E.

Courtenay Arthur Ralegh Radford, Esq.

Howard Montagu Colvin Esq., C.B.E.

Arnold Joseph Taylor, Esq., C.B.E.

William Francis Grimes, Esq., C.B.E.

Sheppard Sunderland Frere, Esq., C.B.E.

Richard John Copland Atkinson, Esq.

Sir John Betjeman, Kt., C.B.E.

Harold McCarter Taylor, Esq., C.B.E.

George Zarnecki, Esq., C.B.E.

John Kenneth Sinclair St Joseph, Esq., O.B.E.

Paul Ashbee, Esq.

Arthur Richard Dufty, Esq., C.B.E.

Mark Girouard, Esq.

Secretary

Robert William McDowall, Esq., O.B.E.

FOREWORD

BY THE CHAIRMAN, THE RT. HON. THE LORD ADEANE, P.C., G.C.B., G.C.V.O.

It is fitting the the Royal Commission's survey of Wiltshire should begin with an inventory of the ancient and historical monuments of Salisbury, the cathedral city, often looked upon as the county town although it is not the seat of administration. Our Inventory of Salisbury will be published in two volumes. The first (which now appears) covers the area of the former Municipal Borough, with the exception of the Cathedral Close, and it includes all monuments from the Norman Conquest to the year 1850. Remains of earlier date are included only for Old Sarum. The second volume (in active compilation) deals similarly with the monuments of the Close and will include a description of Salisbury Cathedral.

The present volume has three main divisions. The first deals with the earthworks and architectural remains, ecclesiastical and secular, of Old Sarum, the predecessor of the present city, now deserted. The second deals with all other ecclesiastical monuments in the city, outside the Close. The third division is concerned with secular monuments and deals first with major and public buildings and then with lesser secular buildings. Under the last heading we have attempted to record, in a separate entry, each surviving building that dates from before the year 1850.

Every monument has been inspected internally and externally by at least two of the Commission's investigators and many have been the subject of repeated inspections and prolonged study. Before being printed the drafted text and illustrations have been closely scrutinised by my fellow Commissioners and, where necessary, amended. Within the limits laid down in the Royal Warrant, I am confident that no significant monument has been overlooked.

To help the reader in the identification of monuments in the crowded central part of the city a number of street-maps have been included. With one exception these are based on the large-scale Ordnance Survey of 1880, thus depicting the city at a date not long after our own terminal date, 1850; the street-map of Fisherton is based on the hitherto unpublished Tithe Map of 1843. Monuments in the outlying parts of the city have been overprinted on the general map of the city, scale 1:10,560, which will be found in the end-pocket. With few exceptions the plans of buildings printed in the Inventory are presented at a uniform scale of 1 inch to 24 feet, and many are shaded to indicate the periods of construction of the several parts.

The history of a number of monuments is illuminated by old drawings, engravings, maps and photographs, and many of these are reproduced. We gratefully acknowledge the courtesy and co-operation of appropriate authorities in the British Museum, Wiltshire and Salisbury Diocesan Record Offices, Salisbury Museum, Devizes Museum, Salisbury Library and Salisbury District Muniment Room, who have kindly allowed access to this material, and permit its publication. Other photographs in the volume are the work of the Commission's own staff.

Our thanks are due to many public authorities and private persons who have helped in the compilation of the Inventory. Individual acknowledgements will be found in our thirty-fifth Official Report, a copy of which appears on pp. xx-xxiii. .

This volume of the Inventory was checked in 1975 and changes that have taken place since that date have been largely ignored. In a work of this nature mistakes can hardly be avoided and the Commission will welcome suggestions for the correction of any errors that come to light. New information will be added to the Commission's archives; these remain accessible to accredited persons who wish to consult them, by arrangement with the Secretary.

ADEANE

THE ROYAL WARRANT

WHITEHALL,
2nd OCTOBER, 1963

The QUEEN has been pleased to issue a Commission under Her Majesty's Royal Sign Manual to the following effect:

ELIZABETH R.

ELIZABETH THE SECOND, by the Grace of God of the United Kingdom of Great Britain and Northern Ireland and of Our other Realms and Territories, QUEEN, Head of the Commonwealth, Defender of the Faith,

To

Our Right Trusty and Entirely-beloved Cousin and Counsellor Robert Arthur James, Marquess of Salisbury, Knight of Our Most Noble Order of the Garter;

Our Trusty and Well-beloved:

Sir Albert Edward Richardson, Knight Commander of the Royal Victorian Order;
Sir John Newenham Summerson, Knight, Commander of Our Most Excellent Order of the British Empire;
Nikolaus Pevsner, Esquire, Commander of Our Most Excellent Order of the British Empire;
Christopher Edward Clive Hussey, Esquire, Commander of Our Most Excellent Order of the British Empire;
Ian Archibald Richmond, Esquire, Officer of Our Most Excellent Order of the British Empire;
Henry Clifford Darby, Esquire, Officer of Our Most Excellent Order of the British Empire;
Donald Benjamin Harden, Esquire, Officer of Our Most Excellent Order of the British Empire;
John Grahame Douglas Clark, Esquire;
Howard Montagu Colvin, Esquire;
Vivian Hunter Galbraith, Esquire;
William Abel Pantin, Esquire;
Stuart Piggott, Esquire;
Courtenay Arthur Ralegh Radford, Esquire;
Arnold Joseph Taylor, Esquire;
Francis Wormald, Esquire,

GREETING!

Whereas We have deemed it expedient that the Commissioners appointed to the Royal Commission on the Ancient and Historical Monuments and Constructions of England shall serve for such periods as We by the hand of Our First Lord of the Treasury may specify and that the said Commissioners shall, if The National Buildings Record is liquidated, assume the control and management of such part of The National Buildings Record's collection as does not solely relate to Our Principality of Wales and to Monmouthshire, and that a new Commission should issue for these purposes:

Now Know Ye that We have revoked and determined, and do by these Presents revoke and determine, all the Warrants whereby Commissioners were appointed on the twenty-ninth day of March one thousand nine hundred and forty six and on any subsequent date:

And We do by these Presents authorize and appoint you, the said Robert Arthur James, Marquess of Salisbury (Chairman), Sir Albert Edward Richardson, Sir John Newenham Summerson, Nikolaus Pevsner, Christopher Edward Clive Hussey, Ian Archibald Richmond, Henry Clifford Darby, Donald Benjamin Harden, John Grahame Douglas Clark, Howard Montagu Colvin, Vivian Hunter Galbraith, William Abel Pantin, Stuart Piggott, Courtenay Arthur Ralegh Radford, Arnold Joseph Taylor and Francis Wormald, to be Our Commissioners for such periods as We may specify in respect of each of you, to make an inventory of the Ancient and Historical Monuments and Constructions connected with or illustrative of the contemporary culture, civilisation and conditions of life of the people in England, excluding Monmouthshire, from the earliest times to the year 1714, and such further Monuments and Constructions subsequent to that year as may seem in your discretion to be worthy of mention therein, and to specify those which seem most worthy of preservation:

And Whereas We have deemed it expedient that Our Lieutenants of Countries in England should be appointed ex-officio Members of the said Commission for the purposes of that part of the Commission's inquiry which relates to ancient and historical monuments and constructions within their respective counties:

Now Know Ye that We do by these Presents authorize and appoint Our Lieutenant for the time being of each and every County in England, other than Our County of Monmouth, to be a Member of the said Commission for the purposes of that part of the Commission's inquiry which relates to ancient and historical monuments and constructions within the area of his jurisdiction as Our Lieutenant of such County:

And for the better enabling you to carry out the purposes of this Our Commission, We do by these Presents authorize you to call in the aid and co-operation of owners of ancient monuments, inviting them to assist you in furthering the objects of the Commission; and to invite the possessors of such papers as you may deem it desirable to inspect to produce them before you:

And We do further authorize and empower you to confer with the Council of The National Buildings Record from time to time as may seem expedient to you in order that your deliberations may be assisted by the reports and records in the possession of the Council: and to make such arrangements for the furtherance of objectives of common interest to yourselves and the Council as may be mutually agreeable:

And We do further authorize and empower you to assume the general control and management (whether as Administering Trustees under a Scheme established under the Charities Act 1960 or otherwise) of that part of the collection of The National Buildings Record which does not solely relate to our Principality of Wales or to Monmouthshire and (subject, in relation to the said part of that collection, to the provisions of any such Scheme as may be established affecting the same) to make such arrangements for the continuance and furtherance of the work of The National Buildings Record as you may deem to be necessary both generally and for the creation of any wider record or collection containing or including architectural, archaeological and historical information concerning important sites and buildings throughout England:

And We do further give and grant unto you, or any three or more of you, full power to call before you such persons as you shall judge likely to afford you any information upon the subject of this Our Commission; and also to call for, have access to and examine all such books, documents, registers and records as may afford you the fullest information on the subject and to inquire of and concerning the premises by all other lawful ways and means whatsoever:

And We do by these Presents authorize and empower you, or any three or more of you, to visit and personally inspect such places as you may deem it expedient so to inspect for the more effectual carrying out of the purposes aforesaid:

And We do by these Presents will and ordain that this Our Commission shall continue in full force and virtue, and that you, Our said Commissioners, or any three or more of you, may from time to time proceed in the execution thereof, and of every matter and thing therein contained, although the same be not continued from time to time by adjournment:

And We do further ordain that you, or any three or more of you, have liberty to report your proceedings under this Our Commission from time to time if you shall judge it expedient so to do:

And Our further Will and Pleasure is that you do, with as little delay as possible, report to Us, under your hands and seals, or under the hands and seals of any three or more of you, your opinion upon the matters herein submitted for your consideration.

Given at Our Court at Saint James's the Twenty-eighth day of September, 1963, in The Twelfth Year of Our Reign.

By Her Majesty's Command,
HENRY BROOKE

ROYAL COMMISSION ON THE ANCIENT AND HISTORICAL
MONUMENTS AND CONSTRUCTIONS OF ENGLAND

REPORT to The Queen's Most Excellent Majesty

MAY IT PLEASE YOUR MAJESTY

We, the undersigned Commissioners, appointed to make an Inventory of the Ancient and Historical Monuments and Constructions connected with or illustrative of the contemporary culture, civilisation and conditions of life of the people of England, excluding Monmouthshire, from the earliest times to the year 1714, and such further Monuments and Constructions subsequent to that year as may seem in our discretion to be worthy of mention therein, and to specify those which seem most worthy of preservation, do humbly submit to Your Majesty the following Report, being the thirty-fifth Report on the work of the Commission since its first appointment.

2. With regret we have to record the retirement from the Commission upon expiry of term of office of Professor Maurice Willmore Barley, Fellow of the Society of Antiquaries.

3. We thank Your Majesty for the appointment to the Commission of Professor Mark Girouard and for the reappointment of Professor Sheppard Sunderland Frere, Fellow of the British Academy, Fellow of the Society of Antiquaries.

4. We have pleasure in reporting the completion of our Survey of the *City of Salisbury* (exclusive of the Cathedral Close) in which we have identified 595 Monuments dating from before 1850. We believe that no relevant Monument known at the time of writing has been omitted from the survey.

5. Following our customary practice we have compiled a detailed and comprehensive Inventory of these Monuments, which we intend shortly to issue as the first volume of a non-Parliamentary publication entitled 'Ancient and Historical Monuments in the City of Salisbury'. (The second and final volume, now in process of compilation, will comprise an Inventory of the Cathedral and other Monuments in the Cathedral Close.)

6. As in our previous publications, the Inventory will be prefaced by topographical and historical notes and by a discussion of the principal stages in the architectural development of the City.

7. Our thanks are due to incumbents and churchwardens and to many custodians, owners and occupiers of secular buildings who have kindly permitted us and members of our staff to enter and investigate the Monuments in their ownership or charge. We acknowledge help freely given by officers of the Wiltshire County and Salisbury District Councils, notably Mr. F.W. Crocker, Controller of Planning Services, Mr. B.M. Little, F.L.A., Divisional Librarian, and Mr. D.M. Frost, A.L.A., Director of the City Library. We are particularly grateful for much valuable assistance from Miss P.Rundle, M.A., Archivist in charge of the City Muniments, Miss P.K. Stewart, M.A., Assistant

Diocesan Archivist, and Mr. P.R. Saunders, B.A., A.M.A., Curator of the Salisbury and South Wiltshire Museum. We acknowledge our indebtedness to the goodwill and learning of the late Hugh de Saumarez Shortt, Curator of the Museum until his death in 1975.

8. We humbly recommend to Your Majesty's notice the following Ancient and Historical Monuments in the City of Salisbury (excluding the Close), as Most Worthy of Preservation:

Earthworks and archaeological remains

(1) OLD SARUM, banks and ditches of an Iron Age hill-fort and remains of a superimposed Norman castle, all now in the guardianship of the Secretary of State for the Environment.

(2) CATHEDRAL AT OLD SARUM and associated remains, comprising foundations of mediaeval building and cemeteries, also in the guardianship of the Secretary of State.

(16) CITY DEFENCES, comprising remains of a 13th-century rampart and ditch which formerly enclosed the E. side of the City of New Sarum.

Ecclesiastical buildings

(3) ST. THOMAS'S CHURCH, of 13th-century origin, but largely rebuilt in the 15th century with a spacious and well-proportioned nave and a highly enriched timber roof; the 15th-century "Doom" painting is noteworthy.

(4) ST. MARTIN'S CHURCH, with a 13th-century chancel, a 14th-century tower and spire, and a 15th-century nave and aisles.

(5) ST. EDMUND'S CHURCH (redundant and closed for worship; leased by Salisbury District Council to St. Edmund's Arts Trust), comprising a large chancel with flanking chapels which was added in the 15th century to a 13th-century cruciform church, since demolished. The tower on the site of the 13th-century crossing is a rare example of Cromwellian Gothic architecture.

(6) ST. LAWRENCE'S CHURCH, of 13th-century origin, but mainly of the 15th century and with an 18th-century W. tower.

(8) ST. ANDREW'S CHURCH, a small 14th-century building associated with the poet George Herbert.

(9) ST. GEORGE'S CHURCH, the early 12th-century church of the adjacent village of Harnham, retaining several original features and a painting of c. 1260.

(10) ST. OSMUND'S CHURCH, designed by A.W.N. Pugin, 1847.

(11) ST. JOHN'S CHAPEL, a well-preserved bridge chapel of 1240, now a house.

Major secular buildings

(14) THE COUNCIL HOUSE, formerly St. Edmund's College, a mansion of late 16th-century origin, altered and refronted c. 1750 and extensively enlarged by S.P. Cockerell in 1790.

(15) POULTRY CROSS, a market shelter of 15th-century origin, extensively restored in 1852.

(17) AYLESWADE BRIDGE, dating from 1240, enlarged in 1774.

(19) MILFORD BRIDGE, including late 14th or early 15th-century material.

(22) GENERAL INFIRMARY, designed by John Wood of Bath, 1767.

(26) ST. NICHOLAS'S HOSPITAL, dating from 1230 and retaining parts of the original fabric, designed to accommodate the sick of both sexes in two parallel wards, each with a chapel.

(27) TRINITY HOSPITAL, of 1702, an almshouse for twelve people, comprising four ranges enclosing a small courtyard.

(33) FROWD'S ALMSHOUSES, erected in 1750.

Other secular buildings

Of mediaeval origin

(40–44) Nos. 15–19 OATMEAL ROW, timber-framed houses dating from the 15–17th century, worthy of restoration.

(63) Nos. 48–52 SILVER STREET, timber-framed houses built in 1471.

(71) WHEATSHEAF INN, comprising a small 14th-century and a larger 15th-century house, the latter well-preserved.

(82) Nos. 52–4 HIGH STREET, a well-preserved row of 14th-century timber-framed houses.

(83–4) Nos. 56–8 HIGH STREET, 15th-century timber-framed houses masked by later features.

(97) CHURCH HOUSE, the largest and best-preserved 15th-century house to remain in Salisbury, with a well-restored open hall, parlour and solar.

(102) No. 91 CRANE STREET, a large house partly of the 14th century and partly of the 16th century, retaining mediaeval roofs and 16th-century plasterwork.

(106) No. 47 NEW STREET, a 14th-century stone-walled house with 16th-century timber-framed additions.

(128) No. 8 QUEEN STREET, a mid 15th-century timber-framed house containing 17th-century carved panelling of good quality.

(129) No. 9 QUEEN STREET, a well-preserved timber-framed house probably built in 1306, the oldest datable house in the city.

(132) Nos. 15–18 QUEEN STREET, formerly the Plume of Feathers Inn, a group of timber-framed buildings dating from the 14th century and including a picturesque 17th-century staircase.

(140) No. 21 MILFORD STREET and adjoining houses incorporating the Bolehall, an important 14th-century merchant's house.

(158) Nos. 2–14 GUILDER LANE, a row of timber-framed 15th-century cottages.

(173) GEORGE INN, the remaining range of a large 14th-century courtyard inn with a picturesque W. facade and much original timber framework. A first-floor room retains a false hammerbeam roof with original carved enrichment.

(174) Nos. 11 and 13 HIGH STREET, two 15th-century houses with interesting interior fittings.

(185) THE HALL OF JOHN HALL, the surviving fragment of a large 15th-century house, with a highly enriched open roof, original heraldic glass and a carved stone chimneypiece.

(203) BELL AND CROWN INN, of the mid 14th century.

(219) RED LION HOTEL, a well-preserved 14th-century timber-framed range containing much original material.

(253) Nos. 3 and 5 ST. JOHN'S STREET, timber-framed 15th-century houses.

(290–1) Nos. 60–66 ST. ANN'S STREET, late 15th and early 16th-century timber-framed houses.

(302) WINDOVER HOUSE, a large house of 14th-century origin with four ranges enclosing a courtyard.

(305) No. 18 ST. ANN'S STREET, a small 14th-century timber-framed house.

(328) No. 8 ST. NICHOLAS ROAD, retaining some part of the 13th-century De Vaux College.

(341) HOUSE, probably of the 14th century, at the S.E. corner of Blue Boar Chequer.

(344) RANGE OF BUILDINGS, once part of the Boar Inn, built in 1444.

(399) PHEASANT INN AND SHOEMAKERS' HALL, timber-framed buildings respectively of the 15th and 17th centuries.

(576) ROSE AND CROWN HOTEL, including a 14th-century range with an original crown-post roof.

(588) HARNHAM MILL, a well-preserved industrial building of c. 1500, with walls of chequered flint and ashlar, containing original windows and doorways of good architectural quality.

Of 16th and 17th-century origin

(36) No. 29 CHEESEMARKET, a fine 17th-century town house with a good carved staircase.

(247) No. 53 PAYNE'S HILL, a small house dating from the last quarter of the 17th century.

(252) KING'S ARMS HOTEL, a timber-framed building, mainly of the 16th and 17th centuries, with interesting features.

(273) BARNARD'S CROSS HOUSE, a substantial late 17th-century house.

(293) JOINERS' HALL, an early 17th-century Guild Hall, a property of the National Trust.

(304) CRADOCK HOUSE, probably of 1619.

(359) No. 47 WINCHESTER STREET, a medium-sized town house of 1673.

(526) HOUSE, in Bemerton, with an interesting cruck roof.

(528) BEMERTON RECTORY, an interesting stone building of 1630.

(549) PARSONAGE FARM HOUSE, a 16th-century country house with interesting original fittings and a pleasing early 19th-century facade.

(557) MAWARDEN COURT, a house of c. 1600 with additions probably of 1673.

(581) OLD PARSONAGE FARM, a 16th-century timber-framed building.

Of 18th and 19th-century origin

(87) No. 47 HIGH STREET, a large house of c. 1700, with interesting fittings.

(99) AUDLEY HOUSE, an early 18th-century town house.

(101) No. 93 CRANE STREET, a handsome town house of *c.* 1700.

(110) No. 33 NEW STREET, a well-preserved 18th-century house.

(133) No. 20 QUEEN STREET, with a fine mid 18th-century staircase.

(199) THE HALL, No. 4 New Street, a substantial mid 18th-century town house with good interior fittings.

(254) WHITE HART HOTEL, a building of *c.* 1820 with a conspicuous portico.

(287) No. 82 ST. ANN'S STREET, an early 18th-century house with late 18th-century extensions.

(289) No. 68 ST. ANN'S STREET, a fine mid 18th-century house incorporating parts of an earlier building.

(299) ROTUNDA, No. 42 St. Ann's Street, now a gallery of Salisbury Museum, comprising a dining room of *c.* 1812 with plasterwork of good quality.

(307) No. 6 ST. ANN'S STREET, a large house of *c.* 1750 incorporating an earlier building.

(419) No. 1 CASTLE STREET, the remaining part of a handsome 18th-century town house with an impressive pilastered facade and good internal fittings.

(427) No. 45 CASTLE STREET, an interesting 18th-century house with fittings of good quality.

Groups of buildings

The facades of certain buildings, not by themselves important enough for inclusion in the list, yet merit preservation because they belong, visually, to groups of buildings generally illustrative of Salisbury in former times. Such groups are: (1) the S. side of Crane Street, from High Street to Crane Bridge; (2) both sides of High Street, from the Crane Street crossing to the Close gateway; (3) both sides of St. Ann's Street.

9. The foregoing lists have a purely scholarly basis. In compiling them we have considered the archaeological and architectural importance of each Monument, its rarity in the national as well as in the local field and the degree of cultural loss that would result from its destruction, always bearing in mind the extent to which the Monument is connected with or is illustrative of the contemporary culture, etc. of the people in England, as required in Your Majesty's Warrant. We have taken no account of attendant circumstances such as cost of maintenance or difficulty of preservation.

10. We desire to commend the work done by our executive staff in the production of the Inventory, in particular by the editor, Mr. G.U.S. Corbett, O.B.E., Ph.D., F.S.A., and by our investigators, Mr. N. Drinkwater, O.B.E., T.D., A.R.I.B.A., F.S.A., Mr. D.J. Bonney, B.A., F.S.A., Mrs. H. Bonney, B.A., Mr. J.A. Reeves, F.S.A., Dr. B.E.A. Jones, M.A., and Mr. N.J. Moore, M.A., M.Phil., by our photographers, Messrs. W.C. Light and R.E.W. Parsons, and by our illustrator, Mr. P.A. Spencer. We are also grateful for help from our investigator, Mr. C.F. Stell, M.A., A.R.I.B.A., F.S.A. The index was compiled by Mrs. H.M. Green.

11. In conclusion we desire to commend our Secretary and General Editor, Mr. R.W. McDowall, O.B.E., M.A., F.S.A., who continues to afford unremitting assistance to us in the discharge of Your Majesty's Commission.

All of which we submit to Your Majesty with our humble duty.

Signed: ADEANE   R.J.C. ATKINSON
         MARGADALE   JOHN BETJEMAN
         H.C. DARBY   H.M. TAYLOR
         C.A. RALEGH RADFORD   G. ZARNECKI
         H.M. COLVIN   J.K.S. ST JOSEPH
         A.J. TAYLOR   PAUL ASHBEE
         W.F. GRIMES   A.R. DUFTY
         S.S. FRERE   MARK GIROUARD

         15th December, 1976   R.W. McDOWALL *(Secretary)*

SALISBURY I

SECTIONAL PREFACE

DOCUMENTARY SOURCES

In compiling the Inventory much use has been made of documentary material, both published and unpublished. Almost all published matter is included in the list of works frequently cited (p. 175), where also early maps are listed. Documents used in connection with particular monuments are identified as far as possible in notes at the end of the relevant entries; however, as new catalogues are now being compiled, these references can only be provisional. Unpublished matter consulted for the Inventory includes mediaeval deeds, wills and account rolls, and many later minute-books, leases, lease-books, surveys, terriers, maps and plans. Most of these are now in the care of the County Archivist, being either in the Record Office at Trowbridge, in the Diocesan Record Office at Salisbury, or among the city archives in the Council House. For the present volume, the last-named has proved the most valuable of the three collections.

The main use of the documents has been in elucidating the history of individual tenements. Inevitably the survival of documents has been as uncertain as that of buildings. At a few sites documentary evidence and architectural evidence are mutually illuminating, but it happens all too often that an interesting building has no documentation while the history of an adjacent site, now vacant or occupied by some modern structure, is illustrated by a long sequence of deeds. It has not been possible to trace the history of any tenement back to a date before the late 13th century. The student of Salisbury history is hampered by lack of early documents, but a lifetime might be spent sorting out evidence which survives from the late 14th century and subsequent periods.

Normally the identification of a tenement is only possible when a considerable number of surviving deeds relates to a known length of street frontage (defined by fixed points, such as two angles of a chequer) or where a notable landmark such as a watercourse or a well-known inn is mentioned; we are able to say little about long frontages such as New Street, the W. side of Castle Street, the N. side of Bedwin Street, or the W. side of Catherine Street. Our method has been to compile the descent of a tenement from owner to owner, making use of evidence from the deeds of neighbouring tenements, of which the owners' names are nearly always mentioned. In general, the research worker is often surprised at the large size of mediaeval tenements and at the persistence of their boundaries over many years and even centuries.

Most of the identifiable tenements belonged at some time to corporate landlords, the continuity of this kind of ownership making such properties easier to identify; the bulk of the records moreover emanate from these corporate bodies. Among the largest mediaeval landowners in Salisbury were the Mayor and Commonalty (the Corporation after 1612), the Dean and Chapter who administered both the Fabric Fund of the Cathedral and the Common Fund of the Canons, the Vicars Choral, the Choristers of the Cathedral, the College of St. Edmund, De Vaux College, Trinity Hospital, St. Nicholas's Hospital, and the trade guilds, especially the Tailors' Guild. From all these bodies some documentation of property has survived, in some cases in great quantity. St. Edmund's College, dissolved at the Reformation, has left few records although it certainly owned important tenements. By contrast a full cartulary survives in the British Library (Add. MS. 28870) for De Vaux College, which owned several tenements in High Street near the Close gate. Lists of 'corporations' appear in seven episcopal quit-rentals from c. 1650 to 1781 and confirm that only minor changes took place in the number and value of their tenements during that period (Sar. D. & C.M., Ch. Commrs. Docs., 13678881–7). The bishop himself owned few tenements, but he collected quit-rent from every householder in the town. The rental for 1455 in Bishop Beauchamp's *Liber Niger* is one of the few surviving documents to provide a general conspectus of the mediaeval town.

By the common mediaeval practice of founding a chantry or *obit* many private owners became benefactors of the corporate landlords, to whom they bequeathed tenements for the endowment of their pious foundations. Their names appear in the obit calendar of the cathedral (Wordsworth, *Statutes*, 3–16), in the bede roll of the merchant Guild of St. George (Benson & Hatcher, 133) and in the bede roll of the Tailors' Guild (Haskins, *Guilds*, 130; *W.A.M.*, xxxix (1916), 375).

Once a tenement had become the property of a corporate landlord (often in the 15th century) its subsequent history was recorded in a great variety of records: leases and lease-books from the 16th century onwards; surveys and terriers from the 17th century onwards; maps and plans of the 18th and 19th centuries. Many plans of individual tenements were made in the 19th century when the property was leased to a new tenant or sold into private ownership. The survey of the city, scale 1:500, made in 1854 by Kingdon & Shearm, engineers, in preparation for the installation of modern sewers, includes a valuable record of the former watercourses.

The documents which have proved most useful in the compilation of the Inventory are listed below.

Salisbury City Archives (Council House muniment room)[1]

1. Records concerning miscellaneous properties:
    Domesday Books. Four MS. volumes containing transcripts of documents, mainly deeds and wills, witnessed in the court of the subdean by the bishop's bailiff, the mayor, other officials and citizens. Vol. i, 1357–68; vol. ii, 1396–1413; vol. iii, 1413–33, together with a register or short list of conveyances from 1317–40 and 1355–1422; vol. iv, 1459–79.
    Deeds, 1270–1830, filed chronologically; also a few wills. Many of these documents refer to tenements which later became city property.
    General Entry Books or *Ledgers.* The minutes of the meetings of the city council from 1387 to 1836 are preserved in eight MS. volumes which supply much general information such as market, watch-and-ward, and building regulations, as well as grants of leases and records of repairing and rebuilding city properties.
    Ward Taxation Lists. A roll of contributors' names with the sums contributed. Formerly dated to the late 15th century, this roll is now firmly assigned on internal evidence to the year 1399 or 1400.[2]

2. Records concerning properties of the Mayor and Commonalty:
    The Chamberlain's Account Rolls, 1444–1527. Eleven rolls.
    Register of Leases (temp. Ed. IV). The register contains several important items, notably a room-by-room list of 'implements and necessaries' belonging to the George Inn in 1474.
    Grammar School Deeds, 1575–1631. Title deeds of the house (423) in Castle Street where the school originated.
    Leases, 1647–1904. Forty-five bundles of leases relating to city properties.
    Surveys and Terriers. A series of volumes containing abstracts of title etc. Vol. 1 contains leases from *c.* 1590 to *c.* 1675; at the end, on unnumbered folios, a complete survey of city lands for 1618 gives dimensions of tenements in poles and feet. Vol. 4 (1672–1716) includes a survey of

---

1. A list of this collection has been published in *Wilts. Rec. Soc.,* Vol. V.

2. The list includes Alicia, widow of John Camel (*d.* 30 Dec. 1398) and Thomas Bowyer (*d.* 1400). The purpose for which the contributions were collected is uncertain; it could have been a donation from Salisbury to Henry IV on his accession (cf. Benson & Hatcher, 123). The lists are valuable for the evidence they contain concerning the trades and relative wealth of the citizens in 1399–1400.

1716 with lists of rooms in each building and dimensions of plots in feet and inches; at the end of the volume are transcripts of deeds of sale of city properties which took place between 1649 and 1657 under the Commonwealth. Vol. 8 (1783–1835) repeats much of the information of vol. 4 in a survey made in 1783. It includes names of 18th and 19th-century lease holders.

Plans of City Properties, c. 1850–70. Two volumes of ground-plans drawn by J.M. and Henry Peniston, County Surveyors. The first volume includes an undated plan of the George Inn by F.R. Fisher (Plate 13), the only known plan of the mediaeval inn. The second volume is largely a fair copy of the first, but it omits Fisher's plan of the George and, unlike the first, it includes an abstract of the Corporation Terrier of 1865; there are also a few additional plans of properties.

3. Records concerning properties of other corporate landlords:

Trinity Hospital. All the records of this ancient foundation are in the Council muniment room, including deeds from 1300, account rolls from the mid 15th century onwards, many late leases and 19th-century terriers. An article by T.H. Baker (*W.A.M.*, xxxvi (1910), 376) contains transcripts of several inventories and other documents.

The Tailors' Guild. This trade guild owned more property in the city than any other and was the only one to retain a sizable corpus of records. Its muniments include deeds from 1307 to 1815, a 'Survey of Lands of the Taylors' made in 1657, and plans (additamenta 29 and 32) of six tenements drawn in 1823 by W. Sleat, architect.

Parish Deeds. Some 19th-century deeds of St. Thomas's parish help to explain various changes made during that period to the churchyard and footpaths around St. Thomas's church.

The Diocesan Record Office

1. Chapter Records (formerly in the Cathedral Muniment Room):

Parliamentary Survey of Church Lands, 1649. From this most useful document it is possible to identify nearly all of the tenements (many described room-by-room and with some dimensions) owned by the four ecclesiastical corporate landlords: the Dean and Chapter or Common Fund of the Canons; the Cathedral Fabric Fund administered by the Clerk of Works; the Vicars Choral; and the Choristers.

Deeds and Wills. Several boxes of mediaeval deeds and wills relating to Salisbury properties and to the tenements of the four corporate landlords (see above) are among the Chapter records. A number of these documents relate to properties of the Harding family, one of whom was Cathedral Clerk of Works in the 15th century. Among the Vicars Choral deeds is a terrier for 1671–2.

Lease Books. The Vicars Choral lease book 1673–1717 includes a copy of the terrier mentioned above. From further study of the Chapter lease books it would be possible to trace the history of some tenements throughout the 18th and 19th centuries, but we have done this only occasionally.

2. Records formerly in the care of the Church Commissioners:

Deeds. These include a few mediaeval deeds and a great number of later leases relating to church properties. They include properties of the bishopric.

Plans. A volume of mid 19th-century plans entitled 'Salisbury Chapter Estates', perhaps by the Penistons, contains useful material. One drawing shows the line of Bridge Street before its widening.

Wiltshire County Record Office

The collection of plans and other papers from the offices of the Peniston family, Surveyors, 1822–64, was of great value in compiling the Inventory. A few mediaeval deeds in W.R.O. have also been consulted.

H.M.B.

HISTORICAL SUMMARY

Salisbury lies at a confluence of rivers: the Nadder from the Vale of Wardour to the W., augmented by the Wylye at Wilton, and the Avon and the Bourne from the chalk uplands of Salisbury Plain to the north. The alluvial plains of the valleys, about 150 ft. above O.D. in the vicinity of the city, are bordered by continuous gravel terraces of varying width from which the Upper Chalk rises, often steeply, to over 300ft. above O.D. in the adjoining spurs and ridges. The pattern of rivers and intervening ridges has led to a concentration of routes, especially upland routes, and river-crossings in the area, while the gravel terraces have provided suitable sites for nearly all the post-Roman settlements and notably for the city of New Salisbury itself.

EARLY DEVELOPMENT

The logical starting point for any consideration of the evolution and development of the various Salisburys is the Iron Age Hill-fort at Old Sarum, the presence of which had so obvious an impact on local history, and the influence of which may be said to have persisted down to the Reform Act of 1832. As a major defensive work the hill-fort presumably functioned as an administrative centre for the surrounding area during the Iron Age, though the limits of the territory under its control and protection remain unknown. After the conquest some element of this administrative role may well have been retained by the Romans. The settlement, which came to be known as *Sorviodunum*, clearly takes the latter part of its name from the hill-fort, [1] but it does not necessarily follow that it lay within the Iron Age defences. The general paucity of Roman finds from the site suggests otherwise, although the raising and levelling of the interior in the Norman period has inhibited exploration of potential Roman levels. The recent discovery of a substantial Roman settlement a short distance to S.W. in the present village of Stratford-sub-Castle raises the possibility that this is *Sorviodunum*. It lies astride the Roman road from Old Sarum to Dorchester at the point where it crossed the R. Avon, and finds indicate that it was inhabited from the conquest down to the 4th century. Other evidence of occupation in the Roman period, in the immediate vicinity of Salisbury, is at present limited; most finds have been made along the ridge extending S.E. from Old Sarum, especially around Paul's Dene.

A number of Roman roads met on the E. side of Old Sarum which, because of its prominent position, served as a sighting point for the Roman surveyors. These roads continued to be used long after the Roman period; even today, in the vicinity of the hill-fort, metalled roads follow the line of the earlier roads to Winchester and Silchester; a third probably corresponds with a road which led northward to *Cunetio*.

The only historical event which may be confidently associated with the Salisbury area in the immediate post-Roman period marks a stage in the growing ascendancy of the Anglo-Saxon settlers over the native Britons. The Anglo-Saxon Chronicle records (*s.a.* 552) 'In this year Cynric fought against the Britons in the place which is called *Searoburh* and put the Britons to flight'. *Searoburh* without doubt refers to the hill-fort at Old Sarum, and a battle there suggests use of its defences, though whether by Briton or Saxon remains unknown. The capacity of the hill-fort to control a major junction of Roman roads immediately outside it may well have been significant in this encounter. Material evidence from the sub-Roman and early Saxon period at Old Sarum is equally sparse, comprising a 5th-century belt-fitting and a 7th-century silver sceatta.

For the Salisbury area generally, however, there is substantial evidence of pagan Saxon occupation, though almost entirely in the form of burials. Most of these occur in cemeteries, and it is cemeteries in particular which indicate the presence of settled communities nearby. The cemeteries at Harnham Hill, St. Edmund's churchyard, Petersfinger[2] and Winterbourne Gunner[3] all lie on the lower slopes of the valleys; along the margins, but usually just above the gravel terraces. Probably all of them were in existence by the early 6th century and some possibly even earlier. Finds[4] from the vicinity of Dairyhouse Bridge suggest the possibility of early Saxon settlement near the con-

1. *Britannia* I, (1970), 79.

2. V.C.H., *Wilts.* i (i), 58, 102–3.

3. *W.A.M.*, 59 (1964), 86–109.

4. *W.A.M.*, 63 (1968), 103–5; 64 (1969), 128.

fluence of the Bourne and the Avon, on or near the site of the former hamlet of Mumworth. Two burials, probably of the late 5th century and perhaps part of a cemetery, were found together in a pipe-trench immediately N.W. of Old Sarum.[1]

The later Saxon period, too, is thinly represented archaeologically at Old Sarum; a circular bronze brooch ascribed to the late 9th century and silver pennies of Athelstan (925–40) and Edgar (959–975) represent the total of finds dating from before the beginning of the 11th century. There is some hint that, by that time, the ravages of the Danes in southern England had made it necessary to refurbish the defences of Old Sarum so that they might serve as a military strongpoint and as protection for those who dwelt in the locality, together with their goods and livestock. The Anglo-Saxon Chronicle (s.a. 1003) records that Swein 'led his army into Wilton, and they ravaged and burnt the borough, and he betook him then to Salisbury and from there went back to the sea . . .'.[2] That Salisbury should have been visited, though the Chronicle is silent about the purpose and the outcome of the visit, raises suspicion that it was more than a few villages on a large rural manor. What is beyond dispute is that immediately after this time a number of moneyers formerly associated with Wilton are to be found coining at Old Sarum, and that a mint continued there until the reign of Henry II. Possession of a mint was one of the normal attributes of a borough, and under Athelstan's laws was one of the necessary qualifications for burghal status. There is a slight suggestion from excavations across the inner rampart on the N.E. side that the defences were remodelled before the Norman Conquest.

A possible date before which any substantial reoccupation of Old Sarum might be regarded as unlikely is A.D. 972. In that year a charter, granting an estate which appears to coincide with the later manor of Little Durnford, refers to a length of the present road between Amesbury and Old Sarum as 'the way which runs from Amesbury to Alderbury'.[3] This old road came as far S. as Old Sarum and then turned S.E. towards the crossing of the R. Bourne at Milford. The description suggests that no place of importance lay along the road between Amesbury and Alderbury.

OLD SALISBURY AND OLD SARUM

By the Norman Conquest the general picture of the Salisbury area appears to have been as follows: Old Sarum was occupied as some kind of borough or fortified settlement which lay, presumably, entirely within the defences and was under royal control. It seems to have been one of the two most important minting-places in the shire and, therefore, probably one of its most advanced trading centres.[4] Stretching on either side of it, to N. and S. along the Avon valley, lay a large estate, nearly nine square miles in extent, in the possession of the Bishop of Ramsbury and Sherborne. Essentially it comprised the later parishes of St. Martin's, Stratford-sub-Castle and Woodford. Of the earlier history of this estate, when it was granted to the Church and whether as an entity or piecemeal, nothing is known. It has been suggested that it was a royal benefaction of a date not later than the early 10th century.[5]

So large an estate must have comprised several settlements or vills, but these did not begin to be recorded by name until the end of the 11th century, by which time many of them must have been in existence for several centuries. In Domesday Book the whole estate, assessed for some 50 hides, is described collectively under Salisbury (Sarisberie)[6] and it is, therefore, impossible to distinguish geographically its component settlements. It is, however, clear from Domesday Book that the essentially riverine pattern of mediaeval and later settlement in the neighbourhood of Salisbury, so characteristic of the chalklands throughout Wessex, was already well developed by the mid 11th century and there is no reason to suppose that this pattern did not continue within the bishop's estate. Its N. part, represented by Woodford, is of no immediate concern. The central part developed into a manor and parish around the settlement of Stratford, a name first mentioned in 1091[7] and one descriptive of a position at or close to the point where the Roman road to the S.W.

1. *W.A.M.*, 65 (1970), 208.
2. *Anglo-Saxon Chronicle*, 86.
3. *W.A.M.*, 64 (1969), 58.
4. V.C.H., *Wilts.* ii, 16–18.
5. *ibid.*. 84.
6. *ibid.* 121–2.
7. *Reg. St. Osmund*, i, 198.

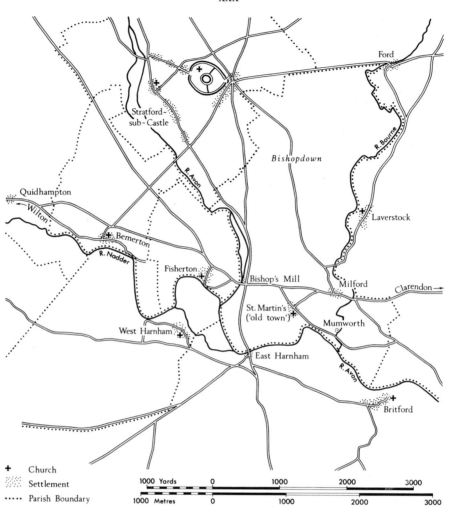

Roads, settlements etc. before 1220.

crossed the R. Avon. The borough at Old Sarum lay within this part of the estate and acquired certain of its lands, probably during the 11th century. The remainder of the bishop's estate lay to the S. and E., between the Avon and the Bourne. Before the foundation of New Salisbury in the early 13th century the whole of this area lay within the parish of St. Martin. It too became a separate manor and from the early 14th century onwards was usually known as the manor of Milford, but it was also known as the manor of Salisbury at least until the late 14th century. The chief settlement of the manor, sometimes referred to as 'the old town', lay close to St. Martin's church, mostly along the way leading to it from the N.W. Further E. lay a second settlement, Milford, on either side of an important crossing-point of the R. Bourne; only that part of it on the W. bank of the river lay within the bishop's estate. A third settlement may well have existed on the W. side of the manor, close to the bishop's mill, beside the R. Avon. These settlements, of which only that at Milford developed a distinctive name, are presumably included among the *veteres Sarisberias* mentioned in a papal bull of 1146, a collective phrase probably intended to describe all the vills on the bishop's estate. Later in the 12th century the term Old Salisbury occurs in the Pipe Rolls; it is used apparently to distinguish the bishop's estate, and perhaps the southern part of it in particular, from the borough of Salisbury at Old Sarum.

The founding of New Salisbury disrupted the existing pattern. St. Martin's church and the old settlement around it were left on the very edge of the new town and soon became a form of extramural suburb; any settlement which might have existed beside the bishop's mill would have been absorbed into the town itself. Milford, on the other hand, lay at a distance from the town sufficient to retain its separate identity.

The history of Old Sarum, by contrast with that of the bishop's estate, was altogether more eventful. The rapid establishment of a royal castle and the seat of a bishop in the years immediately following the Norman Conquest led to substantial changes of both a physical and an administrative nature within the Saxon borough. The castle founded by William I appears to have been in use by 1070 at the latest. It became the sheriff's headquarters and was visited frequently by the early Norman kings. It was here, for example, that the famous meeting of the king's council took place in 1086, at which all the major landholders in England took an oath of allegiance to the king. The castle was built within the hill-fort, on the highest part of the spur, where it dominated the surrounding countryside as do its remains even today. A massive ring motte, set within an impressive ditch, was erected in the centre of the enclosure. The bailey comprised the whole of the E. part of the hill-fort, the defences of which were greatly strengthened. The first castle buildings were almost certainly of wood; the remains of the earliest stone buildings, the Great Tower and the Courtyard House, date respectively from the late 11th and early 12th century.

In 1075 the Council of London decreed that the seats of certain bishops should be transferred from villages to towns; the Anglo-Saxon rural cathedral was an anachronism in Norman eyes. The central churches of the sees of Lichfield and Selsey, for example, were to be moved to Chester and Chichester; and that of the bishop of the combined dioceses of Sherborne and Ramsbury, brought together as recently as 1058, was to be moved to Old Sarum, or rather the Borough of Salisbury as it would have been known at the time. William of Malmesbury, in writing of the event, clearly considered Old Sarum an odd choice for a bishop's seat, declaring it a castle rather than a city.[1]

The transfer to Salisbury took place under Bishop Herman, but the building of the first cathedral church, completed in 1092, was the work of his successor, Bishop Osmund (1078–1099). The new church was sited outside the castle defences but within the N.W. quadrant of the hill-fort, an area which was levelled up to receive it and which appears to have comprised the ecclesiastical precinct, or a substantial part of it. Bishop Roger, nominated in 1102 and consecrated in 1107, planned to rebuild the entire church on a larger and grander scale. He finished the E. end, the transepts and the crossing, but the treasure which he had provided for the completion of the work was siezed after his disgrace in 1139 and the old nave remained standing. Roger also obtained custody of the castle, probably soon after 1130, and is said to have surrounded it with a wall, probably the unfinished stone wall of which foundations remain on the line of the inner rampart of the hill-fort. This effectively enlarged the castle to include the ecclesiastical precinct, an act which was to prove a recurrent source of trouble to the clergy.

Little is known of the civil part of the borough until the 12th century. Coins continued to be minted there until the reign of Henry II and it may be presumed to have possessed a market, although one is not mentioned until 1130. Henry I granted a charter to the burgesses of Salisbury, giving them a guild merchant.[2] There is no evidence that any part of the civil settlement lay within the defences in Norman times; although much of the interior has still to be investigated archaeologically it seems likely that most of the settlement lay outside the defences, on E., S. and W., in the areas of so-called 'suburbs' ((1), p. 12). In support of this is a map of *c.* 1700 which shows the burgages of Old Sarum outside the E. gate and on either side of the Portway, as far as the R. Avon on the south. Bishop Osmund's charter of 1091 provided land for the canons' houses and gardens *ante portam castelli Sarum*.[3]

The borough of Salisbury is likely to have declined in importance as the 12th century advanced.[4] Despite attempts to sustain it in the 13th century, rapid decline set in with the departure of the bishop and clergy, *c.* 1219, and in the face of strong competition from the growing town of New Salisbury. Old Salisbury as it soon came to be known, and eventually Old Sarum, was a military

1. Wm. of Malmesbury, *Gesta Pontificum Anglorum* (Rolls Series lii), 67, 183.
2. Confirmed by Henry II (*Cal. Charter Rolls,* i, 92).
3. *Reg. St. Osmund,* i, 198.
4. V.C.H., *Wilts.* vi, 62.

borough and, unlike its successor in the valley below it, had not been planned and sited with the needs of trade and industry primarily in mind. The Poll Tax returns of 1377 demonstrate the relative positions of the two boroughs: New Salisbury has a recorded (not total) population of 3,226; the comparable figure for Old Sarum is 10.[1]

NEW SALISBURY

Two separate but closely connected aspirations may be presumed to have come together in the removal of the cathedral and clergy from Old Sarum and in the foundation of a new town 1½ miles to the south. The more obvious and pressing was the desire of the clergy to move to a more commodious site from the generally inhospitable environment of Old Sarum, where even water had to be brought at high cost from a distance; and in particular to leave their inconvenient quarters in the castle, where their movements and those of pilgrims were subject to interference by the castellan. Less obstrusive was the wish of the bishop and clergy, presumably supported by many of the citizens of Old Sarum to establish a new town in the fashion of the times, in which the privileges granted to the inhabitants would provide increased incentive to trade and where tolls would make a welcome addition to the revenue. The first of these aspirations may to some extent have provided a pretext for the second.

The idea of removing the cathedral church from Old Sarum to the site by the R. Avon appears to have originated during the episcopate of Herbert Poore (1194—1217) and to have been effected during that of his successor Richard Poore (1217—1228). According to the compiler of St. Osmund's Register, Richard I gave his approval to the scheme. By 1213 precise plans for the layout of the buildings in the Close are evident in the Chapter decrees. Pope Honorius III was petitioned in 1217 and the bull authorizing the transfer was issued in March 1219. Immediately, a churchyard was consecrated and a temporary wooden chapel erected to serve during the construction of the new cathedral, on which work began in 1220. A residence for the bishop, referred to as *ad novum locum*, may have been built by 1219. In the same year a license to hold a market on the new site was obtained from the king, and thereafter was renewed for short periods from time to time; by 1224 it was referred to as the Market of New Salisbury. In 1221 the bishop obtained a grant of an annual fair. Both grants were confirmed in the royal charter of 1227. The latter emphasized the ecclesiastical nature of the foundation and granted the bishop and his successors the right to hold the city as their demesne in perpetuity. It also declared New Salisbury a free city and granted its citizens all the liberties enjoyed by the citizens of Winchester.

In 1225 Bishop Poore granted a charter in which he set out the conditions of tenure within his city. The citizens were to hold their tenements by what amounted to burgage tenure, although it was not so described.[2] The standard plot was to be seven by three perches, or about 115ft. by 50ft. — an ample size, in keeping with the character of the whole scheme — and the standard ground-rent was to be 12d. a year. Tenants who held more or less land than that were to pay more or less rent accordingly, so it is evident that from the very outset the tenements were expected to vary in size. The plan of streets and chequers was in part laid out to accommodate standard plots and a few such plots are still traceable today.

Siting and Layout. As in a number of other new towns of the 12th and 13th centuries, the layout of New Salisbury was on a generous scale, manifest in the ample proportions of its tenements, of its streets and, above all, of its market place. The urban area was unusually extensive; about 260 acres (105 ha) of the bishop's land was set aside for the new city, of which the Cathedral Close occupied approximately 83 acres (34 ha) and the fully-developed urban area a further 120 acres (49 ha). The remainder was low-lying marshy ground known as Bugmore (plan, p. xxxix).

Three factors in particular exerted a strong and obvious influence on the siting and layout of the new town: the presence of existing settlements, routes and river-crossings; the need for an ample water supply; and the need for an ecclesiastical precinct giving both space and privacy. The im-

1. V.C.H., *Wilts.* iv, 306, 311.   2.   Benson & Hatcher, 728.

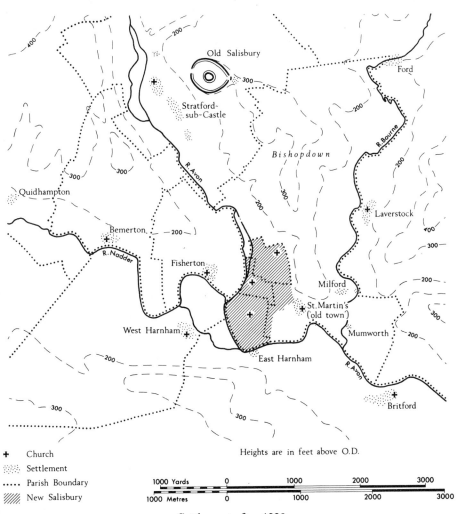

+ Church
::: Settlement
.... Parish Boundary
//// New Salisbury

Heights are in feet above O.D.

1000 Yards 0 1000 2000 3000
1000 Metres 0 1000 2000 3000

Settlement after 1220.

portance attached to the second and third requirements was in large measure a reaction to the conditions experienced at Old Sarum.

The decision to provide the town with a supply of water running in shallow channels down the centres of most of its streets must have been taken at an early stage and was clearly an essential and integral part of the town plan. It was, moreover, probably the most important single consideration in the actual siting of the town. It required a large, nearly flat area close to, but above water-level and for the most part above the level of regular flooding. Within the whole extent of the bishop's manors of Salisbury only one such area, that within the bend of the Avon, E. of its confluence with the Nadder, met that requirement. Here, in addition, the leat or stream supplying the bishop's mill (on the site of the present Town Mill, just N. of Fisherton Bridge) constituted a ready source of water at the correct height above river level to feed the system of street-channels.

The plan of the town (Plate 17) indicates that some attempt was made at a regular layout, but a truly rectangular grid-iron pattern characteristic of many new towns of the period was not possible. To begin with the plan had to take account of certain pre-existing features, in particular routeways. A major road linking Winchester and Wilton descended Milford Hill and proceeded W. to a crossing of the Avon, presumably a ford on or near the site of Upper Fisherton Bridge; the alignment of Milford (formerly Winchester) Street probably follows it closely. A road from N. to S. passed by way of Old Sarum towards a crossing of the Avon near Ayleswade Bridge; Castle Street and High Street mark its approximate line and the continuation of the latter southwards through the Close may have had some influence on the position of the cathedral, the W. front of which abuts it. In the N.E. angle of the intersection of these two routes the large market place of the new town was laid out, and almost at the crossing the first parish church within the town, St. Thomas's, was built.

There were also pre-existing settlements (see p. xxx) within the subdivision of the bishop's manor of Salisbury which coincided with the parish of St. Martin. In addition to Milford, or rather that part of Milford which lay W. of the R. Bourne, there was a settlement in the vicinity of St. Martin's church, and smaller settlements may have existed near the bishop's mill and, less likely, near the river-crossing to East Harnham. The settlement at St. Martin's was probably the most important of these and it appears to have been concentrated along the way or street which leads S.E. towards the church, now known as St. Martin's Church Street. The presence of this street may well have caused St. Ann's Street, which meets its N.W. end, to deviate from an original planned line parallel to New Street, thus giving rise to a peculiar pattern of chequers in this part of the town. It is noticeable that the W. part of St. Ann's Street is parallel to New Street (Ivy Street) and that a continuation of this alignment would have led straight to St. Martin's church.

It was the system of channels, designed to provide water for both household and industrial use, which had the most marked influence on the street plan. Since the channels ran along the centres of the streets it was essential that the latter should be carefully aligned to respect the contours and to ensure a gentle gradient for the water all the way from the mill-stream on the N.W. to the meadows at Bugmore. Water entered the system from the mill-stream by means of two inlets controlled by sluices, one (a) W. of Castle Gate, the other (b) further S., to the W. of Scot's Lane (map, p. xxxv). Water at the level of the mill-stream could be made to flow in surface channels to a point (c) a short distance E. of Endless Street on the N., and as far as the S. side of St. Edmund's churchyard (d) on the N.E. From this crucial latter point the water was taken S. at the foot of the rising ground along the line marked by St. Edmund's Church Street and Gigant Street. That this constituted its absolute eastward limit is indicated by the fact that the alignment of these streets tends to follow the contour rather than a straight line. (It is noticeable that the next street up the slope to E., where no water channel had to be accommodated, is markedly straight.) In all, four streets on the E. side of the town run parallel, or very nearly so, to this most easterly water channel. The interval between them is, understandably, the approximate length of two burgage plots, and they are the most obvious manifestation in the town plan of an attempt at a regular layout. To accommodate the most westerly of these streets it was necessary to impinge on the N.E. corner of the Close. Their divergence from the old line of Castle Street and High Street to the W., however, left an irregular area between and prevented a true grid plan overall. A truly rectangular pattern of streets was achieved only in the most northerly chequers. Further S. the rectangularity is broken by Winchester Street, the direction of which was probably determined by the slope of the ground and the resultant necessary alignment of the water channel along it.

A notable exception to the general pattern of water channels is that which ran S. from point 'c' through Gores chequer, presumably once continued through Three Swans chequer, and reappeared in Cross Keys chequer. It followed no street and was conceivably a later addition to the system. No excavated section of any early water channel in a street has been illustrated or adequately described; the only record is of late date and well after the channels were reconstructed in the 18th century (see p. xlviii).

There were also two much deeper water courses, the Town Ditch (also called New Canal) and the Close Ditch. These took water from the R. Avon below the bishop's mill and therefore flowed at a considerably lower level than the street channels. The Town Ditch was carefully positioned to collect water which passed under the easternmost arch of Upper Fisherton Bridge. This it carried

Watercourses and Ditches. The map on p. xxxv shows water channels and drainage ditches in relation to physical topography and the city streets. Contours based on O.S. spot heights which often represent modern surfaces, cannot be precisely those of the 13th century, but relative heights probably are not much distorted. The watercourses are as on Naish's map (Plate 16), except for a conjectural stretch in Three Swans Chequer which presumably linked the known channels of Gores and Cross Keys Chequers. It is possible that a channel existed in Salt Lane, between Rolleston Street and St. Edmund's Church Street, but the evidence only occurs in Speed's map which contains demonstrable inaccuracies and is of doubtful value. Alteration of the watercourses following the Act of 1737 may explain differences in the two editions of Naish's map. The 1716 version shows no channel in Ivy Street; the 1751 edition shows one, and omits channels in St. John's Street and the W. part of St. Ann's Street.

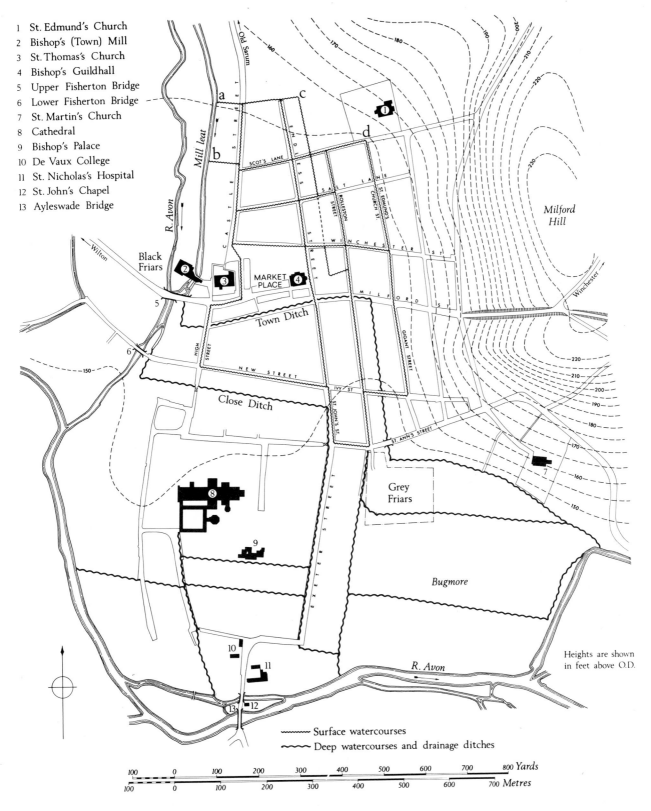

1 St. Edmund's Church
2 Bishop's (Town) Mill
3 St. Thomas's Church
4 Bishop's Guildhall
5 Upper Fisherton Bridge
6 Lower Fisherton Bridge
7 St. Martin's Church
8 Cathedral
9 Bishop's Palace
10 De Vaux College
11 St. Nicholas's Hospital
12 St. John's Chapel
13 Ayleswade Bridge

Milford Hill

Black Friars

MARKET PLACE

Town Ditch

Close Ditch

New Street

Grey Friars

Bugmore

R. Avon

Heights are shown
in feet above O.D.

—— Surface watercourses
⌇⌇ Deep watercourses and drainage ditches

100   0   100   200   300   400   500   600   700   800 Yards
100   0   100   200   300   400   500   600   700 Metres

southwards for a short distance, to maintain the flow, before turning sharply to the east. The Town Ditch defined the S. side of the Market Place, at its fullest extent, and acted as a main drain in that area. Its existence accounts for the notably oblique alignment of the N. side of New Street chequer. Beyond the Market Place, in Milford Street, the Town Ditch turned S. through Trinity chequer and Marsh chequer, where for the whole of its length it served as a property boundary. South of St. Ann's Street it turned E. to flow past the Friary precinct and thence to the Avon once more; it also joined the ditches draining Bugmore. Because of its depth, bridges were necessary to carry the streets over it. It has been suggested[1] that the Town Ditch was built later than the main water system, but this seems most unlikely and the deed of 1345, quoted in support, scarcely constitutes evidence for this (see monument (77)).

The Close, the precinct of the bishop and clergy, was also part of the original town plan and, as such, affected its layout. Bounded on the W. and S. by the R. Avon it occupied much of the low-lying S. part of the site and stood physically separate from the town and largely independent of it. It was bounded by the Close Ditch, a deep wet ditch which took its water from the Avon at Lower Fisherton (Crane) Bridge in a manner similar to that of the Town Ditch further upstream. The Close Ditch provided drainage for the houses of those canons whose tenements backed on to it and it also helped to drain the Close as a whole, much of it wet and subject to flooding. During the first century of its existence it probably also provided the precinct with a measure of defence or protection, until it was supplemented by the building of the close wall in the second quarter of the 14th century.

It is significant that New Street, undoubtedly one of the earliest streets of the new town and first recorded in 1265, was laid out parallel with the N. side of the Close and approximately the length of a burgage plot from it. The name *Novus Vicus* was originally used of the whole street-line, now bearing six names, which extends from Lower Fisherton Bridge on the W. to the town boundary at the top of Payne's Hill on the east. The line of the present Exeter Street and its continuation to Ayleswade Bridge was also conditioned by the presence of the Close.

Mention should be made of Endless Street which, as its name may imply, once continued N. beyond the city boundary, perhaps with the original intention of meeting the main road S. from Old Sarum; Naish's map (Plate 16) shows a length of lane just to the N. of Endless Street and directly in line with it. This line was severed, presumably, by the construction of the city defences in the 14th or early 15th century. It has been suggested that this street line, which continues S. to skirt the Close and so leads to Ayleswade Bridge, was originally intended to be the main thoroughfare through the city, but that it never succeeded in usurping the old route represented by Castle Street.[2] It may be significant that the whole way from Endless Street to Ayleswade Bridge was referred to as *altus vicus* in the early 14th century (but see under).

Street-names etc.[3] Many of the present street-names are of mediaeval origin and some of them were in use within a few decades of the foundation of the city. Over the centuries names have changed, sometimes more than once, and some of the earlier names no longer survive. Such changes appear to have been gradual rather than sudden and they are in consequence not precisely datable. It is not unusual to find two names for a street in use at the same time. The general tendency, however, has been for street-names to become more specific and therefore more numerous. Most early names were originally used of longer lengths of street than they are today; the case of New Street which today bears six separate street-names has already been mentioned. Some examples of different types of name illustrate the various processes at work. (Dates in brackets are those of the earliest known mention of the name.)

In 14th-century deeds the term *altus vicus* appears in combination with certain street-names, and in most instances it refers to streets which served as thoroughfares through the city. It conveyed the sense 'the king's highway' as used of streets in 17th-century deeds rather than any modern connotation of 'high street'. It was used, for example, of the whole way, some seven-eighths of a mile, from

1. V.C.H., *Wilts.* vi, 90.
2. *ibid.* 81.

3. For modern street-names see folding map in end-pocket.

Endless Street to Ayleswade Bridge, and in the early 15th century it was also used of the way from Castle Gate to the Close Gate; but by this period 'le Heystrete' (1420)[1] referred to the modern High Street.

A few streets acquired directional names, notably the original Winchester Street (1316),[2] now Milford Street and New Canal; this was the only street to acquire the name of a distant place in the mediaeval period. Other directional names relate to nearer places; in the 13th century Minster Street (1265)[3] was used of the way leading towards the cathedral, from Castle Gate to the Close Gate in High Street, and in a deed of 1348[4] it was used in the description of a tenement which lay some distance N. of Castle Gate. Castle Street (1339),[5] the way leading towards the castle of Old Sarum, was not commonly used until the 15th century; in a deed of 1342 Castle Street and Minster Street are used of the same frontage.[6] St. Ann's Street (1716),[7] which acquired its present name from St. Ann's Gate at its W. end, was, together with St. Martin's Church Street, originally known as 'the way leading to St. Martin's Church' (1302).[8]

The names of several streets described trades and activities carried on in them. Wynman Street (1316),[9] now Winchester Street, is self-explanatory. Catherine Street, a corruption of *Carterestret*, 'the street of the carters' (1323),[10] originally began in the Market Place and reached some distance S. of St. Ann's Gate. The name Gigant Street (1320)[11] or Gigor Street (1485) is perhaps derived from gigour, a fiddler; it was used of the whole length from Bedwin Street to St. Ann's Street. Culver Street (1328)[12] may suggest the presence of dove-cotes along the E. margin of the town; it extended from the present Winchester Street to St. Ann's Street. Further N. this line, now Greencroft Street, was known as Melemonger Stret (1361),[13] 'the street of meal sellers'. Chipper Lane, formerly Chipper Street or 'the street of the market men' (1323).[14] once continued as far E. as St. Edmund's Church Street.

Streets also acquired personal names: Scot's Lane which once continued E. to St. Edmund's churchyard appears to have been named from John Scot (1269),[15] whose house stood at its W. end. Rolleston Street (1328)[16] is alleged to take its name through Rolveston (1455) from one Rolfe, and its S. extension, Brown Street (*c*.1275),[17] may well be a personal name. Street-corners and the tenements occupying them also acquired personal names in the mediaeval period. *Nuggescorner* (1365)[18] in the angle between Endless Street and Blue Boar Row took its name from Hugh Nugge whose house stood there in 1269.[19] *Florentyn Corner* in the angle between High Street and New Street was occupied by the family of that name in 1297; in 1455 it was known as Old Florentyne Corner (see monument (92)). *Drakehallestret* (1339),[20] or *Dragall Street*, an earlier name for Exeter Street, was apparently named after Drake's Hall, no doubt an important building in the street.

The three bridges giving access to the mediaeval city have all changed their names. Ayleswade Bridge, so called in 1255,[21] was generally known as Harnham Bridge by the later 15th century, but with the building of a modern bridge downstream the older name is returning to use. Fisherton Bridge (1561)[22] and Crane Bridge (1540)[23] were originally known as the upper and lower bridges of Fisherton.

1. *Tropenell Cart.*, i. 225.
2. Sar. D. & C.M., Sarum deeds, 3/13.
3. *Sar. Chart.*, 341.
4. Sar. Corp. MS., deeds, will of Henry Baudrey, 1348.
5. De Vaux Cartulary.
6. Sar. Corp MS., deeds, will of Gilbert le Dubben.
7. Naish map (Plate 16).
8. Sar. D. & C.M., Sarum deeds, 3/8.
9. *ibid.* 1&17.
10. *ibid.*, 2/12.
11. *ibid.*, 1/20.
12. *ibid.*, 4/2.
13. Dom. Bk. i. f 13.
14. Sar. D. & C.M. Sarum deeds, 1/28.
15. Benson & Hatcher, 740.
16. Sar. D. & C.M., Sarum deeds, 4/2.
17. Wordsworth, *St. Nicholas,* 146.
18. Sar. D. & C.M., Sarum deeds, 2/40.
19. Benson & Hatcher, 735.
20. De Vaux Cartulary.
21. *E.P.N.S.* (Wiltshire), 222.
22. Sar. Corp. MS., Ledger A, f 48.
23. Leland, *Itin.*, 261; see Monument (102).

The roughly square blocks into which the mediaeval part of the city is divided by its intersecting streets have been known as 'chequers' since 1603 if not earlier. Most of them, especially those near the centre, were named after their most prominent building, often an inn.[1] The 18th-century names are shown on Naish's map (Plate 16).

Defences. In general the construction of mediaeval town defences, especially walls, was a burdensome, piecemeal and protracted process except in those places, usually the royal boroughs, where the king took a direct interest. Sufficient money was rarely allocated for the purpose and many of the seigneurial boroughs, of which Salisbury was one, received no walls. An additional disincentive was the fact that the slightest barrier was enough to protect a town's rights in its tolls.

For all its great prosperity Salisbury had only earthwork defences. A bank and ditch, the former perhaps surmounted by a palisade, were built along the N. and E. sides of the city; on the remaining sides the R. Avon and the marsh at Bugmore were evidently considered an adequate protection. Work on the defences had probably begun before the end of the 13th century, but it appears to have been pursued only intermittently and despite successive attempts by the mayor and commonalty it seems not to have been completed until shortly after 1440. Bars or barriers, probably constructed mainly of wood, controlled the entrances to the city, which included the three bridges over the R. Avon; only in Wynman (now Winchester) Street and Castle Street were stone gateways built.

From the late 15th century onwards the defences were neglected and allowed to fall into disrepair. By 1716 those on the N. side of the city had been levelled and by the later 19th century only a few fragments were left along the E. side.

Parishes and Wards. Before the end of the 13th century the city had been divided into four wards and three parishes (map, p. xxxix): rapid growth made such administrative divisions desirable. Two aldermen, implying the existence of wards, are mentioned as early as 1249[2] and the four wards appear by name in a list of citizens who signed an agreement with Bishop Simon of Ghent in 1306.[3] The names of the four wards, *Novus Vicus, Forum, Pratum* and *Sanctus Martinus* — New Street, Market, Mead and St. Martin's — sound as if the wards belong to an early phase of the city's development; in particular it is noticeable that St. Thomas's does not appear.

Parish arrangements during the first fifty years are far from clear. St. Martin's, the original parish church of the area, appears to have had no parochial status within the new town, the boundary of which seems to have been drawn deliberately to exclude it. A chapel of St. Thomas had been built by 1238, and the parish of St. Thomas is mentioned in 1246.[4] Already in 1245 Bishop Bingham appears to have given St. Nicholas's Hospital (26), founded by him in 1231, parochial rights over much of the southern and eastern parts of the town.[5] All this changed in 1269 when the collegiate church of St. Edmund was established, presumably to meet the needs of a growing population. So rapidly were the chequers becoming occupied, it seems, that a large enough site to accommodate the new foundation could be provided only in the N.E. corner of the town. St. Edmund's churchyard is as large as a whole chequer, much larger than St. Thomas's. The church was served by a college of priests whose house adjoined the churchyard on the east. St. Edmund's was also to be responsible for the church and parish of St. Martin. The first provost of this grandiose foundation was one of the cathedral canons, Nicholas de St. Quintin, one of the earliest founders of a private chantry in the cathedral, a chantry endowed with property in the town ((86), (91)). The foundation-deed of St. Edmund's[6] sets out in detail the exact boundaries between the three parishes of St. Edmund, St. Thomas and St. Martin, the last now being given parochial status within the city boundary although the church and parish were to be cared for by the new college. At the same time St. Nicholas's reverted to its original function as a hospital, entrusted also with the care and maintenance of Ayleswade Bridge (17) and the chapel of St. John (11), built on the island between the

1. *Arch. J.,* cxx (1963), 238.
2. V.C.H., *Wilts.* vi. 95.
3. Benson & Hatcher, 742.
4. V.C.H., *Wilts.* vi, 147.
5. *ibid.,* iii, 345.
6. Benson & Hatcher, 735.

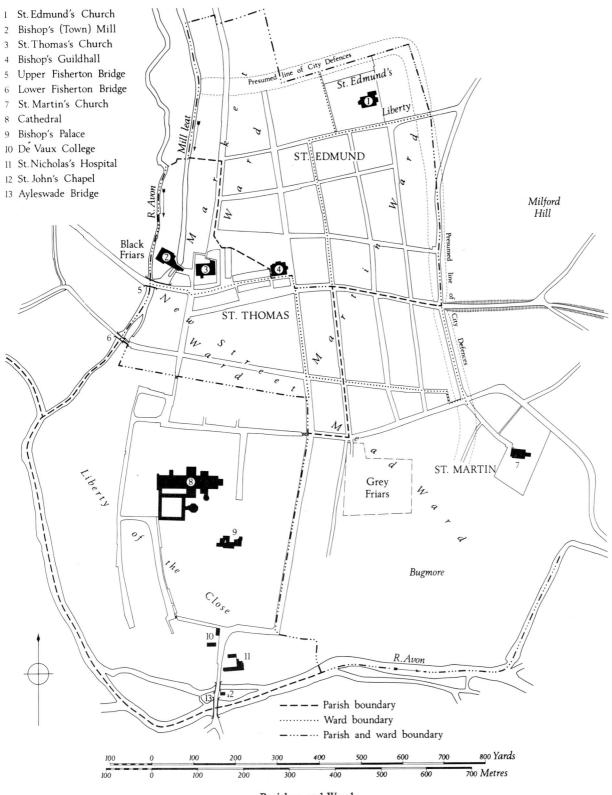

1 St. Edmund's Church
2 Bishop's (Town) Mill
3 St. Thomas's Church
4 Bishop's Guildhall
5 Upper Fisherton Bridge
6 Lower Fisherton Bridge
7 St. Martin's Church
8 Cathedral
9 Bishop's Palace
10 De Vaux College
11 St. Nicholas's Hospital
12 St. John's Chapel
13 Ayleswade Bridge

Presumed line of City Defences

St. Edmund's
Liberty

Milford
Hill

ST. EDMUND

Mill leat

R. Avon

Black
Friars

ST. THOMAS

New Street Ward

St. Edmund's Ward

Martin's Ward

Grey
Friars

ST. MARTIN

Liberty
of
the
Close

Presumed line of City Defences

Bugmore

R. Avon

--- Parish boundary
.... Ward boundary
-·-·-· Parish and ward boundary

| 100 | 0 | 100 | 200 | 300 | 400 | 500 | 600 | 700 | 800 Yards |
| 100 | 0 | 100 | 200 | 300 | 400 | 500 | 600 | 700 Metres |

Parishes and Wards

two arms of the river. Opposite the hospital, in a meadow by the river, lies De Vaux College (327–8), founded in 1261 by Bishop Giles de Bridport. This was an academic institution, designed to cater for the needs of students and scholars associated with the cathedral.[1]

The parish arrangements, the colleges, St. Nicholas's, the bridge, and St. John's chapel, were all episcopal enterprises. However, the growing city attracted two other ecclesiastical foundations, the Friaries, dependent here as elsewhere upon powerful lay patronage. The Franciscans arrived in Salisbury in the very first years of its existence and by 1228 were provided with a house and precinct lying south of St. Ann's Street (see (304)). Royal patronage provided them, both then and later, with timber for building from Clarendon Forest.[2] In 1281 the Dominicans also acquired a site on the edge of the new town, just W. of the R. Avon, near the upper bridge. Their removal from Wilton, where they had arrived in 1245, is a pointer to the relative growth and decline of the rival towns.

D.J.B.

DEVELOPMENT OF THE MEDIAEVAL CITY

Among the provincial towns of England, Salisbury ranked sixth in 1377 and in 1523–7, and as high as third in the 15th century.[3] It is fortunate that, for the early 15th century, both architectural and documentary evidence survives in sufficient quantity to provide a detailed picture of the city at the height of its prosperity, based on the wool trade.

The centre of the town was the Market Place which stretched originally from Blue Boar Row to New Canal and from St. Thomas's Church to Queen Street (Plate 1 and map, p. 60). Around the Guildhall, against the churchyard of St. Thomas's and in much of the area between, were rows of shops and houses, replacing earlier stalls. In contrast to the very large tenements in the surrounding chequers, many of which contained several buildings, courtyards, gardens and even orchards, tenements in the encroachments upon the Market Place consisted only of the few square yards occupied by the actual buildings. Both the 'rows' and the chequer frontages overlooking the market tended to acquire street-names descriptive of the goods sold thereabouts. However, the various trades were by no means rigidly segregated; not all of them were represented among the street-names and many names which were representative have been altered in succeeding centuries.

One market frontage which never had a trade name was the N. side of New Street chequer. Here were some of the largest houses in the town, belonging to wealthy citizens, many of them wool merchants or grocers, for example Henry Russel and John Hall. The tenements were described in the documents as standing 'in Winchestrestret on the Ditch', a description which also applied to houses on both sides of Milford Street as far E. as the point where the Town Ditch turned S. into Trinity chequer. Tenements on the N. side of the Market Place were said to be 'opposite the market where corn is sold', whether they were in Blue Boar Row or Cheesemarket. On the E. side the tenements were 'opposite the market where wool and yarn are sold'; somewhere nearby there stood a stone cross referred to as the 'yarn market' and also the king's weighbeam for weighing sacks of wool.[4] Most of the houses and shops in Guildhall chequer, built up against the Guildhall and round the courtyard there (Plate 12), were occupied by wool merchants, drapers and mercers.[5]

Permanent buildings began to replace the stalls in the rows by about 1300. Some had been built in the *Fysschamels*, later Fish Row, by 1314.[6] The butchers' stalls may have lasted somewhat longer, although a tenement worth 5s. existed in *le Bocherie* by 1328.[7] The name Butcher Row, first used in 1380,[8] applied only to the S. side of the present street; the N. side was *la potrewe* in 1350,[9] *Bothelrewe* or Pot Row in 1385.[10] In 1405 three shops in Pot Row were still said to be

1. V.C.H., *Wilts.* iii, 369–72.
2. *ibid.,* 329.
3. *ibid.,* vi, 129.
4. V.C.H., *Wilts.* vi, 86. Sar. Corp. MS., City Chamberlain's Account Rolls, *passim.*
5. Sar. D. & C.M., Choristers' deeds, *passim.*
6. V.C.H., *Wilts.* vi, 86.
7. Sar. D. & C.M., Sarum deeds, 4/2.
8. W.R.O., 164/1/5.
9. Sar. D. & C.M., will of Joanna Pethen.
10. Sar. Corp. MS., deed.

opposite the butchers' stalls,[1] a phrase used since 1350 at latest.[2] The house at the W. end of Pot Row, *Otemele Corner*, was bequeathed to the mayor and commonalty by Christina Baron between 1418 and 1461;[3] later the name was transferred to Oatmeal Row, the N.–S. row in the E. side of Minster Street. Here too there were buildings by 1314;[4] in 1329 they were said to be 'where the wheelrights live,'[5] in 1365 simply *le Whelernrow*.[6] The two corner houses at the S. end of this row had both cellars and solars in 1351 and were called, after the families who owned them, *Hamptonscorner* and *Powelscorner*.[7] Walter Hampton, baker, already occupied one of them in 1314. *Ironmonger Row* is mentioned in 1366,[8] but the name occurs only rarely; it seems to refer to a few shops in the eastern side of Mitre chequer, opposite *Ironmongercorner*. This last was the S.W. corner shop at the W. end of Butcher Row; it was inhabited by Thomas Blecher, ironmonger, in 1405 and by John Swift, ironmonger, in 1416. The neighbouring house in the N.W. corner was inhabited by butchers in 1405[9] and in 1416.[10]

Regulations have survived from the mid 15th century describing the arrangements made for traders who brought fresh food from outside the town to sell in Salisbury market.[11] Fishermen and butchers were ordered to have their standings along the Town Ditch, behind and separate from the shops of the Salisbury men in Fish Row and Butcher Row. Milk, cheese, fruit and vegetables were sold in Cheesemarket around the Milk Cross or Cheese Cross,[12] in *c*. 1440 said to be newly built (35). Poultry was sold around the Poultry Cross, rebuilt in the 15th century; its predecessor, extant by 1307,[13] was called *la Fayrecroys* in 1351.[14] At that period fruit and vegetables were sold there[15] and the poultry market was in Silver Street,[16] called *la polatrie* in 1405[17] and still known as *Poultry Street* in 1629.[18] Many shopkeepers in this street followed other trades; against St. Thomas's churchyard was *Cordwainer Row* and on the S. at least two of the larger tenements in Mitre chequer belonged to goldsmiths.[19]

Away from the Market Place fewer street-names were descriptive of the many and varied trades of the inhabitants, but clearly, for practical reasons, certain trades tended to congregate in certain areas. On both sides of the High Street, leading to the Close, there were inns and taverns, especially on the W. where the long plots provided space for stabling and the river supplied water for the horses (map, p. 67). In Bridge Street, then called 'the street leading towards the church of the friars preachers' or 'leading to the upper bridge of Fisherton', were tenements belonging to fishermen and dyers who no doubt made good use of the river[20] Dyers also lived on the W. side of Cheesemarket and Castle Street, with room for workshops on the large plots backing on the river and with a plentiful supply of water. In 1512 Nicholas Martin, merchant, had a tenement called the 'Digh House' beside Fisherton Bridge, and in 1523 William Webbe had another near Water Lane.[21] Water Lane, a 'lost' street name, lay opposite Scot's Lane[22] and led to the river-bank and the sluice which controlled the southern inlet of water to the street-channels;[23] traces of this old right of way remain (see monument (427) and map, p. 149). In 1398 the lane was used for taking horses to the river.[24]

Away from the river the streets accomodated a great variety of trades. Many weavers, tailors and tuckers, none very wealthy, appear in the Ward Lists of 1399–1400. The involvement of so many

1. Dom. Bk. ii, f.51[V].
2. W.R.O., 164/1/3.
3. Benson & Hatcher, 94. Sar. Corp. MS., Ledger B, f.27.
4. Sar. D. & C.M., Sarum deeds, 1/15.
5. *ibid.*, 3/19.
6. Dom. Bk. i, f.60.
7. Sar. D. & C.M., Sarum deeds, 1/47.
8. Dom. Bk. i, f.62.
9. Dom. Bk. ii, f.59[V] (John Mannying).
10. Dom. Bk. iii, f.26 (William Halstede).
11. Sar. Corp. MS., Ledger A, ff. 140, 147. Benson & Hatcher, 122.
12. Sar. Corp. MS., Ledger B, f.38.
13. V.C.H., *Wilts.* vi, 86.
14. Sar. D. & C.M., Sarum deeds, 1/47.
15. Dom. Bk. i, f.47 (1361).
16. *ibid.*, f.17 (1348).
17. Dom. Bk. ii, f.60.
18. Sar. D. & C.M., Sarum deeds, 1/99.
19. *Tropnell Cart.*, i, 206. Dom. Bk. i, f.17.
20. Dom. Bk. i, f.1[V] (1391); ii, f.111[V] (1413); iii, f.81[V] (1423).
21. Somerset House, P.C.C. wills, Betiplace 16 and 12 Bodfelde.
22. Dom. Bk. iii, f.33[V].
23. Sar. Corp. MS., Ledger B, f.154[V].
24. Dom. Bk. ii, f.21.

citizens in the manufacture of cloth and clothing is striking, and in the case of the tuckers was no doubt made possible by the city's plentiful water supply. A great number of deeds refer to gardens and other empty plots used as rack-closes for drying cloth, particularly in outlying chequers.[1] Many tanners, parchment-makers and glovers appear in the Ward Lists, most of them living in the S.E. part of the town. In the 16th century 'the way leading to St. Martin's Church, (St. Ann's Street) came to be called Tanner Street, but the name probably came by corruption from St. Ann's chapel over the Close gate at the W. end of the street.[2] The tanners living thereabouts were the last (and one of the dirtiest) industrial users of the water-supply in the Town Ditch.[3] Certain metal industries were located in this part of the town, carried on by smiths, braziers, bell-founders and a few cutlers. Archaeological and documentary evidence relates to a bronze-foundry and bell-foundry pit which may have belonged to John Barber, brazier (*d.* 1403), who lived on the corner of Milford Street and Guilder Lane (see monument (169) and map, p. 94). The pots supposedly sold in Pot Row would have included pots made by braziers as well as clay pots. Brewing and baking seem to have taken place all over the town, not particularly in any one area; there are numerous references in deeds to bakehouses.[4] In 1407 John Hampton, brewer, acquired the S.E. corner tenement in Griffin chequer, known as *Juescornere* from a previous owner, Ralph Juys.[5]

Two members of the legal profession occupied large houses near the S. end of Brown Street. In 1431 William Alessaundre, one of the five legal officers for the city, was living in the house called The Barracks (258), or its predecessor. Windover House (302) was probably built by Edmund Enefeld, clerk, who in 1399–1400 was the richest inhabitant of Mead Ward; his name appears frequently in late 14th-century deeds as a witness to property transactions, or as an executor. In 1455 the most important official in Salisbury, the Bishop's bailiff, John Whittokesmeade, was living as a tenant of the mayor and commonalty in Balle's Place, a 14th-century house with a dignified great hall (351).

The planning of houses was conditioned by the size and position of the tenements they occupied. Some no doubt had been small from the outset, but many tenements were of standard burgage-plot size or larger. Although the relative lack of congestion in the town meant that many tenements remained large and undivided, some in favourable positions were subdivided at an early date, and others were amalgamated and then subdivided later, making irregular-shaped plots, such as that of Pynnok's Inn (77). The grid pattern of streets with the tenements arranged in chequers resulted in there being very few of the back lanes which are so characteristic a feature of other mediaeval towns, providing access to the rear of the tenements when the street frontage is fully occupied by buildings. In Salisbury such access had to be contrived in other ways, most commonly by an arched gateway in the main frontage. In the 19th century these gateways were still a noted feature of Salisbury's streets.[6] Alternatively a back gateway might be provided by annexing an adjoining tenement which fronted on a minor street, either on the opposite side of the chequer or round the corner. Both the 'George' and the 'Leg' inns in High Street had back entries through tenements in New Street, creating L-shaped properties, typical of many. Back-to-back pairs of tenements resulted in very long plots with houses built up along a succession of courtyards and passages; in several chequers these little alleys acquired the name 'abbey' (e.g., monument (131)); an alley in Antelope chequer appears on Naish's map, as does another in New Street chequer. The latter (beside monument (184)) provided access to gardens and orchards surrounded by high walls of flint, chalk and rubble at the centre of this very large chequer. The lane in question is mentioned in 14th-century deeds,[7] but it was obliterated at the S. end in the 18th century when the tenements there were made into an extensive garden for 'The Hall' (199).

---

1. See V.C.H., *Wilts.* iv, 124–8; vi, 125.
2. *ibid.*, vi, 79.
3. See Monument (297).
4. See Monuments (219), (234), (250) and (269).
5. Dom. Bk. ii, f.73.

6. See illustration (Hall, *Memorials*, Pl. xii) of the 15th-century gateway of the New Inn, which was in New Canal, between Monuments (181) and (182).
7. Sar. D. & C.M., Sarum deeds, *passim*, 1331–1365; Dom. Bk. i, f.20ᵛ; ii, f.23ᵛ.

In Cross Keys chequer (plan, p. 81) a sufficient number of mediaeval buildings and boundaries survive to illustrate the diversity in size and shape of the tenements. The W. and S. frontages were more favoured than those to N. and E., with the result that houses and shops were crowded into the S.W. angle while in Brown Street there were only minor tenements, back entries and out-buildings. An unusual feature of this chequer was the small watercourse which bounded the N.E. quarter (map, p. xxxv). Towards the N.W. corner four standard burgage plots are recognisable, over-looking the market and extending back as far as the watercourse. All were large courtyard houses with gateways leading in from the street. St. Mary's Abbey (131) had annexed to it an adjoining tenement in Brown Street, thus creating an alley across the centre of the chequer. The next tene-ment on the S. (129–30) was divided in 1306, making two long, narrow plots. Monuments (126–8), small shops and houses, were crowded into the W. frontage of *Cheesecorner* (on the S.W. angle), a favourable position for wool-merchants and mercers, opposite the Guildhall and wool market. The tenements facing S. to Milford Street were larger, particularly in the centre of the frontage. Near the S.E. angle there were two tenements containing eleven shops; they included the site of (136), all the ground behind it, on the corner and as far N. as the watercourse. The angle tenement must have been contained within the 'L' plan of the inner tenement, and there were two gateways in Brown Street.[1] At the N.E. angle of the chequer there was a similar arrangement, with a squarish corner plot (135) enclosed by a large L-shaped plot now partly occupied by monument (134).

Five large tenements occupied the entire S. frontage of Black Horse chequer (plan, p. 89). All three central tenements were L-shaped, with back entries in Pennyfarthing Street, a small tenement on the site of Grove Place serving Nos. (152) and (153), properties of the Harding family *c.* 1400.

A different arrangement was contrived at the N.E. angle of Trinity chequer, making use of that major amenity, the Town Ditch. *Glastyngburiecorner* was a large irregular tenement which stretched into the interior of the chequer, as far as the ditch and southwards along it. The street frontages to either side of this important house were occupied by smaller tenements, those in Milford Street also having access to the ditch (see monument (234)). There was a similar layout in the N.E. part of Marsh chequer (see monument (270)).

Perhaps the largest tenement of which we have any record is the High Street property, 9 perches and 10 feet long, given to the dean and chapter in 1265[2] by Nicholas de St. Quintin when he made provision for a chantry in the cathedral (see note preceding monuments (86)–(92) on p. 70). Nicholas was a canon of the cathedral and in 1269 became the first provost of St. Edmund's College. He owned all the land on the E. side of the High Street between New Street and the Close Gate, but he excluded from his gift the small angle tenement (92) and another tenement in New Street. His gateway in New Street lay between them, with the solar of one house built above it. It is not clear where the main house stood in 1265, nor whether the High Street frontage was fully built up, but certainly by the later Middle Ages there was a row of narrow, gabled shops (88–91) and a larger house (86), all facing High Street. The shops had only the smallest of back yards whereas to the house there belonged a great garden, still '10 perches of ground' in 1649.[3] This property, held by a canon of the cathedral, invites comparison by virtue of its size and position with some of the extensive sites allotted to the clergy within the Close.

At the other extreme were tenements on the fringes of the urban area which were never fully developed. They might contain cottages, or probably were used merely as gardens or as rack-closes for laying out cloth to dry after dyeing or fulling. There were many such tenements in Friary Lane, both on the E. side, S. of the Friary precinct, and on the W. side where some came to be annexed to tenements in Exeter Street.[4] Others lay in the northern chequers. In 1362 John Richeman gave a group of four tenements in Rolleston Street, on the W. side of Parsons chequer, to the College of St. Edmund to augment the endowment of the Woodford chantry. The property consisted of four

1. Dom. Bks., i, ff.12[V] and 16; ii, ff.64 and 68; iii, ff.11[V], 32 and 42[V] (1361–1419).
2. *Sar. Chart.*, 341.
3. Sar. D. & C.M., Parl. Svy., untitled sheaf (Sar. 11), f.37.
4. Dom Bk. ii, f.68[V].

cottages, each with a curtilage and the racks built there. Also included in the gift was a curtilage without any buildings at the N.W. angle of the chequer. In the town centre, by the 1360s, a corner site such as this would have contained a shop or a jettied house.

The drastic conversion of many town houses into modern shops has destroyed their original plans at ground level, but much can be inferred from roofs and upper floors. In some cases it has been possible to supplement the fragmentary architectural evidence with information from documents which, in the absence of excavation, is the only indication to be had of the existence of out-buildings. Of all the hundreds of workshops, barns, stables, warehouses and other minor buildings which existed in mediaeval Salisbury, none that is datable so early has survived. The tithe barn, presumably mediaeval, which stood on the N. side of St. Martin's Church emphasised the original status of that church within the whole of the large episcopal holding, but it was demolished towards the end of the 19th century.[1] Three parish churches remain, but the two friary churches have disappeared together with their conventual buildings; also the College house of St. Edmund. Only fragments, both large and small, of the more substantial inns and houses exist today.

The grandest buildings were built of stone, but most buildings were of timber framework, often with carved bargeboards to decorate the tall gables, a noted feature even in the 19th century.[2] Roofs were covered with tile after the city council forbade the use of thatch in 1431.[3]

The late 13th-century Bishop's Guildhall had a simple trussed-rafter roof; it is seen in a drawing made while demolition was in progress (Plate 8). Several unusual roof structures survive from the 14th century, including crown-post roofs with stout bracing springing from near the base of the post (e.g. monument (173)), and there is one example of a tall crown-post with coupled rafters (102). Three different types of scissor brace used in conjunction with tie-beams over relatively narrow spans are notable (monuments (82), (132), (219)). Heavy cross-bracing is a repeated feature in 14th-century buildings; it is used not only in roof trusses but also in gables and in wall framing. The customary infilling seems to have been chalk rubble; no doubt this was easier to use in large triangular panels than it would have been between close vertical studding. The latter, together with wattle-and-daub infilling, appears in later mediaeval houses (e.g. monument (80)). Chalk infilling was found *in situ* when the cross-braced gable roof of No. 47 New Canal (177), the heavily braced wall of the Plume of Feathers (132) and the main hall roof truss of No. 9 Queen Street (129) were investigated; since then it has all gone. The truss of No. 9 Queen Street has the shape of a large cusped arch spanning a hall 21 ft. wide. A similar profile appeared in the wider hammerbeam roof of Balle's Place (351), where vertical boarding was applied to fill the spandrels of the truss above the main braces. The form of the hammerbeams in this roof imply that the hall had stone walls about 2 ft. thick, but a similar truss without a crown-post was used a generation later in the timber-framed hall at the Plume of Feathers (132). Hammerbeam roofs of similar date, but without 'aisle' plates and with decorative cross-bracing above the collar, were used over the hall and upper chamber of Windover House (302). The N.E. chamber of the George Inn (173) contains an early example of a false hammerbeam roof, a type which has structural similarities with the arch-braced collar roof. With two or three purlins and with tiered pairs of cusped windbraces both roof-types were used, sometimes in combination, for the fashionable hall roofs of the 15th century.

Many Salisbury merchants lived in courtyard houses, each with an open hall and numerous ancillary buildings. The halls measured, on average, about 23 ft. by 35 ft., which can be compared with the grander scale of the canons' houses in the Close (the Dean's hall was 32 ft. 50 ft.). In the 14th century the halls were heated by open hearths and the roof-timbers became heavily encrusted with soot. Evidence of smoke louvres is found at the Bolehall (140) and at Windover House (302). The latter also contains an example of the new stone fireplaces which became fashionable in the 15th century, usually set into a side wall of the hall. Storeyed hall ranges were then a possibility; an early example was The Barracks (258), built fronting the street with the chimneystack in the front wall and a screens-passage alongside, an unusual arrangement, more common in Devonshire.

1. It appears on O.S., 1880.
2. Parker, *Glossary of Architecture* (1845), i, 42; ii.
3. Sar. Corp. MS., Ledger A, f.96.

In Salisbury it was common for a merchant's house to fill the main street frontage of the tenement. The house was built on the normal mediaeval plan of a hall with one or two gabled cross-wings. The hall was well lit by windows on the street, and the courtyard behind was reached by a through-way in the main range, in the normal screens-passage position. In one case (177) a screens-passage and a through-way wide enough for carts were provided side-by-side, occupying the whole ground floor of the cross-wing. At Church House (97) the through-way has a handsome arched gateway. Here the hall was entered by a doorway (now gone) from the courtyard, and there was no screens-passage.

An alternative plan was to site the main house parallel with the street, but in the interior of the tenement, between the courtyard and the garden. The street front was then occupied by shops or by a minor range of buildings which might be sublet to tenants. A passage or through-way in the front range led to the courtyard, and a screens-passage in the house led through to the garden or back yard. At Windover House (302) the front range may originally have contained shops, but it was rebuilt by William Windover early in the 17th century. At Balle's Place (351) the mediaeval layout of the main house and the street range could both be deduced from the surviving structures and from documents (plan, p. 136). Deeds for a sub-tenement on the corner of the chequer state that it occupied the square of ground between the threshold of the S. entry, leading to the main house, and the kitchen of the main house in Rolleston Street.[1] Evidently the S. entry was the small W. bay in the street range, where a narrow through-passage still existed until demolition; the kitchen would probably have been detached from the main range, but in line with it. Further N. along the street was a gateway wide enough for carts, and in the garden was a dovecot.[2] (A dovecot was often one of the appurtenances of a Salisbury messuage, as at Shoves Corner (p. 120) which had a large garden in the centre of Marsh chequer.) A layout such as that of Balle's Place provided most of the usual advantages of a free-standing house.

A third layout for courtyard houses was to place the hall within the tenement, but at right-angles to the street and alongside the courtyard. John Hall's hall (185) is the best surviving example, but the type was common as it was easily adapted to tenements of various sizes. The frontage could be filled with one or more shops and a gateway to the courtyard, which could be left open at the inner end. This type of plan was often paired, two houses sharing an entry and courtyard. Detailed evidence of such an arrangement is contained in the 'Survey of Radborde's land', dated 1584.[3] As by that date the houses in question were very much decayed it is probable that they were of mediaeval origin. They occupied a tenement with a frontage of 43½ ft. to Blue Boar Row, where they stood on either side of a long narrow courtyard. Each house had a shop with a chamber over it, fronting the street, an open-roofed hall overlooking the yard, a kitchen with a well, butteries, stables, lofts and outbuildings. The eastern house of the pair had, next to the hall, a parlour with an open-roofed chamber over it. At the N. end of the yard, with a small garden beyond, was an open-roofed great hall (22 ft. by 37 ft.) used by the tanners of Salisbury for their guildhall. The relationship of this important building to the others named in the survey can only be conjectural. The mention of wells is typical; many houses in the town had a shallow well excavated in the valley gravel, either in the kitchen or in the courtyard. The well water was better for drinking than the general supply in the street channels.

Occasionally a house with a hall was built with a gable-end towards the street, filling a narrow tenement; the hall was then entered through the shop or room in the front. Side windows in the hall were vulnerable to blocking by any new building on adjoining plots and it is not surprising that the one well-preserved example of this type is relatively early in date (129).

Smaller houses were built either one bay deep and roofed parallel with the street, or two or more bays deep and set gable-end to the street. The subsidiary shops at Balle's Place, dating from the 14th and 15th centuries (only the latter survive), were of the former type. Another group (203), at the S.E. corner of Antelope chequer, comprises an L-shaped range with a crown-post roof; in 1415 it

1.   Dom. Bk. iii, f.171 (1423).   3.   W.R.O., 39/9.
2.   Sar. Corp. MS., Reg. of Demises of City Land, 1477.

contained three shops in Ivy Street and one in Catherine Street. In Guilder Lane a terrace of seven jettied cottages (158) was built on ground which had been empty from 1425 to 1443.

Gabled houses were also built in short rows. A mid 14th-century row of three shops in High Street (82), two bays deep, has three parallel scissor-braced roofs, each three bays long, with steep gables toward the street; a narrow side-passage at the S. end of the building led from the street to a small yard at the back. In Silver Street another group of three gabled houses (63), three storeys high, was built in 1471. Pynnok's Inn (77) was rebuilt in 1491 as four houses, each with two upper floors. Further S., on the corner of Crane Street, a three-storeyed pair of houses (81), also of late 15th-century date, occupies a plot only 22½ ft. by 24 ft.; at one time it was a subsidiary tenement of the Rose Inn.

Single-gabled houses were no doubt common on small sites, especially in the 'rows' and near the town centre, where many were rebuilt in the 16th and 17th centuries. When carried up to three storeys and double-jettied they were substantial buildings; monuments (44), (52), (71) and (92) provide examples. Taller houses gave greater scope for display. No. 58 High Street (84) had a double-jettied gabled front decorated with cusped bracing. Extra space was sometimes provided by making the lowest storey a cellar or half-cellar and by raising the ground floor above it, as in the Wheatsheaf Inn (71), No. 25 High Street (171) and the George Inn (173). Most documentary references to cellars occur in deeds for tenements on cramped sites; when they occur in deeds for large tenements such as monument (132) it can usually be shown that the word is used to refer to storage accomodation above ground. A complete small house, two storeys high and two bays deep, is the 15th-century corner house (57) which was given to Trinity Hospital in 1458 by John Wynchestre, 'barbour'. Other corner houses of similar size are probably not complete houses, but remnants of larger ones; examples are monuments (305) and (341), properties of the Baudrey and Nugge families in the 14th century.

By the late 15th century some prosperous merchants were choosing to live, not in a great court-yard house, but in a compact gabled house two bays wide and two or three bays deep, with windows back and front and with a narrow passage leading from the street to the back yard. Four surviving examples, built on small sites in favourable commercial positions, date from the middle or late years of the 15th century: No. 3 Minster Street (55), No. 56 High Street (83), No. 8 Queen Street (128) and No. 13 High Street (174). The internal arrangements of the first named are clearly described in a detailed 'schedule of implements' accompanying a lease of 1611. The ground floor contained the shop and a half-cellar with a low room over it. The hall occupied one whole bay of the first floor and extended from front to back of the house, with doors leading to a chamber at the front and to a kitchen at the back, the latter overlooking St. Thomas's churchyard. The upper floors contained chambers and attics. Houses of this type required a substantial chimneystack of brick or stone. In plan and profile they were the forerunners of Georgian double-pile town-houses.

Courtyard houses were easily adapted for use as inns and although there are three purpose-built mediaeval inn-ranges in Salisbury (the George (173), the Blue Boar (344) and the White Bear (219)) it is probable that all three were additions to merchant's houses. A 13th-century house formerly occupied part of the S. side of the George Inn courtyard. The surviving 14th-century range of the White Bear was added to a large corner tenement and courtyard house called *Duynescorner* after the Duynes family. The Blue Boar range was built under a contract of 1444 as an addition to *Burfordes-place*, the tenement of Thomas Burford in 1404, when it already extended fully across the chequer from the Market Place to Chipper Lane. The surviving ranges of all three inns contain large chambers in the upper storey. That each party of travellers was accomodated in a separate chamber, furnished both for sleeping and eating, is clear from the inventory of the George Inn made in 1474. This lists the names and furnishings of fourteen chambers, each containing two or three beds, tables, benches and a spere or fixed screen beside the doorway. In addition there were two public rooms for eating and drinking: the Buttery and the Tavern or Wine Cellar, the latter divided into alcoves by latticework screens and furnished with tables and settles. The tuns of ale stood there. This may have been the half-cellar mentioned above. The final entry in the inventory of 1474 concerns the well, equipped with two iron buckets, a pulley and a chain.

LATER HISTORY

The long campaign of the merchant class for freedom from the the Bishop's domination attained success with the incorporation of the city in 1612, just at the period when economic prosperity began to decline.[1] In 1574—5 the Council anticipated their independence by building a new Council House in the Market Place, alongside the Bishop's Guildhall. The earliest known illustration of it is inset in in the corner of John Speed's map of the town (Plate 1). It was a typical Elizabethan civic building, timber-framed, with gabled roofs and a central cupola, containing a large first-floor meeting-room built over an open arcade of pillars and arches. Later the arcade was filled in and new arcades were built, set further out (Plate 2). This Council House was burnt down after the mayoral banquet in 1780, and the adjacent Bishop's Guildhall and surrounding buildings were demolished to make way for a new Guildhall (13), which combined the civic and judicial functions of its two predecessors.

The City Council was not the only organisation to build a new meeting house; several craft guilds already had done so. During the 15th century the Tailors' Guild held meetings in the church of the Greyfriars, but the Dissolution made that impossible and, perhaps foreseeing that eventuality, in 1534 the Tailors built a new hall (165) in Swayne's chequer. Here were kept the 'Giant' and 'Hob-Nob', pageant properties which were taken out each year for the midsummer feast and procession from the hall to the guild chapel of St. John in St. Thomas's church, thence to St. John's chapel on Ayleswade Bridge and back again.[2] The Weavers' hall was in Endless Street in the late 18th century, but how long it had been there is not known.[3] The Tanners were using a hall in Blue Boar chequer in 1569 (above, p. xlv). In 1612, as part of the reorganisation following the granting of the city charter, many mediaeval guilds were reconstituted as Craft Companies.[4] The Joiners' hall (293) in St. Ann's Street, built about this time, has a facade decorated with elaborately carved timber work. In 1638 the Shoemakers were given a house (399) at the S.E. corner of Gore's chequer where they built a large upstairs room for the meetings of their company.

During the 17th century problems of an administrative kind multiplied. The streets were ill-paved, the street channels were neglected and dirty.[5] Poverty increased as the wool trade declined. During the mayoralty of John Ivie in the plague year of 1627 a valiant attempt was made to cope with overwhelming social problems.[6] At St. Thomas's churchyard the piece of city property which lay nearest to the river was used as a Bridewell from 1602 to 1673,[7] and the building now called Church House was made into a workhouse in 1637.[8] Several almshouses are 17th-century foundations. Perhaps the incident most evocative of the decline of Salisbury from its mediaeval prosperity occurred in 1653, when the tower of St. Edmund's church collapsed and the nave was in consequence pulled down.

One of the few houses of any size to be built in the first half of the 17th century occupies part of the site of the Franciscan Friary. Matthew Bee, mayor in 1600, a puritan and an associate of John Ivie, was granted a license to build in the Friary orchard in 1619. His house (304) is one of the earliest brick buildings in the town; the plan, too, was very up-to-date. Most citizens at this time were content to make additions and minor alterations to their mediaeval timber-framed houses, often building at the back, away from the offensive streets. At No. 47 Blue Boar Row (338) a two-storeyed range of this kind survives, although the mediaeval house which stood between it and the street was rebuilt between 1724 and 1740. In St. Ann's Street, William Windover, a benefactor of six of the city companies,[9] was content to occupy the house (302) which had been built for Edmund Enefeld, c. 1400; he inserted a ceiling in the hall and rebuilt the range fronting the street. Between 1663 and 1689 the Eyre family, who owned estates in S.E. Wiltshire and whose prosperity and social standing are attested by elaborate family monuments in St. Thomas's church, built a

1. V.C.H., *Wilts.* vi, 129.
2. Hugh Shortt, *Salisbury Museum Booklet,* 1972.
3. Haskins, *Guilds,* 95.
4. *ibid.,* 79.
5. V.C.H., *Wilts.* vi, 110.

6. P. Slack, *Poverty in Early Stuart Salisbury,* Wilts. Rec. Soc., xxxi (1975); and see Monument (259).
7. Slack, *op. cit.;* Sar. Corp. MS., 0/117/8, f.9.
8. V.C.H., *Wilts.* vi, 111.
9. Haskins, *Guilds,* 252.

completely new brick house (36), tall and square, overlooking the river behind their timber-framed mediaeval house in Cheesemarket. The ownership of such a house in Salisbury was to become fashionable with the country gentry.

One trade which did prosper in 17th-century Salisbury was innkeeping; the city was well placed on the main road from London to the West Country to profit from the increase in traffic. The larger courtyard houses were easily converted to inns. The Plume of Feathers (132) probably became an inn and acquired its name during the years when Prince Henry, eldest son of James I, was a popular Prince of Wales. The Vine (37) became an inn when it was leased to William Vyner in 1647, having belonged to the Webb family during the 16th century and having been occupied as a town house by Sir Edward Penruddock of Compton Chamberlayne. The corporation bought it in 1680[1] and it was included, with a list of rooms, in the Survey of City Lands of 1716; the same survey records the Three Lions at the N.W. corner of Cross Keys (or Three Lions) chequer,[2] and all other properties then owned by the corporation. At the Vine and Three Lions the main rooms were still called in the mediaeval manner by individual names such as Angel, Fox and Fleur-de-Luce. The lists gave a vivid impression of rambling buildings grouped around long courtyards.[3]

The names of the great inns seldom changed, many being adopted for the chequers, the distinctive names of which date at latest from the early 17th century.[4] Not all chequers were called after inns; some were named after families such as the Rolfes, Gores and Vanners who were resident or owned tenements. In 1716 William Naish published the first edition of his map of Salisbury (Plate 16), with the chequer names recorded on it together with street names and a fairly accurate portrayal of the density and distribution of buildings. The third edition (1751) differed only in detail; the parish boundaries were marked, the 'Ditch' had become 'New Canal' and the water-channels on the W. and S. sides of White Hart chequer had been replaced by one on the north.

In 1737 an Act of Parliament created a special body, the directors of highways, with powers to make improvements to the streets. The water-channels were moved to one side and given brick beds; from a later report we learn that they were about 2 ft. wide and 2 ft. deep with up to 1½ ft. of water in them. Between 1820 and 1840 the channels, used increasingly for sewage, were covered over. This rendered them more unhygienic than ever and led to a serious outbreak of cholera in 1849. Soon after this they were filled in and by 1860 all of them had gone.[5]

Other improvements were made or proposed during the 18th century. In 1771 Winchester Gate and in 1781 Castle Gate were taken down to make 'free openings' into the city.[6] In 1762 Fisherton Bridge was rebuilt,[7] and in 1764 a subscription was raised to 'purchase the houses on the left of the way leading from High Street to Fisherton Bridge in order to render that entrance to the city spacious and convenient'.[8] It was about a hundred years before this was actually achieved and the sharp angle between Bridge Street and High Street can still be seen in an undated 19th-century plan.[9] Bridge Street was narrow and at its E. end travellers must have had to turn right and then left again to enter Silver Street, passing around the houses on the S. of St. Thomas's churchyard. The proposed modifications were complete by 1854 when Kingdon & Shearm's map was drawn. Bridge Street was further widened in 1872 and the bridge was again rebuilt.[10]

During the 18th century the town acquired the predominantly Georgian aspect which to some extent it still retains. Many of the richer citizens preferred to live in the Close, but some fine town houses with elegant staircases and elaborate interior plasterwork were built; examples occur in St. Ann's Street and Castle Street. The College (14) was the largest and grandest house of the time. Elsewhere, brick fronts were added to timber-framed houses and framework was also effectively hidden behind facades of 'mathematical' tile. Some very elegant and extensive gardens were created

1. Sar. Corp. MS., Ledger A, f.243ᵛ.
2. See note at end of entry (133), p.
3. Sar. Corp. MS., 0/117/4, ff.54—6 and 64.
4. *Arch J.*, cxx (1963), 236—41.
5. V.C.H., *Wilts.* vi, 89.
6. Benson & Hatcher, 535.
7. V.C.H., *Wilts.* vi, 87.
8. Benson & Hatcher, 525.
9. Sar. D. & C.M., Chapter Estate Book, Ch. Commrs. Recs. 8604/8.
10. V.C.H., *Wilts.* vi, 87.

towards the end of the century by amalgamating the gardens of several tenements; examples were The Hall (199) in New Street chequer, and the garden which lay behind Colonel Baker's house (299) in St. Ann's Street. Considerable ingenuity was displayed in the creation of such gardens. At the College (14), part of the city rampart was removed in the 1790s to make a vista in the picturesque manner, and at No. 45 Castle Street (427) the old right-of-way to the river bank and to the sluices which controlled the water-supply to the street channels was masked by brick walls at the back of the house and along one side of the garden. At the other extreme from such considerations of taste and privacy, courtyards and gardens elsewhere in the city were filled with terraces of small workmen's cottages, for example Finch's Court (145) and Ivy Place (434).

Some handsome Georgian buildings of brick were erected for charitable purposes. In 1702 Trinity Hospital (27) was completely rebuilt, including the chapel, around a paved courtyard. Frowd's Almshouses (33) were built in 1750 and appear on the third edition of Naish's map. The General Infirmary (22) was begun in 1767 and opened in 1771; to pay for it a general subscription was opened, the list being headed by the Duchess of Queensberry and the Earls of Pembroke and Radnor. The architect was John Wood of Bath.

When the new Guildhall (13) was built in 1788—94 the second Earl of Radnor, Recorder of Salisbury, again acted as benefactor, paying for the design and erection of the new yellow brick building. The project entailed much administrative and topographical rearrangement. After the burning of the Elizabethan council house in 1780, the mediaeval council house on the N. side of St. Thomas's churchyard came back temporarily into use (it had been leased from time to time with the adjacent Vine Tavern (37)). In 1785 the Bishop's Guildhall together with all the little tenements of Guildhall chequer (the property of the cathedral choristers, administered by the dean and chapter) was demolished to provide a site for the new hall. In exchange the dean and chapter were given the Vine Tavern (37), a tenement in High Street (77) and six other tenements in New Street.[1] Finally, after the completion of the new Guildhall, the old mediaeval council house in St. Thomas's churchyard was exchanged in 1797 for another tenement in the churchyard, and a new house (38) was built on the site. The ways around the churchyard, then desperately overcrowded, were re-organised in 1835; the remaining properties belonging to the city on the N. side of the churchyard were demolished, the S. side of The Vine was rebuilt, the churchyard was lowered and enlarged, and the present footpath was made. The removal of the N. porch of St. Thomas's church and the sealing up of the N. doorway interrupted an old footpath which formerly passed through the N. and S. stiles of the churchyard and, by way of the N. and S. porches, through the church itself. This old right-of-way probably represented the original (13th-century) alignment of Minster Street, as it passed the W. end of the church before the 15th-century lengthening of the nave (see p. lii). The E. stile into the churchyard is shown in its original position on O.S., 1880; it was moved some 20 feet S. to its present position in 1894.[2] At the N.W. and S.W. corners of the churchyard, the Sunday School and Parish Schools of St. Thomas's (established in 1785 and 1832) were housed in a succession of buildings.

For most of the first half of the 19th century Salisbury remained the quiet cathedral city depicted by Constable and numerous topographical artists, amateur and professional. Of the latter, the two whose picturesque views have proved most useful in the preparation of this inventory are John Buckler, who worked for Sir Richard Colt Hoare during the compilation of the 'History of Modern Wiltshire', and William Twopeny whose drawings of old buildings in the town are incomparable for clarity of detail.

Before 1835, partly because of the great estates which lay on nearly every side, Salisbury expanded little beyond its mediaeval boundaries; some villas, however, were built along Wilton Road and a few Regency town houses appeared. The arrival of the railways in the 1840s and 1850s brought with it the construction of massive embankments along the northern and eastern fringes of

1.   Sar. D. & C.M., Chapter Lease Book (1785), ff.30ᵛ—33.
2.   Sar. Corp. MS., St. Thomas parish, deed of 1894.

the town and filled Fisherton and Bemerton with streets of small brick houses. In 1847 the first railway was opened, the terminus of the L. & S.W.R. at Milford bringing traffic from London and Southampton. In 1856 a branch of the G.W.R. was opened, bringing traffic from Warminster and further west; the terminus partly survives on the N. of the present station. The through-line from London to the West Country by way of Yeovil and Exeter, fully opened in 1860, became possible only when a tunnel had been constructed under Bishopsdown, the L. & S.W.R. station then being built on the present site. In 1859 a short independent branch-line was opened, connecting the station with the new Market House and Corn Exchange (25), with its grandiose facade overlooking the Market Place.

The present administrative boundary of the City of Salisbury encloses an area of 3,640 acres (1,473 ha), which far exceeds that of the mediaeval city. The mediaeval boundaries remained unaltered until 1835, when the area was extended to include growing suburbs on the W., N. and E. of the city. Further enlargements have been made since 1934 and Salisbury now incorporates substantial parts of adjacent former ecclesiastical parishes. These are the whole of Fisherton Anger; much of Fugglestone St. Peter, notably the chapelry of Bemerton; most of Milford (St. Martin's); and parts of Britford, of Stratford-sub-Castle and of West Harnham.

H.M.B.

ARCHITECTURE

ECCLESIASTICAL BUILDINGS

Bishop Osmund's cathedral at Old Sarum (plan opp. p. 15), known only from the foundations excavated in 1913, must have been started soon after 1075 when the *cathedra* was moved to Salisbury from Sherborne. It stood outside the motte-and-bailey castle, but inside the double ring of Iron Age earthworks which surrounded that fortress and which were later used in its enlargement. Osmund's nave was of nine or perhaps ten bays and ended to E. in an apsed presbytery; the narrow N. and S. aisles also probably had small eastern apses; to N. and S. were square transepts, again with apses. The great thickness of the transept foundations suggests that they carried towers; these towers would have flanked the main body of the church in much the same way as do the surviving 12th-century examples at Exeter. A rectangular building N.W. of the northern transept was probably the sacristy.

The plan of Bishop Osmund's cathedral, with five apsed chapels arranged in echelon, is closely paralleled in that of the slightly larger, but almost contemporary church of Shaftesbury Abbey (*Dorset* IV, 57–61) where massive foundations again suggest that there were flanking towers.[1]

Early in the *12th century* Osmund was succeeded in the bishopric by Roger, Henry I's powerful minister who later was entrusted with the custody of the castle itself. Under Roger the cathedral was greatly enlarged. Osmund's presbytery, E. end and flanking towers were taken down to ground level and replaced by larger buildings. With the original nave, which remained, the church then had a cruciform plan, the long E. presbytery and the new N. and S. transepts meeting at a central tower. All arms were flanked by aisles, the double aisles of the transepts evidently imitating those of Winchester. The slope of the hillside made possible the construction of an undercroft to the sacristy which lay at the N. end of the N. transept. This undercroft was probably the first of Bishop Roger's works to be undertaken and is the part which remains best preserved (Plate 28). Elsewhere little more than the footings of the walls and the substructure of some of the floors remain.

On the E., Bishop Roger's presbytery was bounded by an ambulatory beyond which lay three chapels. This part of the cathedral has been demolished more completely than any other, but the scanty foundations uncovered in 1913 show narrow parallel corridors running E. from the ambulatory to separate the central chapel from those to N. and S. These corridors are best explained as passages leading to a small chapel or crypt which lay below the raised floor of a main central chapel. Flights of steps as suggested in the sketch on p. 19 could have given access to the upper level. No

1. The possibility of towers was overlooked in our Survey of Dorset.

doubt the lower chapel contained relics and there may have been a small window or *fenestella* in the E. wall of the ambulatory, through which the relics could be exposed for veneration. Some time in the 12th century the crypt was abolished and the main floor was lowered, but without completely obliterating the original foundations.

In the Norman castle the chapels of St. Margaret and St. Nicholas formed part of the 12th-century Courtyard House, the principal domestic building of the inner bailey. St. Nicholas's was on the first floor and has gone entirely; below it, St. Margaret's occupied a vaulted undercroft entered from the bailey. The excavations of 1910 revealed a simple plan of three rectangular bays defined by shafted pilasters; a square recess for an altar lay at the E. end. A shaft-base with dog-tooth ornament was found, also some fragments of Purbeck marble which may have come from the altar. The pilasters presumably supported groined cross-vaulting.

Two miles S.S.E. of the castle, St. Martin's church, mainly of the 13th century and later, evidently replaces the church which existed in 1091 when its tithes and other possessions were set aside for the maintenance of the canons of Bishop Osmund's new cathedral.[1] Some foundations of *c.* 1100 have been identified.[2]

Another 12th-century church is St. George's, the parish church of Harnham, a settlement on the S. bank of the R. Nadder 2½ miles S. of Old Sarum; it was a separate parish until 1927 when boundary changes brought it into the Municipal Borough. The original church comprised a nave and a slightly narrower chancel (plan, p. 43). The chancel arch was rebuilt in the 14th century, but the remaining niche and *mensa* of an early side altar at the E. end of the nave show that there was originally a narrow chancel arch flanked by altars. The niche, discovered in 1873, retains part of a 13th-century painting.

The *13th-century* was for Salisbury a period of great activity in building. It might be thought that the new cathedral, started in 1220, and the adjacent houses for its clergy would have monopolised the skill of every available mason, but this was not so. At least five other churches were under construction in and around the new city. The chancel of St. Lawrence's with two 13th-century windows and part of a contemporary piscina must be 'the chapel of Stratford' which Bishop Poore bestowed on Master Harvey in 1228[3]. St. Thomas's is mentioned in a document of 1238;[4] the church was largely rebuilt in the 15th century, but 13th-century masonry survives at the E. end. Arcaded corbel-tables of 13th-century character also remain, but are not *in situ*. Later developments (see below) suggest that the original plan was cruciform, possibly without aisles. If aisleless it would have been slightly smaller than the contemporary church at Amesbury, but comparable in the proportions of the plan.

Bishop Bingham's important group of buildings, Ayleswade Bridge, St. John's chapel and St. Nicholas's hospital, date from the the second quarter of the 13th century. St. John's has become a house and many of its well-preserved lancet windows have been blocked up, but the E. window-sill of the S. wall retains a double piscina. St. Nicholas's is classed among secular buildings (p. 54). During the 13th century, St Martin's was provided with a large new chancel (Plate 31); although not precisely dated, it is clearly work of the first half of the century.

Nothing remains visible of the original church of St. Edmund, founded in 1269 by Bishop Walter de la Wyle to serve the northern part of the new city. The surviving 15th-century extensions suggest that the original building was cruciform. John Speed's map of 1616 shows St. Edmund's with a central tower, a nave, and a southern projection, either a large porch or a transept. The central tower and all to the west of it was pulled down in the 17th century.

The most important *14th-century* church building to remain in Salisbury, outside the Close, is the tower and spire of St. Martin's (Plate 36). The E. side of the tower rests on a pre-existing wall of flint, 3¼ ft. thick and up to 25 ft. high, set obliquely to the axis of the church. There is no evidence

1. *Reg. St. Osmund*, i, 198–200. The proof that '*ecclesia de Sarum cum decimis et ceteris ibidem appendiciis*' is St. Martin's church emerges from Bishop Roger's charter of 1228 (*Sar. Chart.*, 191): '*ecclesia S. Martini de manerio nostro Sarum*'. Evidently St. Martin's was the mother-church of the bishop's manor.

2. *W.A.M.*, lvii (1958), 40–9.   3. *Sar. Chart.*, 191.   4. *ibid.*, 246.

that 'the wall was previously associated with the church and for this reason it has not been mentioned before among ecclesiatical monuments.

At St. Thomas's the respond and springing of an early 14th-century arch embedded in later masonry at the N.W. corner of the present S. chapel represent a feature which once spanned the S. transept; such an arch would be needed to contain the thrust of the nave arcade and it may perhaps be inferred that an aisle was built or rebuilt at this time. Later 14th-century responds in the walls assumed to have been the W. walls of both transepts also indicate aisles. In the accompanying plans

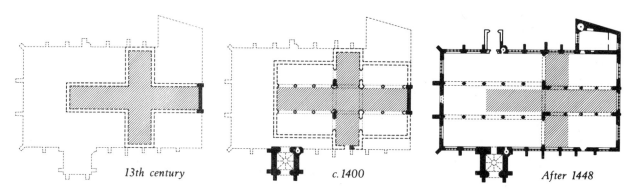

13th century   c. 1400   After 1448

St. THOMAS'S CHURCH, Conjectured development.

the earlier stages are hypothetical, but they accommodate the little that is known about the church before its 15th-century rebuilding. The width of the original chancel is shown by the surviving E. wall; its length before the mid 15th-century rebuilding is recorded in a document of 1448 as 40 ft. 4 ins.[1] The jamb of a 14th-century doorway incorporated with the S. wall of the present S. chapel may indicate the length of the former transept. The tower was being built in 1400.[2]

Although the present nave is later, the 14th-century chancel arch of St. Lawrence's church predicates a nave of that date; the consecration recorded in 1326 presumably relates to it.[3] At St. Andrew's, Bemerton, the earliest datable features are 14th-century windows, but there is mention of a church in the 13th century.[4]

A well-proportioned 14th-century chancel arch at St. George's Harnham (Plate 37), replaces the 12th-century opening; to make room for it the two original nave side-altars were suppressed. A S. chapel was added during the 14th century.

Early in the *15th century* St. Edmund's received the addition of a huge chancel flanked by N. and S. chapels. In size the church was at least doubled and the original nave, which continued to stand, was so far reduced in significance that a will of 1407 refers to 'the newly built church of St. Edmund'.[5] At St. Martin's the nave was rebuilt. The bay nearest the 13th-century chancel was started early in the 15th century, with four-centred arches opening N. and S. to side chapels; later, the rest of the nave was rebuilt with two-centred arches opening into the aisles.

About 1448, following the collapse of the chancel,[6] the E. arm of St. Thomas's was lengthened to include the area of the former transept. Subsequently the nave and aisles also were rebuilt on a larger scale than before (plan on p. 25). St. Thomas's vestry appears to have been added in the 16th century.

St. Lawrence's was extensively repaired in the 15th century. In the chancel the whole E. wall was rebuilt and new windows were put in the N. and S. walls. About the same time, or a little later, the nave was given new windows and buttresses; some of the latter were rebuilt in 1583.

1.   See note 6.
2.   Will of Thomas de Boyton, Dom. Bk. iii, f.30[v].
3.   V.C.H., *Wilts.* vi, 210, n.42.
4.   *ibid.*, 46, n.93.
5.   Somerset Hse., P.C.C. Wills, 14 Marche; will of Wm. Mercer.

6.   The disaster is recorded in a deed of 1448 bound into a Chapter Act book (Sar. D. & C.M., Reg. Burgh. f.2).
   The reason for the collapse is not stated.

Entries in the unusually complete series of churchwardens' annual accounts relating to St. Edmund's bear vivid witness to the decay of that church during the first half of the *17th century*.[1] In 1623–4 the chancel (present nave) roof was in a serious state. In 1638 three buttresses had to be built to support the N. wall. In 1652 the foundations of the S.W. pier of the central tower subsided and, to lighten the weight, the bells and a lead turret were removed. On June 26, 1653 the main pillars 'did bulge out and sensibly shake, and clefts were seen to open and shut with the ringing of the sermon bell'. Next day the tower collapsed. On September 5th the Vestry resolved that 'the E. end of the church shall be repaired and made fit for our meeting' while 'the W. end (nave) which is now likely to fall shall be taken down in convenient time'. On March 5th, 1654 the Vestry decided to rebuild the tower; it was ready to receive the new bells in 1656. The N. and S. transepts of the mediaeval cruciform church are not mentioned in the mid 17th-century accounts, but they must still have existed in order to close the W. ends of the two chancel aisles; they either collapsed with the tower or were taken down at the same time as the old nave. The walls which now close the W. ends of the aisles are integral with the tower of 1656; together with the tower they form a handsome W. front in which mediaeval forms remain surprisingly lively. The central and southern doorways are re-used 15th-century material and the tracery of the W. windows in the aisles may also be partly mediaeval, but other windows with two-centred heads and cusped tracery are 17th-century work. The tall buttresses with ogee-moulded plinths and weathered offsets copy the details of smaller buttresses to the 15th-century aisle walls. The crenellated tower parapet repeats a common 15th-century pattern, but the stringcourse has the mouldings of a classical cornice and ends in 'gargoyles' which are almost classical busts. The crocketed finials have acanthus foliage.

Minor church works of the 17th century include George Herbert's restoration of St. Andrew's, Bemerton, as recorded by Izaac Walton, but nothing of this date is positively recognisable. At St. Lawrence's repairs were executed in 1656.

The W. tower of St. Lawrence's was rebuilt in the *18th century* on the mediaeval foundations at the expense of Thomas Pitt, Governor of Madras. Pitt, a grandfather of the Earl of Chatham, acquired a nearby house in 1686 and represented the borough of Old Sarum in Parliament between 1715 and 1726. The tower, of 1711, is a neat, plain building, mainly remarkable as a very late example of traditional church architecture, here all but extinct, and for the prominence of Pitt's name on the W. front.

The Methodist chapel in St. Edmund's Church Street, a plain brick-built hall with round-headed windows, was built in 1810, but its original character has been obscured by late 19th-century additions and decorations. The wooden columns supporting the gallery are probably original. Of the Primitive Methodists' meeting room in Fisherton (481), two brick walls with round-headed windows survive. It appears to have been a very simple building.

Of greater architectural significance in 19th-century Salisbury is St. Osmund's Roman Catholic church, consecrated in 1848 and one of Augustus Welby Pugin's last works. Externally the fine proportions of the austere flint-faced nave and tower are impaired by the bulky N. aisle added in 1894 by Doran Webb, but Pugin's mature genius is seen in the detail of the original architectural features and in the subtle disposition of the sparse ornament.

At St. Martin's an elliptical chancel arch was replaced in 1838 by a 'gothic' arch of lath and plaster; this in turn was removed in 1885 when a thorough restoration of the whole church was directed by Crickmay & Son, architects.

At St. Thomas's the galleries were removed and the chancel was rearranged in 1865–70 by G.E. Street. At St. Edmund's a chancel which had been added in 1766 was replaced in 1865 by a new chancel with flanking chapels designed by George Gilbert Scott. Restorations at St. George's in 1873 were directed by William Butterfield.

St. Clement's, the mediaeval parish church of Fisherton Anger, was demolished in 1852 and in the following year St. Paul's church, designed by T.H. Wyatt, was opened on a site some 350 yds. to the north. As it was built after 1850 St. Paul's is not described in the Inventory.

1. Swayne, *Accounts, passim*.

CHURCH ROOFS

The sole example of mediaeval stone vaulting to be seen in Salisbury (outside the Close) is in the S. porch of St. Thomas's church, *i.e.* the lowest stage of the S. tower; it dates from *c*. 1400. Elsewhere St. Thomas's has lead-covered timber roofs of low pitch. The chancel of 1448 has an oak roof with stout king-strut tie-beam trusses; at the centre of each tie-beam is a foliate boss. The nave roof, structurally similar but more elaborately carved and painted, is later 15th-century work. The aisles and chapels have flat roofs on moulded and painted beams which intersect to form square panels.

At St. Martin's the N. aisle has a late 15th-century wagon roof rising from enriched cornices supported on moulded and panelled wall-shafts. The shafts stand on stone head-corbels of distinctly classical style (Plate 42); one represents a monk wearing spectacles. The nave and S. aisle have plainer 16th-century wagon roofs. The chancel roof is of the 19th century.

St. Lawrence's has wagon roofs with grotesque bosses at the rib intersections. The chancel roof is of the early 15th century; the nave roof, where the ribs have recently been restored, is probably late 15th-century work.

As St. George's the late 15th-century wagon roof of the chancel has transverse ribs springing from carved head-corbels which project horizontally from the wall-plates.

CHURCH FITTINGS ETC.

Altars: Fragments of Purbeck marble found in 1910 during the excavation of St. Margaret's chapel in the castle of Old Sarum were thought to represent the *mensa* of the 12th-century altar. The remains of a rubble pedestal and imprints on the wall-plaster indicated that the *mensa* had been 5 ft. long and 2½ ft. wide. St. George's church, Harnham, retains *in situ* part of the stone *mensa* of a small side altar at the E. end of the nave, S. of the chancel arch (Plate 37). It is probably an original feature of the 12th-century church although the painting behind it is 13th-century work. When the chancel arch was rebuilt and widened in the 14th century the altar became part of the plinth of the S. respond. The chapel of Trinity Hospital (27) has the *mensa* of a mediaeval altar, discarded at the Reformation, but discovered in 1908 and reinstated. The only other stone altar known in Salisbury is that of 1847 in the S. chapel of St. Osmund's.

Bells and Bellfounders: The oldest known bell in Salisbury is probably of the 14th century,[1] but its history and present whereabouts are unknown and it has not been included in the inventory; until recently it was in the chapel of Newbridge Hospital, a modern Poor-Law Institution. After this the earliest known bell is probably that of St. Andrew's church, thought to have been cast at Reading *c*. 1540—50.[2] In 1581 John Wallis made two small bells for the tower clock of St. Thomas's; other bells by this well-known Salisbury bellfounder are in St. Martin's, St. Lawrence's and St. Clement's. The tenor at St. Martin's, 1624, is John Wallis's last known casting and also bears the initials of his successor John Danton. In 1656 William Purdue and Nathanial Bolter made four bells for the new tower of St. Edmund's, and in 1675 Richard Flower made two for St. Martin's. The tenor at St. Thomas's was cast in 1716 by Abraham Rudhall of Gloucester;[3] others at St. Thomas's were made in 1771 by Robert Wells of Aldbourne,[4] who also made bells for St. Edmund's and St. Lawrence's. St. Martin's, St. Edmund's and St. Paul's have 19th-century bells by Thomas Mears.

Brasses and Indents: Few remain. The most interesting is a worn Purbeck marble slab, probably of the 15th century, in the S. aisle of St. Edmund's church; it has indents for a male and a female figure lying in twin niches under crocketed pinnacles, between which are four shields; the brasses have gone. Another slab with indents for a figure and four shields lies in the churchyard of St. Edmund's, N. of the tower. At St. Thomas's an anonymous mid 15th-century Purbeck marble table tomb of good quality (drawing, p. vii) has indents in the top slab for two principal figures, groups

1.   H.B. Walters, *Church Bells of Wiltshire*, 251.
2.   *ibid.*, 22.
3.   Swayne, *Accounts*, 351.
4.   *S.J.*, 13th May 1771.

of children, a shield, an inscription plate etc., but the brasses have gone, the indents have been filled in, and 17th-century and 18th-century inscriptions are superimposed. A somewhat coarser 15th-century table tomb with indents for brasses stands in the W. porch of St. Martin's. At St. Thomas's the Purbeck marble floorslab of John Webb (mayor 1560) retains brasses depicting Webb and his wife, two groups of children, three shields-of-arms and a brass border with a black-letter inscription. Also at St. Thomas's the floorslab of John and Catherine Baylye, 1600, has a brass inscription plate with neat Roman lettering and a shield displaying Baylye's arms and those of a mercantile house; below, on the same slab, a small brass plate of 1709 commemorates a later member of Baylye's family. A floorslab in the chancel of St. Thomas's has a plain brass plate with a poem commemorating Thomas Eyre's wife, Elizabeth, who died in 1612; she was the mother of nine sons and five daughters. A brass plate in St. Martin's has a Latin inscription in ill-formed Roman capitals incised and filled with white enamel; it commemorates John Sebastian Carpenter, 1632, a wide-ranging traveller and an accomplished linguist who appears to have officiated as minister.

Chairs: An early 17th-century oak arm-chair is preserved in the chancel of St. Thomas's; another, enriched with chip-carving, is in the late 19th-century church of All Saints, Harnham (listed with St. George's). St. Martin's has two good-quality secular ladder-back chairs of the 18th century.

Chests: St. Lawrence's has a mediaeval elm chest with a 17th-century lid. The large 16th-century oak churchwardens' chest at St. Thomas's is remarkable for its iron binding, with hasps and staples for three padlocks (Plate 53). St. Martin's has an iron chest, probably of the late 16th century, painted externally with rosettes; the lid is fastened by nine latches. A cupboard at St. Edmund's has '1697' carved on a panel. Cast-iron register-boxes of 1813 are found at St. Martin's and (formerly) St. Clement's.

Clocks: The tower clock at St. Thomas's is modern, but the wooden dial is 18th-century and the bells are of 1581. Two figures representing men in 16th-century armour formerly struck the bells, but the mechanism no longer works. St. Lawrence's has a clock of *c.* 1711. St. Edmund's has one of 1839.

Communion Rails: Moulded oak communion rails with turned balusters were installed in St. Lawrence's church when it was restored, *c.* 1711. All other Salisbury churches have modern rails.

Communion Tables: Seventeenth-century oak communion tables with stout turned legs, some with chip-carving on the rails, are in St. Thomas's, St. Martin's, St. Edmund's and St. George's.

Fonts: The font bowl at St. Lawrence's was originally a large square block of Purbeck marble with shallow elliptical-headed panels recessed in two of its sides; a third side had a pattern of intersecting circles. It is probably of 12th-century origin and older than the church, which is not mentioned until 1228; the local tradition that it comes from Old Sarum may well be true. St. George's, an early 12th-century parish church, has a plain round font of *c.* 1200. St. Martin's and St. Edmund's have nearly identical 13th-century fonts with octagonal Purbeck marble bowls, cylindrical legs, moulded centre shafts and octagonal bases (Plate 41). The roll-moulded 13th-century tub-font formerly in St. Clement's parish church is now in St. Paul's (Plate 41).

Glass: Reset in a window in the S. chapel of St. Thomas's are three panels of 15th-century stained glass depicting St. Thomas of Canterbury, St. Christopher and probably St. Francis; they were formerly in the E. window of the vestry. Other windows in St. Thomas's have fragments of 15th-century stained glass *in situ* in the tracery, or reset.
A small panel (12½ ins. by 8 ins.) of Swiss glass at St. Edmund's depicts the Creation and Fall in twelve scenes, with the date 1617. It may be no more than a coincidence that the Creation was the subject of the window at St. Edmund's which the puritan Henry Sherfield defaced in 1629, with notorious legal consequences (Benson & Hatcher, 371–4).

Trinity Hospital (27) has mediaeval and later glass fragments reset in the chapel windows; among them is a panel of Stuart Royal arms. St. Osmund's church has glass of 1848 by Hardman.

Hatchments: St. Thomas's and St. Martin's each have seven funeral hatchments earlier than 1850 and St. Edmund's has nine. The earliest appears to be that of John Batt in St. Martin's (*d.* 1723).[1]

Hour-glasses: A swivelling iron bracket attached to the N. respond of the chancel arch in St. Lawrence's church, close to the pulpit, supports a round socket for an hour-glass and is decorated with spear-shaped finials. An hour-glass is mentioned in the churchwardens' accounts for 1652, but the present wood-framed hour-glass is of the 19th century. A brass-framed hour-glass at St. Martin's is inscribed 'St. Martin Sarum 1721'.

Images: A late 14th or early 15th-century carved stone Crucifixion in a cinquefoil ogee-headed recess has been reset in a buttress of the S. chapel of St. Thomas's; its original position is unknown. Above the archway to the S. porch of St. Thomas's (in the base of the tower) are 15th-century stone images of St. Thomas of Canterbury and of the Virgin and Child. In the S. aisle of St. Martin's a double cinquefoil-headed niche discovered in 1886 contains an Annunciation with two standing figures in carved alabaster. The figures have been extensively restored, but the lower parts are 15th-century work and were found *in situ*; a fragment of the same carving was found in the tower.[2]

Inscriptions: The name 'John Nichol . . . the founder of this peler' carved in black-letter on a stone scroll at the head of a column in the chancel of St. Thomas's (Plate 35) no doubt records a large donation to the fund for rebuilding the church after the disaster of 1448. Painted inscriptions on the beams of the adjacent S. chapel roof, praying for the souls of William Swayne and members of his family, are presumably of slightly later date. An inscription in Roman lettering on a cartouche over the W. doorway of St. Edmund's church records the collapse of the old tower in 1653; the names of the two churchwardens of 1655–6 incised below the parapet of the present tower relate to the completion of the rebuilding. A large inscription of 1711 commemorates the donor of the W. tower of St. Lawrence's.

Numerous dated scratchings are noted in the Inventory. One in St. Martin's appears to be of the 15th century.

Lectern: A brass eagle lectern of the second half of the 15th century in St. Martin's church is in good condition except that the usual couchant-lion feet are missing from the pedestal base.[3]

Monuments and Floorslabs: In 1912–3 the excavators at Old Sarum found many graves near the cathedral and recorded details of 22 funerary monuments.[4] In most cases the burial was covered by a large chamfered or weathered slab or by a coffin-lid; stones from Purbeck, Portland and Bath were reported, as well as Greensand. The two earliest graves (Nos. xxi, xxii on the plan opp. p. 15) were assigned to the *11th century*; they were covered by slabs of soft Greensand stone with incised crosses, and each had a vertical headstone and footstone decorated with wheel crosses and crosses paty. Among *12th-century* monuments in the canons' cemetery were two inscribed slabs, one commemorating Alward of Ramsbury, the other Godwin the precentor. Three important 12th-century monuments originally at Old Sarum were moved to the new cathedral in the 13th century. One, a fine mid 12th-century Purbeck coffin-lid with the effigy of a bishop (Plate 30) and a metrical inscription probably commemorates Bishop Osmund; it is thought to come from the tomb in Bishop Roger's enlarged cathedral to which Osmund's body was translated in the 12th century. Another, a slab of Purbeck inscribed in the 16th or 17th century with the date of Osmund's death (*Anno mxcix*), may be from the grave of Bishop Roger. Thirdly, a rich marble coffin-lid with a bishop's effigy surrounded by a vine-scroll frieze (Plate 30) is thought to be from Bishop Jocelyn's tomb at Old Sarum.

1. Baker, *St. Martin's*, 13. Reeves, *Inscriptions*, 88.
2. *ibid.*, 9, 11, 97.
3. Oman, *Arch. J.*, lxxxvii (1930), 117–49.
4. *P.S.A.*, 2nd Ser., xxvi (1914), 111–4.

Of the early *13th century* is a Purbeck coffin with a shaped interior found at Old Sarum in 1912 and removed to the cloisters of Salisbury cathedral. In St. Martin's churchyard is a coffin lid, probably of the 13th century, with moulded and hollow-chamfered sides and a flat top, partly excised, but retaining a cross.

No *14th-century* funerary monuments are known in Salisbury outside the Close. The best *15th-century* monument is a Purbeck table-tomb in St. Thomas's. It has recently been reset at the E. end of the N. aisle; before that it was in the N.E. corner of the N. chapel, but Lyons's plan of 1745

St. THOMAS'S CHURCH. 15th-century table tomb.

shows its original position on the centre-line of the N. chapel, about 15 ft. from the W. end. The focal position implies that the unknown person for whom the tomb was made was the principal contributor to the cost of rebuilding the chapel after its collapse in 1448 (see p. lii). Embossed on the middle shield of each long side is a merchant mark, as yet unidentified; the other shields are recessed for brasses, now gone. The brasses from the top slab have also gone and inscriptions of 1679 and 1727 commemorating members of Chafyn family take their place. St. Martin's has a small and less skilfully worked 15th-century Purbeck table-tomb, also with indents for brasses in the top slab. St. Edmund's has two Purbeck marble floorslabs with indents for brasses, probably of the 15th century; the one in the S. aisle must, when complete, have been especially noteworthy (see brasses).

The only 16th-century funeral monuments in the Inventory are the Purbeck floorslab in St. Thomas's with brasses commemorating John Webb and his wife (brass 3), and a slab in St. Martin's (floorslab 12) with a neatly incised black-letter inscription, only partly legible.

Outstanding among *17th-century* monuments are a pair of large alabaster memorials in St. Thomas's (Plate 49). One commemorates Christopher Eyre (*d*. 1624), the other his parents Thomas and Elizabeth (*d*. 1612) and their fourteen children.[1] Both monuments were set up under the terms of Christopher's will; originally they faced one another across the chancel, but were moved to the S. chapel in the 19th century. Another notable monument in St. Thomas's is the large oak panel, depicting the Sacrifice of Isaac (Plate 47), carved as his own memorial by Humphrey Beckham, *d*. 1671. A smaller version, evidently by the same carver, forms part of the parlour chimneypiece of No. 8 Queen Street (128). Beckham was chamberlain of the Joiners' Company in 1621 and doubtless had much to do with the building of the Joiners' Hall (293). Two plain, solid table-tombs in St. Edmund's churchyard bear dates of the 1640s; a more elaborate example covering the grave of James Townsend in St. Lawrence's churchyard is dated 1679. A small round cartouche of white marble with a neat italic inscription commemorating Richard and Margarett Kent, 1692, 1711, originally in St. Clement's church, but now in St. Paul's, has a scroll border and acanthus enrichment of good quality. Fine carving is also seen in the handsome black slate floorslabs of Jane Eyre, 1695,[2] and Elizabeth (Chester) Eyre, 1705, in St. Thomas's.

1. Thomas, still living at the time of erection, is not named on the monument.
2. Although Jane's husband, Nicholas Eyre (1603–74) does not appear on the various Eyre pedigrees published by Hoare (*Mod. Wilts., passim*) it is probable that he was one of Thomas and Elizabeth's numerous progeny.

The grandest *18th-century* monument in Salisbury was erected by Sir Robert Eyre (Lord Chief Justice 1723; *d.* 1735) on his wife's death in 1724. A wide burial vault at the E. end of the S. chapel of St. Thomas's forms a raised platform with a panelled stone front, upon which is set a barrier of richly ornamented ironwork. The walls behind and at the ends of the platform are masked by oak screenwork including a central feature with Corinthian pilasters supporting a scrolled pediment and a cartouche-of-arms of Eyre quartering Lucy (Plate 45). Two early 18th-century wall-monuments are conspicuously alike (Plate 49). One commemorates Marshall Hill, a young lawyer who died in 1707; the other John Gough of Queen's College, Oxford, who died aged 19 in 1709. Hill's monument is in St. Edmund's; Gough's in St. Thomas's. An impressive marble monument in the chancel of St. Martin's records the extinction in 1748 of a branch of the Swayne family, resident in Milford for several generations (cf. (570)). The best of the smaller 18th-century wall-monuments are illustrated on Plates 50–52. It is notable that most good ones earlier than 1750 are in St. Thomas's, but later examples are nearly all in St. Martin's. No doubt this reflects the increasing unhealthiness of St. Thomas's parish and the removal of the richer inhabitants to other areas. St. Edmund's, which retains only one outstanding 18th-century wall-monument, was cleared of monuments in the 19th century. Monuments seen there early in the 18th century are listed in Rawlinson's *History and Antiquities of Salisbury Cathedral and Bath Abbey* (1719).

The earliest wall-monument on which a sculptor's signature (R. Earlsman) has been found is that of Sir Alexander Powell, 1748, in St. Thomas's; the next in date is an elegant composition of 1796 in St. Martin's, by King of Bath (Baker). A floorslab in St. Thomas's with dates 1737–72 (probably retrospective) is signed Mitcherd, and the same signature appears on a wall-monument of 1800 formerly in St. Clement's, now in St. Paul's. The Mitcherds evidently worked as monumental masons for more than one generation. Louisa Mitcherd's headstone, 1827, in St. Clement's churchyard, is inscribed 'John and Mary Mitcherd her parents' own work'.

There are, of course, many 19th-century wall-monuments, table-tombs, headstones and floor-slabs, but none is particularly notable as a work of art. A high proportion are by the well-known sculptor, William Osmond, whose atelier in St. John's Street (251) is still distinguished by an elegant Grecian facade.

Organ: The organ in St. Thomas's, made by Samuel Green, but extensively modified in the 19th century and later, was given by George III in 1792 to Salisbury cathedral, where at first it occupied a pulpitum erected by Wyatt under the E. arch of the crossing.[1] The pulpitum was dismantled by Scott soon after 1863 and the organ was transferred to St. Thomas's in 1877.

Paintings: A small niche behind an original nave altar in the 12th-century church of St. George, Harnham, retains part of a painting in red outline, *c.* 1260, representing the Virgin kneeling before the Risen Christ.[2] The S. chapel in St. Thomas's, dedicated in 1469 to the Virgin and St. John the Baptist,[3] has on the N. wall paintings representing a wall-hanging powdered with vases of lilies and garter badges; on this background three panels show scenes from the Virgin's life: Annunciation, Visitation. Adoration (Plate 43). The garter badges probably allude to the appointment of Bishop Beauchamp as Chancellor of the Order of the Garter.

Although it has suffered from injudicious restoration, the most important wall-painting in Salisbury is the late 15th-century 'Doom' above the chancel arch in St. Thomas's (Plate 35). Flanked by angels bearing the emblems of the passion, Christ is seated on a double rainbow with the apostles at his feet. Angels sound their trumpets; the dead rise from their graves and are received into heaven or cast by devils into hell.[3]

Piscinae: Thirteenth-century piscinae in trefoil-headed niches remain in St. Martin's and St.

---

1. Dodsworth, 181–2.
2. Tristram, *Eng. Med. Wall-Painting, xiii cent.,* 552.
3. Licence by Edward IV to Wm. Swayne; *Arch. J.,* civ (1947), 152–3.
4. Hollaender, *W.A.M.,* 1 (1944), 351–70.

George's churches and in the former chapel of St. Nicholas's Hospital (Plate 40). At St. John's chapel, a double piscina is sunk in a window-sill. The trefoil head of a small 13th-century niche in the N. wall of the chancel of St. Lawrence's appears to come from a former piscina; the present piscina on the S. of the chancel is of the 14th century. The S. chapel of St. George's has an ogee-headed 14th-century piscina. Fifteenth-century examples occur in the S. chapels of St. Martin's and St. Edmund's.

Plate: Of the rich collections of pre-Reformation silver formerly in Salisbury churches (St. Edmund's had fifteen gilt chalices and patens)[1] only one piece remains: an engraved paten (Plate 55) with the London hall-mark and date-letter for 1533. The maker's mark TW is probably for Thomas Wastell.

St. Martin's has a cup and cover-paten (Plate 54) without assay marks, but corresponding closely to the 'Gillingham' series;[2] an inscription on the foot of the cup names the donor, William Wickham, Bishop of Winchester (the second of that name, who occupied the see in 1595). Other late 16th-century cups are at St. Andrew's church and at the chapel of Trinity Hospital (27). St. Martin's has a large silver flagon of 1669, acquired in 1670 and valued in 1678 at about £13.[3] Even more impressive at St. Martin's is a gilt dish of 1662 with a wide *repoussé* flange (Plate 54); it is engraved with the shield and coronet of Edward Hyde, Earl of Clarendon, who lived at Hatch House, Semley.[4] Valued at £20. 3s. 6d., it was given to St. Martin's in 1686 by Alice Denham,[5] presumably a relative of Clarendon's second wife.

A large plain almsdish at St. Edmund's was made by Gabriel Sleath in 1734 and given in the same year (Plate 55). St. Lawrence's has a massive set of cup, paten, flagon and almsdish made by Benjamin Pyne in 1712 and given by Thomas Pitt. Pewter flagons and patens belong to St. Clement's (now in St. Paul's) and to the chapel of Trinity Hospital.

Pulpits: A polygonal oak pulpit in St. Mark's church (1892) was in St. Martin's until 1884. Some of the woodwork is of the 15th century; other parts were renewed in 1849.[6] The best pulpit in Salisbury is the fine 17th-century example in St. Lawrence's church (Plate 46). A late 19th-century pulpit in the Methodist church (12) includes woodwork from an earlier pulpit, made probably in 1811.

Royal Arms: Entries in St. Thomas's churchwardens' accounts for 1572–3, recording payments to Andrew Marbell for painting the Queen's arms on a newly-built wall at the upper end of the choir, are unlikely to refer to the wooden panel painted with the arms of Queen Elizabeth I which now hangs in the S. aisle (Plate 56); this more probably dates from 1593–4, when payments were made to Roger Lovell 'for making the Queen's arms' and to Reynald Beckham for the frame and for wainscot.[7] A similar, but more coarsely executed panel of Queen Elizabeth's arms at St. Martin's is not dated.[8]

In 1605 the churchwardens of St. Martin's paid £3. 15d. 'for the King's Armes', probably the carved wooden achievement of the Stuart royal arms which now hangs at the W. end of the nave. A larger carved achievement in St. Lawrence's church, showing the arms of Queen Anne, was given in 1713 (Plate 56).

Rood-lofts and Screens: The rood-screen in St. Martin's is modern, but undecorated areas of the panelled stonework flanking the chancel arch, suggest that the opening was originally traversed by a wooden rood-loft. The roof-loft staircase is on the S. side of the S. aisle and an extension of the

1. Nightingale, 14.
2. R.C.H.M., *Dorset* IV, xxxiv.
3. Baker, *St. Martin's*, 59.
4. Hoare, *Mod. Wilts.*, iv, (ii), 23.
5. Baker, *St. Martin's*, 60.
6. Baker, *St. Martin's*, 5.

7. Swayne, *Accounts*, 299, 300.
8. Roger Lovell received £8 for the arms in St. Thomas's, and the payment of 4s. to a painter for 'wrytinge the quene's mties name in letres of gould with a posy', in 1588, cannot be regarded as evidence for the date of the St. Martin's panel.

loft must therefore have passed across the aisle; presumably it formed a screen in front of the S. chapel. Oak screenwork of 15th-century origin (Plate 44) in St. Lawrence's probably comes from a former rood-screen although in its present form the screen is mainly 18th-century. A 17th-century oak screen is in St. George's (Plate 44).

Stalls and Seating: St. Thomas's retains four plain oak stalls of 15th-century origin with hinged seats below which are carved misericords (Plate 46). St. Lawrence's has some 18th-century box-pews together with a number of 19th-century pews made out of 17th-century panelling.

Stoups: Two niches in St. Martin's probably originated as holy-water stoups.

Tables of Creed and Decalogue: on the panelling at the E. end of St. Lawrence's, were erected in the 18th century.

Textile: A frontal in St. Thomas's, of velvet embroidered in gold and silver thread with seraphim, double-headed eagles and fleurs-de-lis surrounding a representation of the Annunciation, is evidently part of a 15th-century cope (Plate 53). Now framed and protected by glass, it was used in the 18th century to cover the top of the communion table and is shown on Lyons's plan of 1745. It may correspond with an entry in the churchwardens' accounts for 1547–8, when 3s. 4d. was received 'for the overplus of a coope cutt for the highe aulter'.[1] The embroidered monogram D E C with a crosier in the E is enigmatic; possibly the first letter should be read as T for St. Thomas of Canterbury.

SECULAR BUILDINGS

Although the Iron Age hill-fort at Old Sarum was occupied in Roman and Saxon times, nothing now is visible of any building erected there before the 11th century. The Norman castle was plundered for stone in the 16th century and although the plan is known, little but corework survives above the foundations. The inner bailey, at the top of a large moated motte which the Normans raised at the centre of the hill-fort, was enclosed at first by a palisade and later by a flint and stone curtain-wall. The Great Tower is of the 11th century. The ashlar-fronted Courtyard House (Plate 27) in the N.W. quadrant of the inner bailey was built early in the 12th century by Bishop Roger, probably replacing 'the king's chamber in Salisbury' mentioned in a document of *c.* 1070. The house is closely comparable with Sherborne Old Castle,[2] another of Bishop Roger's works, but whereas at Sherborne the moated bailey, curtain, gates, keep and house appear to have been planned integrally, at Salisbury the house was built to to give comfort and elegance in what had originally been a military structure. The Sherborne keep may have been modelled on that of Salisbury; it has the same two-cell plan and the same substantial garderobe turret with a cess pit in the lower part. As at Salisbury, the Sherborne keep was only to be entered by means of a stone stairway enclosed within the house. The two houses have much in common. The central feature of each is a square court with a peripheral walk sheltered by roofs, from which the surrounding ranges were entered. The great hall forms one side of each court. In each house the E. part of another range is occupied by a chapel and its undercroft while the W. part contains the main doorway of the house and its vestibule. Each house has projecting wings with garderobes rising over strongly built cesspits. One difference between the two houses results from a difference in terrain. Sherborne stands on level ground and has undercrofts below all four ranges; at Salisbury the made-up ground on the reverse of the bailey defences provides a platform for the N. and W. ranges so that undercrofts only occur in the S. and E. ranges.

A 12th-century building in the N.W. quarter of the outer bailey of Old Sarum was undoubtedly the Bishop's Palace. The foundations, which alone remain, indicate an aisled hall on the E. side of a courtyard enclosed on the other sides by narrower ranges. The foundations of other domestic buildings of undetermined plan, but probably dating from the 12th century, were found W. of the 11th-century cathedral.

1. Swayne, *Accounts*, 275.
2. R.C.H.M., *Dorset* I, 64–6.

Early in the 13th century an additional hall was built in the inner bailey at Old Sarum. It stood near the curtain wall and had a wide porch at the N.W. end, but it was poorly built and little remains; it was in need of repair by the middle of the century. A bakehouse in another part of the bailey is probably contemporary. In the new city, after 1220, a number of secular works were undertaken as well as the church buildings already mentioned. Of St. Nicholas's Hospital (26), started by Bishop Bingham in 1231, much remains, albeit masked by 19th-century restorations. The arches of Ayleswade Bridge (17), built in 1244, are intact behind 18th-century face-work. Part of De Vaux College, founded by Bishop Bridport in 1261, stands a few yards N.W. of the bridge, but its remains are concealed by a 19th-century house (328). The stout flint wall which forms the W. end of St. Martin's church is another building possibly secular in origin; it contains a 13th-century doorway with a two-centred head.

Although few surviving dwellings in Salisbury can be positively dated before the 14th century, the building of the new town must have started early in the 13th century, if not before. A house (95) in Crane Street, mainly timber framed, contains a stone wall on which is part of a painted vine-scroll frieze (Plate 43), attributable to the 13th century and closely paralleled in the Cathedral. Stout flint and ashlar walls marking the boundaries between tenements could be of 13th-century origin; examples occur in monuments (132), (173) and (177). A stone building, destroyed in the 19th century, which formerly stood at the S.W. corner of the George Inn yard (173) would appear to have been of 13th-century origin; it was drawn by Peter Hall and measured by Sir Henry Dryden, both of whom show a typical 13th-century doorway with chamfered and shouldered jambs and a flat lintel.[1]

Eighteen houses in Salisbury can be dated with some confidence to the 14th century; three others described in the Inventory have been pulled down since being investigated by the Commission. Of those that remain, No. 9 Queen Street (129) was almost certainly built in or soon after 1306; remarkably well-preserved, it is the oldest datable timber-framed building in the city. The upper part of the early 14th-century hall has recently been made into the show-room of a shop. The moulded and enriched roof truss, in the form of a large cusped arch, is especially notable (Plate 82).

The Bolehall (140), a house first mentioned in a deed of 1319, has been divided into several parts and its walls (if they exist) are hidden by 17th-century and 18th-century brickwork, but significant parts of the original roof with crown-post and smoke louvre remain *in situ*. The former Plume of Feathers Inn (132) included a timber-framed building datable to the 14th century by the style of its ornament; it probably is identifiable with a house on the site owned in 1340 by Robert de Woodford. Nos. 52–4 High Street (82), mentioned in a lease of 1341 as 'a corner tenement with shops', is a conspicuous timber-framed building (Plate 60) with interesting scissor-truss roofs. A few yards W. of the last named are the remains of a 14th-century house, known in the 15th century as Le Crane (102); it retains two and a half bays of a 14th-century crown-post roof with coupled rafters. Another well-preserved timber-framed building of the first half of the 14th century is the S. range of the Red Lion Hotel (219), formerly the White Bear. With a long room with elaborately moulded timbers in the lower storey and with three large chambers above, it appears to have been designed from the beginning to accommodate travellers. The George (173), also built as an inn, has suffered much destruction, but the upper storeys of the surviving W. range retain something of their original form, including a chamber with a richly carved false hammer-beam roof (Plate 84). Balle's Place (351), a large house contemporary with the George and retaining substantial parts of a three-bay hall roof with hammer-beam queen-post trusses, was demolished in 1962. Other noteworthy 14th-century buildings include one range of the Wheatsheaf Inn (71), a house in New Canal (177), the Queen's Arms Inn (225), part of Windover House (302), No. 11 St. Ann's Street (305), and the Rose and Crown Hotel at Harnham (576).

Most 14th-century houses to survive outside the Close are timber-framed. Party-walls of stone and flint remain in a few instances up to the level of the first floor, and in Le Crane (102) it is

1. Hall, *Memorials*, vignette following plate xv. Dryden collection, Northampton Public Library.

possible that original stonework rises to a higher level, masked by modern facings, but only at No. 47 New Street (106) does an original facade of flint and rubble with ashlar quoins stand exposed to its full height of two storeys and an attic.

About sixty 15th-century monuments are recorded in the Inventory. The majority are of timber-frame construction, but the list includes seven buildings where stone predominates. Poultry Cross (15), an arcaded market shelter, hexagonal in plan, is the most conspicuous (Plate 57). Two large houses have ashlar-fronted great halls: Church House (97) and the Hall of John Hall (185); the latter retains interesting 15th-century heraldic glass and a highly enriched timber roof (Plate 83). Another 15th-century stone-fronted house, the so-called Barracks (258), was demolished during the second half of the 19th century. Late mediaeval masonry in a house (327) near the site of De Vaux College probably represents the college precinct wall and perhaps a fragment of a gate house. Milford Bridge (19) includes late mediaeval masonry. Picturesque chequered flint and ashlar is seen at Harnham Mill (588) (Plate 58).

Good quality moulded and enriched 15th-century timber framework is seen in Nos. 3 and 5 Minster Street (55) and in the Wheatsheaf Inn (71). Nos. 48–52 Silver Street (63) were built in 1471 and appear to be well preserved, but most of the framework is hidden by modern tile-hanging; a richly cusped cinquefoil-headed wooden window is visible. No. 8 Queen Street (128) provides a good example of exposed framework (Plate 63). A range of the former Blue Boar Inn (344) is interesting because an indenture of the carpenter's contract survives; it is dated 1444. No. 88 Milford Street (250), demolished in 1972, may have been part of a larger 15th-century house; it had moulded timbers and two stone fireplaces.

Noteworthy 16th-century buildings in Salisbury are fewer than those of the 15th century. The earliest surviving parts of St. Edmund's College (14), of rendered rubble with stone dressings, appear to be a rebuilding of the collegiate dwelling-house following the Dissolution. The W. range of Church House (98) dates from about the same period, but its original character was obliterated in 1881. In the E. range of Parsonage Farm House (549), Stratford-sub-Castle, which probably is of the mid 16th century, the stone-walled lower storey retains a doorway with a four-centred head, but other features are hidden by 19th-century alterations; the upper storey is probably basically of timber framework. Late in the 16th century No. 91 Crane Street (102) was partly rebuilt and given a new street front, of stone in the lower storey and of jettied timber framework above. The Tailors' Hall (165), a building with a timber-framed upper storey and with its ground-floor walls at least partly of brick and flint, was built in 1534; after years of neglect in recent times the last fragment was finally demolished in 1971. No. 66 St. Ann's Street, mainly of close-studded timber framework, has a Wealden-type upper storey with a central recess, subsequently filled in. A very handsome three-storeyed house at No. 15 Oatmeal Row (44) was originally free-standing and had jetties on all four sides, with moulded timbers; most of the framework is hidden by tile-hanging. At Old Parsonage Farm (581), Harnham, the W. elevation and probably the two western bays of the house are of close-studded timber framework in both storeys. To E., a timber-frame extension dates from c. 1600. Mawarden Court (557), a handsome stone building of c. 1600, originally had a half-H plan, but one wing was demolished c. 1835.

The arches of Crane Bridge (18), faced with ashlar in sandstone from the Upper Greensand, received their present form early in the 17th century although the vaults have since been lengthened for the widening of the roadway. The stone stair tower at Church House (97) was certainly built by 1630 and may well be earlier. George Herbert's house (528) at Bemerton, also c. 1630, is of flint and stone. A stone extension to Mawarden Court (557) in sophistcated classical style is probably of 1673. Timber framework on a large scale occurs only at No. 41 Milford Street (155), in the King's Arms Hotel (252) and, appropriately, in the Joiners' Hall (293); all these are of the first quarter of the 17th century and are the latest major examples to survive. Brickwork as a facing material makes an early appearance in Cradock House (304), c. 1619, and in the adjacent and nearly contemporary house (264) misnamed the 'Priory'. Later 17th-century town houses with brick facades, often embellished with stone dressings, include No. 6 St. Ann's Street (307), No. 29 Cheesemarket (36), No. 47 Winchester Street (359) and Barnard's Cross House (273). In its time No. 29 Cheesemarket was one of the best houses in the town; it appears to date from soon after the Restoration and was built as the residence of one of Salisbury's leading citizens, Samuel Eyre, but it has suffered greatly from neglect and alteration, and the full meaning of the interesting double-pile plan is lost. The handsomeness of the staircase with its twisted balusters (advanced work in comparison with contemporary local joinery and perhaps imported) suggests that the main rooms were on the first floor. No. 47 Winchester Street, on the other hand, is old-fashioned for its period. Although built after 1671 it still has hollow-chamfered stone window-surrounds, roll-moulded and weathered stone copings and an oak staircase with a roll handrail, chamfered newel posts and moulded rectangular finials.

Trinity Hospital (27) provides a good example of Salisbury building at the beginning of the 18th century, with symmetrical but unpretentious brick elevations enhanced with stone dressings and with a pleasant colonnaded loggia and courtyard. Other 18th-century institutional buildings include the workhouse of 1728, now part of Church House (97), Frowd's Almshouses (33) of 1750 and the General Infirmary (22), designed by the younger John Wood of Bath in 1767.

In the 18th century many of the more important inhabitants of Salisbury lived in the Close, but two houses in the city stand apart from the others by reason of their size and richness. The College (14), basically a late 16th-century building, belonged throughout the 18th and for most of the 19th century to the Wyndhams. The house was on the edge of the town and, with a large park-like garden extending to N. and E., had something of the character of a country mansion. About the middle of the 18th century the S. front was rebuilt by an unknown architect working in the manner of James Gibbs, and in 1790 the E. front was built and the interior was remodelled by S.P. Cockerell. The other pre-eminent house, The Hall (199), was built soon after the middle of the 18th century for Alderman William Hussey, mayor in 1758, who represented Salisbury in Parliament from 1774 until his death in 1813. The Hall, on the N. side of New Street, replaced earlier buildings and, unlike The College, was clearly designed as a town house. The architect's name is not known.

Interesting 18th-century town houses in Salisbury include a mirror-image pair (354), built c. 1716 and evidently meant for quite well-to-do families; they provide an early example of a plan-form which was destined to become exceedingly popular. Of 18th and 19th-century family houses with regular sash-windowed facades, classical doorcases and panelled drawing rooms, Salisbury probably has as many examples as any comparable southern English town. After c. 1700 the larger houses were often planned with the principal parlour or drawing room on the first floor, probably in imitation of the fashion then current in London and Bath.

S.C.

CLASSIFICATION OF HOUSE-PLANS

The Commission's use of letters to identify certain plan-types frequently found in small houses, thus enabling the description of such buildings to be shortened, was found of value in the Dorset inventories[1] and has been continued in the present volume although the system is noticeably more useful in the surrounding villages than in the city. The following types occur in the Salisbury area.

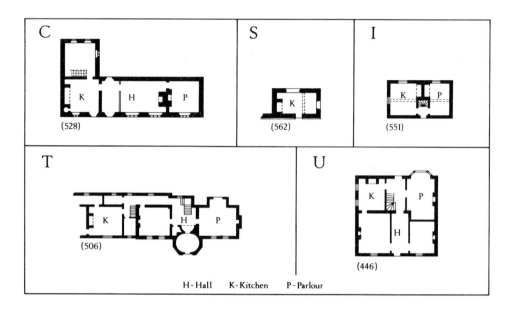

H - Hall   K - Kitchen   P - Parlour

Class C. The traditional mediaeval plan, comprising three rooms (kitchen—hall—parlour) in a row.[2] No mediaeval example occurs in the volume, but the type persisted and Bemerton Rectory (528) supplies a 17th-century example.

Class I. Two ground-floor rooms with a central chimneystack against which there is a lobby entrance and often a stair. The example shown is at Stratford-sub-Castle and dates from early in the 17th century.

Class S. The simplest plan, usually found in very humble dwellings, comprises a single heated living room or kitchen, with the end opposite the fireplace partitioned off to make a store and sometimes accomodating a stair to the upper storey. The example illustrated, a 16th-century cottage (562) at Old Sarum, is now the nucleus of a larger building.

Class T. A range containing a central hall or vestibule with a parlour on one side, a dining room on the other, fireplaces against the end walls, stairs at the back of the hall, and kitchen etc. in a wing behind or an extension beyond the dining room. The plan was commonly used in 18th and 19th-century houses, both in town and in the country. Crane Lodge (506) provides an example.

Class U. Description as for class T, but with two ranges in double pile, giving a square plan with four main compartments as well as the vestibule and staircase. No. 206 Castle Street (446) is of the early 19th century.

1.   R.C.H.M., *Dorset* II, lxi—lxiv.

2.   R.C.H.M., *Cambridgeshire* II, xlii, *E.V.H., chap. 1, passim*

AN INVENTORY OF
THE ANCIENT AND HISTORICAL MONUMENTS
IN THE CITY OF SALISBURY

Vol. 1 of the Inventory covers the area of the former Municipal Borough, exclusive of the Cathedral Close and its walls and gates. It includes all monuments and constructions from the Norman Conquest to 1850. Earlier remains other than Old Sarum (included herein) are reserved for treatment elsewhere.

The present work is divided as follows: *a*. Old Sarum Castle and Cathedral; *b*. Other Ecclesiastical Monuments; *c*. Other Secular Monuments. Under *c*, public buildings are treated first, then lesser secular monuments. The latter comprise the bulk of the Inventory and for convenience are arranged in groups based on municipal divisions as they existed in 1974, the year when compilation began.

Maps are provided for the easy identification of individual monuments. Monuments near the centre of the city are shown on maps at a scale of approximately 1:1600 set as close as possible to the relevant entries; they are based on O.S., 1:500 (1880). A general street plan in the end-pocket also gives the position of many major monuments. Monuments in Fisherton are shown on a copy of part of the Tithe Map of 1843. All other monuments appear on an overlay to the 1:10,000 O.S. which will be found in the end-pocket.

In architectural descriptions of churches, the parts of the building are taken in the order E. to W. and N. to S.; in descriptions of houses the exterior precedes the interior. Architectural plans have a uniform scale of 24 ft. to the inch (except for some key-plans at approximately half that scale). Hatching symbols to indicate dating are uniform throughout the volume. Construction since 1850 is termed 'modern'. The date given in the description of a funerary monument is that of the death of the person first commemorated; if known, the date of erection of the monument is added; surnames in round brackets are maiden names.

OLD SARUM

(1) **Old Sarum**, an Iron Age hill-fort, the defences of which were adapted to form a mediaeval castle, stands in a prominent hilltop position 1½ miles N.N.E. of the city (Plate 24 and map in end-pocket). The site lies between 250 ft. and 300 ft. above O.D. at the N.W. end of Bishopsdown Hill, a westward facing spur overlooking the valley of the R. Avon. The ground slopes steeply to W. and S., and less steeply to N.; eastwards, it dips slightly to the narrowest part of the spur, immediately outside the E. entrance, and then rises to the main ridge. The monument, largely under grass, is in the guardianship of the Department of the Environment. The earthworks are well-preserved, though damaged in places by quarrying. The main E. entrance is disturbed by tracks and partly overlain by a farmyard. Although the mediaeval masonry has been extensively robbed, leaving little but foundations and core-work, in places the lower courses of the ashlar facing survive.

The earliest occupation of the hill-fort is associated with pottery of Iron Age 'A' type. The slender evidence available is not enough to show that the site was continuously occupied, but there was occupation shortly before the Roman conquest and this continued until at least *c*. a.d. 300.[1] The hill-fort gave its name to the Roman settlement of *Sorviodunum*, twice mentioned

in the Antonine Itineraries.[2] It is an important junction of Roman roads and it is probable that there was a Roman fort near by in the early years of the conquest. Mediaeval make-up of the interior has caused earlier levels to be buried under a considerable but varying depth of chalk and soil and there has been no systematic exploration of Roman and earlier levels. The meagre evidence available from these periods comes from finds dispersed over a large part of the site.

The Anglo-Saxon Chronicle records under the year 552 a battle at *Searobyrg* between the Saxons and the Britons, in which the Britons were put to flight.[3] The pagan Saxon cemeteries at Harnham Hill and Petersfinger are evidence of Saxon settlement in the area in the 6th century. Later, the main Saxon settlement in the area was Wilton, which gave its name to the shire and is listed in the Burghal Hidage of the early 10th century.[4] In 1003 the chronicle records a Danish attack on Wilton in which the borough was ravaged and burnt; the record continues 'and he [Swein, king of Denmark] betook him then to Salisbury and from there went back to the sea'.[5] Numismatic evidence proves that moneyers, who had previously been striking at Wilton, at this date began coining at Salisbury which by implication became a borough.[6] It would be natural to look for the borough within the hill-fort, as at Cadbury, Somerset, which became a borough a few years later in consequence of the insecurity of Ilchester and other Somerset mints.[7] Pre-conquest finds are scarce at Old Sarum owing to the lack of systematic exploration of the earlier levels, but it is possible that layers of flint and mortar, found in 1957 at a comparatively low level on the N.E. side,[8] represent the destruction of a wall contemporary with those of Cadbury and Cricklade.[9]

The castle of Salisbury was founded by William I, probably soon after the conquest. A confirmation of land to the monks of St. Florent of Saumur, ascribed to 1069 or 1070, was granted 'in the king's chamber in the castle called Salisbury'.[10] The earliest castle was of motte-and-bailey type. The motte, a massive mound embanked and ditched, was placed in the centre of the

hill-fort, on the highest point of the spur. Banks and ditches running S. and N.E. from the mound define the W. side of the bailey, which covered the E. part of the Iron Age enclosure. The cathedral and its close stood outside the bailey in the N.W. quadrant of the former hill-fort.

The banks of the bailey, and doubtless those surrounding the motte, were palisaded; internal buildings, including the king's chamber, were almost certainly of wood. Apart from the Cathedral (2), consecrated in 1092, the earliest reference to a building which can still be identified occurs in the Pipe Roll of 1130 (31 Hen. I), when it is recorded that the sheriff spent 20s. 'making a doorway to the cellar of the tower'.[11] The Great Tower and the Courtyard House, the latter used in the 14th century to accommodate the sheriff, date respectively

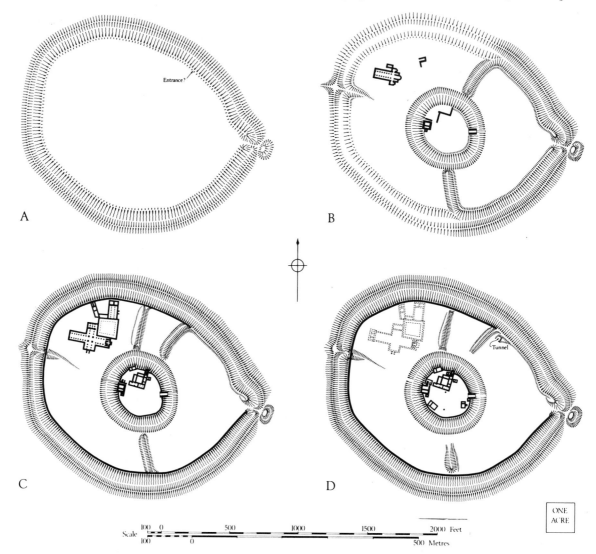

OLD SARUM. A. Iron Age hill-fort. B. Norman castle with early cathedral. C. Castle with outer curtain and later cathedral, c.1140. D. Later mediaeval.

from the late 11th century and the early 12th century.

William of Malmesbury, writing about 1140, states that Bishop Roger of Salisbury had asked for and obtained from King Henry I the custody of the castle, which was surrounded by a wall.[12] This most probably refers to the stone curtain which follows the inner rampart of the hill-fort and includes within its circuit the cathedral and its close. Owing to the fall and death of Roger in 1139 it was never completed.[13] The wall is associated with a massive levelling-up of rammed chalk, providing a flatter surface possibly to facilitate the construction of buildings along the perimeter. In 1153 a writ by King Stephen was addressed to Patrick, Earl of Salisbury, as Sheriff of Wiltshire, ordering the demolition of part of the monastery and church adjoining the castle, and of the castle itself,[14] but the order seems to have been disregarded.

Substantial expenditure was incurred on the castle and the 'king's houses' during the reign of Henry II, particularly between 1170 and 1179.[15] A sum of £24 was spent on the bridge and the castle in 1170–1; £17 was spent on the walls in 1172–3; £47 was spent on the houses, the wall and the gates in 1173–4. Expenditure during this decade totalled more than £250; it included work on the houses and probably also the stone curtain surrounding the inner bailey. In 1181–2 there is a record of work being carried out on the treasury in the Great Tower.[16] In the last years of Henry's reign over £80 was spent on the castle, including a small sum on the chamber over the gate, the first time this apartment is mentioned.[17]

Major expenditure is again recorded between 1201 and 1208,[18] when the total amounted to more than £150; the greater part of this sum was allocated to the repair of the castle, including the bridge and the ditches. The new hall, a 13th-century building needing repair in 1247, was among the works carried out at this time.

The building of the outer curtain brought the cathedral and its close within the perimeter of the castle. As a result there was friction between the king's officers and the ecclesiastical authorities. Matters came to a head at the end of John's reign, probably as a result of security measures put into force during the final struggle. After some years of negotiation the seat of the bishopric was moved to Salisbury in 1219.[19] Part of the cathedral at old Sarum was retained in use as the Chapel of St. Mary, but when the bishop and canons left for the new site their dwellings at Old Sarum passed into the king's hands. At first they were maintained and as late as 1236 the sheriff was instructed to cause the dwellings to be repaired.[20] A year later the order was given that the hall and other buildings within the bailey of the castle, that had belonged to the bishopric of Salisbury, should be taken down without delay and the timber and stone carried to the castle. An exception was made for the chapel, which belonged to the bishop.[21]

The early 13th-century hall was the last important building to be erected. Subsequent records, concerned with repairs, illustrate the use and survival of the buildings. An order of 1246 lists 'the great tower in the king's castle of Salisbury, the tower above the kitchen, the tower of Herlewin,[22] the tower above the great gate, the great gate itself, the great hall of the same castle, the chamber above the wardrobe and the tower above the postern and the bridge of the same postern'; in all these, repairs were to be undertaken as needed. It was further ordered that the cloister or passage between the hall and the great chamber should be rebuilt.[23] In 1247 instructions were given for the repair, among other things, of the king's two kitchens, the new hall and the king's gaol in the outer bailey.[24]

The castle contained a number of chapels. The order of 1246 states that a lamp must be kept burning day and night in the chapel of St. Nicholas. At the same time the sheriff was ordered to find chaplains to officiate in the chapels of St. Margaret and St. Mary, both within the castle, the latter 'where the seat of the bishopric used to be'.[25] A chaplain was also to be found for the chapel of St. Mary Magdalen in the tower.[26] The chapel of St. Cross, above or beyond (*ultra*) the great gate of the castle, was in a dangerous condition in 1246 and the king ordered it to be pulled down and rebuilt.[27]

No attempt was made to modernise the castle to meet the changed needs of the 13th century. It can hardly have been of much military importance after the Barons' Wars in the third quarter of the century, but it continued to serve as the centre of administration for the shire. Many of the buildings were kept in repair throughout the 14th century, though others fell down and were not rebuilt. A hall (probably the New Hall), chamber, kitchen and bakehouse 'fell' in 1307–8, though the walls were still standing in 1330.[28] A survey in 1315 estimated the cost of repairs as follows: to the roof of the great hall which had been damaged by the failure of the lead gutters of the adjoining kitchen and bakery, £50; to the great tower, £600 (*DC libris*); to the chamber near Herlewin's tower and the chapel of St. Nicholas which had been damaged by storm, £20; to the tower above (*ultra*) the gate with the latrine, £20.[29]

Accounts for extensive repairs to the towers and walls of Old Sarum date from 1337–8, when a certain amount was also spent on the houses.[30] In 1366 a detailed indenture was drawn up concerning the repair and improvement of what may be called the Courtyard House and other buildings;[31] it names many of the rooms and enables us to identify the 'hall, chamber and chapel in which the sheriff and his officers dwell', as recorded in a document of 1330.[32]

These seem to have been the last comprehensive attempts to put the castle in order. In 1447 it was granted to Sir John Stourton, Treasurer of the Household,[33] but the grant does not seem to have been effective. Thomas Compton, Groom of the Chamber, received in 1514 'the stone walls and stone called the castle or tower of Old Sarum', with liberty to knock them down and carry away materials.[34] Old Sarum remained a Parliamentary Borough and returned two members to the House of Commons until the Reform Act of 1832.

St. Osmund's charter of 1091 includes among the properties granted to the canons of Salisbury 'land in front of the gate of the castle, on either side of the road, for the needs of the houses and gardens of the canons'.[35] In 1935 and 1958 traces of roads, buildings, cesspits and a cemetery comprising at least twenty-four orientated burials were found about 150 yds. E. of the great gate of the castle;[36] some of the associated pottery dates from as early as c. 1100. This is part of the 'fair suburbe' which Leland records outside the E. gate; there had been a parish church of St. John, of which a chapel was still standing in Leland's day. He also records a suburb outside the W. gate.[37]

Antiquarian interest in Old Sarum began late in the 18th century when severe frost brought about the collapse of the mouth of a tunnel on the N.E. side of the bailey, and its subsequent exploration.[38] Dry weather in 1834 revealed the plan of the cathedral in the N.W. quadrant and led to a superficial exploration of the site.[39] Serious research began in the present century when extensive excavations were carried out by the Society of Antiquaries, between 1909 and 1915, under the direction of Sir William St. John Hope, Lt.–Col. William Hawley and Mr. D.H. Montgomerie. Interim reports were published each year,[40] but no final report appeared. Hawley's MS. daybooks, preserved in Salisbury and South Wiltshire Museum, record the provenance of many architectural finds as well as other details. Montgomerie elaborated certain points, principally in connection with the earthworks, in a short article published in 1947.[41]

In the course of the excavations it was found necessary to carry out repairs for the preservation of the newly exposed walls. The irregular tops of the walls were brought to a common level by flint rubble laid in mortar. No attempt was made to restore the ashlar; when a facing was re-formed coursed flint was used (extensive use of this material is seen on the E. and S. surfaces of the great tower). 'Whenever it was necessary, as occasionally, to insert a worked stone, care was taken to cut upon it the year of our Lord, wherein it was laid'. At some more recent period a few of the fallen facing stones of the ashlar have been replaced without any such date, presumably on the walls beneath which they were found.

The site was laid out by the Office of Works after the first World War and certain explorations were carried out by that Department, both at the time and subsequently. The only systematic excavations undertaken in recent years were directed to specific problems.[42]

The Earthworks. The hill-fort, roughly oval (1,400 ft. by 1,100 ft. internally), is defined by twin banks with a medial ditch enclosing an area of 29½ acres (Plate 26). The banks are massive, but their size is due partly to the scarping of natural slopes. The inner bank varies in height above the interior from less than 3 ft. in places, notably on the S.W. side, to 10 ft. elsewhere. It rises as much as 45 ft. above the present ditch bottom and has an external slope of 38°. The outer bank reaches 27 ft. above the bottom of the ditch and a similar height above the external ground level. Over all, the defences measure some 200 ft. in width.

There are two entrances. The eastern, at the pointed end of the oval, is a gap in the rampart about 15 ft. wide approached by a causeway of similar width. Direct access from the E. is blocked by an outwork, a flat-topped mound (60 ft. by 50 ft. and 6 ft. high) flanked by a ditch on the N., E. and S., almost certainly a secondary feature. The ditch was re-formed in 1173–4 (see note 15). The modern access, following the mediaeval and probably the prehistoric line, skirts the main fosse to the S. of the gate and turns abruptly across it on a causeway which replaces a mediaeval bridge. The W. entrance appears to be mediaeval in origin. It consists of a gap through the inner bank in the form of a hollow-way, 10 ft. wide and up to 12 ft. deep, which falls steadily from the level of the interior. The track is carried across the ditch on a narrow causeway, only 4 ft. wide, which leads to a level platform on the line of the outer rampart. Further W. the outer ditch blocks egress from the castle.

In spite of levelling-up in the middle ages and modern deposits of spoil in places, the interior of the hill-fort, dominated by the mound of the mediaeval castle, remains slightly domed. The castle mound is oval (370 ft. by 320 ft.) and the top (2 acres) is surrounded by a substantial bank which is surmounted by a stone wall, now robbed to the footings; this gives a hollow or dished appearance to the summit of the mound. At the centre, the surface lies some eight feet above the original ground level. The mound is surrounded by a great ditch, about 20 ft. deep and 75 ft. across, spanned on the E. by a modern bridge which follows the line of the mediaeval entrance. On the W., in front of the postern gate, disturbances on the outer face and at the bottom of the ditch indicate the line of another bridge. A ramp leading down to the bottom of the ditch on the S. side is probably modern.

A number of features are visible in the zone between the inner rampart of the hill-fort and the castle ditch:

On the S. side of the castle mound a radial bank up to 5 ft. high and 25 ft. wide extends two-thirds of the way from the inner rampart of the hill-fort to the central ditch. There are traces of a ditch on the W., but a large quarry of uncertain origin has destroyed much of the evidence. This bank has not been tested by excavation.

A radial bank in the N.E. quadrant extends S.W. from the inner rampart of the hill-fort, diminishing in height and fading away some distance short of the castle ditch. It starts opposite the E. end of the stone curtain which was added to the outer defences in the second quarter of the 12th century, under Bishop Roger (p. 3), and it consists of a scarp surmounted by a bank, the whole measuring some 50 ft. across over all. The bank stands 6 ft. above ground level on the N.W. where there remains a slight hollow, possibly representing an original ditch; on the S.E. the difference in level rises to 16 ft., the ground being locally lower on account of a depression which leads to a tunnel passing under the rampart of the hill-fort (p. 12). A trial trench cut in the bank in 1957 disclosed no trace of masonry.

Due N. of the castle a third radial bank extends from the inner rampart of the hill-fort almost to the edge of the ditch surrounding the central mound. It is from 20 ft. to 27 ft. across and it stands up to 9 ft. high. Traces of a ditch about 40 ft. wide occur on the W. side. This bank has not been tested by excavation.

About half-way between the inner rampart of the hill-fort and the ditch of the castle, slight variations of level in the N.E., S.E. and S.W. quadrants suggest an outward-facing circular scarp, possibly the remains of an enclosure earlier than the Iron Age hill-fort. The feature has not been tested by excavation and is not shown on the plans.

No complete section of the rampart of the hill-fort has been cut. The outer bank is shown on the published cross-section[43] as consisting of chalk piled on the natural slope of the hill. The evidence, based on a small trench cut into the outer slope, does not preclude a complex structure of more than one date.

In 1914 the inner rampart was examined N. of the cathedral,[44] showing a sequence of three banks, the two earlier of which were not dated. On the original ground surface, at the forward edge of the visible earthwork, stood a small bank about 4 ft. high and remaining to a width of 16 ft. This bank was sealed by a turf-line over which further material had been piled to enlarge the bank to a maximum height of 14 ft. and to a width of at least 40 ft.; a second turf-line sealed the added material. The final stage was marked by the truncation of the outer face of the two-period bank, by the building of a curtain wall (11 ft. thick at its base) behind the bank, and by the in-filling of the space between the earlier earthwork and the curtain wall with chalk and other materials which added about 19 ft. to the height of the former bank. The loose character of the fill and the fact that the wall-face was left rough leave no doubt that curtain and in-filling are contemporary; they probably date from c. 1135.

Trenches cut in 1957 were designed to test the continuity of the added curtain on the E. side of the hill-fort and to locate the tunnel recorded in 1795. Information bearing on the sequence of earthworks was incidental to the main purposes of the excavation.

In the S.E. quadrant of the defences the curtain was found. It was associated with an internal make-up of rammed chalk which extended as a thin layer under the curtain, showing that the latter was probably contemporary with or later than the make-up;[45] this was excavated to a depth of only 2 ft., but a similar make-up reaching in places to a depth of 14 ft. had been noted in 1914 in the N.W. quadrant. Outside the curtain, the top of the bank of piled chalk was noted in the cross-section; about 4 ft. from the hypothetical face of the curtain, which was not located, the inner face of this bank was cut to a steep angle. The interspace seems to have been filled with chalk debris through which a robber hole had been cut; the hole contained a loose filling. It may be noted that the chalk bank, which was not directly dated, was very different both in material and in scale from the earlier two-phase rampart found in the N.W. quadrant; in scale it resembled the finished 12th-century rampart in that quadrant.

Trenches cut in 1957 in the N.E. quadrant established that neither the internal make-up of rammed chalk nor the curtain wall of stone exists in the sector between the N.E. radial bank and the E. gate; they also showed that the curtain comes to an abrupt end at the point where the N.E. radial bank joins the main rampart.[46] The interpretation of the earlier sequence is difficult, as the cross-sections were not carried down to natural chalk, but the excavators concluded that the main bank, near the centre of the quadrant, was of 'at least three periods, Iron Age, Belgic–Roman and Mediaeval'.[47] The earliest stage of the hill-fort was associated with pottery of Iron Age 'A' type including a very good haematite-coated rim and some coarser black sherds which are identical with sherds from 'a large A2 group found one mile to the E. on Bishopsdown'. This pottery was found lying immediately above the natural chalk, in a gap in the rampart which was interpreted as an original entrance. The 'Belgic–Roman' occupation in this part of the site ran from the 1st century a.d., starting rather before the Roman conquest, to the 3rd century; there was a notable absence of 4th-century material. The mediaeval addition, with a large proportion of chalk in its make-up, was on a massive scale; one large palisade post-hole was recorded on the drawn section.[48] At two places layers of flint and morter, the debris of some mortared structure, were found at a low level; they were post-Roman but are not to be associated with the curtain.[49]

A tentative reconstruction of the development of the earthworks may be based on these records (plans, p. 2). The first Iron Age hill-fort was a simple enclosure with defences on a modest scale, and possibly with an entrance on the N.E. where the approach to the spur becomes easier. It was probably univallate and, like its successor, enclosed an area of 29½ acres. Subsequently the defences were refashioned on a more massive scale and made bivallate, with the main rampart following the former line. The 'original gate' on the N.E. (if correctly interpreted) was blocked and a new gate was formed on the E. side of the hill-fort, on the crest of the spur. The basic form of the present E. gate, with an outwork blocking direct access, probably dates from this period.

Early mediaeval destruction layers, including mortar, found in the N.E. quadrant, hint at the possibility that the borough which came into being c. 1003 was defended by an earthen bank faced by a mortared wall, as at Cadbury (c. 1010).

The embanked and ditched central enclosure comprises the castle motte thrown up by William I; the N.E. quadrant, where the outer curtain was never built, indicates the original scale of the defences of the bailey. The very much smaller and earlier bank in the N.W. quadrant, which was not modified until the 12th century, shows that the Norman castle did not at first include the whole area of the hill-fort. The bailey occupied the E. sector only, being defined on the W. by the radial banks to S. and N.E. of the motte, and on the other sides by the enlarged rampart of the E. part of the prehistoric circuit. The 11th-century defences were completed by timber palisades on top of the banks. The motte would thus have stood in a normal position on the perimeter of the castle and would not have been entirely surrounded by its bailey, as at present.

When Bishop Roger obtained custody of the castle, c. 1130, he initiated the building of a stone curtain to enclose the whole area of the hill-fort, including the W. half where the cathedral stood. In the E. half the foundations of the curtain wall were cut into the bank of the 11th-century bailey, but in the W. sector the curtain was built along the inner margin of the prehistoric rampart, the space between that rampart and the added curtain being filled to form a bank comparable in scale with that of the bailey. At the same time the area within the curtain was levelled-up with a filling of rammed chalk, in places as much as 14 ft. thick. The work was left unfinished when Bishop Roger fell from power in 1139.

Architectural Description.[50] The *Castle Mound*, the motte of the 11th-century castle, has a stone curtain surmounting the older earth bank (Plate 25). The main gate is on the E., opposite the entrance to the bailey; there is a postern on the W. side. The enclosure within the curtain contains a number of buildings, now reduced to low walls, but still retaining in places the ashlar facing of the flint rubble core. The Great Tower stands on the W. side of the inner bailey, immediately S. of the postern. To the N., enclosing the entry to the great tower, is the 'tower above the postern'. Herlewin's Tower and the Kitchen Tower stand across the N. sector of the bank; both towers are older than the curtain, which butts against them. Immediately within the bank on the N. side is the Courtyard House (Plate 27), a building of four ranges enclosing a paved court, with a forebuilding forming a W. extension of the S. range and with an E. range which continues N. to the Kitchen Tower. The New Hall and the Bakehouse are the only recognisable stone buildings in the S. part of the inner bailey, but the ground inside the curtain is terraced in places, apparently for wooden buildings. There is a well near the centre of the mound, S. of the courtyard house; another, unfinished, was found further S. Fugitive traces of other buildings, mostly late, were found in the course of the excavations.

The original defences of the castle mound were mainly of earth and timber, but it is likely that the Great Tower (and perhaps also the East Gateway) was of stone from the beginning. The Pipe Rolls (note 15) suggest that the timber palisade was replaced by a stone curtain in the decade 1170–80.[51]

The *East Gate* was approached by a bridge spanning the ditch of the castle mound. Documentary references to the gate and the bridge, which begin in 1171, are seldom explicit and most of them may equally well refer either to the E. gate of the castle mound or to the E. gate of the bailey. But the order of 1246 to repair the bridge before the great gate, the great gate itself, the tower above the postern and the bridge before the postern[52] can be referred with confidence to the gates of the castle mound. The estimate for £20 for the repair of the gate tower and the latrine in 1315 can likewise be assigned to the E. gate of the castle mound.[53]

The western abutments of the mediaeval bridge with its drawbridge pit can be seen below the modern timber bridge. The masonry shows that the bridge was about 20 ft. wide.

The walls flanking the E. gateway have a core of flint rubble set in hard mortar; they were faced with ashlar rising from a chamfered base, but the facing is mostly gone. The wall-face continues across the whole of the N. side showing that the wall was carried down to secure a good foundation and that the gate tower was in existence before the curtain was built. Walls with clasping buttresses at the inner ends flank the gateway; at the outer ends they project boldly down the slope of the bank. There is no evidence for the rounded outer ends shown on the excavators' plan; more probably they were square. The position of the outer gate is indicated by a draw-bar hole on the S. side, but all dressings have gone. About six feet behind the gate the passage widens to an area 14 ft. by 18 ft., beyond which was an archway 11½ ft. wide. Barrel-vaulted chambers contrived in the thickness of the side walls open out of the gate-passage on each side. Of the superstructure there remains only a large fallen block on the bank to the south. South of the gate, and of one build with it, a latrine turret has a horizontal shelf on the S., marking the level of a floor.

There is no detail which would serve to give a close date to the gate. But the plan — a stone tower above a gate passage which forms the ground stage and is closed with inner and outer gates — is found in conjunction with earth and timber defences in a number of early Norman fortifications. At Exeter the form is foreshadowed in the gate of Rougemont Castle, *c.* 1070; at Ludlow a more developed example dates from the first quarter of the 12th century; the same form is found in the 12th-century city gates of York and Newark.

The *Curtain*, some 8 ft. thick, generally survives only as a foundation or as a rough line of flint rubble, but in places the lowest courses of the ashlar facing remain in position, and occasionally it stands to a greater height;[54] in the S.E. sector a modern kerb indicates the position of the former masonry; on the N., beside the Kitchen Tower, the inside of the curtain is of flint. The outer face has a number of rectangular buttresses irregularly spaced and of varying dimensions. East of Herlewin's Tower the lowest steps of a stair which led up to a wall-walk remain partly recessed in the thickness of the curtain; similar steps occur S. of the E. gate, and E. of the Kitchen Tower there is evidence for a stone stair borne on a half-arch.

Buildings on the W. and N.W. of the inner bailey compose an administrative compound which included, from an early date, a dwelling house of considerable dignity and, at times, a treasury. Within the compound were three separate but linked units; the Great Tower, the Courtyard House and Herlewin's Tower. Attached to the great tower was 'the tower over the postern'. All the main buildings of the compound date from the late 11th or early 12th century.

The *Great Tower* is first mentioned in the Pipe Roll of 1130 (31 Hen. I), where the making of a doorway in the cellar is recorded at a cost of 20s. In 1181–2 the tower is first mentioned as housing a treasury. Repairs are recorded during the 12th and 13th century, the most substantial being the releading of the roof, on which £53 and £60 were spent in 1250–1 and 1269–70 respectively.[55] In 1315 necessary repairs were estimated to cost £600. In 1337–8 work to the value of about £30 was carried out, mainly on the Great Tower.[56]

The tower stands across the W. bank of the castle mound immediately S. of the postern. The walls, 10 ft. thick, are of flint rubble faced with coarsely jointed ashlar, but little remains of the original facings. The E. face has a vertical base, 2 ft. high, above which is a battered plinth of 10 courses (Plate 28). Above the battered plinth no part of the original wall-face remains, but the modern reconstruction in coursed flint seems approximately correct. No doubt the battered plinth was also carried along the W. face, of which nothing survives. The N. face of the tower is carried down vertically to form the S. wall of the gate-hall of the W. postern. Part of the S. face is masked by a later latrine

pit and part has gone. No detail remains on the tower, but a date in the late 11th century is suggested by the simple form of the plinth and by the rough ashlar of the surviving facing.

The interior of the tower is divided into two parts by a wall running E.–W. The only storey now accessible lies about 12 ft. above the level of the inner bailey. The opening at the N.E. corner is roughly broken through and not original, but the rebate of a secondary door-jamb cut in the ashlar wall-face close to the broken aperture appears to be mediaeval; it may well represent the opening upon which twenty shillings was spent in 1130. A few original ashlar facing stones remain, but no other detail. A small latrine pit divided into two parts by an arch running N.–S. originally projected from the S. wall of the tower; part of its ashlar-lined N. and E. sides remains, but the whole of the S. part has gone.

The Great Tower was probably of three storeys, including storage compartments below the rooms now accessible. The top stage has gone, but the surviving masonry shows that there was no original doorway in the N., S. or E. side of either lower storey; hence there must have been an entrance at a higher level. The position of such a doorway in the N. wall is indicated by the surviving lower steps of a broad stone stair on the N. (in the Tower above the Postern); presumably it ascended to a doorway in the upper stage. To judge by the inclination of the remaining steps, the threshold of this doorway would have been some 28 ft. above the inner bailey floor (cross-section in end-pocket). The stair may have replaced an original wooden ladder. If the tower walls were carried up to surround the roof, the total height of the building could have been fifty or sixty feet.

Adjacent to the S. side of the tower is an added latrine turret, divided into two parts by an arch. The battered E. face of the turret is continuous with that of the tower and no joint is visible in the remaining facing work; internally, however, the N. wall of the latrine turret is separated from the S. wall of the tower by a narrow cavity, no longer seen, but noted at the time of excavation.[57] The S. and W. sides of the turret have a multiple chamfered plinth from which rise shallow pilaster buttresses; these have been restored on the S. face on the basis of a single course of original ashlar which remains at the bottom of the W. buttress. The turret dates from the 12th century; if it was approached from the wall-walk of the curtain it may be as late as 1170, though the masonry style of the plinth suggests a rather earlier date.

The *Tower above the Postern* is first mentioned in the Liberate Roll of 1246. It forms the forebuilding of the Great Tower and incorporates the stair which led up to the main entrance of that tower.

The earliest part of the complex is a wall running nearly parallel with and about 8 ft. away from the N.

wall of the Great Tower; it forms the N. side of the postern gate-passage. Draw-bar holes which must have been made while the Great Tower was being built indicate the position of inner and outer gates, one set slightly back from the N.E. angle of the tower, the other in the plane of the curtain. No trace remains of the original means of access to the upper stage of the Great Tower.

The next stage in the evolution of the Tower above the Postern was the erection of a stone stair, rising from the N. and crossing the postern gate-passage to reach an upper stage of the Great Tower. The lower steps remain in position and part of the original ashlar is preserved in the outer face of the W. side: the style of masonry indicates a date in the mid 12th century. The side wall is not parallel with the adjacent curtain, as might be expected had it been contemporary or later.

Finally, probably in the late 12th or early 13th century, the middle part of the postern gate-passage was blocked with rubble faced with reused ashlar. After the insertion of the blocking wall the postern entrance led N. from the W. end of the gate-passage, between the inner side of the curtain and the stair to the upper storey of the Great Tower. A recess hollowed-out under the stair was lined with ashlar to serve as a gate-keeper's lodge (the base of the recess is filled with modern masonry, presumably to prevent the undermining of the stair). When the foot of the stair was reached the passage turned E., between the steps and a wall forming the N. side of the tower. A N. doorway here led into a court on the W. of the courtyard house. Opposite, steps led down, alongside the stair, to a passage which traversed the inner end of the blocking and gave access to the Great Tower through the secondary doorway noted above. At the end of the N. passage a third doorway led to a room on the E. side of the Tower above the Postern; this probably provided a direct link between the Great Tower and the courtyard house. These alterations appear to belong to a single period and may be connected with the work on the treasury in the Great Tower in 1181–2, reflecting the need to provide greater security, and a means of access from the W. bailey for the use of clerks and chamberlains working in the treasury.[58]

The *Courtyard House*,[59] the principal domestic building on the castle mound, dates from the early 12th century. The courtyard plan has been compared with that of Bishop Roger's complex in Sherborne Old Castle, with the implication that the house at Old Sarum was erected by that prelate late in the reign of Henry I, when the castle was in his custody.[60] The style of the roughly jointed ashlar suggests, however, an earlier 12th-century date. Any connection with Bishop Roger must be explained by the fact that he was, for the greater part of the reign, Henry I's principal and most trusted minister; he could therefore be expected to have a dominant voice in any building erected for his royal master in a castle so near his own episcopal palace.

The 12th and early 13th-century accounts record substantial expenditure on the king's house in the castle of Salisbury, but the entries do not allocate the money to particular buildings. The courtyard house figures in 1246, the repairs then ordered (note 23) including work on the tower above the kitchen (at the N. end of the E. range) and on the cloister or pent-roofed passage between the hall and the great chamber. In the same year there are references to the chapels of St. Margaret and St. Nicholas, which can be identified as occupying the S.E. corner of the house, on the lower and upper storeys respectively. That St. Nicholas's was the upper chapel is clear from a document of 1315 (note 29), which states that it, along with the great chamber (i.e. the N. range), had suffered damage from storm. The courtyard house is referred to again in 1330 when it is particularised as 'the hall, chamber and chapel in which the sheriff and his office dwell' (note 32). A detailed indenture of 1366 names the hall (W. range), the great chamber near Herlewin's Tower (N. range), and the chamber between the kitchen and the chapel (E. range).[61]

The house consists of four ranges enclosing a rectangular inner court. The court itself, together with the ranges to W. and N., are at first-floor level compared with the surviving rooms of the S. and E. ranges; these are at the level of the inner bailey.

The forebuilding at the W. end of the S. range of the Courtyard House is separated from the Tower above the Postern by a space, 12 ft. wide, which now provides a route from the W. part of the inner bailey to the raised area W. of the house. A substantial foundation at the lower (S.) end of the space links the S. wall of the fore-building with the tower. It can be inferred that in the 12th century the space contained steps or, less probably, a ramp rising from the lower to the upper level. The entry was probably closed by a gate and perhaps was spanned by a room or bridge linking the two buildings. The E. range is prolonged N. to end in a massive tower, the Kitchen Tower, which stands across the castle bank and projects beyond the curtain wall.

The N. wall of the court and the N. end of the hall are built on an older foundation, 7½ ft. thick, which extends beyond the N.W. corner of the hall and appears to have been at least 76 ft. and perhaps as much as 90 ft. long; it serves as a foundation for the walls of the courtyard house. The older structure appears to have been a retaining wall for the rear slope of the castle bank. Coeval with it may be a wall, at right-angles and of equal thickness, marking the W. side of the hall; it is also possible that the same structure continues, turning yet again, to form the N. side of the postern gateway. The 'King's chamber at Salisbury', mentioned in 1069 or 1070 (note 10), was probably timber-built and set on the platform which these walls supported; or it could have been at a lower level, in the shelter provided by the re-entrant angle.

The walls of the Courtyard House are built with a core of flint rubble set in a hard mortar and faced with ashlar (Plate 27). At intervals along the S. and E. faces of the lower storey there are pilaster buttresses rising from a chamfered plinth. The walls of the S. and E. ranges are preserved to a height of several feet, though only the lower courses of the ashlar facing remain. The inner court and the walls of the N. and W. ranges have been robbed almost to ground level, though enough remains to show the plan. The house was richly ornamented and the excavations produced much 12th-century detail, but little of it can now be precisely located. 'The roofs were covered with stone shingles with ornate ridge-tiles glazed with various shades of red and green';[62] it is possible that some of these tiles represent works of repair. Tile, generally set on edge, was also used for the inserted hearths and fireplaces, some of which probably date from 1366.

A S. doorway, now blocked, is indicated by the projecting step of its threshold in the E. part of the S. wall of the forebuilding. Blocks of rubble within the building indicate that stairs to the upper storey of the courtyard house turned W., then N. and finally E. along the outer walls, probably with landings at each turn. At the back of the E. part the remains of ashlar facing indicate a recess (? a door-keeper's lodge) contrived under the top flight of steps. The upper stage of the forebuilding has entirely gone, but there would have been space between the top flight of stairs and the S. wall to accommodate a bridge leading from the postern tower, across the intervening space, to the main storey of the courtyard house. Subsequently the S. doorway was sealed (the lowest course of blocking remains) and the stair became accessible only from within the S. range.

East of the forebuilding, the lower storey of the S. range is in two parts. To the W., a large room was spanned by an arch of two orders, six feet thick, with a span of 13 ft.; this feature probably supported the main entrance on the upper floor. A bench runs along the N. wall of the room. In the N.E. corner, 2 ft. above the original floor level, is an added hearth of tiles set on edge; W. of the arch are an external doorway and a window of which only the sloping sill remains; E. of the arch is another window. The chapel of St. Margaret, in the E. part of the S. range, is of three bays defined by shafted responds; originally the bays were vaulted. The chancel is narrower than the other bays and has an inset altar recess originally covered by a barrel vault. The altar is represented by its base; fragments of a thick slab of Purbeck marble found nearby may have been from the *mensa*. The only detail recorded in the chapel was a moulded wall-shaft base with dog-tooth ornament; it was found in the S.W. corner.[63] There is an external doorway in the W. bay of the nave, and windows were

recorded in the eastern bay and in the chancel. Benches run along the side walls of the nave, above which is a band of ashlar. The upper part of the walls is of coursed flint, formerly plastered.

Originally, the E. range comprised a single ground-floor room (50 ft. by 16½ ft.) with a wooden ceiling supported on a central row of posts; some of the stone post-bases remain. The room communicates with the chancel of St. Margaret's chapel through a secondary doorway, and there is an external door at the N. end of the E. wall; there were also three windows in the E. wall. The walls were of flint and rubble, plastered, with a double chamfered string, now largely gone, along the E. wall at the level of the window sills. The S. part of the room was subsequently cut off by a cross-wall, presumably to form a room for the priest serving the chapel.

The original fireplace near the centre of the E. wall retains a stone kerb, a rounded back and side pilasters to carry the hood. The hearth and the fire-back were repaired, possibly in 1366, with tiles set on edge. A narrow doorway in the N. wall leads to a square room identified as a kitchen.[64] The adjacent circular stone stair is a secondary insertion; it appears to replace an original stone stair in the adjoining E. turret and it may incorporate some of the original stone steps.

The Kitchen had a large fireplace against the N. wall, with a double hearth spanned by an arch (now gone) which sprang from a respond of ashlar and a central pier; the ashlar is laid in alternating courses of white limestone and greensand (Plate 28). The chimney bressummers sprang from the side walls and from the central pier, of which only the lightly moulded base remains *in situ*. An arch spanning from the pier to a respond in the S. wall carried the floor of the room above.

The East Turret, containing latrines, cesspits and originally a spiral stair, projects at a slight angle, overlapping the wall between the kitchen and the room to the S.; it is contemporary with the E. range. A doorway in the S.E. corner of the kitchen, later blocked, led to the stair and so down to a latrine which was floored on a level about 1 ft. below that of the kitchen. Slots for beams to carry the latrine floor can be seen on the E. and W. sides of the W. pit, indicating the position of seats along the S. side. The E. pit of the turret must from the beginning have served upper rooms in the E. range and perhaps the Great Chamber also.

The upper storey of the courtyard house is largely ruined and little detail remains, but the general plan is clear. A porch at the head of the stair in the forebuilding occupied the S.W. corner. Thence a N. doorway probably led into the lower end of the hall, but the main entrance of the house was doubtless on the E., directly over the archway in the lower storey; it probably led to a square ante-chamber from which there was on the E. a doorway to St. Nicholas's Chapel and on the N. a doorway to the courtyard. The court had a pent-roofed passage or cloister on one or more sides; this was renewed in 1246 (note 23).

The Hall occupied the whole of the W. range. The only details remaining are a doorway at the N. end of the E. wall and, near the middle of the same wall, a feature which probably is the base of a serving hatch. The doorway which gave access to the dais end of the hall has jambs with reversed rebates showing that it was an entrance from the hall to the courtyard and the rest of the house, rather than *vice versa*. Both doorway and hatch appear to be late features, possibly dating from 1366 when alterations were carried out. There is no chimney; an open hearth with hanging ironwork was provided in 1366. Traces of later walls (not shown on the accompanying plan) remain at the N. end and on the W. side of the hall.

The Great Chamber, so called in 1246, but named 'the high chamber near Herlewin's Tower' in 1366, has a doorway in the S. wall and, in the middle of the N. wall, a fireplace with a rounded back; the latter was set with tiles in 1366. The position of the fireplace is probably original as many stones belonging to an ornate early 12th-century chimney, with smoke-holes and bands of decoration, were found outside.[65] An open hearth of tiles set on edge, found near the W. end of the chamber, doubtless heated this part of the chamber which was separated by a wooden partition in 1366. Only the footings of the S. wall of the chamber remain exposed; the outline of the rest of the structure is indicated by turf-covered mounds.

Nothing remains of the Chapel of St. Nicholas in the E. part of the upper stage of the S. range, or of the chamber between the kitchen and the chapel[66] at the same level in the E. range. The size of the chimneybreast outside the E. wall suggests that there was a fireplace on the first floor. The repair of the fireplace in the upper chamber is recorded in 1366, when a partition was inserted in this room and a timber-built solar was added, reached by a wooden stair.

The *Kitchen Tower*, at the N. end of the E. range, named the Tower above the Kitchen in 1246 and the High Tower in 1366, is of one build with the E. range. It has walls 8 ft. thick at the base, and there probably were battered plinths to N. and E. Two latrine pits on the S. are integral with the tower; on the tower side they are lined with ashlar; on the other sides they are of well-built rubble with ashlar quoins. The E. pit has an arch 2 ft. wide on the E. side, perhaps to carry a passage linking the tower and the E. range; a central arch spanning the W. pit shows that it served garderobes in two upper storeys. Subsequently the two latrine pits were closed in and the space above them was added to the room over the kitchen, forming a chamber 24 ft. by 18 ft. with a three-sided fireplace in its W. wall. The

alteration probably dates from 1366, when work was carried out in the chamber of the knights. Three windows are mentioned at this date. The compartment seen on the plan at the centre of the tower was accessible only by a narrow stair from above; it may have been a cistern. S.E. of the tower, chamfered capping on a block of masonry built beside the adjoining curtain suggests the springing of a half-arch such as might have supported a stone stair going up from the curtain wall-walk to a doorway at the S.E. corner of the tower. A secondary wall closes the recess below the supposed stair, possibly to make another cistern. The closing of the latrines on the S. of the Kitchen Tower necessitated the provision of further latrines (only the pits remain) in the angle between the tower and the Great Chamber.

A number of latrine pits were cleared during the excavations; those explored were found to have been carried down through the made-up ground to the natural gravel which caps the chalk. The pits had been used for the deposit of waste material and contained many layers of quicklime, thrown in for sanitary reasons. The percolation of this lime and of iron in solution gave the natural gravel at the base the appearance of a 'foundation of about 2 ft. of gravel concrete'.

Herlewin's Tower, with an adjacent chamber to the N.E., stands across the castle bank near the N.W. corner of the courtyard house. The building, similar in construction to the kitchen tower, is probably of the early 12th century; on either side the curtain is butted against the masonry. Herlewin's tower is mentioned in the list of 1246 as needing repair; it also figures in 1315 and 1366, when the lead roof was made good. Both tower and chamber are badly ruined, the walls standing only 4 ft. or 5 ft. high at most. The N.W. side had a heavy foundation carried some distance down the slope of the bank, with a battered plinth. A doorway opens in the S.E. wall of the chamber.

A number of fragmentary walls, not forming any coherent plan, were found at a high level in the space between the courtyard house and the curtain.[67] They are no longer visible and are not shown on the accompanying plan. They must include, among other things, the walls of the kitchen and bakery, adjacent to the hall, which were causing trouble in 1315 through the decay of the lead gutters. They probably represent a redevelopment of this area which may have taken place after the fall of the new hall, early in the 14th century. Several orientated burials were recorded in the space between the great chamber and the curtain.

A rectangular saw-pit was found S. of the Great Tower. It was revetted with reused building stones, including some with 12th-century ornament set with the decorated face inwards. The pit was later used as a latrine.

The *New Hall* is first mentioned in 1246 when it needed repair. It 'fell' in 1307–8, but the walls were still standing in 1330; an associated chamber, kitchen and bakehouse are recorded as having fallen at the same time.[68]

The hall was on the S.W. of the inner bailey, close to the curtain. When excavated in 1911 only the base of the S.W. wall and the return of the N.W. end were found; the position of the other walls was indicated by ridges of rammed chalk.[69] At the N.W. end was a porch, probably about 12 ft. wide, with a central doorway; the club-shaped S.W. jamb of the entrance remains, with moulded internal and external shaft-bases of early 13th-century character. Masonry in the S. corner of the porch may be the foundation of a stair going up to a gallery. Inside, the hall has a stone bench following the S.W. wall. Other ridges of rammed chalk were found near the hall, but no plan survives.

A *Well* is sunk at the centre of the castle mound, 11 ft. S. of the courtyard house. The upper part (the top courses were rebuilt in 1910) was steined, with a diameter of 5 ft. near the surface expanding to 8 ft. at a depth of 28 ft.; below this the shaft in the solid chalk was unlined. Only the top 2 ft. of the chalk-cut shaft were excavated.

A second, but unfinished, well was found in the southern part of the inner bailey, about 45 ft. from the curtain. Within a pit 20 ft. across, a steined shaft 7 ft. in diameter was carried down to a depth of 18 feet; below this the shaft was cut through solid chalk for a further depth of 3 feet and then abandoned, the bottom being left irregular. The space between the steining and the side of the pit was packed with loose soil and rubbish, including building stones and tiles.

In 1911, galleries dug out of the well-shaft at original ground-level brought to light a storage pit of Iron Age type, 9 ft. in diameter. Only the top 3 ft. were excavated and no datable objects were found. At original ground-level, and partly built over the storage pit, were walls of a Roman building with a cobbled floor.[70]

Levelled platforms, from 7 ft. to 14 ft. wide, in places with a border of stone blocks acting as a retaining wall, were noted against the inner faces of the S. and S.E. curtain; they mark the position of auxiliary buildings, probably of timber.

The *Bakehouse* lies in the S.E. of the inner bailey, close to the E. curtain. The poorly built walls stand 4 ft. or 5 ft. high at the S. end, but elsewhere are ruined or missing. The bases of two circular ovens were found near the centre of the W. wall and a third oven stood almost opposite, against the E. wall. At the N. end is a separate room with traces of a fireplace at the E. end. On the E., the remains of a much ruined third room extend to the curtain. The bakehouse, probably built at the same time as the new hall, 'fell' in 1307–8.

The *Lower Bailey* comprised, in the 13th century and later, not only the bailey of the 11th-century castle but the whole area between the castle mound and the peri-

meter of the former hill-fort.[71] For the greater part of the circuit it was enclosed by a stone curtain with turrets, still kept in repair in the early 14th century.[72] There was an East Gate with a chamber over it, of which no trace remains, and a West Postern. Within the bailey, the only structures recorded in modern times are various earthworks, the tunnel, and the Cathedral with its Close (below (2)). Of the King's Gaol [73] and other structures that might be expected to have stood there, no trace remains; most of them were probably of timber framework.

The *Outer Curtain*, a flint wall 10 ft. to 12 ft. thick, without towers, was begun by Bishop Roger in the later years of Henry I; it was unfinished when he was forced to surrender the castle in 1139 and the N.E. sector, between the N.E. radial cross-bank and the E. gate, was never built. Where investigated, the wall was found to be built on the natural chalk and its face was covered externally to a depth of as much as 20 ft. by the bank of the earlier bailey, or by material piled against it at the time of construction. Internally, the building of the wall appears to have been associated with a levelling-up of the immediately adjacent areas. In the S.E. quadrant the levelling is composed of rammed chalk. In the N.W. quadrant, in the area of the cathedral, part of the fill is of looser material (mainly chalk) and considerable differences of level remain, suggesting that much of the filling was in place before the building of the curtain. The greatest recorded depth of fill, in the area W. of the bishop's palace, is 14 ft.

North of the cathedral part of the curtain remains visible; it stands some 12 ft. high over a length of about 15 ft. When this stretch of wall was examined in 1914 it was stated to be 'of later date than the Norman city wall, on which it rests'. About 10 ft. above the present ground level, and probably rather more above the mediaeval level, two beam slots (13 ins. square) penetrate the flintwork horizontally to a depth of 6½ ft. from the outer face. They lie 6 ft. apart. These slots probably housed the lower beams of the brattices which were put up in time of war. Their position suggests that the height of the curtain, from the ground inside to the level of the wall-walk, was about 15 ft. The dimension may be exceptional, as the secondary character of the masonry may indicate that the present wall belongs to one of the turrets which are mentioned in the accounts of repairs carried out in 1337–8.

The *West Gate*, excavated in 1912, proved to be little more than a postern.[74] Gate and passage, about 9 ft. wide, were set in the solid chalk (Plate 27). The bases of the side walls were found, surmounted by traces of plaster on the vertical faces of the chalk. A row of green-sand blocks formed the threshold of the gateway. 'Inside the gate the ground was level for a yard or two and then sloped quickly up into the bailey.' The threshold lay nearly 5 ft. below the 12th-century ground level and neither the description nor the photographs taken at the time suggest 12th-century work. The original curtain with its plinth was found at a higher level on the S. side, but on the N. the whole wall had gone. 'There was no indication of a gate tower on this side [of the city] and it was possible that the wall simply crossed the gully and that a plain arched recess in its base formed the gate passage.'

The *Tunnel*, first recorded in 1795 when a severe frost caused the mouth to fall in, extends from a hollow beside the N.E. radial cross-bank to an unknown point outside the outer rampart; it is probable that the radial bank is composed, in part at least, of spoil from the tunnel. It may be compared with the more elaborate system at Dover where, in 1229–30, £100 was spent on making a 'tunnel to go out of the castle towards the field'.[75]

The tunnel, cut through the solid chalk, passes under the filled-in gap (above, p. 5) in the early Iron Age rampart. It descends steeply and varies in size; an average cross-section is 7 ft. to 8 ft. wide and as much in height, with the roof forming a flattened semicircle. The explorers of 1795 penetrated between 90 ft. and 114 ft. from the entrance, to a point which would bring them under the ditch. The excavators of 1957 could only proceed 57 ft., to a point where the tunnel dipped sharply and was filled with chalk scree. The pitch of descent varies; in 1795 unworn steps were found cut in the chalk. There are numerous graffiti on the walls, none demonstrably earlier than 1795.[76]

The *Church of St. Cross*, of which there is now no trace, is often mentioned in the records. In 1236 it was in need of repair,[77] and it was at this period described as lying above or beyond (*ultra*) the gate.[78] The nave was stated to be ruinous and the sheriff was instructed to pull it down and build a new one.[79] Further repairs were needed in 1315 when documents describe the chapel as above or beyond (*ultra*), or outside (*extra*) the gate of the castle.[80]

There is, for the Norman period and after, both documentary and archaeological evidence of occupation outside the defences of Old Sarum. It is customary to refer to this *Extra-mural Settlement* as 'suburbs', following Leland who in 1540 wrote that outside both E. and W. gates there had formerly been 'a fair suburbe'.[81] It is questionable, however, if the term 'suburb' is entirely appropriate. With the castle mound and bailey occupying the E. part of the former hill-fort and the ecclesiastical precinct (2) much of the W. part there would have been little room within the defences to accommodate a developing civil settlement; perhaps from the beginning most or all of it lay outside the defences on E., S. and W. The idea receives support from a map of *c.* 1700 (though it is late evidence) showing that the burgages of Old Sarum lay outside the E. gate and on either side of the Portway, extending as far as Stratford-sub-Castle

and the R. Avon on the south.[82]

Most of the available information relates to the area outside the E. gate of the castle, where much has been brought to light as a result of road realignment, building, pipe-trenching and ploughing, as well as by deliberate archaeological excavation. Leland records that there had been 'houses in tyme of mind inhabited in the est suburbe' but that it was deserted at the time of his visit. He also mentions a chapel which still stood and which belonged to the former parish church of St. John. The latter may have been one of two buildings discovered in 1933, during excavations N. of the Old Castle Inn (562), just W. of the old main road from Amesbury to Salisbury (SU 14143261).[83] The buildings were incompletely excavated and retained little but their plaster floors. The more easterly of the two was aligned E.–W.; within it were found fragments of carved stonework of 13th-century date and a carefully constructed stone-lined pit, possibly a base for a font. An earlier cess-pit beneath the floor was not excavated. A number of burials, part of an extensive cemetery (see below), were found immediately outside the building on the S. side, but none within it. The floor of the second building was cut into by several graves; it overlay two large rectangular cess-pits, 19½ ft. deep and 12 ft. deep respectively, both of which contained much late 11th and 12th-century pottery.

Excavations immediately to W. and S.W. of this area in 1958 revealed several more cess-pits, most of which were not excavated; remains of a building of several phases, perhaps 12th to 14th-century; and a junction of roads or tracks which merged and continued N. and W. towards the E. gate of the castle. One track led S.E. to Bishopdown, the old road to Milford, Laverstock and Clarendon.[84] More recently a trench cut for a modern pipe-line cut through cellars, floors and cess-pits nearby (SU 141326).[85] To N. and S. of the old road from Amesbury to Salisbury more cess-pits have been found, together with shallow chalk quarries, some associated with lime burning.[86] At SU 142327 floors of two timber buildings aligned on Ford Lane were discovered.[87] There is some evidence of further extra-mural settlement in the field immediately below the ramparts on the S.E. side (around SU 140325) where ploughing has revealed the outlines of further cess-pits.[88]

The *Cemetery*, presumably one of the main burial-grounds of the borough, also lay on either side of the old Amesbury–Salisbury road, just N. of the Old Castle Inn. Discovery of burials is first recorded in 1834 and excavations in 1855,[89] 1931–3,[90] and 1960[91] have revealed at least 70 graves. Most of the graves contained single burials, were 1½ ft. to 4 ft. deep and were generally orientated N.W. to S.E.; only one yielded evidence of a coffin. Some of the graves were too small for the bodies, which had apparently been forced into position. Two shallow group-graves found E. of the old road, one with nine the other with at least five burials, were thought to be among the latest interments in the cemetery. In this area, too, ploughing in the late 19th century and in more recent years has disturbed numerous burials over a fairly large area.

There is evidence of occupation outside the W. gate of the defences. A scatter of domestic refuse and large fragments of Greensand stone, probably wall-footings, were found in the field immediately below the entrance.[92] Further material was found on either side of the present road which goes from Dean's Farm (559) towards the West Gate, especially along the N. side, where a number of cess-pits and ditches yielded 12th and 13th-century pottery and some building stones.[93] Perhaps some of this material marks the site of 'Newton Westgate', a name first mentioned in 1353,[94] which might well refer to extra-mural urban growth.

1. *W.A.M.*, lvii (1960), 364–70.
2. O. Cuntz, *Itineraria Romana*, i (1929), 74–5; *E.P.N.S.*, xvi (1939), 18.
3. *A.S.C.*, (trans. D. Whitelock, 1961), s.a. 552.
4. A.J. Robertson, *Anglo–Saxon Charters* (1939), 246–9. *Med. Arch.*, xiii (1969), 84–92.
5. *A.S.C.*, s.a. 1003 (text C(DE)).
6. R.M. Dolley, *Nordisk Numismatisk Unions Medlemsblad* (1954), 152–6.
7. L. Alcock, *By South Cadbury is that Camelot ......* (1972), 194–201.
8. *W.A.M.*, lvii (1960), 353–70, trenches B and H.
9. *ibid.*, lxvii (1972), 61–111.
10. H.W.C. Davis, *Regesta Regum Anglo–Normannorum*, i (1913), No. 46. See also No. 227, ascribed to 1075–86; cf. *Cal. Doc. France*, ed. Round, No. 1135.
11. *Magnum Rotulum Scaccarii de anno 31 Hen. I* (ed. J. Hunter, 1833), 13: *in uno ostio faciendo ad Cellarium Turris Sar' 20s.*
12. Wm. of Malmesbury, *Hist. Novella.* (Rolls Ser. xc), 547: *Castellum Salesberiae, quod cum regii juris proprium esset, ab Henrico rege impetratum, muro cinctum custodiae suae attraxerat.* cf. *Annales Wintoniae*, s.a. 1138 (*Ann. Mon.*, Rolls Ser. xxxvi, 51).
13. For the history of Salisbury Castle, see *V.C.H., Wilts.* vi, 53–60; also *King's Works*, ii, 824–8. Only documents which bear directly on the castle buildings are cited here.
14. Benson & Hatcher, 32.
15. *Pipe Roll* 1171 (P.R.S., xvi), 23: *in operatione Pontis et Castelli £24. 4s. 10d.*; 1173 (P.R.S., xix), 96–7: *in operatione Castelli £17. 4s.*; 1174 (P.R.S., xxi), 29: *in operatione domorum et muri et portarum £27. 5s. 5d.*; 1176 (P.R.S., xxv), 175: *Summa denariorum quos misit in operatione domorum et castelli £33. 17d.*; 1177 (P.R.S., xxvi), 103: *Summa denariorum quos misit in*

operationem domorum regis in Castello £61. 13d.; 1179 (P.R.S., xxviii), 57: *in reparatione domorum castelli Regis £17. 4s. 1d.* These figures for the reign of Henry II are listed by R. Allen Brown (*Eng. Hist. Rev.*, lxx (1955), 353–98) in Table B. The only expenditure for the years 1170–80 specifically allocated to the outer bailey is the small sum of 61s. for the making, or more probably the re-formation, of the ditch of the earthwork covering the main gate (*Pipe R.* 1173 (P.R.S., xix), 96–7): *pro faciendo attractu ad claudendum magnum ballium castelli 61s.*

16. *Pipe R.* 1182 (P.R.S., xxxi), 84: *in operatione domus thesauri in turri .... £9. 1s.* For Salisbury as a provincial treasury in the reign of Henry II, see *Studies presented to Sir Hilary Jenkinson* (ed. J. Conway Davies, 1957), 44–6.

17. *Pipe R.* 1188 (P.R.S., xxxviii), 14: *in operatione camere super portam castelli et in emendatione turris £1. 7s.*

18. *Pipe R.* 1201 (P.R.S., n.s. xiv), 75: *in operatione castelli £29. 6s. 8d.*; 1202 (P.R.S., n.s. xv), 119: *in operatione castelli £16. 5s. 2d.*: 1206 (P.R.S., n.s. xx), 182: *ad reparandum castrum £44. 7d*; 1208 (P.R.S., n.s. xxiii), 193: *in reparatione pontis et fossatorum castelli S........et domorum £63. 18s. 6d.* Compare *Rot. Litt. Claus.*, i (Rec. Com., 1883), 61 (1205–6) and 111 (1208) for repair of bridge and ditch. These figures are taken from Table A in the article by Allen Brown cited in note 15, but with the addition of the entry from *Pipe Roll* 1202, not there included.

19. *Reg. St. Osmund*, ii, 3–14; *Sar. Chart and Doc.* (Rolls Ser., xcvii), 266–70.

20. *Cal. Close Rolls*, 1234–7, 280.

21. *Cal. Lib. Rolls*, 1226–40, 281. The phraseology perhaps reflects the earlier status of the cathedral close, when it lay outside the castle; cf. *ibid.*, 305.

22. There is a strong possibility that the name was given out of respect for the memory of Abbot Herluin (984–1078), founder of the abbey of Bec-Hellouin in Normandy. He died not many weeks after Osmund's consecration to the bishopric and if, as is likely, the ceremonial *dedicatio* of the new cathedral took place about the same time, the occasion would almost certainly have been attended by Archbishop Lanfranc and others who revered Herluin as their master and teacher. Osmund and his contemporaries may have agreed to commemorate a great figure of the older generation by giving his name to a building, perhaps even then under construction. The tower with its attached chamber seems residential rather than military. Its position within the administrative compound suggests that it, or perhaps a wooden predecessor, may have been designed for the use of Bishop Osmund himself, providing a retreat more secure than a palace in the close which lay outside the castle defences.

23. *Cal. Lib. Rolls*, 1245–51, 65 (P.R.O., C. 62/22,

m.6): *mandatum est........quod magnam turrim in castro Regis Sar', turrim ultra coquinam, turrim Herlewin, turrim ultra magnam portam, et eandem magnam portam, magnam etiam aulam eiusdem castri et cameram ultra garderobam regis et turrim ultra posternam et pontem eiusdem posterne........ reparari faciat, claustrum etiam inter aulam et magnam cameram ibidem de novo refici.*

24. *ibid.*, 1245—51, 156.

25. *ibid.*, 65.

26. *ibid.*, 97. Salisbury is queried in the calendar.

27. *ibid.*, 96. The writ of 8 June 1249 mentions five chaplains ministering within and without the castle of Salisbury. One was perhaps associated with the church of St. John in the E. suburb (*ibid.*, 239).

28. *Cal. Inq. Misc.*, ii, No. 1158 (1330).

29. *ibid.*, No. 210.

30. P.R.O., E 101/593/11 and 12(1).

31. P.R.O., E. 101/593/31(1). For text, see appendix, p. 173. The convenience of the descriptive term 'Courtyard House' in this account is self-evident.

32. P.R.O., C 145/114(1), quoted in *King's Works*, ii, 828, n.4.

33. *Cal. Pat. Rolls*, 1446—52, 35.

34. *L. & P. Hen. VIII*, i, No. 5715, 26 Dec. 1514.

35. *Reg. St. Osmund*, i, 198—200: *ante portam castelli Sarum terram ex utraque parte viae in ortorum domorumque canonicorum necessitate.*

36. See p. 12.

37. Leland, *Itin.*, i, 260—1.

38. Summarised in *W.A.M.*, lvii (1960), 359.

39. *Gentleman's Magazine*, 1834 (ii), 418; 1835 (ii), 143—6 and 640. *P.S.A.*, xxv (1913), 95.

40. *P.S.A.*, xxiii (1910—11), 190—201 and 501—18; xxiv (1912), 52—65; xxv (1913), 93—104; xxvi (1914), 100—19; xxvii (1915), 230—40; xxviii (1916), 174—83.

41. *Arch. J.*, civ (1947), 129—39.

42. *W.A.M.*, lvii (1960), 352—70.

43. *P.S.A.*, xxvii (1915), illustration opp. 236.

44. *ibid.*, xxvii (1915), 236—8. *Arch. J.*, civ (1947), 134—5.

45. *W.A.M.*, lvii (1960), 355—6 (trench A).

46. *ibid.*, 356—7 (trenches B and H).

47. *ibid.*, 356 and 364—7.

48. *ibid.*, 365—6 (trench B).

49. *ibid.*, 357—8 and 364 (trenches B and H).

50. In the Architectural Description a number of details not now visible on the site are included on the basis of the excavation reports; these are the source of any passage directly quoted.

51. *P.S.A.*, xxiii (1910), 192.

52. *Cal. Lib. Rolls*, 1245—51, Nos. 31, 65.

53. *Cal. Inq. Misc.*, ii, No. 210.

54. The best preserved stretch appears to be S. of the

Great Tower. When uncovered in 1910 it was recorded as being 'about 8½ ft. thick and still some 8 ft. high, with its inner side faced with ashlar' (*P.S.A.*, xxiii (1910—11), 511).

55. *Pipe R. 35 Hen. III: in turri castri Sarum plumbanda de novo £48. 4s. ....in turri castri Sarum plumbanda £4. 17s.; Pipe R. 54 Hen. III: in turri castri predicti plumbo cooperienda et de novo gistanda £60. 5d.* (P.R.O., E 372/114, m.4).

56. P.R.O., E 101/593/12(1).

57. Hawley MS., 19 October, 1910.

58. For example, *Pipe R. 1184* (P.R.S., xxxiii), 92: *in liberatione clericorum et camerariorum........ ad deferendum thesaurum per diversa loca........*

59. The document of 1330 (note 32) shows that this was the Sheriff's house in the 14th century. The excavators identified the building as the Great Tower or Keep and it has also been explained as Bishop Roger's episcopal palace, but neither term can be justified.

60. *Arch. J.*, civ (1947), 139—40.

61. The indenture of 1366 is printed in full at the end of the volume (p. 173).

62. *P.S.A.*, xxiii (1910), 509.

63. *ibid.*, 503.

64. Cf. 12th-century kitchens in the tower of Orford Castle.

65. *P.S.A.*, xxii (1910), 505. The stones are in Salisbury Museum.

66. So named in 1366.

67. *P.S.A.*, xxiii (1910), 510.

68. See notes 24, 28, above.

69. *P.S.A.*, xxiv (1912), 54.

70. *ibid.*, 57—8.

71. For example Lib. Roll, 15 July 1237 (P.R.O., C 62/11 m.b.): *maeremium aule quod fuit de episcopatu, infra baillium castri nostri Sarr'.*

72. P.R.O., E 101/593/12(1), (1337—8): *In vadiis....... cimentariorum emendantum et reparantum muros inferioris ballii dicti castri et turrellos eorumdem murorum et murum et tecturam camere ultra portam castri.......*

73. *Cal. Lib. Rolls*, 1245—51, 156: order to repair the king's gaol within the outer bailey. Cf. *Close Rolls*, 1237—42, 153, where the building is likely to have been of wood rather than masonry.

74. *P.S.A.*, xxv (1913), 99—100.

75. *King's Works*, ii (1963), 636, quoting *Pipe Roll 13 Hen. III: bova ad exeundum de castro versus campum.*

76. *W.A.M.*, lvii (1960), 359, quoting earlier literature.

77. *Cal. Close Rolls*, 1234—7, 280.

78. *Cal. Lib. Rolls*, 1226—40, 374.

79. *ibid.*, 1245—51, 96.

80. *Cal. Close Rolls*, 1313—8, 171: estimate of 10 marks to repair the chapel of Holy Cross outside

the gate of the castle. *Cal. Inq. Misc.*, 1307—49, No. 210: defects of chapel of Holy Cross beyond the gate can be amended for 10 marks.

81. Leland, *Itin.*, i, 261.
82. *V.C.H., Wilts.* vi, 66—7.
83. *Ant. J.*, xv (1935), 174—92.
84. *W.A.M.*, 59 (1964), 130—54.
85. *ibid.*, 69 (1974), 187.
86. *ibid.*, 57 (1959), 179—91.
87. *ibid.*, 68 (1973), 136.
88. See note 83.
89. *Arch.*, xxxvi (1855), 182—4.
90. See note 83.
91. See note 84.
92. *W.A.M.*, 59 (1964), 141—2.
93. *ibid.*, 65 (1970), 208.
94. *V.C.H., Wilts.* vi, 64.

(2) **The Cathedral at Old Sarum**, and associated buildings within the cathedral close, are represented by foundations in the N.W. sector of the bailey between the castle mound and the rampart of the former hill-fort (Plate 26). Originally the area lay outside the castle, but with the erection of the outer curtain the close came inside the enlarged bailey.

The second council of Archbishop Lanfranc, held in London in 1075, decreed the removal of the see of Sherborne to Salisbury.[1] Herman, consecrated Bishop of Ramsbury in 1045, had held the see of Sherborne (with which Ramsbury was united) since 1058. He became the first Bishop of Salisbury and is said to have started building a new cathedral; but he was already an old man and when he died, 20th February, 1078, the work cannot have proceeded very far.[2]

The builder of the first cathedral, Bishop (later Saint) Osmund, was consecrated on June 3rd, 1078, and held the see for 21 years. Osmund was a man of noble birth; his mother was a daughter of Robert, Duke of Normandy and a sister of the Conqueror.[3] He had been Chancellor of the Kingdom and was an able administrator and a friend to learning.[4] He organised the body of canons serving the cathedral and endowed them with a substantial part of the lands of the bishopric.[5] His charter, dated 1091, states that he built the church of Salisbury; it was consecrated on April 5th, 1092.[6] To Osmund also is attributed the beginning of those customs which became the Use of Sarum, the most widely adopted order of service in mediaeval England.

Bishop Osmund's cathedral had an apsidal east end with narrow north and south aisles flanking the presbytery, north and south transepts carried up as towers, and an aisled nave (plan, opposite). Five days after the dedication a violent thunderstorm destroyed the roof of a tower and fractured much of the masonry,[7] but the damage was probably repaired before Osmund's death

in 1099. He was succeeded by Bishop Roger, who also had been Chancellor before his nomination to the bishopric in 1102. Roger's consecration was delayed for five years on account of the king's quarrel with Anselm.

Bishop Roger was described by his contemporary, William of Malmesbury, as a proud man, never sparing expense, who carried to completion whatever he took in hand, especially buildings. Among his many projects was the rebuilding of Bishop Osmund's cathedral on a larger scale than before: 'He made the new church of Salisbury and adorned it with furnishings so that it yielded place to no other in England, but surpassed many'.[8] This passage in the *Gesta Regum*, completed in 1125, must refer to the new east end, presumably well advanced if not finished by that date.

Roger's first work at the cathedral was a building of two storeys sited immediately N. of the old N. transept. The vaulted undercroft with its floor 13 ft. below the pavement of the transept contained the treasury;[9] above was the vestry.[10] The new building was designed with the future N. transept in mind, the bays of the undercroft corresponding closely with the spacing of the projected transept arcades. The small amount of architectural detail to survive in the undercroft is consistent with a date of *c.* 1110.

The east end of the enlarged cathedral comprised an aisled presbytery, with three chapels opening off the ambulatory which linked the E. ends of the aisles; aisled north and south transepts were also built, and provision was made for a central tower over the crossing. The new building was 12 ft. wider than Osmund's nave and aisles. The plan of the W. piers in the crossing shows that Roger intended to rebuild the nave also,[11] and in his last days, when already in disgrace, he made provision for this work; but after his death King Stephen carried off 'all the money and precious relics he left, which he had placed on the altar for the completion of the cathedral'.[12]

After the completion of the east end a cloister was formed in the angle between the E. arm and the N. transept, linking the cathedral with the bishop's palace to the north. None of this work is closely datable, but cloister and palace are part of a single plan and both are later than the east end. At the same time differences of level and of filling in this part of the site show that there was no general levelling of the area within the defences, as was found on the S.E. side of the bailey; the work must therefore belong to the period before the building of the curtain. This work, together with the building of the curtain (above, p. 11), probably accounts for Roger's failure to complete the rebuilding of the whole cathedral.

The last major addition to the cathedral is an annexe at the W. end, carried on very heavy foundations, which alone survive. This new narthex, laid out in conformity with the 11th-century plan, marks the abandonment of

Bishop Roger's grand design. The published records of excavation provide no closer dating,[13] but the narthex is clearly the work of Bishop Jocelyn de Bohun; at this period twin towers flanking a main west door are likely to have been favoured. A number of other alterations date from the episcopate of Bishop Jocelyn (1142–84); they include the pulpitum, which may perhaps be connected with a charter ascribed by the editors of the *Register of St. Osmund* to *c*. 1179 (below, p. 20). The church as completed during the second half of the 12th century formed the setting for the order of service known as the Use of Sarum, the earliest recension of which dates from *c*. 1210.[14]

The location of the cathedral within the bailey of a royal castle gave rise to difficulties. These were intensified during the troubles at the end of John's reign and matters came to a head in 1215 when the Constable barred the castle gates against the return of the Rogationtide procession after mass at St. Martin's Church (4), two miles S.E. of the castle.[15] Bishop Herbert Poore, who had begun negotiations for a transfer of the *cathedra*, died in January 1217, but the canons proceeded with a petition to the Pope asking that they be allowed to move elsewhere. On 19th March the petition was referred to Gualo, the papal legate,[16] and papal consent to the removal was given a year later, on 29th March 1218.[17] In 1219 a cemetery was consecrated and a wooden chapel was built near the site of the present cathedral. Mass was first celebrated in this chapel by Bishop Richard Poore on Trinity Sunday, 1219.[18]

The removal from Old Sarum left the cathedral and other buildings within the close in the king's hands. In the cathedral itself, a chapel named in honour of St. Mary remained in use. In 1246 the sheriff was ordered to find two chaplains to celebrate in the chapels of St. Margaret and St. Mary, both in the castle, the latter 'where the seat of the bishop used to be'; he was also instructed to find books and ornaments.[19] St. Mary's chapel probably lay in the nave of the former cathedral; it may perhaps be associated with a blocking-wall and an altar at the E. end of the S. aisle. Finally, in 1331 the Bishop and Chapter of Salisbury were granted the use of the stones of the old cathedral for the repair of their church and for the building of the precinct wall.[20] A chapel was still required, for in the following year the canons, pleading that they were bound to find a chantry within the old cathedral, were allowed to build a chapel at any other suitable place within the castle;[21] this chapel remained in use until the 16th century.[22]

The remains of the cathedral first attracted antiquarian interest in 1834 when a dry summer disclosed the major elements of the plan.[23] Superficial excavations were then carried out. The whole area of the close was systematically uncovered in 1912–14 in the course of excavations sponsored by the Society of Antiquaries.[24] The cathedral site was marked out by the Office of Works in the years following 1920, the older foundations with flint and the later with packed chalk. Subsequently concrete was used to mark the position of the foundations.

Architectural Description.[25] The Cathedral Close at Old Sarum lies in the N.W. sector of the outer bailey of the castle (plan, opp. p. 15). It was bounded on the E. by a straight bank with an internal depression which runs almost exactly at right-angles to the cathedral axis and parallel to the E. walk of the cloister. On the S., buildings associated with the cathedral extend only slightly beyond a line linking the W. postern of the castle mound with the W. gate of the city; a road linking the two gates probably marked the S. boundary of the close. To N.W. the close extended to the rampart of the former hill-fort, later amplified by the 12th-century curtain and heightened bank (above, p. 11).

The cathedral occupies the centre of the close, having the canons' cemetery S. of the choir and a cemetery for lay persons further S. and E., with an extension W. beside the nave. To N.E., partly bounded by the E. arm and partly by the E. side of the N. transept, was the cloister, an irregular quadrilateral. The bishop's palace stood N. of the cloister and had a garden to the west. Traces of walls and foundations remaining from structures of uncertain use lay W. of the cathedral, near the surrounding curtain wall.

In the later middle ages the cathedral was robbed of its stonework almost to ground level, and with very few exceptions the only masonry that now stands above ground is core-work, composed of flint rubble. Well-preserved ashlar face-work is found in the angle between the N. transept and the E. arm, where Bishop Roger's building stands several courses high; the stone is quarried from the Upper Greensand. Pavements identified in the excavations had a pattern of alternating slabs of green Hurdcote and white Chilmark stone. The roofs were of stone-slate with glazed clay ridge tiles. All these details (with the possible exception of some small areas of pavement in the nave) belong to the second building period and are datable to the first quarter of the 12th century or later. Architectural fragments, many with decorative sculpture of high quality (Plate 29), are preserved in Salisbury Museum and in a modern building on the castle mound.

First Period (*c*. 1078–92). The foundations of Bishop Osmund's late 11th-century church are of strong flint rubble set in white mortar and carried down to the solid chalk; the wall-core which survives near ground level is similar. A few stones of the ashlar facing remain *in situ* in the S. wall of the nave.

The foundations of the main apse are 7 ft. wide, but have been cut through at each end by later foundations. Inside, a rectangular footing (8 ft. by 4 ft. widening to 4½ ft.) marks the position of the bishop's throne. The position of the high altar is not recorded; probably its foundation was destroyed in the construction of the sleeper wall for the E. side of the later crossing, which cuts across the 11th-century presbytery 15 ft. W. of the throne. The side walls of the presbytery itself were probably solid, but there is no basis for the opinion that they continued W. as far as the centre-line of the transepts;[26] the fragmentary foundations which remain can be interpreted as sleeper walls. The aisles are square-ended externally, but analogy suggests that the chapels within were apsidal.

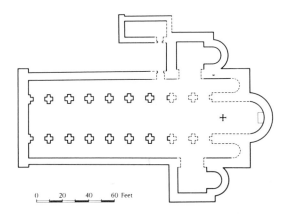

In the 11th-century church the nave arcades must have continued uninterrupted as far as the presbytery; the cruciform piers, of which the bases of two remain embedded in the later pulpitum, are too light to have carried a central tower. On the other hand the thick footings of the transept walls (at least 6½ ft. wide) suggest that these were designed to carry twin towers, as in the early 12th-century cathedral of Exeter. The foundations of the apses projecting E. from the transepts have a normal breadth of 5 ft.

Although the masonry of the nave is generally ruined to a level below that of the original floor, the outer wall of the S. aisle retains its core, standing up to 1 ft. high, with a few stones of the lowest course of ashlar remaining both outside and in. The side walls had no buttresses. The thicker foundations of the W. wall project at both ends, perhaps to carry stair turrets. The nave arcades are of seven equal bays, with two more in the crossing; the piers of cruciform plan show that the arches were of two orders. No pier remains above floor level, but the edges of the pavement and the later step to the platform in front of the pulpitum preserve the matrix of the easternmost pier in the S. nave arcade. The pavement, composed of green and white stone blocks set either in rows or diagonally, is of the same type as that of the early 12th century found in the E. part of the church and may be a later 12th-century renewal. Several areas were revealed during the excavations and one remains exposed in and beside the second bay of the S. nave arcade.

There is no evidence that the aisles were vaulted. Trenches cut across the nave during the excavations disclosed no evidence of an earlier building on the site.

During the exploration of the area N. of the cathedral, a building (30 ft. by 12 ft.) with broad foundations of stone and flint rubble was found lying parallel with the nave and 21 ft. distant. The S. wall was 'in line with, and of the same date as the N. end of Bishop Osmund's transept'. This building, destroyed when Bishop Roger's treasury was erected, is likely to have been the vestry or sacristy of Bishop Osmund's church; like its successor it probably had a treasury in the lower storey.[27] Communication with the cathedral may have been through a pent-roofed passage following the W. side of the transept and leading to a doorway in the E. part of the N. aisle. Nothing is now visible.

Second Period (c. 1110–25). In Bishop Roger's enlargement of his predecessor's church the *Vestry* and *Treasury* formed a building of two storeys; its S. wall was intended from the outset to constitute the N. end of the projected transept. No trace remains of the upper storey, containing the vestry, and the lower storey (Plate 28) is much ruined. The E. and W. walls are 10 ft. thick; the N. wall 12 ft. and the S. wall 8 ft. thick. The bays were marked externally by shallow pilaster buttresses. A short length of external wall facing, recorded at the W. end, had a battered plinth rising from a chamfered base. The building is set in a deep excavation carried down into the natural chalk. The wall-cores are of flint rubble set in white mortar similar to that used in the 11th-century cathedral. The remaining ashlar is finely jointed.

The treasury is divided into two aisles, each of four bays. The vaults supporting the vestry floor sprang from three circular piers and from semicircular responds projecting from the walls. The E. pier (5 ft. in diameter) has a chamfered plinth and an ashlar-faced shaft; a wall respond of similar form remains on the S. side. The other piers and responds retain only formless core-work, but some facing stones remain in the walls. The floor, 13 ft. below the level of the transept pavement, was reached by a stair descending from the E. aisle of the transept. There was a door at the bottom, but its drawbar hole, recorded in 1913, can no longer be seen. A narrow loop set in a deep embrasure with a stepped base occupies each bay of the E., W. and N. walls. A small ashlar-lined recess with an arched head of rough voussoirs is set in the W. bay of the S. wall and traces of a similar recess remain in the adjacent bay. In front of the next bay of the S. wall is a well, 6 ft. in diameter, with two courses of ashlar lining the head of the shaft; below this it is cut through the solid chalk.

Bishop Roger's enlarged *East End* consisted of an aisled presbytery with an eastern ambulatory from which opened three chapels, and north and south transepts, also aisled; the crossing was made strong

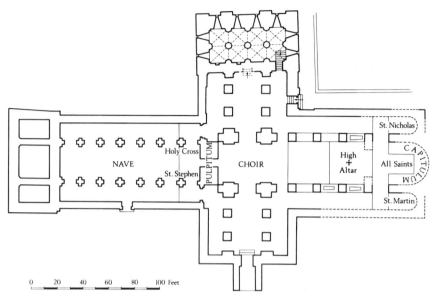

OLD SARUM. The 12th-century cathedral.

enough to support a central tower. The new building is on the same axis as the old, but wider, the central part of the presbytery being 8 ft. wider than the old eastern arm. The new walls were of flint rubble 'characterised throughout by the use of a mortar of a bright yellow colour, instead of the white mortar of the older work', faced with finely jointed Greensand ashlar, almost all of which has been robbed. The best preserved stretch of external ashlar is in the E. wall of the N. transept and the adjacent N. wall of the E. arm; here the base of the walls has been preserved owing to the cloister being at a lower level than the church. The walls have continuous chamfered bases from which rose pilaster buttresses corresponding with the bays of the interior; between the buttresses two courses of a battered plinth remain. A small fragment of similar face-work remains on the W. wall of the same transept, adjacent to the remaining face-work of the treasury. Elsewhere 'hardly any of the 12th-century building remains above floor level, and in the presbytery not a fragment is left of pillar or respond. It is nevertheless possible to recover many of its details and, what is more extraordinary, most of the pattern and colouring of the floor'.

The pavement of which the design was recovered is the earliest known example of the flooring of a major English church. As it is no longer in evidence the excavators' account is repeated in full: 'The whole of the new work, except in one or two places, was paved throughout with squared blocks of stone, either of white Chilmark or the delicate green from Hurdcote. These blocks were faced on one side only, leaving the other side rough; in order, therefore, to obtain a level surface, the blocks were laid in a very thick bed of mortar. When the church was dismantled these blocks were taken up,

leaving the mortar bed exposed, with here and there embedded chips of the displaced stones. By diligent brushing of the dust and rubbish out of the hollows we have been able to recover from these beds the disposition of the blocks, and Lt. Col. Hawley noticed one damp day the alternating colours of the stone chips' (*P.S.A.*, xxvi (1914), 107).

The *North Chapel*[28] (St. Nicholas) is the same width as the aisle (12½ ft.). It was raised one step above the level of the aisle and had a further two steps to the altar. Externally the chapel is square-ended; internally it was probably apsidal.

The *Central Chapel* (All Saints), as described by the excavators, was 15 ft. wide at ground level and at least 30 ft. long. Externally the chapel may have been apsed or square-ended; internally it was apsed. Passages 3 ft. wide flanked the chapel and extended W. to the ambulatory. There were steps across the chapel floor 20 ft. and 23 ft. E. of the ambulatory. The position of the altar, as shown on the excavators' plan, was outlined in front and on the N. side by the matrix of the paving of 'rows of stone blocks, alternately white and green'; a few stones have been set in position to indicate an altar. The paving on the altar level and on the step in front was of the same type as that in other parts of the E. end. In front of the step 'the chapel floor also retained the mortar bed of a curious pavement of interlacing circles, but not of the same material as the altar platform, the stones comprising it having been flat and not rough underneath'. Elsewhere in England elaborate pavements like that described in front of the step are not known before the last quarter of the 12th century;[29] this example shows that the present arrangement of the chapel floor is secondary.

The thick walls show that the flanking passages were vaulted and the plan indicates that they cannot have extended beyond the line of the step in front of the altar, which retained traces of its original paving. These factors, together with the disproportionately small size of the recess containing the altar, again with traces of its original pavement, indicate that the central part of the E. end originally had two storeys: at ground level a low crypt entered from the flanking passages; above, a main chapel opening W. to the ambulatory. A crypt of this kind, presumably containing the altar of the relics, would normally have had a small window or *fenestella*

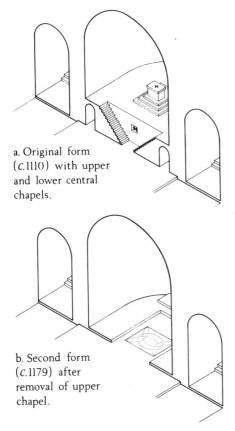

a. Original form (*c*.1110) with upper and lower central chapels.

b. Second form (*c*.1179) after removal of upper chapel.

OLD SARUM. Possible form of the E. chapels at two periods.

looking W. to the ambulatory. No trace of such a feature was recorded, but the excavators did not search below the mortar bed of the later pavement. The main chapel on the upper storey would have been approached by steps, probably twin flights rising to right and left of the *fenestella*; its altar, directly over that of the relics, might have been flanked by platforms extending W., upon which relics could have been exposed for veneration by pilgrims passing through the ambulatory. East of the altar, the upper stage (the *capitulum*) is likely to have been the meeting place of the chapter;[30] it was probably apsidal.

The *South Chapel* (St. Martin) was like that of St. Nicholas on the N. side.

The *Ambulatory* was raised one step above the aisles; evidence for its paving remained in a small area at the S. end. When excavated, the passage was found to be blocked at the S. end by a mass of rubble masonry (about 8 ft. square), now removed; it was thought to be mediaeval, but it does not appear on any plan and its purpose is unexplained. As the ambulatory was completely blocked, the masonry probably dates from after the transfer of the Cathedral.

The rectangular *Presbytery* is flanked by low walls, now preserved in rubble to a height nowhere more than 2 ft.,[31] on which stood the piers of the arcades. Nothing remains of these, but their arrangement in three equal bays with a narrower bay on the W. is established by the position of tombs in the first and second bays on the S. side, and by the evidence of pavement in the openings of the westernmost bay, the *ostia presbyterii*. The form of the E. end is uncertain; presumably there was a central archway flanked either by narrower arches, or, more probably, by solid responds; the upper part rising above the roof of the ambulatory could have provided space for windows.

The pavement of the whole E. bay and the E. half of the second bay in the presbytery, the *gradus altaris*, was at a higher level than elsewhere and has perished entirely. There is no record of the position of the high altar. The line of destruction in the second bay, indicating the position of a step, cuts across the pattern of the pavement and suggests that this rearrangement dates from the time of Bishop Jocelyn.[32] Westwards the pavement continued as far as the last pair of piers, where another step, the *gradus presbyterii*, descended to the pavement of the choir; this lay at the same level as that of the aisles. In the middle bay of the presbytery, near the centre of the third bay, is a stone socket for a lectern.

The plan published by the excavators shows tombs, now represented by flat-bottomed sinkings in the rubble, in the first and second intercolumniations of the S. side. The easternmost tomb had been opened in 1835 and found empty; the second was largely destroyed, only the foot remaining. That these were the tombs of Bishop Roger and Bishop Jocelyn is certain. Their bodies together with that of Bishop Osmund were translated from Old Sarum to the present cathedral on Trinity Sunday, 1226.[33] Of Bishop Osmund the excavators wrote that he was 'no doubt first buried in a place of honour in his own church, but when the eastern parts were demolished he was most likely taken up and translated to the north side of the altar in the new presbytery, where there are some indications of another tomb'. In a later paper Hope wrote 'north of the altar, under the first arch, probably stood the tomb of St. Osmund, with the Easter Sepulchre in the arch west of it'.[34] The tomb-slab (6½ ft. by 2½ ft.), with the effigy of a bishop

(Plate 30) and a metrical inscription which identifies it as that of Bishop Osmund,[35] is now in the nave of Salisbury Cathedral, on the S. side near the W. end. The opening words of the inscription 'Flent hodie.........' indicate that the verses (quantitative hexameters with internal and tailed rhymes) were composed at the time of the bishop's death. But the effigy can hardly be earlier in style than the middle of the 12th century and it must have been made after the relics were translated into the new choir, perhaps at the time of the changes made under Bishop Jocelyn.[36] The adjacent effigy (Plate 30), more advanced in style, but lacking any inscription, may appropriately be ascribed to Bishop Jocelyn. Bishop Roger, whose treasure designed for the completion of the cathedral was seized by King Stephen, is probably commemorated in the new cathedral by the plain coffin lid which was once attributed to the grave of Bishop Osmund and upon which 'anno mxcix' was inscribed, probably in the 16th or 17th century.

The *North Transept* is of three bays with E. and W. aisles. The arcades are marked by square plinths partly outlined by the surviving indications of the pavement; they probably carried circular columns. The central bay of the E. wall has a doorway opening into the cloister while the N. end of the E. aisle contains the head of the stairs leading down to the treasury. The steps up to the vestry were probably at the centre of the N. wall. The position of the doorways makes it certain that there can have been no altars against the E. wall.

The *Crossing* is delimited by four compound piers, of which the core of that to the N.W. was found standing 3 ft. high. The massive cruciform footings were evidently designed to carry a central tower. The inner faces of the piers on N. and S. were flattened to accommodate the stalls of the choir, the positions of which were outlined by the pavement.

The *South Transept* resembles that on the north. The pavement is indicated more fully than elsewhere by the underbedding of the slabs, and its continuity along the E. aisle and in front of the piers of the E. arcade shows that there were no altars in any of these positions. There is a doorway at the centre of the S. wall.

The *Nave* of the late 11th-century church remained in use. It was of seven bays and 8 ft. narrower than the 12th-century presbytery. The arches and piers were of two orders.

A number of additions and alterations were made to the cathedral left incomplete by Bishop Roger. As not all are datable, they are described in topographical order.

The *Chapel of All Saints* was re-formed at one level (drawing, p. 19) and the W. part was repaved during the later part of the 12th century. Probably it continued to be used for chapter meetings, with seats set on floors which covered the remains of the demolished passage walls. It was suggested above that the original lower

chapel contained the altar of relics, and the change should probably be explained by the growing importance of the Feast of the Relics. In *c.* 1210 this feast, celebrated on the 17th September, was among the *duplicia*[37] and the relics were housed in a chest near the high altar.[38] The date was changed by Bishop Jocelyn, and the confirmation of the change by Archbishop Theobald (1138–61), who granted an indulgence of 40 days, states that the feast had formerly been celebrated at an inconvenient season 'in which neither could the people assemble nor the relics be duly venerated'.[39] A transfer of the relics, from an altar approached only by narrow passages to a position in the presbytery (possibly on a lofty beam) where they could be seen from the ambulatory, would be a normal development. The pavement seen in the western part of the chapel belongs to a type which was much in favour at Rome, where examples are found dating from as early as *c.* 1100. The connection is further illustrated by the discovery, in the course of the excavations, of fragments of *verde antico* marble and of red porphyry, materials which were often used in Rome in the 12th century for the inlay of church furnishings, including altars.

A *Porch* was added outside the doorway in the S. wall of the S. transept. The door was approached by three steps leading up from the pavement of the transept. Fragments of ornamental gables outlined with mouldings, including a capstone surmounted by two lions, were found lying outside the transept. They date from the late 12th century and indicate that the porch was added by Bishop Jocelyn.

The *Pulpitum*, which formed the W. end of the choir, is represented by a solid base traversing the nave and filling the bay between the crossing and the easternmost piers of the nave. Altars were set against the W. face of the pulpitum, and the pavement of the nave in front of them is raised by two steps above the level further west. The pulpitum and the choir stalls are later than Bishop Roger's crossing. As the heavy stone base engulfs the easternmost piers of Bishop Osmund's nave it must date from a period when the intention to rebuild this part of the cathedral had been abandoned; that is, from the episcopate of Bishop Jocelyn. Its erection should probably be connected with provision made in a charter issued by Jocelyn, charging the prebend of Bedwyn with the provision of three lights to burn nightly in the cathedral, one of them by the doorway to the choir.[40] The charter is not dated, but it is ascribed to *c.* 1179 by the editors of St. Osmund's Register.

A *Blocking Wall*, closing the E. end of the S. aisle of the nave, extends from the easternmost pier of the arcade to the S. wall; there are traces of an altar against the W. face. The Sunday procession and other processions laid down in the Use of Sarum all passed along this aisle; hence the blocking must date from after the transfer of the *cathedra* to Salisbury, *c.* 1219. This part of the S.

aisle is probably the chapel of St. Mary, mentioned in a number of 13th and 14th-century documents.

A *Doorway* cut through the wall of the fourth bay of the S. aisle cannot be closely dated; it is, perhaps, the 'new south doorway' of an inventory of 1214.[41]

The *West Towers* and *Narthex* are built of 'flint rubble with yellow mortar .... originally faced with ashlar. [The structure] is noteworthy for the massiveness of its foundations'.[42] These were carried down to the solid chalk and are therefore of varying depth. The overall width of the structure and the position of its internal foundations are related to Bishop Osmund's nave and therefore must belong to a period when there was no longer any intention of rebuilding the whole church; it can hardly date from before 1150. At this date a design with paired towers flanking a large west door is likely to have been favoured.

The *Canons' Cemetery* lay S. of the E. arm of the cathedral. It formed a separate area within the main cemetery and was bounded on the S. by a wall running E. from the corner of the S. transept. The wall ended in a square stone base which is thought to have been the foundation for a cross; it may have marked the position of the first station in the Palm Sunday procession, when the main procession was met by a smaller group of clergy carrying the Host.[43]

The *Lay Cemetery* was further S., beyond the wall; it extended E. of the church and also W. in the area S. of the nave; it was probably bounded on the S. by the road which formed the S. side of the close. Other graves of laity were found N. of the nave.

Gravestones etc.: Many graves came to light during the excavations of 1909–16, and the plan of the N.W. quarter of the city drawn by D.L. Montgomerie records 28 burials which had substantial stone coffins, coffin-lids etc. On the plan opposite p. 15 these graves are numbered in correspondence with the report on the excavations.[44] Twenty-two of the stones are described and ten are illustrated in the excavation report, which forms the basis of the following list.

East of the eastern chapels, (i) grave retaining only greensand bearer stones; (ii) slab with middle rib and roll-moulded edges, footstone with cross paty; (iii) plain Purbeck marble slab; (iv) slab with double chamfered sides, slightly curved, with cross formy; (v) rough slab with chamfered end and sides; (vi) oolite, partly destroyed; (vii) flat oolite slab with six square depressions, perhaps for pillars supporting an upper slab.

In canons' cemetery, S. of presbytery, (viii) oolite slab carved in high relief with wheel crosses (report, fig. 7); (ix) greensand coffin with shaped interior (report, fig. 7); (x) untapered chamfered greensand slab with inclined E. and W. ends; (xi) greensand bearers only; (xii) similar to (ii); (xiii) coped greensand slab with oolite end-stones; (xiv) greensand slab with chamfered edges (report, fig. 6); (xv) similar to (xiv), but inscribed

'Ecce tvis Alward ervas Ramnesberiarvm........' etc.[45] Adjoining Alward's grave on S., (xvi) large oolite coffin lid with deeply chamfered sides (report, fig. 6); further S., (xvii) cracked and worn soft oolite coffin lid (report, fig. 8) inscribed, as well as could be deciphered, 'Proditvs a pvero Godwinvs .... vita' etc.[46] To N.W. near church wall, (xviii) greensand coffin with shaped interior; (xix) foundations only; (xx) fine Purbeck marble coffin with shaped interior (report, fig. 4), brought to light in 1912. On S. of nave, 12 yds. W. of S. transept, (xxi–ii) pair of soft greensand coffin-lids with crosses paty on top and with end-stones with wheel crosses and crosses paty (report, fig. 5).

Tombs ii–iv were still visible in 1972 and were found to be made, respectively, of Portland stone, Purbeck marble and Bath stone; No. v, of greensand, remains (1974) partly visible. No. xx was taken in 1912 to the present cathedral where it is exhibited in the S. walk of the cloisters. The others are reburied.

The *Cloister* lies N.E. of the cathedral, with the S. and W. sides bounded in part by the E. arm of the church and in part by the N. transept. It is an irregular quadrilateral with walks on all four sides. In the central bay of the E. aisle of the transept several steps led down to a landing on which opened the outer door; beyond the door more steps went down to the level of the cloister walk. The difference in level led to the preservation of the outer face of the church wall in this area. In the N.W. corner of the cloister a door led to a porch at the S. end of the W. range of the bishop's palace, and also to a garden. This doorway must also have served for the passage of processions circumambulating the church. In the N.E. corner of the cloister there was space for a doorway leading to a porch on the E. side of the bishop's hall, doubtless the main entrance to the palace. The S.E. corner, which was destroyed to ground level, must have included a fourth doorway through which processions passed to the cemetery.

Below the N.E. corner of the cloister an older building was found; it lay partly under the cloister walk and projected obliquely to N.E. The building was not fully exposed and nothing is now visible. Two rooms were found, divided by a thick wall extending E.N.E.–W.S.W. At the N.E. end of the more northerly room, outside the cloister, was an added *Well-house* with doorways to N.W. and S.E. The house was probably built to accommodate a large wheel operating the winding gear; the well itself was immediately outside the S.E. doorway. The masonry was of 12th-century character and probably contemporary with Bishop Roger's palace.

The *Bishop's Palace* dates from the time of Bishop Roger (1102–39); latrines at the N. end of the W. range are complete in themselves and antedate the adjacent curtain wall. The palace consisted of four ranges enclosing a paved court, an irregular quadrilateral. Only foundations survive; they are carried down to original ground level and are built of flint rubble set in yellow mortar. The spaces between the foundation walls were filled with loose chalk and soil. To the W., a levelled garden was contained by a retaining wall 2 ft. thick at the base and ashlar-faced on the W., but left rough on the inside, extending from the N.W. corner of the treasury to the curtain.

The E. range, set approximately at right-angles to the N. side of the cloister, was entirely occupied by an aisled *Hall* with later additions at its N. end. The central part of the hall (90 ft. by 21 ft.) was flanked by aisles (11 ft. to 12 ft. wide). Fragments of masonry found in the excavation suggested that the piers of the aisles were rectangular, with twisted shafts at the angles, and that the arches had moulded orders and ornamental hood-mouldings. A 'corbel with setting-out lines upon its upper surface suggests that the aisles were vaulted, and this rather points to a clearstorey above the middle division'.[47] A dais 8 ft. wide, raised 2 ft. above general floor level, lay at the S. end. The floor was of plaster. In the second bay from the N., in the body of the hall 'a large square section [of the floor] bore some traces of an enclosing curb, and was blackened to such an extent as to suggest that it marked the place of a brazier or hearth of logs, by which the building was warmed'. Solid external foundations near the middle of the E. wall indicated a porch covering the main entrance. The two rooms on the N. were later than the hall; their foundations included squared and moulded stones of the 11th and 12th centuries laid in white mortar. These rooms had served as kitchens.

The S. range of the palace was set against the N. wall of the cloister. On the ground floor it formed a gallery linking the dais of the hall with the W. range. There was a latrine in the internal angle between the N. wall and the hall. The solid foundations indicate that the range had two storeys, the upper one possibly containing the bishop's chapel.

The W. range, probably containing the *camera* and private apartment of the bishop in the upper storey, was set obliquely to the cloister and extended to the curtain wall, which was built against the latrine block at the N. end. The ashlar lining of the two latrine pits had been removed, except for a few stones in the lowest courses. Two projections from the W. wall of the range were explained by the excavators as the foundations of a chimneybreast and of a vice, the latter standing opposite the cross wall which divides the range into two parts, 'but of neither of these was there any direct evidence'.[48]

The ground to S.W. and W. of the cathedral, extending as far as the W. gate of the city, was occupied by a number of small buildings with latrine pits set against the inner face of the curtain wall and therefore later than it in date. The best preserved of these buildings, S.W. of the cathedral nave, had a chamber with a doorway on the S. side and with a latrine at the W. end; the hall lay on the N. side. This building, apparently more substantial than others adjacent, was perhaps the Deanery, mentioned in the Use of Sarum.[49] Most of these buildings probably had timber-framed walls set on stone bases.

Dedications of Altars in the Cathedral at Old Sarum

The archaeological evidence is sufficient to show that in the final form of the church there were places for six altars: the high altar, three in the E. chapels and two on the W. side of the pulpitum, these last being attested by steps at the E. end of the nave. The pattern of the pavements shows that there were no altars in the S. transept and doorways show that there can have been none in the N. transept. Correspondingly, six altars are named in documents dating from before the transfer of the *cathedra* in 1219.[50]

The high altar (*magnum* or *authenticum*) stood in the E. part of the presbytery, away from any wall; the earliest recension of the Use of Sarum (*c.* 1210) shows that it could be circumambulated: *Deinde sacerdos ponat thus in thuribulo .... procedat ad altare .... illud incensat, primo in medio, deinde dextera parte, postea in sinistra; exinde imaginem beate Marie, postea archam in quo continentur reliquie, deinde thurificando altare circumeat.*[51]

In a charter ascribed to *c.* 1179 Bishop Jocelyn charges the prebend of Bedwyn with the nightly provision of three lights, to burn: *unum mortarium ante altare Sanctae Crucis, alterum juxta magnum altare ante imaginem Sanctae Mariae, tertium ante altare Omnium Sanctorum.*[52] In view of the connection between All Saints and the cult of relics, and considering that the main altar in the central E. chapel of the new cathedral was dedicated in honour of All Saints and the Trinity,[53] it may be taken that the corresponding chapel in the old cathedral was named in honour of All Saints.

The Use of Sarum shows that the treasurer in *c.* 1210 was bound to provide each night a mortar by the altar of St. Martin and another before the W. doorway to the choir: *praetera unum mortarium tenetur thesaurarius administrare singulis noctibus per annum coram altare Sancti Martini et alium ante januas ostii chori occidentalis.*[54] Altars dedicated to St. Nicholas and St. Stephen are mentioned in the early Use of Sarum in the rules for the Christmas procession, which visited every altar in the cathedral.[55] The procession passed through the N. door, circumambulated the presbytery in a clockwise direction and re-entered the choir through the W. doorway. Assuming that St. Nicholas and St. Stephen were the first and last altars visited, the former would be at the E. end of the N. aisle and the latter would be against the W. side of the pulpitum, S. of the choir doorway.

The altar of the Holy Cross was probably the parochial altar, standing against the W. face of the pulpitum on the N. of the choir doorway. The remaining chapel, at the

E. end on the S. side, must therefore have been that of St. Martin. The deduction is borne out by the order for the Easter procession with the cross from the sepulchre. Starting from the treasury the procession went into the choir by the S. door and passed out through the W. door;[56] it then went clockwise around the choir to end at the alter of St. Martin where the final anthem *'surrexit dominus de sepulchro'* was sung and the participants dispersed to reassemble for matins.

1. Wm. of Malmesbury, *Gesta Pontificum Angl.* (Rolls Ser. lii), 67–8.

2. *ibid.*, 182–3: *illic inchoata novi operis ecclesia, morte senili tempus dedicationis praevenit. A.S.C.,* s.a. (text E).

3. *Sar. Chart*, 373.

4. He may have continued in the chancellorship after his appointment to the bishopric (H.W.C. Davis, *Regesta Regum Anglo–Normannorum* (1913), xvii and No. 188).

5. *Reg. St. Osmund*, i, 190–200. V.C.H., *Wilts.*, iii, 156–8.

6. Simeon of Durham, *Historia Regum*, v, 2 (Rolls Ser. lxxv, 219).

7. Wm. of Malmesbury, *Gesta Regum Anglorum* (Rolls Ser. xc), ii, 375: *tectum turris ecclesiae omnino disjecit, multamque maceriam labefactavit.*

8. *ibid.*, 484.

9. *Cal. Chanc. Wts.* i, 30: Mandate for a writ to the sheriff to deliver the stones of the cellar which was the treasury of the great church in the castle of Salisbury to Friar Solomon (1291).

10. The list of ornaments in 1214 includes: *cortinae iii a parte aquiloni ante vestiarium* (*Reg. St. Osmund*, ii, 134).

11. A corresponding failure to complete the planned nave has been noted in the Abbey Church of Sherborne, with which Bishop Roger was also concerned (R.C.H.M., *Dorset* I, xlix).

12. Wm. of Malmesbury, *Historia Novella* (Rolls Ser. xc) ii, 559.

13. *P.S.A.*, xxvi (1914), 110–11.

14. Frere, *Use*, xx. In *Arch.* lxviii (1917), 111–26, Hope showed that the early recension of the Use relates to Old Sarum and not to the present cathedral.

15. The 15th-century narrative (*Sar. Chart.*, 266–70) is based on older records; it has here been collated with the earliest extant documents (cf. Frere, *Use*, 173).

16. P. Pressutti, *Regesta Honorii Papae III*, No. 441; *Cal. Papal Letters*, i, 46.

17. *Reg. St. Osmund*, ii, 5–7; Pressutti, *op. cit.*, No. 1194.

18. *ibid.*, ii, 10.

19. *Cal. Lib. Rolls*, 1245–51, 65.

20. *Cal. Pat. Rolls*, 1330–4, 82.

21. *ibid.*, 1330–4, 234.

22. Leland, *Itin.*, i, 260.

23. *Gentleman's Magazine*, 1834 (ii), 418; 1835 (ii), 143–6, 640.

24. *P.S.A.*, xxv (1913), 93–104; xxvi (1914), 100–19; xxvii (1915), 230–40; xxviii (1916), 174–83.

25. The Architectural Description is based on the remains visible in 1974, but a number of details not then visible have been included on the basis of the excavators' published reports and Colonel Hawley's day-books, the latter now in Salisbury Museum.

26. A.W. Clapham, *English Romanesque Architecture after the Conquest* (1934), 22. Fig. 4, showing the presumed end of the solid wall at the point where the sleeper wall is overlain by the latter pulpitum, is based on a misreading of the excavation plan.

27. William of Malmesbury probably refers to the lower storey in his description of the Ascension Day procession in the time of St. Osmund: *proferuntur reliquiae ex conditoriis* (*Gesta Pontificum Anglorum* (Rolls Ser. lii), 430).

28. For the dedication of the six altars, deduced from passages in the *Use of Sarum* and the *Register of St. Osmund*, see p. 22.

29. Clapham, *op.cit.*, 161, gives comparable examples in the S. transept at Byland (*c.* 1180).

30. Frere, *Use*, i, xiv.

31. Cf. *P.S.A.*, xxvii, 108.

32. Fragments of glazed floor tiles were found in this area (Hawley MS., 26 July, 1913).

33. *Reg. St. Osmund*, ii, 55. Benson & Hatcher, 24.

34. *Arch.*, lxviii (1917), 116.

35. *Arch. J.*, civ (1947), 146–7. The identification is disputed by H. de S. Shortt (*W.A.M.*, lvii (1959), 217–9) who assigns the slab in question to Bishop Jocelyn.

36. The slab could have covered a small receptacle as the bones would have been disarticulated in the intervening 20 years; this might account for the slight traces of the tomb discovered in the E. bay of the N. arcade, if it really contained St. Osmund's bones. On the other hand the bones might equally well have been placed in the presbytery, in front of the high altar. Of the Easter Sepulchre no trace is recorded. The best text of the Use of Sarum indicates that it was set up in the treasury and lighted by candles (*Praeterea in die parasceues post repositum corpus domini in sepulcro, duo cerei dimidie libre ad minus in thesauraria tota die ante sepulchrum ardebunt;* Frere, *Use*, 6). Hope, in the article cited above, prefers other early texts which say that the candles were supplied from the treasury (*de thesaurario*) and leave the location of the sepulchre uncertain. But an Easter Sepulchre in the presbytery is difficult to reconcile with the order for the Easter morning procession (*deinde crucem de sepulchro tollant........ et sic eant, per*

ostium australe presbiterii incedentes, per medium chori regredientes........ ad altare sancti Martini canentes........ Deinde........ inchoentur matutine; Frere, *Use,* 153—4).

37. Frere, *Use,* 29.

38. *ibid.,* 44: *in eminencia coram reliquiis et crucifixo et imaginabus ibi constitutis* (cf. *ibid.,* 4).

39. *Reg. St. Osmund,* i, 227; ascribed to *c.* 1150.

40. *ibid.,* i, 252.

41. *ibid.,* ii, 134: *cortinae duae ad crucem versus novum hostium a parte australi.*

42. *P.S.A.,* xxvi (1914), 109.

43. *In primis circa claustrum et ita exeant per portam cimiterii laicorum usque ad locum prime stacionis que sit in extrema orientali parte cimeterii laicorum........* (Frere, *Use,* 60).

44. *P.S.A.,* xxvi (1914), 111—4.

45. This may be the Alward whose holdings in Salisbury are mentioned in a bull of Eugenius III (1146) confirming the Church's possessions (*Sar. Chart.,* 12). The excavators suggested Ailward who witnessed a charter of Bishop Roger, *c.* 1108 (*Reg.*

St. Osmund, i, 381). It is possible that they are the same person. An early 12th-century date is indicated by the proximity of Godwin (tomb xvii).

46. He may be identified with Godwin the chancellor who witnessed a charter of Bishop Roger, *c.* 1108 (*Reg. St. Osmund,* i, 381).

47. *P.S.A.,* xxvii (1915), 233—4.

48. *ibid.,* 232.

49. Frere, *Use,* 124.

50. Hope (*Arch.,* lxviii (1917), 119) mistakenly uses in this connection a document of 1222 (*Reg. St. Osmund,* ii, 127—36). It is probable that the altars which he adduces were in the temporary chapel on the site of the new cathedral.

51. Frere, *Use,* 44.

52. *Reg. St. Osmund,* i, 252.

53. *ibid.,* ii, 38—9.

54. Frere, *Use,* 6. These probably correspond with the third and first, respectively, named in the charter of *c.* 1179.

55. *ibid.,* 124.

56. *Reg. St. Osmund,* ii, 153—4.

ECCLESIASTICAL BUILDINGS

(3) **The Church of St. Thomas of Canterbury** (Plates 32–35) stands in a churchyard between the Market Place and the R. Avon. The walls are partly of ashlar and partly of flint and rubble with ashlar dressings; in places they are rendered; occasionally brickwork has been used for repairs. The roofs are lead-covered.[1]

There is no mention of St. Thomas's in Bishop Richard Poore's grant of 1228 and presumably it was at that time numbered among the churches and chapels to be built *(ecclesias et capellas constructas et construendas)* in Salisbury, but ten years later a chapel is spoken of and in 1248 'the church of St. Thomas of Sarum' is mentioned.[2] About 1448 the chancel collapsed; a document of that date records its length as 40 ft., 4 ins.[3] The present *Chancel,* rebuilt soon after 1448 to the original width, but extending further W. than the recorded length, retains at the E. end a weathered ashlar plinth, a stretch of flint walling and two small ashlar buttresses, all of 13th-century origin. Arcaded corbel-tables of 13th-century style now seen in the N. and S. chapels are at too low a level to be *in situ.* Their unworn condition shows that they have been protected from the weather since an early date, probably by the roofs of added aisles; after 1448 they were reused as internal corbels to support the chapel roofs. There is some reason to think that the 13th-century church was cruciform (plan, p. lii). The present chancel is just long enough to accommodate the original chancel to-

gether with a square crossing, suggesting that at the rebuilding of 1448 the former crossing was taken into the chancel. The respond, capital and springing of an early 14th-century arch, exposed by the removal of later masonry at the N.W. corner of the S. chapel, remain from an arch which spanned the presumed S. transept. Large archways at the W. ends of the N. and S. chapels have 14th-century responds. The arches have been rebuilt and the openings widened, but the 14th-century responds still remain, those on the outside re-sited to suit the width of the 15th-century chapels; originally it seems that these openings were in the W. walls of the transept. A 14th-century door jamb built into the S. wall of the S. chapel indicates the length of the former transept. The *South Tower* was being built in 1400;[4] its position suggests that plans had already been made for the widening of the nave. When the chancel was rebuilt after the disaster recorded in 1448 the roof of the *North Chapel* was provided by William Ludlow[5] and the *South Chapel* was rebuilt by William Swayne.[6] Also about the middle of the 15th century the *Nave* was rebuilt and lengthened westwards, perhaps extending over an area where there had formerly been a N.–S. thoroughfare, linking Castle Street and High Street.[7] Flanking the 15th-century nave are wide *North* and *South Aisles,* that on the S. extending to the tower so that the lowest storey of the tower forms a *South Porch.* On John Lyons's engraving dated 1745,[8] in which the

THE CHURCH OF
ST. THOMAS OF CANTERBURY

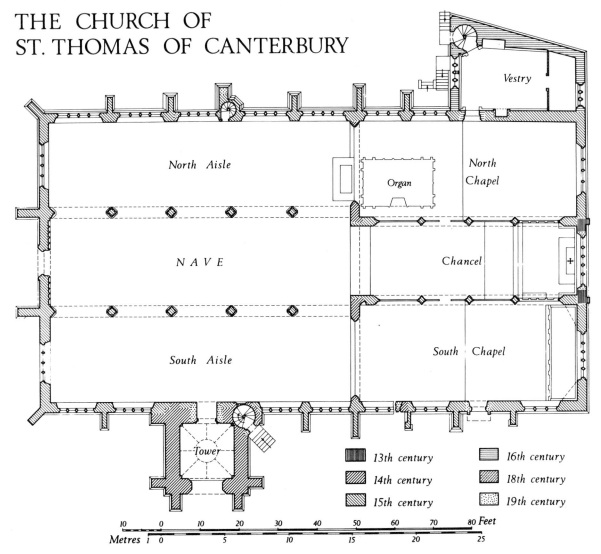

Tower

▓ 13th century	▤ 16th century
▨ 14th century	▧ 18th century
▨ 15th century	▒ 19th century

10　0　10　20　30　40　50　60　70　80 *Feet*

Metres 1　0　　　　5　　　　10　　　　15　　　　20　　　　25

ground plan of the church and two perspective views are presented, a N. doorway and porch are seen immediately opposite the S. tower; the porch is also seen in a drawing of 1805.[9] In 1835 the N. doorway was replaced by a window and the porch was demolished, leaving only the stair turret which had given access to a room over the porch. The three-storeyed *Vestry* wing was added early in the 16th century. Restorations in 1819 revealed a large 15th-century painting of the Last Judgement above the chancel arch. In 1865–70, under the direction of G.E. Street, the galleries were removed, the chancel was rearranged and new seating was provided.[10]

The nave and aisles afford a good example of medieval architecture at the beginning of its latest phase, with the masonry reduced as far as possible to tracery, whether glazed or blind. The highly enriched 15th-century timber roofs are noteworthy, and the contemporary 'Doom' painting is a rare survival.

Architectural Description – Below the 19th-century E. window the E. wall of the *Chancel* is faced with 13th century knapped flint interspersed with a few rough ashlar blocks. Most of the original ashlar plinth has a 15th-century moulded capping, but the steeply weathered 13th-century capping remains at each end. The corners of the chancel are defined by small 13th-century ashlar buttresses capped by 15th-century weathering. The E. window has five transomed lights with curvilinear tracery and is of the late 19th century. Benson & Hatcher (engraving opp. p. 588) show a four-light window with vertical tracery of 15th-century style, but John Buckler (1805) agrees with John Lyons in showing a five-light opening.[11] Above the window is a low 15th-century gable with a moulded stringcourse. The N. and S. sides of the chancel have uniform 15th-century arcades with moulded four-centred arches rising from piers and responds in which attached shafts with foliate capitals and moulded bases alternate with hollow-chamfers. Some capitals have undercut carving with fruit, animals and birds as well as foliage; one on the S. has two shields charged with merchant's marks as illustrated:

WL probably stands for William Lightfoot;[12] IW may be for John Wyot. Another capital has angels bearing a scroll inscribed 'Jhon Nichol John Nichol John the founder of this peler wt. a part of this arche & Jhne the wif of the seyde John' (Plates 35, 42). Above, each side of the chancel has six square-headed clearstorey windows, each with three trefoiled-headed lights; externally they have plain labels and between them are small weathered buttresses with diagonal pinnacles; Lyons's engraving of 1745 shows crocketed finials, but these have gone. The chancel arch is two-centred and of two orders, the inner order with ogee and roll-mouldings, the outer order with hollow-chamfers. The inner order springs from angel corbels. On the W. side the outer order continues on the responds; on the E. it dies into the N. and S. walls. Adjacent, in the S. wall of the chancel is the blocked square-headed upper doorway of a former rood-loft. A segmental-headed recess on the N., now blocked, may be associated with a former pulpit (Lyons's engraving).

The mid 15th-century roof of the chancel has seven stout moulded king-strut tie-beam trusses braced with moulded and traceried quadrant braces to oak wall-posts; these stand on carved stone corbels, two on the E. with crowned heads, two on the W. with shields, the others representing angels bearing musical instruments. The mouldings on the underside of the tie-beams continue on the braces. At the centre of each tie-beam is a carved wooden boss; one depicting a woman's head is probably 14th-century work and perhaps was salvaged from the earlier roof. The moulded principals support purlins and ridge-pieces and these carry hollow-chamfered rafters with run-out stops. Cusped tracery fills the spaces between the tie-beams and the principals.

The E. wall of the *North Chapel* is faced externally with ashlar chequered with knapped flint; the plinth has ogee-moulded capping; the flat roof has a low weathered parapet. The E. window has four trefoil-headed lights (the inner pair ogee-headed) with vertical tracery in a four-centred head under a hollow-chamfered label with plain stops. The doorway to the vestry has a moulded four-centred head with continuous jambs, stone panelled responds with a traceried intrados, and a moulded square

label with bishop and king stops; the carved stone spandrels below the label have quatrefoils with leaf centres. In the upper part of the N. wall a small square-headed loop communicates with the room above the vestry. The N. windows of the chapel are each of three cinquefoil-headed lights under a two-centred outer head; vertical tracery fills the space over the centre light, and the side lights have quatrefoil tracery lights and mouchettes. Externally above each window is a hollow-chamfered label with defaced head-stops. The buttress between the windows is of three weathered stages. On the S. side of the chapel, the wall above the chancel arcade has a stone corbel-table in the style of the 13th century with chamfered two-centred archlets springing from ogee-moulded brackets and supporting a hollow-chamfered stringcourse. The origin of this feature is uncertain, but it probably capped the walls of the original church and was reset at its present level in the 15th century, when the chancel was rebuilt. The stonework is crisp and it cannot have been exposed for long externally. The corbel-table supports one side of the 15th-century chapel roof. At the W. end of the chapel is a wide two-centred arch of two chamfered orders springing from hollow-chamfered responds with moulded and enriched capitals and chamfered bases. The responds are of the 14th century, but that on the N. appears to have been moved in the 15th century from its original position, presumably to widen the archway; the arch voussoirs are larger than is normal in 14th-century work and the thin N. buttress is evidently a 15th-century feature. It thus appears that the 14th-century aisle was narrower than the present one.

The 15th-century roof of the N. chapel, of five bays, is almost flat and rests on four cambered main beams, heavily moulded and mitred to similarly moulded wall-plates. Moulded longitudinal beams divide each bay into four compartments; each compartment is subdivided by a rafter into two square panels closed with boarding; moulded cross-fillets attached to the boarding further subdivide each panel into four parts. The intersections of each main beam with the central longitudinal beam and with the side wall-plates are masked by wooden shields borne by carved angels (in many cases the wings have gone); the intersections of the cross-fillets are masked by foliate bosses. The larger beams are enriched with colour in diagonal bands and many of the shields are painted heraldically:[13] from E. to W., i Stourton, ii France quartering *gules a lion passant or*, iii Audley, iv? Willoughby, v Bourchier, vi *argent a fess gules* impaling Ludlow, vii Hungerford; others blank, missing or inaccessible.

The *South Chapel* is nearly uniform with that on the north. The E. window has five gradated trefoil-headed lights and vertical tracery in a four-centred head; the lower part is blocked with brickwork. As on the S. side of the N. chapel, the N. side has a corbel-table of 13th-century style above the 15th-century arcade. An opening in the masonry in the N.W. corner of the chapel reveals the remains of an earlier arch of two chamfered orders springing from a polygonal respond with a roll-moulded and hollow-chamfered capital; it appears to be of the late 13th or early 14th century and its impost lies 4 ft. below that of the 15th-century arcade. It has been suggested (p. lii) that this arch spanned the opening to a former S. transept. The S. wall has windows and buttresses generally similar to those of the N. chapel; externally the labels have carved head-stops. The second window from the E. has been blocked in the lower part to accomodate a late 19th-century S. doorway with a four-centred head and a stone hood. Beside the third buttress from the E. is the jamb of a 14th-century doorway with an ogee moulding ending at a broach stop; the opening is now blocked, but it is shown as a doorway on Lyons's engraving of 1745. If our conjectures about earlier plans are correct the opening will have been formed in the S. end of the original S. transept. The W. end of the S. chapel has an archway uniform with that of the N. chapel. In the arch, many small 14th-century voussoirs are seen together with larger ones which attest the 15th-century enlargement of the opening. The S. buttress is of the 15th century.

The S. chapel roof (Plate 47) closely resembles that of the N. chapel. Black-letter inscriptions painted on the sides of the main beams ask for prayers for the souls of William Swayne (mayor 1454, 1477), Chrystian his wife and James his father. Carved angel busts at the intersections of the main beams and the central longitudinal beams bear shields painted with—i Five Wounds, ii indecipherable, iii *argent a cross gules*, iv pelican vulning, v Swayne's merchant mark, vi and vii emblem of Trinity, viii–x *azure a chevron between three pheons or* (Swayne).

 William Swayne's merchant mark painted in roof of S. chapel.

The *Nave* (Plate 34) has uniform N. and S. arcades with two-centred arches of three orders; the moulded inner and outer orders rest on attached shafts with undercut foliate capitals and moulded polygonal bases; the wave-moulded intermediate orders continue on the piers. At the E. end the inner orders spring from head-corbels and the outer orders die into the wall; at the W. end there are shafted responds. Above the arches, internally, the N. and S. clearstorey walls are of panelled stonework, each bay having six transomed trefoil ogee-headed panels surmounted by vertical tracery within an elliptical-headed casement-moulded surround. Between

the bays, attached wall-shafts with shield capitals support the woodwork of the roof. In each bay the four middle panels of the upper height are perforated and glazed, forming clearstorey windows with trefoil ogee-headed lights and vertical tracery. Externally the clearstory windows have elliptical labels; between the windows diagonally-set pinnacles resting on worn head-corbels continue upwards, passing through hollow-chamfered stringcourses to terminate in embattled parapets with continuous moulded coping. Lyons's engraving shows crocketed finials, but these have gone. At the E. and W. ends of the clearstorey wall, small two-stage buttresses rise above the end-walls of the aisles. At the W. end of the nave stout buttresses of four weathered stages retain the thrusts of the arcades. The W. doorway has a moulded two-centred head and continuous jambs in a square-headed surround with quatrefoils in the spandrels. Flanking the doorway, internally, are two heights of panelled stonework, the panels having cinquefoil two-centred heads and hollow-chamfered and roll-moulded tracery. The W. window is of seven transomed lights with cinquefoil heads in each height; above, vertical and curvilinear tracery fills the casement-moulded two-centred head. The two-centred head only appears externally and an elliptical transom divides the true lights of the window from false lights in the pointed upper part. Above the window, the embattled parapet forms a low gable with a cross finial.

The nave roof has six king-strut tie-beam trusses with moulded and cambered ties, enriched above and below with brattishing and on the sides with spaced bosses; inverted brattishing below each tie-beam continues on segmental braces which rise from wooden wall-shafts with moulded capitals. Other segmental timber braces springing from the same wall-shafts outline the surrounds of the clearstorey windows and support wall-plate cornices enriched in the same way as the tie-beams. The heavily moulded principal rafters are of equal size with the purlins, ridge-beams and intermediate rafters, forming eight large panels in each bay; moulded secondary rafters and purlins divide each panel into four parts. The triangles between the principals, the king-posts and the tie-beams contain cusped and crocketed wooden tracery. At the centre of each tie-beam, facing E. and W., and at the centre of the wall-plate cornice in each bay, the roof is embellished with a carved wooden angel bearing a shield or a scroll; many shields are charged with sacred emblems carved in relief. The intersections of the moulded timbers are covered by wooden bosses, foliate and heraldic. Centrally in the second bay from E. a shield is carved in relief with the arms of Courtenay quartering Redvers; nearby, on the N. wall-plate, is a carved shield-of-arms of Hungerford.

The windows of the *North Aisle* are approximately uniform with those described in the N. chapel, but taller and of four instead of three lights; the middle window replaces the former N. doorway, abolished in 1835. Each window has a moulded label with defaced stops; above is a hollow-chamfered stringcourse and a low parapet with roll-moulded capping. The stair turret between the second and third bays originally gave access to a chamber over the former porch; at the foot of the stair is a doorway with a chamfered 'Tudor' head. The square-set buttresses between the other bays are each of three weathered stages, as also is the diagonal buttress at the N.W. corner. Part of the E. side of the former N. porch has been formed into a buttress of two weathered stages; in it the doorway of the former porch chamber, a square-headed opening with a moulded label, now has ogee-headed tracery and is used as a window. The stair continues above this level in an octagonal turret to give access to the aisle roof; the W. side of the turret rests on a 19th-century squinch supported on a corbel carved to represent the head and shoulders of a bishop. The W. wall of the N. aisle, rendered externally, has a window uniform with those on the north. The nearly flat wooden roof of the aisle, extensively restored, is similar to that of the N. chapel and externally the lead covering is continuous. Inside, the roof has seven bays. Carved angel bosses at the intersections of the main members and at the centre of each bay of the N. and S. wall-plates bear shields with the following painted charges: from E. to W., i *gules, two keys in saltire or*; ii a page of writing; iii *sable, a cross paty*; iv *gules, a harp or*; v, vi and vii quarterly France and England; viii Bourchier; ix See of Salisbury; x *gules, a cross argent*; xi uncharged; xii *gules, in a border azure semy of crosses paty, three lions passant or*; xiii Five Wounds; xiv Beauchamp; xv Fitzalan quartering Matravers; xvi emblem of Trinity; xvii as v; xviii Stourton; xix *argent, a chevron gules*; xx Edward the Confessor; xxi Montacute quartering Monthermer; xxii Fitzalan; xxiii Audley; xxiv Bourchier; xxv Neville; xxvi *argent a chevron sable*; xxvii *gules a chevron sable*; xxviii *argent a cross gules*.

The *South Aisle* is similar to that on the N. In the middle bay the lower part of the S. tower forms the S. wall. Above the S. doorway a blocked window of three trefoil-headed lights in a chamfered square-headed surround formerly opened into a chamber over the porch. In the next bay, a blocked doorway to the tower vice has a hollow-chamfered two-centred head; above is a blocked window of two square-headed lights. The four large S. windows in the S. aisle are uniform with those of the N. aisle, as also is the W. window and the buttresses. The roof, uniform with that of the N. aisle, has painted shields charged as follows: from E. to W., i indecipherable; ii ?Fitzgerald; iii St. George; iv Gorges; v *sable a chevron between three lilies argent, quartering ermine*; vi *gules a chevron between three catherine wheels or*; vii *argent a chevron between three roses gules*; viii *argent a fess between three moorhens*; ix indecipherable; x *argent a cross gules*; xi perhaps Brereton; xii Audley;

xiii *argent a chevron gules*; xiv Ludlow; xv Clifford (*checky, a fess*); xvi Clifford (*barry*); xvii *sable a chevron ermine between three hurdles argent*; xviii Hungerford; xix Fitgerald; xx *argent a chevron gules*; xxi as xii; xxii *argent a bend engrailed sable*; xxiii ? Talbot; xxiv *gules six drops argent*; xxv *gules a pallium azure impaling argent a chevron gules*; xxvi *argent a chevron gules*; xxvii Stourton; xxviii Beauchamp.

The *Vestry*, of two storeys and a cellar, has ashlar walls and a lead-covered roof. The plinth of the E. wall is uniform with that of the N. chapel; the wall-head has a hollow-chamfered string-course and a low gabled coping. The ground storey has a window with three trefoil-headed lights in a casement-moulded square-headed surround; the upper storey has a similar window of two lights without casement moulding. The N. wall has modern upper windows of one and two lights; the N.W. corner is splayed in the upper part and contains a square-headed niche. The W. wall has a modern doorway near the N. end, a four-light window (as before) in the ground storey, and a similar three-light opening above. An external stair goes down to the cellar doorway, which has a four-centred head of three recessed orders under a hollow-chamfered label; beside it is a square-headed window with double-chamfered jambs. Inside, the ground-floor vestry is lined with oak wainscot with fielded panelling in two heights; it was installed in 1734.[14] The centre mullion of the W. window has a detached hollow-chamfered shaft which supports two four-centred rear-arches. The upper room has a fireplace surround with a hollow-chamfered four-centred head and continuous jambs with splay stops. The cellar is said to have contained a beam with an inscription naming William Swayne (cf. S. chapel roof),[15] but this was not necessarily *in situ*.

The *South Tower*, of four stages, has a moulded plinth, weathered string-courses between the stages, and an embattled parapet above a moulded string-course with gargoyles (Plate 32). The parapet is decorated with trefoil-headed stone panelling. The three lower stages have angle buttresses with weathered offsets, except that the lower parts of the northern buttresses are omitted or have been removed where they would otherwise obtrude into the S. aisle. The stair turret at the N.E. corner ends at the top of the third stage; its S.E. doorway, with a chamfered two-centred head, is of the 19th century. The lowest stage of the tower forms the *South Porch* and has a S. archway with a restored two-centred, double ogee-moulded, casement-moulded and hollow-chamfered head, and continuous jambs ending in run-out stops above hollow-chamfered plinths; the moulded label has square stops. Inside, the porch is vaulted, with hollow-chamfered wall, diagonal and ridge ribs rising from angle shafts with moulded caps and cylindrical bases. Foliate bosses cover the junctions between the wall and ridge ribs. The centre of the vault has a circular bellway. On the N., an archway with a roll-moulded and hollow-chamfered two-centred head and continuous jambs, perhaps of the 18th or early 19th century, opens into the S. aisle. The second stage has E. and W. windows, each of one trefoil-headed light with blind spandrels under a square label. On the S. a similar window of two cinquefoil-headed lights is flanked by cinquefoil-headed niches with shafted jambs, each shaft having a foliate corbel and a crocketed finial. The ashlar of the W. wall retains the outline of the steeply pitched roof of a house which formerly stood in the angle between the tower and the S. wall of the aisle; it appears in Buckler's S.W. view of the church.[16] The third stage has a single-light S. window uniform with those on E. and W. in the second stage. Each side of the top stage has a belfry window of two cinquefoil-headed lights with a cusped tracery light under a two-centred head, with a hollow-chamfered label with head stops. The lower part of each main light is closed by a stone slab pierced with quatrefoils; the upper part has wooden louvres, except on the E. where the upper part of the window is masked by a clockface (see fittings). The steep lead roof, in the form of a hexagonal pyramid, has a metal finial and wind-vane. Within the belfry each corner of the tower has a two-centred squinch of four chamfered orders, suggesting that a stone spire was originally intended.

Fittings – *Bells:* eight; 1st–4th by R. Wells of Aldbourne, 1771, M. Bailey, T. Ogden, churchwardens; 5th given by John Windham, 1683, recast by Wells 1771; 6th and 7th as 1st–4th; tenor by Abraham Rudhall of Gloucester, 1716, Nathl. Sturidg, Tho. Hales, churchwardens, Wm. Naish, mayor. *Clock-bells:* two, by I.W., 1581, Symon Nelle, Willym Yonge church wardens, Robart Ellyt mayor, with monogram SN.

Benefactors' Tables: In vestry, above cornice of 18th-century panelling, records of benefactions from 17th century onwards, probably painted in 19th century.

Brasses and *Indents. Brasses:* In chancel, in floorslab on N., (1) of Elizabeth Eyre, 1612, plate with verses in Roman capitals (concealed by choir-stalls); (2) of Robert Eyre, 1638, similar to foregoing; on S., (3) of John Webbe, 1570 (Plate 48), with black-letter inscription on margin, male and female figures in attitude of prayer, two smaller brasses of children, three shields-of-arms (Webbe quartering Abarough, Webbe impaling Abarough, and Webbe quartering Abarough impaling Wylford) and indent for fourth shield. In N. chapel (4) inscription-plate of John and Catherine Baylye, 1600, with shield-of-arms of Merchant Adventurers of Hamburg impaling Baylye; (5) inscription-plate of Dorothea Ballard, 1709. In S. chapel, reset on N. screen, (6) of William Viner, 1680, inscription-plate and shield-of-arms of Viner. *Indents:* In chancel, on N., (1) for two rectangular plates, 26 ins. by 17 ins. overall. In N. aisle, on top slab of table-tomb (see monument (2)), indents (2) for two

figures bearing scrolls, two groups of children, one shield, one rectangular panel, four corner roundels and continuous margin strip in moulded edge of slab, mid 15th century, all filled in and partly obliterated by later inscriptions; on floorslab No. 10, indent (3) for plate, 2½ ins. by 13 ins., surmounted by figure 11½ ins. high. In S. aisle, near W. end, (4) for plate, 3 ins. by 8 ins.; adjacent (5) for plate, 4½ ins. by 20½ ins.; at S. doorway, (6) for plate 2¼ ins. by 11 ins., and shield 4½ ins. high.

Chairs: In chancel, one, of oak, with turned legs, panelled back, shaped armrests, early 17th century. In vestry, ten uniform oak chairs with turned legs, leather seats and backs, mid 17th century.

Chests: In N. chapel, of oak, with iron straps and handles, 19th century. In S. aisle, of oak, heavily bound with ten strap-hinges, two hasps and staples, and end lifting-handles (Plate 53), early 16th century. In vestry, of oak with panelled sides, late 18th century.

Clocks: In tower (modern movement), with square wooden dial with moulded border, probably 18th century, with added churchwardens' inscriptions of 1843; below, two small wooden striking jacks representing men in late 16th-century armour, probably 1581 (cf. *Bells*). In vestry, oak longcase clock by Francis Shuttleworth, Salisbury, 18th century.

Communion Table: Oak, with bulbous turned legs, 17th century.

Door: In doorway from N. chapel to vestry, of oak with four-centred head and six fielded panels, 1734.

Fonts: Loose in S. porch, circular stone bowl with roll-moulded base, 13th century; octagonal stone shaft with panelled sides, 16th century; moulded base, 19th century.

Glass: In N. chapel, in tracery of E. window, some original stained glass *in situ*, also reset fragments, 15th century; in N. windows, in mouchette openings of tracery, 15th-century leaf patterns; in heads of lateral lights and tracery quatrefoils, 15th-century foliage. In S. chapel, in cusped heads of E. window, fragments of canopy finials; in tracery lights, fragmentary shields with merchant marks, an irradiated figure and other fragments, 15th century. Reset in second S. window from E., formerly in vestry, St. Christopher, perhaps St. Francis, St. Thomas of Canterbury, fragmentary, 15th century.

Hatchments: Seven with shields-of-arms: Spooner impaling Burt; Long; Hawes impaling Hawkins; Long impaling Blackall (*bis*); Powell quartering Priaulx, with inescutcheon of Burrough; Hayter impaling Egerton; 18th and 19th century.

Images: In niches in S. elevation of tower, (1) Virgin and Child, emblem of the See of Salisbury, (2) St. Thomas of Canterbury, patron; 15th century. Reset in easternmost buttress of S. chapel, (3) ogee cinquefoil-headed recess enclosing relief of Crucifixion with St. Mary and St. John; late 14th or early 15th century.

Monuments and *Floorslabs. Monuments:* In chancel, at W. end of N. wall, (1) of William Wroughton, 1770, and Dorothy (Musgrave) his wife, 1799, variegated marble tablet in shaped surround (Plate 50), with arms of Wroughton impaling Musgrave.

In N. aisle, reset at E. end (Lyons shows it centrally in W. part of N. chapel), (2) Purbeck marble table-tomb (illustrated on p. lvii) with moulded top, panelled sides.

Unidentified merchant mark on table-tomb in N. chapel.

six blank shields and two with a merchant mark, plinth with quatrefoil enrichment; top originally with brasses (see *Indents*); mid 15th century. Inset in top slab of foregoing and partly masking indents, alabaster inscription-panels of (3) Thomas Chafin, 1679, and (4) Thomas Chafin Markes, 1727.

In N. chapel, on E. wall, (5) of Thomas Ray, 1670, and Margaret his wife, 1682, marble cartouche with baroque surround and arms of Ray impaling an unidentified coat; on N. wall (6) of John Gough, 1709/10, slate panel in marble surround representing draped archway in architectural surround (Plate 52), arms of Gough on tympanum; (7) of Sara Hersent, 1741, marble tablet in classical surround; (8) of Sir Alexander Powell, 1748, Catherine (Willes) his wife, 1772, and others of the same family, marble monument by R. Earlsman, with obelisk-shaped finial, urns and cartouche-of-arms (obliterated) impaling Willes (Plate 50).

In S. chapel, reset in N.E. corner (Plate 49), (9) of Christopher Eyre [1624], with two kneeling figures in double aedicule with three Corinthian columns under entablature and cresting with shield-of-arms of Eyre and of Eyre impaling Smithies; in S.E. corner, (10) of [Thomas Eyre] and Elizabeth (Rogers) his wife, 1612, painted monument erected *c.* 1624 resembling foregoing and formerly also in chancel, with kneeling figures in double aedicule between obelisks; above, shield-of-arms of Eyre flanked by urns; below, figures of eleven children and three infants.

Below the foregoing monuments and occupying the full width of S. chapel, monument (11) of Sir Robert Eyre (Plate 45), authorised by Vestry in 1724,[17] consisting of low platform (presumably containing burial vault) with ashlar front of fielded panels between panelled pilasters and with moulded capping surmounted by wrought-iron screen, richly worked with scrolls and leafwork, with shaped central gates, eight scrolled uprights, shields-of-arms of Eyre, and a central cresting with arms of Eyre quartering Lucy; top of vault patterned with slate and ashlar; behind, N., E. and S. walls of S. chapel lined with oak wainscot with round-headed panels between fluted pilasters supporting moulded cornices; large central panel with Corinthian pilasters and scrolled broken pediment enclosing carved swags and cartouche-of-arms of Eyre quartering Lucy; Ionic lateral pilasters with smaller pediments. Also in S. chapel, on S. wall, (12) of Thomas Harrington, 1828, marble tablet by Osmond.

In nave, on N. respond of chancel arch, (13) of Richard Earlsman, 1831, marble tablet by Cave; on S. respond, (14) of Joan Popple, 1572, marble tablet (1826) by Osmond. In S. aisle, reset on S. wall, (15) of Humphrey Beckham, 1671, oak panel with biblical scenes carved in high relief (Plate 47); on W. wall, (16) of members of the Long family, 1723–1824, marble tablet by Osmond with shield-of-arms of Long.

In churchyard, 8 paces S. of 3rd buttress of S. chapel, (17) of Ann, 1785, and Benjamin Banks, 1795 (maker of musical instruments), flat stone.

Floorslabs: To the number of 133, few if any *in situ*, include the following: In chancel, (1) of John Webbe, 1570, see *Brasses* (3). In N. chapel, (2) of Mary (Ray) Barnaby, 1724, slate, with long inscription neatly carved; (3) of John Powell, 1737, and his daughter Catherine, 1757, Purbeck with bold lettering and sculptor's signature Mitcherd; (4) of Catherine Powell, 1772, also by Mitcherd. In S. chapel, near S. wall, (5) of Thomas Hawker, 1636, and his wife; (6) of John Conant, 1653, 'orthodox and faithfull minister of this parish'; (7) of Mary Viner, 1682, small slate slab. In nave, near W. doorway, (8) of Henry Long, 1727, Purbeck marble with shield-of-arms of Long. In N. aisle, (9) of Lieut. Francis le Breton, R.N., 1798, Purbeck marble with bold lettering; (10) of Margaret Hele, 1672, Purbeck marble, with indent for antecedent brass, also with inscription of Richard Eyre, 1725. In S. aisle, reset (1975) near E. end, (11) of Jane Eyre, 1695, and (12) of Elizabeth (Chester) Eyre, 1705, two similar black slate slabs with richly carved cartouches-of-arms and moulded margins; near S. doorway, (13) of Anne, 1683, and Richard Minifie, 1706, also Anne (Minifie) Knight, 1709, double slate slab with two shields-of-arms (Knight quartering Page, Minifie and Stoning).

Organ: In N. chapel, by Samuel Green, 1792, in panelled wood case with gothic enrichments, given by George III to Salisbury Cathedral and transferred, with some alteration, in 1877. Previously, a large organ by Thomas Swarbrick, 1739, had been at the W. end of the nave.[18]

Paintings: In nave, on E. wall, Last Judgement (Plate 35), late 15th century; whitewashed 1593, discovered 1819 and re-whitewashed; exposed and restored 1881;[19] at base, on N. of chancel arch, nimbed figure in canopied niche, perhaps St. James; on S., in plainer niche, mitred figure with crosier, perhaps St. Thomas of Canterbury or St. Osmund. In S. chapel, on N. wall, above arcade, three late 15th-century panels (Plate 43) depicting Annunciation, Visitation and Adoration; background painted to simulate red hangings powdered with garter badges and vases of lilies. In vestry, reset on E. wall above panelling, part of biblical scene on canvas, probably remains of a large 'Transfiguration' by Douglas Guest, 1809.[20]

Rainwater Heads: On S. wall of S. chapel, 1682; ditto S. aisle, 1682; on S. wall of chancel clearstorey, 1748; ditto nave clearstorey, 1751, with city badge (eagle).

Royal Arms: In S. aisle, formerly over chancel arch, panel (6 ft. by 6 ft.) in moulded surround with arms of Elizabeth I (Plate 56); probably 1593 (Swayne, 299).

Screens: In E. bay of chancel, on N. and S., of stone, each with four trefoil-headed panels with carved spandrels enclosing blank shields; above, coved cornice with four angel busts carrying scrolls and upper frieze of quatrefoils; late 15th-century. In S. chapel, in E. bay, see monument (11).

Stalls: In chancel, four, of oak with moulded tops and shafted sides; misericords with foliate carving, two with heads (Plate 46), 15th century.

Sundial: On tower, near top of S. elevation, painted, with large wrought-iron gnomon, perhaps 1672.[21]

Table: In vestry, of oak, with circular drop-leaf top and eight legs, late 17th century.

Miscellanea: Mace-rest, of wrought-iron painted and gilded, with central cresting repainted with arms and cypher of George III, and side plaques with civic emblems, 1643.[22] *Textile* (2ft. 10 ins. by 4 ft. 6 ins.), velvet with gold and silver embroidery (Plate 53); at centre, Annunciation, above (?) T E C with crosier, surround powdered with fleurs-de-lis, seraphim and double-headed eagles, 15th century.

For fittings formerly at St. Edmund's, moved to St. Thomas's in 1973–5, see Monument (5).

1. For the history of the church, see Swayne, *Accounts, passim*; V.C.H., *Wilts.* vi, 147–50; *W.A.M.*, xxxvi (1910), 1–12; *Arch. J.*, civ (1947), 150–4.
2. *Sar. Chart.*, 191, 246, 315.
3. Indenture of 1448 preserved in Chapter Act Book (Sar. D. & C.M.), Reg. Burgh., f.2.
4. Will of Thomas de Boyton, Dom. Bk. ii, f.30[v].
5. *Tropenell Cart.*, i, 274: 'William Ludlow of Hill Deverell, boteler to Kyng Harry ivth, vth and vith, which is buried in S. Thomas church in New Salisbury, under a marble tombe atte ende of the Hygh auter in the north side thereof; the ile of the which the seid William Ludlow hathe late new siled, and paynted and sette with scochyn of armes of himself, his wyf, and his children'. Benson & Hatcher render 'siled' erroneously as 'seated'. Ludlow's tomb appears on Lyons's plan (B), but it was removed *c.* 1840 (B & H, 590).
6. *W.A.M.*, xxxvi (1910), 3.
7. See Preface, p. xxxiii.
8. Swayne, *Accounts*, frontispiece.
9. Devizes Mus., Buckler album ix, 18.
10. Faculty petitions, Sar. Dioc. Regy.
11. Devizes Mus., Buckler album ix, 18.
12. Lightfoot was buried in St. Thomas's (P.C.C. Wills, 17 Stockton); the mark ascribed to Wyot occurs again in the hall of Church House (97), for which Lightfoot paid rent in 1455 (*Liber Niger*).
13. According to Benson & Hatcher (p.588) the painted heraldry is unreliable.
14. Swayne, *Accounts*, 352.
15. *W.A.M.*, xxxvi (1910), 10.
16. Devizes Mus., Buckler album ix, 21.
17. Swayne, *Accounts*, 351.
18. Lyons's engraving; also Glyn, 1824, in *W.A.M.*, xlii (1923), 288.
19. *W.A.M.*, 1 (1944), 351–70.
20. *S.J.*, 13 Mar., 1809. *Gentleman's Magazine*, 1810, 581; 1830, i, 409.
21. Swayne, *Accounts*, 341.
22. *ibid.*, 322.

(4) St. Martin's Church, in the S.E. quarter of the city, has walls of flint and rubble with ashlar dressings, and tile-covered roofs; the tower and spire are of ashlar.

At the Domesday Survey of 1086 the bishop's estate in Salisbury comprised the greater part of the Hundred of Underditch. Valued at £47 a year it included the site of the present cathedral, Stratford and Milford, and it nearly surrounded the king's holding which included the castle.[1] No church is mentioned in Domesday, but in 1091 when Bishop Osmund set aside part of the episcopal property for the endowment of the cathedral canons he included 'the church of Sarum with its tithes and other possessions'.[2] In the context this can only mean the church of the manor, identified as St. Martin's in an episcopal charter of 1228 which refers to 'the church of St. Martin of our manor of Salisbury'.[3]

The earliest structural remains yet identified are foundations, perhaps of a *South Transept*, excavated in 1956 just S. of the present S. aisle; they are dated *c.* 1100 by associated pottery.[4] Also of an early date is an obliquely-set flint and rubble wall at the W. end of the present nave and S. aisle. An inclined creasing course in this wall suggests a former roof (Plate 36), but its significance is not altogether certain and there is no proof that the wall was originally part of the church building. The obliquely-set wall is pierced by an early 13th-century doorway with a two-centred head under a roll moulded label; the rebates show that it was the entrance to a building on the site of the present tower and porch.[5]

The long *Chancel* is datable by style to the first half of the 13th century. Early in the 14th century the *West Tower* was built, the lower part of its E. side incorpor-

ST. MARTIN'S CHURCH

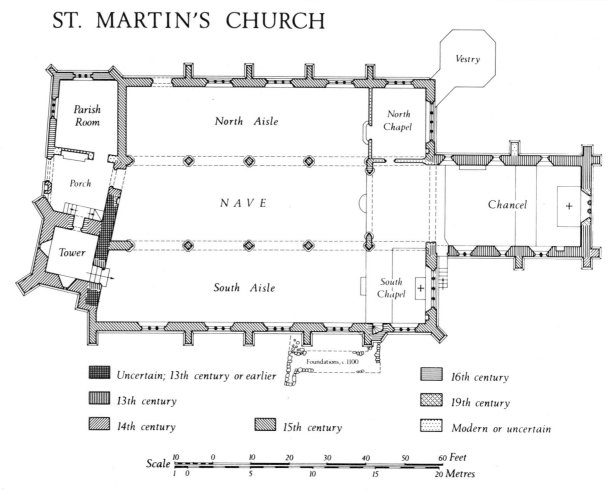

Uncertain; 13th century or earlier

13th century

14th century

15th century

16th century

19th century

Modern or uncertain

Scale

ating the oblique wall with its 13th-century doorway. A 14th-century doorway at the N. end of the oblique wall shows that this wall then served as the W. end of the nave.

Early in the 15th century work began on the *North* and *South Chapels* and on the reconstruction of the *Nave* with *North* and *South Aisles*. The chapels opened off the chancel through archways with four-centred heads, but as work proceeded westwards the design was changed and loftier two-centred arches continued the same alignment in the arcades flanking the nave. The oblique wall at the W. end of the church with its 14th-century nave doorway was retained, but a new W. window was provided.

Before the middle of the 16th century a transverse arch was erected to mark the division between nave and chancel, its responds being set against the piers of the nave arcade at the point where the design of the arches changes. Below the chancel arch was a roof-loft, but this has gone (the present rood-screen is modern) and there only remains the turret stair inserted in the wall at the S.W. corner of the S. chapel. The *West Porch* and adjoining *Parish Room* are of the 16th century; the latter is

sometimes called the Chapel of Corpus Christi.

In the 17th or 18th century the 13th-century chancel was given a lower ceiling and an elliptical arch was placed at its W. end, in line with the E. walls of the N. and S. chapels. In 1838 this elliptical arch was removed, a 'gothic' arch of plaster and lath was put in its place and the chancel ceiling was replaced by a timber and plaster wagon roof. The E. window of the chancel was inserted in 1849[6] in place of one which appears to have been of the 15th century.[7] In 1886 the church was extensively restored and the plaster arch of 1838 was replaced by one of oak.[8]

Architectural Description — The gabled E. wall of the *Chancel* (Plate 31) is built of small flints mixed with some rubble and has original scaffolding holes outlined in rubble; at the base is a chamfered plinth. The window of 1849 has three gradated lancets; above is a circular loop with cusping. The original ashlar angle-buttresses on the N.E. are of one weathered stage; those on the S.E. have two weathered stages and are of the 14th century. The N. wall, of flint and rubble, has three chamfered and rebated lancet windows with moulded labels and stiff-leaf stops. Ashlar at the W. extremity of the wall may suggest the re-entrant angle of a former N. chapel. Inside, the lancet windows have hollow-chamfered rear-arches with labels as on the outside; below the window sills is a restored roll-moulded stringcourse. The S. wall, similar in build to the E. and N. walls, has restored lancet windows of one and two lights, as described, and a two-stage 15th-century buttress. On the W. is an original doorway with a chamfered two-centred head, partly restored, chamfered jambs and a roll-moulded label; the roll moulding is repeated transversely on the E. label-stop; that on the W. is covered by the wall of the S. chapel. Inside, the S. chancel windows have rear-arches as on the N. and the sills have a roll-moulded stringcourse which also forms a label over the segmental-pointed rear-arch of the S. doorway.

The W. bay of the chancel has early 15th-century four-centred N. and S. arches, each with two ogee-moulded orders rising from hollow-chamfered and shafted responds with moulded caps and bases. The N.E. respond has small head-stops in the hollow-chamfers; the N.W. respond, originally a free-standing column, is masked by the N. respond of the chancel arch. The E. respond of the S. arch rests on a shafted bracket with a carved head-corbel; the S.W. respond is similar to that on the N.W. The 16th-century chancel arch is two-centred and of two ogee and roll-moulded orders separated by a casement-moulding; it springs from hollow-chamfered and shafted responds with polygonal caps and bases.

In the *Nave* (Plate 39), the W. face of each respond of the chancel arch, masking the shafting of the former nave columns, has two heights of ogee-headed stone panelling. The upper panel on the S. contains a bracket for an image. Plain ashlar above the panels suggests the level of the 16th-century rood-loft. The N. and S. arcades are nearly uniform, with two-centred arches of two ogee-moulded orders rising from hollow-chamfered and shafted piers similar to those in the W. part of the chancel. Polygonal shaft-caps and bases in the S. arcade suggest that that side was built after the N. side, where most but not all of these features are circular. The oblique W. wall, of flint and rubble with ashlar dressings, has a 14th-century doorway with a chamfered two-centred head and continuous jambs, and a double roll-moulded label with head-stops. The upper part of the W. wall contains a restored 15th-century window of five transomed cinquefoil-headed lights with vertical tracery in a two-centred head (Plate 36).

The nave has a 16th-century wagon roof of eight bays with moulded ribs springing from carved wooden corbels on moulded cornices; the corbels represent angels, demons etc. in various attitudes. Leaf-bosses cover the intersection of the ribs. The regular spacing of the E. bay suggests that the wagon roof is later than the inserted chancel arch.

The *North Aisle* (including the *North Chapel*) has two-stage buttresses of ashlar and flint. The E. window has four cinquefoil-headed lights with vertical tracery and a cusped roundel in a two-centred head; the hollow-chamfered rear-arch springs from male and female head-corbels. The four N. windows are uniform, each having three cinquefoil-headed lights with vertical tracery in a four-centred head. The hollow-chamfered rear-arches spring from corbels carved to represent heads of monks, priests, ladies, a queen, a king and a pope (Plate 42). The N. doorway has a chamfered two-centred head and continuous jambs with rounded stops. In the W. wall, a window uniform with that on the E. opens above the roof of the adjoining building; its two-centred rear-arch has male and female head corbels. The richly decorated late 15th-century wagon roof has moulded ribs with leaf bosses at the intersections; the moulded wall-plate cornices have hollow-chamfers with spaced flowers and carved enrichment above (Plate 44). Alternate cross-ribs rest on polygonal oak wall-shafts with moulded caps and bases; these stand on stone brackets carved to represent male, female and grotesque heads, one with eye-glasses (Plate 42). The intervening cross-ribs spring from oak brackets.

The *South Aisle* (including the *South Chapel*) has ashlar buttresses of two weathered stages. The E. window has four cinquefoil-headed lights with vertical tracery in a two-centred head with a label. The five S. windows are uniform, each having three cinquefoil-headed lights and tracery as described; the hollow-chamfered two-centred rear-arches die into the splayed jambs. The polygonal rood-vice turret, not integral with the adjacent buttress, has a weathered head and a chamfered plinth; on the W. side of the buttress the upper part of the turret rests on a grotesque corbel. The lower doorway of the vice has a four-centred rebated and roll-moulded head and mitred spandrels in a chamfered square surround; the upper doorway has a chamfered four-centred head. The W. end of the aisle (Plate 36) is formed mainly of the E. side of the 14th-century tower, itself incorporating the remains of the earlier oblique flint wall with its 13th-century doorway. In 1886, when the masonry was restored, several fragments of 12th-century carving were exposed and reset; their provenance is unknown. The 13th-century doorway has a chamfered two-centred head and continuous jambs, and a roll-moulded label with returned stops. In adapting the earlier flint wall to form the base of this side of the 14th-century tower the masonry was provided with inclined creasing, bonded to the ashlar of the tower. The inclination of the creasing stones suggests a roof-line and has led to the hypothesis of a 14th-century aisle, but the evidence is inconclusive. The 16th-century wagon roof, similar to that of the nave, was extensively restored in 1886.

The *West Tower* (Plate 36) has diagonal N.W. and S.W. buttresses of three weathered stages and a similar square-set buttress on the S.E.; the windows are in three storeys, but the walls are without offsets. The base has a weathered plinth and the top has a plain parapet with a moulded stringcourse and coping. In the lower storey the N. side has an inserted doorway with a rounded head; the E. side comprises the antecedent wall with the 13th-century doorway already described; the S. and W. sides have small trefoil-headed loops with moulded labels. In the middle storey the N., S. and W. sides have taller loops. In the upper storey the same sides have each a belfry window of two trefoil-headed lights with a cusped tracery light in a two-centred head with a moulded label. Above the W. belfry window is a small loop. The octagonal spire, of ashlar 7½ ins. thick at the base, has weathered broaches, roll-moulded arrises and moulded stringcourses defining four stages. Unlike the cathedral spire (see *Salisbury*, II) it has no internal timber framework.

The *West Porch* and *Parish Room* (Plate 36) have ashlar walls with moulded stringcourses and modern parapets. The N.W. corner has a weathered single-stage buttress. The flat roof lies below the sills of the W. windows of the nave and N. aisle; old pictures show that the roof was formerly pitched and tiled. The room has N. and W. windows of three cinquefoil-headed lights with square labels continuous with the stringcourses. The W. doorway of the porch has a two-centred head of two hollow-chamfered orders and continuous jambs; a small ogee-headed niche beside the S. jamb was probably for a stoup. A narrow ogee-headed window immediately to the S. resembles those of the W. tower and has probably been reset. The wall which divides the porch from the parish room is of uncertain date; it contains a tomb recess with a moulded elliptical head probably of the early 16th century, but not *in situ*; reset within it is a 15th-century table-tomb. Recess and tomb were drawn in 1811 by J. Buckler.[9] The walls of the parish room are lined with modern woodwork. Below is a 19th-century heating chamber.

Fittings – *Bells:* eight; treble and 2nd modern; 3rd and 4th by Mears, 1842–3; 5th and 6th by Richard Flower or Florey of Salisbury, William Smith and Walter Pope churchwardens, 1675; 7th by John Wallis, 1582, 'Be mec and loly to heare the word of God'; tenor by John Wallis and John Danton, 1624, 'Call a solemne assemblie gather the people'.

Brasses and *Indents. Brasses:* In S. aisle, on S. wall, of John Sebastian Carpenter, 1632, plate (13½ ins. by 21 ins.) with inscriptions in Latin, Greek and English and representation of the commemorated, kneeling. In N. aisle, in paving slab near W. end, of M. Godwin, 1785. *Indents:* In S. aisle, near W. end, Purbeck marble floorslab with indents for two rectangular plates. In W. porch, on top of table-tomb, indents for two figures and rectangular plate, 15th century.

Chairs: pair, mahogany, with plain legs, leather-covered seats, shaped arm-rests and serpentine 'ladder' backs, 18th century. *Chests:* two, one iron-bound and painted externally with rosettes, with complicated and highly enriched lock mechanism inside lid, probably late 16th century; another of cast iron with panelled sides, 1813 (old vestry book).

Communion Table: In chancel, of oak, incorporating carved bulbous turned legs and chip-carved rail, 17th century, made up with modern work.

Cross: In churchyard, octagonal stone shaft with spurred foot, mediaeval; finial and pedestal modern.

Doors: In W. doorway of W. porch, of oak planks with cover-fillets, iron ring-handle and scalloped scutcheon, early 16th-century. In N. doorway of N. aisle, doors as described, late 15th century. In parish room, to closet, two reused oak pew doors with shaped tops and fielded panels, 18th century.

Font: (Plate 41) of Purbeck marble, octagonal, with two trefoil-headed panels on each side, moulded central shaft, eight plain corner shafts, hollow-chamfered plinth, and chamfered base; mainly 13th century.

Hatchments: In N. aisle (1) of H.P. Baker, 1794; (2) of John Fuller, 1777; (3) of Mary Thomas, 1781. In S. Aisle, (4) of John Batt, 1723; (5) of . . . . Gooding; (6) of Edward Baker, 1796; (7) of Jane (Phipps) Baker, 1800.

Hour-glass: mounted in brass, inscribed 'St. Martin Sarum, 1721'.

Images, see *Niches*.

Inscriptions and *Scratchings:* In chancel, on E. respond of N. arch, 'Westbury', cursive, 15th century. In N. aisle, on 3rd pier of N. arcade, 'WS 1675'. On E. jamb of N. doorway, outside, 'TI MR 1631'. In tower, on 2nd-storey window jamb, '1535 TS'; 'IS 1627 September the 17'. On N. face of tower, below parapet, '....aird .... churchwardens'; on N.W. tower buttress, 'this spire.... the year of 1794'. (On p.167 Baker records 'This spire was repaired in the year of our Lord 1791: T. Adams J. Young Churchwardens.)

Lectern: (Plate 53) of brass, with eagle and turned pedestal, feet gone, second half of 15th century.[10]

Monuments and *Floorslabs. Monuments:* In chancel, on N. wall, (1) of Richard Earlsman, 1831, tablet by Cave; (2) of William Ludlow of Clarendon, and his daughter Anne, 1749, Purbeck marble tablet with enriched surround and shield-of-arms (Plate 51); (3) of Bennet Swayne, 1748, and Thomas Swayne, 1747, grey and white marble monument (Plate 50) with sarcophagus, urns, shield-of-arms, portrait medallion, cherubs and festoons; on S. wall, (4) of John Chester Pern Tinney, 1832, tablet by Osmond; (5) of Daniel and Edward Hales, 1645, small black marble tablet with emblems of mortality and shields-of-arms of Hales and Hales impaling Gantlet; (6) of Mary Thomas, 1781, marble tablet with scroll cresting (Plate 51). In N. aisle,

(7) of Joseph and Jane Willis, 1772, 1777, slate tablet with marble surround (Plate 51); (8) of Edward Hinxman, 1807, and others of his family, marble tablet by Osmond; (9) of Henry Chester, 1786, and his wife Hetty, 1812, small tablet with arms; (10) of Henry Hinxman, 1829, and others of his family, sarcophagus-shaped tablet with shield-of-arms and crest, by Osmond; (11) of James Bartlett, 1768, and others of his family, marble tablet with pediment (Plate 52). In S. aisle, (12) of Edward Baker, 1796, and his wife Jane (Phipps), 1800, marble wall monument with urn, and arms of Baker impaling Phipps, by King of Bath (Plate 51); (13) of Thomas Snow, 1776, and Elizabeth Tatum, 1798, marble tablet (Plate 51); (14) of Mary Edgar, 1770, slate tablet in marble surround (Plate 51); (15) of John, 1803, and Margaret Blake, 1812, marble tablet with shield-of-arms; (16) of Laetitia Lee, 1800, marble tablet with arms of Lee impaling another coat, by Reeves of Bath; (17) of Goldwyer family, 1748–1812, marble tablet with shield-of-arms and crest. In W. porch, reset in recess in N. wall, (18) Purbeck marble table-tomb with arcaded sides and hollow-chamfered capping, top with indents for brasses, 15th century. In churchyard on S., several headstones and table-tombs, 18th century; 40 paces S. of the tower, (19) stone coffin-lid with hollow-chamfered and roll-moulded sides and cross carved on top, defaced, probably 13th century; 40 paces S. of nave, (20) of William Garlick, 1796, and others, table-tomb with carved panels and moulded top.

Floorslabs: In chancel, 10 reset slate and Purbeck marble slabs include: (1) of Catherine Egerton, 1743, and Elizabeth Grevile, 1745, with lozenges-of-arms of Egerton and Grevile (Plate 50); (2) of Ann (Goddard) Reaves, 1754, with lozenge-of-arms of Goddard; (3) of Sarah Slater, 1797, with lozenge-of-arms of Slater; (4) of Rev. Peter Terry, 1727, and his wife Mary, 1739, with arms of Terry impaling Prince; (5) of John Greenhill, 1674, with arms of Greenhill impaling another coat. In nave and aisles, 46 reset inscribed slabs of slate, marble and Purbeck marble, ranging from 1645 to 1839 include: (6) of Thomas Hancock, 1725, with arms and crest; (7) of William Wastfield, 1735, with arms and crest; (8) of John Rolfe, 1735, with arms and inescutcheon, impaling another coat; (9) of William Goldwyer, 1748, with arms; (10) of Edward Windover, 1645, with arms; (11) of Elizabeth Payne, 1734, with arms of Payne and inescutcheon. In N. aisle, at W. end, (12) of Purbeck marble with worn black-letter inscription, *orate pro natu Johannis . . . . . Jacob . . . . .,* probably early 16th century.

Niches: In N. chapel, in E. wall, with square head and rebated jambs, containing hollow-chamfered shelf; probably 15th century. In S. aisle, in S. wall, with moulded stone surround and coupled cinquefoil head with miniature vaulting, containing Annunciation with two standing figures in alabaster, discovered and restored

1886.[11]

Piscinae: In chancel, in S. wall, with double roll-moulded trefoil head and continuous jambs, shelf, and plain sill with quatrefoil basin, 13th century (Plate 40). In S. chapel, in E. wall, with trefoil head in ogee-moulded square surround, with plain shelf and moulded corbelled sill with octagonal basin, late 15th century (Plate 40).

Plate: Elizabethan silver cup and cover-paten (Plate 54), without assay or maker's mark, but similar in design to 'Gillingham' series,[12] inscribed 'Ex dono Gulielmi Wickham episcopi Vintonia' (Wm. Wickham, 1595). Two patens, one inscribed 'Christopher Horte Thomas Chiffinch church wardins of St. Martins Anno Domini 1620'. Stand-paten by Gabriel Sleath, 1728. Silver flagon, 10 ins. high (Plate 55), with assay mark of 1669 and inscription 'This flagon belongeth to the Parish Church of St. Martins in Sarum, William Antrum, William Ginaway, Churchwardens 1670'. Silver-gilt dish, 18 ins. diam. (Plate 54), with repoussé border; assay mark of 1662 and maker's mark DR with pellets above and below (punch with serrated outline); central shield-of-arms of Edward Hyde, Lord Clarendon, surrounded by donor's inscription of Alice Denham, 1686.[13]

Pulpit: Formerly in St. Martin's[14] now in modern church of St. Mark, of oak, much restored, with tapering panelled base and five panelled sides with cusped arcading and brattishing (Plate 46), late 15th century.

Royal Arms: Of Elizabeth I, painted on panel (Plate 56). Of James I, of carved and painted wood, with arms in garter, crowned, flanked by lion and unicorn carved in the round; probably 1605.[15]

Stoups: Externally on W. wall of porch, with hollow-chamfered ogee head under weathered hood and with continuous jambs ending in broach stops, bowl replaced by weathered ashlar, probably 14th century, reset. In nave, beside W. doorway, with chamfered four-centred head and continuous jambs, chamfered sill and quatrefoil bowl, early 16th century.

Sundials: On S.W. buttress of S. aisle, inscribed *hora porrigit*, with bronze gnomon, 18th century; on S.E. buttresses of chancel and S. aisle, two mediaeval scratch-dials.

Miscellanea: Reset in S. aisle, in W. wall, two carved stones, probably 11th century; in S. wall, carved stone four-petalled flower, similar to examples in Cathedral Close wall reputed to be from Old Sarum; externally in the E. wall of S. aisle, carved mediaeval fragments.

1. V.C.H., *Wilts.*, ii, 121–2.

2. *Reg. St. Osmund*, i, 198–200.

3. *Sar. Chart.*, 191.

4. *W.A.M.* lvii (1958), 40–9.

5. The oblique wall could survive from the church of 1091 and it is possible to construct a sequence of church plans to accomodate the known facts, but

it is also possible that the wall did not become part of the church until the 14th century.

6. *Builder*, 22 Dec., 1849, vii, 605.

7. Drawing of 1838–9 in vestry, also S. Glyn in *W.A.M.*, xlii (1923), 289.

8. Baker, *St. Martin's*, 10.

9. Devizes Mus., Buckler album, ix, f.20.

10. Oman, *Arch. J.*, lxxxvii (1930), 131.

11. Baker, *St, Martin's*, 11.

12. *Dorset* IV, xxxiv.

13. Possibly a relation of Clarendon's second wife, Francis Aylesbury, whose mother was a Denham.

14. Hall, *Memorials*, vignette following plate xxv.

15. Baker, *St. Martin's*, 30.

ST. EDMUND'S CHURCH

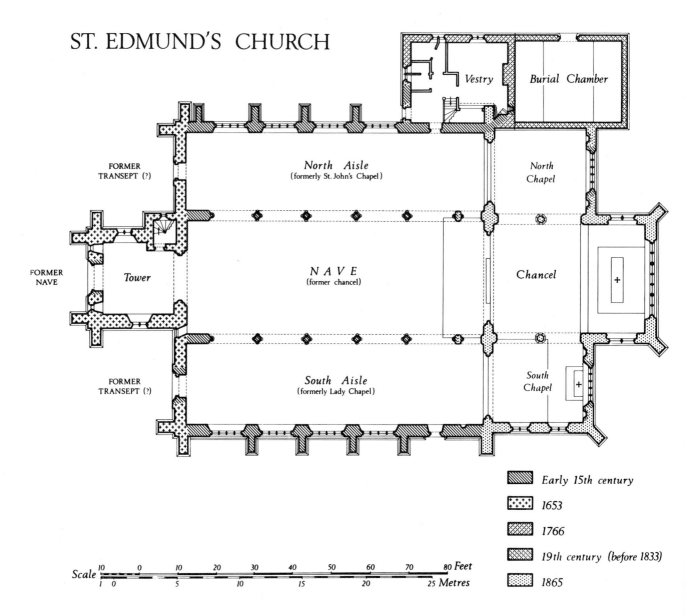

Scale / Legend:
- Early 15th century
- 1653
- 1766
- 19th century (before 1833)
- 1865

(5) St. Edmund's Church, in the N.E. quarter of the mediaeval town, was the church of St. Edmund's College, founded by Bishop Walter de la Wyle in 1269 for a provost and thirteen priests whose duties included the service of a parish.[1] Of the 13th-century building nothing is seen. In the 15th century a large aisled chancel was built, the N. aisle containing a Chapel of St. John and the S. aisle a Lady Chapel.[2] The 15th-century aisled chancel still exists as the present nave; the will of Wm. Mercer (*d.* 1407) probably refers to it when it mentions the newly built church of St. Edmund.[3] As the 15th-century chancel is flanked by aisles the 13th-century church may well have been cruciform, with a central tower and four aisleless arms; the main compartment of the 15th-century chancel would thus have replaced the original chancel while the chancel aisles would have extended E. from the transepts. John Speed's map of Salisbury (Plate 1) shows the church with a nave, a central tower, a S. arm and a wide chancel.

In 1653 the central tower collapsed and it was resolved 'that the E. end of the church now standing shall be repaired' while the W. end 'which is now likely to fall, be taken down in convenient time'.[4] It is probable that the walls then taken down included the remains of the 13th-century building. By 1656 the *Tower* had been rebuilt in the original position and the W. ends of the former N. and S. chapels had been closed with new walls; the 15th-century E. end thus became a *Nave* with *North* and *South Aisles*. There is no clearstorey. A chancel built in 1766[5] is known from a drawing by J. Buckler,[6] and from the plan in Benson & Hatcher (opp. p. 592); it was demolished in 1865 to make way for the present *Chancel* with *North* and *South Chapels*.[7] The lower storey of the *North Vestry* dates from 1766 and the upper storey from 1809,[8] but the W. wall of the vestry incorporates mediaeval masonry. The *Burial Chamber* on the E. of the vestry was added before 1833 (Reform Act map); above it on the first floor is an additional vestry room. In 1973 the church became redundant and was converted to secular uses. Many of the movable fittings were transferred to St. Thomas's (3), but the present inventory records things as they were *c*. 1970.

The walls of the building are mainly of Chilmark ashlar. The nave and aisle roofs are tiled. The tower is a noteworthy example of the survival of the mediaeval style in the middle of the 17th century (Plate 33).

Architectural Description – Reset in the E. walls of the 19th-century N. and S. chapels are two 15th-century windows, probably transferred in 1865 from the E. ends of the aisles. Each window is of five transomed lights with cinquefoil two-centred heads in each height and with vertical tracery in a two-centred outer head. The chancel windows are of 1865.

The chancel arch of 1865 stands approximately in the same position as that of 1766. The 15th-century chancel, now the *Nave*, has N. and S. arcades with uniform two-centred arches, each of two hollow-chamfered orders resting on piers and responds in which attached shafts alternate with hollow-chamfers; the shafts have moulded capitals and bases. Narrow arches at the E. end of each arcade appear to be of 1865.

The *North Aisle* (formerly St. John's Chapel) has five uniform windows, each of four trefoil-headed lights with vertical tracery. The main tracery lights have upper and lower cusping; the four-centred outer heads have moulded labels with head-stops; the rear-arches are seg-

mental-pointed. The easternmost window is masked externally by the vestry building, but it is seen inside; below is a doorway with a double ogee-moulded four-centred head and continuous jambs with broach stops. The N. wall has a plain weathered parapet with a chamfered stringcourse and two worn gargoyles. Each of the four 15th-century N. buttresses has a double plinth and three stages with weathered offsets. The N.W. angle buttresses are of 1656 and have three weathered stages somewhat taller than those of the N. buttresses; their hollow-chamfered plinths are continuous with those of the W. wall and the tower. The W. doorway of the N. aisle has a wave-moulded and hollow-chamfered two-centred head, continuous jambs and a moulded label with square stops; it opens in a plain ashlar projection with a moulded cornice. Above, the W. window has five cinquefoil-headed lights with vertical tracery in a two-centred outer head; the tracery appears to be mediaeval and presumably is reset.

The *South Aisle* (formerly the Lady Chapel) has windows, buttresses and parapet similar to those on the N. An angel is carved on the S.E. corner of the parapet and the stringcourse has three worn gargoyles. The doorway below the easternmost window has a moulded label and continuous jambs ending in run-out stops. The W. doorway has a double ogee-moulded, casement-moulded and hollow-chamfered two-centred head flanked by panelled and cusped spandrels, and continuous jambs with run-out stops; it is of the 15th century and reset. As in the N. aisle the doorway is set in an ashlar projection of 1656 with a moulded cornice. Above is a five-light window uniform with the W. window of the N. aisle.

The *West Tower* (Plate 33) has three stages defined by moulded stringcourses; at the base is a hollow-chamfered plinth; at the top is an embattled parapet above a stringcourse with classical mouldings and corner gargoyles; the corners have pinnacles with crocketed and foliate finials (one missing). The tower buttresses are similar to the N.W. and S.W. angle-buttresses of the aisles, but taller. The N.E. corner of the tower has a plain stair turret. The tower arch, two-centred and of three chamfered orders with continuous jambs, was 'raised' in 1865 and appears to be wholly of that date.[9] In the lower stages the N. and S. walls have square-headed windows of two trefoil-headed lights with cusped tracery lights under moulded labels with eroded stops. The W. doorway is similar to that of the S. aisle and must be reset 15th-century material; flanking the doorway are single-light windows with cusped tracery. Above is a W. window of four trefoil-headed lights with tracery similar to that of the N. and S. windows of the aisles; the two-centred head has a moulded label with head stops. The middle stage has no openings in the E., W. and S. sides; the N. side has a square-headed window of one light. In the top stage each face of the tower has a belfry window of two trefoil-headed lights with a quatrefoil tracery light in a two-centred head; above is a moulded label with head stops; the lower part of each window has a stone closure slab pierced with quatrefoils.

The lower storey of the W. part of the *North Vestry* was mainly built in 1766, but the southern part of the W. wall remains from the 15th century; above the head of the modern doorway is a weathered and hollow-chamfered stringcourse. John Buckler shows a single-storeyed building in this place with a window of 15th-century form in the N. wall. The upper storey was added in 1809 and has two N. windows, each of three lights with plain intersecting tracery in a two-centred head. Nineteenth-century head-corbels flank each opening at springing level, but there are no labels. A straight-joint divides the N. wall of the vestry from that of the added burial chamber. In the lower storey the burial chamber has a doorway with a four-centred head; above are two windows uniform with those of the room over the vestry. Reset at the N.E. corner of the burial chamber is a stone carved to represent an angel; it is similar to the one in the parapet of the S. aisle and no doubt comes from a corresponding position in the N. aisle parapet. The S.E. corner of the burial chamber has another worn mediaeval carving.

Fittings — *Bells:* eight; 1st and 2nd 1884; 3rd, 5th, 7th and tenor by William Purdue and Nathanial Bolter, August 1656, with inscriptions of Richard Grafton, 'friend to the worke', John Percevall, churchwarden, John Stricland, minister, and William Stone, mayor; 4th by Wells, Aldbourne, 1773, 'Mr Wilkins church-warden'; 6th be Mears, 1846. Bell-frame *c.* 1656.

Brackets: In nave, two, reset at W. end on N. and S., stone angel busts with scrolls, 15th century (Plate 42).

Brass and *Indents. Brass:* In tower on N., plate (9 ins. by 6 ins.) of Henry Dove, 1616, mayor, with verses, city shield and dove crest. *Indents·* In S. aisle, Purbeck marble floorslab with indents for male and female figures, double canopy and four shields (Plate 48), probably 15th century. In churchyard, 3 paces N. of tower, Purbeck marble floorslab with indents for figure with inscription and for four shields, probably 15th century.

Chairs: two, oak, with 'pointed' backs with cinquefoil-headed panels and reeded borders, reeded arm-rests and legs, early 19th century.

Chest: Oak, with panelled front and ends, late 18th century.

Cupboard: Deal, painted white, incorporating panel inscribed '1697, George Fort, William Staples, church-wardens'; ventilation holes in door suggest cupboard for dole-bread.

Clock: In tower, by James Phillips, donor Wadham Wyndham, 1839.

Communion Tables: two, with turned legs and

moulded rails, 17th century.

Font: Purbeck marble, with octagonal bowl with two shallow trefoil-headed recesses in each face, 13th century; moulded central shaft with eight plain surrounding shafts, restored; chamfered octagonal base, modern.

Glass: Panel (8 ins. by 12½ ins.), loose, Swiss, 1617.[10]

Hatchments: nine, (1) Wyndham impaling Hearst, 1736; (2) Ivy? impaling Hearst, 18th century; (3) Wyndham impaling Penruddock, 1788; (4) unidentified impaling Eyre, *c.* 1780; (5) Whitchurch? impaling Francis, probably 1822; (6) Hawes, 1820; (7) Wyndham quartering Hearst, impaling Slade, 1844; (8) Wyndham quartering Campbell, 1845; (9) as (8), 1846.

Inscriptions etc.: On tower, below W. parapet, 'John Hilary, John Perceval, churchwardens'; on jamb of W. belfry window 'James Berber 1762'; on N. of central W. doorway, scratched dove; over W. doorway, on oval cartouche with segmental pediment, 'The Lord did marvelously preserve a great congregation of his people from the fall of the tower in this place upon the sabbath day being June 26th 1653' (Plate 20).

Mace-stand: Mahogany, with shaped legs with acanthus enrichment supporting Corinthian columns and segmental pediment; above, double-faced achievement of royal arms (1714–1801) carved in the round (unicorn on reverse of lion and vice versa), painted and gilded, mid 18th century (Plate 56).

Monuments and *Floorslabs. Monuments:* In chancel on N., (1) of Herbert Hawes, 1837, tablet by Osmond. In nave on N., (2) of Wyndham family, 1668–1868, marble tablet, probably 19th century. In N. aisle, (3) of Sydenham Burrough, 1782, Francis Powell, 1746, Anna Powell, 1825, marble tablet by Croome; (4) of Robert Cooper, 1778, and others of his family, marble tablet by Osmond; (5) of Anne and John Baskerville, 1749, 1761, and Thomas and Mary Baskerville, 1781, 1768, pair of alabaster monuments with architectural surrounds; (6) of Elizabeth White, 1833, tablet by Osmond; (7) of John Wych, 1805, and others, oval plaque by Brown. In tower, (8) of Marshall Hill, 1707, marble wall-monument with architectural surround (Plate 52) and shield-of-arms of Hill. In churchyard, 30 paces N. of tower, (9) worn stone table-tomb inscribed 'Here lieth the body of Mr. Peter . . . . ., 164 . .'; adjacent, (10) stone table-tomb with moulded top and panelled sides, inscription indecipherable, 1649. *Floorslabs:* In nave, five slate slabs of members of Long family, 1724–1787, with shields-of-arms of Long and other coats. See also *Indents, s.v. Brasses.*

Niches: In N. and S. chapels, reset on E. walls, remains of eight, with vaulted and canopied recesses, mediaeval. In S. aisle, with imitation vaulting and moulded pedestal for image, hacked back to wall-face, 15th century.

Piscina: Reset in S. chapel, with moulded cinquefoil head, stone shelf at half height and octagonal bowl, 15th century.

Plate: includes silver gilt paten (Plate 55), 6 ins. diam., with date letter 1533 and maker's mark T.W., inscribed in black-letter on rim 'benedicamus patrem et filium cum sancto'; also large silver almsdish with maker's mark G.S., assay mark 1734 and donor's inscription of Edith Naish, 1734 (Plate 55).

Recess: In S. aisle, with moulded four-centred head and continuous jambs, early 15th century.

Royal Arms: see *Mace-stand.*

Woodwork: Incorporated with modern choir-stalls, carved oak bench-ends, 15th century; built into organ case, oak panels carved to represent window tracery etc.

and two with linenfold decoration, 15th century.

1. V.C.H., *Wilts.* iii, 385.
2. Swayne, *Accounts,* xxix.
3. Somerset Hse., P.C.C. wills, 14 Marche.
4. Swayne, *Accounts,* 228.
5. Sar. Corp. MS., St. Edmund's Churchwardens' Accounts, 1757–99, f.20.
6. Devizes Mus., Buckler album ix, f.17.
7. Faculty Petition, Sar. Dioc. Regy.
8. Churchwardens' Accounts, f.42.
9. Sar. Dioc. Regy., Faculty.
10. *W.A.M.,* 1 (1942), 18–23.

ST. LAWRENCE'S CHURCH
Stratford-sub-Castle

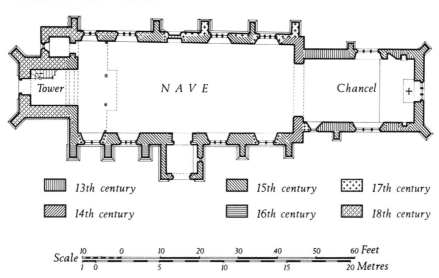

▓ 13th century	▨ 15th century	▦ 17th century
▨ 14th century	▤ 16th century	▨ 18th century

Scale — 10 0 10 20 30 40 50 60 *Feet*

1 0   5   10   15   20 *Metres*

(6) **St. Lawrence's Church**, Stratford-sub-Castle, has walls of flint, rubble and ashlar, and tiled roofs (Plate 38). Although patched and refaced, the N. and S. walls of the *Chancel* are of 13th-century origin and probably represent the Chapel of Stratford mentioned in 1228;[1] there is also a fragment of a 13th-century piscina. The 14th-century chancel arch predicates a nave of that date, and the record of consecration in 1326[2] probably refers to this part of the building; nevertheless the *Nave, Tower Arch* and *South Porch* are of the 15th century. Three nave buttresses were rebuilt in 1583–4.[3] In 1711 the *West Tower* was rebuilt, using the 15th-century plinth and tower arch. Drawings by J. Buckler, *c.* 1808, in Devizes Museum[4] show the church very much as it is today. Restorations were undertaken in 1904 and further repairs date from 1926 and later. The church,

very well maintained, is interesting for the many periods represented in its structure and especially for the continued use of a 'mediaeval' style in 1711. Many fittings are notable.

Architectural Description – The E. end of the *Chancel* was rebuilt during the first half of the 15th century and has masonry of banded flint and ashlar with ashlar dressings. The N.E. and S.E. buttresses are each of two weathered stages. The E. window has three cinquefoil-headed lights and vertical tracery in a two-centred head. The N. wall has a square-set buttress as described and a 15th-century window of three cinquefoil-headed lights. The original masonry is hidden by 15th-century refacing, but the 13th-century origin of the wall is attested internally by the widely splayed reveal of a former window. The S. wall has a window and a buttress uniform with those on the N.; a tall square-headed window at the W. end retains the rebated E. jamb of a 13th-century lancet; its W. jamb and square head are of the 17th century. The 14th-century chancel arch, built with small voussoirs, is two-centred and of one lightly chamfered order springing from hollow-chamfered abaci on chamfered responds; in the N. respond the W. chamfer rises from a convex stop.

The N. wall of the *Nave* is reported to have been 'rebuilt' in 1656,[5] but the wall cannot have been wholly renewed as little more than £8 was spent and an earlier roof remains *in situ*. Externally the wall is of chequered flint and ashlar and the E. part has a chamfered plinth. All five buttresses are of ashlar and of two stages with weathered offsets; the 1st and 3rd are plain and probably of 1656; the 2nd and 4th have wave-moulded weathering and are of the 15th century; the 5th is of the 18th century. In the eastern bay is a 17th-century window of three square-headed lights; the adjacent 15th-century window has cinquefoil-headed lights in a square-headed surround; the blocked N. doorway has a lightly chamfered 'Tudor' head; the two western bays have 18th-century windows uniform with those of the tower. The S. wall of the nave has two original windows with cinquefoil-headed lights; the S. doorway, probably of the 16th century, has a chamfered segmental head and continuous jambs. All the S. buttresses are of two stages with moulded plinths and weathered offsets; the three which were rebuilt in 1583–4 are identified on the W. of the porch by their uniformity and superior masonry.

The *Tower* is of two stages and has walls of flint and squared rubble with ashlar dressings. The ogee-moulded plinth survives from the 15th century. The ashlar N.W. and S.W. buttresses have two weathered stages and do not continue into the upper stage of the tower. The base of the upper stage is defined by a weathered and hollow-chamfered stringcourse. The embattled parapet has a moulded stringcourse, moulded coping and angle pinnacles with finials serrated to suggest crockets. A plain square turret adjoining the N. side of the tower was probably built for a staircase, but the lower part is now a vestry. The tower arch is two-centred and of two deeply chamfered orders dying into the responds. The W. doorway has a lightly chamfered 'Tudor' head upon which is carved in large Roman letters ERECTED ANNO 1711; above, in the lower stage, is a window with two chamfered round-headed lights in a square surround; above this and below the stringcourse is the inscription THO. PITT ESQ. BENEFACTOR. The upper stage of the tower has two storeys. The lower of these has a W. window uniform with that of the lower stage and, on the S. side, a square clock-face. On W. and S. the belfry storey has two-light openings as before, but with louvres; the N. and E. sides have louvred belfry windows of one light.

The *South Porch* is single-storeyed; its flint walls with ashlar dressings are continuous with the S. wall of the nave. The E. side has a small square-headed window. The S. doorway of the porch, with rebated jambs and a chamfered segmental head, is of the 18th century.

The *Roof* of the chancel has a wagon ceiling with moulded wooden ribs, probably of the first half of the 15th century; the wall-plates are masked by fascia boards with classical mouldings. Fifteenth-century wooden bosses cover the intersections of the ribs and the longitudinal members; two of them represent human heads and the others foliage. More elaborate bosses reset at the springing of the transverse ribs (Plate 47) include a mermaid, a king's head, birds, IHS, a collared bear, a man's head and a double eagle. The nave roof, also of wagon form, probably dates from later in the 15th century, but many members have recently been renewed. The wall-plate has double ogee mouldings. The rib intersections are masked by bosses, mostly foliate, but three have heads. At the springing of each transverse rib the wall-plate bosses (Plate 47 centre) are carved with grotesque or human busts, praying or carrying emblems, some of them heraldic.

Fittings — *Bells:* two; treble inscribed Prays God I.W., 1594; tenor by R. Wells, Aldbourne, 1767, I. Blake, W. Randall churchwardens. *Bellframe:* of oak, 1711.

Chairs: In chancel, pair, with turned legs and fiddle backs, mahogany, walnut and elm, late 17th century.

Chests: Three; one of elm with a locking compartment at one end, mediaeval, with 17th-century oak lid; one of oak with panelled sides, early 17th century; one, in vestry, with drawers, oak, early 18th century.

Clock: In W. tower, 1711.

Coffin-stools: One, of oak, with shaped rails and turned legs, *c.* 1600; another, large, of elm, crudely made, perhaps 17th century.

Communion Rails: Of oak, with turned balusters and moulded rails, *c.* 1711.

Doors: In tower archway, oak, incorporating pierced panels with trefoil-headed openings; 15th century. In S. doorway, with fielded panels and round head; in porch doorway, with iron-spiked top; in W. doorway, similar to that in S. doorway; all of pine, *c.* 1711.

Font: Purbeck marble, originally square, but sawn into an octagon, with shallow arcading on two original faces and circles on a third; 12th century. Pedestal, cylindrical with moulded octagonal cap and base, probably 17th century.

Gallery: At W. end of nave, wooden, with fielded panelling above wooden pillars with modern elliptical arches; late 18th century.

Hour-glass bracket: wrought-iron, probably 1652 (ch. wdns. books).

Inscriptions and *Scratchings:* On jamb of S. doorway, initials and dates from 1619; on jambs of porch doorway, from 1728; in tower on W. window, 'I. Borough, C. warden, 1711'; on jamb of N. doorway, 16...

Monuments and *Floorslabs. Monuments:* In chancel, on N. wall, (1) of Anne (Halswell) Bowreman (*sic*), 1630, wall-monument with segmental broken pediment, emblems of mortality and cartouche-of-arms of Bowerman impaling Halswell; (2) of Anne, daughter of Andrew Bowerman, D.D., 1652, small marble tablet; on S. wall, (3) of Josiah Nisbet of Nevis, M.D., 1781, marble wall-monument by H. Hunter, with pediment and shield-of-arms of Nisbet; (4) of Joseph Webb of Nevis, 1779, monument similar to foregoing. In nave, (5) of Harriet Sarjeant, 1831, and others of same family, sarcophagus-shaped tablet by Osmond. In churchyard, 10 paces E. of chancel, (6) of James Townsend, 1679?, table-tomb with panelled sides, scrollwork on pilasters, shields on ends, and moulded top and base (illustration below); one shield with arms of Townsend, another with arms of Davies. *Floorslabs:* In chancel, (1) of Sara Young, 1652; (2) of Andrew Bowerman, 1655; (3) of John Duke, 1670, and Avis his wife, 1687; (4) of Elizabeth Duke, 1692; (5) of Bridget, wife of Bishop Earle, 1696, with lozenge-of-arms of Earle impaling another coat; (6) of Jane Arny, 1650. In nave, (7) of Elizabeth Bewde, 1662; (8) of Catherine Tompson and her son John, both 1702.

Paintings: In nave, over chancel arch, fragment of scroll border in red below illegible black-letter inscription; in porch, over S. doorway of nave, fragment of black-letter inscription and red border; both probably late 16th or early 17th century.

Piscinae: In chancel, two; one on N., presumably reset, with chamfered trefoil head grooved for shelf, 13th century, lower part restored; one on S., with chamfered two-centred head, jambs grooved for shelf, and round basin, probably 14th century, W. half restored.

Plate: Set of silver cup, flagon, paten and almsdish engraved with sacred emblems and cartouches-of-arms of Pitt, with crescent for difference; London assay marks, 1712.

Pulpit: Oak, octagonal (Plate 46), with panelled and arcaded sides in two heights, with chip-carving and other enrichment, also enriched sounding-board with turned pendants, early 17th century; stairs 19th century.

Reredos: Oak, with lower zone of fielded panelling in two heights between Corinthian pilasters, circular central panel with delicately carved and undercut foliate enrichment, and entablature with broken segmental pediment; above, E. window surrounded with moulded oak architrave flanked by fielded panels and round-headed tables of decalogue; at top, frieze of foliate scrollwork surmounted by cartouche flanked by foliate swags; early 18th century.

Royal Arms: Over S. doorway, of Queen Anne (Plate 56), carved in full relief; given by Thomas Pitt, 1713 (ch. wdns. recds.); colour renewed.

Screen: Below chancel arch, of oak (Plate 44), 18th-century assemblage of 15th-century pieces including stout, moulded and casement-moulded beam with foliate bosses, pierced cinquefoil-headed arcading with tracery, and lower panels with cusped and sub-cusped cinquefoil heads below frieze of fretted tracery. Central opening with panelled pilasters and semicircular arch, 18th century.

Seating: In chancel, low box-pews with fielded panelling, oak, 18th century. In nave, 19th-century assemblage of late 17th-century panelling from former box-pews.

Tables of Decalogue: see *Reredos.*

Miscellanea: Carved stonework of 12th century, probably from Old Sarum (Monuments (1)-(2)), built into S.E. nave buttress and N. wall of nave; also one loose arch voussoir.

1. *Sar. Chart.*, 191.
2. *V.C.H.*, *Wilts.* vi, 210.
3. Parish records. Churchwardens' Book, 1572–1728, f.13.
4. Buckler album i, f.30.
5. Churchwardens' Book, *s.a.*

 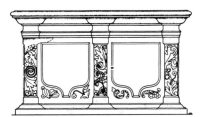

St. LAWRENCE'S CHURCH.
Monument of James Townsend.

(7) **St. Clement's Church,** Fisherton Anger, was demolished in 1852, but some of its fittings were transferred to St. Paul's church, erected in the same year, 350 yds. to the north. Views of the former church are preserved in Salisbury Museum and in Devizes Museum.[1] There is a description of *c.* 1824 by Sir S. Glynne.[2] Part of the old churchyard remains as a garden. Ashlar angle-buttresses of three stages with weathered offsets in the S.W. tower of St. Paul's include masonry brought from St. Clement's.[3] Other masonry from the old church is said to be incorporated with the arches and piers at St. Paul's.

Fittings (in St. Paul's unless otherwise stated) – *Bells:* eight; 3rd by Robert Beconsall, inscribed 'Gev God the glory, R.B., 1616'; 4th and 6th by T. Mears, 1832; 5th by T. Mears, 1842; 7th by John Wallis, inscribed 'Prayse the Lord, I.W., 1609'; others modern.

Benefactors' Tables: Reset in tower, (1) of John Nowes of Lee, wooden panel with painted inscription and shield-of-arms of Nowes, 1819; (2) of General

George Michell, plain wooden panel, 1831; (3) of John Woodward, 19th-century wooden panel with painted architectural border; (4) of Edmund Lambert, plain 19th-century wooden panel.

Book: Incomplete copy of Foxe's Book of Martyrs, black-letter, n.d.

Chest: For registers, cast-iron, panelled, with lion-mask bosses; 'Bramshaw Foundry, 1813'.

Font: Round stone bowl with roll-mouldings above and below, on cylindrical pedestal with roll-moulded and chamfered plinth (Plate 41), 13th century.

Monuments: In chancel, on N. respond of chancel arch, (1) of Richard Kent, rector, 1692, and his wife Margarett, 1711, small white marble cartouche with scrolled surround and acanthus enrichment. In nave, at W. end of S. wall, (2) of Martha, 1801, and William Moulton, 1803, marble tablet surmounted by sarcophagus and urn, with arms of Moulton impaling another coat; at W. end of N. wall, (3) of Sarah d'Oyly, 1800, and others later, marble tablet by Mitcherd, Fisherton. In N. aisle, on S. wall, (4) of Amelia Calder, 1830, marble tablet with lozenge-of-arms of Calder impaling Michell, by Osmond; on W. wall, (5) of Thomas Atkinson, 1838, and his wife Charlotte, 1845, marble tablet by Osmond. In S.W. tower, on S. wall, (6) of William Boucher, 1676, and others of his family, white marble tablet with broken pediment enclosing cartouche-of-arms of Boucher, erected late in the 18th century and subsequently inscribed 'Removed from old church. Osmond, Sarum'; on N. wall, (7) of John Woodward, 1828, marble tablet by Osmond. In St. Clement's churchyard, (8) of Joseph Turner, 1833, table-tomb with panelled sides; (9) of Robert, 1814, and Thomas Askew, 1831, table-tomb with reeded pilasters; (10) of Louisa Mitcherd, 1827, headstone 'carved by John and Mary Mitcherd, her parents'; (11) of Mary Keene, 1841, tomb-slab with lozenge-of-arms of Keene impaling another coat.

Plate: includes pewter flagon inscribed 'the pot of Fisharton Anger church: George Heely, John Marchant, churchwardens, 1660', also two pewter patens inscribed 'Fisherton Parish', with maker's stamp of John Ingles, 1672.

Royal Arms: Above chancel arch, on ogee-headed wooden panel in moulded frame, painted arms of George III.

1.   Devizes Mus., Buckler album i, f.27.
2.   *W.A.M.*, xlii (1923), 199.
3.   V.C.H., *Wilts.* vi, 192.

(8) **St. Andrew's Church**, Bemerton, about 1½ miles W. of the city, has flint and rubble walls with ashlar dressings, and tile-covered roofs. Consisting of a *Nave*, with a small *South Porch* and a wooden *Bellcote*, the building appears to have originated during the second half of the 14th century, but it has been extensively altered. It was restored *c.* 1630,[1] *c.* 1860 and in 1895.[2] Two drawings by J. Buckler, 1808, are in Devizes Museum.[3]

The building is notable for its association with the poet George Herbert who had the benefice from 1630 until his death in 1632.

ST. ANDREW'S CHURCH, Bemerton

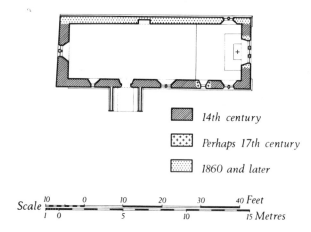

▨	*14th century*
▦	*Perhaps 17th century*
▢	*1860 and later*

Scale   10   0   10   20   30   40 Feet
      1   0   5   10   15 Metres

Architectural Description — The E. window is of three gradated lancet lights in 13th-century style, inserted *c.* 1860. The N. wall, rebuilt *c.* 1860, includes a blocked square-headed doorway with a round-headed rear-arch; it is of uncertain origin but probably of 1860. The S. wall has at the E. end a 14th-century window of two trefoil ogee-headed lights with a chamfered segmental rear-arch. Adjacent on the W. is a small rectangular opening with a chamfered and rebated ashlar surround, probably of the 17th century. Further W. is a well-proportioned 14th-century window of two trefoil ogee-headed lights with a quatrefoil tracery light in an ogee head; an oak beam serves as a rear-arch. The S. doorway has a chamfered two-centred head with continuous jambs; it may be partly original, but the large stones composing the head suggest 17th-century restoration. Near the W. end of the S. wall is a very worn window of one chamfered, square-headed light with an oak lintel internally. The S.W. angle of the nave is of ashlar. The W. window, probably of the late 14th century, has two trefoil-headed lights and a quatrefoil tracery light in a two-centred head under a hollow-chamfered label with head-stops.

The roof includes five pairs of trussed rafters, perhaps of the 17th century; other trusses were renewed *c.* 1860 and in 1895. The louvred *Bell-cote* over the W. gable is probably of *c.* 1800,[4] but it no longer retains its original form (cf. Buckler drawings); the sides are tile-hung.

The *Porch*, of timber on a stone plinth, is of the late 19th century.

Fittings — *Bell:* inscribed A B D C E F G, probably from a Reading foundry, *c.* 1550.

Door: In S. doorway (Plate 46), of oak, with upright planks masked externally by moulded fillets simulating nine panels, and with an enriched rounded head; ? 1630.

Monuments: In nave, on N. wall, (1) of G[eorge] H[erbert], 1632, modern tablet; (2) of John Norris, 1711, slate tablet flanked by white marble Ionic pilasters and surmounted by cartouche-of-arms of Norris impaling Goddard; (3) of Anna Maria (Paulet) Piggot, 1851, marble tablet in form of paper scroll by T. Gaffi; (4) of John Hawes, 1787, and others of his family, oval tablet in architectural surround of variegated marbles with shield-of-arms of Hawes impaling Hawkins; (5) of Margaret, 1820, and Herbert Hawes, 1837, sarcophagus-shaped tablet by Osmond. On S. wall, (6) of William Coxe, 1828, and his wife Eleanor, 1830, marble tablet in moulded frame by Osmond.

Plate: includes two silver communion cups, one with cover-paten the other without, neither dated, probably late 16th century; silver paten with simple incised scrollwork on rim, no assay mark, maker IF, probably *c.* 1700; silver paten with pie-crust rim, Irish assay mark, no date, probably late 18th century.

Miscellanea: Oak panelling with chip-carving, perhaps 17th century, incorporated in modern chest. Iron-strap-hinges on shutter to small S. opening, perhaps 17th century.

1. I. Walton, *Life of George Herbert.*
2. Report by C.E. Ponting; Wilts. Tracts, Vol. 29, Devizes Museum.
3. Buckler album i, f.24.
4. V.C.H., *Wilts.* vi, 48.

(9) **St. George's Church,** Harnham, has walls mainly of flint with ashlar dressings, but partly of ashlar and partly of brick, and is roofed with tiles. The church of Harnham is mentioned in a document of *c.* 1115.[1] The *Chancel* and *Nave* are of the early 12th century and retain N. windows and a N. doorway of the period. The original chancel arch was narrower than at present and was flanked on N. and S. by side altars backed by round-headed recesses. The surviving portion of the S. recess shows that it was originally about 4 ft. wide. In the 13th century new windows were inserted in the S. wall of the chancel and in the nave. Early in the 14th century the chancel arch was rebuilt, larger than before, and the side altars were removed to make room for the wider opening. Also in the 14th century the *South Chapel* was built and the S. doorway was made; probably this is the chapel of Holy Trinity for which provision was made in 1349.[2] A porch outside the original N. doorway has angle buttresses of 14th-century form, albeit rebuilt; they suggest that the porch was intended from the

outset to act as the base of a *North Tower.* In the 15th century the chancel roof was rebuilt and the tower was completed. The tower of this date no longer exists, but it appears in a view by J. Buckler (Plate 11).[3] Shortly before 1835 the 15th-century tower was rebuilt, partly in stone and partly in brick chequered with knapped flint.[4] In 1873 extensive restorations by William Butterfield included the rebuilding of the E. end of the chancel, the W. wall of the nave and the nave roof. The N. porch, at the base of the tower, was turned into a vestry and a new porch was provided on the S. of the nave.

The church retains interesting 12th-century features and a painting of *c.* 1260. The 14th-century chancel arch is well proportioned.

ST. GEORGE'S CHURCH, Harnham

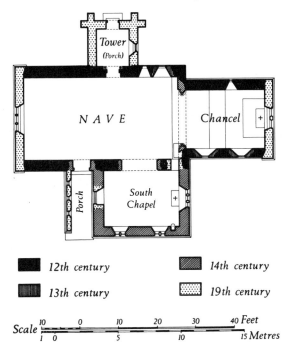

■ 12th century		▨ 14th century	
▥ 13th century		⬚ 19th century	

Scale

Architectural Description — The modern E. window of the *Chancel* has two trefoil-headed lights under a quatrefoil in a two-centred head; that depicted by Buckler appears to have been of similar form. The N. wall, mainly of flint, has a narrow 12th-century window with a round head and wide splays. The re-entrant angle between the N. wall of the chancel and the E. wall of the nave is of ashlar, much of it original. The S. wall has two 13th-century lancets with chamfered surrounds, wide internal splays and segmental-pointed rear-arches; the E. window is set higher than that on the W. to accommodate a contemporary piscina below the sill.

The late 15th-century wagon roof has moulded wall-plates and ogee-moulded ribs with foliate or mask bosses at the intersections. At the springing of the major ribs, busts project horizontally from the wall-plates.

The 14th-century chancel arch (Plate 37) is two-centred and of two wave-moulded orders springing from triple-shafted responds with moulded caps and bases; the bases are set on high plinths. The N. respond has been extensively restored, but that on the S. is original; its base rests on the *mensa* of a 12th-century altar. Tooling on the W. face of the respond suggests the removal of a fourth shaft. Beside the respond, the S. part of a shallow recess for the original side altar is exposed, the N. part truncated by the 14th-century masonry. The corresponding N. recess has gone.

Externally, the E. wall of the *Nave* is of ashlar. The flint N. wall contains a late 13th-century window of one trefoil-headed light with plate tracery in a two-centred head; the tracery comprises a quatrefoil and pierced spandrels. Adjacent on the W. is a round-headed 12th-century window similar to that of the chancel, but wider. Further W. is a 12th-century doorway (Plate 38) with restored plain jambs and square head under an original round-headed recessed tympanum; the voussoirs of the round head rest on original capitals with hollow-chamfered abaci; the shafts and bases have been restored. The S. side of the nave has, at the E. end, a modern squint to the S. chapel; further W. is a 14th-century archway of two chamfered orders, the inner chamfer dying into the responds, the outer chamfer continuous and ending in broach stops. The S. doorway is of 14th-century origin, but restored; it has a chamfered two-centred head and chamfered jambs with broach stops. The W. wall has an ashlar plinth chequered with knapped flintwork above a single course of ashlar; the upper part of the wall is of brick. The plain ashlar at the base is perhaps of the 14th century; the rest of the W. wall is of 1873.

The *North Tower* has stout N.E. and N.W. buttresses of two stages with weathered offsets rising no higher than the ground storey. Similar buttresses drawn by Buckler in 1803 were probably of 14th-century origin, but the present buttresses, N. doorway and E. window are 19th-century work. Above the ground stage, the tower of *c.* 1835 has brick walls chequered with knapped flintwork.

The *South Chapel* is faced externally with ashlar. The E. wall has a window of three gradated trefoil-headed lights with a segmental-pointed rear-arch. The S. windows, each a pair of trefoil-headed lancets, differ from Buckler's drawing which shows square-headed openings. The W. wall contains a wide squint of uncertain origin, with chamfered jambs and lintel; the splayed reveals support a cambered and ovolo-moulded rear-arch.

Fittings (including items in late 19th-century Church of All Saints) – *Altar:* In nave, in recess on S. of chancel arch, chamfered *mensa* on ashlar pedestal, central and two S. consecration crosses preserved, N. part cut away, 12th century.

Bells: Two; 1st modern; 2nd by Clement Tosiear, 1692, Richard Baxter and James Samells churchwardens.

Chairs: Two, of oak, with moulded and carved framework and cane panels, late 17th century. One (in All Saints) of oak, with turned legs, chip-carved stretchers and highly enriched back panel with scroll cresting, early 17th century.

Chests: Oak bible-box with chip-carving and initials MW, 17th century. (In All Saints) oak chest with chip-carving on stiles, 17th century.

Communion Table: In S. chapel, of oak, with turned legs and chip-carving on rails, 17th century.

Font: Plain round stone bowl on roll-moulded stem, *c.* 1200.

Inscriptions and Scratchings: Externally on N.E. quoin of chancel, fleur-de-lis and Here Lyeth . . . . .; on W. wall of S. chapel, dates and initials from 1810; on E. jamb of S. doorway, I H D and crosses, perhaps 17th century.

Monuments: In nave, on W. wall, (1) of Maria, 1791, and Ann Kirkman, 1799, marble tablet with architectural ornament; (2) of Maria Kirkman, 1805, tablet uniform with the foregoing. In churchyard, N. of chancel, (3) of Thomas Ingland, 1709, headstone; (4) of Mary, 1810, and James Precey, 1822, headstone with foliate enrichment; (5) of Sarah Precey, 1787, and William Precey . . . . ., headstone; (6) of Ann White, 1797, and (7) of John White, 1815, pair of shaped headstones with foliate enrichment.

Painting: In recess above side altar on S. of chancel arch, Resurrection with fragmentary kneeling figure with vase and (r) nimbed figure, in dark red outline, *c.* 1260 (Tristram, *Eng. Med. Wall Painting*, XIII cent., 552).

Piscinae: In chancel, on S., hollow-chamfered trefoil-headed recess (Plate 40) with shallow circular basin and roll-moulded corbel; 13th century. In S. chapel, restored ogee trefoil-headed recess with double ovolo-mouldings ending in broach stops, with scalloped bowl and octagonal stepped corbel; 14th century (Plate 40).

Screen: In archway to S. chapel, of oak, with panelled lower zone, arcaded and columned upper zone, and strapwork frieze (Plate 44); early 17th century.

Sundial: On S.W. corner of S. chapel, with hole for gnomon, probably mediaeval.

1. *Reg. St Osmund*, ii, 201–2.
2. *Wilts. I.P.M.* (1327–77), 216.
3. Devizes Mus., Buckler album ii, f 35.
4. Hoare, *Mod. Wilts.*, iii, Pt.2, Cawdon, 63.

(10) **St. Osmund's Church**, designed by A.W.N. Pugin and built in 1847–8 has flint walls with ashlar dressings and roof coverings of slate and of tile (Plate 38). The

ST. OSMUND'S CHURCH

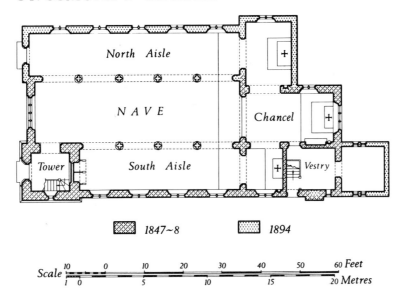

North Aisle

N A V E

Chancel

Tower   South Aisle   Vestry

1847~8   1894

Scale [10 0 10 20 30 40 50 60 Feet / 1 0 5 10 15 20 Metres]

original building comprised *Chancel, Nave, South Aisle, South Chapel, S.W. Tower* and *Vestry*. The N. aisle and the N. chapel were added in 1894.

Fittings include a carved stone *Altar* in the S. chapel, with a hollow-chamfered *mensa* enriched with foliate bosses, set on a square pedestal with a panelled front composed of quatrefoils enclosing fleurs-de-lis; 19th century.

Glass: in chancel and S. chapel windows, by Hardman (*Builder*, Oct. 7, 1848); that in the S. chapel presented by Pugin.

Monument: in churchyard, of John Peniston, 1848, tomb-slab with foliate cross.

(11) **St. John's Chapel**, Ayleswade Bridge, now a dwelling, has rendered rubble walls with ashlar dressings, and a slate-covered roof. The building dates from *c.* 1240 and was founded by Bishop Bingham at the same time as the Bridge (17) and adjacent Hospital (26). Benson & Hatcher (1843) refer to the conversion of this building into a house as 'recent' (p.49, note) but chimneystacks and walled-up windows depicted by Buckler show that changes had already been made *c.* 1808.[1] The dwelling is now three-storeyed, the steep mediaeval roof-pitch having been altered and the walls heightened since Buckler's time, but probably during the first half of the 19th century. Shortly before 1914 the lower part of the building, now containing cellars, was to some extent restored.[2]

Architectural Description – Of the three original gradated lancet windows in the E. wall, the middle one is blocked by a chimneybreast and its position is merely

outlined externally. The two lateral windows, fitted with modern casements, have chamfered two-centred heads under roll-moulded labels with returned stops. Inside, they have widely splayed jambs and hollow-chamfered segmental-pointed rear-arches. A square-headed doorway inserted below the southern E. window has an 18th-century panelled doorcase and acanthus consoles supporting a flat hood, but the woodwork does not appear in Buckler's drawing and presumably comes from elsewhere. The N. wall retains the greater part of four original lancets with sills at a lower level than those on the E.; two have been altered to receive modern case-

ST. JOHN'S CHAPEL

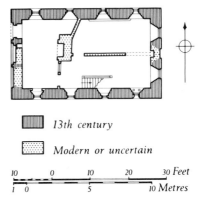

13th century

Modern or uncertain

[10 0 10 20 30 Feet / 1 0 5 10 Metres]

ments and two are bricked up. They have wide splays, stepped sills and hollow-chamfered rear-arches as on the east. Below the sills, part of a roll-moulded interior stringcourse survives. The S. wall retains the sills and splays of four corresponding lancets and traces of a former stringcourse, hacked away. The most easterly window sill contains the plain circular bowls of an original double piscina. The W. wall, largely masked by 19th-century alterations, originally had three openings at ground level. The nothernmost, a doorway with a two-centred head of two chamfered orders under a roll-moulded label and with continuous jambs in which the outer order ends at broach stops, is well preserved; the threshold lies some 8 ft. below the level of the present road. The central and southern openings have been blocked, but the remains of chamfered surrounds indicate former windows with sills some 4 ft. above the doorway threshold; the window heads are obliterated.

Inside, the early 19th century house has simple joinery of the period, including two chimneypieces with neo-classical ornament. Reset in the lower storey is a well preserved 13th-century head corbel (Plate 42). Fragments of 13th-century glazed floor tiles with geometric patterns and of mediaeval window glass are also preserved. A fragment of 13th-century leaf carving is built into a modern wall near the W. doorway.

1. Devizes Mus., Buckler album i, f.26.
2. C. Wordsworth in *Festival Book of Salisbury* (Salisbury Museum, 1914), 37–46.

(12) **Methodist Church**, in Griffin Chequer, has brick walls and slate-covered roofs and was built in 1811.[1] The site had been leased by the congregation in 1758 and in the following year John Wesley preached in 'the new chapel in Church Street',[2] but of this building nothing remains. In 1835 the building of 1811 was extended westwards and vestries were added. In 1870 the W. front was rendered; further alterations to the facade were made early in the present century. Internally, the chapel has galleries on four sides and there are windows in two storeys; the lower ones are segmental-headed and those of the gallery have round heads. In the N. elevation the disposition of the original windows in three bays can be seen; one of them has been blocked and replaced by a smaller opening a little further W.; another is masked by an addition. Further W., upper and lower windows uniform with the original openings have been added to light the 1835 extension. The N. end of a cement plat-band which decorated the W. facade of 1811 remains in the N. elevation.

Inside, the gallery is supported on wooden columns with Roman-Doric capitals, probably of 1811, but the cast-iron parapet is late 19th-century work. The ceiling has late 19th-century enrichment.

Fittings – *Monuments:* (1) of Richard Earlsman, 1831, black marble tablet by Cave; (2) of Joseph Sanger, 1846, sarcophagus-shaped tablet.

Pulpit: mainly of *c.* 1870, incorporates wooden pilasters and front panel, probably from a pulpit of 1811.

1. *S.J.*, 17 June; 1 July.
2. *ibid.*, 24 Sept., 1759.

Presbyterian Meeting House, see Monument (356).
Primitive Methodist Chapel, see Monument (481).

MAJOR SECULAR BUILDINGS

(13) **The Guildhall**, at the S.E. corner of the Market Place, is mainly of two storeys with cellars and has brick walls with stone dressings, and slate-covered roofs. It was erected in 1788–94 on the site of the former Bishop's Guildhall, demolished to make room for it. The demolished building was probably of early 14th-century origin.[1] A drawing in Salisbury Museum (Plate 8) depicts the mediaeval hall in the course of demolition; a plan by Buckler (Plate 12) is in Devizes Museum. The drawing shows the scars of the roofs of a row of low buildings which formerly adjoined the hall on the S.; no doubt they formed the N. side of a courtyard which lay S. of the hall, as shown on Naish's map (Plate 16).

The present building, containing a council chamber, a banqueting room, mayor's parlour etc. and a court of justice, was designed by Sir Robert Taylor and erected with some changes by his pupil, William Pilkington.[2] The foundation-stone was laid on 14 Oct., 1788.[3] A view by E. Dayes, engraved by Frederick Jukes (1795), shows the building with a recessed portico on the N. and a projecting portico on the west.[4] In 1829 the building was enlarged by Thomas Hopper, the N. portico being rebuilt in projecting form with a room above it for the grand jury.[5] In 1889 the W. portico was demolished and a wing containing rooms associated with the law-courts was built in its place. Internally, the building was extensively refitted in 1896–7.

In the N. front (Plate 18), the two main lateral bays, with large round-headed windows with vermiculated archivolts and quoins, are of 1794. The Roman-Doric portico of 1829 probably incorporates four columns and part of the entablature of the original N. portico; above are the three round-headed windows of the grand jury room. The central stone panel, with dedicatory inscription of 1794, appears to have been in the parapet of the original portico. The E. elevation retains its original form, with a large projecting bay with three round-headed windows. In the S. elevation the two main lateral bays of the N. front are repeated, but with simpler details; the central bay, altered in 1829 and later, has round-headed windows in the lower storey and three square-headed windows above, the latter lighting the council chamber.

Inside, the entrance hall contains a reset chimney-piece of *c.* 1580; it was brought from the former Council House, burnt down in 1780[6] and demolished in 1800, which stood some 40 yds. N. of the Bishop's Guildhall. The jambs of the chimneypiece have coarse Ionic pilasters; the frieze has strapwork panels and centrally the arms of the city, *barry of eight, or and azure*, supported by double-headed eagles ducally gorged.

The banqueting room has plaster enrichments and joinery of 1794. Joins in the dado and skirting of the W. wall show the original position of the doorways, before the enlargement of the entrance hall in 1829 allowed the present more spacious arrangement. The fireplace surround is of grey marble with the city arms on a white marble panel; above is a replica of Winterhalter's portrait of Queen Victoria in coronation robes, and over this a trophy with the royal arms as borne from 1707–1714. According to Britton,[7] the Corporation's portrait of Queen Anne by Dahl formerly hung in this position.[8]

The grand jury room has a marble fireplace surround of 1829. A carved oak chair in the mayor's parlour (Plate 21) bears the date 1585, initials TB. HH, and RBM for Robert Bower, mayor, 1584; a similar chair has the date 1622, WM. II, and MGM for Maurice Green, mayor in 1621. Another chair, richly carved in mahogany (Plate 21), has the initials I T M for Joseph Tanner, mayor, and the date 1795.

The inventory of civic plate compiled in 1895 by L. Jewitt and W. St. John Hope,[9] remains unchanged in respect of pieces earlier than 1850. The great mace of 1749 is illustrated on Plate 21. A collection of bronze standard weights and measures, engraved 'New Sarum, 1825' with the city arms and supporters, is now in Salisbury Museum (Plate 21).

1.   V.C.H., *Wilts.* vi, 86.
2.   Colvin, 603.
3.   *Salisbury Journal*, 20 Oct.
4.   V.C.H., *Wilts.* vi, illustration opp. p. 87.
5.   Contract; Sar. Corp. MS., Box 10, No. 32.
6.   *Salisbury Journal*, 20 Nov.
7.   *Beauties of Wiltshire*, I (1801), 88.
8.   Haskins, *Salisbury Corpn. Pictures*, 31.
9.   *Corporation Plate of England and Wales*, 314–20.

THE GUILDHALL

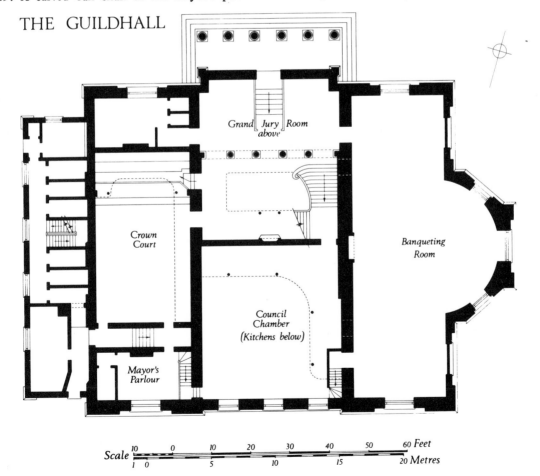

Grand Jury Room
above

Crown
Court

Banqueting
Room

Council
Chamber
(Kitchens below)

Mayor's
Parlour

Scale
10   0   10   20   30   40   50   60 *Feet*
1 0   5   10   15   20 *Metres*

ST. EDMUND'S COLLEGE

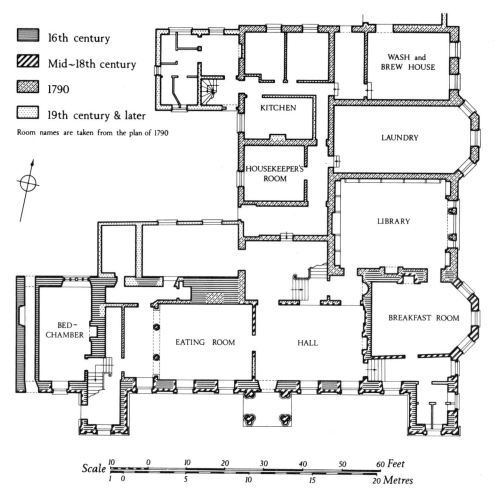

16th century

Mid~18th century

1790

19th century & later

Room names are taken from the plan of 1790

WASH and BREW HOUSE

KITCHEN

LAUNDRY

HOUSEKEEPER'S ROOM

LIBRARY

BED~CHAMBER

BREAKFAST ROOM

EATING ROOM　　　HALL

Scale 10 0 10 20 30 40 50 60 Feet

1 0 5 10 15 20 Metres

(14) **St. Edmund's College,** now **The Council House,** is of two storeys with a cellar and in part with a mezzanine floor; it has rubble and brick-faced walls with stone dressings, and slate-covered roofs. The present building presumably takes the place of the College of St. Edmund which was founded in 1269;[1] stonework in the cellar below the W. part of the S. range may be mediaeval. In 1546 the college was surrendered to the Crown and sold first to William St. Barbe, three years later to John Beckingham, and in 1575 to Giles Estcourt. The S. range, which appears to be of late 16th-century origin, retains plasterwork in which the Estcourt arms occur. In 1660 the college was bought by Wadham Wyndham of Norrington, whose heirs retained possession until 1871.[2] Known as The College throughout this period, it was the largest and handsomest private house in the town. In 1873 it became a school and additions were made on the north. In 1927 it was acquired by the City and converted to local government offices and committee rooms.

A drawing dated 1670 in the possession of the City Council[3] shows the S. front of the 16th-century building as approximately symmetrical and of seven bays, with projecting bays at the centre and at each end of the facade and with an eighth bay on the W., beyond the western projection. The same features are shown on a drawing dated 1690 in Salisbury Museum (Plate 3). The centre bay contained a porch and had a gabled roof; the lateral projecting bays had flat roofs with ball finials at the corners. A stable range stood on the W. of the court in front of the house. The original windows of the S. front were square headed and of three to five lights, many of them with transoms. Above the first-floor windows there were six gables containing attic windows; similar gables occurred on the E. elevation.

About the middle of the 18th century the S. front, perhaps originally of rubble and ashlar, was cased in brickwork with ashlar dressings in a style showing the influence of James Gibbs. The attic storey was removed and new roofs of shallow pitch were masked by brick parapets with ball finials above a moulded stone cornice

(Plate 18). In the projecting end bays, mezzanine windows with elliptical heads replaced the former ground and first-floor openings. A single-storeyed stone porch with Roman-Doric details and clustered columns replaced the former two-storeyed porch bay. In the main plane of the S. front the fenestration was completely changed and the place of four bays of transomed casements was taken by six tall sashed openings with rusticated classical surrounds. In the E. elevation a two-storeyed bay window was added at the end of the original range.

In 1790,[4] under the ownership of Henry Penruddock Wyndham, the N. wing was added, containing the staircase, library, kitchens and service rooms on the ground floor, and bedrooms in mezzanine and upper storeys. The architect was S.P. Cockerell; plans for the projected works, signed S.P.C., 1788, are preserved (Plate 3).[5] Although adapted to new uses the rooms still remain much as originally planned. The large Venetian window of the library and the adjacent bay window, which together with the mid 18th-century bay window to S. make the E. front into a symmetrical composition, are not shown in the plans of 1778, but probably were added to the design before construction took place. Buckler's watercolour of 1811[6] shows the building almost as it is today.

The westernmost bay of the S. range, beyond the W. projection of the S. front, has rendered walls and the windows are asymmetrically disposed. A panel in the W. elevation, with a two-centred head simulating a blocked mediaeval window, appears in Buckler's drawing of St. Edmund's church, 1805[7] and dates probably from c. 1790. The rendered N. front of the W. bay retains, in the lower storey, a late 16th-century stone window of four transomed square-headed lights with ogee-moulded and hollow-chamfered surrounds; doubtless the windows seen in the drawings of 1670 and 1690 had similar details. The N. wall of the S. range also retains a 16th-century stone stringcourse with a strong cyma recta profile.

Inside, the main staircase has cast-iron balustrades and mahogany handrails of 1790; the staircase window has a stained glass panel with the arms of Wyndham. The oak stair in the W. projecting wing of the S. front, with fluted column-shaped newel posts and turned balusters (Plate 89), dates from earlier in the 18th century; on the plans of 1788 it is shown as already in existence. The W. ground-floor room of the S. range (bed-chamber) has a late 16th-century ceiling with interlacing moulded plaster ribs and small panels of foliate enrichment. The 16th-century N. window noted above lights this room, and the embrasure of a similar window, now partly blocked, occurs further E. in the same wall; the remains of a third window are seen in the plan of 1788. A large 16th-century chimneybreast, attested by the thickness of the walls, but hidden by 18th-century and later plasterwork, is shown on the plans of 1788. On the first floor, a room near the W. end of the S. range has a late 16th-century ceiling with interlacing moulded ribs with foliate enrichment and a moulded wall-cornice with a frieze in which shields-of-arms of Estcourt alternate with arabesques. Elsewhere, the principal rooms have decoration of c. 1790 with neo-classical plasterwork of good quality. Francis Bernasconi was employed at the house in 1804, but his bills[8] relate to exterior work and cannot be used as evidence that he was engaged on the interior.

A 15th-century stone *Porch* in the garden 150 yds. E. of the house (Plate 59) was removed from Salisbury cathedral during Wyatt's restorations and rebuilt here in 1791; it formerly sheltered a doorway at the N. end of the N. transept[9] and was known as St. Thomas's Porch.[10] The plain E. buttresses evidently take the place of the cathedral wall. The octagonal spire and pinnacles seen in John Buckler's perspective views of the rebuilt porch[11] were added in 1791; engravings show that the porch at the cathedral was flat-roofed. Inside, the two-centred arches have spandrels heavily enriched with 15th-century leaf carving and are outlined by casement mouldings with spaced flower bosses. The shallow elliptical vault with false ribs is of 1791.

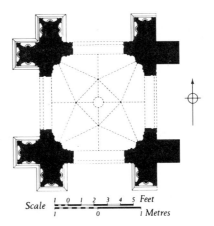

Scale

Porch from Salisbury Cathedral rebuilt at St. Edmund's College in 1791.

In the garden is part of a stone *Urn*, probably of the 17th century, with guilloche decoration; the neck and foot are missing. In 1774 it was set on a pedestal inscribed to record the discovery near that place of bones and rusty armour,[12] supposed to be evidence of Cynric's victory over the British, A.D. 552.[13]

Part of the *City Rampart* survives in the garden (see Monument (16)).

1. V.C.H., *Wilts.* iii, 385–9.
2. Haskins, *Salisbury Charters and History of St. Edmund's College* (Salisbury, 1927), 33–40.
3. Haskins, *op. cit.*, opp. p.30.
4. *Gentleman's Magazine,* 1790, ii, 692.

5. Salisbury Museum, Edwards Collection, I, 191–3.

6. Devizes Mus., Buckler album x, f 32;

7. Devizes Mus., Buckler album ix, f 17.

8. Sar. Corp. MS., Wyndham papers.

9. Benson & Hatcher, engraving opp. p. 524.

10. Frere, *Use*, plan opp. p. 1.

11. Devizes Mus., Buckler album ix, ff, 26, 27.

12. E. Easton, *Salisbury Guide*, 1774, 39.

13. Benson & Hatcher, 5; also *Salisbury Journal*, 16 Mar., 6 Apr., 1722.

(15) **The Poultry Cross** (Plate 57), of Chilmark ashlar with a lead-covered timber roof, stands at the corner of Minster Street and Butcher Row. The hexagonal arcade has piers with weathered and pinnacled buttresses supporting ogee-moulded and hollow-chamfered segmental-pointed arches with ogee labels; above is a moulded stringcourse and a pierced parapet with a canopied niche at the middle of each side. The monument thus far described is datable by style to the end of the 15th century; it cannot be the cross mentioned in the reign of Richard II.[1] The upper part, with flying buttresses surrounding a central pinnacle with six ogee-headed niches and a cross finial, was designed by Owen Carter following a proposal published in 1834 by Peter Hall;[2] the work was executed by W. Osmond in 1852–4;[3] the masonry of the lower part of the monument was restored at the same time. Pictures of the Poultry Cross as it was before 1852 include two drawings in Salisbury Museum,[4] Buckler's view of 1810 (Plate 2), a drawing by A.W. Pugin,[5] and an oil painting of *c*. 1850.[6] Other views are in Salisbury Museum.[7]

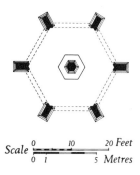

Scale 0 10 20 Feet
0 1 5 Metres

Inside, the hexagonal central shaft and the re-entrant angles of the buttresses retain traces of former vaulting. Each vault rib sprang from a carved corbel; those which survive represent angels holding shields. There are traces of heraldic colouring, *barry of eight, or and azure*.

1. *Arch.*, ix (1789), 373–7.

2. *Picturesque Memorials*, plate xiii.

3. Council Minute Book, 1851–5, 402. *Ills. Lndn. News*, 26 Mar., 1853.

4. One is reproduced in V.C.H., *Wilts*. vi, opp. p.138.

5. R.I.B.A. collection, 1965–16.

6. Shortt (ed.), *City of Salisbury*, Pl.35.

7. Edwards Collection, I, 127, 306.

(16) **City Defences.** The royal charter of 1227 granted the bishop the right to enclose the city with adequate ditches (*fossatis competentibus*). The expression presumably means 'defences' since a ditch with an accompanying bank or wall, or a combination of both, would have been normal, and without it would scarcely constitute an effective defence.[1] Although work may have begun in the 13th century it was certainly unfinished in 1306–7.[2] A deed of 1331 concerning a tenement at the N. of Endless Street speaks of *novum fossatum*, presumably a newly built part of the town defence, on its N. side.[3] In 1367 Bishop Wyvil gave the citizens permission to fortify the town with four gates and a stone wall with turrets and also 'to dig in his soil on every side to the width of eight perches for a ditch'.[4] Such an enterprising scheme was altogether too ambitious and it remained unrealised. In 1378 the citizens sought help of the king to complete the ditch around the city and also a wooden fence or palisade, presumably to surmount the rampart. Despite a grant and subsequent levies on property-owners within the city, the work was still unfinished as late as 1440, but it was probably completed soon after that.

On the W. and S. of the city the R. Avon formed a natural defence; on the E., where the ground rises steeply, and on the N., earthwork defences were constructed. From the marsh at Bugmore on the S. a rampart and ditch extended along the E. side of the city to a point N.E. of St. Edmund's Church (5), where it turned and continued westwards to the E. arm of the R. Avon, in reality the leat of the Town Mill. The marshy nature of the ground foiled an attempt to carry it as far W. as the R. Avon proper. Two fragments of the rampart still survive, immediately N.E. and S.E. of the Council House (14). The bank (Plate 17) is about 60 ft. wide at the base and stands up to 18 ft. high; the surrounding land, and especially the ditch, has been much altered by shallow quarrying and by garden landscaping. Along the W. side of Rampart Road, remains of the bank (6 ft. to 8 ft. high) were revealed and demolished during the construction of a road in 1970; evidence of 13th-century occupation was found in a number of places under the bank. An incomplete section of the ditch (at SU 14852982) showed that it had been recut once and suggested that it was 40 ft. across and nearly 20 ft. deep at that point.[5]

There were eight entrances to the city (Plate 16 and map on p. xxxix) and control over some of them is evident as early as 1269 when there is mention of 'the eastern bars of the city' and of a bar in Castle Street.[6] Bars or barriers, presumably mainly of wood, served to protect most of the entrances even in the 15th century, and formal gateways appear to have been built only in Wynman Street (modern Winchester Street) and Castle Street. The gateways are shown on Speed's map (Plate 1) as rectangular towers with embattled parapets. *Wynman Gate* was demolished in 1771, but part of its N. side may have survived until late in the 19th century, appearing as a rubble wall in an old photograph (Plate 15). An 18th-century painting (Plate 9) shows the round-headed archway. The ground was excavated in 1971 for the building of the inner ring-road, but no trace of the former gateway was found. *Castle Street Gate* was partly demolished in 1788,[7] but the E. abutment remained until 1906; its thick walls are recognisable in a 19th-century plan preserved in the City

Upkeep of the defences seems to have been neglected from the end of the 15th century, but precise information on the stages of their demolition is lacking. Encroachment on the ditch had started by 1499 and in the following century parts of it on the E. side of the city were regularly leased out. Excavations on the S. side of Milford Street have shown that the ditch was filled with rubbish in the 15th and 16th centuries.[10] Naish's plan of 1716 (Plate 16) shows defences only on the E. side of the city; those on the N. had presumably been levelled already. By 1880 (O.S.) about 150 yds. of rampart on the E. side of Barnard's Cross Chequer and the present fragments near the Council House were all that survived.

1.   For a fuller account of the history of the defences, see V.C.H., *Wilts.* vi, 88–9.
2.   Benson & Hatcher, 740 '. . . . *fossatum . . . . olim inceptum*'.
3.   Sar. Corp. MS., deeds 1331.
4.   Benson & Hatcher, 83.
5.   *W.A.M.*, 68 (1973), 137.
6.   Benson & Hatcher, 53, 736.
7.   *S.J.*, 21 July, 1788.
8.   Council Mins., Ledger C, f 408.
9.   Council Mins., Ledger 4, f 133[v].
10. *W.A.M.*, 68 (1973), 137.

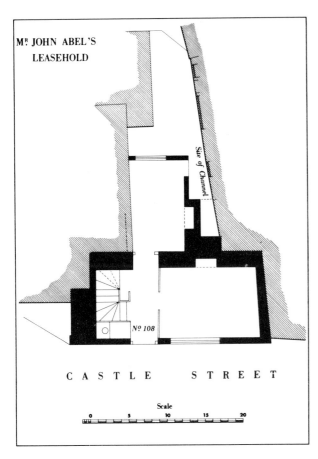

No. 180 Castle Street, demolished in 1906, including the E. side of Castle Street Gate.

Engineer's office. In the upper part of the abutment was a stone panel with the royal arms (Plate 20); presumably it was originally over the archway. Since 1908 the panel has been reset in an adjacent building. It probably dates from 1638,[8] and it appears to have been taken down during the Commonwealth and re-erected in 1662,[9]

(17) **Ayleswade Bridge,** (Plate 19) spanning the R. Avon on the S. of the city, was built by Bishop Bingham, *c.* 1240,[1] at a point where the river is divided by an eyot into two channels. The wider channel on the S. is spanned by six two-centred arches of Chilmark stone; that on the N. has three arches; the northernmost arch is now blocked. The intrados of each original arch is plain and the end voussoirs have double chamfers. The arches rise from stone piers with up-stream and down-stream cutwaters and support a roadway originally some 17 ft. wide. In 1774, to widen the roadway, supplementary arches were built on top of the cutwaters, thus adding 3 ft. to each side of the six S. spans and about 6 ft. to the W. side of the three N. spans. A semicircular pedestrian refuge was built in 1774 on the E. side of the N. part of the bridge; a triangular refuge on the adjacent pier is of the 19th century. Late 18th-century inscriptions record the building of the bridge by Bishop Bingham and its widening in 1774.

1. V.C.H., *Wilts.* iii, 344.

(18) **Crane Bridge,** crossing the R. Avon at the W. end of Crane Street, is of ashlar quarried from the Upper Greensand and has four segmental arches springing from piers with up-stream and down-stream cutwaters. On the N. side (Plate 19) the E. arch has two rings of chamfered voussoirs and may be partly mediaeval. The other

arches have wide chamfers and keystones and are probably of the 17th century. In the 16th century a former bridge had six arches.[1] The S. side of the bridge was rebuilt when the road was widened in 1898, and again in 1970. To the E. of the supposed mediaeval arch, a smaller opening, now blocked, admitted water to the Close Ditch (see p. xxxvi).

1.   Leland, *Itin.*, i, 261.

(19) **Milford Bridge**, of squared rubble and ashlar, carries a narrow and apparently ancient road across two distinct channels of the R. Bourne on the E. boundary of the city. The road probably led to Clarendon Palace,[1] but the present bridge appears to be no older than the late 14th or early 15th century. As the watercourse is divided, the bridge has two pairs of arches separated by a length of causeway (Plate 19). The most westerly arch is semicircular; the others are two-centred. On the S. side the voussoirs of all four arches are mediaeval, with chamfered and hollow-chamfered mouldings. On the N., unmoulded voussoirs indicate rebuilding and lengthening of the vaults for the widening of the road, probably in the 18th century; the semicircular W. arch of the S. side was presumably rebuilt at this time. The piers between both pairs of arches have cutwaters with weathered heads. Road-level is indicated on the N. and S. sides of the bridge by a continuous roll-moulded and hollow-chamfered stringcourse, evidently mediaeval and no doubt partly reset. The ashlar parapets have 18th-century torus-moulded and weathered coping.

1.   Hoare, *Mod. Wilts.*, v. Pt.1, 112.

(20) **Laverstock Bridge**, crossing the R. Bourne on the E. boundary of the city and comprising three spans of cast-iron girders on ashlar piers, was built in 1841 to replace the bridge swept away by floods in that year (*Salisbury Journal*, 25 Jan, 4). The girders are embossed with the maker's name 'Figes Sarum'.

(21) **Dairyhouse, Mutton's** and **Hatches Bridges**, carrying the Southampton road over the R. Bourne and adjacent conduit, S.E. of the city, have been altered in the course of modern roadworks, but retain original features. *Dairyhouse Bridge*, spanning the main stream, consists of a segmental brick arch between ashlar abutments; the parapets are of wrought-iron with twisted uprights and ball finials. The ashlar coping at road level is inscribed J S 1836. *Mutton's Bridge*, about 60 yds. to the W., is of ashlar and has two segmental arches. The S. side has been rebuilt in modern times, but the ashlar parapet includes a date-stone of 1732. *Hatches Bridge*, 250 yds. E. of Dairyhouse Bridge, is of the first half of the 19th century and has two segmental brick arches springing from an ashlar pier with a rounded cutwater.

Inside the W. arch are the voussoirs of an ashlar arch, presumably part of an earlier and narrower bridge.

(22) **General Infirmary**, of five storeys with brick walls and tiled roofs, was designed by 'Mr. Wood of Bath' in 1767 and opened to patients in 1771.[1] Attribution to the younger John Wood is confirmed by analogies at Standlynch House, Downton, where he was active in 1766. Four plans (reproduced on p. 53) and a N. elevation by T. Atkinson, 1819, show the original form of the building. Although somewhat altered and masked by extensions, the 18th-century structure is still in use (Plate 23).[2]

Wood designed a tall building with symmetrical elevations capped by crenellated parapets. Turrets projecting on the E. and W. contained privies and nurses' bed closets. The main entrance was originally at first-floor level, the inconvenience of an exterior stair being mitigated to some extent by artificial heightening of the forecourt; an old photograph (Plate 15) shows the arrangement. The principal administrative rooms and the chapel were on the first floor, with the chapel just inside the main entrance. (The entrance has now been transferred to what originally was the basement level, and the forecourt has been lowered.) The three wards were named after the principal benefactors of the hospital, the Duchess of Queensberry and the Earls of Pembroke and Radnor. Queensberry Ward survives nearly in its original form.

The foundation stone was laid in September, 1767 and tenders from contractors were invited early in 1768. Robert Surman was appointed bricklayer and tiler; Robert Schafflin plasterer; Minty & Godwin glaziers, painters and plumbers; carpentry and joinery was undertaken by Mr. Edmund Lush who also was Clerk of the Works; James Kellow of Tisbury was stonemason.

In 1819 the chapel was converted into an accident ward and the former committee room became the chapel. In 1822 part of the old city gaol (see (476)), which stood between the Infirmary and the R. Avon, was converted into a fever ward, but it was dilapidated and inconvenient and in 1845 it was replaced by a new three-storeyed wing named for a Mr. Bartlett who in 1818 had left money for extensions. In 1846 the accident ward was restored to its original use as a chapel and fitted with a columned and pedimented 18th-century reredos from Warminster parish church. The silver-gilt communion vessels have assay marks of 1793, donor's inscriptions of William Batt, 1794, and shields-of-arms of Batt quartering Clarke.

1.   Governors' Minute Books.
2.   C. Haskins, *History of Salisbury Infirmary*, Salisbury 1922, *passim*.

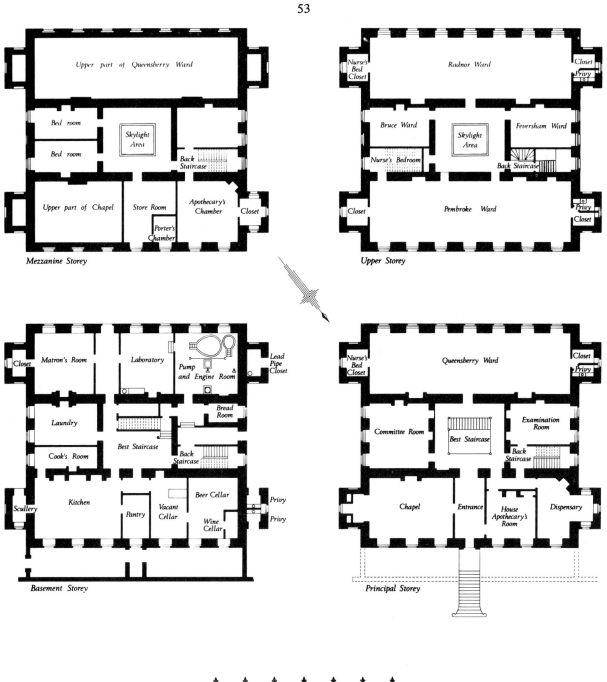

Mezzanine Storey

Upper part of Queensberry Ward

Bed room

Bed room

Skylight Area

Back Staircase

Upper part of Chapel

Store Room

Porter's Chamber

Apothecary's Chamber

Closet

Upper Storey

Nurse's Bed Closet

Radnor Ward

Closet

Privy

Bruce Ward

Skylight Area

Feversham Ward

Nurse's Bedroom

Back Staircase

Closet

Pembroke Ward

Privy

Closet

Basement Storey

Closet

Matron's Room

Laboratory

Pump and Engine Room

Lead Pipe Closet

Laundry

Bread Room

Cook's Room

Best Staircase

Back Staircase

Scullery

Kitchen

Pantry

Vacant Cellar

Beer Cellar

Wine Cellar

Privy

Privy

Principal Storey

Nurse's Bed Closet

Queensberry Ward

Closet

Privy

Committee Room

Best Staircase

Examination Room

Back Staircase

Chapel

Entrance

House Apothecary's Room

Dispensary

Scale of 10   0   10   20   30   40   50 Feet

(22) GENERAL INFIRMARY. Early 19th-century plans.

(23) **Police Station and Lock-up,** near the S. end of Devizes Road, are of two storeys with brick walls and slated roofs; they do not appear on the Reform Act map of 1833, but they are on Botham's plan and probably were built before 1850. The station, now shops, comprised dwellings and offices and has a symmetrical W. front of six bays. The lock-up on the E. has been stripped of floors and partitions and is now a warehouse. The scars of the dismantled brickwork indicate ten vaulted cells in each storey, each cell having a lunette window set high above the floor, with an iron grille in an ashlar frame.

(24) **Former County Gaol,** 100 yds. S.E. of (23), was of three storeys with cellars and had rendered brick walls and slate-covered roofs. Built between 1818 and 1822,[1] the administrative building (a) and the chapel (c) were still in existence in 1959, but were demolished soon afterwards. From 1875 to 1901 the administrative building was in private occupation; thereafter it was used as military headquarters.

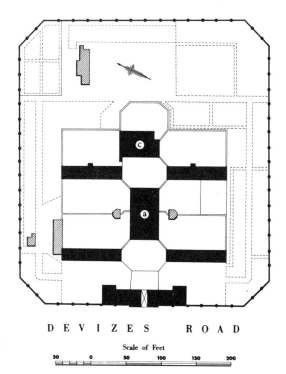

D E V I Z E S   R O A D

Scale of Feet

50   0   50   100   150   200

The former COUNTY GAOL. From a drawing of 1854 (City Surveyor's records).

The administrative building had a symmetrical W. front of three bays with a central doorway, round-headed sashed windows in the two lower storeys and square-headed upper windows. The N. and S. elevations were similar but respectively of six and five bays; the E. side was masked by a later building. Inside, the

stone stairs had plain iron balustrades. The cellar had brick vaults.

The chapel had long been converted to secular use and in 1959 was much altered from its original form. At the time of demolition it had a basement and two upper storeys; a single-storeyed projection on the E. was probably the former chancel.

1. V.C.H., *Wilts.* vi, 182.

(25) **The Market House,** or Corn Exchange, with walls of ashlar and of brick, with an iron and glass roof, was built in 1858 and thus falls strictly outside the scope of this inventory, but it is included because of its prominence as a public building. A Corn Exchange was mooted in 1854 and at first it was intended to build it on the site of the old Council House, in the E. part of the Market Place,[1] but in a revised project the site was transferred to the W. side of Castle Street, whence a 'tram road' might connect it with the newly constructed London and South Western Railway.[2] A plan of the site by Peniston, *c.* 1855, is in W.R.O. (451/222). The Market House Railway was opened in 1859 with the Corn Exchange as its E. terminal.[3] The E. front of the Exchange, designed by John Strapp, Chief Engineer of the L.S.W.R., is ashlar-faced. It has three bays defined by rusticated pilasters, and three large round-headed archways; the middle bay has a pediment. In 1975, when much of the building was pulled down, the facade was incorporated with the structure of a new public library.

The site, between Cheesemarket and the R. Avon, was occupied in mediaeval times by a large courtyard house. Early in the 15th century it belonged to a dyer from Longbridge Deverill and was called Deverell's Inn. In 1423 it passed to John Porte (mayor, 1446) and his wife Juliana.[4] By 1721 the building had become the Maidenhead Inn and it so remained until demolished to make way for the Market House.[5] The 18th-century E. front of the inn is seen in an old photograph (Plate 14). The remains of a 15th-century hall roof and a stone chimneypiece, discovered during demolition, were saved and re-erected in a school (475) near St. Edmund's church.

1. Council Mins., vol. 2, 386.
2. *ibid.*, vol. 3, 24.
3. For an account of the opening ceremonies, see *Salisbury Journal*, 28 May 1859, p. 6.
4. Dom. Bk.iii, f.17[v], 68, 77.
5. Haskins, *Guilds*, 334.

(26) **St. Nicholas's Hospital,** of one and two storeys, with walls mainly of flint and rubble with ashlar dressings, and with tiled roofs, dates from the second quarter of the 13th century. Although the buildings were extensively restored and altered between 1850 and 1884,[1] the outlines of the original structure are clearly distinguishable. In the 13th century there were two

parallel buildings; to the N. a range 62 ft. long (E.—W.) and 24 ft. wide; to the S. a much larger building, 146 ft. long and 48 ft. wide. The N. building was probably two-storeyed. The S. building was single-storeyed and comprised two aisles parted by a central arcade of seven arches (Plate 58); each aisle had its own pitched roof. A chapel was contained within the E. end of each aisle, and each probably had its own W. porch although that of the S. aisle alone remains. The dual nature of the S. building presumably reflects the obligation of the hospital to care for the sick and poor of both sexes. It was built by Bishop Bingham, probably in 1231 when royal grants were made of timber 'for building the hospital'.[2] Bishop Bingham's reference to 'the old hospital towards the

north' suggests that the smaller N. building may be an earlier hospital of St. Nicholas which occurs in documents of 1227.[3] When the S. building had come into being the N. building was probably retained as accommodation for the warden and chaplains.

Enough of the hospital survives to afford a particularly interesting example of mediaeval planning: a single building designed for the separate needs, both spiritual and physical, of men and of women.

Architectural Description – The *North Building* was restored in 1860 and its masonry repointed, but original stonework is seen in the lower part of the walls. In the S. wall are jambs of four blocked doorways. That on the

ST. NICHOLAS'S HOSPITAL

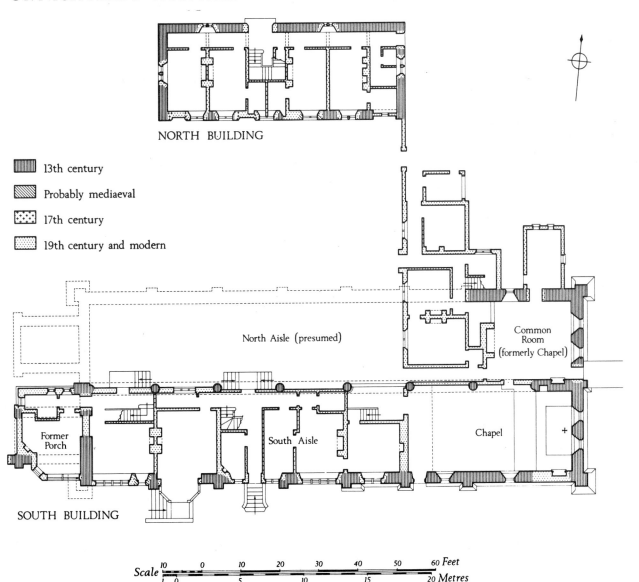

NORTH BUILDING

▦ 13th century

▨ Probably mediaeval

▧ 17th century

▦ 19th century and modern

North Aisle (presumed)

Common Room (formerly Chapel)

Former Porch

South Aisle

Chapel

SOUTH BUILDING

Scale

10   0   10   20   30   40   50   60 *Feet*

1   0   5   10   15   20 *Metres*

E., with a chamfered two-centred head springing from square jambs, is probably original; the next doorway corresponds with a modern window, but the threshold and chamfered jambs are partly mediaeval; further W. a blocked doorway with a chamfered elliptical head and continuous jambs is perhaps of the 17th century; a similar blocked doorway occurs near the W. end of the wall. A weathered stringcourse below the first-floor window sills is of the 19th century, but it may replace a mediaeval feature. Above, at the W. end of the S. elevation, a blocked first-floor window of two trefoil headed lights in 13th-century style, but wholly restored, presumably represents an original opening. The other windows in the S. elevation are modern. The W. wall of the range has a ground-floor window of two pointed lights, perhaps partly original; the upper window is modern. At the E. end of the N. elevation a blocked first-floor window of two pointed lights, fully restored, probably replaces an original opening. In the E. wall the trefoil heads of two 19th-century first-floor windows may echo mediaeval features. Inside, the building has been modernised, but the reveal of a mediaeval S. window is indicated by a niche near the middle of the S. wall.

In the *South Building*, restored by Crickmay in 1884, the two E. chapels are preserved; that on the N. is used as a common-room by the pensioners of the hospital; the southern remains a chapel. The E. wall has a steeply chamfered plinth and clasping corner buttresses of two stages with moulded plinths and weathered offsets. In the square-set middle buttress the weathered offset is roll-moulded. The E. windows of the chapel have chamfered lancet-headed surrounds, wide splays and hollow-chamfered two-centred rear-arches with moulded labels. Above, the gable has a round window of eight lobes with foliate cusps; this is modern, but a drawing by J. Buckler, 1803,[4] shows a similar feature. The N. chapel or common-room has a restored N. lancet and two lancets on the E., all similar to those of the S. chapel. The gable has been rebuilt.

The S. wall of the S. range has a plinth as before and pilaster buttresses of one weathered stage. The remaining original windows have lancet heads, chamfered surrounds and hollow-chamfered segmental-pointed rear-arches. In the second bay from the E. is a small original doorway with a chamfered two-centred head, continuous jambs and run-out stops. Buckler's drawing shows a pair of lancet windows near the S.E. corner, but these have gone. The W. part of the S. wall retains elements of four single-stage buttresses and the jamb of another window, but the masonry has been rebuilt and much altered. A small window near the W. end has a chamfered square head and continuous jambs.

The W. gable of the S. aisle has two restored lancets and a loop, as shown on another Buckler drawing (Plate 11). Further W., the W. wall of the former porch con-

tains a blocked archway with a two-centred head and continuous jambs of two orders, chamfered and hollow-chamfered, under a moulded label without stops.

The N. side of the S. aisle is composed of the original seven-bay arcade in which most of the arches have been closed by modern or 19th-century walls. The arches, two-centred and of two chamfered orders with roll-moulded labels, spring from moulded capitals on cylindrical shafts with moulded bases; the latter are now below ground. Inside, the part of the S. aisle which lies W. of the chapel has been converted into the Warden's residence and other rooms. The former W. porch of the S. aisle is likewise used as part of a dwelling. West of the common-room the N. aisle has gone.

Fittings — *Aumbry:* In S. chapel, in N. wall, with rebated two-centred head and stone shelf, 13th century. *Bell:* At entrance to S. chapel, by John Wallis, 1623. *Benefactor's Table:* In S. chapel, on S. wall, marble tablet in stone frame with four-centred head, recording benefactions of Edward Emily, 1795. *Piscina:* In N. chapel (common-room), in S. wall, with moulded trefoil head, shafted jambs and three-lobed basin (Plate 40), 1231; in S. chapel, replica of foregoing, 19th century. *Table:* In common-room, of oak (11½ ft. by 2½ ft.), with moulded rails, six turned legs and plain stretchers, 17th century. *Tiles:* Reset in S. chapel, thirty, with slip decoration including bowman, deer, griffin etc., 14th century; *Wall-clock:* In common-room, with painted wooden case, by Hugh Hughes, c. 1760.

1. *W.A.M.*, xxv (1891), 156; V.C.H., *Wilts.* iii, 354; Wordsworth, *St. Nicholas*, passim; Charity Comm'rs Report, xxix (1835), 1415–31.
2. V.C.H., *Wilts.* iii, 344.
3. *ibid.*, 343.
4. Devizes Museum, Buckler Collection.

(27) **Trinity Hospital**, founded in 1379 for twelve inmates,[1] was entirely rebuilt in 1702. It is of two storeys with attics and has brick walls with stone dressings and tiled roofs. The chapel was refurnished in 1908. Modernisation in 1950 reduced the number accomodated from twelve to ten.

The symmetrical S. front (Plate 22) has a central doorway with a stone architrave and a broken pediment surmounted by a stone panel with a sundial. The doorway opens into an arcaded loggia at the S. end of the central courtyard. At the N. end of the courtyard (Plate 22) a doorway to the chapel, with a bolection-moulded timber surround and acanthus brackets supporting a broken pediment, has above it two reset stones formerly carved and thought to be relics of the original building.[2] In 1968 the lower stone retained a fragment of a relief suggestive of the decoration seen on

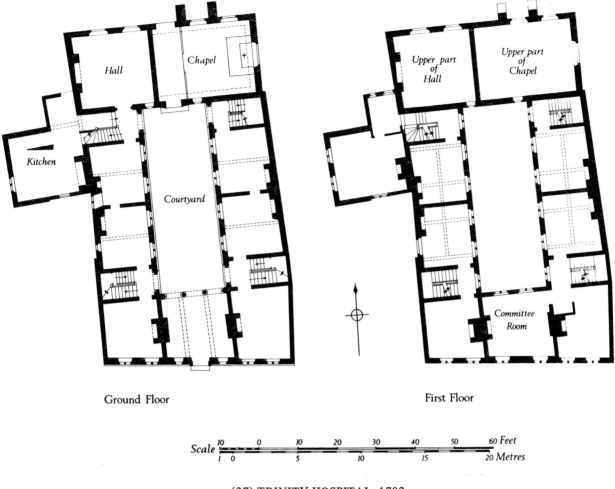

Ground Floor

First Floor

Scale

(27) **TRINITY HOSPITAL, 1702.**

some 13th-century coffin slabs,[3] but this has since perished. Centrally on the roof of the N. range is a square timber bellcote with a clock and a concave lead roof with an octagonal finial. This bellcote, a prominent feature in 18th-century drawings (cf. Plate 9 and the view on Naish's plan, Plate 16), seems to perpetuate the memory of a small spire which may have been a feature of the mediaeval building (Plate 1).

Inside, the chapel has the height of two storeys. The plain walls have heavy moulded plaster cornices with acanthus brackets; above is an elliptical plaster vault. The windows are round-headed. The hall, of equal height with the chapel, has a draught-lobby with early 19th-century fielded panelling; the fireplace is modern. The adjacent kitchen has a wide fireplace with a cambered and chamfered oak bressummer.

The four staircases have plain oak newel posts and close strings; the balustrades have been boarded in. The committee room on the first floor at the centre of the S. range has a moulded plaster cornice and, above the fire-place, a panel with the arms of Queen Anne, in a bolection moulded frame.

Fittings – *Altar:* of stone with consecration crosses, mediaeval, discovered and reset in chapel, 1908. *Bell:* unmarked. *Chairs:* in hall, six, of oak with turned legs and leather-covered seats, *c.* 1702. *Clock:* in bellcote, probably 1702. *Glass:* reset in chapel windows, late mediaeval and 17th-century fragments including royal shield-of-arms (1603–89). *Plate:* in chapel, includes silver cup with engraved strapwork, probably late 16th century; silver stand-paten with Britannia assay marks, 1706; pewter flagon with donor's inscription of William Waterman (mayor 1702) and date 1707. *Table:* in hall, oak, with six turned legs, *c.* 1702.

1. V.C.H., *Wilts.* iii, 357–61; *W.A.M.*, xxxvi (1909), 376–412.

2. Benson & Hatcher, 598.

3. e.g., *Arch J.*, cxxi (1964), pl.xix, a.

(28) Blechynden's Almshouses, No. 75 Winchester Street, are a 17th-century foundation, but the present group of single-storeyed brick cottages, with tiled roofs, appears to result from total reconstruction in 1857. A stone tablet reset in the S. gable of the E. range bears an inscription of 1683 (not 1663).[1] Another tablet records the rebuilding in 1857.

1. Benson & Hatcher, 599.

(29) Culver Street Almshouses, Nos. 28–32 Culver Street, of two storeys with brick walls and slate-covered roofs, were built in 1842 to replace almshouses said to date from the reign of Elizabeth I.[1] They were demolished in 1972.

1. V.C.H., *Wilts.* vi, 169.

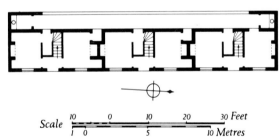

(29) CULVER STREET ALMSHOUSES.

(30) Hayter's Almshouses, near the W. end of Fisherton Street, on the N. side, demolished and rebuilt in

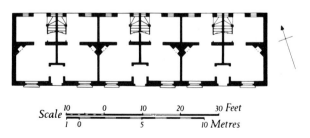

(30) HAYTER'S ALMSHOUSES.

1964, comprised a range of six two-storeyed dwellings with rendered walls and tiled roofs. A segmental-headed plaque was inscribed 'This Asylum built and endow'd for six poor women by Mrs. Sarah Hayter, lady of this manor, 1797'.

(31) Thomas Brown's Almshouses, Nos. 129–135 Castle Street, of two storeys with brick walls and tiled roofs were demolished in 1971. The seven dwellings appeared to be of *c.* 1800 although the charity was not formally established until 1852 (V.C.H., *Wilts.* vi, 171).

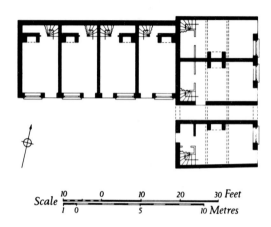

(31) THOMAS BROWN'S ALMSHOUSES.

(32) Taylor's Almshouses, at the N.E. corner of Parsons Chequer, are two-storeyed and have brick walls with ashlar dressings and tiled roofs. Founded in 1695 and first built in 1698, the building was entirely reconstructed in 1886. Stone tablets with inscriptions of 1698 are preserved.

(33) Frowd's Almshouses, at the N.W. corner of Parsons Chequer, are two-storeyed with brick walls and tiled roofs (Plate 23); they were built in 1750 to accommodate 24 pensioners.[1] The middle bay of the symmetrical N. front has brick quoins and a moulded timber open pediment. The round-headed doorway is set in an oak doorcase with rusticated Tuscan pilasters supporting a segmental open pediment within which, on a panel with a rococo carved border, is inscribed 'Built and Endowd by the Liberality of Mr. Edward Frowd, Merch't late of this City, 1750'; above is a Palladian window. Centrally on the roof is an octagonal lantern with a lead cupola. The S. elevation has an arcaded loggia in the lower storey and circular windows lighting a corridor in the upper storey. Inside, the oak stairs have close strings, square newel posts, plain hand rails and Tuscan-column balusters. The vestibule and some lodging rooms retain moulded and coved cornices. The Audit Room at the centre of the upper storey has bolection-

moulded oak panelling. In 1974 the building was adapted for use as a hostel and the interior was extensively altered.

1.   *Charity Comm'rs Reports,* xxvi (1833), 418–22.

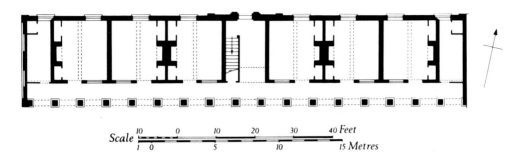

Scale

(33) FROWD'S ALMSHOUSES.

LESSER SECULAR BUILDINGS

ST. MARTIN WARD

The secular monuments of St. Martin Ward are divided for convenience of presentation into groups based mainly on the chequers which the mediaeval streets define. To assist in the identification of monuments, small maps based on O.S. (1880) are inset in the text. The maps are conventionally orientated and are printed at a uniform scale, approximately 1:1,600.

MARKET PLACE

For monuments on the N. side of the Market Place, see p. 132; for those on the E., p. 81. For notes on the evolution of the Market Place and surrounding streets, see p. xl.

(34) **House,** No. 32 Cheesemarket, of three storeys with brick and ashlar walls and with slate-covered roofs, dates from the second half of the 18th century. The lower storey of the four-bay facade has 19th-century stone rustication; the brick upper storeys retain original stone quoins, plat-band, cornice and parapet. The square-headed sashed windows and other original woodwork remain. A photograph (Plate 14) taken before

1859 depicts the facade of No. 32 very much as it is today.

(35) **House,** No. 31 Cheesemarket, of three storeys with a modest 18th-century brick facade and a tiled roof, is substantially a timber-framed building of 14th-century origin. Described in mediaeval leases as a messuage with shops and cellars, it was owned in 1396 by Nicholas Taillour, citizen and draper of London and Sarum; 1396–1417 by William Baly, draper; 1417–22 by Richard Oword; then by Richard Gage.[1] A market regulation of *c.* 1440 orders 'that victuallers bringing cheese, milk, grapes, plums, apples, pears and other fruits to the city shall be constrained in future to keep the place assigned them opposite the tenement once of Richard Oword, now of John (*sic*) Gage, where the new cross is built'.[2] The mediaeval tenement occupied the sites of Monuments (35) and (36) and perhaps also (34). In 1541 it was sold by Sir Henry Lang to Robert Eyre, with a garden which lay across the river, behind the mill.[3]

During the second half of the 17th century, when Sir Samuel Eyre built a large house (36) on land immediately to the W., part of the lower storey of the old house was opened up to make a carriage through-way. The S. wall of the original building, with very stout

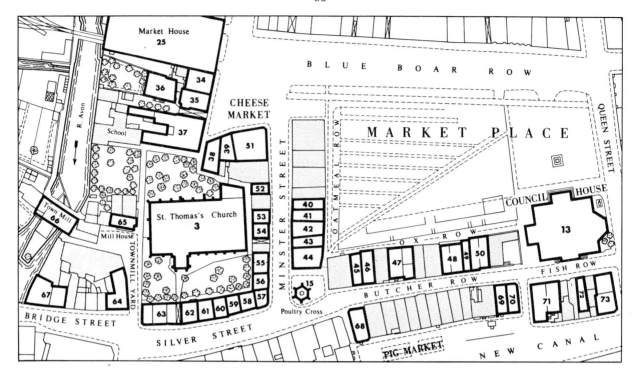

Monuments W. and S. of the Market Place. Map based on O.S. 1880.

chamfered posts and curved braces, is visible on the S. side of the through-way. Inside the house a few chamfered beams, stout posts and braces are exposed, but the 14th-century structure is largely masked by plaster. In the roof a collar purlin and some curved braces are seen. For a time during the 19th century the building was the Post Office.[4]

1. Dom. Bk. ii, ff 1, 140[v]; iii, ff 33[v], 79[v].
2. Sar. Corp. MS., D/32, Ledger A, ff 147–8. Benson & Hatcher (p. 122) mistakenly assign the regulation to an earlier date.
3. Eyre Papers, Newhouse, Redlynch.
4. Kindon & Shearm.

(36) **House**, No. 29 Cheesemarket, a large town house of the latter part of the 17th century, is of two storeys with cellars and attics and has brick walls and tiled roofs. After being acquired in 1541 by Robert Eyre (see (35)) the tenement remained with the Eyre family until 1780. The house was built by Sir Samuel Eyre between 1663 and 1689. A lease of 1697 granted by Robert Eyre to Ferdinand Younge, apothecary, provides a schedule of goods and a list of rooms, including a withdrawing room and a great parlour; it also mentions a bridge with two doors leading to a garden on the other side of the river.[1] The old house (35) was used for service rooms, but there were 'two wainscot rooms' over the coach

house, wood house and coal house.

The symmetrical five-bay S. front has been partly covered by additions, but the rusticated brick quoins, plaster eaves cove and moulded cornice remain visible. The central doorway has gone. Many windows have 18th-century sashes, but the staircase window in the N. elevation retains an original oak mullion and transom with leaded iron casements. Inside, the 17th-century oak close-string staircase (Plate 87) has panelled newel posts, turned and twisted balusters, stout moulded handrails and dados with fielded panelling. Some first-floor rooms

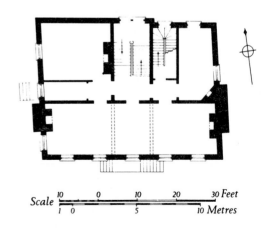

Scale [10] [0] [10] [20] [30 Feet] / [1] [0] [5] [10 Metres]

(36) No. 29 Cheesemarket. First-floor plan.

have moulded plaster cornices, panelled dados and bolection-moulded chimneypieces. The attic stairs have original turned balusters and moulded handrails. Beams with 15th-century mouldings in the cellar are presumably reused.

1.   Eyre papers, Newhouse, Redlynch.

(37) **Offices and Shops**, formerly the Vine Inn, Nos. 28 Cheesemarket and 2–4 St. Thomas's Square, are mainly two-storeyed and have walls partly of brick and partly of timber framework, tile-hung to simulate brickwork; the roofs are slate-covered and tiled. Although the buildings appear to be mainly of late 18th and early 19th-century origin the plan indicates a large mediaeval courtyard house, and this is confirmed in several documents. In 1400 Thomas Boyton, bowyer, bequeathed the tenement to his wife Gunnora[1] and in 1421 his executor sold it to Robert Okebourne. Many later deeds survive.[2] Early in the 17th century, when the house belonged to the Webb family, it was occupied as a town house by Edward Penruddock of Compton Chamberlayne. The lease included a schedule of 'thinges to be left att the end of his tearme' listed room by room. The document shows that the house comprised nine ground-floor rooms including a hall, a large parlour hung with pictures, and a study; there were eleven upper chambers. Subsequently the house declined in status and later tenants were a tanner, a clothier and a goldsmith. In 1637 Sir John Webb sold the house to William Joyce. In 1647 Joyce let it to William Vyner, vintner, again with a room-by-room schedule; a new staircase rising through three storeys is mentioned. Henceforward the building was called the Vine Inn. A trade token issued by Vyner in 1657 shows the device of a bunch of grapes;[3] he was mayor in 1668 and died in 1677. In 1679 John Joyce or his executors sold the property to the Corporation. A survey made in 1716 shows that some of the main rooms overlooked the street while others, including the hall, lay on the N. of a courtyard and extended as far as the river;[4] eleven chambers had names such as Lyon, Dolphin and Vine (the latter on the first floor at the N.E. corner of the house, overlooking Cheesemarket). A range on the S. of the courtyard contained kitchens and stables.

In 1795, as part of an exchange made when the Guildhall (13) was built, the Vine Inn became the property of the Dean and Chapter.[5] In 1835 a row of buildings adjoining the Vine Inn was pulled down for the enlargement of St. Thomas's churchyard and the S. range of the inn was refronted.[6] In 1861–2 the part of the tenement adjacent to the R. Avon was leased to the Church for the construction of a school.[7] The school was pulled down in 1974 to make way for two new houses, one of them St. Thomas's Rectory.

Of this extensive inn, the yard and the carriage through-way leading into the yard from Cheesemarket are still distinguishable. The through-way has become a shop (No. 28). The jettied first floor can be seen in the northern part of the E. front (No. 28a) behind 19th-century and later facings. Inside, an 18th-century close-string staircase with a moulded handrail and turned balusters, on the N. of the former through-way, is probably the 'substantial staircase up to a room called the Vine' covenanted for in a lease of 1702.[8]

1.   Dom. Bk. ii, ff. 30ᵛ–31.
2.   Sar. Corp. MS., Deeds, W.205.
3.   Rowe, *Coinage*, 32.
4.   Sar. Corp. MS., 0/117/4.
5.   Sar. Corp. MS., 0/117/8, f.39.
6.   *ibid.*, 0/108/3, 1835, June 9.
7.   Sar. Corp. MS., St. Thomas's deeds (with plan).
8.   *ibid.*, Deeds, W.205.

(38) **House**, No. 27 Cheesemarket, of three storeys with late 18th-century walls of ashlar and brick and with a modern flat roof, occupies the site of the mediaeval Council House (1416–1584). It was built in or soon after 1797 by H. Jeffrey, who acquired the tenement from the Corporation in that year. In 1783 the former building was still known as 'the old council house'.[1]

The W. front, of ashlar in the lower storey, has three bays. A 19th-century shop window occupies the N. bay. The middle bay has a doorway of *c.* 1797 with a panelled doorcase with reeded pilasters and an open pediment hood with a wreath in the tympanum (cf. (415)). The S. bay has a plain sashed window. The brick-faced upper storeys have plain sashed windows with gauged brick heads and keystones, or blind recesses. At the top is a moulded and bracketed wooden cornice and a plain parapet. The two-bay N. elevation and the S. elevation have similar features. Inside, the stairs have open strings and scrolled spandrels ornamented with guttae. Several rooms have panelled dados.

1.   Sar. Corp. MS., 0/117/8, f 11.

(39) **Warehouse**, of three storeys with brick walls and slate-covered roofs, is of the early 19th century.

(40) **House**, No. 19 Oatmeal Row, of three and two storeys with timber-framed walls and tiled roofs, is of 15th or 16th-century origin but has been much altered. The jettied E. front is hung with mathematical tiles and has sashed windows. Inside, the E. first-floor room retains some original plasterwork with roses and estoiles. The winding stairs are largley modern, but retain an original circular oak newel post and some original oak steps.

(41) **House,** No. 18 Oatmeal Row, demolished 1958, was timber-framed and of three storeys·with an attic; it probably dated from late in the 16th century. The E. front was jettied at the second floor. The building had been altered inside and the roof had been renewed, but the moulded barge-boards of the E. gable were probably original. Being of later date than the houses on each side, the building had no lateral walls.

(42) **House,** No. 17 Oatmeal Row, of three storeys with attics, with timber-framed walls and tiled roofs, is of the first half of the 17th century. Above a modern ground-floor shop window the gabled E. front has an original two-storeyed bow window with moulded timber mullions and transoms and a flat roof supported on shaped brackets with turned pendants; between storeys the mullions continue, enclosing plaster panels with fleur-de-lis enrichment. The roof is of five bays.

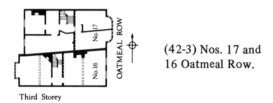

(42-3) Nos. 17 and 16 Oatmeal Row.

(43) **House,** No. 16 Oatmeal Row, with characteristics as in (42), is of the late 16th or early 17th century. The gabled E. front is jettied at the second floor. Inside, the E. first-floor room has 17th-century oak panelling and a contemporary chimneypiece with shafted uprights and chip-carving. At the W. end of the W. room the posts of a former outside wall retain mortices for a window which projected under the second floor jetty. In the third storey the W. elevation has a rectangular projecting window of seven lights. The S. wall of this house comprises the former N. front of the adjacent house (44), an earlier building.

(44) **House,** No. 15 Oatmeal Row, perhaps originally two houses, each three-storeyed with attics, has tile-hung timber-framed walls and tiled roofs and is of the mid 16th century. The building was originally isolated and the upper storeys are jettied on all four sides; where revealed, the jetties have heavily moulded oak sills. Mortices for the mullions of projecting windows, now gone, are seen on the underside of the jetties. The two lower storeys have been combined by the removal of the first floor and the space so formed is occupied by a shop. On the N. side the two upper storeys are seen inside the adjacent house (43).

(45) **House,** No. 14 Ox Row, of three storeys and attic, with brick walls and a tiled roof, is of the early

18th century. In the upper storeys the original stairs have close strings and turned balusters. The roof has collared trusses with cruck-shaped principals.

(46) **Warehouse,** No. 13 Ox Row, demolished in 1962, had a four-storeyed N. front of brickwork, with three bays of plain sashed windows; externally the building appeared to be of the late 19th century. Inside, however, there was an early 18th-century staircase with square newel posts, moulded close strings and twisted balusters. The N. room on the first floor had contemporary bolection-moulded panelling in two heights. Removal of this panelling revealed a two-storeyed late mediaeval building with timber-framed walls with wattle-and-daub infilling.

(47) **City Arms Inn,** of two storeys with tile-hung timber-framed walls and tiled roofs, is of 16th-century origin, but considerably altered. Inside, a ground-floor room retains a moulded beam and a stone fireplace surround with a moulded four-centred head and jambs with shaped stops. Scratchings on the fireplace fascia include a unicorn, a stag, other animals and numerous initials; these appear to the of the 17th century or earlier.

(48) **Houses,** two, Nos. 6–7 Ox Row, now united and used as a shop, are three-storeyed and have brick walls and tiled roofs; they are probably of mid 18th-century origin, but retain few original features. On the S. front each building has an early 19th-century elevation, but on the N. they are united by a common facade with a wide pediment-like gable with a moulded wooden cornice, often a conspicuous feature in early views of the Market Place (e.g. Rowlandson, *c.* 1800, V.C.H., *Wilts.* vi, opp. p.138). In the top storey the facade retains three original windows with false round heads, the lateral windows being of Palladian form. The two lower storeys have modern windows. Probably reset at the W. end of the ground floor is an original pedimented doorcase, the entablature of which includes a window.

(49) **Shop,** No. 5 Ox Row, of three storeys with cellar and attic, with rendered and tile-hung timber-framed walls and a tiled roof, is of the early 18th century. In the first and second storeys the N. front has original bow windows, each of three bays with hung sashes, curved on plan.

(50) **Duchess of Albany,** former inn, demolished in 1973, was of three storeys with cellar and attic; it had brick walls and slated and tiled roofs. It was partly of the late 18th and partly of the mid 19th century.

MINSTER STREET

Monuments on the E. side are described above (40)–(44).

(51) **Houses**, four adjoining, now combined to make bank offices, are of three storeys with brick walls and slated roofs. The two E. houses in Minster Street are of the early 19th century; those on the W., fronting Cheese-market, are somewhat earlier. All retain original sashed windows in the upper storeys. Inside, there is some contemporary joinery.

(52) **House**, No. 15, of three storeys with attics, with timber-framed walls and a tiled roof, dates from late in the 15th century. By removal of the first floor the two lower storeys have been combined to make a modern shop. The upper part of the E. front is masked by a tile-hung facade. The W. elevation is jettied at second-floor level and retains a moulded sill and original corner posts with curved brackets. Inside, the three-bay roof has two tie-beam trusses with chamfered arch-braced collars, curved windbraces and butt purlins.

(53) **House**, No. 11, of four storeys with brick walls and a slate-covered roof, is largely of the late 18th century. The two-bay E. front has plain sashed windows. The tile-hung top storey is modern.

(54) **House**, No. 9, of two storeys and an attic, with timber-framed walls on a stone plinth and with a slate-covered roof, is of the early 16th century. A first-floor room has intersecting beams. The two-bay roof is ridged N.–S. and has a yoked and collared tie-beam truss with lower angle braces and clasped purlins.

(55) **House**, Nos. 3 and 5, originally one, divided in 1680 into two tenements but now in part reunited, is of three storeys with attics and has timber-framed walls and tiled roofs. The house appears to date from late in the 15th century and comprises two parallel ranges with roofs ridged E.–W. and with a two-gabled E. front. In 1611, when Robert Jole leased the house from Robert Holmes,[1] a schedule of rooms and fittings mentions a cellar, a shop, a hall, various chambers and two cock-lofts. In 1632 Holmes sold the property to Richard Mason, shoemaker. In 1680 Henry Mason divided it into two parts, settling the S. range on Thomas Cooper; in 1687 Cooper also acquired some rooms in the N. range. In 1741 both parts were bought by Samuel Fawconer, hosier, who owned the adjoining Haunch of Venison Inn (56). There are plans of c. 1850 by Peniston.[2]

In the E. elevation the lower storey has a modern shop-front, but above first-floor level many original features remain (Plate 100). In the N. range the first-floor room has a projecting window with a moulded sill and shafted wood mullions; the corresponding window

First Floor

Attics

Ground Floor
Haunch of Venison Inn   No.3   No.5
MINSTER STREET

Second Floor

10   0   10   20   30   40 *Feet*
Metres 1 0   5   10   15

(55) Nos. 3 and 5 Minster Street. (56) Haunch of Venison Inn.

in the S. range is modern. The walls on either side of the projecting windows were originally pierced by continuous rows of segmental-headed windows, now blocked. Moulded posts at the centre and corners of the facade have brackets for the jettied second floor. The third storey has projecting windows as described, but smaller. The cusped barge-boards are of the 19th century. In the W. elevation both ranges are jettied at the first and second floors, but the framework is masked by tile-hanging and all windows are modern.

Inside, jowl-headed posts and heavy beams are exposed. The ground-floor rooms have no notable features. On the first floor, a doorway (a) has a hollow-chamfered four-centred head and foliate spandrels enclosing a shield with a merchant mark as shown. The adjacent fire-place has moulded stone jambs and an overhanging oak bressumer (Plate 90). The second-floor rooms retain some original doorways and partitions. In the attic storey the roof of the N. range has three collared tie-beam trusses with mortices for former arch-braces; the roof of the S. range is concealed.

1. W.R.O., 897.
2. W.R.O., 451/73.

(56) **Haunch of Venison Inn,** (see plan with (55)), of three storeys with rendered and tile-hung timber-framed walls, and with a tiled roof ridged N.–S., is of the mid 15th century. The E. front has 18th-century windows and is jettied at the second floor (Plate 100); the W. front retains no early features. Inside, original timber framework is exposed. In the E. ground-floor room the former first-floor jetty, now underbuilt, is shown by cuttings in the first-floor joists. The S.W. ground-floor room has an open fireplace with an original cambered and chamfered timber bressummer. The two-bay roof has double-collared tie-beam trusses with purlins at two levels and curved wind-braces.

SILVER STREET

(57) **House,** on the corner of Silver Street and Minster Street, is of three storeys with attics and has timber-framed walls and a tiled roof (Plate 100). Of 15th-century origin, it probably is the building which John Wynchestre bequeathed to Trinity Hospital in 1458 (Haskins, *Guilds*, 363). Extensive alterations and internal refitting have taken place. The two-bay roof has curved wind-braces.

(58) **House,** No. 38, of three storeys with attics, with timber-framed walls and tiled roofs, was built early in the 18th century. The three-bay N. front (Plate 100) is faced with mathematical tiles and has sashed windows

and a wooden cornice. The dog-leg staircase with close strings and turned balusters is original.

(59) **House,** No. 40, of three storeys with attics, with timber-framed walls and tiled roofs, is of the early 18th century. The two-bay N. front is faced with mathematical tiles.

(60) **House,** No. 42, originally of two low storeys with an attic, but now without the first floor, has timber-framed walls and a tiled roof and probably is of 15th-century origin.

(61) **House,** No. 44, of two storeys with an attic, with timber-framed walls and a tiled roof, was built in the 17th century. The gabled S. front has 19th-century sashed windows.

(62) **House,** No. 46, of two storeys with attics, with timber-framed walls and tiled roofs, is of 16th-century origin, but it was extensively altered and refaced in the 19th century.

(63) **Houses,** three adjoining, Nos. 48–52, are each three-storeyed with an attic and have walls partly of flint and ashlar, but mainly of timber framework; the roofs are tiled. A drawing of 1813 by W.H. Charlton is in Salisbury Museum (Plate 10). The present houses, built in 1471, replace three buildings which were given to the Dean and Chapter by John Waltham, a favourite of Richard II, who was Bishop of Salisbury in 1388 and Chancellor of England in 1391. Although buried at Westminster in 1395 (brass in chapel of Edward the Confessor), he established a chantry in Salisbury cathedral and endowed it with a rent of 60s. from these properties. In 1455 the three dwellings were occupied by chantry priests.[1] In 1471, being ruinous, £160 was given for their rebuilding by John Cranborn and John Stokes, canons of the cathedral, who thereby founded their own *obit*.[2] The new houses were complete in 1473. In 1649 all three had shops facing Silver Street: No. 48 and part of No. 50 was occupied by Walter Comb, hosier; Henry Whitmarsh, public notary, had the rest of No. 50; Henry Steward, grocer, had No. 52.[3] A through-passage in the E. part of No. 48 perpetuates an ancient right-of-way from High Street to Castle Street through St. Thomas's churchyard (see p. xxxiii); the passage is entered through elliptical-headed archways, doubtless added in the 18th century. Further W., the lower part of the N. wall of No. 52 is of chequered flint and ashlar with an ogee-moulded plinth; elsewhere the N. wall is timber-framed, and an original dragon-post with a plain bracket above a moulded capping remains at the N.W. corner. Each house is jettied to N. and S. at first and second-floor levels and each has a gabled roof with a N.–S. ridge; the W. house, No. 52, is also jettied westwards at the same

levels. The N. front of No. 50 retains in the second storey an original oak window of two ogee-headed lights with tracery, as shown. In the three-bay roofs, collared and angle-braced tie-beam trusses support chamfered single through-purlins, with wind-braces.

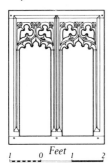

Feet

1. *Liber Niger*, 69.
2. Sar. D. & C.M., Ch. Commrs. Deeds, Chap. 64a.
3. Parl. Svy., untitled (Sar. 11), ff.28—30.

BRIDGE STREET

(64) **Shoulder of Mutton Inn,** demolished in 1962, was two-storeyed with brick walls and tiled roofs and appeared to be of late 18th or early 19th-century origin. A plan of 1849 by Peniston is in W.R.O. (451/187).

(65) **House,** now a shop, is two-storeyed with brick walls and a tiled roof and dates from the middle of the 18th century. The S. front was formerly symmetrical and of five bays with a central doorway and sashed windows, but the openings of the lower storey have been replaced by shop-windows. The plan, formerly of class T, has been obliterated.

(66) **Town Mill,** of three storeys with lofts and having brick walls and tiled roofs, probably occupies the site of a mill built by Bishop Richard Poore in the 13th century (V.C.H., *Wilts.* vi, 90). The present mill dates from 1757. Extensions with walls of flint and ashlar and with mullioned and transomed stone windows were added in 1898. The 18th-century building, oblong on plan and plain in elevation, spans a branch of the R. Avon; its S.W. corner rests on an ashlar substructure with a wide chamfered plinth, possibly mediaeval. The date 1756 is carved on the keystone of a relieving arch in the N. wall. The five-bay roof has tie-beam trusses with lower angle struts.

(67) **Houses,** three adjoining, Nos. 12—14 Bridge Street, of three storeys with brick walls and slated roofs, appear to be of the first half of the 19th century. A plan of 1849 by Peniston (W.R.O., 451/187) designates the two western houses 'London Inn', as also do Kingdon & Shearm.

BUTCHER ROW

(68) **House,** No. 33, is mainly two-storeyed with an attic and has rendered and tile-hung walls and tiled roofs. It probably is of the 15th or 16th century. Most early features have been obliterated, but old photographs (Lov. Cn., 17, 164) show a gabled N. front jettied at the first floor. The bases of early stone and flint walls were exposed below the ground floor in 1972, and part of a mediaeval fireplace was found.

(69) **House,** No.11, of three storeys and a cellar, with brick walls and a tiled roof, was advertised in 1784 (*S.J.* 13 Dec.) as built 'not many years'.

(70) **House,** No. 9, of two storeys and a cellar, with brick walls in the lower storey and of timber framework above, and with a tiled roof, is of the 17th century. Early in the 19th century the walls of the upper storey were slate-hung and a fluted frieze with paterae was applied below the eaves. The upper storey is jettied on the east.

FISH ROW

(71) **Wheatsheaf Inn,** Nos. 7—9, comprises two houses with rendered timber-framed walls and tiled roofs. No. 9 has two storeys and an attic and is of the 14th century; No. 7, of three storeys with attic and cellar, is of the 15th century. An extension on the S. of No. 9 is of *c.* 1800.

No. 9 has a gabled and jettied N. front; the original S. front is masked by the extension; the W. elevation has no notable features. Inside, the N. first-floor room has a

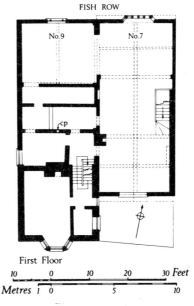

FISH ROW

No.9   No.7

First Floor

Feet

Metres

(71) Wheatsheaf Inn.

beam with roll and ogee mouldings. The roof has braced collared rafters with a collar purlin. A crown-post remains in the roof at the position indicated (cp).

No. 7 has first and second-floor jetties in the gabled N. front (Plate 64) and restored bow windows in the second and third storeys. Inside, although the partitions of the rooms in the two lower storeys have gone, the beams define three main bays. A 15th-century stone fireplace (Plate 90) is not *in situ*; masonry in the cellar suggests that it formerly stood on the E. side of the S. bay. In the third storey, where original partitions remain, the S. chamber has a beam and wall-plates with ogee and triple roll-mouldings.

A mediaeval house of two storeys and an attic, adjoining the Wheatsheaf Inn on the E., appears in an old photograph (Lov. Cn., 107).

(72) **House**, No. 3, of two storeys with an attic, has timber-framed walls and tiled roofs and is of the 15th century. The gabled N. and S. elevations are largely masked by modern extensions. Inside, original timber framework indicates a plan with two square rooms on each floor, each room having two bays. Mortices indicate the position of former partitions, windows etc. A chimneystack occupies the middle of the E. wall. The four-bay roof has three tie-beam trusses with cambered collars, lower king-struts and clasped purlins; the gable trusses have lower angle braces.

(73) **House**, of three storeys with attics, with rendered early 16th-century timber-framed walls and with tiled roofs, was extensively damaged by fire in 1973, especially at the S. end. The wide plan comprises two parallel original ranges with roofs ridged N.–S., each range having four bays; the first and second floors are jettied N. and E. A fifth bay added on the S., perhaps *c.* 1800, concealed the original S. front which came to light in 1973. The N. elevation has two equal gables; on the S. the roof is hipped. Above modern shop windows the second and third storeys had early 19th-century windows, now renewed. In the second storey the N.E. corner retains a moulded dragon post and bracket; elsewhere the second-floor jetty is supported by hollow-chamfered brackets. The two four-bay roofs have tie-beam trusses with lower angle-braces and cambered collars. The date 1664 is punched on the bressummer of a first-floor fireplace.

HIGH STREET

(74) **House**, No. 12, of two storeys and an attic, with brick walls and a tiled roof, is of the early 18th century. The two-bay E. front has sashed windows in the upper

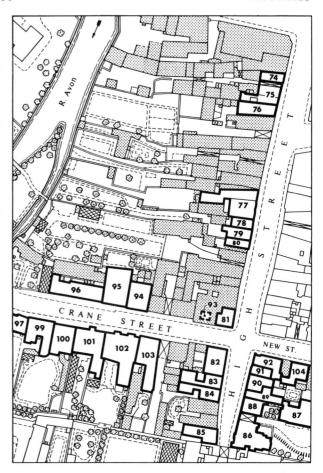

Monuments in High Street and Crane Street.

storeys and a cornice with dentils. Part of the original staircase with turned balusters remains.

(75) **Houses**, two adjoining, Nos. 14–16, of three storeys with brick walls and tiled roofs, are superficially of the mid 18th century, but the interior plasterwork masks timber framework, probably of 16th-century origin. The rendered E. front is of the 19th century.

(76) **House**, No. 18, of two storeys with brick walls and tiled roofs, is of the early 18th century. The gabled W. elevation has a moulded brick plat-band. The roof has original collared tie-beam trusses.

(77) **Houses**, two adjoining, Nos. 32–4, recently demolished, were substantially mediaeval although the original structures were masked by 17th-century and 18th-century alterations. No. 34 was pulled down in 1958; No. 32 in 1976.

No. 32, of three storeys with timber-framed original walls, probably dated from 1491 (see below), but it had been extensively altered in the 18th century. The lower storey of the brick-built E. front had been obliterated; the second storey had a projecting window with three sashed lights and a domical lead roof; the upper storey had two plain sashed windows. A lead rainwater head was dated 1773. Inside, the 18th-century staircase (Plate 88) was surprisingly large for a house of this size. The E. room on the first floor had 18th-century pine panelling in two heights. The corresponding second-floor room had a panelled dado.

No. 34, also timber-framed, but of four storeys, was probably of the 16th century. The E. front had two shop windows at ground level, a bow window similar to that of No. 32 on the first floor, and two plain sashed windows in each of the two upper storeys. A cornice and parapet masked the roof. Inside, the W. room on the ground floor had panelling of *c.* 1700 in three heights with a frieze and cornice. The stairs to the first floor were of the late 18th century and had slender turned balusters and column-shaped newel posts. The E. room

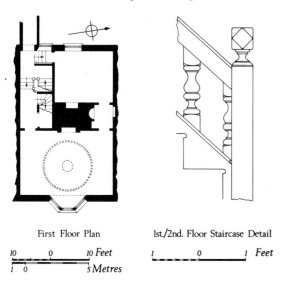

First Floor Plan

1st./2nd. Floor Staircase Detail

(77) No. 34 High Street.

on the first floor had moulded and fielded oak panelling and a late 18th-century enriched plaster ceiling. The stairs above first-floor level were of the 16th century with square newel posts with polygonal finials, closed strings and bulbous balusters. The W. room on the second floor had reset oak panelling in five heights with carved enrichment in the top height; the chimneypiece was flanked by pilasters with strapwork enrichment. The W. room on the third floor had some late 16th-century panelling. The two-bay roof had a plain collared tie-beam truss.

The two houses stood in the S.E. corner of a mediaeval tenement, Pynnok's Inn, to which many documents in the city archives relate.[1] William Pynnok, the first recorded owner, died in 1270 bequeathing his dwelling-house to his brother Richard, and an annual rent of 15s.

from an adjacent house to the Vicars Choral 'to make our obit'.[2] Richard, parliamentary representative in 1295,[3] died in 1310 and bequeathed the house to his wife with reversion to his son John; the will mentions a new chamber.[4] By 1333 John Pynnok had leased the N. part of the property to John and Alice le Taverner, the lessees agreeing to make good any damage done to the property by themselves or their guests; the deed states that the Town Ditch defined the N. side of the tenement.[5] The Pynnoks continued to own the property for most of the 14th century. In 1385 when another John Pynnok leased part of the Inn to William and Edith Fuystour the lease included a ruined building (42 ft. by 21 ft.) and an adjoining chamber;[6] set back from the street (the deed reserves the right to cross an adjoining plot), it is possible that the ruined building was William Pynnok's original dwelling. John Pynnok, a benefactor of the Tailors' Guild, died abroad *c.* 1386 and left the property to his sister Isabella Fyns.[7] In 1428–31 Pynnok's Inn and four other properties were purchased under royal licence by the mayor and commonalty,[8] the purchasers agreeing to maintain the annual payment of 15s. for William Pynnok's original obit. Thereafter the inn appears in the city chamberlain's rent rolls.[9]

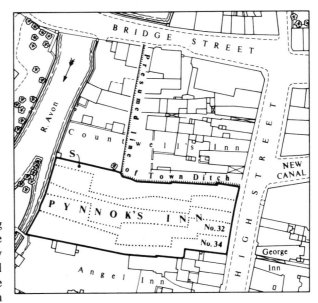

(77) Pynnok's Inn. Mediaeval boundaries.

The boundaries of the tenement are easily recognisable on O.S., 1880. A curved recess in the N. boundary probably marks the elbow of the Town Ditch, which flowed S. from a pool below Fisherton Mill and turned E. to pass along 'New Canal'. An indenture of 1345,[10] devising a small plot of land to a 'way to the river bank . . . . for a watercourse', has been held to date the construction of the Town Ditch, but it is more probable that it alludes to a narrow strip of ground (S) in the N.W. corner of the tenement, between the elbow of the ditch and the bank of the Avon; the ditch already occurs in the lease of 1333 mentioned above. The city let the property in several parts: an inn called the Helme in the 15th century, and at least three houses.[11] In 1455 quit rent of 3s. 7½d. was paid 'pro hospitio vocato Pynnokes Inn'.[12] From time to time efforts were made to rebuild the inn, notably in 1434 and 1484.[13] In 1491 four houses were built with shops and two upper storeys.[14] By 1618 there were five separate plots between the Town Ditch on the N. and the garden of the Angel Inn on the south.[15] The southernmost plot, No. 34 High Street, was sold in 1649 to Richard Banks; later it belonged to the Eyre family.[16] The northernmost plot was given to the Dean and Chapter, *c.* 1785, in exchange for land upon which to build the Guildhall (13).[17] All leases of the N. tenement include a covenant allowing access to the Town Ditch. The three middle tenements remained city property until 1876 and plans by Peniston are preserved.[18] Plan No. 4 corresponds with No. 32 High Street.

1. Haskins, *Guilds*, 296—9.
2. Sar. Corp. MS., Deeds, drawer A.
3. V.C.H., *Wilts.* vi, 81.
4. Sar. Corp. MS., Deeds, drawer A, *s.a.* 1310.
5. *ibid.*, drawer B.
6. *ibid.*, drawer E, 1385, iii/26.
7. *ibid.*, drawer G, deed of 1424.
8. *ibid.*, drawer H.
9. *ibid.*, 0/103 *passim.*
10. *ibid.*, Deeds, drawer C.
11. *ibid.*, D/32, Ledger B, f 154.
12. *Liber Niger*, 76.
13. Sar. Corp. MS., D/32, Ledgers A, f 102; B, f 154.
14. V.C.H., *Wilts.* vi, 81.
15. Sar. Corp. MS., 0/117/1, f 32.
16. *ibid.*, 0/117/4, ff 4 and 154.
17. *ibid.*, 0/117/8, f 1.
18. *ibid.*, V/204, Nos. 2—4.

(78—9) **Houses**, two adjacent, Nos. 36—8, demolished *c.* 1958, were of three storeys with attics and had timber-framed walls and tiled roofs. They were of late 16th-century origin. In each house the two lower storeys of the E. front had been obliterated by a modern shop window; above, the jettied upper storey and gable remained visible. Inside, in the upper part of each house jowl-headed posts and chamfered beams were exposed.

(80) **House**, No. 40, of two storeys with an attic, has timber-framed walls and a tiled roof and is of the mid 15th century. The gabled E. front has a modern shop window in the lower storey and a 19th-century bow window above; in the second storey and jettied attic storey timber framework is exposed. The three-bay roof has cambered tie-beam trusses.

(81) **House**, No. 50, at the corner of Crane Street, is of three storeys with walls mainly of tile-hung timber framework and with tiled roofs. Of late 15th-century origin, it must be a rebuilding of part of the inn called La Rose or La Hotecorner which was given in 1410 to the Vicars Choral by John Gowayn of Norrington, bishop's bailiff 1399—1408.[1] The inn extended N. into the area now occupied by No. 48, a modern building. By 1649 No. 50 had been separated from the inn and was described as two tenements which once belonged to the Rose, comprising two shops, two chambers, three garrets and a cellar; the plot measured 22½ ft. by 24 ft. overall and was leased to Silvester Pope, tailor.[2] The properties are also described in a Vicars Choral terrier of 1671.[3]

The S. and E. elevations of the 15th-century house are jettied at the first and second floors, but the S. jetty of the first floor is enclosed in a modern shop window. The two parallel roofs, ridged E.—W., are now hipped, but no doubt were formerly gabled. Inside, an arch-braced collar-beam truss is visible in the S. roof. Reset in a first-floor room is a mediaeval oak head-corbel (Plate 84).

1. Benson & Hatcher, 804.
2. Parl. Svy., untitled (Sar. 11), f 22.
3. Sar. D. & C.M.

(82) **Row of three Houses**, Nos. 52—4 High Street, now a bookshop, of two storeys with walls of timber framework and with tiled roofs, is a well-preserved 14th-century structure (Plate 60). In 1341 the 'corner tenement with shops adjoining' was leased by John of Shaftesbury, spicer, to Walter de Upton. In 1356 it passed (perhaps only briefly) into the ownership of the Hungerfords;[1] later it belonged to the Vicars Choral, remaining their property until 1815.[2] In the Parliamentary Survey of 1649 the description of the S. part of the building is lost, but the two N. houses were occupied by John Langley, watchmaker. Langley still had them in 1671 when he added the S. house to his lease.[3] The building consists of three parallel ranges, each of two bays in the lower and of three bays in the upper storey. In one place the surviving external posts of the lower storey retain mortices for the horizontal beams of a wall panel. Before underbuilding, the first floor was jettied on N. and E., the jetties being supported on plain

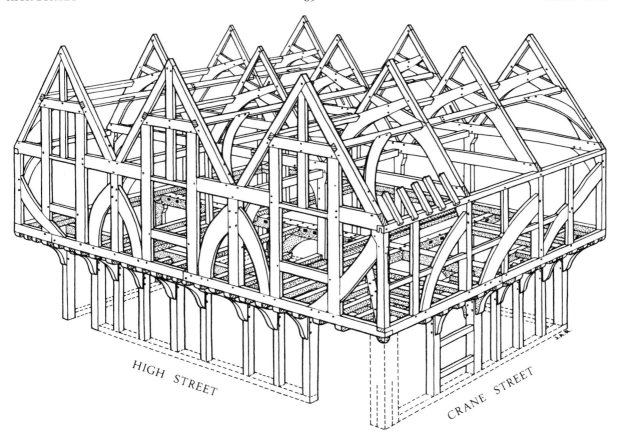

(82) Nos. 52—4 High Street. Timber framework.

brackets; two of these remain and others are attested by mortices. On the S., the first floor extends over a ground-floor passage which formerly followed the side of the S. range. A fireplace with a 16th-century brick chimneybreast occupies the width of the passage in the W. bay; whether it blocks an original passage or replaces an earlier chimneybreast is unknown. Other fireplaces are modern. On the first floor the three ranges are separated by original partitions; a plaster panel in the middle range has 16th-century painted decoration.

The roofs have continuous tie-beams spanning the ranges, with scarfed joints in the middle of the middle range; above, each range has three scissor-trusses with upper principals. The gables have plain framing, probably for windows. An attic dormer window on the N. side of the N. range (not shown on drawing) is a 16th-century addition. There is no evidence of an original attic floor.

A 19th-century photograph shows the building when the timber framework was hung with slates.[4]

1. W.R.O., 164/1, No. 2; 490/35.

2. Sar. D. & C.M., Ch. Commrs. Deeds, Vic. Ch., 28/1—5.

3. *ibid.*, Press iii, Vic. Ch. deeds, terrier, 1671; Vic. Ch. lease bk. 1673—1717, f.15[v].

4. Lov. Cn., 135.

(83) **House**, No. 56, of three storeys with tile-hung timber-framed walls and tiled roofs, is of the 15th century. The upper part of the E. front, originally of two gabled bays, is masked by a 19th-century tiled facade with sashed windows and a plain parapet. In the lower storey the S.E. corner post (p) retains the moulded jamb of an original doorway and a curved and chamfered bracket supporting the jettied first floor. Inside, the layout of the lower storey has been obliterated in the formation of a shop, but the former plan is recorded in a survey of 1849,[1] here reproduced. A doorway (d) in the S. part of the original W. wall has a chamfered elliptical head and continuous jambs. To W., a kitchen of *c.* 1800 (still with fittings of that date) was formerly separated from the 15th-century house by a small court, now roofed over. The stairs of *c.* 1800 encroach on the adjoining house (84). There are two

parallel roofs, ridged E.–W., each with collared tie-beam trusses and butt purlins; the tie-beams are continuous across the two ranges.

1. Peniston papers, W.R.O., 451/73 (xviii).

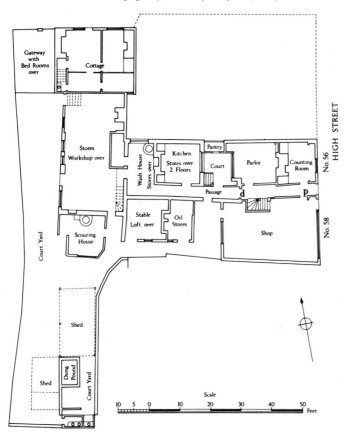

Nos. 56–8 High Street. Peniston's plan, 1849.

(84) **House**, No. 58, of three storeys with tile-hung timber-framed walls and tiled roofs, is of the 15th century. The E. front, originally jettied at the first and

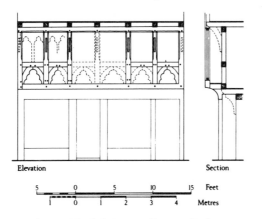

(84) No. 58 High Street. Former E. front.

second floors, is now concealed by an early 19th-century tiled facade in the plane of the third storey and continuous with the facade of No. 56 (83). Inside, enough remains of the original E. front to show that the second storey had cinquefoil cusped bracing in the lower panels, and windows (perhaps originally with trefoil-headed lights) in the upper panels. Mortices remain for brackets to the jettied second floor. The roof has collared tie-beam trusses with lower angle-braces and clasped purlins. For a plan of 1849, see monument (83).

(85) **House**, No. 64, of three storeys, has walls of timber framework hung with mathematical tiles and a tiled roof. Of the late 18th century, it is likely to be the 'neat dwelling house' advertised in *Salisbury Journal*, 14 Jan. and 21 Apr., 1788. In the E. front the lower storey is rendered and rusticated. The doorway has panelled pilasters and an open pediment with *carton-pierre* enrichment. The 19th-century shop window probably replaces sashed windows. Inside, the principal rooms have late 18th-century dados, chimneypieces and moulded cornices.

Monuments (86)–(92)

In 1265 Nicholas de St. Quintin, the first Provost of St. Edmund's College, endowed his chantry in Salisbury Cathedral with rents from property in High Street (Minstrestrete) extending from the Close wall on the S. to two tenements in New Street (*Sar. Chart.*, 341). There was a gateway between the two New Street tenements. The length of the property from E. to W. was 9 perches and 10 ft. (158½ ft.). It was valuable land and by 1535 its rents constituted nearly a third of the canons' total receipts from city properties (Benson & Hatcher, 807). The endowment explains the fact that in 1649 monuments (86)–(91) were all in the possession of the Dean and Chapter, paying rent to the canons' common fund (Parl. Svy.). Monument (92) was also Chapter property, but its rent went to the fabric fund, indicating a separate endowment.

(86) **Shops and Offices**, formerly an **Inn**, Nos. 49–51, are of two storeys with attics and have brick and ashlar walls and tiled roofs. In style the W. front is of the second half of the 17th century, but earlier walls are found internally and at the rear of the building. In a lease of 1609 the tenement is described as 'a capital messuage and garden adjoining, sometyme an Inne called the Horseshoe, afterwards the White Horse'; it was let to John Lowe.[1] In 1649 when it was let to James Underhill, vintner, the following rooms were listed: hall, parlour, kitchen, solar, 2 butteries, coalhouse, taphouse, 2 drinking rooms, stable, woodhouse, a fair dining room, 4 fair chambers, 3 chambers for servants, a shop and a

garden of 10 perches; there was also a little tenement adjoining, 'next unto the close wall', containing a shop with a chamber over it.[2] In 1682, as 'the sign of the Sunn', the building was led to Robert Westbury, vintner.[3] The rebuilding of the facade must date from about this time although it is not mentioned in the leases.

The W. front, originally symmetrical and of five bays with the middle and end bays set slightly in front of the intermediate bays, has ashlar piers between the modern shop windows and doorways, an ashlar plat-band at the first-floor windowsills and a moulded and coved plaster cornice at the eaves. A brick-fronted dormer window over the central bay, with flanking pilasters and a flat roof, was formerly pedimented; centrally behind is a chimneystack with panelled sides. The central opening of the second storey retains an original wooden casement of two lights, but other openings have modern fittings or are blocked. The bay beyond the S. end of the W. front, adjoining the Close gateway, obviously corresponds with the 'little tenement' of the Parliamentary Survey. The corresponding bay beyond the N. end of the facade is occupied by a carriage through-way leading to a garden on the E.; above the through-way are two projecting storeys with large sashed windows. A 17th-century brick chimneystack with shafted angles and a moulded cornice stands against the party-wall between this bay and the adjoining building (88). Inside, several rooms retain stout moulded beams of late 16th or early 17th-century date. A large ground-floor fireplace has a moulded, cambered and shouldered oak bressumer above brick jambs. A room in the E. wing has a heavily moulded early 17th-century beam, and an adjacent room has walls lined with panelling of c. 1700 with bolection mouldings.

1. Sar. D. & C.M., Ch. Commrs. Recs., 67209.
2. Parl. Svy., untitled (Sar. 11) f.37.
3. Sar. D. & C.M., Ch. Commrs. Recs., 67212.

(87) **House**, No. 47, of three storeys and a cellar, has brick walls and tiled roofs; it was built towards the end of the 17th century perhaps by Dr. John Ballard who, with his heirs, appears to have held the ground lease from 1698 to 1733.[1] Previously the site was occupied by stables let to William Collyer.[2] In 1736 the lease was renewed to Walter Long.[3]

The S. front is approximately symmetrical and of six bays with two moulded brick plat-bands and brick quoins. The eaves have a late 18th-century wooden soffit with coupled brackets. The upper storeys have regularly spaced plain sashed windows. In the lower storey the central doorway has Tuscan columns supporting a bracketed cornice and pediment; on the W. is an original service doorway; the windows and the projecting bay are modern.

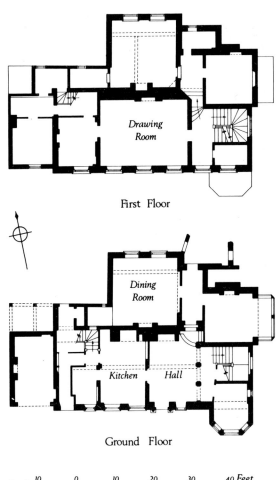

First Floor

Ground Floor

Scale (87) No. 47 High Street.

Inside, the hall has a late 17th-century screen of three arches with fluted Ionic pilasters (Plate 97); the contemporary oak stairs have spiral balusters and coupled newel posts. The stairs W. of the kitchen have turned balusters in the lower flights and serpentine splats above. The dining room has plain 18th-century panelling in two heights, with a moulded dado rail. The N.E. room is lined with reset early 17th-century small-panelled oak wainscot with a guilloche frieze. The first-floor drawing room (Plate 96) has 18th-century decoration.

1. Sar. D. & C.M., Ch. Commrs. Recs., 69214; Chap. leases x, xi, *passim*.
2. Parl. Svy., untitled (Sar. 11), f 43.
3. Sar. D. & C.M., Chap. leases, xi, 190.

(88–90) **Houses**, range of three, Nos. 41–5, originally of two but now of three storeys with attics and cellars, have walls partly of brick and partly of tile-hung timber framework, and tiled roofs. In 1649 the site was registered as comprising four tenements although only three tenants are named;[1] the present building, however, dates from later in the 17th century. In the 18th century the building was heightened from two to three storeys and refronted in a manner to suggest, deceptively, a single house with a symmetrical five-bay facade (Frontispiece). Since then the fenestration has been altered and the effect of uniformity has gone. Former roof trusses embedded in partitions on the second floor show that the third storey replaces an attic. Late in the 18th or early in the 19th century a new attic storey was added above the third storey and a 17th-century chimneystack was heightened. Inside, No. 45 (88) has an original close-string dog-legged staircase with twisted balusters. Nos. 43 and 41 (89—90) have 18th-century staircases.

    1.   Parl. Svy., untitled (Sar. 11), f 43.

(91) **House**, No. 39, of two storeys with an attic, has tile-hung walls and a tiled roof and appears to be of the 18th century.

(92) **Houses**, two adjacent, Nos. 37 High Street and 79 New Street, now combined as a shop, are each three-storeyed with cellars and attics and have walls of stout timber-frame construction, with some flint, brick and rubble; the roofs are tiled. Both houses are of the early 16th century, but differing floor levels suggest that they were not built at the same time. By 1620 they were combined as an inn, the Holy Lamb; later (1742—c. 1760) it was the Sun and Lamb, a name still remembered in 1807.[1] In 1649, when Charles Snook was tenant, the rooms were listed.[2] It is customary for bishops of Salisbury to use No. 37 as a robing-place before their enthronement, hence the modern name Mitre House.[3]

In No. 37 the first floor is jettied N. and W. (the jetties are now underbuilt) and the second floor is jettied on the N. only. In the third storey there are three original N. windows, each of two lights with a moulded oak frame. In No. 79 the first and second floors are jettied N. at higher levels than in No. 37. The three-bay roof of No. 37, ridged E.—W., has four tie-beam trusses, each with two collars and clasped purlins. No. 79 has an 18th-century roof.

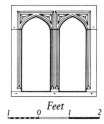

Feet
1   0   1   2

In 1297 this corner tenement belonged to Robert, son of Nicholas de St. Quintin (see note on p. 70), but it was occupied by William and Agatha Florentyn.[4] It

was still called Florentyne's Corner in 1363.[5] In 1455, when it was called Old Florentyne Corner, the clerk of the Cathedral fabric fund paid 20 d. quit rent.[6]

    1.   Haskins, *Guilds*, 310.
    2.   Parl. Svy., Foy 56 (Sar. 8), f.20.
    3.   Wordsworth, *Salisbury Processions*, 127.
    4.   Sar. D. & C.M., Sarum deeds, 3/5.
    5.   Dom. Bk. i, ff.42ᵛ, 44ᵛ.
    6.   *Liber Niger*, 69.

CRANE STREET

(93) **House**, recently rebuilt, formerly part of the Crown Inn, was of two storeys with a cellar and had a symmetrical three-bay S. front with sashed windows, and a central doorway with a flat hood on scroll brackets. The house appeared to be mainly of the early 19th century, but it contained a cellar (11½ ft. by 20½ ft.) with walls of ashlar and knapped flint, probably mediaeval. Reset in a ground-floor room was a small late 13th-century stone carving of a female head;[1] there were also two 14th-century oak brackets carved with curvilinear tracery panels. In 1649 (Parl. Svy., untitled sheaf (Sar. 11), f.10) the site contained two cottages leased to John Batten.

    1.   Now in Salisbury Museum.

(94) **Houses**, pair, Nos. 82—4, of three storeys with cellars, with brick-faced and tile-hung timber-framed walls and with tiled roofs, appear originally to have been one house, probably of the 16th century. Late in the 18th century the house was divided into two parts and the S. front, jettied originally at the first and second floors, was masked by a four-bay facade set in the plane of the top storey (two bays to each house). The facade is of brick in the lower storey and hung with mathematical tiles above the first floor; at the top is a plain cornice and parapet. Inside, the 16th-century timber-framed walls of the upper storeys include large members, probably reused. The roof, ridged E.—W., is of three

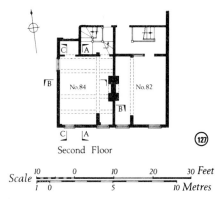

Second Floor

Scale
10 0 10 20 30 Feet
1 0   5   10 Metres

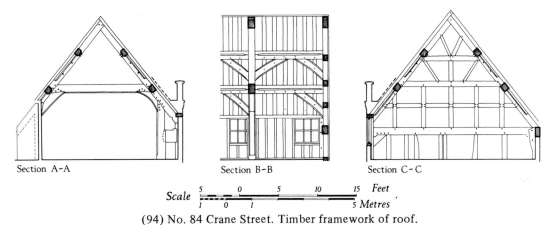

Section A-A   Section B-B   Section C-C

Scale 5 0 5 10 15 *Feet* / 1 0 1 5 *Metres*

(94) No. 84 Crane Street. Timber framework of roof.

bays resting on two heavy collar-beam trusses with 12″ x 9″ principals, spere-posts of the same size, and curved braces; speres, braces and collars are lightly chamfered. Tenoned to the outside face of one spere is a massive stub tie-beam (9″ x 16″). The trusses carry chamfered purlins (10″ x 6″) with chamfered wind-braces. Demolition of an adjacent building in 1969 exposed the E. gable of No. 82; it had a collared tie-beam truss with a lower king strut and two curved braces.

(95) **House,** No. 86, of three storeys with timber-framed walls and tiled roofs, appears to be mainly of the 16th century; the wall dividing it from No. 88 on the W. is, however, of the 13th century and the S. front is of the late 19th century. The gabled N. wall and the E. side of the N. wing have exposed 16th-century timber framework. Inside, there are several exposed beams and posts. The 19th-century stairs have close strings and turned balusters. A panel (8½ ins. by 2 ft. 2 ins.) of 13th-century mural decoration (Plate 43) is exposed on the W. wall of a first-floor room in the N. wing. The decoration resembles contemporary work in the Cathedral and consists of *rinceaux* of dark ochre on a cream-coloured background.

(96) **Cottages,** range of four, Nos. 90–96, are two-storeyed with brick walls and tiled roofs and date from the first half of the 19th century. The ground-floor rooms are now shops.

(97) **Church House, North and West Ranges,** now the administrative offices of the diocese, are of two storeys with attics and have walls of ashlar, flint and brick, and tiled roofs. The *North Range* appears to be of the second half of the 15th century and is probably the house called 'le Faucon' which William Lightfoot owned in 1455 (*Liber Niger*).[1] In 1523 the house belonged to Thomas Coke who bequeathed it to his daughter Scholastica, wife of Thomas Chafyn; the *West Range* probably dates from this period. From *c.* 1559 the house belonged to Piers Harris and by 1578 it had been

bought by John Bayley. Early in the 17th century the hall was chambered over and a stair tower was built in the angle between the two ranges. In 1630 John Bayley's heirs sold the house to Lord Castlehaven, and in 1634 it was acquired by the city and became a workhouse. It so remained until 1881, when it was bought by the Church of England and restored (Crickmay and son, architects).[2] The *South Range* (98) was added in 1728, as shown on a plan of 1742 (Plate 12) in the possession of the Diocesan Board of Finance.

Architectural Description – In the N. elevation of the *North Range* a large 15th-century archway, leading by a carriage through-way to the courtyard on the S., has a moulded segmental-pointed head with continuous jambs and a moulded label with octagonal stops (Plate 59). The oak gates have trefoil-headed panels in two heights; much of the woodwork is original. The original facade E. of the arch has an 18th-century sashed window in each storey. Over the archway is a window of two square-headed lights, perhaps of the 17th century, under an original label. To the W. the hall has two windows, each of four transomed cinquefoil-headed lights; their state before Crickmay's restoration is shown in a drawing dated 1833 by W. Twopeny (Plate 9). Further W. each storey has a restored window of two cinquefoil-headed lights; beside these is a large chimneybreast with weathered offsets. The gabled bay projecting N. at the W. end of the N. front is largely of the late 19th century although Twopeny's drawing shows that there was a projection there in 1833; from the plan of 1742 we know that the ground floor in this part of the building contained a larder and two prison cells, and that the lean-to building depicted by Twopeny contained an oven. The S. elevation of the hall is now flint-faced with ashlar dressings, but both Buckler (Plate 11) and Twopeny[3] show it as faced with ashlar. The S. arch of the through-way has a chamfered segmental-pointed head, continuous jambs and no label; above is a window of two cinquefoil-headed lights. As on the N. side, the hall windows were restored after 1881, presumably to their

CHURCH HOUSE *Crane Street*

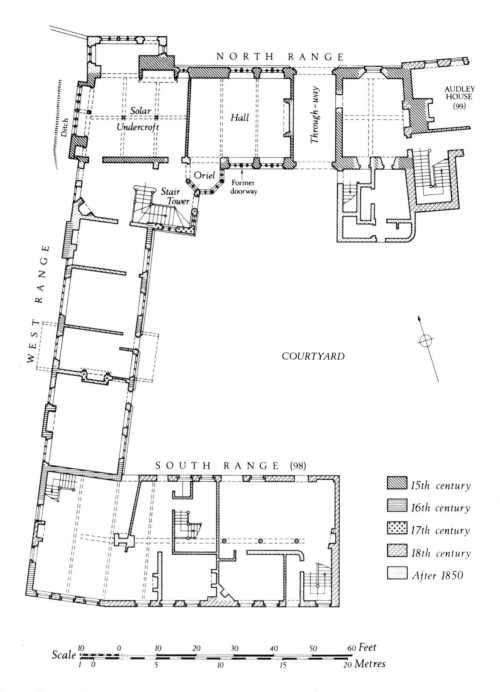

Scale

| 15th century |
| 16th century |
| 17th century |
| 18th century |
| After 1850 |

original form. Twopeny's drawing shows first-floor windows with ovolo-moulded stone surrounds under cambered lintels; they appear to be of the early 17th century and probably indicate the date of the chambering-over of the hall. An original doorway below the sill of the W. window, with a four-centred head and carved spandrels under a square label, was

removed in 1881. Further W. is a two-storeyed oriel with cinquefoil-headed windows in each storey; those of the lower storey are transomed. The three sides of the oriel which face the courtyard are of the 15th century; the two sides within the stair tower are of 1881. There may originally have been a small stair beside the oriel, giving access to the solar and oriel chamber (cf. Bingham's Melcombe, *Dorset* III, 164); presumably it was removed in the 17th century when the stair tower was built. The plan of 1742 shows a fireplace in the W. part of the oriel recess, and Twopeny shows its chimney.

The *Stair Tower* (Plate 59) remains externally much as depicted by Buckler except that the present doorway has carved spandrels and a label, perhaps taken from the former S. doorway of the hall. The windows with ovolo mouldings and cambered lintels are evidently of the early 17th century. The E. elevation of the *West Range* has been extensively rebuilt, but the modern casement windows with transomed square-headed lights and ovolo-moulded oak frames are similar to those shown by Buckler and no doubt their design is based on those removed in 1881. The W. elevation of the range was rebuilt at the same time. The plan of 1742 shows that the Close Ditch formerly ran below the wall, and for a short length at the N. end of the elevation the depression of this watercourse remains visible. Projecting on brackets over the former ditch, the solar undercroft has a restored 15th-century stone window of six transomed cinquefoil-headed lights; beside it to S. is a 15th-century privy. On the first floor, above the projecting window and privy, a 16th-century wood-framed window of seventeen transomed square-headed casements gives light to the solar. Further S. in the W. elevation, two 16th-century chimneystacks, partly of ashlar and partly of brick, correspond with fireplaces shown on the plan of 1742. Elsewhere the W. elevation is of 1881.

Inside, the *Hall* was restored in 1881, the inserted first floor being removed and the transomed windows reinstated. The chimneypiece (Plate 91) reset at the E. end of the hall was brought from a 15th-century house in Mere.[4] Above first-floor level the E. and W. end-walls are of timber frame construction, extensively restored. The N. and S. walls are capped by moulded oak wall-plate cornices.

The four trusses of the three-bay timber roof rise from moulded timber wall-posts which rest on carved stone corbels (Plate 85). Two of these represent angels with shields and one an angel with a scroll, two are men in 15th-century secular dress, one is a monk, another is a grotesque figure in workman's dress, the eighth has been defaced. One of the angels' shields is uncharged; the other bears a merchant mark similar to that in St. Thomas's church (p. 26) which we ascribe tentatively to John Wyot. Wrongly associated with John Webb it has given rise to the belief that the hall was built by a member of that family. The two intermediate roof trusses are arch-braced collar trusses with collar yokes; trefoil-headed tracery above the collars is of uncertain origin. The trusses in the plane of the E. and W. walls have the same features, together with timber studwork (Plate 83).

The lower storey of the *Oriel* opens from the hall through a moulded four-centred archway with continuous jambs, partly modern; below the first-floor ceiling is a roll-moulded and hollow-chamfered stringcourse. The upper storey consists of a gallery opening into the hall through an archway of 1881.

The *Solar Undercroft* has a ceiling of six panels defined by moulded beams and wall-plates; the posts are modern. The W. window has two moulded three-centred rear-arches resting on a centre pier which is joined to the centre mullion by a cusped arch; on the S. is the former privy. The 14th-century chimneypiece (Plate 90) comes from a house in Fisherton Street and was set in its present place in 1881. That another fireplace originally occupied the same position is attested by the large external chimneybreast (Plate 9).

The *Solar* on the first floor has a late 16th-century plaster ceiling with moulded ribs forming geometric panels. Corbels in the moulded oak cornices on N. and S. mark the position of two roof trusses, originally exposed; they are plain collar-beam trusses with chamfered arch-braces and upper angle-struts. The asymmetrical arrangement of the lights in the timber 16th-century W. window suggests that the S. part of the embrasure, over the ground-floor privy, originally contained another privy. The stone chimneypiece decorated with quatrefoils (Plate 90) is original. The projecting N. bay behind the chimneybreast is of 1881. The window E. of the fireplace contains fragments of mediaeval glass, reset.

The ground-floor room E. of the carriage throughway, at one time joined to the next house (99), has 18th-century bolection-moulded panelling in two heights. In the corresponding first-floor room the S. wall retains traces of a blocked 15th-century window with a moulded label. The three-bay roof over this part of the 15th-century range appears to be continuous with that of the hall although retiling has occasioned a slight change of level externally. The easternmost truss has a collar and scissor-braces; mortices in the principals show that the next truss originally had an arch-braced collar-beam; the third truss, corresponding with the E. side of the carriage through-way, has scissor-braces above the collar and vertical and curved braces below; the fourth truss has been described in the hall.

The stairs in the 17th-century stair tower are of 1881; reset in the ground-floor stair-hall to the W. is a 15th-century stone chimneypiece (Plate 90) from the house in Mere which also supplied the hall chimneypiece.

The *West Range,* extensively remodelled c. 1881, retains few noteworthy features. In a large first-floor room the openings to E. and W. bays with projecting windows have 16th-century moulded oak lintels and jambs. Two ground-floor rooms are fitted with stone chimneypieces brought from elsewhere in 1881. One in Renaissance style is from Longford Castle (Plate 91). Another, bearing insignia of Henry Serryge, mayor in 1508, was discovered in 1788 on the site of the Guildhall (13).[5] The four shields on the traceried frieze are charged with HS intertwined; IHS; a dolphin embowed; a merchant mark (below). A similar chimney-piece, but with six panels, appears in the foreground of the drawing (Plate 8) which shows the demolition of the old Guildhall.

1. For the history of the tenement, 1455–1634, see C.R. Everett, *W.A.M.*, xlix (1941), 435–79.

2. For a description of the building in 1881, see *The Builder*, xl (1881), 698, and two pages of drawings (not numbered).

3. B.M. (Prints & Drawings) 1874–2–14–443.

4. For an account of this and other chimneypieces reset *c.* 1881, see *W.A.M.*, xxxvi (1910), 370–2.

5. *Gentleman's Magazine*, 1788, i, 224.

John Wyot?

Henry Serryge

Merchant marks at Church House.

(98) **Church House, South Range,** of three storeys with brick walls and tiled roofs, was erected in 1728 for the enlargement of the former workhouse. A plan of 1742 (Plate 12) shows the lower storey as a workshop, without partitions and with a row of seven posts to support the first floor; there were stairs in the N.W. and S.E. corners. The plan on p. 74 shows the arrangement of rooms before 1881 and is taken from Crickmay's survey published in *The Builder* (see above, n. 2); further changes have been made since. The N. elevation has nine bays with plain sashed windows in each storey, ashlar plat-bands marking the first and second floors, and a moulded eaves cornice. The S. elevation is similar, but less regular and partly hidden by outbuildings; the E. and W. elevations have plain sashed windows. Inside, two ground-floor rooms contain reset 15th-century chimney-pieces; one (Plate 91) has shields charged respectively: RP, France quartering England, and an unidentified coat (27, p. 183); another has shields charged with the letters W and P. The first chimneypiece was brought from a house in St. Ann's Street opposite monument (299);[1] the source of the other is unknown. Reset in a first-floor room is a 16th-century fireplace surround with a moulded four-centred head and continuous jambs with shaped stops; its source too is unknown.

1. *W.A.M.*, xxxvi (1910), 370.

(99) **Audley House,**[1] No. 97 Crane Street, is of two storeys with a cellar and attics and has brick walls with stone dressings, and tiled roofs. It was built early in the 18th century, probably for Benjamin Wyche who acquired the tenement in 1701.[2] Until late in the 19th century the eastern rooms in the N. range of Church House (97) were annexed to Audley House, probably providing the service wing (plan, p. 74).

The symmetrical five-bay N. front has a central door-way with a pedimented hood on acanthus brackets, and plain sashed windows in both storeys; the windows in the upper storey are taller than those below (Plate 74).

Inside, several rooms have early 18th-century panelled dados and other joinery of the period. The main staircase is of oak, with twisted balusters. The first-floor drawing room is fully lined with bolection-moulded pine panelling in two heights under a moulded cornice.

1. Church House (97) at one time bore the name and is so designated on many maps.

2. *W.A.M.*, xlix (1941), 475.

(100) **House,** No. 95, of two storeys with attics, with rendered brick walls and a slate-covered roof, was built in 1812 on land which had previously contained a yard or outbuildings of No. 97.[1] The three-bay N. front (Plate 103) has plain sashed windows and a round-headed doorway under a flat hood; a parapet with a

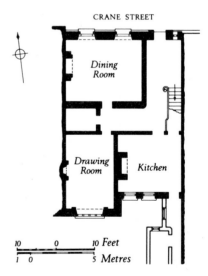

(100) No. 95 Crane Street.

moulded cornice masks the roof. Inside, the upper part of the staircase is oval on plan. The large S. window in the drawing room is flanked by pilasters with neo-classical enrichment.

1. *W.A.M.*, xlix (1941), 476.

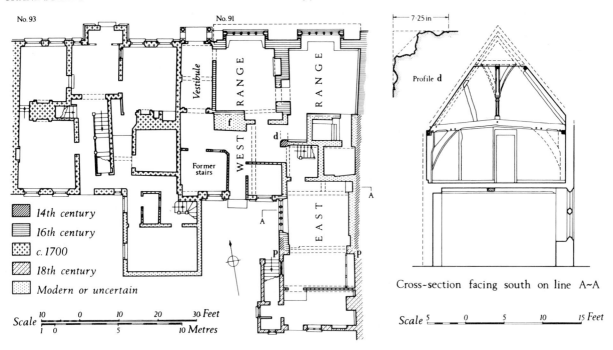

(101-2) Nos. 93 and 91 Crane Street.

Within the plan:
No. 93   No. 91   Vestibule   WEST RANGE   EAST RANGE   f   d   Former stairs   A   A   P   P

Legend:
- 14th century
- 16th century
- c. 1700
- 18th century
- Modern or uncertain

Scale — 10 0 10 20 30 Feet / 1 0 5 10 Metres

Profile d — 7·25 in

Cross-section facing south on line A~A

Scale — 5 0 5 10 15 Feet

(101) **House**, No. 93, of two storeys with a cellar and attics, has brick walls with ashlar dressings, and tiled roofs (Plate 73). It appears to have been built late in the 17th or early in the 18th century on ground, probably open, belonging to No. 91, a much earlier house (102). The N. front of No. 93 is approximately symmetrical and of six bays with stone plinths, quoins and moulded stringcourses and with a plaster eaves cove. One bay projects to form a two-storeyed porch. The porch doorway has a flat hood on wooden acanthus brackets; over it, a stone plaque inscribed STEYNINGS is perhaps a 19th-century insertion. Most of the plain sashed windows were renewed in the 19th century, but two original windows remain in the upper storey. At the E. end of the six-bay facade a seventh bay, integral with those described, fronts the vestibule of No. 91 and its corresponding first-floor room, but the continuity has been obscured by modern paintwork. Evidently the N. front of No. 93 was designed to accommodate the entrance to No. 91.

Inside, several rooms have dados with fielded panelling. The staircase opens from the entrance hall through an elliptical archway with panelled jambs (Plate 96). The stairs have turned balusters and newel posts. The S.W. ground-floor room has bolection-moulded panelling in two heights. Reset in the corresponding first-floor room are a richly carved early 17th-century oak chimneypiece (Plate 92) and panelling of the same period; their provenance is unknown.

(102) **House**, No. 91, includes part of the tenement of 'Johne Lysle milite. . .., vocato le Crane', recorded in Bishop Beauchamp's rental of 1455.[1] In the following year it was owned by Robert Newman, mercer, and it remained with his descendants until William Newman sold it to Anthony Weekes some time between 1562 and 1572.[2] The house is mainly of two storeys with cellars and attics, but partly three-storeyed; it has walls of stone, timber framework and brick, and tiled roofs (Plate 71). Apart from a narrow bay containing the vestibule, the plan consists of two parallel ranges at right-angles to the street. The middle part of the E. range dates from the 14th century and retains two and a half bays of an original crown-post roof. The northern parts of both ranges and also the N. front are of the 16th century. The S. part of the W. range and the narrow vestibule on the W. are contemporary with No. 93 (101) and date from c. 1700. The S. extension of the E. range is of the late 18th century.

The 14th-century E. range formerly extended further N., but the mediaeval structure now ceases some 20 ft. from the street. The S. end of the same structure is represented by two timber corner posts (p) about 33 ft. further south. The W. wall of the range, of rubble with ashlar dressings, extensively refaced in brickwork, ends in a stone quoin beside the S.W. corner-post; close to this the lower storey contains a late 16th-century stone window of five transomed square-headed lights. At the northern extremity of the surviving mediaeval W. wall there remains the S. jamb of a stone doorway (d) with 14th-century wave mouldings (see profile); the mouldings are continuous on an arched head, of which no more than the springing remains (Plate 91). The E. wall of the mediaeval E. range can only be seen in the upper storey, where it is of timber framework. The features so far described indicate an original 14th-century range with a W. front of stone containing a handsome doorway. Presumably the doorway opened into a hall, but we do not know if the hall was in the E. range or at right-angles, parallel to Crane Street; if the latter, the E. range must be regarded as a cross-wing.

The present northern parts of the E. and W. ranges were built during the last quarter of the 16th century when the property belonged to the Weekes family. A graffito, recorded in a photograph,[3] indicates that this part of the house was in existence in 1578. The N. front is of two bays. The lower storey, of rendered rubble with ashlar dressings, has two projecting windows with ovolo-moulded stone mullions and transoms; beneath them are two blocked four-light windows of former cellars, rendered useless at an unknown period by the lowering of the ground floor. The jettied upper storeys, of rendered timber framework, were remodelled c. 1700 and have sashed and semicircular windows of that date. The sashed windows are uniform with those of No. 93.

The entrance vestibule was built at the same time as the facade of No. 93, presumably because the construction of that house rendered the former access to No. 91 unusable. The porch has Italian-Doric columns and pilasters and a low pediment.

Inside, the vestibule contains an elliptical archway of c. 1700 with panelled wood spandrels and pilasters supporting a pulvinated entablature. The E. wall of the vestibule has been stripped of plaster to expose the stone plinth and timber-framed W. wall of the 16th-century W. range. An 18th-century staircase formerly in the S. part of the W. range was dismantled c. 1935 and removed to Salisbury House, Des Moines, U.S.A. A fireplace (f) on the N. of the stairhall, also removed to Des Moines, had a 15th-century stone chimneypiece which until c. 1860 had been in The Barracks (258) in Brown Street.[4] The N.–S. wall between the two 16th-century ranges formerly had two ground-floor and two first-floor fireplaces; three with ovolo-moulded 'Tudor' heads were taken to Des Moines; the fourth is lost. The N.E. first-floor room has a 16th-century plaster ceiling with moulded ribs arranged geometrically. The 14th-century roof over the middle bays of the E. range has braced, chamfered and cambered tie-beams, octagonal crown-posts with moulded caps and chamfered braces, and coupled rafters. The 16th-century ranges have collared tie-beam trusses.

1. *Liber Niger*, 70.
2. *W.A.M.*, xlix (1941), 437.
3. Lov. Cn., 56.

4. Benson & Hatcher, opp p.602; Hall, *Memorials*, following Pl. xxvi.

(103) **Houses**, two adjacent, Nos. 87, 89, of two storeys with slate-hung timber-framed walls and tiled roofs, are perhaps of 16th-century origin but they have been extensively altered and retain no notable features. The gabled N. fronts have jettied upper storeys with 19th-century cusped bargeboards. Some roofs with plain collared tie-beam trusses with clasped purlins and straight windbraces have recently been demolished.

NEW STREET

The position of monuments (104)–(117) is shown on the map of New Street Chequer, p. 95.

(104) **Houses**, two adjacent, Nos. 73 and 71, of three storeys with brick walls and tiled roofs, were built early in the 19th century. The N. front of each house comprises a modern shop window in the lower storey and a sashed window in each upper storey.

(105) **Houses**, two adjacent, Nos. 63 and 61, of two storeys with brick walls and slate-covered roofs, date from c. 1820. The N. fronts have square-headed doorways and plain sashed windows.

(106) **House**, No. 47, of two storeys with attics, has walls partly of flint and rubble and partly of timber framework; the roofs are tiled. Of 14th-century origin, the building was enlarged and altered late in the 16th century and further enlarged in the 18th century.

Mediaeval rubble masonry in the N. front rises through two storeys in the eastern bay and extends into the gable; the lower part has large ashlar quoins. Wall thicknesses suggest that the rendered lower storey of the western bay and also the E. wall are contemporary. The upper storey and gable of the western bay of the N. front are now tile-hung but a photograph taken before 1948 shows timber framework, perhaps of the 16th century. A lead rainwater head is dated 1569.

In the timber-framed S.E. wing the first floor is jettied on the W., but the overhang is masked by the 18th-century stair bay. The W. ground-floor room of the N. range has an open fireplace with hollow-chamfered stone jambs and a later timber bressummer. The N.E. room has 18th-century panelling. (Illustration, p. 79.)

(107) **New Inn**, of two storeys with timber-framed walls and tiled roofs, is of the late 15th or early 16th century; the S.W. wing was added late in the 18th century. In the three-bay N. front (Plate 62), jettied at the first floor, the arrangement of doorways and windows suggests that the range was once divided to form three cottages, but this was not the original arrange-

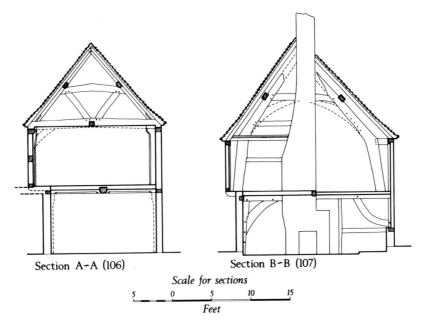

Section A–A (106)   Section B–B (107)

Scale for sections

5   0   5   10   15

Feet

NEW STREET

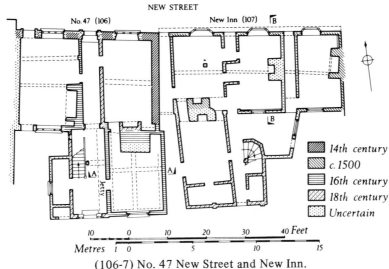

No. 47 (106)   New Inn (107)

14th century
c. 1500
16th century
18th century
Uncertain

10   0   10   20   30   40 *Feet*

Metres 1 0   5   10   15

(106-7) No. 47 New Street and New Inn.

ment. The roof, with four upper-cruck trusses, has peg-holes and mortices which show that the second truss from the E. was originally arch-braced (section B–B) whereas the other trusses are closed with studwork and wattle; it thus appears that the two E. bays of the range originally contained a first-floor hall.

Inside, the ground-floor room of the middle bay has an original chamfered ceiling beam. The E. and S. fire-places have chamfered timber bressummers. The S.W. wing contains a large first-floor room lined with pine panelling and lit by a Palladian window in the S. wall.

(108) **Cottages,** pair, Nos. 37–9, originally one, are two-storeyed with brick-faced and rendered timber-framed walls and tiled roofs. The two-bay N. range,

probably of 15th or 16th-century origin, is masked by a 19th-century facade. The small brick S. wing is of the 18th century. Inside, some chamfered timbers are seen. The roof retains an original tie-beam truss with a cambered collar and upper struts.

(109) **House,** No. 35, of two storeys with attics, with brick walls and tiled roofs, is of the early 19th century. Now communicating with No. 33 by doorways cut through the party-walls, it appears originally to have been a separate dwelling. The N. front has two round-headed recesses flanking a central doorway with a pedimented doorcase. Each recess originally contained two storeys of three-light sashed windows but in the W. recess these have now been altered.

(110) **House**, No. 33, mainly of two storeys with attics, but with a three-storeyed N. range, has brick walls and tiled roofs and was built about the middle of the 18th century. The four-bay facade has moulded brick plat-bands and cornice and a classical door-case with Tuscan columns and entablature. Inside, the staircase hall has plaster vaulting and the stairs have turned newel posts and plain balusters. A ground-floor room is lined with fielded panelling in two heights. Several 18th-century chimneypieces are preserved. Additions on the S. date from early in the 19th century.

A mid 19th-century block-plan of monuments (108)–(110), by Peniston, is in W.R.O. (451/179).

(111) **House**, No. 31, of two storeys with attics, has brick walls and tiled roofs. The tenement belongs to St. Nicholas's Hospital (26) and is probably mentioned in 13th-century records,[1] but the present structure is not earlier than the first half of the 18th century. The three-bay N. front has moulded brick plat-bands and plain sashed windows; three of the latter on the first floor form a three-sided projecting bay. Inside, several rooms have panelled dados and moulded cornices. Three rooms have 18th-century carved wooden chimneypieces (Plate 94).

1. Wordsworth, *St. Nicholas*, 142–5.

(112) **Cottage**, No. 29, of two storeys with rendered timber-framed walls and a tiled roof, is of the early 16th century.

(113) **Houses**, three adjoining, Nos. 27, 25 and 21, of three storeys with brick walls and slate-covered roofs, are of the early 19th century. The unified N. front forms an approximately symmetrical four-bay facade in which the two middle bays of the first floor are occupied by a three-sided projecting window. Elsewhere there are plain sashed windows or modern shop fronts.

(114) **Houses**, pair, Nos. 11 and 9, now united as offices, are three-storeyed with brick walls and slate-covered roofs and date from *c*. 1840.

(115) **House**, No. 7, of two storeys with an attic, has rendered timber-framed walls and tiled roofs and probably is of 15th-century origin. The two-bay N. front, jettied at the first floor, has sashed windows and a plain doorway. Inside, the N. ground-floor room has 18th-century panelling.

(116) **Houses**, two adjacent, Nos. 5 and 3, formerly a single dwelling, are three-storeyed with brick walls and slate-covered roofs and were built *c*. 1840. The N. front is of five bays.

(117) **House**, No. 1, of two storeys with an attic, has brick walls and tiled roofs. The N. range is of the early 16th century; the stairs and S.W. wing were added in the 17th century. A large original fireplace in the gabled E. wall is blocked internally, but the brick chimneybreast remains. Inside, some rooms in the N. range have plain 18th-century panelling; 17th-century panelling remains in the S.W. wing.

For the N. side of New Street, see New Street Chequer, pp. 95, 105-7.

MITRE CHEQUER

For location of monuments (118–125), see plan, p. 95.

(118) **House**, No.1 High Street, of three storeys with brick walls and slate-covered roofs, probably dates from the third quarter of the 18th century. In the W. front the storeys are defined by plat-bands and there is a heavy stone cornice with modillions. Each upper storey has two plain sashed windows with keystones; below is a modern shop window. The interior has been modernised. Old photographs show that No. 3, formerly adjacent on the S. but demolished *c*. 1920, had a four-bay facade uniform and continuous with that of No. 1;[1] an advertisement of 1770 for a 'large new-built house' is likely to refer to No. 3.[2]

Another photograph (Plate 15) shows the demolition, *c*. 1930, of a mediaeval house at the N.W. corner of the chequer.[3] It was three-storeyed and had scissor-braced timber framework with jetties to N. and W.

1. Lov. Cn., 130.
2. *S.J.*, 26 Mar., 1770.
3. Lov. Cn., 244.

(119) **House**, No. 61 Silver Street, recently demolished, was of four storeys with timber-framed walls and tiled roofs; it probably was of the late 16th century. The gabled N. front was jettied at the second floor and had one sashed window in each upper storey; the ground floor had a modern shop window. Inside, chamfered beams and posts were exposed. The three-bay roof had tie-beam trusses with queen-struts and windbracing. The tie-beams were braced to the uprights of the fourth storey.

(120) **Shop,** No. 53 Silver Street, and **Warehouse** extending S. to New Canal, are of three storeys with brick walls and slate-covered roofs and were built early in the 19th century. The front to Silver Street has four bays of plain sashed windows in the upper storeys and modern shop windows below. The S. front is of eleven bays, mostly with windows with small-paned cast-iron casements, but the centre bay has doorways in each storey served by a hoist with a wrought-iron crane.

(121) **House and Shop,** No. 21 Silver Street, of four storeys with brick walls and slate-covered roofs, is of the mid 19th century. Above a modern shop front the N. elevation has three plain sashed windows in each storey, and a moulded stone cornice.

(122) **House,** No. 41 Silver Street, of three storeys with brick walls and a slate-covered roof, is of the late 18th century. The two-bay N. front has a modern shop window in the ground storey and sashed windows with triple keystones in the upper storeys. Above is a moulded stone cornice and a brick parapet. Inside, plain 18th-century stairs are preserved above first-floor level.

(123) **House and Shop,** No. 39 Silver Street, of three storeys with brick walls and a slate-covered roof, is of the 18th century. The four-bay N. front has a modern shop window in the ground storey and plain sashed windows in both upper storeys. Above is a moulded timber cornice with dentils, and a parapet. Inside, the upper storeys retain original joinery of good quality. As the lowest step and curtail of the main staircase is at first-floor level it appears that the ground floor was designed to be a shop.

(124) **House,** now incorporated with and enclosed on three sides by a modern shop, is of three storeys with an attic and has brick walls and a tiled roof. It is of the 17th century. The E. front, rebuilt in the 18th century, has three sashed windows in each upper storey and a moulded brick stringcourse and cornice. Inside, the third storey has chamfered ceiling beams with shaped stops. The stairs from this storey to the attic have a closed string, stout square newel posts, a moulded handrail and shaped splats in lieu of balusters.

(125) **Cottage,** No. 18 New Canal, formerly concealed by modern walls but discovered during demolition, was of two storeys with timber-framed walls and a tiled roof ridged E.–W.; it was of the 14th or 15th century. The first floor was jettied on the S. and a roll-moulded bracket projected from the S.E. corner post of the lower storey.

CROSS KEYS CHEQUER

Of the monuments recorded, a number were demolished for the rebuilding of the N. half of the chequer in 1976. The remains of two 14th-century houses (131–2) and an 18th-century staircase (133) were preserved and incorporated with the new buildings. The facades to Queen Street were partly preserved and partly reproduced in facsimile.

Monuments in Cross Keys Chequer.

(126) **House,** No. 5 Queen Street, of two storeys with tile-hung timber-framed walls and a tiled roof, is probably of 16th-century origin, but extensively altered. The W. front is jettied at the first floor. An early photograph[1] shows this house together with a timber-framed mediaeval building on the S.W. corner of the chequer, now gone. The large corner tenement facing W. to the Guildhall and S. to Milford Street belonged throughout the 14th century to the Chese, Chuse or Juwys family,[2] and was known by 1420 as Cheesecorner. Although the westward-facing houses of Cheesecorner (126–8) had at times been occupied separately, they all belonged to Robert Cove by the middle of the 15th century.[3]

1. Lov. Cn., 146.
2. Sar. D. & C.M., Sarum deeds, 3/40. W.R.O., 164/1; 9, 10, 12, 13.
3. *Liber Niger*, 68.

(127) **Pair of Houses**, Nos. 6–7 Queen Street, originally one, but divided before 1854 (Kingdon & Shearm), were built *c.* 1785. A drawing of *c.* 1790 (Plate 8) shows the three lower storeys of the existing W. front, but in the engraving of the old council house, *c.* 1780 (Plate 2), an older building appears. In *c.* 1790 the ground floor was 'Shorto's Cutlery'. The houses are now four-storeyed with brick walls and slate-covered roofs. Above modern shop windows each upper storey of the W. elevation has four plain sashed windows. The original top-lit oak staircase survives in the N. house, above first-floor level. Two rooms have 18th-century fireplace surrounds.

(128) **House**, No. 8 Queen Street, of three storeys with timber-framed walls and tiled roofs, is probably of the mid 15th century. The site was once part of the Cheesecorner tenement (see monument (126)). Of the several shops formerly built along the W. side of this large tenement, at least two facing the Guildhall were acquired in 1397 by John Cammell, grocer.[1] Cammell died in 1398[2] leaving this property to another John Cammell (mayor 1449) who retained it until after 1450.

The W. front (Plate 63), retaining much original timber framework, was jettied at the first and second floors, but only the second-floor jetty remains; the casement windows are modern. The tile-hung E. elevation has 18th-century sashed windows, that in the lower storey having three lights with gothic heads.

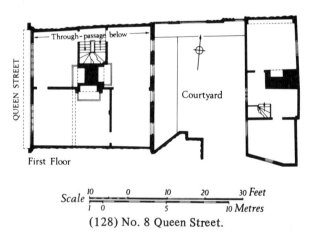

(128) No. 8 Queen Street.

In plan the main part of the house is square, the rooms being grouped around a single chimneystack which may be an early 17th-century insertion. A narrow through-passage on the ground floor gives access from the street to a courtyard on the E. The partitions between the ground-floor rooms have gone, but jowl-headed posts and chamfered beams with moulded stops remain. The N.E. ground-floor room, extended in the 18th century and lined with fielded panelling of that

period, has a fireplace with chamfered stone jambs and a timber bressummer. The stairs are of the 18th century with plain balustrades and a moulded mahogany handrail. On the first floor, the long E. room has 18th-century panelling and a 17th-century fireplace with moulded stone jambs and a timber bressummer. The S.W. room is lined with 17th-century oak panelling *in situ* and has a stone fireplace (Plate 92) with a carved oak chimneypiece in which the Sacrifice of Isaac, evidently by Humphrey Beckham (cf. his own monument in St. Thomas's, Plate 47), is flanked by busts of a king and a queen and by caryatids probably representing Religion and Innocence. The N.W. room has an enriched cornice of *c.* 1800. The roofs have collared tie-beam trusses with clasped purlins.

A two-storeyed service range with timber-framed walls and a tiled roof, E. of the courtyard, is of the late 16th or early 17th century; it has a central chimneystack with a fireplace on each floor.

The popular association of this house with John Port (mayor 1446) is due to misinterpretation of documentary evidence. Port's house was in the Cheesemarket (see (25), p. 54).

1. Dom. Bk. ii, f 8.
2. W.R.O., will, 164/1/6.

(129) **House**, No. 9 Queen Street, of three storeys with timber-framed walls and a tiled roof, dates mainly from early in the 14th century and is remarkably well preserved. In 1306 Roger Hupewell, the holder of the land now occupied by Nos. 9 and 10 (130), sold a piece of ground 39 ft. long (other dimension unspecified) to William Russel with permission for Russel to build a wooden house beside that which already stood on the site of No. 10.[1] Russel, who owned adjoining land, presumably the rest of that which now is No. 9, agreed to maintain an efficient gutter between the two buildings. In 1314 Hupewell gave Russel permission to heighten the house, but reserved the right to make his own house higher still if he so wished; the heightening may explain the tiered fenestration of Russel's hall. The owners of the house throughout the 14th and 15th centuries are identifiable.[2] Being opposite the Guildhall and Wool Market it was often owned by wool merchants; these included Henry Russel (before 1354), Henry Fleming (1354–60), Thomas Hyndon (1363–98) and members of the Harding family (1398–1459). In 1435 Thomas Harding, draper of London, let the house to Richard and Alice Walker; the Walkers lived there until 1459 when the house was given to the cathedral by William Harding, clerk of the cathedral works. In 1649 the house comprised a shop, a kitchen, a buttery, a hall above stairs, four chambers, a garret, a courtyard and a stable.[3]

Apart from the roof and the W. front, both rebuilt between 1780 and 1790 (cf. Plates 2 and 8), William

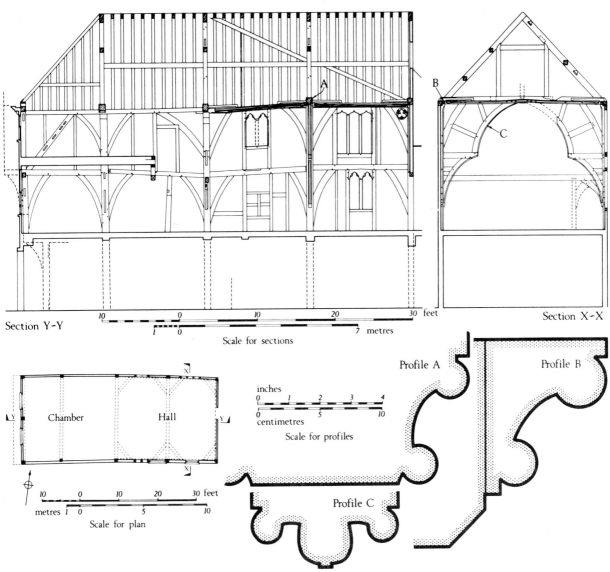

Section Y-Y

Section X-X

10   0   10   20   30 feet
1 0   7 metres
Scale for sections

Chamber   Hall

inches
0   1   2   3   4
0   5   10
centimetres
Scale for profiles

Profile A   Profile B

Profile C

10   0   10   20   30 feet
metres 1 0   5   10
Scale for plan

(129) WILLIAM RUSSEL'S HOUSE, No. 9 Queen Street, *c.* 1306.

Russel's house of 1306–14 survives virtually intact. The 18th-century W. front, faced with mathematical tiles, has a modern shop window below and plain sashed windows in the upper storeys; the hipped roof rises over a wooden cornice with brackets. The N., S. and E. elevations are largely concealed by adjoining buildings. Inside, the lower storey is masked by modern wall-linings, but in the second and third storeys the original structure is exposed. The mediaeval house is four bays long. The two western bays are three-storeyed, but the two eastern bays comprise a hall (26 ft. by 21 ft.) originally open from ground to roof. In 1975 an inserted second floor was removed and the upper part of the hall was restored (Plate 82). The original cambered and moulded tie-team (A) of the hall roof is braced by timber framework in the form of a large cusped arch (C),

decorated with continuous triple roll-mouldings, the middle roll keeled. Until recently the radial timber framework of the spandrels was filled in with chalk rubble, but this has now been removed. At the apex the upper arch-braces clasp a carved timber boss; in the original roof a crown-post may well have stood over this boss. The tie-beam has double roll-mouldings with foliate stops on each side. Similar mouldings are applied to the wallplates on the N., S. and E. of the hall. Above the wall-plates, the four corners of each bay in the hall have chamfered horizontal braces. Mediaeval timbers reused in the 18th-century roof probably come from the original structure.

The hall was lit by timber windows, each originally of two lights with cusped two-centred heads. These windows occur at levels corresponding with the second and third storeys. On the N. side in the third storey the W. bay has an original window, but the E. bay has a widened window of three lights with ogee heads, probably a 15th-century modification. High up at the E. end of the N. wall is a small circular opening with trefoil cusping. The second storey on the N. side has an original window in the E. bay, but the W. bay has no opening, probably because Roger Hupewell's house covered it externally. On the S. side an original cusped two-light window remains in the W. bay of the hall; it is partly covered by the 15th-century roof of No. 8 (128). The E. bay of the S. side has 18th-century sashed windows in both upper storeys.

The first-floor chamber in the W. half of the house communicated with the hall through a doorway with a chamfered two-centred head; the chamfer remains on the brace of the second-floor beam. If there was no gallery the doorway may have opened directly from the stairs.

In the W. wall the reset wall-plate of the third storey (moved some 3 ft. E. of its original position when the jetty was removed, c. 1780) has ogee mouldings and mortices on its underside indicating two windows, each of three square-headed lights.

A two-storeyed brick building adjoining the E. end of the mediaeval hall appears to have been added during the 18th century. It has no noteworthy features.

1. Sar. Corp. MS., 1/249, Nos. 2 and 3.
2. Sar. D. & C.M., Sarum deeds, 3 and 4; Harding deeds, passim.
3. Parl. Svy., Foy 56 (Sar. 8), f.13.

(130) **House**, No. 10 Queen Street, of three storeys and an attic, with brick walls and a tiled roof, appears to be of the mid 18th century. In the W. front the lower storey is modern; the second storey has a projecting window of three sashed lights with an ogee-shaped lead roof; the third storey has two plain sashed windows; the attic is masked by a shaped parapet with elliptical-headed panels. Inside, some rooms retain 18th century joinery and moulded cornices. The stairs have turned balusters and moulded handrails.

The history of the long, narrow tenement can be traced in deeds of the Tailors' Guild.[1] In 1306 (see (129)) it was the property of Roger Hupewell; by 1386 it belonged to William More, tailor, and his wife Susanna; from 1432 to 1464 it belonged to Edward Goodyer, tailor, and his wife Dionisia. Both the Mores and the Goodyers appear in the bede roll of benefactors of the Tailors' Guild, William More (d. 1424) having endowed his obit with funds from the tenement, while the Goodyers gave the tenement to the guild in 1464.[2] In a deed of 1432 Susanna More leased the front shop and rooms over it, together with the kitchen, upper rooms and outbuildings at the rear of the tenement, to the Goodyers, but she retained the hall and parlour for

her own use. The house remained with the Tailors' Guild until the 19th century. Lessees include Thomas Goddard, cutler, in 1791 and 1831, and John Munday, a warden of the guild, in 1834.[3]

1. Sar. Corp. MS., 1/249, passim.
2. Haskins, Guilds, 130.
3. ibid., 209—15.

(131) **House with Shop** and another **Building**, Nos. 14 and 13 Queen Street, were part of the former Cross Keys Inn. In 1341 the tenement was described as extending 'from Carterstrete (Queen Street) along the alley opposite the Market to Brown Street'.[1] The W. part of the area, approximately 50 ft. by 110 ft., evidently corresponds with a standard burgage plot of 3 by 7 perches as laid down in the city charter of 1225. In the 14th century the tenement belonged to the elder William Teynturer who, dying in 1363, endowed his chantry at the cathedral with the revenue.[2] The arrangement of the mediaeval buildings 'along the alley' is suggested in a lease of 1403 wherein the N. part of the tenement (No. 14) is described as a shop with chambers newly built and a stable with chambers over it adjoining the said shop; the tenant had access to the yard by way of the entry, and to a well and a latrine in the yard.[3] In 1465 the property was called Seynt Mary-abbey, probably because it belonged to the cathedral.[4] The first-floor plan of No. 14 appears with the plans of Nos. 15—18 (132) on p. 85.

The survey of 1649 gives a more detailed picture. The Queen Street frontage then comprised three shops and an entry. No. 14, the largest of the three, was described as a part of the inn called The Cross Keys. The E. part of the tenement contained stables surrounding 'the great yard or court situate in the middle of the said abbey and parcel of the same, through which court there hath been and now are ways and passages to and from the said tenements and stables'.[5]

No. 13, formerly on the S. of the court (see map, p. 81) but demolished in 1965, was two-storeyed with timber-framed walls and an iron-covered roof; it probably was of the early 15th century. The roof, originally of collar-rafter construction without purlins, was strengthened by the addition of four collared tie-beam trusses. The two W. trusses had chamfered and cambered tie-beams braced to the walls with chamfered curved members; the two E. trusses had lower angle-braces and supported purlins. The timbers were smoke-blackened and the ceiling of the first-floor rooms had probably been inserted in the 18th century, as also had two brick chimneystacks set against the S. wall. The building formerly extended further west.

No. 14 was on the N. side of the former court. Much of the range was demolished in 1974 during the redevelopment of the N. part of the chequer, but the timber framework of the four W. bays was preserved; it is of the late 14th-century (witness the lease of 1403 cited above) and of three storeys. The gabled W. front (Plate 101), partly rendered and partly tile-hung, was originally jettied in both upper storeys. The roof of the original four-bay structure has a central tie-beam truss and two intermediate collar-trusses, with clasped purlins and curved windbraces. The eastern half of the 14th-century building appears originally to have had no second floor, the roof timbers being smoke-blackened. The large chimneystack and the four two-storeyed bays E. of it were probably of the 16th century. The easternmost bay was of the 18th or 19th century.

1. Sar. D. & C.M., deeds, Box I.
2. Sar. Corp. MS., Dom. Bk. I, f 37.
3. Sar. D. & C.M., *loc. cit.*
4. Sar. Corp. MS., Tailors' Guild deeds, No. 84.
5. Parl. Svy., Foy 56 (Sar. 8), ff. 3–5.

(132) **Plume of Feathers,** Nos. 15–18 Queen Street, formerly an inn,[1] but at the time of investigation (1965–74) partly shops and partly unoccupied and since 1974 extensively altered in the redevelopment of the N. part of the chequer, occupied a rectangular burgage plot (A, B, C, D, on the plan) equal in size to the adjacent plot (131). When investigated the plot contained seven distinct structures (*i–vii* on the drawings and in the following description), ranging in date of origin from the 14th to the 19th century; they surrounded a narrow yard entered from the Market Place by a through-way in

the W. range (*i–ii*). The W. front (Plate 101, *r.*), preserved in the redevelopment, comprises two facades, No. 15 of three and No. 18 of four storeys, each two bays wide. On the ground floor there are modern shop fronts; the upper storeys of No. 15 are faced with 18th-century mathematical tiles; No. 18 is brick-fronted. The facade of No. 18, with plain triple sashed windows, must be later than 1795 as a drawing published in that year shows in its place a timber-framed elevation with two gables.[2] Before the alterations of 1974 the elevations surrounding the yard were tile-hung, rendered, weatherboarded, of brick and of timber framework. A picturesque 17th-century staircase (Plate 86) occupied the S.E. corner of the yard. A lead rainwater head was dated 1689. The whole site had been badly neglected for many years.

Described in mediaeval deeds as 'opposite the market where wool is sold', the tenement belonged in the 14th century to rich wool merchants. Robert de Woodford, mayor 1322, collector and receiver of the King's wool for Wiltshire in 1343–5, owned the house from 1340 at latest.[3] In 1362, after the deaths of Robert and his brother John, the tenement was sold to William de Wichford, mayor 1359.[4] Later it belonged to Nicholas le Taillour, draper, mayor 1373, and by 1400 to Thomas Castleton, mercer. In 1420 Castleton sold it for £140 to William Harnhalle, barber, who since 1393–4 had been a sub-tenant, occupying a shop with solar and a building named 'le celer' behind the shop; Harnhalle also enjoyed right of access to a well and to a latrine in

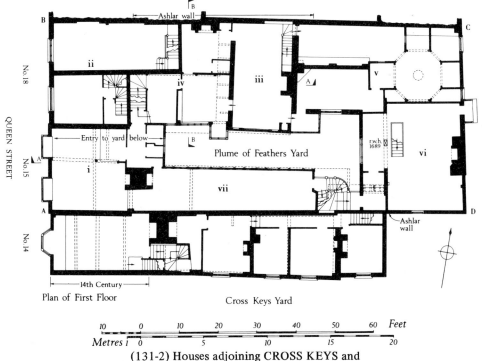

(131-2) Houses adjoining CROSS KEYS and
PLUME OF FEATHERS YARDS. First floor plan.

the courtyard.[5] It is not clear when the house became an inn, but at least part of the plot was called the Plume of Feathers by 1635; it retained the name throughout the 17th and 18th centuries.[6] In 1752 it was reported that 'the Plume of Feathers in the Market Place is now completely fitted up and made commodious'.[7]

In 1974, while the buildings were being prepared partly for demolition and partly for incorporation in a modern structure, the following facts were confirmed.

i. The building (No. 15) at the S.W. corner of the burgage plot is timber-framed and of three storeys with attics. It was in existence when No. 14 (131) was built and must therefore be earlier than 1403; almost certainly it is of the 14th century. The heavily strutted timber framework of the gabled S. wall is illustrated below; between the timbers the wall was of chalk blocks. There is evidence in the surviving members that the mathematical-tiled 18th-century W. front replaces an original street front which was jettied at the first and second floors. That the building formerly extended into the N. part of the plot is shown by two panels of its stout timber-framed E. wall which survived until recently in the lower storey of No. 18 (*ii*), between the two S. staircases; the heavy cross-braced framework

(drawing below) was certainly of the 14th century. A mortice for further bracing in the N. side of an upper post provided additional evidence of the northward continuation of the building. It probably extended to the N. side of the plot.

The roof of building *i* (partly preserved in the modern structure) has two main bays, each bisected by an arch-braced open truss. The truss between the bays has framework similar to that of the S. gable and probably corresponded with a partition between two second-floor chambers. There are long mortices for horizontal braces between the wall-plates and the tie-beam.

ii. The N.W. corner of the burgage plot was occupied in 1965–74 by a plain brick building of *c*. 1800. It comprised two shops, one longer than the other, each with three upper storeys. As stated above, the E. wall of the S. shop was partly of the 14th century. The northern shop extended into the area formerly occupied by building *iv*.

iii. In the middle of the N. side of the burgage plot a three-storeyed timber-framed range, with the first floor jettied S. and the second floor originally jettied S. and W., is also of 14th-century origin. The stone N. wall of the lower storey continues to E. and W. and is probably

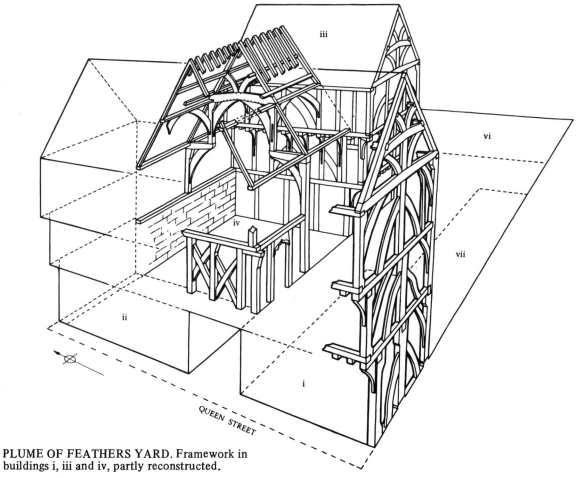

PLUME OF FEATHERS YARD. Framework in buildings i, iii and iv, partly reconstructed.

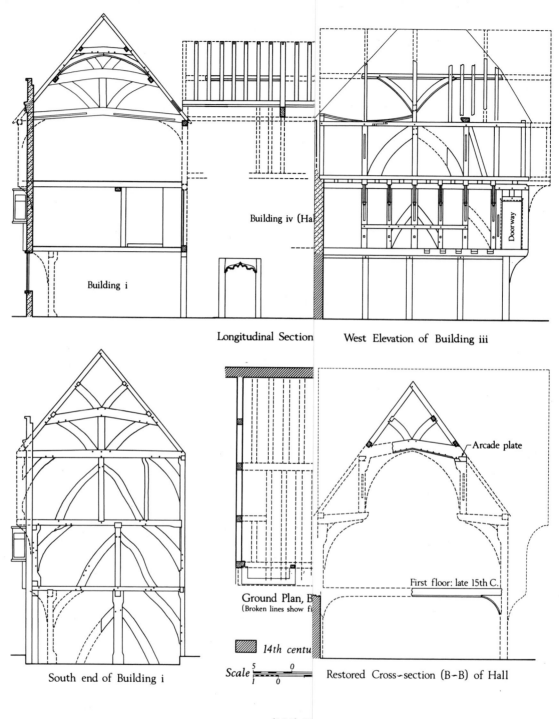

Longitudinal Section

West Elevation of Building iii

Building iv (Ha

Doorway

Building i

South end of Building i

Building i

Ground Plan, B
(Broken lines show f

14th centu

Scale 5 0
      1 0

Arcade plate

First floor: late 15th C.

Restored Cross-section (B-B) of Hall

(132) H

the original plot boundary; above first-floor level this wall is of 18th-century brickwork. Timber framework in the N. wall of the third storey retains the rebates of a former window. The E. wall has a large chimney-breast of brick and ashlar, apparently an early 17th-century feature; on the ground floor it is blind and merely supports the first-floor fireplace. In the S. front, originally gabled, the 14th-century lower jetty remains, but that of the second floor has been cut back. In the W. elevation the second-floor jetty is supported on six 14th-century brackets with curved and chamfered braces rising from small wall-shafts with ogee-moulded capitals. Although it came to be enclosed in building *iv*, the W. wall of *iii* must originally have been external. A rebated doorway at first-floor level in the S. part of the west elevation must be an original feature as building *iv* blocks it up; it may have been approached originally by an outside staircase or it may have given access to a balcony sheltered by the ornamental W. jetty. Inside, building *iii* originally had a single room on each floor. The large second-floor room, open to the roof, has chamfered jowl-headed wall-posts. The slightly cambered central tie-beam has mortices for horizontal bracing. The 14th-century roof has been severely mutilated, but surviving members indicate an original four-bay structure with a collared tie-beam truss with haunched principals and lower angle-braces, near the middle, and with two intermediate trusses with ogee scissor braces; only one of the latter survives and its upper part has perished (see drawing; the cruck strapped to the base of one ogee member has obviously been brought from elsewhere).

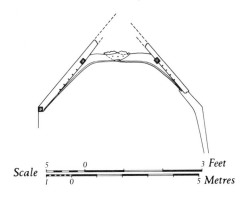

Scale
5   0   3 *Feet*
1   0   5 *Metres*

The removal of the S. jetty of the second floor in building *iii* and the substitution of hipped roofs for the original N. and S. gables probably took place in the 17th century.

iv. Early in the 15th century the space between the W. side of building *iii* and the E. side of the northern end of building *i* was filled by a lofty hall, two bays long from W. to E. and corresponding in height with the three-storeyed buildings at either end. The N. side of the hall rested on the stone boundary wall of the plot; the E. end consisted of the W. side of building *iii* with its orna-

mental jetty; the W. end was the E. side of building *i*. Nothing remains of the S. wall except a timber doorway with a cusped and sub-cusped ogee head. The hall

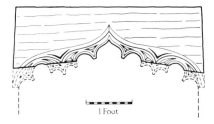

1 Foot

roof is represented by a number of members remaining *in situ*, including a large chamfered collar-beam with upper principal rafters and V-struts, purlins and stout common rafters. Mortices and peg-holes in the collar-beam show that it is the main transverse member of a former hammer-beam collar truss from which all other members have gone (cross-section B–B opposite). The main supporting wall-posts have also gone, but the S. post was attested by a vertical recess in a brick wall which formerly encased and ultimately replaced it. Resting on the W. eaves-plate of building *iii* is the E. end of a moulded arcade-plate; the mortice for its brace is seen in the 14th-century post directly underneath, and the housing of the W. end of the plate is seen in the S. part of the collar beam. The soot which encrusts the surviving roof timbers shows that the hall originally had an open hearth, but this cannot have remained long in use because an ovolo-moulded first-floor beam, resting on a curved brace which must once have been morticed into the missing S. wall posts, shows that the hall was chambered over, perhaps towards the end of the 15th century. In the 17th century a second floor (not shown on drawing) was inserted, converting the hall into a three-storeyed range. This floor was jettied southwards and the lower part of the hall roof was cut away and replaced by two hipped roofs, ridged N.–S.

v. Originally the E. part of the burgage plot contained stables, but nothing remains of these. Towards the end of the 19th century a Turkish bath of two storeys with brick walls and flat roofs was built in the N.E. corner. The octagonal bath hall was top-lit. This building was demolished in 1974.

vi. South of the baths, the E. part of the plot was occupied by a 17th-century building (perhaps the original Plume of Feathers inn) of two storeys with attics, with brick walls and tiled roofs. Greatly altered in the 19th century, it was demolished in 1974. The W. front was masked by a two-storeyed late 19th-century extension with a lean-to roof, and the former plan of both floors had been obliterated, but the 17th-century roof with two W.-facing gables remained. A lead rain-water-head between the gables had billeted capping, baluster-shaped corners and SE (?Samuel Eyre) 1689 embossed on the front; below were two flowers.

vii. The S. side of the plot contains a narrow two-storeyed building, mainly of the 18th century, but incorporating earlier work. Blocks of ashlar reused in the S. wall probably came from the original burgage plot boundary wall. Elsewhere the walls are of slender timber framework with brick nogging. The roof is tiled. The narrow first-floor room is jettied over the yard. At the E. end of this range, in the space between buildings *vi* and *vii*, an early 17th-century staircase (Plate 86) has panelled, moulded and fretted newel posts, plain close strings, stout balusters and a plain handrail. The original flight of steps gave access to the first floor of building *vi* and may well have been the principal entrance to the inn. Early in the 18th century a second flight of steps was added, branching from the 17th-century flight some 4 ft. above ground level and curving round to serve the upper storey of building *vii*. The added staircase has moulded close strings, slenderer turned balusters than the original ones, moulded handrails and stout plain newel posts with ball finials and turned pendants.

1. Haskins, *Guilds*, 330.
2. Drawing by Edward Dayes, engraved by F. Jukes; reproduced in V.C.H., *Wilts.*, vi, opp. 87.
3. Sar. D. & C.M., deeds, I, 38.
4. Dom. Bk. i, ff.25, 35–6.
5. Dom. Bk. iii, ff.49ᵛ–50. A later owner was John Hall (Duke, *Prolusiones*, viii; see monument (185)).
6. Haskins, *Guilds*, 330.
7. *S.J.*, Sept. 18, 1752.

(133) **House,** No. 20 Queen Street, largely demolished in 1974, was three-storeyed with brick walls and tiled roofs and was mainly of the 18th century although earlier features came to light at demolition. The site was described in 1400 as 'a tenement and three shops opposite the Wool Market' when Thomas Boyton, bowyer, the owner since 1361, bequeathed it to his cousin William who kept it until *c.* 1420.[1]

The W. range, parallel with the street, retained elements of a timber-framed building perhaps of 15th-century origin; it had been altered in the 17th century and was refronted in the 18th century. The drawing room, stair hall and N. range were added about the middle of the 18th century. The staircase (partly preserved) is of outstanding quality (Plate 88). Lastly, *c.* 1840, the W. range was remodelled internally, but this work was much inferior to that of the 18th century; probably at this time the ground-floor rooms were turned into shops. It appears that an 18th-century scheme for the modernisation and enlargement of the house on a rather grand scale was abortive and that internal alterations in the W. range were not executed until after the house had declined in status. At demolition in 1974 the W. front and the stair hall were preserved for incorporation with modern buildings.

The northern doorway in the six-bay W. front (Plate 101) opened into a passage which led to the stair hall through a doorway below the N.W. quarter-landing of the staircase. Another doorway further S., which led from the stair hall to the shop, may originally have communicated with a vestibule centrally placed in the W. range. The preserved staircase has carved and inlaid step-spandrels, column-shaped newel posts and balusters, and marquetry enrichment in the quarter-landings. The N. window has glass mainly of the late 19th century, but including the arms of Walmsley, perhaps a reset 16th-century fragment; a 19th-century inscription commemorates Maude Walmsley, 1591. The staircase ceiling has 18th-century enrichment. The doorway from the stair hall to the first-floor drawing room has fluted pilasters and an entablature with a segmental broken pediment. The demolished drawing room chimneypiece was flanked by tall wooden pilasters with carved capitals; the overmantel had carved foliage surrounding an acanthus bracket (Plate 95). The ceiling had a heavily moulded cornice and panelled enrichment.

Two first-floor rooms on the N. of the courtyard

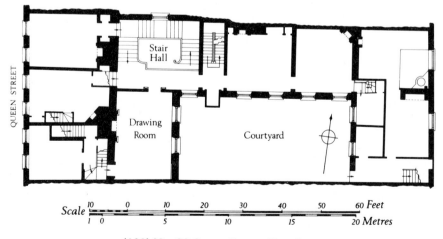

(133) No. 20 Queen Street. First floor.

were lined with pine panelling in two heights, with moulded cornices, fielded panels and moulded dado-rails. A fireplace surround had a pulvinated entablature with laurel leaf enrichment.

A building of 1879 on the corner tenement adjoining monument (133) was largely demolished in 1975, but its N. and W. fronts were preserved. In 1409 the tenement, a burgage plot called Grandonescorner, was sold by John Grandon to Thomas Bover, draper.[2] In the 17th century the Three Lions Inn, a corporation property, occupied the site. For a description of 1716, *see* Sar. Corp. MS., 0/117/4, f.64. In 1879 Pinkney's Bank was built to designs by H. Hall, some rooms being fitted with 17th-century woodwork brought from elsewhere.[3]

1.   Dom. Bk. i, f. 14; ii, ff 30^v–31, 56^v, 74.
2.   Dom. Bk. ii, ff. 30^v, 80; iii, ff 74, 130.
3.   *Building News*, 6 Sept. 1878.

(134) **Building**, Nos. 6 and 8 Winchester Street, recently demolished, was of two storeys with brick walls and a tiled roof. It was built in the late 18th or early 19th century. The lower storey contained shops and had no notable features. In the upper storey the N. front had eight plain sashed windows and a moulded eaves cove. Inside, the stairs and fireplaces were of the 19th century.

(135) **Houses**, two adjacent, Nos. 14 and 16 Winchester Street, are each three-storeyed with brick walls and slate-covered roofs. They were built during the first half of the 19th century.

(136) **Houses**, two adjacent, Nos. 15 and 17 Milford Street, now combined, are two-storeyed with attics and have slate-hung timber-framed walls and tile-covered roofs; they are of 16th-century origin, but much altered. Inside, some original beams are seen; a first-floor room in the E. house has an original doorway with chamfered jambs. No doubt the roofs were formerly gabled on the S., but the upper part of each gable is now hipped; they have collared tie-beam trusses with queen-struts or lower angle braces, and clasped purlins.

(137) **House**, No. 13 Milford Street, of three storeys with timber-framed walls hung with mathematical tiles and with a tiled roof, is of the late 18th or early 19th century.

(138) **House**, No. 11 Milford Street, of three storeys with brick walls with cement quoins and with a tiled roof, is of the early 18th century. In the S. front, above a modern shop window, the second storey has a Palladian window and the third storey has a sashed window of three lights.

(139) **Cathedral Hotel**, of four storeys with brick walls and tiled roofs, is mainly of the 19th century and later, but it incorporates a nucleus dating from the second half of the 18th century. In the S. front the five middle bays of the three lower storeys are original. Inside, some ground-floor rooms have original wooden dados with fielded panels. The oak staircase (Plate 89) is original. Two first-floor rooms are lined with fielded panelling in two heights, with moulded skirtings, dado-rails and cornices. Old photographs (Lov. Cn. 145, 152) show the S. front before the fourth storey was added.

BLACK HORSE CHEQUER

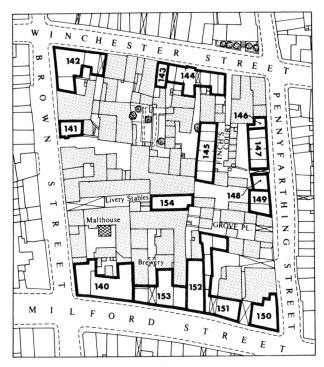

Monuments in Black Horse Chequer.

(140) **Houses**, No. 21 Milford Street and No. 13 Brown Street, of two storeys with brick outer walls and tiled roofs, are mainly of the 17th and 18th centuries, but they occupy the site and include part of the roof of The Bolehall, an important mediaeval dwelling identifiable through numerous documents.[1] The outline of the mediaeval tenement, some 113 ft. (N.–S.) by 75 ft., is recognisable in the boundaries on O.S., 1880; it was considerably larger than the normal burgage plot.

In 1319 Philip Aubyn, city coroner in 1303, transferred 'the tenement called the Bolehall in Wynchestret' to Henry Borry (mayor 1323).[2] The surviving roof probably belongs to Aubyn's house and is therefore, one of the oldest documented domestic buildings in the city. Later the house was associated with John Buterlegh, draper, collector of Customs and Subsidy at Southampton, 1385–90.[3] Buterlegh owned the Bolehall from 1390 at latest and his name was still connected with it in 1466–7.[4] In 1396 Buterlegh's executors transferred the property to John Camel, grocer,[5] who bequeathed it to his widow Alice as her 'free bench'.[6] In 1400 Alice Camel was one of Salisbury's most highly assessed tax-paying citizens.[7] The Camels still had an interest in the property in 1455 when quit rent was paid by Johanna Camyl and two others.[8] The house may by this time have been divided into two or more parts.

The correspondence between the surviving mediaeval hall roof and a plan of the building made *c.* 1850 by J.M. Peniston,[9] here reproduced, indicates an aisled hall in the S. part of the tenement, parallel with Milford Street, with cross-wings to E. and W. According to the plan, the E. cross-wing and half of the former hall comprised Mr. Miles's house; the other half of the hall was 'late Burden's dwelling house'; the W. cross-wing was Mrs. Maton's house. Today, the six E. bays of the S. elevation have 17th-century brick facades with wooden cornices and hipped, tile-covered roofs. There are two 18th-century windows; the others are modern. The E. cross-wing has a modern roof. The W. cross-wing (Mrs. Maton's) appears to have been rebuilt in the second half of the 18th century; it has an approximately symmetrical W. front of five bays with a square-headed central doorway and plain sashed windows.

Inside, in the part of the building formerly occupied by Burden and Miles, the lower storeys have been obliterated by modern shop fittings and nothing of note is found on the ground and first floors. In the attics, however, in the area where shading has been added to Peniston's plan, three main trusses and 20 pairs of collared rafters survive from the 14th-century hall roof.

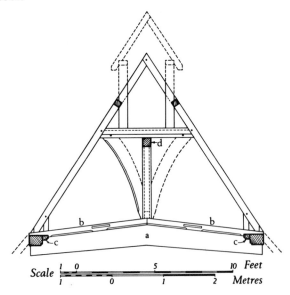

Scale

Only the upper part of the roof is visible and it is uncertain how much of the lower part may be concealed by partitions. The main trusses are represented by three

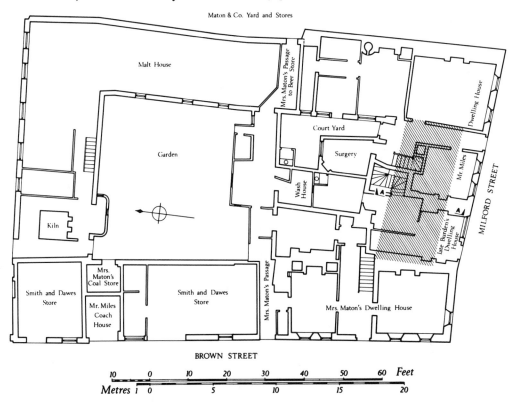

(140) No. 21 Milford Street, formerly THE BOLEHALL. Plan of *c.* 1850. (Shading shows area of mediaeval roof.)

91

massive cambered collar-beams (a), some 20 ft. above ground level. The middle truss probably had arch-braces and principal rafters which presumably rested on the N. and S. walls of the former hall. Lying on the collar-beams and overhanging them on either side are hollow-chamfered upper members (b) morticed to receive horizontal diagonal braces. Large hollow-chamfered arcade-plates are housed into the collar beams at either end; smaller hollow-chamfered members (c) attached to them have mortices for the diagonal braces. The central collar-beam carries a chamfered crown-post with curved and chamfered braces supporting collar-purlins (d). The pair of common rafters immediately E. of the middle collar-beam is cut and trimmed at the top to receive the uprights of a former smoke-louvre.

1. Sar. D. & C.M., Harding deeds, 1390—1466, *passim*.
2. Dom. Bk. iii, register, f. 5.
3. V.C.H., *Wilts.* iv, 128; vi, 104.
4. Harding deeds, *passim*.
5. Dom. Bk. iii, register, f. 53.
6. W.R.O., 164/1/6, will 1398—9.
7. Sar. Corp. MS., Z/238.
8. *Liber Niger*, 87, 89.
9. W.R.O., 451/143.

(141) **House**, No. 5 Brown Street, of two storeys with brick walls and slate-covered roofs, is of the first quarter of the 19th century.

(142) **Houses and Shops**, Nos. 1 Brown Street and 18—22 Winchester Street, respectively of two and of three storeys with brick walls, plain sashed windows and tiled roofs, are the W. and N. ranges of the former Black Horse Inn;[1] they were built *c.* 1770.[2] Part of the brick pavement of the inn yard remains between the two ranges, and the walled-up carriage entry from Winchester Street is indicated by an elliptical arch in the N. front of No. 18. Inside, some 18th-century joinery remains.

1. Plan by J. Peniston, W.R.O., 451/73 (xlviii).
2. Advt., *S.J.*, 5 Feb., 1776.

(143) **House**, No. 32 Winchester Street, of three storeys with brick walls and a slated roof, is of the first half of the 18th century. In the two-bay N. front the original doorway has been reset beside a modern shop window. The upper storeys have sashed windows, a wooden plat-band and a bracketed eaves cornice.

(144) **Houses**, five adjoining, Nos. 34—42 Winchester Street, are three-storeyed with brick walls and slated roofs and date from the first half of the 19th century.

(145) **Finch's Court**, range of six uniform cottages of two storeys with attics, has brick walls and tiled roofs.

Built towards the end of the 18th century, the cottages are now uninhabited.

(146) **Cottage**, No. 6 Pennyfarthing Street, of two storeys with an attic, has brick walls and a tiled roof and was built *c.* 1830.

(147) **Houses**, range of four, Nos. 8—14 Pennyfarthing Street, are three-storeyed with brick walls and slated roofs and were built *c.* 1830.

(148) **House**, No. 16 Pennyfarthing Street, of two storeys with brick walls and a tiled roof, was built *c.* 1800. The three-bay E. front has a pentice at the level of the first floor.

(149) **Cottages**, pair, now a workshop, No. 18 Pennyfarthing Street, are two-storeyed with brick walls and tiled roofs and date from early in the 19th century.

(150) **House**, now shops and three dwellings, Nos. 35—9 Milford Street, is of two storeys with brick walls and tiled roofs and was built *c.* 1800. Above modern shop fronts the S. elevation has five sashed windows symmetrically arranged under a brick cornice and parapet. Inside, nothing noteworthy remains.

(151) **Catherine Wheel Inn**, Nos. 31—3 Milford Street, partly of one and partly of two storeys, has rendered and tile-hung timber-framed walls and tiled roofs. In the single-storeyed S. range (No. 33), parallel with the street, a mutilated two-bay hall roof with a hammer-beam truss (A on the drawing) is probably of the 15th

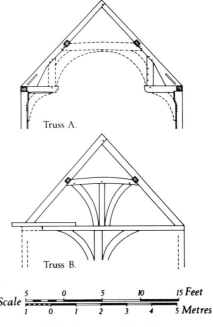

(151) Catherine Wheel Inn.

Site Plan
1968

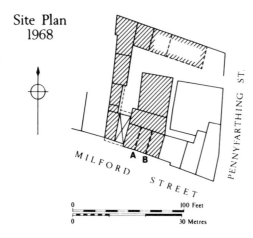

MILFORD STREET

PENNYFARTHING ST.

A B

0   100 Feet

0   30 Metres

century. The sides of the hall have been rebuilt in recent years. Its E. end is defined by a partition truss (B).

The cross-wing (No. 31) at the W. end of the hall is jettied N. and S. at the first floor; the structure is hidden by mathematical tiling, but it probably is of 17th-century origin. In 1968 the lower storey contained a carriage through-way to the inn-yard on the N., as shown on the plan, but the opening is now walled up. A narrow range continuing the line of the cross-wing northwards on the W. of the yard is also of the 17th century; its first floor is jettied on the east. Further N. are 18th-century outhouses. The N. side of the yard was defined by a 16th-century stable range of which the W. bay remains; its collared tie-beam roof has a lower king-strut with curved braces.

The occupants of the five major tenements on the S. side of Black Horse Chequer in 1399–1400 are known from the taxation list;[1] the site of the Catherine Wheel belonged to Richard Spencer, grocer, in his time probably one of the three richest men in Salisbury. In 1414 it passed to his widow Edith as her 'free bench'.[2] Edith then married William Cambrigg of London and in 1418 the tenement passed to Cambrigg's son, John Warbilton, and to John Pervys, alderman and fishmonger of London.[3] In 1419 the owner was Stephen Lythenard.[4] In 1455 it was one of the many Salisbury properties of William Ludlow.[5]

1.   Sar, Corp. MS., Z/238; (see p. xxvi).
2.   Dom. Bk. iii, f. 11[v].
3.   Dom. Bk. iii, f. 62; Thrupp, *Merchant Class of Mediaeval London*, 327, 360.
4.   Sar. D. & C.M., press iv, will of Nicholas Harding.
5.   *Liber Niger*, 79.

(152) **House**, No. 29 Milford Street, of three storeys with rendered walls and tiled roofs, is of the late 18th century. The ground-floor rooms have been altered for conversion to a shop, but rooms on the first floor retain original joinery.

(153) **Milford Arms Inn**, No. 25 Milford Street, of two storeys with timber-framed walls and tiled roofs, is of 15th-century origin; the S. range is masked by a 19th-century six-bay facade of rendered brickwork. The drawing shows the upper part of an original partition which is visible between the 4th and 5th bays from W. An eastward continuation of the 15th-century S. range may be concealed by plaster etc. in No. 27. The N. wing of No. 25 appears to be of the 16th century; it has timber framework in the upper storey and a roof with a collared tie-beam truss with chamfered purlins and curved windbraces.

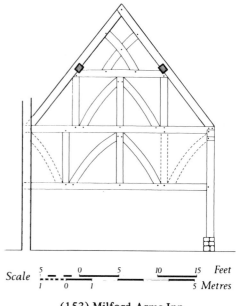

Scale   5   0   5   10   15   Feet

1   0   1   5 Metres

(153) Milford Arms Inn.

In 1390 the site of monuments (152–3), together with Grove Place (see map, p. 89), was occupied by two tenements belonging to Isabel, widow of John Cole; from her they were acquired by Nicholas Harding 'Webbe' and they are clearly described in the will (1419) by which Webbe bequeathed them to his sons Thomas and William. A shop stood between the Hardings' dwelling, next to the Bolehall, and the other tenement. The garden (Grove Place) extended to 'Gigorstrete' (Pennyfarthing Street) where there was a gateway flanked by cottages. Thomas Harding died in 1446 and in 1459 William sold the whole property to the Dean and Chapter. In 1466, to refute the claims of his bastard son, William made a statement concerning these transactions.[1]

1.   Sar. D. & C.M., press i, Sarum deeds, box iv, *passim*. Press iv, will of Nicholas Harding.

(154) **Warehouse**, of two storeys with brick and weatherboarded walls and slate-covered roofs, is of the first half of the 19th century.

SWAYNE'S CHEQUER

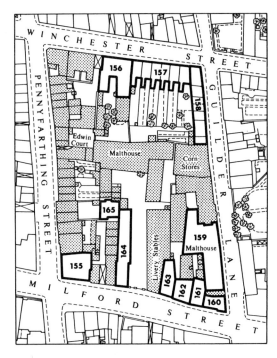

Monuments in Swayne's Chequer.

(155) **House**, No. 41 Milford Street, of three storeys with tile-hung timber-framed walls and tile-covered roofs, dates from early in the 17th century (Plate 66). The S. and W. fronts are jettied at the first and second floors. The ground-floor rooms retain stop-chamfered beams, but the walls have been rebuilt. In the second and third storeys a considerable quantity of original framework survives. The roofs have tie-beam trusses with collars and queen-struts, two butt-purlins on each side, and small plain windbraces. In 1972, while the building was being remodelled, the timber framework was temporarily exposed.

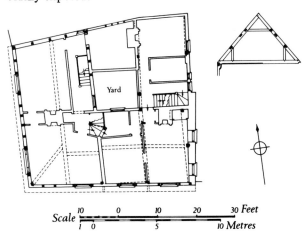

Scale

(155) No. 41 Milford Street. First floor.

(156) **House**, Nos. 62–4 Winchester Street, is of two storeys with attics and has brick walls and tiled roofs. Built about the middle of the 18th century as a town house of medium size, it now is divided into several dwellings and has shops in the ground-floor rooms. The N. front retains the principal doorway with a rounded

hood supported by Tuscan columns; in the upper storey are six plain sashed windows. Inside, on the first floor, the original stairs remain. Room *a* is lined from floor to ceiling with fielded panelling in two heights. Room *b* has a chimneypiece with a scroll frieze.

(157) **Houses**, range of six, Nos. 66–76 Winchester Street, are three-storeyed with brick walls and slated roofs and were built early in the 19th century. The facade of each house has one sashed window in each storey and a plain doorway at street level.

(158) **Cottages**, range of seven, Nos. 2–14 Guilder Lane, are two-storeyed with timber-framed walls set on rubble plinths and with tiled roofs. They date from the second half of the 15th century and replace a corner house with a shop and four cottages repeatedly mentioned in earlier mediaeval deeds (Sar. D. & C.M., Sarum deeds, boxes 1 and 2, *passim*). One deed records that the corner site was vacant in 1443. In the present buildings the first floor is jettied W. and E., but the W. side has been underbuilt and the original wall of the lower storey removed. The E. side retains a jetty with curved brackets. Former casements have been replaced by 18th-century sashes.

(159) **Malthouse**, now demolished, was of two storeys with brick walls and tiled roofs and was built late in the 18th century. The eight-bay E. elevation had shallow buttresses between the bays and openings with flat arches of guaged brick. (Plan of 1849, W.R.O., 451/207.)

(160) **Houses**, two adjacent, now combined, No. 61 Milford Street, are single-storeyed with attics. The corner house has timber-framed walls and dates from the 15th century; the adjoining house has brick walls and is of the early 18th century; both have tiled roofs. The 15th-century house has an early 19th-century shop window facing Milford Street. (Plan of 1849, W.R.O., 451/207.)

(161) **House,** No. 59 Milford Street, of two storeys with attics, with tile-hung timber-framed walls and a tiled roof, was built early in the 18th century, but has been extensively altered.

(162) **House,** No. 57 Milford Street, of two storeys with brick walls and a tiled roof, is of the late 18th century. The S. front is symmetrical and of two bays with a central doorway. (Plan of 1849, W.R.O., 451/207.)

(163) **House,** No. 55 Milford Street, of two storeys with rendered brick walls and a tiled roof, is of the mid 18th century. The S. front has a doorway and a three-light sashed window in the lower storey, and three sashed windows in the upper storey. (Plan of 1849, W.R.O., 451/207.)

(164) **Crystal Fountain Inn,** of two and three storeys with brick walls and slate-covered roofs, was built *c.* 1840 and demolished in 1969. The plan of 1849 (W.R.O., 451/207) indicates an extensive brewery.

(165) **Tailors' Hall,** demolished in 1971, was of two storeys and had walls partly of flint and rubble, but mainly of timber framework, and a tiled roof. The demolished structure was of 16th-century origin and must have been a surviving fragment of the 'conveny-ant mansion house' erected by the tailors' craft guild in 1534.[1] A plan dated 1823 by W. Sleat, architect, is preserved among the guild records.[2]

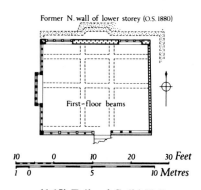

(165) Tailors' Guild Hall.

Up to the first floor the W. wall was of flint, patched with stone and brick; above that level it was of weather-boarded timber framework (Plate 67). In the upper storey was a projecting window with five transomed lights on the W. and with narrower lights on N. and S.; the oak mullions and transoms had ovolo and hollow-chamfered mouldings. The N. wall had been rebuilt in brickwork late in the 19th century; O.S. (1880) shows it about 3 ft. further north. In the lower storey the E. wall was of stout timber stud-work; above the first floor it was of modern materials. In the upper storey the S.

wall retained a few uprights from a former partition.

Inside, the first floor rested on large chamfered beams which intersected to form nine panels of unequal size. Some fragments of 17th-century oak panelling were found in the first-floor room.

1. Haskins, *Guilds*, 160; V.C.H., *Wilts.* vi, 134.
2. Sar. Corp. MS., *Additamenta*, 32.

CHEQUER ON E. OF GUILDER LANE

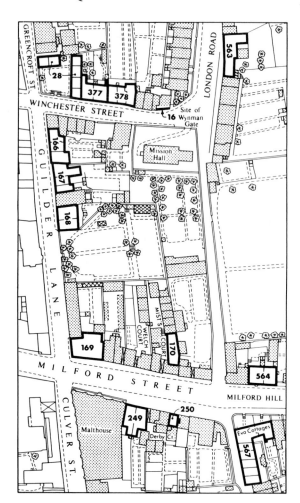

Monuments in Guilder Lane and adjacent streets.

(166) **Cottages,** three adjacent, Nos. 1–5 Guilder Lane, of two storeys with brick-faced walls and tiled roofs, contain some stout timber framework and probably are of 16th-century origin.

(167) **Cottages,** pair, Nos. 7–9 Guilder Lane and one adjacent, No. 11, are two-storeyed with brick walls and tiled roofs and date from the middle of the 18th century. In plan each dwelling has a front and a back room in each storey. No. 11, later than the other two and with

higher rooms and superior joinery, has recently been combined with No. 9.

(168) **Cottages**, two adjoining, Nos. 15–17 Guilder Lane, are two-storeyed with attics and have timber-framed walls set on brick plinths, and tiled roofs; they are of the 15th century. The timber framework is masked externally, but the N.W. corner-post of No. 15 and the bracket of a former first-floor jetty are seen inside an adjacent workshop. No. 15 is one bay wide (N.–S.) and No. 17 has two bays. Inside, stout posts and chamfered beams with curved brackets are seen. The roofs have collared tie-beam trusses with lower king-struts and curved angle-braces, upper scissor-braces, chamfered clasped purlins and curved chamfered wind-braces.

(169) **House with Shop**, No. 65 Milford Street, of two storeys with brick walls and a tiled roof, is of 18th-century origin, but was extensively rebuilt in 1975.

Early in the 15th century, houses on or near this site, including workshops and a gateway, belonged to the bell-founder John Barbor and his wife Alice.[1] The remains of mediaeval foundries have recently been uncovered.[2]

1. *W.A.M.,* xxxv (1908), 355.
2. *W.A.M.,* lxvii (1973), 137.

(170) **Warehouse**, formerly in Mist's Court, demolished in 1972, was two-storeyed with brick walls and a tiled roof and was built in the second half of the 18th century. The mansard roof had collared tie-beam upper trusses with queen-struts resting on lower purlins supported by curved upright members.

NEW STREET CHEQUER

(171) **Houses**, four adjoining, Nos. 25–31 High Street, of three storeys with brick and tile-hung walls and with slate-covered roofs, were built early in the 19th century. All the ground-floor rooms have been obliterated to make shops. Nos. 29–31 were originally a pair of houses, but have been combined; they have a common W. front of two bays with plain sashed windows in each upper storey. No. 27, of *c.* 1830 and with a two-bay

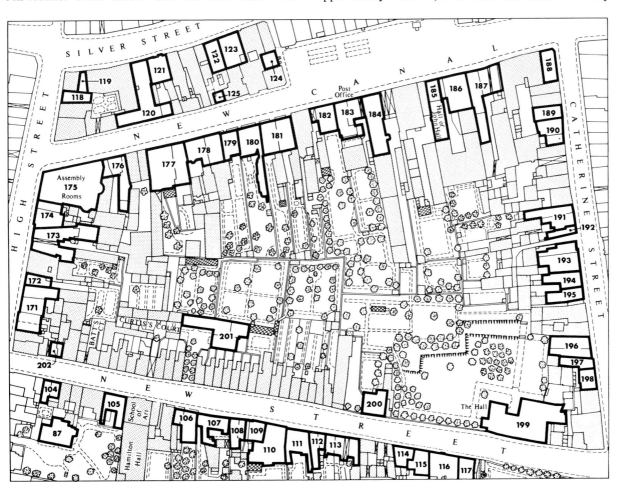

Monuments in Mitre Chequer, New Street Chequer and New Street.

THE GEORGE INN
(Survey, 1965)

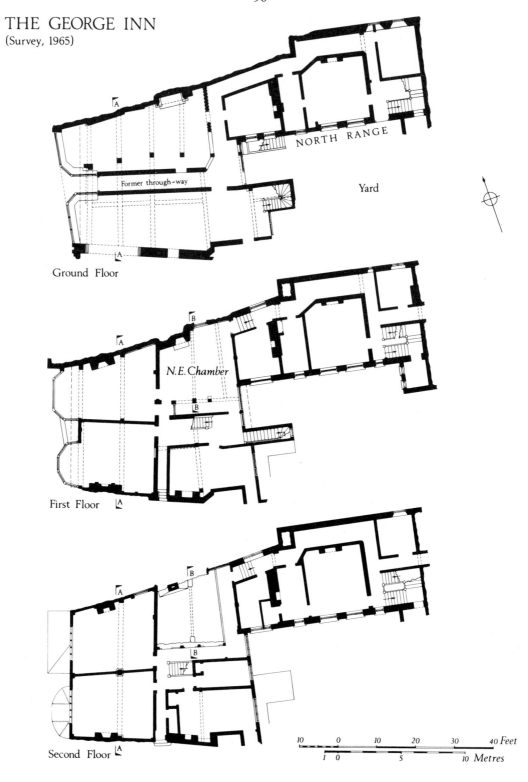

Ground Floor

First Floor

Second Floor

Former through-way

NORTH RANGE

Yard

N.E. Chamber

10 0 10 20 30 40 *Feet*

1 0 5 10 *Metres*

facade, now contains two ground-floor shops. No. 25, demolished and rebuilt in 1975, had a two-bay facade of *c*. 1800 with a single sashed bow window at first-floor level. Inside, all four houses had plain 19th-century joinery and plasterwork. Below the ground floor, No. 25 retained the lower part of a former cellar with N., E. and S. walls of coursed stonework, perhaps mediaeval.

(172) **House**, No. 23 High Street, demolished in 1967, was of three storeys and had rendered timber-framed walls, jettied in the W. front, and tiled roofs; it was of 16th-century origin. The lower storey contained a modern shop front; the second storey had two 18th-century bow windows under the jetty; the jettied third storey had two 19th-century sashed windows, each with three lights (Plate 102). The roof had collared tie-beam trusses with lower angle struts and clasped purlins.

In mediaeval times the site was part of a tenement called The Leg, of which the history is traceable through deeds dating from 1364.[1] In 1455, when it belonged to William White of Mere, another tenement owned by him in New Street provided a back entrance.[2] Subsequently the whole property belonged to Sir Thomas Audeley, and in 1495 part of it was leased to John Godfrey, tailor. Audeley's property included a kitchen and a barton. The kitchen and barton appear again in a deed of 1533 together with shops, solars and a cellar. During the 16th century the whole tenement passed to the Tailors' Guild, which retained it until late in the 19th century. A description is included in the survey of guild lands made in 1657.[3] The extent of the tenement in 1823 is shown on a plan by W. Sleat.[4]

1. Sar. Corp. MS., I/249, *passim*.
2. *Liber Niger*, 76.
3. Sar. Corp. MS., Additamenta, 29.
4. *ibid.*, 32.

(173) **The George Inn**, as it survives, is of two and three storeys with walls mainly of timber framework and with tiled roofs (Plate 61). The existing W. range is only a small part of an important inn, mainly built during the third quarter of the 14th century, but also making use of antecedent buildings. A strong wall of rubble and ashlar on the N. side, parallel with New Canal and therefore joining High Street front obliquely, probably dates from the 13th century. A stone doorway and window in the S. range, now gone, but attested in 19th-century drawings (below, p. 98), was perhaps of the same period.

The inn belonged to the corporation from 1413 to 1858, but after *c*. 1760 it was occupied not as an inn, but as dwellings. In 1858 the buildings again became a hostelry, but were extensively altered, everything being pulled down except the W. range. About the same time, the N. range was built. In 1967 the N. range was demolished and the lower storey of the W. range was re-modelled, the carriage through-way which led from High Street to the inn yard being replaced by a wider passage as the pedestrian entrance to a modern shopping precinct (Old George Mall). The upper rooms of the W. range were adapted as a restaurant.

A detailed history of the inn might be compiled from the numerous deeds, leases and surveys preserved in the city archives. William Teynturer the younger (mayor 1361 and 1375), a merchant of great energy and enterprise who left much property when he died in 1377,[1] bought three properties in High Street in 1357 and 1361.[2] All of these may have become part of the inn site, especially one acquired from the family of John de Homyngton, cook, which included a shop with solars beside an entry which led to the hall of another house, then occupied for life by Peter Moundelard who had been living there since 1342. It is possible that Moundelard's house contained the stone doorway and window mentioned above. In 1371 Teynturer added a curtilage which lay 'behind the tenement and wall of William Mountagu in Wynchestrestret' (now New Canal; i.e. the site of monument (176), an 18th-century building).[3] A document of 1401 mentions a barn and a laundry in the S. part of the ground obtained from Mountagu;[4] this probably corresponds with the barn at the George leased with other buildings to Thomas Allesley, 'osteler', in 1427.[5] The earliest use of the name 'Georgesin' occurs in a deed of 1379 relating to the adjacent house (172).[6] The name recalls the merchant guild of the city, dedicated to St. George, and it is not unlikely that Teynturer from the beginning of his ownership meant the inn to become city property.[7] The purchase of the property by the city took place in 1413 when royal and episcopal licences permitted the city to acquire property to the value of 100 marks;[8] thereafter the George appears in the chamberlain's account rolls.[9] Some idea of the inn's furnishings and movable fittings may be obtained from the list of goods and utensils which were left for sale by the last private owner, Sir George Meriot, who died in 1410.[10] The inn came to him through his wife Alice, previously married to William Teynturer. The most interesting of numerous later documents is a lease of 1474 to John Gryme, which includes an inventory of permanent fittings.[11] Fourteen lodging chambers are listed, each with a distinctive name and all furnished with beds and tables; the principal chamber was the only room in which a fireplace is mentioned. There is no mention of a hall (the word *aula* denotes a small lobby adjoining the Fitzwareyne chamber); the tavern or wine cellar and the buttery were used as public rooms. The surviving building, with only five chambers, is insufficient in relation to the known extent of the mediaeval inn for any identification of rooms to be possible. Later descriptions of the George occur in surveys of city property made in 1618, 1716 and 1783.[12] The extent of the buildings in the 19th century is recorded on a plan of *c*. 1850 by F.R. Fisher (Plate 13);[13] it shows the inn's narrow frontage to High Street, with the through-way leading to a narrow courtyard surrounded by buildings; further E. were other yards and stables.

The picturesque quality of the buildings attracted many 19th-century artists whose work affords some idea of the former appearance of the street front and of the courtyard (Plates 4–7). Buckler's drawing of 1805 shows the remains of the pargeting which was applied in 1593.[14] Inside the yard, the W. part of the N. range, near the E. end of the through-way from High Street, comprised a tall building with first and second-floor jetties; it was drawn thus by W.H. Charlton in 1813 (Plate 6), but the top storey had been removed when the view by Goodall and Surgey was painted, *c*. 1850 (Plate 4). Closing the E. end of the courtyard, Sir Henry Dryden in a watercolour dated 1859 (Plate 6) shows a three-storeyed building with two gables with elaborately cusped bargeboards; the same building is shown in a drawing of 1833 by William Twopeny (Plate 7). A passage on the N. of this building led to the stable yard. The drawings show that the eastern part of the S. side of the courtyard was overlooked by an open first-floor gallery projecting on curved brackets, a feature which made the yard suitable for plays as ordained in 1624.[15] Further W., the S. side of the courtyard had a three-storeyed building, jettied at the second floor. Measured sketches of 1863 by Dryden (Northampton Public Library) show that the lower storey of this building contained a stone doorway with chamfered jambs shouldered at the top to support a flat lintel, characteristic of the 13th century; beside it was a small chamfered square-headed window. Hall illustrates the same features.[16] Neither opening appears in Dryden's watercolour of 1859, but they are seen in Charlton's drawing, although here the doorway is shown as round-headed. Adjacent, in the S.W. corner of the courtyard, Charlton, Dryden and Goodall-Surgey all show a square, tower-like structure of two storeys, apparently of brick with ashlar dressings, with a pyramidal tiled roof; a classical entablature lay just below the upper window-sill and the square-headed E. doorway had a classical architrave. By its style this structure dated from about the middle of the 17th century. Dryden's sketch plan of 1863 shows that it contained a newel stair.

The three-storeyed W. front has modern shop windows in the lower storey. Since the photograph on Plate 61 was taken, the 14th-century oak N.W. pier of the former carriage through-way, seen in Buckler's drawing of 1805 and in Twopeny's drawing of 1833, has been exposed (Plate 84) and a modern replica of its S.W. counterpart has been supplied. The large 17th-century bow windows in the second storey remain as depicted in the 19th-century drawings, except that the pargeting has gone. The third-storey windows are modern restorations of original lights closed in the 17th century. Removal of

the plaster has revealed cross-braced timber framework. Because the ground plan is trapeze-shaped, the E. elevation of the 14th-century range is three bays wide in contrast to the two bays of the W. front; the entire E. elevation is, however, hidden by modern tile-hanging. The demolished 19th-century N. range had a three-storeyed S. elevation of brick, with plain sashed windows in each storey and with plat-bands marking the floor levels. (Plan on p.96.)

Inside, the irregular N. wall is built to the height of the first floor in ashlar with panels of knapped flintwork, the latter including some tile. A former fireplace set at a high level, and corresponding beam-holes in the masonry, now blocked, show that the ground floor was once about 2 ft. above present street level, thus making room for a basement storey on the N. of the through-way. An entrance to this basement appears in an old photograph (Plate 104).

Before the alterations of 1967 the N. side of the through-way was represented by a row of free-standing timber posts braced to the first floor with curved brackets. The corresponding posts which once formed the S. side of the through-way had gone, but their positions were shown by mortices in the first-floor beams (cross-section A–A).

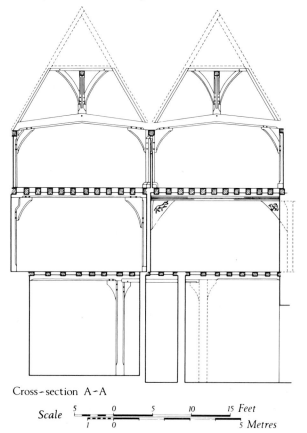

Cross-section A-A

Scale   5   0   5   10   15 *Feet*
          1   0   5 *Metres*

(173) The George Inn. Section, looking E.

On the first floor, the N.W. room retains original chamfered wall-posts, wall-braces, and a large N.–S. beam joined to the wall-posts with chamfered braces. In the embrasure of the 17th-century window are seen the overhanging members of the original second-floor jetty. In the S.W. room the beam and its braces are encased in 17th-century plaster enriched with a frieze of griffins (Plate 93).

While the W. part of the range is of three storeys, the E. part is two-storeyed, with a large N.E. chamber open to the roof. As in the W. rooms, the walls of this chamber have massive 14th-century timber uprights with cross-bracing (cross-section B–B). The central wall-posts on

1. Will, Dom. Bk. iii, reg., f. 36; Cal. Close Rolls, 1349–54, 344–573.
2. Dom. Bk. iii, reg., ff. 15, 19; also Sar. Corp. MS., deeds, drawers B, C and D.
3. Dom. Bk. i, f. 39ᵛ.
4. Sar. Corp. MS., deeds, drawer F.
5. *ibid.*, drawer G.
6. *ibid.*, I/249, No. 21.
7. Haskins, *Guilds*, 288–303; Benson & Hatcher, 100.
8. Dom. Bk. ii, ff. 112–3.
9. Sar. Corp. MS., O/103, *passim*.
10. Dom. Bk. ii, ff. 89ᵛ–90ᵛ.
11. Sar. Corp. MS., Z/240, F. 305.
12. *ibid.*, O/117/1, 4 and 8.
13. *ibid.*, V/204/2, No. 1.
14. *ibid.*, Ledger Book C, f. 139.
15. Haskins, *Guilds*, 295.
16. *Memorials*, following Pl.xv.

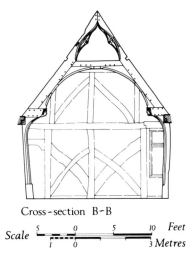

Cross-section B–B

Scale (5 0 5 10 Feet / 1 0 3 Metres)

(173) George Inn. N.E. chamber.

N. and S. have moulded sides and curve out at the top to support a false hammerbeam truss; the ends of the horizontal members are carved to represent a bearded king's and a queen's head (Plate 84); above, there are moulded arch-braces. Over the collar the principals are enriched with ogee mouldings and traceried cusps. The collar-purlin and the original rafters have been replaced by later through-purlins and common rafters. The 14th-century moulded wall-plates remain, with carved flowers at the ends of the mouldings. Original doorways with shouldered lintels occur in the N. part of the E. wall and in the W. part of the S. wall.

On the second floor, each of the two W. chambers is spanned by a cambered and roll-moulded beam supporting a crown-post and a collar-purlin (Plate 83). Mouldings on the gable tie-beams show that the present modern windows replace original openings. The wall-plates are moulded and enriched.

In the 19th-century N. range, demolished in 1967, the thick N. wall was probably mediaeval. Reset in the E. part of the range was an early 17th-century staircase (Plate 87); since 1967 its balustrade has been reused in monument (174).

(174) **Houses**, two adjoining, Nos. 11 and 13 High Street, are of three storeys with attics and have tile-hung timber-framed walls and tiled roofs. Both buildings are now combined with the George Inn (173) to make shops and restaurants. No. 11 is of mid 15th-century origin. No. 13, of 1476, takes the place of two mediaeval cottages which were given to the Dean and Chapter in 1459 by William Harding, canon and clerk-of-works to the cathedral.[1] In 1476 the work of rebuilding occasioned a legal settlement concerning encroachment on the George Inn.[2] By 1649 the houses had been united and were occupied by John Joyce, apothecary.[3]

The W. front of No. 13, remodelled in the 18th century, is jettied at the second floor and at first-floor level has a pentice, but no jetty (Plate 102). The N. bay in the second storey has a bow window with an ogival lead roof. Originally the facade had two gables, but the

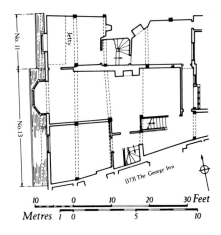

(174) Nos. 11 and 13 High Street. First floor.

valley between them was roofed-in during the 18th century and the former gables were concealed by tile-hanging. Inside, the lower storey has been modernised. On the first floor, although partitions have been removed, it is clear that there were formerly two W. rooms and one to N.E.; that on the N.W. retains some 17th-century oak panelling in four heights and a modelled plaster ceiling; the panelling is mentioned in the Parliamentary Survey. The beam at the head of the former partition between the N.W. and N.E. rooms has a 17th-century black-letter inscription: 'Have God before thine eies, who searcheth hart & raines, and live according to his law, then glory is thy gaines'. The chimneypiece in the N.E. room is composed of reset pieces of enriched oak panelling, some of it 16th-century work. Since 1967 the balustrade of the 17th-century staircase from the N. range of monument (173) has been reset in No. 13.

The W. front of No. 11 is of the 17th century, with a small jetty at the second floor and with an 18th-century window in each upper storey. The 15th-century W. front, however, stood some 8½ ft. behind the present facade; its alignment is indicated by the outline of the original second-floor jetty, seen in the W. room of the first floor. The position of the former street-front falls on a straight line drawn from the S.W. corner of Mitre chequer to the original ground-level front of the George Inn (173). Inside, the E. room on the ground floor had, until 1967, a chimneypiece composed of reset early 17th-century oak panels with arabesque enrichment. The E. room on the first floor had a handsome mid 17th-century chimneypiece (Plate 92), now gone. In the third storey the original street-front gable, with king and queen struts, now forms an internal roof truss.

1. Sar. D. & C.M., Harding deeds, *passim*.
2. Sar. Corp. MS., D/32, Ledger B, f 126.
3. Parl. Svy., Foy 56 (Sar. 8), f.27.

(175) **Assembly Rooms**, now a shop, on the corner of High Street and New Canal, are of two storeys with brick walls and tiled roofs. The building dates from 1802 (*S.J.*, 1 Nov. 1802; 26 Aug. 1804). The three-bay W. elevation with a projecting porch and tall round-headed windows is seen in an early photograph (Plate 104). The lower storey has been completely modernised. On the first floor (plan, O.S., 1880), the main Assembly Room is used as a warehouse. Original neo-classical plaster enrichment survives.

(176) **House**, No. 53 New Canal, the Spread Eagle Inn in 1854 (Kingdon & Shearm), demolished 1966, was of three storeys and had walls mainly of brick, but with some tile-hung timber framework, and a tiled roof. Most of the structure was of the late 18th century, but the timber-framed W. wall probably represented an earlier building. The four-bay N. front had modern shop

windows in the lower storey and plain sashed windows above. Inside, some rooms had panelled dados. The stairs had closed strings and turned balusters.

(177) **Houses**, Nos. 47–9 New Canal, of two storeys with timber-framed walls and tiled roofs, were to a large extent demolished in 1966 and the small part which survives was 'restored' and altered. Before demolition the houses contained remains of a substantial 14th-century dwelling in which there had been a lofty hall with a two-storeyed cross-wing at its W. end. The lower storey of the cross-wing contained a carriage through-way. South of the hall and E. of the through-way there had been a courtyard, and beyond this there was a 16th-century S. range. After 1966 the N. part of the cross-wing was incorporated with a modern shop; the rest was demolished.

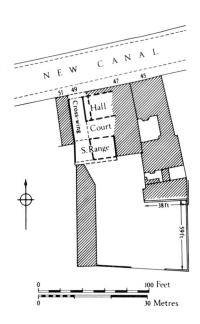

The site is identifiable with a tenement held successively by Richard Todeworth and Henry Russel, mayors during the period 1320–40;[1] In 1365 Russel's executor, Henry Fleming, sold it to William Teynturer, owner of the George Inn (173). On Teynturer's death it passed with the George to his widow Alice and so to her second husband, John Byterlegh, wool merchant. Byterlegh died in 1397,[2] and Alice married Sir George Meriot. On Meriot's death in 1410 the tenement passed to William Alisaundre, who still had it in 1428.[3] The deeds repeatedly mention a stone-walled garden measuring 59 ft. by 38 ft.; a piece of ground approximately this size, partly defined by stone walls, was still identifiable in 1961 (see plan). The deeds also mention two two-storeyed shops W. of the house. These possibly explain the restricted plan, wherein the carriage through-way

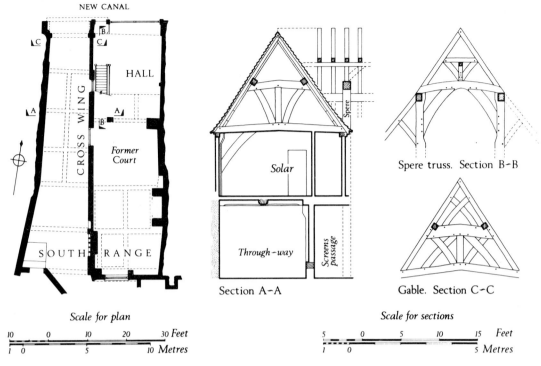

NEW CANAL

CROSS WING

HALL

Former Court

SOUTH RANGE

Solar

Through-way

Screens passage

Section A–A

Spere truss. Section B–B

Gable. Section C–C

Scale for plan

10   0   10   20   30 Feet
1   0   5   10 Metres

Scale for sections

5   0   5   10   15 Feet
1   0   5 Metres

(177) Nos. 47-9 New Canal. Ground plan and cross-sections.

and the hall screens-passage lay side-by-side in the cross-wing, underneath the solar.

Until 1966 the whole of No. 47 and the E. part of No. 49 were fronted by three-storeyed 18th-century facades with sashed windows in the upper storeys and with a continuous dentil cornice below a plain parapet; the ground storeys had shop windows. The cross-wing in the W. part of No. 49 was two-storeyed, gabled and jettied at the first floor (Plate 60); it remained very much as drawn by William Twopeny in 1833 (Plate 7). The lower storey of the cross-wing contained two openings: on the W. was the entrance to the carriage through-way; on the E., where Twopeny depicts a wall, there was a 19th-century doorway. The gate to the through-way was flanked by stout ovolo-moulded posts with brackets to support the jetty. The gateway occupied little more than two-thirds of the width of the cross wing and the N.E. corner of the upper storey was supported on a dragon beam. (Since 1966 the E. spur-post has been moved and an intermediate post has been supplied.) Cross-braced timber framework, now seen in the upper storey and gable, was revealed in 1967 and is original (section C–C). The cusped bargeboards remain as drawn by Twopeny and are the only surviving example of a mediaeval feature once common in Salisbury.

Inside, the ground and first-floor rooms of No. 49 had no notable features, but in the roof over the N.

room mediaeval timbers were found *in situ*. Parallel with the carriage through-way and about 3½ ft. to the E. was a well-preserved spere truss with posts 14 ins. thick supporting massive purlins and a cambered tie-beam with curved braces; above these were trussed rafters and a braced collar-purlin (sections A–A, B–B). Without doubt the spere truss marked the W. end of the hall; its timbers were smoke-blackened on the E. side only.

At ground level, the 3½ ft. gap between the E. side of the carriage through-way and the place where the spere-posts must originally have stood was evidently a screens-passage; it was entered by a door from the through-way (described below). The E. end of the hall may have been marked by the wall between Nos. 47 and 49, where a moulded post came to light during demolition, or the hall may have extended as far as the E. side of No. 47.

The timber-framed wall seen by Twopeny on the E. side of the through-way was revealed during demolition; the doorway had ogee-moulded and hollow-chamfered jambs, but the shaped head seen in Twopeny's drawing had gone. The W. wall of the through-way was of stone and flint to the level of the first floor. Over the through-way, stout chamfered transverse and longitudinal first-floor beams remain in position. Above the first floor the W. wall, now largely rebuilt, was of timber framework, and at this level there were three windows: near the N. front was a small 14th-century loop with a trefoiled

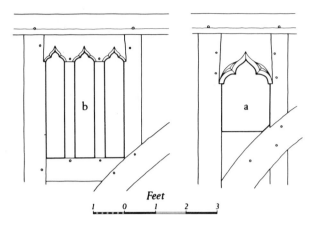

(177) First-floor windows in cross-wing.

ogee head (a); about 25 ft. further S. was a 14th-century three-light window with three trefoiled heads cut in a single beam (b); beside the latter was a 16th-century opening of three square-headed lights with ovolo-moulded oak mullions. The wide interval between the first and second windows probably accommodated the pitched roof of the two-storeyed shop, mentioned in the deeds as being next-door.

A top-lit ground-floor room to the S. of the area of the hall replaced the former courtyard; probably it was roofed over in the 19th century. Further S. was a two-storeyed 16th-century range, parallel with the hall, its upper storey bridging the S. part of the through-way. The ground-floor room had intersecting ceiling beams cased in 17th-century moulded plaster. On the E. was an open fireplace with chamfered stone jambs and a stone lintel with a raised centre. In the timber-framed W. wall, an unglazed window of five lights with diagonally-set oak mullions originally looked over the carriage through-way, but it had been blocked internally. The first floor was jettied southwards. The upper storey contained a single large room with a roof of three bays. Enough of the roof remained to show that it originally had two false hammerbeam collar trusses with arched braces. There were clasped purlins above the collars, and chamfered windbracing between the purlins and the wall-plates.

1.   Dom. Bk. i, f. 59.
2.   Dom. Bk. ii, ff. 13^V and 14, wherein the tenement is called 'once Henry Russel's'.
3.   Dom. Bk. ii, f. 89^V; iii, f. 109.

(178) **Houses**, two adjacent, Nos. 45 and 43 New Canal, demolished in 1967, were two-storeyed with attics and probably dated from *c.* 1600, but they had three-storeyed 18th-century brick facades. Some timber framework was seen inside.

(179) **House**, No. 39 New Canal, demolished in 1967, was of two storeys with an attic and was built late in the 18th century.

(180) **House**, No. 35 New Canal, of three storeys with brick walls and tiled and leaded roofs, was a late 18th-century town house ingeniously planned to make the most of a restricted site. In 1967 the N. front was remodelled to make it suitable for a shop and the rest of the building was demolished. The W. front of the narrow single-storeyed S. range had gauged-brick dressings and a pedimented central feature with a round-headed window. Inside, the E. passage retained fragments of a plaster vaulted ceiling, removed for the insertion of a later staircase. The principal stairs had mahogany handrails and a plain balustrades; above was an oval sky-light with a moulded cornice. On the first floor, the two N. drawing rooms had moulded and enriched cornices, and that on the E. contained a neo-classical chimneypiece of wood with *carton-pierre* enrichment.

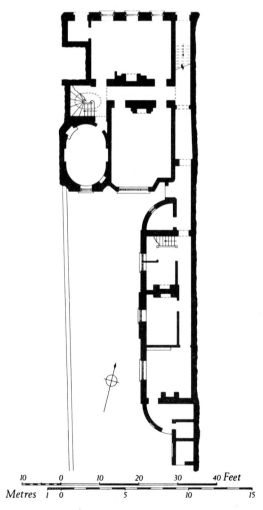

(180) No. 35 New Canal. Ground floor.

(181) **Houses**, pair, Nos. 33 and 31 New Canal, of three storeys with attics, with brick and tile-hung walls and with tiled roofs, were demolished in 1967; they had been built about the middle of the 18th century. Each house had a uniform three-bay N. front with modern shop windows below, sashed windows in the two upper storeys and a cornice with modillions. The windows had flat gauged-brick heads with stone keys and shoulders. Inside, the main rooms had panelled dados and each house had a staircase with a 'Chinese' lattice balustrade (Plate 89).

(182) **House**, No. 27 New Canal, demolished in 1967, was of three storeys with attics and had brick walls and tiled roofs. The N. front, of five bays with modern shop windows in the lower storey, plain sashed windows above and segmental-headed windows in the third storey,[1] was of the 18th century, but the house itself was of the late 16th or early 17th century. Inside, the main rooms had 18th-century joinery, but the stairs from the second floor to the attics were of oak, with close strings, moulded handrails and turned balusters. The roof had three collared tie-beam trusses with two purlins on each side.

1.   Photograph, *c*. 1920, Lov. Cn.

(183) **House**, No. 25 New Canal, demolished in 1967, was three-storeyed with attics and had walls partly of timber framework and partly of brick, and a tiled roof. Of late 15th-century origin it had been extensively altered in the 18th century. The N. front had modern shop windows at ground level and sashed windows symmetrically arranged in five bays in the upper storeys. The original roof, ridged E.—W., was of four bays with collared and arch-braced tie-beam trusses supporting two purlins on each side.

(184) **House**, No. 19 New Canal, now a shop and offices, is of two and three storeys with rendered brick walls and slated and tiled roofs. The N. part of the building is of the 19th century. The two-storeyed S. wing has an E.—facing early 17th-century window of six transomed square-headed lights with chamfered stone mullions and a moulded stone label with returned stops. Adjacent is an 18th-century bow window with six sashed lights. Inside, the S. ground-floor room retains part of an early 17th-century moulded plaster ceiling and an open fireplace with a moulded stone surround. The roof, with collared tie-beam trusses with two purlins on each side, retains some glazed ridge tiles with ribbed decoration.

(185) **Hall of John Hall**, now the vestibule of a theatre, but originally part of a merchant's house, has walls of ashlar and flint, and tiled roofs. It is certainly of the late 15th century although the precise dates proposed by Edward Duke relate to another of John Hall's properties.[1] It occupies the N.W. corner of a large plot (210 ft. by 60 ft.) which extended E. to Catherine Street and S. as far as the garden of Nos. 26–8 Catherine Street (191).

In 1455 John Hall already held property on the Ditch (New Canal) and in Carternstrete (Catherine Street).[2] The hall, built some years after this date, stands testimony to his success as a merchant.[3] In 1669 Aubrey wrote 'as Greville and Wenman bought all the Coteswold, soe did Halle and Webb all the wooll of Salisbury plaines'. Hall was deeply involved in the famous dispute between the commonalty and Bishop Beauchamp.[4] He was mayor in 1450, 1456 and 1464–5, and parliamentary representative in 1460 and 1461; he died in 1479. His political aspirations appear to have been inherited by his son William, aged 24 in 1479, who was involved with Walter Hungerford and others in Buckingham's rebellion of 1483.[5] William became M.P. for Salisbury in 1487; his sister Christian (*d*. 1504) married Sir Thomas Hungerford (*d*. 1494). Stained glass decorated with heraldic roses and with the arms of Hall, Hungerford etc., was probably installed in the hall windows early in the reign of Henry VII.

The axis of the hall lies at right-angles to New Canal. To the E., where two houses (186) now stand, there was formerly a courtyard entered from the street through a gateway with a pointed arch.[6] To the N., between the

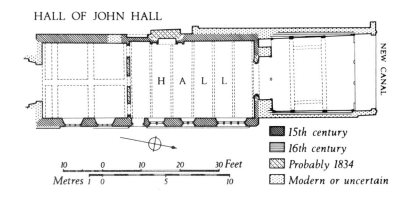

HALL OF JOHN HALL

HALL

NEW CANAL

10   0   10   20   30 Feet

Metres 1 0   5   10

■ *15th century*
▤ *16th century*
▨ *Probably 1834*
▦ *Modern or uncertain*

street and the end of the hall, there is a three-storeyed, 16th-century timber-framed building. From 1816 to 1819 the hall was part of the printing offices of the 'Wiltshire Gazette'.[7] In 1834 it was restored by A.W. Pugin and F.R. Fisher. The N. front, by Frederick Bath, was added in 1880.[8]

The E. elevation of the hall (Plate 59) is of ashlar and has casement-moulded windows of two and four transomed lights with cinquefoil two-centred heads. In the S. window, two lights below the transom are omitted to make room for a doorway with a moulded two-centred head in a square-headed casement-moulded surround. Further S. the ashlar elevation is two-storeyed, but the windows are modern. The W. wall of the hall is mainly of flint and rubble with some tile lacing courses and also with later brick patching. A blocked opening in the S. part of the wall has a four-centred brick head and is perhaps of the 16th century. The brick chimneybreast appears to be of the 19th century. A stone window set at a high level on the N. of the chimneybreast has two cinquefoil-headed lights and is evidently of 15th-century origin, but almost certainly is not *in situ*.

Inside, the hall has a roof of six bays with four arch-braced collar-trusses springing from false hammerbeams at the ends and between each pair of bays, and with three intermediate trusses springing from carved angel corbels. There are three purlins on each side and four tiers of cusped windbraces (Plate 83). The false hammerbeam brackets rest on wall-shafts set on carved stone corbels, some with human heads, others with angel busts bearing shields (the latter were probably painted in 1834 in repetition of the original coats of arms in the window glass). The fireplace, with an original stone chimneypiece decorated with a shield-of-arms of Hall and a merchant mark (Plate 90), is not certainly *in situ*.

Merchant mark of John Hall.

A stone archway with a moulded four-centred head in the N. end of the hall is of 1834. The S. end has three modern doorways and, above, a cartouche-of-arms painted by Pugin.[9] An inscription records the restorations of 1834, when the building belonged to Sampson Payne, merchant of china and glass.

The window glass, extensively restored in 1834 by J. Beare, includes quarries inscribed 'Drede' in black-letter, the initials I and H, and shields-of-arms etc. as follows — E. windows, N. to S., upper lights: i Hall with *estoil* impaling merchant mark; ii (square) France modern and England with label of three points; iii (shield) France modern and England undifferenced;

iv as i but with *mullet* in place of *estoil*; v Monthermer; vi Hall with *estoil* impaling Hall undifferenced; vii Campbell; viii *ermine, a lion regardant or*; ix *ermine a lion or*; x Fitzhugh. Lower lights: xi Hungerford; xii Montacute and Monthermer quartering Neville; xiii quarterly of seven, Beauchamp, Montacute, Monthermer, Neville, Clare, Warwick and Spencer (Ann Neville, wife of Richard III); xiv Hungerford with label impaling Hall with *estoil*; xv Hall (altered) impaling merchant mark; xvi See of Winchester impaling Montague (James Montague, Bp. of Winchester 1616–9); xvii red rose; xviii red rose superimposed on white rose, crowned. The W. window contains: i figure of man bearing banner with arms of France modern and England quarterly; ii shield charged with *seated, chained and collared bear holding axe*.

The ground-floor room at the S. end of the hall has reset heavy oak ceiling-beams with roll, hollow-chamfered and ogee-mouldings forming a ceiling of four square and two oblong panels. The first-floor room contains nothing notable.

The three-storeyed 16th-century house to N. of the hall has been much altered. The N. wall is entirely of 1880. In the lower storeys the E. and W. walls have stout original posts, but a gallery-like opening in the first floor is modern. The third storey has two original W. windows, each of four lights with ovolo-moulded oak mullions. The roof has three collared tie-beam trusses.

1. *Prolusiones*, 44. The deed of 1467 is now seen to relate to Monument (132).
2. *Liber Niger*, 88–9.
3. V.C.H., *Wilts.*, vi, 125–7.
4. *W.A.M.*, xxxix (1915), 233.
5. Benson & Hatcher, 206.
6. Benson & Hatcher, 595–7; Hall, *Memorials*, text following Pl. xii.
7. *W.A.M.*, xl (1917–19), 41–2.
8. *Builder*, 23 Apr. 1881.
9. B. Ferrey, *Recollections of A.W. Pugin*.

(186) **Houses**, pair, Nos. 13 and 13a New Canal, of three storeys with brick and tile-hung walls and tiled roofs, were built *c.* 1800. The symmetrical N. front, rebuilt *c.* 1970, was formerly of timber framework hung with mathematical tiles. Each upper storey had five bays of plain sashed windows, the central windows being narrower than the others, and false. Kingdon & Shearm indicate a central through-passage in the ground storey, now obliterated by a shop.

(187) **Houses**, three adjacent, Nos. 11, 9 and 7 New Canal, demolished in 1962, were three-storeyed with walls of brickwork and of timber framework hung with mathematical tiles; they dated in the main from the

second half of the 18th century. The offices of William and Benjamin Collins, printers of the *Salisbury Journal*, had been on or near the site since 1748,[1] and in 1962 the newspaper still occupied No. 7 and the long back range of No. 11. The E. elevation had 18th-century doorways and sashed windows. The third edition of Naish's town plan, printed by Collins in 1751, names the site 'printing office'. During demolition the W. wall of No. 11 was found to be of mediaeval timber-framed construction on a plinth of rubble and ashlar.

1. *W.A.M.*, xli (1920), 53.

(188) **Houses**, two adjoining, Nos. 2 and 4 Catherine Street, three-storeyed, with rendered walls and slate-covered roofs, are of timber-framed construction and perhaps late mediaeval in origin, but they were re-modelled early in the 19th century. Above modern shop windows the N. and E. elevations have plain sashed and casement windows symmetrically arranged.

(189) **Houses**, three adjoining, Nos. 6–10 Catherine Street, are four-storeyed with brick walls and tiled roofs and were built late in the 18th or early in the 19th century. In each, the E. front is of two bays with modern shop windows at ground level and plain sashed windows above. Nothing noteworthy remains inside.

(190) **Houses**, two adjoining, Nos. 12 and 14 Catherine Street, now combined, are of three storeys with timber-framed walls hung with mathematical tiles and with tiled roofs. They were built during the first half of the 18th century, but were refronted early in the 19th century. The stairs are of the 19th century.

(191) **Houses**, two adjacent, Nos. 26 and 28 Catherine Street, are three-storeyed and have walls, probably of light timber framework, hung with mathematical tiles; the roofs are tiled and slated. The houses date from early in the 19th century and the E. front of No. 26 has first and second-floor balconies with wrought-iron railings, and a projecting first-floor window.

(192) **Cottage**, No. 30 Catherine Street, is two-storeyed with an attic and has timber-framed walls hung with slates and mathematical tiles, and a tiled roof. It is of the 16th century. The first floor is jettied on the S. side.

(193) **Houses**, originally two, Nos. 32 and 34–6 Catherine Street, now three shops, are two-storeyed with brick walls and tiled roofs. They were built about the middle of the 18th century. Originally the E. fronts were continuous, the N. house having two and the S. house four plain sashed windows in the upper storey, with a

continuous modillion cornice and plain parapet above. The lower storeys have been obliterated by modern shops. The S. house was divided into two parts after 1880 (O.S.).

(194) **Warehouse**, No. 38 Catherine Street, is of two and three storeys with brick and timber-framed walls and tiled roofs. The three-storeyed brick building on the E. is of the 19th century. Behind, a six-bay E.–W. range with rough-hewn timber-framed walls and with braced and collared tie-beam roof trusses is probably of 16th-century origin.

(195) **Building**, No. 40 Catherine Street, demolished *c*. 1970, was of two storeys with an attic and had timber-framed walls hung with mathematical tiles. The 19th-century E. front masked a building which retained elements of a 14th-century rafter roof with a collar purlin.

(196) **House**, No. 46 Catherine Street, of three storeys with brick walls and slated roofs, appears to be of the 18th century.

(197) **House**, No. 50 Catherine Street, of two storeys and an attic, has timber-framed walls and a tiled roof and probably is of the 16th century. The E. front is jettied at the first floor. In the 19th century a mathematical tile facade was added, with plain sashed windows at first-floor and attic levels.

(198) **Cottages**, pair, Nos. 52–4 Catherine Street, demolished *c*. 1970, were originally two-storeyed with attics and had timber-framed walls and slate-covered roofs; they were of the 16th century. In the 19th century the E. fronts were heightened to three storeys and rendered, and the jettied first floors were underbuilt.

(199) **'The Hall'** (O.S., 1880), No. 4 New Street, now offices, is of two storeys with attics and has brick walls with stone dressings, and tiled roofs; the E. wall contains mediaeval flint and tile work and 17th-century brick-work. Built soon after the middle of the 18th century for Alderman William Hussey,[1] a wealthy clothier, on the site of the old Assembly House,[2] it is the second largest dwelling house in Salisbury, being surpassed only by The College (14). Hussey represented the city in Parliament from 1774 to 1813. His great-grandfather, Robert Hussey (*d*. 1710), also alderman of Salisbury, was descended from the Husseys of Shapwick, Dorset.

The symmetrical S. front (Plate 76) has a projecting central bay with a porch in the lower storey and bow-windows above. In the three-bay flanking elevations the

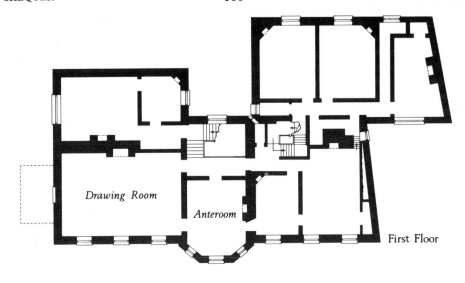

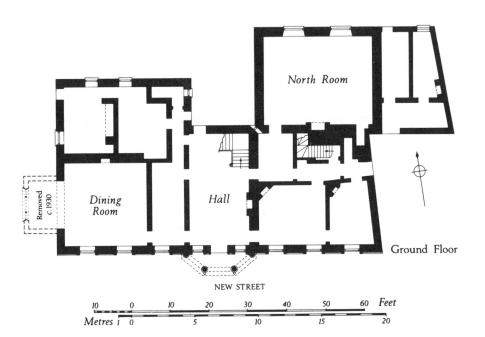

(199) THE HALL, No. 4 New Street.

window architraves of the lower storey are designed as if for doorways.

Inside, the hall fireplace has a pedimented stone chimneypiece. The main stairs have stone steps with cyma-shaped soffits, a plain balustrade with twisted iron newels and a mahogany handrail. The large North Room, added later in the 18th century, has walls and ceilings enriched with neo-classical plasterwork. On the first floor the drawing room has bolection-moulded panelling in two heights and a high coved ceiling which rises into the attic; the chimneypiece (Plate 94) has a rococo frieze panel. The anteroom has panelling with fielded centres

and a rococo chimneypiece of pinewood (Plate 94). Several other rooms have carved wood chimneypieces and enriched plaster ceilings.

1. Haskins, *Sar. Corpn. Pictures* (1910), 55–7.
2. Naish, edition of 1751; not shown on earlier editions.

(200) **House**, No. 8 New Street, demolished in 1967, was three-storeyed and had brick walls and a slate-covered roof. It dated from the first quarter of the 19th century. The S. front was symmetrical and of three bays.

(201) **House**, No. 42 New Street, demolished in 1964, was of two storeys with attics and had brick walls and tiled roofs. The W. part of the building, of mid 18th-century date, had an asymmetrical S. front of seven bays. Towards the end of the 18th century cottages were added at the E. end of the range and other additions were made on the S.E.; the cottages were subsequently incorporated in the house. Inside, the stairs had plain balustrades and turned newel posts. The S.W. room on the first floor had fielded panelling.

(202) **Cottage**, No. 76 New Street, demolished in 1964, was two-storeyed with timber-framed walls and a tiled roof. Of 16th-century origin, the interior had been destroyed to make a garage, but the roof retained collared tie-beam trusses with queen-struts.

ANTELOPE CHEQUER

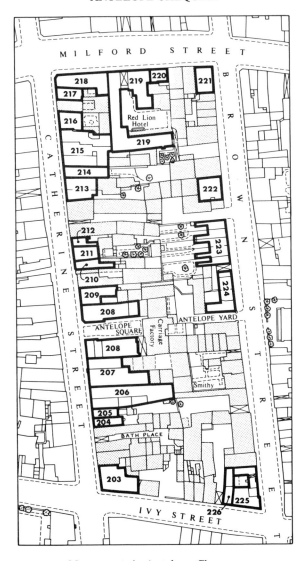

Monuments in Antelope Chequer.

(203) **Bell and Crown Inn**, of mid 14th-century origin, has walls of timber framework faced with brick in the lower and with mathematical tiles in the upper storey, and tiled roofs. The first floor is jettied to W. and S. A brick chimneystack until recently in the re-entrant angle between the two ranges was probably a 17th-century addition. The roof of the S. range has original

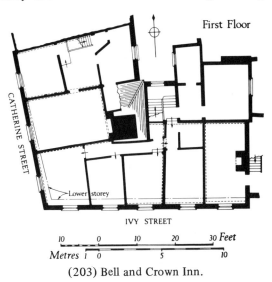

(203) Bell and Crown Inn.

collared rafters with collar-purlins resting on two crown posts. In 1415 the tenement (comprising three shops in Ivy Street and another in Catherine Street, the latter occupied by John Clerk, tanner) was bequeathed by Thomas Chapelyn junior to the Dean and Chapter, to sell for the endowment of his chantry at the cathedral, where he was buried.[1] Drawings of 1831–2 and a specification for stables are preserved.[2]

1. Dom. Bk. iii, f. 28.
2. W.R.O., 451/73 (xlii).

(204) **Cottage**, No. 49 Catherine Street, recently demolished, was two-storeyed with an attic and had timber-framed walls and a tiled roof. Built early in the 16th century, it originally had a single room on each floor; the first floor was jettied to the west. Additional rooms were built on the E., probably in the 17th century. The roof, ridged N.–S., had collared tie-beam trusses with curved V-struts.

(205) **Cottage**, No. 47 Catherine Street, recently demolished, was two-storeyed with an attic and had timber-framed walls and a tiled roof. Of the early 16th century, it must have been older than the adjoining cottage (204) as the masked S. gable retained external rendering. Additions on the E. were of the later 16th and of the 18th century. A 16th-century oak doorway with a four-centred head, at the street entrance, was not *in situ*.

(206) **House**, now two shops, Nos. 45 and 43, of two storeys with brick walls and a slate-covered roof, was built *c.* 1840.

(207) **Houses**, two adjoining, Nos. 39 and 41, of three storeys with brick walls and tiled roofs, are of the first half of the 19th century. The W. fronts are united in a symmetrical composition of five bays with segmental-headed sashed windows.

(208) **Warehouses**, Nos. 37 and 35, of two storeys with rendered walls and slate-covered roofs, partly demolished in 1973, stood respectively S. and N. of a yard called Antelope Square and were formerly two ranges of the Antelope Inn. Having a back entrance from Brown Street, the tenement can probably be identified with one called The Abbey (alley) in 1415–26, when it belonged to William Dondyng, merchant, and his widow Cristina.[1] During the 17th century the site was occupied by the Antelope Inn, from which, by the 18th century, the chequer came to be named. Fragments of Jacobean carved woodwork are recorded by J. Buckler and others.[2] A plan of the inn, *c.* 1830, is preserved.[3] Before demolition the two ranges appeared to be contemporary and of *c.* 1830, but while the N. range was being demolished three partitions between first-floor rooms were found to contain tie-beam trusses with cambered collars, curved lower angle-braces and principals cut to receive clasped purlins; they probably dated from the 15th or 16th century and were heavily sooted. Oak posts and other timber framework were found in the N. wall of the same range.

1. Dom. Bk. iii, ff. 23, 108.
2. Devizes Mus., Buckler album ix, f 15; Benson & Hatcher, opp. 318.
3. W.R.O., 451/137.

(209) **House**, No. 33, of three storeys with brick walls and a slate-covered roof is of the first half of the 19th century.

(210) **House**, No. 29, of two storeys with an attic, has timber-framed walls and a tiled roof. It is of the 17th century, but the W. front is modern.

(211) **House**, No. 27, of two storeys with an attic, has walls probably of timber framework hung with mathematical tiles, and a slated roof. It is of the late 17th or early 18th century.

(212) **House**, No. 25, of two storeys with an attic, has rendered walls and a tiled roof. It probably is of the late 16th or early 17th century.

(213) **House**, Nos. 19 and 17, of three storeys with tile-hung timber-framed walls and with a tiled roof, is of 16th-century origin. Late in the 18th century it was provided with a three-bay W. front faced with mathematical tiles and with plain sashed windows in both upper storeys, one on the first floor projecting. In the 19th century the house was divided into two parts and the ground-floor rooms were fitted as shops.

(214) **House**, No. 15, of three storeys with brick walls and slated roofs, is of the early 19th century. Above a modern shop window the W. front has two plain sashed windows in each storey.

(215) **Houses**, three adjoining, Nos. 13, 11 and 9, of three storeys with brick and tile-hung walls and with slated roofs, are of the early 19th century, but modernised internally. A terrier of 1822 mentions Nos. 9 and 11 as 'newly erected'.[1]

In 1406–7 John Chaundeler, a major benefactor of Trinity Hospital and its first master, bequeathed to the hospital his own dwelling house which stood on the site of monuments (215) and (216).[2] By 1480 the tenement had been divided, John Burnham, wax chandler, and Peter White, joiner, each paying 20s. a year to the hospital.[3] Chaundeler endowed a chantry at the cathedral.[4]

1. T.H. Arch., *s.a.*
2. V.C.H., *Wilts.* iii, 357; Dom. Bk. ii, f. 33[v].
3. *W.A.M.*, xxxvi (1910), 387.
4. Sar. D. & C.M., press I, Sarum deeds, 2/48.

(216) **House**, No. 7, of three storeys with brick walls and a tiled roof, is of the second half of the 18th century. From 1754 to 1850 it was occupied by William Snook, cutler, and his descendants.[1] The lower storey of the three-bay W. front contains a modern shop window; each upper storey has three bays of plain sashed windows. Inside, there are no notable features. The stairs are of the late 19th century. In 1625 an antecedent house, newly erected at a cost of £120, was leased to William Ray.[2] For earlier history of site, see (215).

1. T.H. Arch., deeds.
2. *ibid*.

(217) **House**, No. 3, of three storeys with brick walls and a slate-covered roof, has a two-bay W. front continuous with that of the adjoining building (218). In 1880 (O.S.) the plot of No. 3 extended S. to include the area now occupied by No. 5, a modern building.

(218) **Warehouse**, No. 2 Milford Street, is of three storeys with brick walls and slate-covered roofs. A 'house and shop on the corner of Catherine and Milford

Streets' were advertised in *Salisbury Journal* in 1785 (21st Feb.), but it is doubtful if this refers to the existing building, which appears to be of the 19th century. Above modern shop windows the W. front has four and the N. front has seven uniform sashed windows in each storey. In the 17th century this corner tenement was part of the White Bear inn (219).

(219) **Red Lion Hotel**, formerly the White Bear, of two and three storeys with walls of timber framework and rendered brickwork and with tiled and slated roofs, is partly of the 14th century. The inn was called Red Lion in 1756, but it was the White Bear throughout the 17th century (when it belonged to the Ray family) and as late as 1701.[1] Significantly this also was the name by which the chequer was then known.[2] In 1483 the tenement at the N.W. corner of the chequer was called Berecorner[3] and later deeds relating to adjoining tenements show that the buildings were part of the inn.[4] The Berecorner tenement probably extended E. to include the present inn yard and through-way. The same tenement in the 14th and 15th centuries had been called Duynescorner after Agnes la Duynes who owned it in 1327. From 1338 to 1350 Duynescorner belonged to Henry Burry (mayor 1323), but by 1361 it belonged to the Buterleghs,[5] and in 1395 it passed with other properties (including a bakehouse in Brown Street) from John Buterlegh to John Camel, grocer.[6] In his will (1399) Camel left property including Duynescorner and a Brown Street tenement occupied by Henry Chubbe, baker, to his daughter Agnes, wife of Lawrence Gowayn of Norrington.[7] Duynescorner still belonged to the Gowayns in 1455, but the bakehouse tenement had been given to the Vicars Choral, who retained it until the 19th century.[8] In the 17th century the 'great hall of the White Bear' stood W. of the bakehouse.[9] For plan and section of the 14th-century building see p.110.

The three-storeyed 19th-century N. range (Plate 80) has a carriage through-way with a semicircular arch; the iron inn-sign standard is dated 1823, a probable date for the building. The yard to which the archway gives access has, on the S., a timber-framed range of two storeys with an attic which dates from the first half of the 14th century. Externally it is masked by 19th-century and later additions, but much of the framework is exposed inside. Transverse beams in both storeys divide the range into ten bays, of which four on the W. are narrower than the others. On the ground floor a partition and perhaps a passage leading to the great hall separated these narrower bays from the E. part of the range. The beams in the W. bays are chamfered; those in the E. bays are hollow-chamfered and retain traces of ovolo-mouldings; the mouldings continued on braces formerly attached to the wall posts and on the wall posts themselves. On the ground floor, in a modern window recess near the E. end

of the N. wall, two original wall posts support a moulded wall-plate on which rest the joists of the jettied first floor. An original window of four lights is indicated by mouldings on the posts and by mortices for mullions in the underside of the wall-plate.

In the upper storey, ignoring modern partitions, the ten bays are separated into three chambers by stout 14th-century timber framework. The west chamber is of four bays and has roughly worked timbers. In the middle and east chambers, each of three bays, the timber posts, beams and wall-plates have ovolo mouldings and hollow chamfers. Placed near the centre of the partition on the W. of the middle chamber was a large opening, now blocked, with chamfered jambs and a round head formed by chamfered timber spandrels (see cross-section); to the S. was a narrower opening with a chamfered elliptical head. The partition dividing the middle chamber from the east chamber has a similar narrow opening on the S., but there is no central opening. A chimneybreast which intrudes in the middle chamber is possibly of the 16th or 17th century; the partition on the W. side of the adjacent staircase retains traces of painted decoration.

The 14th-century roof is constructed with collared rafters. The collar beams have mortices for a collar purlin and the pairs of rafters which correspond with the tie-beams are strengthened with scissor braces. From the height of the collars above the tie-beams it may be inferred that the attic was designed for habitation.

1. Haskins, *Guilds*, 328, 333.
2. *W.A.M.*, xxxvi (1910), 427.
3. Sar, Corp. MS., D/33, f. 24.
4. T.H. Arch., terrier 1822; deeds for No. 7 Catherine Street, 1625–1850, *passim*.
5. Sar. Corp. MS., W/205, Deeds. Benson & Hatcher, 695.
6. Dom. Bk. iii, reg. f. 52–3. For additional data on Buterlegh and Camel, see (140).
7. W.R.O., 164/1/6.
8. *W.A.M.*, xxxvii (1911), 67, 70. Benson & Hatcher, 820.
9. Parl. Svy., Foy 83 (Sar. 12), f. 19. Sar. D. & C.M., press III, Vic. Ch. terrier, 1671.

(220) **Oddfellows' Arms Inn**, of two storeys with attics, with rendered timber-framed walls and tiled roofs (Plate 80), is of 16th-century origin. Inside, the ground-floor room has a stout chamfered ceiling beam; timber framework is seen in the upper storeys. The roof has collared tie-beam trusses. This small tenement is the remaining part of a property belonging to the Godmanston family, *c.* 1400. In 1419 they sold it to Richard Foster of Staunton Drew, Somerset.[1]

1. Dom. Bk. ii, f. 45ᵛ; iii, ff. 41, 77.

THE RED LION HOTEL
FOURTEENTH-CENTURY RANGE

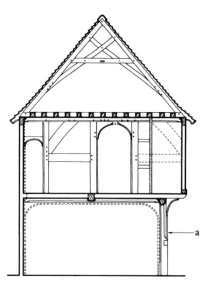

Cross~section (composite) x~y

Scale

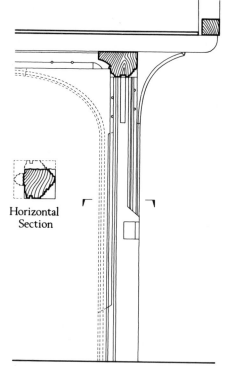

Horizontal Section

Detail of Post 'a'

Scale

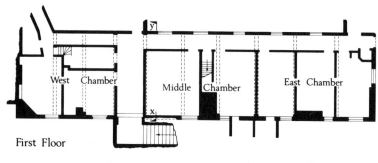

West Chamber   Middle Chamber   East Chamber

First Floor

Scale for Plans

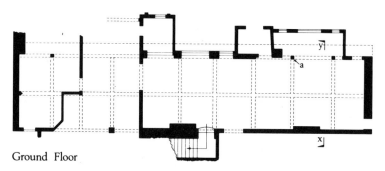

Ground Floor

(221) **House**, at the N.E. corner of the chequer, of two storeys with attics and with brick walls and a tiled roof, appears to be of the 18th century. Above modern shop windows the N. elevation has four and the E. elevation five bays with plain sashed windows.

(222) **House**, No. 34 Brown Street, now part of the Red Lion Hotel, is two-storeyed with attics and has timber-framed walls and tiled roofs. It is of the 16th century and has a four-bay roof with collared tie-beam trusses with queen-struts and clasped purlins.

(223) **Houses**, row of five, Nos. 38–46 Brown Street, demolished *c.* 1967, were three-storeyed and had brick walls and slate-covered roofs. They were built early in the 19th century.

(224) **Warehouses**, Nos. 48 and 50 Brown Street, demolished *c.* 1967, were of two storeys with brick walls and tiled roofs. They were built late in the 18th or early in the 19th century.

(225) **Queen's Arms Inn**, at the S.E. corner of the chequer, is of two storeys with brick walls, partly rendered, and with slate-covered and tiled roofs. The E. range, of 14th-century origin, is part of the dwelling of John Caundel, clerk, who died in 1400 and bequeathed his house, once Alice Restehale's, to the Dean and Chapter; they owned it in 1455.[1] The survey of 1649 describes it as a corner tenement leased to George Mustin, innholder, with a little court 20 ft. square, a hall and other rooms;[2] presumably it was already an inn. It was called by its present name not later than 1732.[3]

The S. range was rebuilt in the 18th century; a noteworthy feature is the shell-shaped hood over the S. doorway. The E. range is brick-faced, but timber framework is seen inside; the roof retains seven pairs of 14th-century collared rafters and parts of two crown-posts. No. 7 Ivy Street (226) was formerly integral with this building, the whole tenement measuring about 80 ft. by 55 ft.[4]

1. Sar. D. & C.M., press I, deeds 76, 82. Dom. Bk.ii, ff. 30, 92. *Liber Niger*, 69.
2. Parl. Svy. untitled (Sar. 11), f. 5.
3. Haskins, *Guilds*, 333.
4. For 17th and 18th-century deeds and a 19th-century plan of the tenement, see Sar. D. & C.M., Ch. Commrs. Rec., 67176; also 86048, pp. 11, 18.

(226) **House**, No. 7 Ivy Street, is two-storeyed with timber-framed walls, now largely replaced in brickwork, and with a tiled roof. It is of the late 15th or early 16th century. A central chimneystack was inserted probably in the 18th century. The roof, ridged N.–S., has collared tie-beam trusses with cambered tie-beams and curved V-struts. The wall-posts below the trusses are jowl-headed.

TRINITY CHEQUER

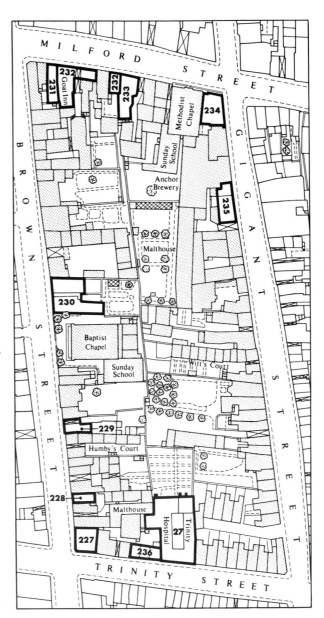

Monuments in Trinity Chequer.

(227) **Star Inn**, at the S.W. corner of the chequer, is two-storeyed with rendered and tile-hung walls and with tiled roofs. Of mid 16th-century origin, but extensively rebuilt in recent years, it replaces the 14th-century Rydedore (Raie d'or) inn. The earliest deed, 1331, indicates that the tenement of Clement atte Rydedore extended from the street corner to the town ditch (here spanned by Blakebrigge). In 1390 the corner tenement was bought for 60 marks by John Chaundiler, sen.; it

probably passed from him to Trinity Hospital.[1] Part of the roof has collared tie-beam trusses with clasped purlins. Plans of *c.* 1850 are preserved.[2]

1. Haskins, *Guilds*, 306. T.H. Arch., leases. Sar. Corp. MS., deeds.
2. W.R.O., 451/73 (xii).

(228) **House**, No. 65 Brown Street, is two-storeyed with attics and has brick walls and tiled roofs; it dates from *c.* 1700. The close-string dog-leg staircase has stout moulded oak handrails, fretted and shaped splats and beaded newel posts.

(229) **Cottage**, No. 49 Brown Street, demolished in 1972, was a 16th-century building of two storeys with slate-hung timber-framed walls and a tiled roof. The through-passage on the N. retained its original W. door. Inside, some chamfered beams and jowl-headed posts were seen. The back wing was of the 19th century.

(230) **Houses**, pair, Nos. 39 and 37 Brown Street, demolished in 1965, were two-storeyed with attics and had brick walls and tiled roofs. The main range was of the mid 18th century (Plate 73); the service wing on the

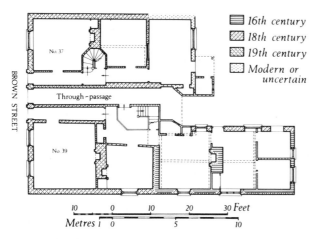

16th century
18th century
19th century
Modern or uncertain

No. 37

BROWN STREET

Through-passage

No. 39

10   0   10   20   30 Feet
Metres 1   0   5   10

(230) Nos. 37-9 Brown Street. Ground floor.

E. of the S. house was of 16th-century origin. The W. front was originally symmetrical, but during the 19th century a ground-floor window in No. 37 was suppressed and the doorway was moved northwards to make way for the entrance to a through-passage formed between the two houses.

Inside, the W. rooms in both storeys of No. 39 retained 18th-century panelling in two heights, with moulded

skirtings, dados and cornices. An 18th-century staircase with close strings and turned balusters in No. 37 may have been moved when the through-passage was formed. The E. wing of No. 39 had timber-framed walls. The first floor was originally jettied on the north, but the jetty had been under-built.

(231) **House**, No. 20 Milford Street, of two storeys and an attic, has rendered walls and a tiled roof and is of the 18th century although much altered in recent times. The building occupies part of 'the angle tenement opposite the Bolehall', the rent of which (30s. p.a.) was given to the city in 1370 by Wm. Wichford.[1] The tenement appears in the earliest survey of city lands (1618), but was sold during the Commonwealth.[2]

1. Dom. Bk. iii, reg., ff. 31, 32.
2. Sar. Corp. MS., O/117/1, f. 12; 4, f. 143.

(232) **Houses**, Nos. 24, 26 and 30 Milford Street, are of three and two storeys with brick walls and slated roofs. No. 24 was formerly the Goat Inn and is mentioned in a document of 1618;[1] it still bore the name in 1880 (O.S.). Building work in 1976 revealed that the three-storeyed N. range of No. 24, parallel with the street, had been rebuilt *c.* 1820, probably after a fire (charred timbers). The previous N. range had been two-storeyed and probably of the 16th century; a collared tie-beam truss with clasped purlins remained in the E. party wall together with the independant roof truss of No. 26. On the ground floor, to E., the N. range of No. 24 had a narrow carriage through-way leading to a small yard. On the W. of the yard the first three bays of the S. range of No. 24 retained timber framework, perhaps of *c.* 1500; the range was originally two-storeyed, with the first floor jettied to E. Early in the 18th century the jetty was under-built and the S. bay of the range was added. The two middle bays of the range probably became a dining room; the S. fireplace in this room had an eared timber surround, an enriched frieze and a moulded cornice. In *c.* 1820 the upper storey of the S. range was rebuilt and a third storey was added.

1. Sar. Corp. MS., O/117/1, f. 12. Haskins, *Guilds* 326–33, *passim*.

(233) **Inn**, No. 32 Milford Street, of two storeys with brick walls and tiled roofs, dates from late in the 15th century. The walls were originally timber-framed and a few timbers remain in the upper storey. The roof has three original collared tie-beam trusses with curved braces and king-struts.

The Town Ditch, coming from the W. along Milford

Street (map, p. xxxv), turned at this point to flow S. through the middle of the chequer and passed beneath the house. In 1416 the reversion of the property was left to the mayor and commonalty by John Beckot, to keep his obit, whence Beckot's name appears in the bede roll of St. George's Guild.[1] In 1431, when the city acquired the property by royal licence, it was occupied by Walter Short and was described as the tenement 'where the water of the common ditch runs under the chamber'.[2] In the chamberlain's accounts (1475–85) the lessee was John Wyse, vintner.[3] The next house to E., also Beckot's, was described in 1418 as a tenement with a small garden and within the tenement, a building with a solar next to the watercourse;[4] both houses evidently made use of the Town Ditch, a major amenity. Both tenements had belonged to Gilbert de Wychebury in 1357 and to his son Nicholas in 1361. Nicholas Wychebury 'dictus Bakere' died in 1391 leaving the properties (one of which he inhabited) to his son John Bakere, grocer, otherwise known as John Salisbury. John Salisbury's contribution to the Taxation List of 1399–1400, the largest of any citizen's, indicates his great wealth. He was mayor five times and died in 1405.[5]

1. Dom. Bk. iii, f. 26. Benson & Hatcher, 133.
2. Sar. Corp. MS., W/205, deeds.
3. Sar. Corp. MS., O/103, 5 and 6.
4. Dom. Bk. iii, ff. 26, 27.
5. Dom. Bk. i, f. 18^V; ii, f. 60; iii, f. 89. Sar. Corp. MS., Z/238. Benson & Hatcher, 695.

(234) **House**, No. 34 Milford Street, with brick walls with ashlar dressings and with tiled roofs, appears to be the surviving part of a larger building. The elevations are of the 18th century, but 17th-century plasterwork inside appears to be *in situ*.

The N. front, with stone quoins, a moulded cornice and stringcourses between the storeys, is in two parts: on the E., two bays with plain sashed windows in the upper storeys have a modern shop-front below; on the W., a single bay slightly set back has a sashed window in each storey. Evidently the facade has been truncated; if symmetrical it would have had seven bays, i.e., a recessed central range of three bays flanked by two-bay projections. The E. elevation has a pedimented doorway flanked by Tuscan columns and sashed windows in three storeys. Inside, the N.E. ground-floor room has 17th-century oak panelling and a ribbed plaster ceiling (Plate 93) of four panels defined by intersecting beams. Other ground-floor rooms have 18th-century fittings.

In 1366 Wm. Teynturer junior acquired this corner tenement, then called Stratfordescorner, from Edward Glastyngbury.[1] From 1397 to 1410 it was occupied by William Hull and in 1416 it was called 'Glastyngburie-

corner sive Stratfordescorner'.[2] Teynturer in 1366 already owned the land adjacent on the W.; it was acquired by the city in 1413 under royal licence and appears in the earliest city rental (1412–3) as 'the tenement near the angle tenement formerly of Wm. Hull in Wynchestrestret – rent 20s. p.a.'.[3] In the chamberlain's account rolls (1475–85) it is called 'le bakehouse formerly held by William Martyn, baker, for 20s. p.a., now leased to John Wyse, vintner'.[4] It does not, however, occur in the 17th and 18th-century surveys of city lands. The Methodist Chapel shown on O.S., 1880 occupies parts of both tenements acquired by William Teynturer in the 14th century. The still recognisable westward projection of the 'bakehous' tenement to the Town Ditch is, no doubt, an original feature.

1. Dom. Bk. i, f. 67.
2. Dom. Bk. ii, f. 16; iii, f. 21^V.
3. Dom. Bk. ii, f. 113. Sar. Corp. MS., D/32, Ledger A, f. 49.
4. Sar. Corp. MS., O/103, 5 and 6.

(235) **Anchor Inn**, of two storeys with walls originally of timber framework, but largely rebuilt in brickwork, and with a tiled roof, is of 16th-century origin. Inside, a first-floor room has an 18th-century fireplace surround.

(236) **Cottages**, three adjacent, Nos. 13–17 Trinity Street, are two-storeyed with attics and have timber-framed walls faced with brickwork, and tiled roofs. Of early 17th-century origin, they were altered in the 19th century when the roofs were rebuilt at a higher level. Inside, a jowl-headed post and an original cambered tie-beam are built into the partition between No. 13 and No. 15.

Six shops on the W. of 'the ditch of the house of Holy Trinity' were given to Trinity Hospital by John Chaundeler in 1400. In 1638 a tenement in this position was leased to John Trewman, tailor.[1]

Plate 14 includes a copy of an early photograph in Salisbury Museum showing the destruction in 1878 of a 15th-century hall with an elaborately decorated false hammerbeam collar-truss roof. The building stood immediately E. of (27) Trinity Hospital, on ground now occupied by Nos. 19–21 Trinity Street. In 1384 a house adjoining the hospital on the E. had been owned by Thomas and Alice le Eyr; they agreed never to obstruct the E. window of the hospital chapel. In 1452 and 1473 the 'capital tenement' next to the hospital belonged to William Pynkebrygge. In 1767 it appears to have been Sir John Webb's.[2]

1. T.H. Arch., *passim*.
2. *Ibid*.

ROLFE'S CHEQUER

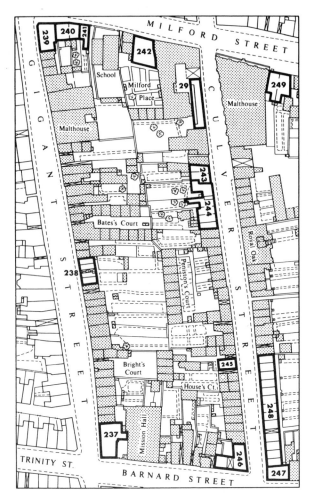

Monuments in Rolfe's and Barnard's Cross Chequers.

(237) **Inn,** at the S.W. corner of the chequer, is three-storeyed with brick walls and slate-covered roofs and was built *c.* 1840.

(238) **Cottages,** range of four, Nos. 91–7 Gigant Street, are two-storeyed with attics and have rendered brick walls and tiled roofs. They appear to be of the early 19th century.

(239) **House,** No. 40 Milford Street, demolished in 1958, was of two storeys with tile-hung timber-framed walls and tiled roofs; it was of the late 16th or early 17th-century. The S. wing, of *c.* 1800, occupied a plot shown empty on Naish's map of 1716. The original building comprised two parallel N.–S. ranges, each three bays long. The first floor was formerly jettied to N. and W., but the jetties had been underbuilt.

(240) **House and Cottage,** Nos. 42 and 44 Milford Street, are respectively of three and two storeys and have brick walls and tiled roofs. They are largely of the late 17th century, but the ground floor of No. 42 appears to include the remains of a 15th-century structure. In the N. front plaster rustication masks the lower storey of No. 42; above, a projecting window with a shaped lead roof with a ball finial, symmetrically arranged sashed windows and a moulded eaves cornice provide a facade of some dignity for what may originally have been a humble dwelling. Inside, the ground-floor room of No. 42 is spanned by a deeply chamfered beam. The N. room on the first floor has a moulded plaster cornice and late 17th-century joinery. The roof of a two-storeyed rear wing, demolished in 1974, had a collared tie-beam truss with a king-strut. In No. 44, a large chimneybreast against the E. wall of No. 42 was built with reused ashlar blocks. A chamfered oak beam supporting the first floor was also reused. Both dwellings were modernised in 1974.

(241) **Cottage,** No. 46, of two storeys with timber-framed walls faced with brickwork and with a tiled roof, is of early 15th-century origin. It was much altered in the 19th century and again in 1974. The roof has been raised, but an original gable truss surviving at the W. end has a cambered tie-beam and curved angle braces.

(242) **House,** Nos. 56–8 Milford Street, of three storeys with brick and timber-framed walls and with tiled roofs, is of late 16th or early 17th-century origin. The four-bay N. front, with plain sashed windows in each storey, was added in the 18th century; a modern shop window replaces two bays of the lower storey. Inside, some stout timber posts and fragments of 17th-century panelling are seen, also an 18th-century bolection-moulded fireplace surround. In the 19th century the building was divided into several tenements. It is now a workshop.

(243) **House,** Nos. 42–4 Culver Street, demolished in 1973, was two-storeyed and had brick-faced timber-framed walls and a tiled roof. The building was probably of 16th-century origin, but it had been extensively rebuilt in the 18th century when it was divided into two dwellings.

(244) **Houses,** range of five, Nos. 46–54 Culver Street, demolished in 1973, were of three storeys with brick walls and slated roofs. They were of the first half of the 19th century.

(245) **House,** No. 80 Culver Street, demolished in 1973, was of two storeys with brick walls and a tiled roof and was of late 18th or early 19th-century origin.

(246) **Factory**, demolished in 1974, of two storeys with a cellar, had brick walls and an iron roof. Although much altered the building was probably of 18th-century origin. The cellar had an elliptical brick vault.

BARNARD'S CROSS CHEQUER

(247) **House**, No. 53 Payne's Hill, is of two principal storeys with a basement and dormer-windowed attics and has brick walls with ashlar plinths and quoins and a tile-covered roof (Plate 74). It appears to date from the last quarter of the 17th century. Inconsistencies in the N. part of the W. elevation suggest that the building may originally have extended further N., or perhaps that it incorporated an earlier adjacent house, now gone. Inside,

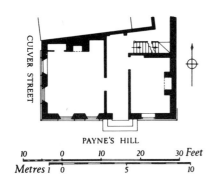

(247) No. 53 Payne's Hill. Ground floor.

several rooms are lined with pine panelling in two heights and have original wooden chimneypieces and moulded cornices. The stairs are of the 19th century. The house was restored in 1972.

(248) **Invicta Terrace**, row of thirteen cottages, Nos. 83–107 Culver Street, demolished in 1976, were two-storeyed with rendered brick walls and slate-covered roofs. They were built during the first half of the 19th century. Demolition of buildings N. of Invicta Terrace in 1972 revealed traces of an early bell-foundry. Associated pottery was of 14th–16th century date; fragments of moulds were perhaps of the 17th or 18th century.[1]

1. *W.A.M.*, lxviii (1973), 137.

(249) **Houses**, pair, Nos. 80–82 Milford Street, built early in the 19th century and demolished in 1971, were two-storeyed with cellars and attics and had brick walls and tiled roofs. A house called Halstedsplace on this site was acquired by 1417 by Walter Halstede, butcher, from Thomas Bystone who had owned it since 1405.[1] In 1464 it was sold by Richard Walker to the

major and commonalty, who exchanged it in 1482 for a house in Castle Street belonging to Henry Penkere.[2]

1. Dom. Bk. ii, f. 68[v].
2. Sar. Corp. MS., W/205, deeds; D/33, ledger B, f. 145.

For location of monument (250) see map on p. 94.

(250) **House**, No. 88 Milford Street, demolished in 1972, was of two storeys and had timber-framed walls and tiled roofs. Although somewhat altered in 1914 when extensions were built to S. and E., the N. range was of the 15th century and retained interesting features.

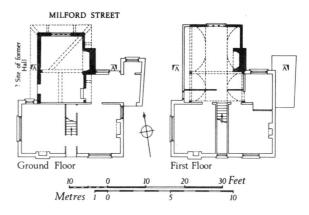

(250) No. 88 Milford Street.

In 1396 a tenement next to Milford Bars and the city rampart, with a street frontage of 42 ft. 2 ins., was acquired from Alice Buterlegh by Wm. Isaac, baker.[1] Isaac occupied it in 1405 and in 1417 and his name was still associated with it in 1464.[2] In 1479 the tenement belonged to Wm. Marchy, tailor.[3] The house which survived until 1972 was probably built by Marchy.

O.S. 1880 shows No. 88 as one of a group of buildings called Derby Court. In 1914 the buildings to the W. were demolished, leaving No. 88 isolated. The form of No. 88 suggests the cross-wing of a hall house and it is possible that the demolished buildings contained remains of a former hall.

In the N. front (Plate 65) the windows and the brick nogging were modern, as also were the N.W. corner post, bracket, upper post and the whole western panel in the upper storey. Presumably this panel was added in 1914 to correct the visual imbalance caused by the removal of the adjoining buildings. The other timbers in the N. front, including the N.E. corner post and bracket and intermediate brackets for the jettied first floor, were original. The E. side of the 15th-century range included an original brick chimneystack with ashlar quoins; to N. and S. the jettied first floor rested on timber brackets. The W. side was rendered externally in the lower storey; the jettied upper storey was of 1914.

Inside, the ground-floor room contained a stone chimneypiece with a moulded square-headed fireplace opening; a moulded cornice was returned at the N. end and had a carved head-stop on the south. The ceiling had a hollow-chamfered beam supported by a shafted W. wall post with a moulded capital. The dragon beam was chamfered. The first-floor room had a similar but smaller stone fireplace, with no head-stop. The butt-purlin roof had a collared truss with hollow-chamfered cruck-shaped principals, the chamfer continuing on the collar; below the purlins were curved windbraces. A mediaeval glazed terracotta ball finial and two crested ridge tiles from the tiled roof are now in Salisbury Museum.

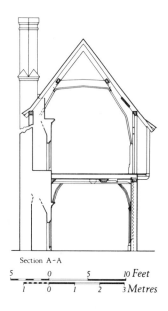

Section A–A

5 0 5 10 Feet

1 0 1 2 3 Metres

After demolition in 1972 the timber framework was removed to Lockeridge, near Marlborough, for re-erection.

1. Dom. Bk. ii, f. 13[V].
2. Dom. Bk. ii, f. 68[V]; iii, f. 31[V]. Sar. Corp. MS., W/205, deeds.
3. Somerset Hse., P.C.C. wills, 1 Logge.

WHITE HART CHEQUER

(251) **House and Shop**, No. 13 St. John's Street, of two storeys with ashlar walls and a slate-covered roof, was built *c.* 1820 as the *atelier* of William Osmond, statuary and monumental mason. The elegant W. facade in the grecian style has Doric columns flanking the central doorway, and an entablature with triglyphs. The upper storey has a three-light sashed window.

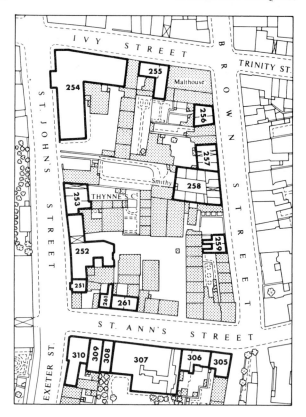

Monuments in White Hart Chequer and St. Ann's Street.

(252) **King's Arms Hotel**, of two and three storeys with attics, has timber-framed walls and tiled roofs. A two-bay range on the W. of the court appears to be of the late 16th century. The N. range is of the first half of the 17th century and possibly corresponds with a 'newly erected house .... heretofore seven tenements commonly called the Seven Deadly Sins' leased by the Dean and Chapter in 1638 to William Symonds.[1] In 1649 the house was leased to Sir Giles Mompesson and occupied by Henry Hewett.[2] North of the N. range, a large 19th-century first-floor dining room with three windows overlooking St. John's Street is now divided up and partly in separate occupation. The low ground-floor shops under the former dining room are likely to be of earlier date and may be integral with the adjoining building (253), but only one chamfered post and a bracket are visible. In Plate 66 the jettied and gabled W. end of the 17th-century N. range is seen between the N. gable of the 16th-century range and the S. end of the dining room.

Inside, the buildings have been extensively remodelled, but timber framework remains exposed. The court has been roofed over in the lower storey and encroached upon by corridors on the first floor. The first-floor room at the W. end of the N. range retains a moulded

First-floor plan

stone fireplace (Plate 92) and oak panelling of *c.* 1638; the stone shield over the fireplace, with arms of Mayne of Teffont, quartering Barnes, Mompesson and Hele, appears to be of the 19th century. The middle room on the first floor of the N. range has a plain stone fireplace with a cambered and chamfered head on which are scratched initials and dates (the earliest decipherable 1651) and six merchant marks as illustrated. In the third storey of the N. range, the W. chamber has a stone fireplace-surround with a moulded four-centred head and jambs with shaped stops. The staircase is mainly of

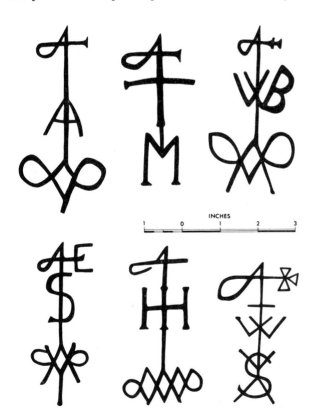

INCHES

'Merchant marks in King's Arms Hotel.

the 18th century, but the top flight retains a stout 17th-century balustrade. A 17th-century stone fireplace at the S. end of the dining room shows that there was an earlier room in this position.

1. Sar. D. & C.M., Eccls. Commrs. deeds, Chap., 45/2, 8th Sept., 1638.
2. Parl. Svy., loose folio.

(253) **Houses**, now shops, Nos. 3 and 5 St. John's Street, are two-storeyed with attics and have timber-framed walls and tiled roofs. The three-bay W. range, with exposed timber framework jettied on the first floor, is of the 15th century. Adjacent on the E. of No. 3 is an early 17th-century two-storeyed timber-framed addition comprising one room on each floor and a spiral staircase. The lower room has an original window with ovolo-moulded oak mullions. The upper room, lined with 17th-century oak panelling, has a stone fireplace with a moulded four-centred head and continuous jambs with shaped stops. The 16th-century roof has collared tie-beam trusses with clasped purlins.

(254) **White Hart Hotel**, at the N.W. corner of the chequer, of three storeys with brick walls and slate-covered roofs (Plate 81), appears to be mainly of *c.* 1820 although an inn of this name existed on the site in 1635.[1] The W. front has a handsome Ionic portico. A two-storeyed E. extension of the N. range contains a large first-floor assembly room of *c.* 1840, now divided into bedrooms.

1. Haskins, *Guilds*, 328.

(255) **Houses**, two adjacent, Nos. 2–4 Ivy Street, of two storeys with rendered timber-framed walls and tiled roofs, date from the 16th century. The first floor is jettied on the north. No. 4 has an 18th-century S. extension.

(256) **Houses**, pair, Nos. 82–4 Brown Street, are two-storeyed with attics and have brick walls and tiled roofs. They were built during the second half of the 18th century, originally as one house, with an E. front of four bays, with plain sashed windows in each storey and with a dentilled eaves cornice. The gauged brick lintel of the original N. ground-floor window is seen above the doorway of No. 82.

(257) **Houses**, two adjoining, Nos. 90–2 Brown Street, are two-storeyed with attics and have rendered and tile-hung walls and tiled roofs. Of the early 18th century, the two dwellings seem originally to have been one, but it also appears that the range was at one time divided into three parts.

(258) **The Barracks**, a stone-fronted two-storeyed 15th-century house, almost entirely demolished during the second half of the 19th century, is represented by part of its S. wall. Drawings by John Buckler, *c.* 1808,[1] and by William Twopeny (Plate 9), 1833, show an E. front of some pretension. Interior views of two rooms published by Benson & Hatcher in 1843 (opp. p. 602) are based on drawings by William Capon, 1819, now in Salisbury Museum (Edwards collection); notes on the drawings prove that the rooms occupied the middle of the E. range, one on each floor. Kingdon & Shearm's map of 1854, here reproduced, shows the E. range with

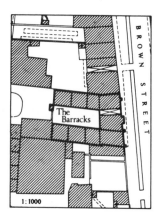

its projecting buttresses and, to W., a courtyard with N. and S. ranges. By 1880 (O.S.) the E. range had been replaced by four two-storeyed cottages. When the 15th-century range was demolished an ornate chimneypiece from the lower room was moved to No. 91 Crane Street (102); later it was taken to America.

The surviving S. wall of the S. range (now the boundary of a car-park) is of rubble and flint with ashlar dressings. It contains a stone window of two square-headed lights with chamfered surrounds and another window of three lights with ovolo mouldings; both are blocked.

To W. of the house, a garden originally extended across the chequer as far as St. John's Street. Adjoining properties to S. belonged either to the city or to the cathedral, and deeds record the names of many owners of the Barracks tenement. In 1431, when the house must have been quite new, it belonged to William Alessaundre, one of the city's five legal officers.[2] Later owners are recorded by Benson & Hatcher.[3] In 1649 the owner was Sir Gabriel Dowse.[4]

1. Devizes Mus., Buckler album ix, f. 7.
2. Sar. Corp. MS., deed 1431, relating to monument (259).
3. Benson & Hatcher, 602.
4. Parl. Svy., loose folio.

(259) **Cottages**, pair, Nos. 104–6 Brown Street, are two-storeyed with brick walls and slate-covered roofs and were built *c.* 1850. Adjacent to S., O.S. 1880 shows a row of five small buildings beside the street, extending to within 30 ft. of the street corner. Demolished early in the present century these five cottages were city property,[1] remaining from a much larger property (the whole S.E. quarter of the chequer) which had been bequeathed to the city in 1416 by William Ashleigh, chaplain, and acquired by royal licence in 1431. Deeds of *c.* 1290 show that the property comprised shops, cottages and a gateway facing Brown Street, a house on the corner and, to W., another house, the principal dwelling of the tenement.[2] The ground further W. belonged to the church. Throughout the first half of the 14th century Ashleigh's properties had been owned first by the Baudrey family, then by William le Frend (*d.* 1361), and from 1366 by Wm. Ashleigh sen.[3] Descriptions occur in 16th-century deeds and in the city survey of 1618. In an area called Storehouse Yard, N. and W. of the buildings, the boundary between city and church lands was ill-defined, but the yard was usually held by the innkeeper of the King's Arms Inn (252), a property of the Dean and Chapter. In 1649 the yard was sold to Edmond Edmonds, linendraper, who in 1663 also obtained the lease of the inn.[4]

1. Sar. Corp. MS., V/204/1, 2, No. 40 (plan); surveys in O/117/4, f. 74; O/117/8, f. 47.
2. Dom. Bk. iii, f. 20[V]; Council Mins., Ledger A, f. 56; Sar. Corp. MS., deed, 1431; Benson & Hatcher, 113.
3. Sar. Corp. MS., deeds, 1290–1416, *passim*. Dom. Bk. i, f. 7[V]; ii, f. 67[V].
4. Sar. Corp. MS., O/117/1, f. 84. Survey of 1618, f. 12. O/117/4, f. 165. Council Mins., Ledger C, ff. 190, 408, 416[V], 417[V]. Sar. D. & C.M., Chap. lease bk. 3. Storehouse Yard was probably so named because it was close to the public storehouse established by John Ivie in his experiment in Poor Relief, *c.* 1620–40 (P. Slack, *Poverty in Early Stuart Salisbury*, Wilts. Rec. Soc., xxxi, *passim*).

(260) **Houses**, pair, Nos. 5 and 3 St. Ann's Street, now united, are two-storeyed with attics and have timber-framed walls and tiled roofs; they are of the 16th century. The first-floor jetty in the S. front was underbuilt in the 19th century. The N. elevation of No. 3 retains, at the W. end, an original flint and tile chimney-breast with ashlar dressings, a moulded stone plinth and weathered offsets. Inside, the fireplace has moulded stone jambs; beside it on the W. is a chamfered loop with a two-centred head. A first-floor partition in No. 5 has planks with moulded muntins, perhaps of the 17th century. The roofs have collared tie-beam trusses with

queen-struts, butt-purlins and curved windbracing. In 1649 the tenement was occupied by Robert Smith, baker (Parl. Svy., Foy 83 (Sar. 12), f. 18).

(261) **House**, No. 1 St. Ann's Street, two-storeyed with an attic, with brick walls and tiled roofs, is of the 18th century.

MARSH CHEQUER

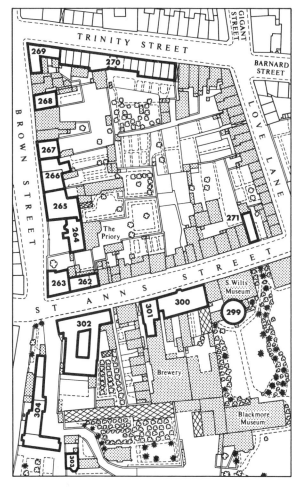

Monuments in Marsh Chequer and St. Ann's Street.

(262) **Houses**, two adjoining, Nos. 11 and 13 St. Ann's Street, are two-storeyed with attics and have brick walls and tiled roofs; they were built early in the 19th century.

(263) **House**, at the S.W. corner of the chequer, is of three storeys with brick walls and a slated roof and was built *c.* 1840.

(264) **'The Priory'**, house, of three storeys with brick walls with ashlar dressings and with tiled roofs, is of early 17th-century origin. The third storey was built in the 18th century, replacing former attics and making use of 17th-century ovolo-moulded stone windows with square-headed lights. In the 19th century the two lower storeys of the W. front were remodelled and windows of 16th-century style were supplied, but an original ashlar-faced two-storeyed porch was retained; at the same time additional rooms were built on the E. of the original range. Inside, the ground-floor rooms and stairs have 19th-century fittings in Jacobean style. The N.W. room on the first floor retains 17th-century oak panelling and an enriched chimneypiece of the period; in the S.W. room the chimneypiece and flanking alcoves are of the 18th century. On the second floor the E. wall of the W. range retains blocked 17th-century windows, presumably of former gables.

(265) **House**, No. 93 Brown Street, is three-storeyed with brick walls and tiled roofs. Although mainly of late 18th-century date, the S. wall is of the 17th century and contains blocked windows which correspond in level and size with those of 'The Priory' (264). Presumably this wall originally fronted a wing of 'The Priory' on the N. of the forecourt. Inside, the plan is of class U.

(266) **Houses**, two adjoining, Nos. 91 and 89 Brown Street, are two-storeyed with attics and have brick walls and tiled roofs. They date from the first half of the 18th century. Although No. 91 is larger, with four bays instead of three in the W. front (Plate 79), the two dwellings were built at the same time and the plat-band and coved eaves cornice are continuous. The enlarged doorway and the first-floor bow window of No. 91 are of the 19th century. Beside the chimneybreast in the W. ground-floor room of No. 89 is a shell-headed niche with carved enrichment and shaped shelves (Plate 95).

(267) **House**, No. 87 Brown Street, of two storeys with an attic, has brick walls and a tiled roof and is somewhat later in date than No. 89 (266), which it adjoins (Plate 79). Inside, the W. ground-floor room is lined with fielded softwood panelling in two heights; other rooms have dados and the hall has a reset 17th-century panelled oak dado. The stairs are of the 18th century.

(268) **House**, No. 81 Brown Street, of two storeys with an attic, with brick walls and a tiled roof, probably dates from early in the 18th century. The four-bay W. front has plain sashed windows and a moulded brick plat-band. Inside, the plan is a variant of class U, with no corridor between the two W. rooms. The stairs are original. The S.W. room, lined with fielded panelling, has a shell-headed niche with shaped shelves.

(269) **Houses**, Nos. 71–5 Brown Street, at the N.W. corner of the chequer, are two-storeyed with timber-framed walls and tiled roofs and appear to be of the mid 16th century. The first floors are jettied to N. and W. and there is a dragon beam at the N.W. corner. The roof truss at the N. end of the S. range (Nos. 73–5) is closed, suggesting that these houses were not originally an extension of No. 71. The roof of No. 71, ridged E.–W. and with a gable to Brown Street, is of four bays with collared tie-beam trusses, queen-struts, clasped purlins and curved windbraces. For history, see monument (270).

(270) **Cottages**, twelve uniform dwellings, Nos. 14–20 and 26–40 Trinity Street, are two-storeyed with attics and have brick walls and tiled roofs; they date from late in the 18th or early in the 19th century. No. 22/4, a house of three storeys with brick walls and a slated roof, takes the place of two former cottages and is of the first half of the 19th century.

The tenement (269) at the N.W. corner of the chequer and others on the site of these cottages, extending E. as far as the Town Ditch, were owned in 1455 by the Vicars Choral;[1] they had been given under the will of Thomas Chapelyn junior (*d.* 1415) to maintain a perpetual chantry for himself and his parents in the cathedral.[2] The property then comprised five dwellings and still did so in 1649, but by 1671 there were six, with gardens and a passage to 'a common house of office' over the ditch.[3] In 1649 the E. tenement of the group was a bakehouse; in 1794 it was leased to Robert Wood, baker.[4] It still is a baker's shop.

The N.E. corner of the chequer, now occupied by late 19th-century dwellings, was formerly called Shove's Corner. The history of the tenements can be traced through deeds of the Tailors' Guild from 1369 to 1854.[5]

1. *Liber Niger*, 70.
2. Dom. Bk. iii, ff. 23, 28, 42^v.
3. Parl. Svy., Foy 56 (Sar. 8), f. 24; Foy 39 (Sar. 4), f. 1; untitled sheaf (Sar. 11), f. 14. Sar. D. & C. M., Vic. Chor. terrier, 1671.
4. Sar. D. & C.M., Vic. Ch. Deeds, 33/1–4, 33/2 with plan.
5. Sar. Corp. MS., I/249. Haskins, *Guilds*, 171.

(271) **House**, No. 45 St. Ann's Street, is of two storeys with an attic and has brick walls and tiled roofs. The rendered S. front is of *c.* 1900, but chamfered beams and some original joinery seen inside indicate a small dwelling of *c.* 1700. In plan each storey has a front room and a back room with a central chimneystack between them. The stairs, with turned balusters and a moulded handrail, rise E. of the chimneystack.

POUND CHEQUER

(272) **Cottages**, seven adjacent, in two ranges converging at the N.W. corner of the chequer, are two-storeyed with attics and have brick walls and tiled roofs; they are of *c.* 1800. The corner tenement contains a shop and has two rooms on each floor; the others are approximately uniform and have only a living room and a small scullery on the ground floor. A common yard on the S.W. serves all seven dwellings.

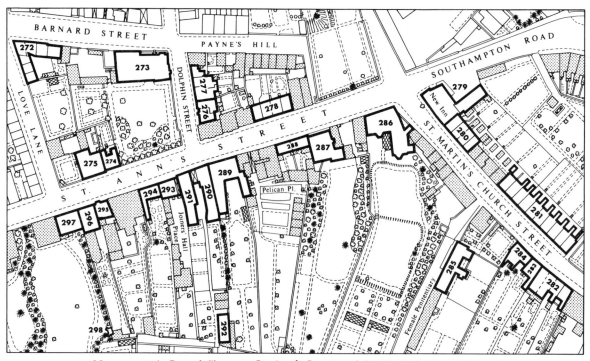

Monuments in Pound Chequer, St. Ann's Street and St. Martin's Church Street.

(273) **Barnard's Cross House**, of two storeys with basement and attics, has walls of brickwork with ashlar dressings, and tiled roofs. The E. part of the house was built late in the 17th century; the obliquity of the drawing room suggests that earlier foundations were used. The original staircase appears to have been in the passage between the two N. rooms. During the first half of the 18th century a small extension was built for a new staircase on the W. of the drawing room, and shortly after this more extensive additions were made to the W.; these include a large dining room, a kitchen and other ground-floor service rooms. Originally the service rooms were in the basement. The house is now part of a college hostel.

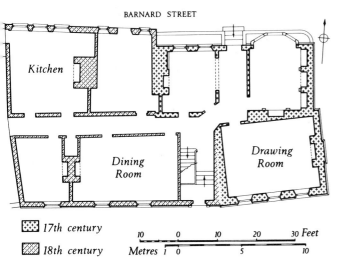

BARNARD STREET

Kitchen

Dining Room

Drawing Room

▨ 17th century
▨ 18th century

10 0 10 20 30 Feet
Metres 1 0 5 10

(273) Barnard's Cross House. Ground floor.

The N. elevation (Plate 72) retains original sashed windows, a panelled entrance doorway and a wooden bow window in which the lower lights could formerly be closed by vertically-sliding panelled shutters. There are two blocked basement windows. Further W., the 18th-century extension has plain sashed windows and a doorway with a flat hood. The S. front has, on the E., the three-bay drawing room range with tall sashed windows in both storeys, a moulded stone stringcourse and a wooden eaves cornice with heavy modillions. On the W. is the 18th-century staircase and dining room extension; a perpendicular joint in the brickwork shows that the staircase was completed first.

Inside, the basement rooms have elliptical brick barrel vaults; one vault bears a scratching of 1740. The ground floor drawing room is lined with original bolection-moulded panelling in two heights; the pedimented doorway and the enriched plaster ceiling appear to be of the mid 18th century; the original fireplace surround has gone. The N.E. room has 18th-century panelling with fluted pilasters. The 18th-century staircase (Plate 89) has newel posts in the form of fluted Tuscan columns.

Above the first floor part of the original staircase survives; it has close strings and spirally turned balusters. Several first-floor rooms have dados of fielded panelling. The roofs have collared queen-strut trusses supporting two butt-purlins on each side.

(274) **House**, No. 51 St. Ann's Street, of two storeys with an attic, has brick walls and a tiled roof and dates from the first half of the 18th century. The three-bay S. front is symmetrical, with a central doorway and plain sashed windows.

(275) **House**, No. 49 St. Ann's Street, of three storeys with brick walls and tiled roofs, was built about the middle of the 18th century. The S. front is of four bays, with sashed windows in each storey and with a pedimented doorway in the E. bay; the third-storey windows have segmental heads; above is a moulded brick cornice and a panelled parapet. On the E. is a slightly lower three-storeyed bay, possibly an addition. Inside, the rooms have 18th-century joinery.

SOUTH—EAST CHEQUER

(276) **Houses**, two adjacent, Nos. 117–9 Dolphin Street, are two-storeyed with timber-framed walls and tiled roofs. They are of 16th-century origin. In both dwellings the first floor is jettied to the W., but that of No. 117 has been underbuilt. Both houses have 18th-century sashed windows, and No. 119 contains an 18th-century chimneypiece.

(277) **Cottages**, range of three, of two storeys with rendered brick walls and tiled roofs, are of the 18th century. In 1854 they formed part of the Dolphin Inn (Kingdon & Shearm).

(278) **Houses**, row of four, Nos. 59–65 St. Ann's Street, are two-storeyed with attics and have brick walls and tiled roofs. They were built c. 1700 and originally were uniform.

ST. MARTIN'S CHURCH STREET

(279) **Toll Gate Inn**, the 'New Inn' in 1880 (O.S.), is of two storeys with brick walls and tiled roofs. The S.W. range dates from early in the 18th century; the parallel N.E. range was added before 1854 (Kingdon & Shearm). A barn to E., with walls partly of brick and partly of cob, could perhaps be of 17th-century origin.

(280) **Cottages**, range of four, Nos. 1–7, are of two storeys with brick walls and slated roofs and stylistically are of c. 1830. Some original casement windows have panes with 'pointed' heads.

(281) **Cottages**, range of ten, Nos. 17–35, are of two storeys with brick walls and slated roofs and date from c. 1840.

(282) **Houses**, range of four, Nos. 18–24, are three-storeyed with brick walls and slated roofs and date from *c.* 1840.

(283) **House**, No. 16, of two storeys with an attic, with brick walls and a slated roof, was built *c.* 1830.

(284) **House**, No. 14, of two storeys with an attic, has brick walls and a tiled roof and was built *c.* 1830. The N.E. front is symmetrical and of three bays, with a central doorway and with sashed windows with keystones.

(285) **The Retreat**, in 1880 (O.S.) a Female Penitentiary, is of two storeys with attics and has brick walls and tiled roofs. The N. part of the building originated *c.* 1810 as a house or pair of houses. By 1850 it had become a penitentiary, and additions were made on the south. Later in the 19th century further additions were made and the W. elevation was rebuilt.

ST. ANN'S STREET

For monuments on the N. side of the street, see White Hart, Marsh, Pound and S.E. chequers. The position of monuments (286)–(298) is shown on p. 120.

(286) **Moorland House**, No. 84, demolished in 1964, was of three storeys with attics and cellars and had brick walls and tiled roofs. The N. part of the building was of the first half of the 18th century. Extensive additions on

the S., built during the second half of the 19th century, replaced an earlier S. wing (Kingdon & Shearm).

The N. front was symmetrical and of five bays, with the three middle bays set forward; the E. and W. ends were emphasised by pilasters in the two upper storeys. The lower storey, with 19th-century plaster rustication, had at the centre an original stone doorway with Roman-Doric columns, entablature and pediment. Between the two upper storeys was a moulded brick stringcourse and at the top was a heavy brick cornice. Above, the roof was masked by a 19th-century parapet with a large curvilinear gable at the centre. The E. and W. elevations had no notable features. The S. elevation was rebuilt between 1854 (Kingdon & Shearm) and 1880 (O.S.).

Inside, the hall had 18th-century pine panelling in two heights, with console-headed pilasters and a dentil cornice. The lower part of the stairs (Plate 88), of oak with twisted balusters, probably came from elsewhere. The 19th-century drawing room was lined with reset 18th-century panelling in two heights with Corinthian pilasters and a moulded cornice. Several first-floor rooms were panelled.

(287) **House**, No. 82, of three storeys with cellars, has walls partly of brick banded with flint and partly of brick alone; the roofs are tiled. Of early 18th-century origin with a class-T plan, the N. range was formerly

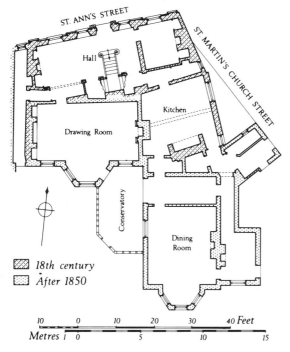

(286) Moorland House. Ground floor.

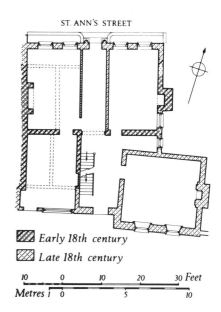

(287) No. 82 St. Ann's Street. Ground floor.

two-storeyed and less spacious than at present, but about the end of the 18th century it was heightened and the N. front was rebuilt 5 ft. N. of the former alignment. The late 18th-century N. front (Plate 75) has a central doorway with Tuscan columns supporting a semicircular hood with a reeded frieze. In the E. elevation the outline of the original range (with flint-banded walls) can be distinguished. The S. elevation is tile-hung. Inside, the main rooms have late 18th-century joinery and plaster-work. The elegant open-string stairs have scrolled spandrels and turned balusters. J.M. Peniston made a plan of the house in 1853 (W.R.O., 451/191).

(288) **Houses**, pair, Nos. 78–80, are two-storeyed with brick walls banded with flint, and with tiled roofs; they were built during the first half of the 18th century. Each house has a symmetrical facade of two bays with a central doorway. Two original three-light casement windows remain, but during the 19th century the other windows were made taller and narrower and were fitted with sashes. Inside the plans are of class T.

(289) **House**, No. 68, of two storeys with cellars and attics, is mainly of the mid 18th century, but the S.W. wing is earlier, perhaps 1610.

The N. front (Plate 78) is symmetrical and of five bays with plain sashed windows and a round-headed doorway in a pedimented doorcase (Plate 98). An extension at the E. end of the facade contains a service doorway in which one jamb and part of the adjacent quoin is hinged to make the opening wider than appears; the passage leads to a S.E. wing which formerly contained stables.

Inside, the 18th-century part of the house has a class-U plan. The main N. rooms have 18th-century joinery and plasterwork of good quality. The stairs in the S.W. quarter of the plan have Tuscan-column balustrades and cut strings with scrolled spandrels. The kitchen in the S.E. quarter adjoins the stable wing. Beyond the staircase, the S.W. wing has timber-framed walls with brick nogging; a ground-floor room contains a beam dated 1610. A 17th-century doorway in the cellar under the main N. range suggests that the 18th-century building replaces an earlier range.

(290) **House**, No. 66, of two storeys with timber-framed walls and tiled roofs, is of the early 16th century. In the upper storey of the three-bay N. front (Plate 62) the outer bays are jettied and the middle bay has the arch-braced eaves-plate of a class-C 'wealden' house.[1] The recess was filled in, perhaps in the 16th century. The lower storey now has shop windows in the two E. bays and a carriage through-way in the W. bay. Mouldings with run-out stops on the beam which spans the through-way show that its W. part originally spanned an external alley beneath the W. jetty of the first floor, while its E. part spanned an internal passage, perhaps the screens-passage of a hall (cf. (177)). The S. wing, contemporary with the street range, contains a kitchen with a large fireplace with brick jambs and a stout timber bres-

summer. Further S. is a range of two bays in which the first floor is jettied on the W.; the S. wall is of the 19th century. The roofs of the N. range have collared tie-beam trusses with king-struts and angle-struts.[2]

1. R.C.H.M., *Cambridgeshire* I, xlvi.
2. *Salisbury Times*, 1 Aug. 1969, p.4.

(291) **House**, No. 60, of two storeys with timber-framed walls and having a tiled roof continuous with that of No. 66 (Plate 62), is probably of the late 15th century. The jettied E. wall (with which the jetty of No. 66 originally combined to form a through-way) has recently been underbuilt, but part of the original flint E. wall of the lower storey remained *in situ* until 1969. Inside, chamfered beams and a doorway with a four-centred oak head are preserved. An inscribed date '1450' is bogus. On the first floor, the W. bay of No. 66 (290) has now been joined to No. 60.

(292) **House**, No. 8 Prospect Place, of two storeys and an attic, with rendered brick walls and a tiled roof, was built early in the 19th century. The W. front is symmetrical and of three bays.

(293) **Joiners' Hall**,[1] Nos. 56 and 58, is of two storeys with attics. The lower storey has walls of rendered brickwork and rubble; the main storey is of timber framework; the roofs are tiled. In style the building is of the first quarter of the 17th century. Much of the original N. front survives (Plate 67) with two first-floor windows, each of seven double-transomed square-headed lights with moulded and panelled mullions, projecting on grotesque brackets. The fascia board of the first-floor jetty has low relief carving of good quality. John Buckler drew the facade in 1805.[2] William Twopeny's drawing

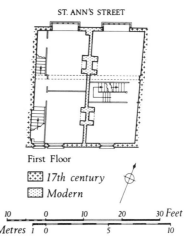

ST. ANN'S STREET

First Floor
▦ *17th century*
▨ *Modern*

10   0   10   20   30 Feet
Metres 1   0   5   10

(293) Joiner's Guild Hall. First floor.

of 1833 (Plate 10) shows an original doorway with a chamfered stone surround and a four-centred head, and a large 18th-century sashed window; both of these have gone. In the 19th century the lower storey of the N. front was remodelled and the interior of the building was extensively altered when a partition and fireplaces were inserted, making two houses. The accompanying plan was made in 1963 before reconversion to single occupation occasioned further changes. The hall now belongs to the National Trust.

1. Haskins, *Guilds*, 339—62.
2. Devizes Mus., Buckler album ix, f. 4.

(294) **House**, No. 54, of three storeys with cellars and attics, has brick walls and tiled roofs. The building appears to be mainly of the late 18th century, but earlier fittings are incorporated. The three-bay N. front has a central doorway under an elliptical hood with acanthus brackets, perhaps of the early 18th century. Inside, the oak staircase has slender turned balusters, plain column-shaped newel posts and moulded handrails of late 18th-century style. Some rooms have dados composed of reset 17th-century panelling. A brick wall on the E. of the garden has a stone panel inscribed 'T. Cooksey built it 1751'. There was a house here in 1649, but nothing of it is visible in the present structure.[1]

1. Parl. Svy., Foy 56 (Sar. 8), f. 11.

(295) **House**, No. 48, of two storeys with brick walls and a tiled roof, was built early in the 18th century. The W. bay of the three-bay N. front has a three-sided bow window in each storey; the E. bay has a doorway with a pediment-shaped hood. Inside, a first-floor room has a heavy plaster cornice and some plank-and-muntin panelling.

(296) **House**, No. 46, of three storeys and a cellar, has brick walls and a slated roof. The two lower storeys are of the early 18th century; the top storey was added in the 19th century. Inside, the N. ground-floor room, presumably the dining room, has fielded oak panelling in two heights. The first-floor drawing room occupies the whole width of the N. front. The stairs from the ground to the first floor are original.

(297) **Vale House**, No. 44, of three storeys with attics, with brick walls and tiled roofs, was built towards the end of the 18th century, perhaps in 1784, the date on a lead rainwater head. The N. front (Plate 76) is symmetrical and of five bays with a round-headed central doorway in a Roman-Doric doorcase with an open pediment (Plate 98). Inside, the plan is of class-U, but with the staircase set against the S. wall. The vestibule between the two N. rooms has plaster cross-vaulting. Three original chimneypieces are preserved.

The land on which the house stands is probably the tenement recorded in 1361 as a property of the cathedral choristers;[1] it was leased by them in 1400 to Robert Tavel and in 1460 to John Crise, a tanner.[2] In 1649, when occupied by John Snowe a parchment-maker, it comprised a hall, a kitchen, a buttery, two chambers and a 'work-house' (the deed of 1400 mentions a 'newly built house called workhous').[3] Nothing remains of these buildings, but the persistent occupation of the tenement by men engaged in tannery is notable since St. Ann's Street was Tanner Street in the 16th and 17th centuries.[4]

1. Dom. Bk. i, f. 19[v].
2. Sar. D. & C.M., Choristers' deeds, 1400, 1460.
3. Parl. Svy., Foy 56 (Sar. 8), f. 9.
4. V.C.H., *Wilts.* vi, 79.

(298) **Doorway** and **Buttresses**, of ashlar, reset in a garden some 50 yds. S. of Vale House (297), are of the late 15th or early 16th century. The doorway has a moulded elliptical head and continuous jambs and is set in a casement-moulded square-headed surround; the spandrels have quatrefoil roundels and cusped mouchettes. On each side are diagonal buttresses with weathered offsets. The origin of the doorway is unknown, but it was probably introduced as a feature in the extensive garden (see O.S., 1880) of a neighbouring house (see (299)). Near by is the N.E. angle and E. wall of the former Friars' Orchard (see (304)); the wall, about 300 ft. long, is mainly of 17th-century brickwork, but it has flint banding in the lower courses. The N. return has a thick flint base, perhaps mediaeval.

Monuments (299)—(304) appear on the map of Marsh Chequer, p. 119.

(299) **Rotunda**, now a gallery in Salisbury Museum, was built *c.* 1812 as the dining room of a large house which formerly stood immediately adjacent on the E.; most of the house was demolished in 1864 to make room for the museum.[1] The rotunda, 29½ ft. in diameter, has Corinthian pilasters internally and a coffered dome with rich foliate plasterwork (Plate 95).

1. *W.A.M.* lii (1948), 312—3. For a photograph of the demolished house, a large 18th-century building, see F. Stevens, *Salisbury Museums 1861— 1947* (Salisbury, 1947). An elevation by Peniston is in W.R.O. (451/74 (xxxiv)).

(300) **Houses**, two adjoining, Nos. 36 and 38, of two storeys with attics, with tile-hung timber-framed walls and tiled roofs, are of 16th-century origin. In the second half of the 18th century the two dwellings appear to have been united, and the jettied N. front (Plate 78) was remodelled and cased in mathematical tiles. Inside, the rooms of No. 38 have 18th-century joinery and plaster-

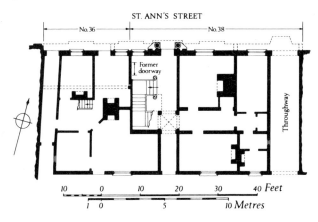

(300) Nos. 36-8 St. Ann's Street. Ground floor.

work. A ground-floor room is lined with 17th-century oak panelling. The first-floor drawing room in No. 38 has a shallow barrel-vaulted ceiling with end lunettes containing late 18th or early 19th-century allegorical paintings; in 1807 the house was occupied by B.C. Collins, the Salisbury printer.[1] In No. 36 the decorations are simpler than in No. 38.

The land on which the house stands belonged to St. Edmund's College from 1361, at latest, until the reformation.[2]

1.   Map, W.R.O., 451/331.
2.   Dom. Bk. i, f. 19ᵛ.

(301) **Albion Inn**, No. 32, of three storeys with brick walls and a slated roof, is of *c.* 1840.

(302) **Windover House**, Nos. 22–6, is mainly of two storeys with attics and has timber-framed walls, partly tile-hung, and tiled roofs. The single-storeyed hall was built late in the 14th century; scarfed purlin-ends and mortices for windbraces show that the hall range originally extended further W., where there now is work of *c.* 1600. The W. range also is of *c.* 1400 in origin, but it has been extensively altered and the S. end is incorporated with the later rebuilding of the W. part of the hall range. The E. range was built in the 16th century. The N. range, of the late 16th or early 17th century, was probably built by William Windover, a Salisbury merchant who died in 1632; it was refaced in the 19th century. The theory that the house includes part of the former

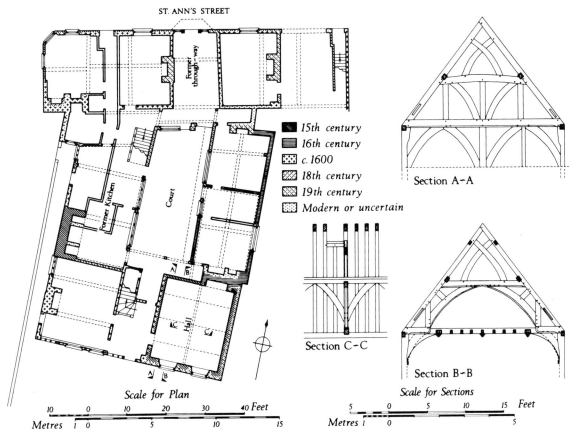

(302) WINDOVER HOUSE. Ground floor plan and details of hall roof.

Franciscan convent cannot be sustained.[1] In 1400 it belonged to Edmund Enefeld, clerk, the richest inhabitant of Meadow Ward, who died in 1403.[2] The messuage is clearly described in a deed of 1423 when, after the death of Enefeld's widow and her later husbands Richard Spencer and William Cambrigg (see (151)), it was sold to William Westbury;[3] it then extended from the street on the N. to the Friars' precinct wall on the S., and from the gateway and entrance leading into the Friary on the W. to a property of the Vicars Choral on the east. Documents relating to the last named property (now vacant) record that Windover House was occupied in 1549 by John Younger, in 1671 by Mrs. Denham, and in 1865 by Isaac White.[4]

The N. front of the *North Range* has mathematical-tile facing and 19th-century sashed windows. The middle bay of the lower storey was originally a carriage throughway, but it is now closed by doorways; above the N. doorway is a projecting window. Inside, the ground-floor rooms are spanned by stout beams with wide chamfers. On the first floor the three W. bays, originally one room, have beams cased in moulded and enriched early 17th-century plasterwork (Plate 93). The W. bay of this room has a 17th-century fireplace with a moulded stone surround with a four-centred head; the other fireplaces and chimneys in the N. range are of the 18th or 19th century.

In the lower storey of the *West Range* three main bays are defined by two stout chamfered beams supporting the first floor. These bays formerly comprised one large room and a big mediaeval fireplace on the W. of the S. bay, with chamfered stone jambs and a timber bressummer, indicates that it was a kitchen. On the first floor, partitions now form several small rooms, but original roof trusses indicate three chambers, each of two sub-bays. The middle chamber, originally open to the roof, was spanned by a hammerbeam and scissor-brace truss similar to that of the hall (see below); the flanking chambers were probably ceiled at collar-beam level. In the S. chamber, a late 16th or early 17th-century stone fireplace with a moulded four-centred head is built against the chimneybreast of the kitchen fireplace.

The W. part of the *South Range*, rebuilt c. 1600, has an oak staircase with massive newel posts with bulbous finials (Plate 87). The chimneybreast at the W. end of the range has, on the ground floor, a plain fireplace with brick jambs and a timber bressummer; it may once have been decorated with a panelled stone fascia of 1630 (see fittings). A window has moulded oak mullions. The corresponding first-floor fireplace has a stone four-centred head.

Although the two structures are contiguous, the timber framework of c. 1600 in the staircase vestibule is independant of the framework in the W. wall of the hall. The details of the latter with original wattle-and-daub infilling preserved behind glass, are shown on p. 125

(section A–A). The hall has a coved plaster ceiling of c. 1600 divided into panels by oak beams with multiple roll mouldings; originally, however, it was open to the roof and above the 17th-century ceiling is a roof truss of c. 1400 (section B–B) with hammerbeams supporting chamfered arch-braces below a collar-beam which is surmounted by crossed struts. The common rafters immediately W. of the hammerbeam truss are trimmed for a former smoke-louvre. The stone fireplace in the hall is of the late 15th or early 16th century and has a hollow-chamfered four-centred head in a roll-moulded square-headed surround.

The first floor of the *East Range* is jettied on the west. The S. ground-floor room has heavily moulded 16th-century beams and wall-plates; the fireplace is modern. The N. room and both first-floor rooms have chamfered beams. Windows in the first-floor rooms have ogee-moulded oak mullions. The roof has collared tie-beam trusses with queen-struts.

Fittings — A half-length portrait in oil on panel, preserved in the house, represents a man in early 17th-century dress holding a letter inscribed 'to my loving friend Mr. William Windover merchant in Hamburg'; at the corners of the panel are four shields: i arms of Windover with a scroll 'I breed him'; ii arms of the Merchant Adventurers of Hamburg with a scroll 'I fedd

Merchant mark of William Windover.

him'; iii arms of the Salters' Company with a scroll 'I made him free'; iv cartouche with date 1633 and merchant mark, with a scroll 'yet knowne by mee'.[5]

Three fragments of a carved stone slab found at Windover House and now in Salisbury Museum are probably part of a chimneypiece. Assembled, the fragments make up a frieze of five panels alternating with small trefoil-headed niches. The square central panel has a vase filled with flowers and the figures 30 on the right, presumably for 1630; the left-hand part of the panel is missing. The four flanking panels contain cusped roundels with painted shields: i arms of the Drapers' Company with a scroll 'I made him free'; ii as iv above, but without date; others defaced. A similar stone fragment preserved in Windover House has a shield-of-arms of the Salters' Company and two other shields, defaced; although carved with trefoil-headed niches and cusped roundels, precisely as described, these panels cannot be combined with those in the museum and therefore must come from a second chimneypiece.

The plot on which the house stands is bounded to E., W. and S. by a stout wall of flint, rubble and brick, in places some 6 ft. high. A partly defaced inscription records that it was built by William Windover in 16....[6] The wall on the S. is probably a replacement or a rebuilding of the Friars' wall, mentioned in 1423 (see above).

1. *W.A.M.*, xlvii (1935), 36–54.
2. Taxation list, 1399–1400 (Sar. Corp. MS., Z 238); Will, Dom. Bk. ii, f. 132.
3. Dom. Bk. iii, f. 80[v].
4. Parl. Svy., untitled (Sar. 11), f. 12. Sar. D. & C.M., Vic. Ch. terrier, 1671. Vic. Ch. deeds, 40/9.
5. *W.A.M.*, xxxix (1917), 502–4.
6. *W.A.M.*, xlvii (1935), 50 and plan opp. p. 40.

(303) **Cottage**, of two storeys with brick walls and a slate-covered roof, was built *c.* 1840. The symmetrical three-bay E. front is partly masked by a slightly later addition.

(304) **Houses and Stables**, Cradock House, Friary Court and Friary Cottages, probably date from 1619 when Matthew Bee (mayor 1600) was licensed to build on this site.[1] Cradock House is two-storeyed with an attic and has brick walls with ashlar dressings. Friary Court is three-storeyed with brick walls. Friary Cottages were originally single-storeyed. All have tiled roofs.

The E. front of *Cradock House* (Plate 70) retains early 17th-century windows with moulded stone

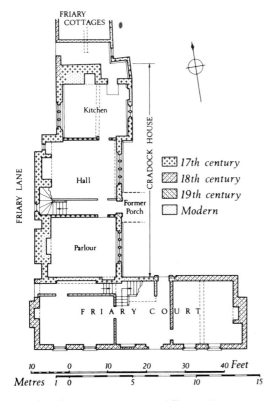

(304) Cradock House and Friary Court.

mullions, transoms and labels. The rendered bay near the centre indicates a former two-storeyed porch (cf. (264)). The W. elevation has two original chimneystacks ending in square-set and diagonally-set brick flues; they flank a gabled stair tower. Inside, the parlour retains an original plaster ceiling with moulded ribs in geometric panels with foliate terminals. The partition between the parlour and the hall is of timber framework and original, that on the N. of the entrance passage is later. The original dogleg stairs have chamfered newels and are continuous from the ground floor to the attic. First-floor rooms have moulded plaster cornices and the S. room has an original stone fireplace with a hollow-chamfered four-centred head.

Friary Court, mainly of the early 18th century, was originally an extension of Cradock House and probably replaces a former S. cross-wing; some 17th-century brickwork remains in the lower part of the N. wall. The range was originally two-storeyed. The top storey was added late in the 18th century and the range probably became a separate house at the same time, the stairs being of this period. The S. front is rendered and of six bays with plain sashed windows in each storey. In the E. elevation, which has no openings, the gable of the early 18th-century two-storeyed range is distinguishable in the brickwork. The N. elevation has an 18th-century doorcase uniform with that of Cradock House. Inside, the E. ground-floor room and the corresponding first-floor room have heavily moulded early 18th-century cornices; elsewhere the decorations are of the late 18th and early 19th century. Early 17th-century oak panelling and a richly carved chimneypiece, formerly in this house, are now at Upp Hall, Braughing, Herts.

Friary Cottages, of 17th-century origin, were extensively altered early in the 18th century to provide stables, coach house and coachman's cottage for Cradock House. The range now forms two dwellings.

The name *Friary* alludes to the Franciscan convent which stood a short distance to S.E. from its foundation in 1230 until its dissolution in 1538.[2] Little remains of the former convent, but the position and extent of its precinct can be deduced from documents and maps. Naish (Plate 16) indicates a rectangle about 130 yds. by 170 yds. containing gardens and a paper mill; a watercourse flowing under the mill may originally have provided drainage for the extensive convent buildings described in 1539.[3] The precinct walls were on N., W. and E. The N. wall probably corresponded with that on the S. of Windover House (302). The W. wall is mentioned in a deed of 1413.[4] Referring to the E. wall, city surveys mention in 1618 'the Friars' wall now Mr. Bee's', and in 1672 and 1716 the 'wall of the Friars' garden'.[5] There were two gateways. The main entrance from St. Ann's Street was at the N.W. corner.[6] A gateway in 'Frerenstrete'[7] may have been some 40 yds. S. of the main gate, possibly in the position where a narrow road appears on a sketch map of the area made in 1807.[8] Friars' Orchard, as the E. part of the precinct was still named in 1807, was subsequently attached to the large house in St. Ann's Street which was demolished in 1864 to make room for the museum (299). Foundations of flint walls found in 1968 about 100 yds. S. of the museum probably represent the mediaeval convent.[9]

A buttressed and apsed building shown on O.S. (1880) some 30 yds. E. of Friary Court was an early 19th-century *Aviary*. It was pulled down in 1961, but photographs are preserved in N.M.R.

1. Sar. Corp. MS., Ledger C, f. 268[V].
2. V.C.H., *Wilts.* iii, 239.
3. *W.A.M.*, xlvii (1935), 36.
4. Dom. Bk. iii, f. 4.
5. Sar. Corp. MS., O/117/1 and 4, f. 52. See also monument (298).
6. Dom. Bk. iii, f. 80[V], 1423.
7. Sar. Corp. MS., deed 1396.
8. Map of Miss Edward's Estate, Peniston papers, W.R.O., 451/331.
9. *W.A.M.*, 64 (1969), 129; *Med. Arch.*, 13 (1969), 248.

Monuments (305)–(310) appear on the map of White Hart Chequer, p. 116.

(305) **House**, No. 18 St. Ann's Street, of two storeys with an attic, has timber-framed walls and tiled roofs and is of 14th-century origin. In 1413 it was referred to as the angle tenement, once John Baudrey's, now John Becket's. In his will (1416) Becket left his 'angle tenement with shops opposite the friars manor' to be sold, and his executors sold it in the same year to Wm. Phebis.[1] By 1618 it was a property of the mayor and commonalty and was described as a 'corner messuage, tenement and gardens near Friars Bridge where are divers tenements and gardens holden by divers poor people at will'.[2] It occurs in later surveys of city lands,[3] and appears in outline on a plan of 1854 by Peniston.[4] The E. range is of the 14th century; on the W. is an 18th-century

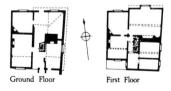

Ground Floor   First Floor

brick-fronted extension. In the gabled N. front of the original house (Plate 60) the first and attic floors are jettied; the first floor is also jettied on the east. Original timber framework with 'St. Andrew's cross' bracing survives in the upper storey, but in the lower storey it has been supplanted by 18th-century brickwork. Inside,

the 14th-century house comprises two rooms on each floor. Between them is a stone chimneybreast, probably inserted, with ground and first-floor fireplaces. The ground-floor fireplace is partly blocked and partly cut away. That on the first floor retains chamfered stone jambs and a later timber lintel; beside it is an 18th-century round-headed recess with shaped shelves. The roof retains many 14th-century members including a collared truss with an upper king-strut supporting a ridge-purlin.

1. Dom. Bk. iii, ff. 4, 26, 27[V].
2. Sar. Corp. MS., O/117/1; Survey, 1618.
3. Sar. Corp. MS., O/117/4, ff. 80–9; O/117/8, ff. 52–3.
4. W.R.O., 451/192 (Mrs. Tinney's leasehold).

(306) **Cottages**, three adjoining, Nos. 12–16, are of two storeys with brick walls and tiled roofs. Nos. 14 and 16, shown as one house on O.S., 1880, are mainly of the 18th century, but they include earlier materials; the W. end of No. 14 (visible in No. 12) incorporates the remains of a cruck truss. The fireplace in No. 14 has a moulded timber bressummer. No. 12 was rebuilt in the 19th century, but it retains 17th-century beams. Plans by J.M. Peniston, 1855, are preserved (see (307)).

(307) **House**, No. 6 St. Ann's Street, partly of three storeys, partly two-storeyed with a cellar and partly single-storeyed, has brick walls and slate-covered roofs. The part of the house W. of the stairs was built *c.* 1750. It is three-storeyed and has a N. front of four bays with plain sashed windows and a round-headed doorway in a classical surround with wooden columns and pediment.

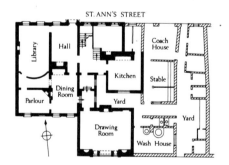

ST. ANN'S STREET

Further E. the middle part of the house has a 17th-century N. elevation of three bays with a weathered plinth, a rounded brick stringcourse and heavy brick quoins; it has rebated stone cellar windows, each of two square-headed lights, transomed mezzanine windows of similar construction and timber two-light windows in the upper storey. To S. of the mezzanine room the single-storeyed kitchen and drawing room are of the early 19th century; probably they were built *c.* 1812 by J.C.P. Tinney, a prominent solicitor.[1] To E. of the service rooms and drawing room, Peniston's plan of 1855 shows a coach house, stables, wash-house etc.;[2] these, shown here in a light tone, have recently been converted to a modern house with a 'Georgian' facade.

Inside, the oak stairs in the 17th-century part of the house appear to be of that period, having close strings, fretted splats instead of balusters and newel posts with shaped finials (Plate 87). The curved S. wall of the 18th-century library is fitted with original bookshelves and has a disguised door; other rooms have fielded panelling and 18th-century joinery of good quality. The drawing room has polished mahogany doors and a columned window (Plate 96).

1. *W.A.M.*, 52 (1947–8), 312; Benson & Hatcher, 657.
2. W.R.O., 451/192.

(308) **House**, No. 4, of three storeys with tile-hung timber-framed walls and a tiled roof, was built about the middle of the 18th century. The N. front has mathematical tiling and there is a projecting sashed window in the second storey.

(309) **House**, No. 2, of three storeys with brick walls and a slate-covered roof, was built during the first quarter of the 19th century. A date stone of 1814 is set in the S. part of the E. boundary wall of the site.

(310) **Old Bell Inn**, mainly of three storeys, has walls faced with 18th-century brickwork, and tiled roofs. The brickwork conceals a 16th-century timber-framed structure, originally jettied N. and W. at the first floor and W. at the second floor. In 1972 when the W. facade was stripped of rendering the sawn-off second-floor jetty beams were exposed. The first-floor jetties are under-built. Inside, original beams and posts remain. A two-storeyed stable range on the S. is probably contemporary with the inn.

EXETER STREET

The location of monuments (311)–(332) is shown on the general map in the end-pocket.

(311) **Houses**, pair, Nos. 76–7, two-storeyed with attics, with brick walls and tiled roofs, were built during the second half of the 18th century. The W. fronts have plain sashed windows and round-headed doorways with wooden pediments. Inside, original fittings remain.

(312) **Houses**, pair, Nos. 81–2, are of three storeys and have brick walls with ashlar plinths and quoins and slate-covered roofs. They appear to be of the first quarter of the 19th century. The entrance doorcases appear to be early 18th-century material reused.

(313) **Houses**, range of three, Nos. 83–5, of three storeys with brick walls and slated roofs, appear to be slightly later in date than Nos. 81–2. The combined facade is approximately symmetrical and of five bays, No. 84 having one window in each storey, the others two. A projecting first-floor window forms a central feature. Adjacent, Nos. 86 and 87 are of *c.* 1850.

(314) **Houses**, pair, Nos. 90–1, of two storeys with attics, with brick walls and tiled roofs, are of *c.* 1700. The W. fronts have a brick plat-band and a moulded brick cornice. The front ground-floor room of No. 90 is lined throughout with softwood panelling in two heights.

(315) **House**, No. 95, the presbytery belonging to St. Osmund's Church (10), is of two storeys with brick walls and tiled roofs. The symmetrical late 18th-century five-bay W. front, with a round-headed central doorway, plain sashed windows and a small pediment over the central bay, conceals two 16th-century houses. Inside, the N. house has intersecting ceiling beams in both storeys. The three-bay roof, ridged N.–S., has collared tie-beam trusses with clasped purlins; the S. tie-beam is moulded. The S. house has 18th-century panelling in the front ground-floor room and a dado of 17th-century panelling in the room above. The two-bay roof is similar to that of the N. house although the two roofs are not continuous.

(316) **House**, No. 96, of two storeys with brick and timber-framed walls and with a tiled roof, is of 16th-century origin. The early structure is masked by a symmetrical late 18th-century three-bay facade similar to that of No. 95. Inside, the S. ground-floor room has an open fireplace with stone jambs and a cambered oak bressummer. The corresponding chamber has a smaller fireplace.

(317) **Cottages**, pair, Nos. 99–100, of two storeys with timber-framed and brick walls and with tiled roofs, are of 16th-century origin. They were refronted in the 18th century.

(318) **Houses**, row of four, Nos. 101–4, of three storeys with timber-framed walls and tiled roofs, are mainly of the early 17th century, but the top storey and the rendered W. fronts are of the 18th century. The first floor is jettied on the west.

(319) **Houses**, row of three, Nos. 105–7, of three storeys with attics, with brick walls and tiled roofs, are of the late 18th or early 19th century.

(320) **Crown and Anchor Inn**, of two storeys with timber-framed walls, partly brick-faced and partly hung

with mathematical tiles, and with tiled roofs, is of 16th-century origin. The W. front has 18th-century sashed windows and is jettied on the first floor. Inside, there are original timber-framed partitions. The roof has collared tie-beam trusses with clasped purlins, windbraces and queen-struts.

(321) **Houses**, two adjacent, Nos. 109–9a, are two-storeyed with attics and have rendered timber-framed walls and tiled roofs; they were built as one house in the 16th century. The rendered W. front now has 18th-century sashed windows and a 19th-century shop window.

(322) **Houses**, three adjoining, Nos. 110–2, are three-storeyed with brick walls and tiled and slate-covered roofs. They were built early in the 19th century.

(323) **House**, No. 114, demolished *c.* 1965, was of two storeys with brick and tile-hung walls and tiled roofs; it was built during the second half of the 18th century.

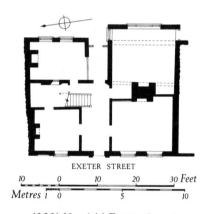

EXETER STREET

10   0   10   20   30 *Feet*

Metres 1 0   5   10

(323) No. 144 Exeter Street.

The lower storey of the four-bay W. front had segmental-headed sashed windows, and a doorway with a wooden doorcase with Tuscan pilasters and a moulded entablature. Inside, there was some fielded panelling; two first-floor rooms had coved ceilings.

(324) **St. Elizabeth's School**, house, of three storeys with brick walls and a slated roof, was built early in the 19th century. The W. front is symmetrical and of three bays with stone plat-bands and a moulded stone cornice. The central doorway (with a later porch) is flanked by three-light sashed windows and there are corresponding windows in the upper storeys. Inside, the plan is a variant of class U.

ST. NICHOLAS' ROAD

(325) **House**, demolished in 1964, was of two storeys with brick walls and tiled roofs; it dated from the first quarter of the 19th century. The nearly symmetrical three-bay E. front had a central doorway and segmental-headed sashed windows.

(326) **Myrfield House**, of three storeys with brick walls and slate-covered roofs, was advertised as new-built in 1813 (*S.J.*, 4 Oct.); until recently it was the property of the Dean and Chapter. The symmetrical three-bay S. front, of grey brick in contrast to the red brick sides and rear, has a central doorway enclosed in a scrolled wrought-iron porch which partly supports a three-sided first-floor bow window; elsewhere in the S. front there are plain sashed windows. The N., E. and W. walls are without any openings, probably because they overlook the gardens of the former Bishop's Palace. The ground plan, constricted by a narrow site, comprises a central vestibule with one room to E. and one to W. The elliptical staircase at the N. end of the vestibule is lit by a window in the roof. To E. and W. of the house, single-storeyed ranges with cellars are of the 18th century and originally were cottages and shops.

(327) **De Vaux House**, of two storeys with an attic, with walls of ashlar, flint and brickwork and with tiled roofs, is mainly of *c.* 1700, but it incorporates late mediaeval walls which probably survive from a building associated with De Vaux College, *Domus de Valle Scholarium* (1260–1542).[1] A plan of *c.* 1825 names the site 'Magdalen Penitentiary'.[2]

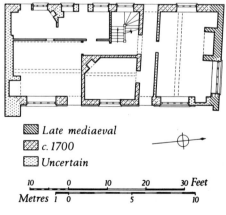

░ *Late mediaeval*
▨ *c. 1700*
▢ *Uncertain*

10   0   10   20   30 *Feet*

Metres 1 0   5   10

(327) DE VAUX HOUSE. Ground floor.

The N. wall, mainly of flint with some original tile coursing, includes a mediaeval chimneybreast. The N.E. corner has an ashlar quoin and a small square-set buttress of one stage with weathered capping. The brick-faced E. front has an ashlar plinth of uncertain date and several 18th-century windows; a doorway with a pointed head is of the 19th century. The W. elevation, of rubble and brick, was rebuilt in the 18th century. The tile-hung S. wall is of uncertain date.

Inside, the N. fireplace has jambs partly stone and partly brick, and a chamfered oak bressummer. Beams and joinery throughout the house are of c. 1700 and later; one room has an oak chimneypiece made up with early 17th-century carved panelling and uprights. The roof has a collared tie-beam truss with queen-struts.

1. *W.A.M.*, xlvi (1934), 637–51; V.C.H., *Wilts.* iii, 369–85.
2. W.R.O., 451/170.

(328) **House**, No. 8 St. Nicholas' Road, is of two storeys and has walls partly of brick and rubble and partly tile-hung. The roofs are tiled. The walls and roof include mediaeval material which probably survives from the *Domus de Valle Scholarium* (see (327)), but the row of mediaeval windows shown in an engraving of c. 1834 is no longer seen.[1] Nevertheless, Hall's assertion that 'the whole edifice is now demolished' is inaccurate.

The lower part of the S. front, of flint and rubble with bands of tile laid in herringbone coursing, includes the chamfered jambs and sill of a former window, probably mediaeval; the upper storey is masked by mathematical tiles. In the gabled E. wall a three-light stone window, probably of the 17th century, has been made into a doorway. An ashlar quoin at the N.E. corner is probably mediaeval. A brick bay projecting near the middle of the N. elevation is of the 17th century. Inside, the rooms have nothing earlier than the second quarter of the 19th century, but the roof includes stout smoke-blackened rafters with mortices in positions to suggest a former scissor-braced rafter roof; they are probably of the 13th century. Two undated 19th-century plans are preserved.[2]

1. Hall, *Memorials*, plate xvii; *W.A.M.*, xlvi (1934), opp. 650.
2. W.R.O., 451/170; 451/174.

(329) **House**, adjoining the foregoing on the W., is partly two-storeyed and partly single-storeyed with an attic and has brick walls and tiled roofs. The two-storeyed N. elevation, probably of the first half of the 18th century, is symmetrical and of three bays with a square-headed central doorway flanked by gauged brick pilasters and with segmental-headed sashed windows in both storeys; all openings have brick flat arches with key-stones; the window sills in the upper storey have brick aprons. Flanking the elevation are two giant Roman-Doric pilasters of gauged brickwork with stone capitals supporting triglyph frieze-blocks and a moulded stone cornice. The modern S. elevation includes reset fragments of an 18th-century stone frieze of unknown provenance. To the W. is a modern extension. Inside, a room is lined with 17th-century oak wainscot brought from elsewhere.

(330) **De Vaux Place**, terrace of six houses, each of three storeys with attics and with rendered brick walls and slate-covered roofs, was built c. 1830 probably by John Peniston; site-plans for the project are among Peniston's papers in W.R.O.[1] Inside, the houses have simple joinery and plasterwork of the period, but the westernmost contains an oak staircase balustrade of c. 1730 with a fist-shaped curtail and fluted column-shaped newel posts and balusters, evidently brought from elsewhere.[2] A stone in the garden wall of the adjoining house is inscribed 'Queene .....eth 1585'.

1. W.R.O., 451/170.
2. cf. R.C.H.M., *Dorset* III, lxii.

(331) **Cottages**, pair, Nos. 16 and 18, of three storeys with attics, with walls partly of timber framework and partly of brick (Plate 19), were originally one house; it was built late in the 16th or early in the 17th century. The embankment of Ayleswade Bridge causes the entrances to be at first-floor level. The second floor is jettied on the east. Inside, an original chimneybreast occurs about the middle of the W. wall, but its openings have been blocked; the existing fireplaces in the gabled N. and S. ends of the range are of the 19th century.

(332) **Houses**, two adjacent, Nos. 9 and 11, of three storeys with brick and tile-hung walls and with slate-covered roofs, were built early in the 19th century. In the S. elevation the W. part of the lower storey, of ashlar, is of 1774 (*see* monument (17)).

St. John's Chapel, see (11), p. 45.

Ayleswade Bridge, see (17), p. 51.

St. Nicholas's Hospital, see (26), p. 54.

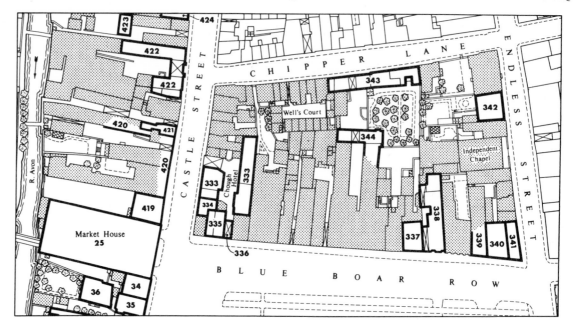

Monuments in Blue Boar Chequer, Castle Street and Cheesemarket.

ST. EDMUND WARD

The monuments in this ward (333–475) are grouped, as in St. Martin Ward, under the names of chequers and streets (see p. 59).

BLUE BOAR CHEQUER

(333) **Chough Hotel**, comprising E. and W. ranges flanking a courtyard, has timber-framed walls extensively cased with brickwork, and tiled roofs. The buildings are of 16th-century origin but have been greatly altered. The E. range, of three storeys with attics and cellars, has an 18th-century W. front of rendered brickwork. Inside, winding stairs with turned balusters and square newels with turned pendants appear to be of the late 17th century. The two-storeyed W. range is faced with modern imitation timber framework, but 16th-century chamfered beams and a little original framework are seen internally.

(334) **House**, No. 2 Castle Street, of three storeys with brick walls and slate-covered roofs, was built *c.* 1820. In the symmetrical three-bay W. front the lower storey contains modern shops; the upper storeys have plain sashed windows and, on the first floor, a projecting window.

(335) **Houses**, Nos. 34–5 Blue Boar Row, are three-storeyed with attics and have brick walls and slate-covered mansard roofs; they were built early in the 19th century. A photograph of 1856 is in Salisbury Museum.

(336) **House**, No. 36 Blue Boar Row, of three storeys with rendered walls and a slate-covered roof, is probably of the early 19th century. The lower storey comprises a through-way leading to the yard of the Chough Hotel (333); above is a projecting sashed window.

(337) **House**, No. 45 Blue Boar Row, of three storeys with an attic, with brick walls and slate-covered roofs, dates from the first half of the 19th century. The symmetrical three-bay S. front was built after 1857 in replacement of the original facade seen in old photographs (Lov. Cn., 142; also Plate 14). Inside, a plain staircase survives above first-floor level.

(338) **House with Shop**, No. 47 Blue Boar Row, is of two and three storeys with rendered brick walls and tiled roofs. The main building, of three storeys, dates from the second quarter of the 18th century; Thomas Cooper obtained the lease in 1724 and a terrier of 1740 mentions 'Mr. Cooper's new-built house'.[1] The present front is of the late 19th century, but the original four-bay facade with plain sashed windows appears in early photographs (Plate 14).[2] On a drawing of *c.* 1790 the same facade is labelled 'Parade Coffee Tavern' (Plate 8).

Inside, the ground floor has been extensively altered to make a modern shop, but the first-floor rooms have moulded plaster cornices and 18th-century joinery. The oak staircase has three turned balusters to each tread, a stout moulded handrail and a dado with fielded panelling. A plan of 1852 is preserved.[3]

The N. part of the plot is occupied by a mid 17th-century two-storeyed building. In the terrier mentioned above, its ground and first-floor rooms are named under the heading 'old building'. They are also named in a survey of 1716 where one first-floor room is called a 'parlour wainscotted all round up' and another 'a large dining-room wainscotted'.[4] The two panelled rooms still exist.

1. Sar. Corp. MS., O/117/1, f. 91.
2. Lov. Cn., 142.
3. W.R.O., 451/191; 451/73 (xi).
4. Sar. Corp. MS., O/117/1, f. 90.

(339) **House**, No. 49 Blue Boar Row, is of three storeys and has an early 19th-century S. front of brick-work with stone quoins and a moulded stone cornice. The lower storey has a modern shop window; above, each storey has three plain sashed windows. Inside, the rooms have been much changed in the construction of a shop.

(340) **House**, No. 50 Blue Boar Row, of three storeys with brick walls and a tiled roof, is of the second half of the 18th century. Above modern shop windows the five-bay S. front has plain sashed windows in each storey, a rendered plat-band and a moulded cornice. Inside, the pine staircase has turned balusters, moulded handrails and a panelled dado. A first-floor room is lined with fielded panelling in two heights and has a moulded wood cornice. A round-headed niche has shaped shelves and fluted pilasters.

(341) **House**, at the S.E. corner of the chequer, is of two storeys with an attic and has tile-hung timber-framed walls and a tiled roof; it appears to be of 14th-century origin. A document of 1268 records that this corner site was the property of Hugh Nugg[1] and it was still called Nuggscorner in the 15th century.[2] In 1649 the lessee was Thomas Hooper.[3]

In the upper storey of the E. elevation, formerly jettied, but now underbuilt with modern shop windows, an original two-light oak window with hollow-chamfered jambs and cusped ogee heads is blocked internally, but exposed externally behind glass. The gabled S. front has no noteworthy features. Inside, the first-floor rooms have defaced roll-moulded and ogee-moulded longitudinal beams morticed centrally to the plain tie-beams of the roof trusses. The four-bay roof has collared tie-beam trusses in which there are mortices to indicate lower angle-braces and lower king-struts, now gone.

1. Benson & Hatcher, 52, 735.
2. *Liber Niger*, 68.
3. Parl. Svy., Foy 39 (Sar. 4), f.9; Foy 83 (Sar. 12), f. 15.

(342) **House**, No. 13 Endless Street, of three storeys with brick walls and tiled roofs, if of *c.* 1800. The interior has been made into modern offices and of the original building only the roof and the symmetrical five-bay E. front remain. The central doorway is flanked by wooden three-quarter columns supporting a hood, elliptical on plan, with a moulded neo-classical entablature and a delicate gothic cornice (Plate 99). Elsewhere there are plain sashed windows. The roofs have collared tie-beam trusses with queen-struts and butt-purlins.

(343) **Houses**, five adjoining, Nos. 26–34 Chipper Lane, are of three storeys with brick walls and tiled roofs and date from late in the 18th century; a lead rainwater-head in No. 32 bears the date 1788. The N. fronts are asymmetrical and have plain doorways and sashed windows; a carriage through-way between Nos. 28 and 30 leads to the yard of the former Boar Inn (344). Inside, the houses have simple 18th-century joinery. Two of these houses probably correspond with those advertised in 1790 as 'new-built, fit for small families' (*S.J.*, 25 Oct.).

(344) **Building**, once a wing of the Boar Inn and now part of a shop, is of two storeys and has walls partly of flint with ashlar dressings, but mainly of timber frame-work extensively replaced by or cased in modern brick-work, and an original timber roof covered with modern tiles. A written contract of 1444 between William Ludlow and John Fayrbowe, carpenter,[1] almost certainly relates to the construction of this range.[2] In 1404 a tenement with shops, cottages and gardens on this site, extending from the Market Place to Chipper Lane, was given by Thomas Burford to William Toyl on Toyl's marriage to Burford's daughter Joanna.[3] Deeds dated between 1424 and 1662, among the Eyre papers at Newhouse, Redlynch, show that the messuage called Burfordesplace (1424) belonged to the Ludlow family by 1448 and was called the Blue Boar by 1451. In 1455 William Ludlow paid rent *pro hospitio suo vocato Boore prius Thome Burford*.[4] In 1595, when the inn belonged to Anthony Parry of the Close, and George Story was innkeeper, the buildings comprised a hall, two parlours, kitchen, buttery, cellar, seventeen chambers, eight shops or warehouses, other small rooms, and a garden on the N. By 1662 the property belonged to the Eyres. The inn continued to exist under its original name until early in the 19th century.[5]

In the lower storey (obliterated *c.* 1970) the few original wall-posts formerly seen had chamfered corners with run-out stops; they rose from a timber sill on an ashlar plinth. Chamfered beams supported the first floor. In the two E. bays of the N. side a flint wall with ashlar dressings replaced or masked the timber framework; against it was a chimneybreast with a chamfered plinth and weathered offsets; the fireplace was blocked. In the

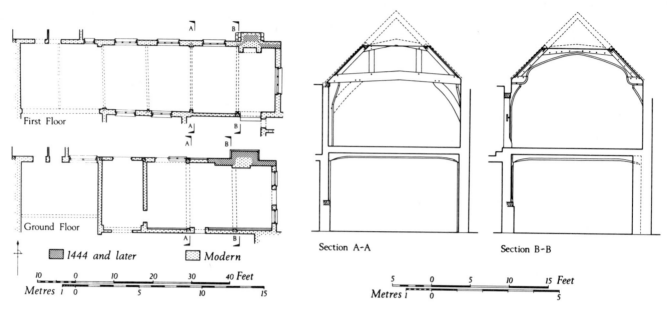

(344) Remains of The Boar Inn.

upper storey (now a restaurant) the two E. bays of the range appear at one time to have comprised a separate room, the second tie-beam from the E. having mortices for the studs of a partition. The 1st and 3rd roof trusses are false hammerbeam collar trusses; the 5th, now hidden, is probably the same; the 2nd and 4th trusses have braced and cambered tie-beams, cambered collars and queen-struts.

To the S., a building at right-angles to the range of 1444 has a brick E. wall with two stone windows, perhaps of the late 17th century.

Three round stones, each about 11 ins. in diameter, set close together in a triangle in the pavement of the yard on the N. of the 15th-century range, two with iron studs set centrally, are said to mark the place of the execution of the Duke of Buckingham in 1483.[6]

1. W.R.O., 164/1/14.
2. *Arch. J.*, cxx (1964), 236—41. Salzman, *Building*, 516—7.
3. Dom. Bk. ii, f. 99.
4. *Liber Niger*, 79.
5. Haskins, *Guilds*, 314.
6. Benson & Hatcher, 207.

THREE SWANS CHEQUER

(345) **Warehouse**, No. 5 Winchester Street, formerly part of the Three Swans Hotel,[1] is of three storeys with brick walls and tiled roofs and was built probably *c.* 1770.[2] The five-bay S. front has, on the E., the opening to a carriage through-way; above it are Palladian windows in both upper storeys; elsewhere there are plain sashed windows. Above are a heavy brick cornice and a shaped pediment. Inside, some 18th-century chimney-pieces remain.

1. Kingdon & Shearm. O.S., 1880.
2. *S.J.*, 23 Mar., 1772.

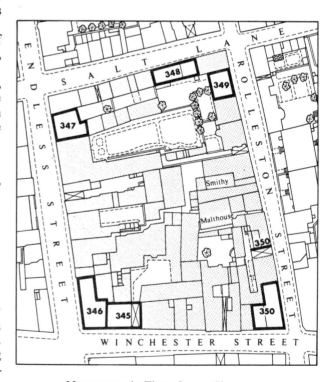

Monuments in Three Swans Chequer.

(346) **House**, No. 2 Endless Street, now a shop and warehouse, is three-storeyed with brick walls and tiled roofs and appears to be mainly of the first half of the 18th century; a two-storeyed wing on the N. is of 17th-century origin. Above modern shop windows the four-bay S. front, flanked by large pilasters, has two storeys of plain sashed windows. Inside, some rooms have moulded cornices and panelled dados. The S. wall of the N. wing is of 17th-century timber framework.

(347) **House**, No. 12 Endless Street, now two-storeyed but formerly of three storeys, has brick walls and tiled roofs; it is of mid 18th-century origin, but has been much altered. The five-bay W. front was originally symmetrical, with a central doorway with a wooden pediment and with sashed windows with keystones. Several of the windows have been blocked and two have been raised and enlarged to correspond with altered floor-levels. Inside, some original panelled dados remain.

(348) **Warehouses**, two, standing end-to-end on the S. side of Salt Lane, are two-storeyed with brick walls and tiled roofs. Some internal timber framework, with jowl-headed posts supporting collared tie-beam trusses, suggests that the buildings are of 16th-century origin. Late in the 18th century the exterior was rebuilt in brickwork, with plain segmental-headed openings. (Demolished, 1978.)

(349) **House**, of two storeys with brick walls and a tiled roof, dates from the second half of the 18th century. In the E. front the upper storey retains six uniform sashed windows; below, the openings have been altered and the position of the original doorway is unknown. The interior has been entirely modernised.

(350) **Old George Inn**, at the S.E. corner of the chequer, is two-storeyed with attics and has rendered brick walls and tiled roofs. Some beams and roof-trusses appear to be of c. 1500; the facades were rebuilt about the middle of the 17th century and the windows were remodelled c. 1800 (Plate 79). The central doorway in the approximately symmetrical S. front has fluted wooden columns supporting a flat hood with foliate enrichment. Some ground-floor windows have keystones with human masks. The E. gable of the S. range has two blocked 17th-century oval windows with hollow-chamfered stone surrounds. Inside, the first-floor rooms in the W. range have chamfered ceiling beams with shaped stops. The oak stairs from the first floor to the attic are of the 17th century, with heavy turned balusters, close strings and plain newel posts (Plate 87); lower, the staircase is of c. 1800. The roofs have collared tie-beam trusses supporting chamfered purlins.

THREE CUPS CHEQUER

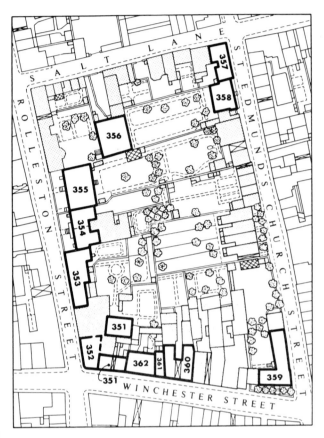

Monuments in Three Cups Chequer.

(351) **Balle's Place**, demolished in 1962,[1] comprised the remains of a substantial 14th-century courtyard house and associated tenements. The timber-framed buildings had been extensively remodelled and many walls were rebuilt in 18th and 19th-century brickwork, but much of the original three-bay hall roof survived, together with a range on Winchester Street.

The hall was built during the third quarter of the 14th century by John Balle (d. 1387), a wool merchant who appears to have come to Salisbury from elsewhere and who held no public office in the town. Soon after 1416 the property was acquired by Walter Shirley (mayor 1408, 1416). In 1455 the tenant was the bishop's bailiff, John Whittokesmeade, the place having by then become city property.[2] Between 1477 and 1565 documents are lacking, but after 1591 when the tenant was Zachary Lyming (mayor 1598) the sequence of leases preserved in the city archives is almost uninterrupted.[3] During the 17th–19th centuries the buildings were divided among numerous tenants. The accompanying plan of the property as it was in the middle of the 19th century is taken from surveys of 1851–5 by J.M. Peniston;[4] it shows that the original walls had by then largely gone. Nevertheless, in the two areas where shading has been added by RCHM to Peniston's survey, mediaeval roofs remained *in situ*. The middle part of No. 27 Winchester Street, a two-storeyed house with brick walls and tiled roofs, was spanned by the original hall roof; to S., Nos. 25 and 29 Winchester Street also enclosed mediaeval timber framework.

Apart from the roof, No. 27 had few notable features. The oak stairs were of 18th-century origin, but early in the 19th century deal lattice work imitating 'chinoiserie' of the 1750s had been put in place of the balustrades;

at the same time pairs of elliptical wooden arches with square pilasters were inserted in both storeys, doubtless to strengthen the staircase floors and ceilings. In the attic (Plate 83) the middle part of the 14th-century hall roof remained, with stout cambered tie-beams supporting crown-posts, collar-purlins and collar-rafters. Below, in the party-wall which divided the former hall between two tenements were the chamfered arch-braces, queen-posts, hammerbeams and lower braces of a hammerbeam queen-post truss. The spandrels of the truss were filled with vertical boarding. Mortices in the queen-posts indicated longitudinal arch-braces to support arcade plates. The W. truss survived because it was built into the party-wall; that on the E. had perished below the level

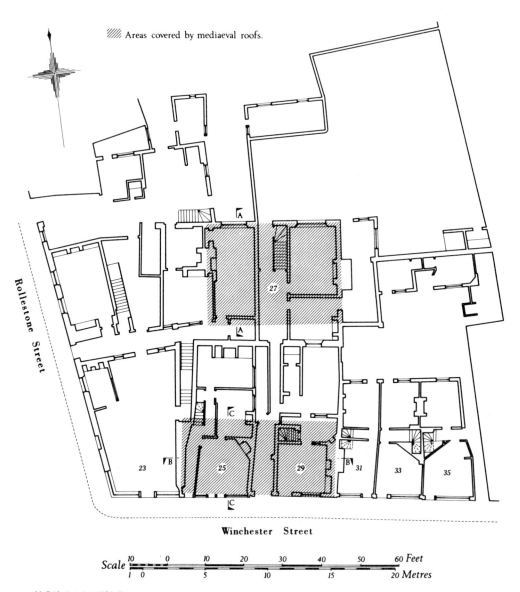

(351) BALLE'S PLACE. Plan of houses in Three Cups Chequer, 1851-5 (after Peniston).

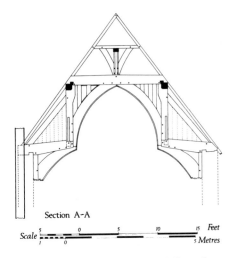

Section A-A

Scale (Feet / Metres)

(351) BALLE'S PLACE. Hall roof.

of the tie-beam. The arcade plates rested on the jowled heads of the queen-posts and had moulded oak cornices. In the W. end truss of the hall, large vertical speres in place of the queen-posts indicated the probable position of the original hall screens. A stout brick chimneybreast at the E. end of the former hall was probably added in the 16th century.

To S. of the hall, Nos. 25 and 29 Winchester Street were small two-storeyed houses with brick walls and tiled roofs. Demolition revealed that the early 19th-century brickwork masked a 14th-century timber-framed range with chamfered posts, about 10 ins. square, braced to a crown-post rafter roof in which the crown-posts were braced longitudinally, but not laterally. The

first floor was jettied on the S., but had been underbuilt. The range was of four bays, but that to W. was narrower than the others; doubtless the narrow bay was an original through-way to the courtyard, presumably corresponding with the S. entrance mentioned in a document of 1423.[5] Another entrance, wide enough for carts, led into the tenement from Rolleston Street. The garden contained a dovecot.[6]

During demolition some mediaeval ridge-tiles with glazed and serrated cresting were found.

1. Upon demolition the hall roof was dismantled and the timbers were stored for eventual reuse.
2. *Liber Niger*, 85.
3. *W.A.M.*, 59 (1964), 155–67.
4. W.R.O., 451/185–6.
5. Dom. Bk., iii, f. 171.
6. Sar. Corp. MS., Reg. of Demises of City Land, 1477.

(352) **House and Shop**, Nos. 23 Winchester Street and 2 Rolleston Street, occupying ground originally part of Balle's Place (351), were demolished in 1962. Most of the building was three-storeyed with brick walls and slate-covered roofs; it dated from the first half of the 19th century. There is a plan of 1851 by J.M. Peniston (W.R.O., 451/185).

(353) **Storehouse, Cottages and Shop**, Nos. 4–8 Rolleston Street, were demolished in 1962. Of two storeys with brick walls and tiled roofs they appeared to have been built early in the 19th century.

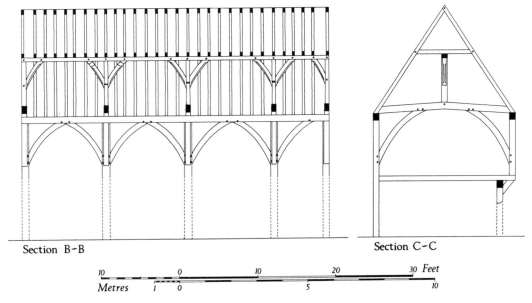

Section B–B   Section C–C

Feet / Metres

(351) BALLE'S PLACE. Nos. 25-9 Winchester Street.

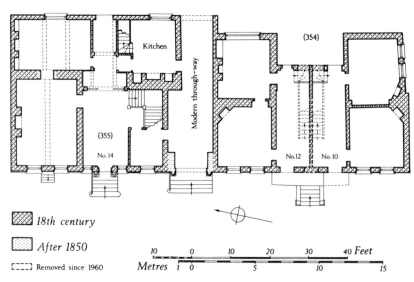

18th century

After 1850

Removed since 1960

10   0   10   20   30   40 Feet
Metres 1   0   5   10   15

(354-5) Nos. 10-14 Rolleston Street.

(354) **Pair of Houses**, formerly Nos. 10 and 12 Rolleston Street, now united and converted to offices, is of two storeys with basement and attic and has brick walls and tiled roofs. The building is of the early 18th century and in its original form was interesting as an early example of 'semi-detached' planning. It is mentioned in the city land survey of 1716 as 'Col. Kenton's new tenement and garden'.[1] The W. front (Plate 15), originally symmetrical and of seven bays, the central bay blind, has sashed windows in both main storeys, a first-floor plat-band and a prominent eaves cornice with modillions. Of the two original doorways, that on the S. has gone; that on the N., with a flat hood on scroll brackets with acanthus enrichment, remained in its original position until 1970 when it was moved to the middle of the facade. A flight of stone steps leading to a platform from which both doorways formerly opened is shown on O.S., 1880; only the N. part of the platform existed in 1970 and that part has now been removed. Inside, the stairs of the N. house remain, with turned and twisted balusters and a stout handrail, but the curtail has been altered.

The two houses are shown as separate on the plan of 1854, but they had been united by 1880 (O.S.). Since 1970 the blind recess in the upper storey has been opened and furnished with sashes, and a window has been put in place of the former N. doorway.

1. Sar. Corp. MS., O/117/1, f. 25. Probably Francis Kenton (1634–1720), alderman and chairman of the committee for rebuilding Trinity Hospital in 1702.

(355) **House**, No. 14 Rolleston Street (plan with (354), of two storeys with cellars and attics, has brick walls and tiled roofs; it dates from about the middle of

the 18th century. The facade was evidently designed to combine with that of Nos. 10–12 to form a 'terrace', but the effect of uniformity has been diminished by the recent removal of the cornice. In the seven-bay W. front the main doorway with narrow flanking windows is arranged to occupy two bays; the wooden doorcase has Tuscan three-quarter columns supporting a semicircular hood with a modillion cornice. In the lower storey the two S. bays of the facade are now occupied by a late 19th-century opening with columns supporting an entablature and a rounded pediment; it was made to give access to an industrial building erected in the garden E. of the house. In place of this opening, O.S. (1880) indicates an ordinary service or office doorway with a narrow flight of steps.

Inside, although used for offices, the main rooms retain joinery of very good quality. The entrance vestibule is spanned by an elliptical archway flanked by Corinthian pilasters with elaborate capitals (Plate 95). The stairs have turned balustrades and panelled dados. The N.W. rooms of each main storey are fully lined with fielded panelling in two heights. In the kitchen, part of the machinery for a turn-spit projects from the chimney-breast and there are traces of a former bread oven.

(356) **Salvation Army Citadel**, originally a Presbyterian Meeting House, is of one storey with rendered brick walls and a slate-covered roof. The E., S. and W. walls were built in 1702;[1] the N. wall is modern. In 1815 the hall became the Methodists' Sunday School and in 1882 it was acquired by the Salvation Army. The building is approximately square (45 ft. by 39½ ft.) and originally had two segmental-headed windows in each wall and a central doorway on the north (O.S., 1880). An old photograph (copy in NMR) shows the roof

supported by two timber posts placed axially, and by two more in the S. which also supported the gallery. The present roof is modern.

1.   Indentures etc., Salisbury Methodist Church.

(357) **Cottages**, four adjoining, Nos. 24–6 Salt Lane and 17–9 St. Edmund's Church Street, rebuilt in 1973, were two-storeyed with attics and had brick walls and slated roofs. The buildings were mainly of the 19th century, but during demolition the wall between Nos. 17 and 19 was revealed as timber-framed. Probably it was the S. end of a 16th-century house.

(358) **House**, No. 15 St. Edmund's Church Street, of two storeys with attics and cellars, with brick walls and tiled roofs, dates probably from the third quarter of the 18th century. Naish's maps show the site empty. The E. front is symmetrical and of three bays with a central doorway with a pedimented doorcase and with plain sashed windows; the eaves have a modillion cornice. A join in the W. elevation shows that the S.W. room is a later addition. Inside, the plan is of class U. The two N. ground-floor rooms are fully lined with fielded panelling in two heights; the hall and stairs have panelled dados, so also have the E. rooms on the first floor. Several original chimneypieces remain. In 1975 the house was extensively restored and a late 19th-century shop-window was removed.

(359) **House**, No. 47 Winchester Street, at the S.E. corner of the chequer, is of two main storeys with cellars and attics and has brick walls and tiled roofs; the S. front is faced with mathematical tiles. The house was built *c.* 1673 on city land which had been leased in 1671 to Gyles Naish;[1] in the lease Naish covenanted to pull down old buildings and rebuild within two years. The history of the former building, the Three Cups Inn, goes back to 1431.[2] Gyles Naish's house seems to have been designed as a private dwelling. Thomas Naish, Clerk of the Cathedral Works, was lessee in 1694 and 1705. In 1748 an inn licence was issued to Richard Sanborn, wine merchant, whose tenancy began in that year.[3] In 1773 John Wyche (mayor 1783) took possession,[4] and it was probably during his tenancy that the S. front was refaced in a contemporary style and the main rooms were replastered. In 1849, when the house was leased to John Finch, J.M. Peniston made a ground plan showing the S. and E. ranges, which still exist, together with a stable range on the W. of the court.[5] In 1877 the freehold was sold to William Hicks. After many years misuse as a warehouse for machinery, the building is now (1976) empty.

The 18th-century S. front is approximately symmetrical and of five bays with plain sashed windows; the central doorway has a pilastered wooden doorcase with fluted capitals and a frieze with garlands. The E. eleva-

tion, presumably of 1673, but old-fashioned for that date, has mullioned and transomed windows with hollow-chamfered stone surrounds below brick relieving arches in which some bricks are set forward to give the effect of rustication (Plate 70). The E. end of the S. range is defined by pilasters of rusticated brickwork; a moulded brick plat-band marks the first floor; the gables have moulded and weathered stone coping. In the courtyard, the 17th-century N. and W. elevations have features similar to those of the E. elevation.

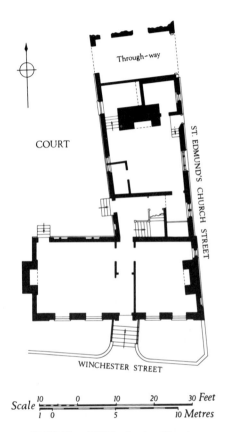

(359) No. 47 Winchester Street.

Inside, the rooms in the S. range have 18th-century moulded cornices and panelled dados probably installed by John Wyche. The staircase appears to be of the 17th century, with close strings, stout balustrades, square or chamfered newel posts and heavy moulded handrails; many of the newel posts have been truncated, but some retain square vase-shaped finials.

1.   Sar. Corp. MS., O/117/1, f. 59[V].
2.   Haskins, *Guilds*, 303–6.
3.   Sar. Corp. MS., O/117/7.
4.   *ibid.*
5.   W.R.O., 451/155.

(360) **Coach and Horses Inn**, No. 39 Winchester Street, two-storeyed with walls largely of brick, but with some original timber framework and with tiled roofs, appears to be of late 15th or early 16th-century origin. Behind a modern facade of imitation timber framework the S. range has an original roof of three bays with collared tie-beam trusses, clasped purlins and curved windbraces. An original chamfered post is visible at the S.W. corner of the range. The first-floor jetty is masked by the modern S. front. The N. wing at the E. end of the S. range is probably contemporary; that at the W. end, with brick walls, is of the late 18th century. Both wings were extended N. in the 19th century.

(361) **House**, No. 37 Winchester Street, of three storeys with brick walls and slate-covered roofs, is of *c.* 1800. The two-bay S. front has a shop window in the lower storey, a projecting window on the first floor and plain sashed windows on the second floor. The plot on which the building stands forms the S.E. corner of the mediaeval Balle's Place tenement (350). It is mentioned in the will of Walter Shirley, 1429,[1] and it certainly corresponds with the plot, 12½ ft. wide, held by William Kent in the city land survey of 1618.[2]

1.   Dom. Bk. iii, transcr., ff. 243–4.
2.   Sar. Corp. MS., O/117/1.

(362) **Houses**, range of three, Nos. 31–5 Winchester Street, are of two storeys with attics and have rendered timber-framed walls and tiled roofs; a few glazed mediaeval ridge tiles remain. The building appears to be of the 15th century and probably corresponds with Walter Shirley's legacy (1429) to John Park.[1] The upper storeys are jettied on the S. and the roofs are of collar-rafter construction.

1.   Dom. Bk. iii, transcr., ff. 243–4.   *W.A.M.*, lix (1964), 164.

GRIFFIN CHEQUER

(363) **Houses**, row of three, Nos. 2–6 St. Edmund's Church Street, are three-storeyed and have brick walls and slate-covered roofs. They were built early in the 19th century and in elevation resemble monument (157).

(364) **Houses**, pair, Nos. 8 and 10, are of two storeys with attics and have brick walls with stone dressings and tiled roofs. They date probably from late in the 17th century and appear to have originated as one house with a W. front of five bays. The central openings are masked by rendering, but part of the former first-floor window is seen internally. The house was divided into two dwellings about the middle of the 19th century.

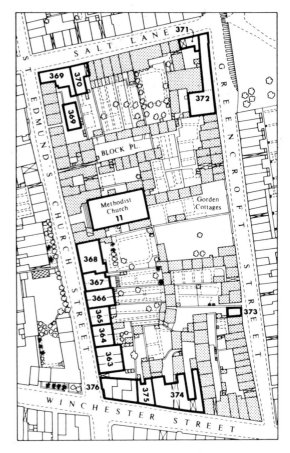

Monuments in Griffin Chequer.

(365) **House**, No. 14, of two storeys with timber-framed walls and tiled roofs, is of 16th-century origin, but it has been much altered. Divided at one time into two cottages, they were united *c.* 1930.

(366) **Cottages**, pair, Nos. 16 and 18, of two storeys with attics, with brick walls and tiled roofs, date from early in the 18th century. Inside, chamfered beams and some original joinery remain.

(367) **Cottages**, two adjacent, Nos. 20 and 22, have been formed from a single house with brick walls and tiled roofs which remained undivided until 1880 (O.S.). The building is of the late 18th century.

(368) **House**, No. 24 St. Edmund's Church Street, of two storeys with attics, with brick walls and tiled roofs, is mainly of *c.* 1700. The central doorway of the symmetrical five-bay W. front (Plate 72) and the projecting window over it are of *c.* 1800, as is an additional bay on the S.; the moulded timber eaves-cornice with

modillions is original. Inside, the stairs have original close strings, moulded handrails and square newel posts, but the plain balustrades are modern. The S.W. ground-

floor room of the original house has a moulded timber cornice; first-floor rooms have contemporary plaster cornices. A first-floor room has a chamfered beam with shaped stops. The roof has collared trusses with two purlins on each side.

(369) **Five Bells Inn**, at the N.W. corner of the chequer, is of two storeys with brick walls and tiled roofs. The elevations have been refaced, but beams inside suggest that the building is of 18th-century origin. Stables to the S. are of *c.* 1800.

(370) **House**, No. 30 Salt Lane, of two storeys with attics, has timber-framed walls and tiled roofs and dates from the 16th century, but it has been extensively altered. The N. front is modern. The N. range of the L-shaped plan, parallel with the street, originally had a carriage through-way in the E. bay leading to a yard, but all three bays of the lower storey have now been obliterated to make a shop. In the upper storey the W. wall of the N. range retains timber framework with curved braces; above, the gable has a collar-beam, lower angle-braces and a king-strut. The S. range contains a large chimneybreast, perhaps original, against the W. wall. Timber framework with curved braces is exposed internally.

(371) **Cottage**, No. 48 Salt Lane, demolished *c.* 1970, was two-storeyed with brick walls and a tiled roof. It was of the early 19th century.

(372) **Barley Mow Inn**, partly of two and partly of three storeys with cellars, has brick walls and slated and tiled roofs, it was built early in the 19th century. A single-storeyed range on the N., formerly a malthouse, is probably of 18th-century origin.

(373) **Cottage**, No. 31 Greencroft Street, of two storeys with brick walls and a tiled roof, is of *c.* 1850.

(374) **Anchor and Hope Inn**, Nos. 59–61 Winchester Street, of two storeys with timber-framed walls and tiled roofs, is of 16th-century origin. The four-bay S. range was rebuilt in the 19th century. At the rear, wings

flanking a narrow court retain much timber framework; the first floor of the E. wing is jettied on the west. The adjacent house on the E., No. 63, a two-storeyed brick building of *c.* 1800, appears originally to have contained stables associated with the inn.

(375) **House**, No. 57 Winchester Street, of two storeys with brick walls and tiled roofs, dates from *c.* 1800.

(376) **Cottages**, range of three, Nos. 51–5 Winchester Street, are two-storeyed with brick walls and slated roofs. Externally they appear to be of the 19th century, but recent stripping of plaster in No. 55 has revealed earlier features. The party-wall between No. 53 and No. 55 contains the timbers of a cruck truss, probably of the 15th century. The N. cruck blade cannot be seen, but

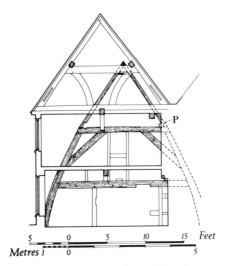

(376) No. 55 Winchester Street. Section, looking W.

the other main members are exposed. The S. purlin has wholly gone; that on the N. is represented by a short length of original beam (P) clasped between the collar-beam and the upper rafters; its deeply weathered W. extremity shows that the ground to W. was originally open, hence the truss in question is the W. end of a former building on the site of No. 55, not the E. end of No. 53. Nos. 51–3 were added, probably late in the 15th or early in the 16th century; internally, however, all timbers are cased and no significant features are seen. In the 16th century the cruck house was replaced by the existing No. 55 which has a two-bay roof with three smoke-blackened collared tie-beam trusses. A chimney-stack was inserted at the E. end of No. 55 in the 17th century.

GREENCROFT

Monuments (377–8) appear on the map on p. 94.

(377) **Cottages**, two adjoining, Nos. 77–9 Winchester Street, are of two storeys with attics and have brick walls and tiled roofs; they were built *c.* 1800.

(378) **Cottages**, range of three, Nos. 81–5 Winchester Street, are of two storeys with attics and have walls mainly of brick, but encasing some timber framework. They appear to be of 16th-century origin, but were re-modelled late in the 18th century. Inside, the first floor of No. 81 rests on a chamfered beam and some 17th-century joinery survives. No. 83 has an original post at the N.W. corner. No. 85 has a stout oak wall-plate.

(379) **Houses**, terrace of five, Nos. 4–8 Greencroft, are of three storeys with brick walls and slate-covered roofs and were built during the second quarter of the 19th century. In the E. front each house has one window in each storey and a doorway at ground level. The first-floor windows have large french casements, but without balconies.

(380) **Houses**, terrace of four, Nos. 14–17 Greencroft, are of two storeys with brick walls and slate-covered roofs and were built *c.* 1850. In the E. front, the lower storeys of Nos. 15 and 16 are recessed and the upper storey rests on a beam supported by iron posts.

Blechynden's Almshouses, see (28).

WHITE HORSE CHEQUER

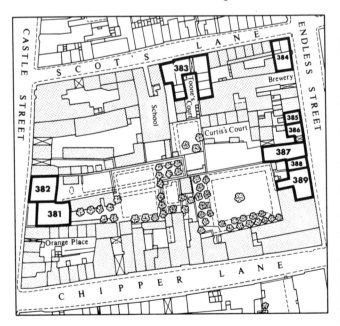

Monuments in White Horse Chequer.

(381) **House**, No. 26 Castle Street, of three storeys with brick walls and slate-covered roofs, was built early in the 19th century; the Rate Books indicate occupation from 1808. The three-bay W. front is separated from the road by a narrow forecourt defined by original iron railings; scrolled ironwork over the gate is modern. The

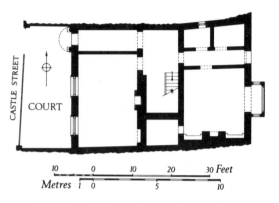

(381) No. 26 Castle Street. Ground floor.

round-headed doorway has a semicircular flat hood supported on Tuscan columns (Plate 99). Inside, the stairs have mahogany handrails and plain iron uprights. The main rooms have plasterwork and joinery, often with reeded decoration.

A plan of 1849 by J.M. Peniston[1] shows a service range and a garden to E., and other buildings flanking a courtyard which extended S. to Chipper Lane. Old photographs are preserved.[2]

1. W.R.O., 451/148.
2. Lov. Cn., 42–4.

(382) **Hotel**, of three storeys with brick walls and slate-covered roofs, was built *c.* 1850. The three-bay W. front has plain sashed windows.

(383) **Toone's Court**, a group of 16th-century buildings recently demolished, comprised Nos. 12, 14 and 18 Scot's Lane together with five small tenements flanking a court on the S. (Plate 65). The buildings were of one and two storeys and had timber-framed walls, partly rendered and partly hung with mathematical tiles; in places 18th-century brickwork replaced the timber framework. The roofs were tiled. The W. part of No. 12 was of the 19th century; the E. part was contained in the westernmost bay of a 16th-century two-storeyed range of five bays, jettied N. at the first floor, but with the jetty partly underbuilt in the lower storey. No. 14 comprised the second and third bays of the 16th-century range, but in the lower storey a through-passage giving access to the court occupied part of the third bay. The fourth and fifth bays of the range, constituting No. 18, had been refronted in brickwork in the 18th century, but part of the original framework remained inside. At

SCOT'S LANE

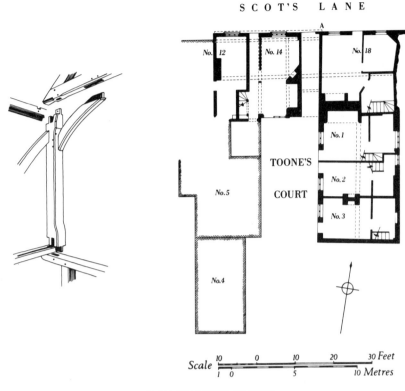

Scale

(383) TOONE'S COURT.

right-angles to the street range, on the E. side of the court, a 16th-century range containing three cottages (Nos. 1–3) had originally been a single-storeyed building, probably a workshop. In the 18th or 19th century it was converted into cottages by inserting partitions, the S. chimneystack, the upper floor and the staircases; in the roof, two original tie-beams were cut away and their ends were stiffened by sling-braces. Nos. 4 and 5, on the W. side of the court, had been largely rebuilt in the 19th century, but they retained elements of original timber framework. Timbers in the roof of No. 12 suggested that the roof of Nos. 4 and 5 formerly extended northwards to a gable on the street front.

Inside, the open fireplace in No. 14 had a reused stone lintel, moulded underneath and probably taken from a 15th-century fireplace. The masonry of the chimneybreast incorporated a number of carved stones brought from elsewhere (probably Old Sarum), with 12th-century chevron decoration etc.; some of the stones had originally been voussoirs. A small 12th-century capital with volutes was reset at the S.W. corner of the through-passage. Reset in the lower part of the stairs of No. 14 was a 16th-century doorway with a chamfered ogee lintel. The large open fireplace in No. 1 had chamfered stone jambs and a chamfered oak bressumer; it was evidently a feature of the original single-storeyed range, serving the presumed workshop.

The roof of Nos. 12, 14 and 18 had collared tie-beam trusses with king-struts and lower angle-struts. The tie-beams were tenoned and braced to the jowl-headed posts and dovetailed into the wall-plates (see sketch).

(384) **House**, No. 37 Endless Street, of three storeys with brick walls and a tiled roof, was built during the first half of the 18th century. The E. front has a 19th-century shop window on the ground floor and five bays of plain sashed windows in the two upper storeys. Inside, the pinewood stairs have open strings, turned balusters and moulded handrails.

(385) **House and Shop**, No. 29, of three storeys with brick walls and a slated roof, is of c. 1850. In 1977 a 15th-century timber-framed wall came to light between this house and No. 27 (386).

(386) **House**, No. 27, of three storeys with brick walls and a slated roof, is of c. 1830. Incorporated with the two-bay E. front, an elliptical-headed archway formerly gave access to Curtis's Court, demolished c. 1965. Further S., the facade of No. 27 covers part of the E. front of the adjacent house (387), including its doorway.

(387) **House**, No. 23, of two storeys and an attic, has brick and tile-hung walls and slate-covered roofs. Of early 17th-century origin it retains a six-bay roof of that period. Inside, plasterwork and joinery are of the mid 18th century.

(388) **House**, No. 21, of two storeys and an attic, with walls of brick, rubble and flint and with tiled roofs, is of the late 17th century.

(389) **House**, No. 19, of three storeys with brick walls and a slated roof, was built *c.* 1800. The E. front is of three bays with plain sashed windows in each storey; in the N. bay of the lower storey is a round-headed doorway with a pedimented hood. Inside, the stairs have a mahogany handrail, turned newels and plain balusters.

Photographs of No. 17 Endless Street, a substantial 18th-century house which formerly occupied the S.E. corner of the chequer, are in the Lovibond Collection (Nos. 71–85).

GORE'S CHEQUER

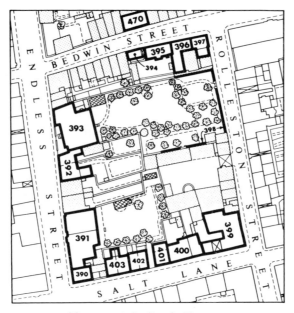

Monuments in Gore's Chequer.

(390) **House**, No. 14 Endless Street, of two storeys with an attic, is probably of the early 17th century; the walls, entirely of 18th-century and later brickwork, presumably replace timber framework. The steeply pitched two-bay roof, ridged E. – W., has original trusses with chamfered purlins and straight windbraces.

(391) **Loder House**, mainly two-storeyed, with brick walls and tiled and slated roofs, was in an advanced state of decay when investigated in 1962; since then it has been extensively altered. The N. part of the house, comprising two ground-floor rooms and three on the first floor, is of *c.* 1750; until 1962 the W. room on each floor retained very handsome decorations. The S. part, containing the entrance vestibule, stairs and service rooms, was of *c.* 1850 and had plainer fittings.

The 18th-century part of the W. front had two sashed windows in each storey and a pediment above a heavy

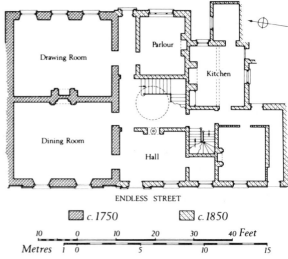

(391) LODER HOUSE. Ground floor.

brick cornice. The windows and eaves of the 19th-century wing were at a lower level than in the earlier building.

Inside, the 19th-century staircase had cast-iron balusters and rounded mahogany handrails. In the 18th-century part of the house the dining room had panelled walls with an acanthus scroll frieze, a bracketed cornice and a panelled plaster ceiling with classical enrichments. The chimneypiece (Plate 94) had a scrolled pediment enclosing a gilded eagle with a garland in its beak. The doorways had pulvinated entablatures. A panel on the N. wall contained a painting on canvas ascribed to the Roman Mannerist school of *c.* 1550, probably a fragment of a larger work. The drawing room had decorations of *c.* 1850. On the first floor, the W. chamber had rococo wall decorations in plaster (Plate 95), and a modelled plaster ceiling of *c.* 1750. The N.E. chamber was lined with 18th-century fielded panelling in three heights. The small S.E. dressing-room had no notable features. In the S. part of the house several rooms had 18th-century joinery, presumably reset.

Since 1962 the building has been divided into shops and offices, and the rich interior decorations have gone.

(392) **Cottages**, pair, Nos. 22–4 Endless Street, are of two storeys with brick walls and slated roofs and were built early in the 19th century. In each cottage the W. front is of two bays with plain sashed windows and a square-headed doorway.

(393) **House**, No. 26, now Local Government Offices, is partly of two and partly of three storeys with brick walls and low-pitched slate-covered roofs; it dates from early in the 19th century. The E. front is asymmetrical, with plain sashed windows and a square-headed doorway in a doorcase with reeded decoration. The porch, largely modern, includes early 19th-century wooden columns of elegant design with clustered shafts and flared capitals. Inside, the original staircase has slender turned balusters.

(394) **Warehouse**, No. 20 Bedwin Street, recently remodelled, was of three storeys with brick walls and a tiled roof and dated from early in the 19th century. It was built as an extension of No. 20a (395).

(395) **House**, No. 20a, of three storeys with brick walls and a tiled roof, was built in the 18th century. Until 1967 it had a symmetrical N. front of three bays with a central doorway, but it has since been remodelled.

(396) **House**, No. 22, mainly of three storeys with brick walls and a tiled roof, was built *c.* 1800. The N. front is symmetrical and of three bays, with a round-headed central doorway and with plain sashed windows or blind recesses. To the S., a two-storeyed wing with walls of rubble and flint in the lower storey and of timber framework above is the W. bay of a 16th-century range which originally extended as far as Rolleston Street; part of the lower storey remains as the garden wall of No. 26 Endless Street (398). The 16th-century roof has a collared tie-beam truss with lower angle braces, a king-strut and clasped purlins. The house of *c.* 1800 has a class—U plan.

(397) **House**, No. 24 Bedwin Street, of three storeys with brick walls and tiled roofs, dates from *c.* 1800. The N. doorway (Plate 99) has a segmental hood, a Greek-fret frieze, and jambs with clustered shafts and leaf capitals. In the E. elevation a first-floor room has a projecting sashed window curved on plan. Inside, the rooms have 19th century joinery of good quality.

(398) **Walls**, bounding the garden of No. 26 Endless Street (393) on E. and S., are of brick with weathered brick copings and appear to be of the early 17th century. Additional brickwork above the coping is probably of the 18th century. Piercing the E. wall is an ashlar doorway with a four-centred head and an original oak door studded with iron nails. A similar doorway occurs in the S. wall of the same garden. In 1975 the brickwork was extensively renewed. On the N. the garden is partly bounded by a 16th-century wall (see (396)).

(399) **Pheasant Inn** and **Shoemakers' Hall**, of two storeys with timber-framed walls and tiled roofs, are respectively of the late 15th and the mid 17th century. In 1638 Philip Crew, a schoolmaster, bequeathed his house at the corner of Rolleston Street and Salt Lane to the Shoemakers' Company, recommending them to build a guild hall.[1] A large 17th-century first-floor room to N.W. of the 15th-century house, with a kitchen below it, evidently results from the bequest.

Externally the lower walls of the 15th-century building have been rebuilt in brickwork, and internally many ground-floor partitions have been removed, but in the upper storey much original timber framework remains

(Plate 64). The roof of the E. range has tie-beam trusses with cambered collars, curved angle-braces and clasped purlins with windbraces. In the S. range the gabled E. wall is jettied at the first floor. Coupled roof trusses in the W. part of the S. range suggest that the range originated as two houses. The division has been obliterated below by the widening of a carriage throughway.

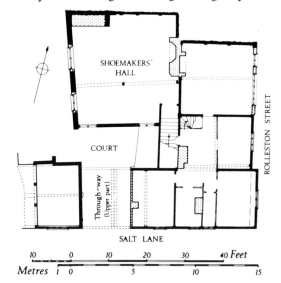

(399) Pheasant Inn and Shoemaker's Hall. First floor.

The 17th-century guild hall has walls partly timber-framed and partly of brick. The lower storey has been modernised, but the first-floor hall retains its original form. The timber-framed S. wall contains two windows, each of two double-transomed lights with ogee-moulded timber surrounds; the openings, now partly blocked, originally reached from the floor to the wall-plate. An original fireplace in the N.W. corner of the hall has been blocked up and a modern fireplace has been built on the E., using old bricks. A 17th-century full-length portrait of Philip Crew hangs in the hall.

1.   Haskins, *Guilds*, 228–30.

(400) **Cottages**, two adjoining, Nos. 11 and 13 Salt Lane, are of two storeys with walls of timber framework and of brick, and with tile-covered roofs. They are of the 16th century but have been much altered. Inside, No. 13 retains an original flint and ashlar chimneybreast.

(401) **Cottage**, No. 9, of two storeys with rendered brick walls and a tiled roof, is of the early 19th century. Two dormer windows in the S. front have wood heads imitating mediaeval window tracery.

(402) **Cottages**, pair, Nos. 5 and 7, of two storeys with brick walls and slate-covered roofs, are of *c.* 1850.

(403) **Cottages**, pair, Nos. 1 and 3, of two storeys with brick walls and slate-covered roofs, are of *c.* 1850.

PARSONS CHEQUER

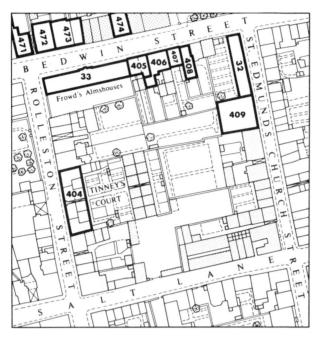

Monuments in Parsons Chequer.

(404) **Rolleston Place**, terrace of four cottages, is two-storeyed with brick walls and slate-covered roofs. On O.S., 1880 it appears as the W. range of Tinney's Court. A tablet with an inscription of 1844 (?) at the centre of the W. front indicates the probable date of erection.

Frowd's Almshouses, see (33).

(405) **Houses**, two adjoining, Nos. 26–8 Bedwin Street, are three-storeyed with brick walls and slate-covered roofs and were built during the first quarter of the 19th century. In each house the N. front is of one bay. No. 28 has a mid 19th-century bow window in the second storey.

(406) **House**, No. 30, of two storeys with brick walls and tiled roofs, appears to date from early in the 18th century. The N. front is symmetrical and of three bays, with a central doorway, plain sashed windows and a blind recess over the doorway. A moulded brick string-course marks the level of the first floor. Inside, several rooms are lined with 18th and early 19th-century panelling.

(407) **House**, No. 32, of three storeys with brick walls and slate-covered roofs, was built *c.* 1840.

(408) **House**, No. 34, of two storeys with rendered timber-framed walls and tiled roofs, is of 16th-century origin, but it has been extensively altered. The N. front is jettied at the first floor. Inside, some original ceiling beams are exposed.

Taylor's Almshouses, see (32).

(409) **House**, No. 42 St. Edmund's Church Street, of two and three storeys with brick walls and tiled roofs, dates probably from 1787, the date on a lead rainwater-head on the N. wall. The E. front is approximately symmetrical and of seven bays, with a round-headed central doorway and plain sashed windows; a doorway in the N. bay presumably gave access to the original service range. Inside, the two-storeyed E. range has a class–T plan. The three-storeyed W. range was added in the 19th century. Several rooms in the E. range have original chimneypieces; one has neo-classical enrichment. The stairs are of the 19th century.

VANNER'S CHEQUER

City surveys mention a number of small tenements on the W., N. and S. sides of the chequer.[1] They were humble dwellings with small gardens or with no gardens at all and fringed a large property at the centre of the chequer. The property, clearly shown on Naish's map (Plate 16), had a large isolated house towards its N. end.[2] In 1504 this 'capital place' with a gateway, together with a barn and a stone house facing St. Edmund's Church, belonged to Richard Freeman.[3]

1. Sar. Corp. MS., O/117/1, ff. 2–4; O/117/4, ff. 35–44; O/117/8, ff. 19–27; V/204/1 and 2 (plans by Peniston).
2. Kingdon & Shearm show a large house in much the same position. By 1880 (O.S.) it had been replaced by the present house, now local government offices.
3. Sar. Corp. MS., will of Richard Freeman, 1504.

(410) **Cottages**, Nos. 58–60 St. Edmund's Church Street, are two-storeyed with attics and have brick walls and tiled roofs. They were built early in the 19th century.

(411) **Cottages**, pair, Nos. 68–70, of two storeys with brick walls and tiled roofs, appear to be mainly of the 18th century, but they incorporate a single-storeyed timber-framed building of 16th-century origin; this came to light in 1974 while the interior was being replastered. The 16th-century roof has a braced tie-beam truss with a cambered collar and lower angle braces.

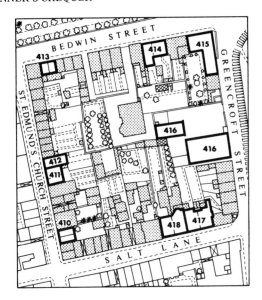

Monuments in Vanner's Chequer.

(412) **Cottage**, No. 72, is two-storeyed with an attic and has brick walls and a tiled roof; the W. front is rendered. The building appears to be mainly of the 18th century. Beams and joists inside are probably 17th-century material, reused.

(413) **Cottages**, pair, Nos. 36–8 Bedwin Street, are two-storeyed with attics and have timber-framed walls and tiled roofs. Of 17th-century origin, they provide a late example of exposed timber framework. The common gable in the attic storey of the symmetrical four-bay N. front is a 19th-century addition; the roof purlin retains mortices for rafters removed when the gable was added. A carved corbel set centrally in the gable is of the 19th century. Inside, some reused chamfered beams are exposed. (Rebuilt, 1977.)

(414) **Houses**, two adjacent, Nos. 54–6 Bedwin Street, are two-storeyed and have timber-framed walls faced with brickwork, and tiled roofs. They are of late 16th-century origin, altered in the 18th century. Inside, stout timber framework and chamfered beams with shaped stops are seen. The roof has collared tie-beam trusses with lower angle struts; some members are notably smoke-blackened, but there is no evidence of a former louvre. Originally the building is likely to have comprised a single house.

(415) **Croft House**, at the N.E. corner of the chequer, is partly of two storeys with attics and cellars and partly three-storeyed; it has brick walls and tiled roofs. The N. range, with a symmetrical three-bay front to Bedwin Street, is of the early 18th century; the central doorway

has a late 18th-century moulded wooden surround with an open pediment on shaped brackets and a tympanum with swags and paterae. The E. range, flanking Greencroft Street, was added towards the end of the 18th century on ground which Naish's town plan (Plate 16) shows unoccupied. The N. bay of the E. range contains a staircase; the next two bays are three-storeyed and have sashed windows with keystones, plat-bands at two levels, and a modillion cornice; the two S. bays are two-storeyed. During the 19th century two more two-storeyed bays were added at the S. end of the range.

Inside, the N. range originally had a class-T plan. In the lower storey the original staircase has gone, but part of it remains between the first floor and the attic. The staircase in the late 18th-century extension is of oak, with slender turned balusters and a dado with fielded panelling. The first-floor room in the three-storeyed part of the E. range has late 18th-century joinery and a carved wood chimneypiece.

(416) **Coach House**, **Stables** and **Dwelling**, Nos. 83–5 Greencroft Street, partly two-storeyed, with brick and flint walls with ashlar dressings and with tile-covered roofs, were built early in the 18th century. Several openings have ashlar surrounds with elliptical heads, keystones etc. resembling those on the S. front of the Council House (14). Presumably these were the stables of that house, built when it was a private residence.

(417) **Houses**, pair, Nos. 49–51 Salt Lane, are two-storeyed with attics and cellars and have timber-framed walls faced with brickwork, and tiled roofs. Of 16th-century origin, they were refronted and extensively altered in the 18th century. No. 49 has recently been demolished. Previously the S. front was symmetrical and of five bays, with plinth, plat-band and coved eaves-cornice, and with plain sashed windows in both main storeys. The doorways were coupled in the middle bay, the corresponding first-floor window belonging to No. 51. The gabled N. wall of No. 49 retained original timber framework. Inside, the ground-floor rooms have stop-chamfered beams.

(418) **Houses**, pair, Nos. 45–7, demolished c. 1967, were of the 16th-century and had characteristics similar to the adjoining pair (417), but they were slightly lower in elevation and the S. fronts had no plinth and no cornice. Inside, No. 45 had an open fireplace with an oak bressummer. The first-floor rooms of both houses had fireplaces; some chamfered ceiling beams had shaped stops. The roofs had collared tie-beam trusses with cambered tie-beams.

CASTLE STREET

Monuments (419)–(423) appear on the map of Blue Boar Chequer, p. 132.

(419) **House**, No. 1, of three storeys with attics, has brick walls and tiled roofs. The surviving structure represents about two thirds of a substantial town house, built during the first half of the 18th century and altered and redecorated towards the end of the same century. In 1858 the southern third was demolished to make room for the Market House (25). From 1861 to 1864 the remaining part accommodated the Brodie collection of antiquities, the nucleus of Salisbury Museum.

The E. front (Plate 77) is decorated with giant Doric pilasters, each capped by an independant triglyph and supporting a bracketed cornice. The doorway in the S.

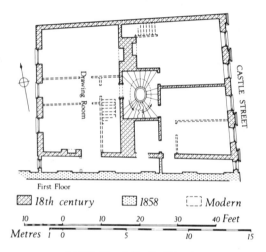

Metres
(419) No. 1 Castle Street.

bay has Ionic columns and a pedimented entablature. A photograph taken before 1858 (Plate 14) shows a fifth pilaster.

Inside, the late 18th-century staircase (removed in the lower storey) is of oak with spiral open-string steps, slender turned balusters, a moulded handrail and a panelled dado; it is lit by an oval glass dome rising from an enriched frieze and culminating in an acanthus boss. The mezzanine drawing-room ceiling has delicate neo-classical plaster enrichment; the fireplace surround is of white marble inlaid with pink. In the N.E. first-floor room the ceiling has rococo decorations, perhaps of papier-maché. Kingdon & Shearm indicate a S.W. wing, now gone.

(420) **Shops**, Nos. 3–9, of two and three storeys with brick walls and slate-covered roofs, demolished in 1975, appear to have incorporated the upper part of the brick facades of three late 18th-century houses, all with plain sashed windows. Inside, nothing noteworthy remained. A range of early 19th-century buildings on the

N.W. of No. 9 were formerly malthouses belonging to Pain's brewery (see (422)). A plan of 1834 is preserved (W.R.O., 451/73 (xlix)).

(421) **House**, No. 11, of three storeys with attics, with brick walls and slate-covered roofs, is of the late 18th century. The E. front has a projecting bow window in the second storey and a sashed window above. The third storey is faced with mathematical tiles.

(422) **Houses**, Nos. 19–25, and ranges of buildings flanking a courtyard on the W., mainly two-storeyed with attics, were demolished in 1968. Before demolition the buildings were used as offices and auction rooms (Plate 80), but in 1854 (Kingdon & Shearm) the site had been a brewery, part of which extended into the area of (420). Although mainly of the 19th century, the complex included earlier buildings. Behind its simple one-bay 18th-century brick facade, No. 19 (not illustrated) had timber-framed walls and was perhaps of 16th-century origin. No. 21 (*l.* in the photograph) was three-storeyed with brick walls and a tiled roof and appeared to be of the early 19th century. Adjacent on the N. was the entrance to No. 23, a conspicuous two-storeyed gateway with turrets in the 'Tudor' style, probably of *c.* 1865. No. 25 had a rendered late 18th-century two-bay elevation of two storeys with plaster quoins and a bracketed cornice. Behind No. 25 the range on the N. of the courtyard was found on demolition to be of 16th-century origin. Some 20 ft. from the E. end the roof of the range had an arch-braced collar truss. Further W. the walls were partly of timber framework and the first floor rested on intersecting chamfered beams with run-out stops. A large chimneybreast of rubble and brick had a 16th-century fireplace, facing E., with chamfered ashlar jambs and a chamfered oak bressummer; another fireplace was on the first floor. Adjacent on the W. was a smaller chimneybreast with a S.-facing fireplace, probably of the 17th century. Here the roof had collared tie-beam trusses with lower angle braces.

(423) **Workshop**, of two storeys with attics, formerly with brick walls and a tiled roof, is of 17th-century origin. It has been extensively remodelled and now is used as offices. The upper floor rests on stout chamfered beams with run-out stops. Truncated tie-beams in the four-bay roof are tenoned into queen-struts which rise from the attic floor beams. On a plan in the city archives, probably by Peniston, *c.* 1850, the building is called 'stores and coach-builders workshop'; in the surveys of city lands dated 1716 and 1783 it is called the New Stable.[1] The whole tenement, including a gateway to Castle Street, houses on each side of the gate, and land stretching W. to the Avon, was sold to the city in 1630 by Dr. John Mosely.[2] Naish's maps show a Free School in this position and the plan of *c.* 1850 designates as 'school-room' a large first-floor room overlooking

Castle Street. Doubtless this was Salisbury's first free school, established elsewhere in 1559 and transferred to this site in 1624.[3] The school-room no longer exists, the E. part of the tenement having been rebuilt about the end of the 19th century.

1. Sar. Corp. MS., V/204/1 and 2; O/117/4, f. 59; O/117/8, f. 36.
2. Sar. Corp. MS., Z/231 A.
3. Benson & Hatcher, 285. Haskins, *Guilds*, 295.

(424) **House**, No. 31, of three storeys with rendered walls and slated and tile-covered roofs, is probably of the second quarter of the 18th century. The four-bay E. front has plain sashed windows in the upper storeys. Beside modern shop windows the lower storey retains an original doorway with fanlight, flat hood and scrolled acanthus brackets. Inside, several rooms have bolection-moulded panelling in two heights, and heavy moulded cornices.

(425) **House**, No. 35, has an E. front similar to and continuous with that of No. 31 (424). Inside, however, it is clear that the two buildings are not contemporary. No. 35 was originally two-storeyed, with timber-framed walls, probably of 16th-century origin. The S. elevation, facing a carriage through-way, has exposed timber frame-work and is jettied at the attic floor.

An outbuilding to W., with brick and tile-hung walls and with a tiled roof, appears to be of the 18th century.

(426) **House**, No. 41, of three storeys and a cellar, has brick walls and a slate-covered roof. Of early 18th-century origin it was remodelled during the first half of the 19th century, the E. front being rebuilt with ashlar quoins, a cornice and a plain parapet; there is a shop-window with Tuscan columns in the lower storey and three bays of plain sashed windows in each upper storey. Inside, a ground-floor room has an original stone chimney-piece with a moulded head and keystone.

(427) **Houses**, Nos. 43–5, now united and used as solicitors' offices, are mainly of three storeys and have brick-faced walls and tiled and slated roofs. From mediaeval times the ground of No. 45 was bounded on the N. by a conduit taking water from the mill-leat to the channels in the city streets; the 18th-century part of the house extends over this conduit.[1] In 1751, when No. 45 belonged to Alexander Powell (deputy recorder 1766–85), a deed recorded the extinction of a right-of-way which formerly passed from Castle Street across Powell's garden to a sluice-house in the N.W. corner of the garden; in exchange Powell granted right-of-way to the S. of the adjoining house (No. 43).[2] The deed states explicitly that Powell had 'enclosed the former passage and taken it into his parlour'. In 1792 the house was acquired by Joseph Tanner,[3] and in 1796 it was adver-tised to let, 'having been in great part new-built within

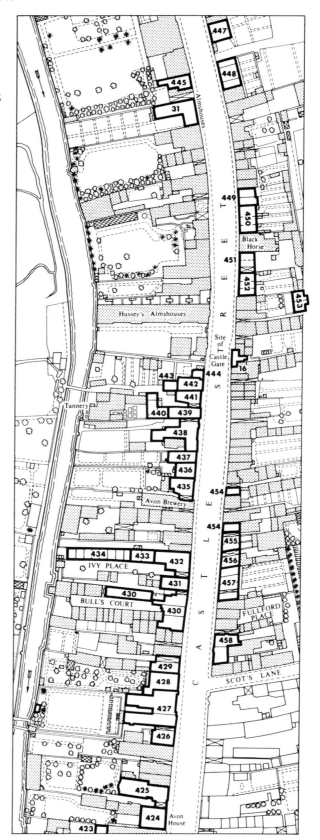

Monuments in N. part of Castle Street.

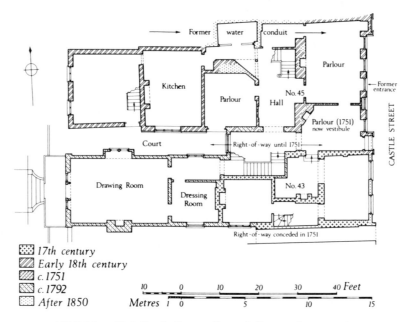

17th century
Early 18th century
c. 1751
c. 1792
After 1850

(427) Nos. 43-5 Castle Street. Ground floor and mezzanine.

the last four years'. It then comprised, on the ground floor an entrance hall, three parlours, kitchen etc.; on the first floor a drawing-room, a dressing-room and five bedrooms; in the attic storey five more bedrooms. A walled garden backing on the Avon measured 72 ft. by 132 ft.[4]

No. 43 is basically timber-framed and probably of 17th-century origin, but much of the framework was replaced by or cased in brickwork in the 19th century. An early but undated photograph (Plate 14) shows its plain E. front with a shop window in the lower storey.

No. 45, a town house consistent with Powell's standing, appears to have been built early in the 18th century. The E. front (Plate 75) is symmetrical and of five bays. Brick pilasters flanking the two upper storeys rise unconventionally from the apexes of the pedimented side porches, that on the N. blind, the other now containing the main entrance to the building. In the early photograph both side porches are blind and a doorway with a flat hood takes the place of the existing centre window. (The same photograph shows that the present coarse brick cornice replaces a more delicately modelled feature, probably of Roman cement.) In the original facade the S. porch probably gave access to the former passage to the sluice-house; the blind N. porch is likely to have been put there for symmetry and perhaps partly in recognition of the conduit which must once have emerged at this point below the 18th-century facade. Presumably the brickwork which closes the S. porch in the old photograph was inserted by Powell, c. 1751. We do not know when the central doorway was abolished, but O.S. (1880) seems to suggest that it was still in existence at that date.

On the W., the house consists of two parallel ranges divided by a narrow court. The 18th-century kitchen range possibly incorporates the brick walls of a somewhat earlier building (ignored on the plan). On the S., where the garden of No. 43 must once have been, a range of c. 1792 comprises a drawing-room or music room,[5] with a triple W. window opening to a terrace from which formal steps descend to a large garden (map, p. 149). Low cellars raise the drawing-room to mezzanine level. A passage which passes from N. to S. in the basement storey may have been designed to accommodate the second right-of-way to the sluice-house. Some brickwork in this part of the building may be reused 17th-century material; it occurs below the level shown on the plan.

Inside No. 45, the early 18th-century oak staircase on the N. of the hall (Plate 88) has twisted Tuscan column balustrades and stout moulded handrails. A large chimneybreast in the N.W. parlour, now partly removed, suggests that this was once a kitchen. On the first floor, a round-headed doorway from the staircase landing to the large, panelled N.E. room indicates that the latter ranked originally as a drawing-room.

The S.E. ground-floor room in No. 45, now the vestibule, is evidently the parlour formed in 1751 by Alexander Powell; it has pine panelling in two heights and a bold wood cornice. The S. staircase in No. 45 was inserted in 1792 primarily to give access to Joseph Tanner's mezzanine drawing-room; part of a back room in No. 43 was taken to make room for it. The staircase is of oak with slender turned balusters and scrolled step spandrels. The mezzanine drawing-room has a carved wooden chimneypiece of c. 1720, presumably reset, with a pulvinated laurel-leaf frieze capped by a broken pediment. The ceiling is heavily enriched with baroque plasterwork, probably of *c.* 1900.

To W., axially laid out with regard to the drawing room window, a brick-walled garden extends to the mill stream. Centrally on the stream bank is a small garden-house of *c.* 1792 with rendered brick walls and a tiled roof.

1. Preface, p. xxxiv.
2. Sar. Corp. MS., W. 205.
3. Rate books, *s.a.*
4. *S.J.*, 29 Aug., 1796. The schedule of rooms together with the dimensions of the garden confirm that the advertisement relates to No. 45.
5. See Lawrence Tanner, in Shortt, *Salisbury*, 6.

(428) **House**, No. 47, of three storeys with brick walls and slate-covered roofs, was built during the second half of the 18th century. Above modern shop windows the three-bay E. front has uniform sashed windows in each upper storey. The moulded wooden cornice and brick parapet have recently been renewed. Inside, the altered ground plan implies a former through-passage on the north. The stairs, with turned balusters and a cast-iron newel-post at the foot, are of the 19th century. The first-floor rooms retain original cornices and dado rails, and a wooden chimneypiece with leaf enrichment, swags and paterae.

(429) **House**, No. 49, of three storeys with brick walls and a tiled roof, is probably of 1755. The three-bay E. front is asymmetrical, with a shop window in the S. part with paired sashed windows in the upper storeys, and with a carriage through-way on the N. with a single sashed window in each upper storey. The eaves have a moulded brick cornice. The date 1755 appears on the keystone of an arch in the through-way.

(430) **Houses**, three adjacent, Nos. 57–61, and an adjoining **Loom House** were demolished in 1965. The houses were two-storeyed with attics and had timber-framed walls, partly faced with brickwork and partly tile-hung, and tiled roofs. No. 57 was of late 15th-century origin; Nos. 59 and 61 were of the 16th or 17th century; all three had been refronted in the 18th century and had pedimented doorways and sashed windows. Inside, the ground-floor room of No. 57 had 18th-century fielded panelling in three heights, elliptical-headed niches flanking the fireplace and a moulded stone chimneypiece. The roof of No. 57 was of four bays with two plain collared tie-beam trusses and, at the centre, a truss with arched braces. Nos. 59 and 61 had no notable features. The loom-house (15 ft. by 65 ft.), some 15 ft. W. of No. 61 but originally connected with it, was two-storeyed with brick walls and a tiled roof. It is said to have been built in 1738 by the clothier Joseph Hinxman.[1] The N. front had twelve segmental-headed openings in the lower storey and four above.

1. G. Fulford, *Festival Book of Salisbury* (ed. Stevens), Salisbury 1914, p. 70.

(431) **House**, No. 63, of two storeys and attics, with timber-framed walls subsequently faced with brickwork and with tiled roofs, was built early in the 16th century. The symmetrical three-bay E. front is of the late 18th century, with a 19th-century shop window. Inside, there is evidence for a large fireplace, now blocked. Several rooms have chamfered beams. The roof of the E. range, ridged N.–S., has collared tie-beam trusses with lower king and queen struts, and clasped purlins; that of the W. range, at right-angles, has lower angle struts.

(432) **House**, No. 63, of two storeys and attics, has timber-framed walls faced in part with brickwork, and tiled roofs. Reset in the E. range is a rebated and chamfered beam from a panelled ceiling, perhaps of 15th-century origin. Elsewhere the timber framework appears to be of the 16th century with later additions. The five-bay E. front was built early in the 18th century, but the shop windows in the lower storey are modern. Inside, some 18th-century joinery remains.

(433) **House**, now two dwellings, Nos. 2 and 3 Ivy Place, is of two storeys with attics and has tile-hung timber-framed walls and tiled roofs. The building is of the 17th century and retains an original brick chimney-stack. Inside, joinery and fittings date from the mid 18th century, when the house was divided. The roof was altered in the mid 18th century.

(434) **Cottages**, row of eight, Nos. 4–11 Ivy Place, are three-storeyed with rendered brick walls and tile-covered roofs; they were built *c.* 1800. Inside, each dwelling has one room on each floor.

(435) **House**, No. 77, of two storeys and attics, has rendered brick walls and tile-covered roofs and was built about the middle of the 18th century. The E. front has an original doorway with a pedimented hood on shaped brackets. Inside, the large entrance vestibule contains a close-string staircase with column-shaped balusters.

(436) **House**, No. 79, of two and three storeys with tile-hung timber-framed walls and tiled roofs, is of the early 17th century. The E. front is jettied at the first floor and in the second storey has a projecting window, partly original, with ogee corbels. Inside, the ground-floor rooms have been obliterated to make a shop. The E. first-floor room retains original panelling and has a chimneypiece composed of 17th-century carved woodwork, reassembled.

(437) **House**, No. 81, of two low storeys with timber-framed walls and a tiled roof, is probably of 17th-century origin, but all original features are hidden by modern tile-work and internal fittings.

(438) **George and Dragon Inn**, together with **No. 83**, adjacent to S., are of two storeys with attics and have rendered timber-framed walls and tiled roofs. They were built early in the 16th century and probably were originally united. The E. fronts are jettied at the first floor. The main roof is ridged N.–S., but the middle bay (the S. bay of the inn) is part of a cross-range and is gabled to E. The E. doorway (d) of the through-passage

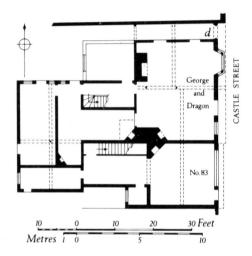

(438) No. 83 Castle Street and George & Dragon Inn.

has a moulded oak surround with a three-centred head and spandrels with cusped mouchettes. Other openings in the E. front are of the 18th century and later. Inside, the two E. ground-floor rooms of the inn (now united) have hollow-chamfered beams with shaped stops. The roof has collared tie-beam trusses with lower angle struts and clasped purlins. The W. wing retains original timber framework, but it was altered and added to in the 18th century.

(439) **House**, No. 87, of two storeys with attics, with timber-framed walls and tiled roofs, dates from early in the 16th century and may originally have been one with the adjoining building (438). The gabled E. front has modern windows. The N. wall of the lower storey, visible in a through-way, contains a blocked doorway with an ogee-headed timber surround. Inside, timber framework is exposed.

(440) **Warehouse and Cottages**, adjacent to No. 87 on the W., are two-storeyed and have timber-framed walls with brick nogging, and tiled roofs; probably they are of the 16th century. The warehouse is two-storeyed and of four bays. In the upper storey, jowl-headed wall-posts support cambered tie-beams with curved braces. The roof, ridged N.–S., hsa trusses with queen-posts, collars, clasped purlins and curved windbraces. A cottage adjoining the warehouse on the E. has a two-bay plan; inside, the rooms have 18th-century joinery of poor quality. Another cottage has been formed in the two N. bays of the warehouse.

(441) **House**, No. 91, of two storeys with walls partly timber-framed and partly of brick, and with tiled roofs, is of 15th-century origin. The E. part of the house was rebuilt in the 18th century and the E. front, of brickwork, has a shop-window below three plain sashed windows; above is a moulded cornice with dentils. The W. part of the house retains original timber framework and is jettied W. and S. at the first floor. The lower storey contains an original fireplace with ashlar jambs and an oak bressummer. The corresponding first-floor room is of two bays; the open roof has an arch-braced collar-truss, purlins and curved windbraces. A blocked doorway with an ogee-headed wooden lintel in the N. wall suggests that Nos. 91 and 93 (442) were originally one dwelling.

(442) **House**, No. 93, of two storeys with timber-framed walls fronted with brickwork and with a tiled roof, is mainly of the 15th century. The mid 18th-century E. front has a classical doorcase (Plate 98) in which the entablature incorporates a window; the first-floor room has a projecting sashed bow window. Inside, the E. ground-floor room has a large original fireplace with ashlar jambs and an oak bressummer. On the first floor the E. room has a stone fireplace corresponding with that below. The roof has collared tie-beam trusses with lower angle braces.

(443) **Hall**, formerly adjacent to No. 93 on the W., was ruinous when investigated and recently has been largely demolished although part of the E. end remains. The single-storeyed building had timber-framed walls with wattle-and-daub infilling and a tiled roof. It probably was of 16th-century origin. Latterly used as a warehouse, the original purpose of the building is unknown.

(444) **House**, No. 95, of two storeys and an attic, with brick walls and a tile-covered roof, is of the early 19th century.

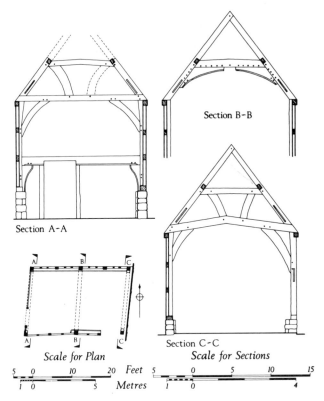

Section B-B

Section A-A

Section C-C

Scale for Plan   *Scale for Sections*

(443) Late mediaeval hall adjoining No. 93 Castle Street.

(445) **House**, No. 137, of two storeys and an attic, with brick walls and a tiled roof, was demolished in 1970. It was of the early 18th century and retained joinery of that period. During demolition the S. wall was seen to include vestiges of antecedent buildings.

(446) **House**, No. 206 Castle Street, of two storeys with attics, has brick walls and slate-covered roofs and was built early in the 19th century. The W. front is symmetrical and of three bays, with a round-headed central doorway under a segmental hood which rests on wood columns; the latter are carved to represent palm trees and reputedly come from Fonthill Abbey (Plate 99). The class-U plan appears on p. lxiv. The dining-room chimneypiece is enriched with a trophy of musical instruments. The stairs have graceful mahogany handrails and turned newel-posts.

(447) **Cottages**, pair, Nos. 184–6, of two storeys with attics, have brick walls and slate-covered roofs and were built *c.* 1800.

(448) **Cottages**, range of four, Nos. 172–8, are two-storeyed with brick walls and slate-covered roofs and were built *c.* 1840.

(449) **Cottages**, two adjacent, Nos. 142–4, are of two storeys with attics and have timber-framed walls partly encased in brickwork, and tile-covered roofs. Probably of 17th-century origin, remodelled *c.* 1850, they were originally one house.

(450) **Cottages**, range of three, Nos. 136–40, are of three storeys with attics and have brick walls and slate-covered roofs; they were built *c.* 1840.

(451) **Cottages**, two adjacent, No. 132, now united and much altered, are two-storeyed with brick walls and slate-covered roofs and are of early 19th-century origin.

(452) **Cottages**, three adjacent, Nos. 124–8, are of two storeys with attics; they have brick walls and tiled roofs and were built *c.* 1850.

(453) **Cottages**, pair, Nos. 1 and 2 Bellvue Place, are two-storeyed with brick walls and tiled roofs; they are of *c.* 1830.

(454) **Cottages**, Nos. 74 and 66, of three storeys with brick walls and slate-covered roofs, were built *c.* 1840. Similar intervening cottages (Nos. 68–72) have recently been demolished.

(455) **Houses**, pair, Nos. 62–4, are three-storeyed with rendered brick walls and slate-covered roofs. They were built *c.* 1840.

(456) **House**, No. 60, of three storeys with brick walls and a slate-covered roof, was built *c.* 1840.

(457) **Cottages**, four adjacent, Nos. 52–8, of two storeys with brick walls and slated roofs, were built *c.* 1840 and demolished in 1970.

(458) **Houses**, two adjacent, Nos. 42–4, demolished in 1970, were of 14th-century origin and originally were probably one house. Each house was two-storeyed with attics and had tile-hung timber-framed walls and a tiled roof; 18th-century street-fronts encompassed the attics and were three-storeyed. No. 44 had a N. wall of flint and stone with tile banding, and a 14th-century three-bay crown-post rafter roof, ridged E.–W. The first floor, jettied on the W., rested on a moulded 15th-century beam. No. 42, of two bays at right-angles to those of No. 44 and thus parallel with Castle Street, included 15th or 16th-century material, but it had been extensively rebuilt in the 18th century.

For monuments in the S. part of Castle Street, on the E. side, see Blue Boar Chequer (p. 132) and White Horse Chequer (p. 142).

ENDLESS STREET

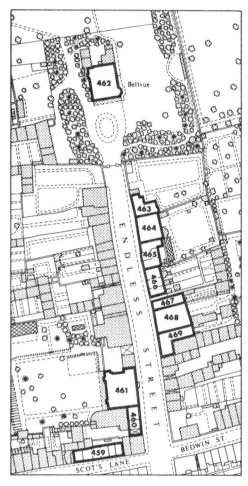

Monuments in the N. part of Endless Street.

(459) Cottages, row of six, Nos. 21–31 Scot's Lane, demolished *c.* 1960, were two-storeyed with attics and had timber-framed walls and a tile-covered roof. They were perhaps of 18th-century origin, but interior fittings were of the 19th century and later.

(460) Houses, two adjoining, Nos. 43–5 Endless Street, of three storeys with brick walls and tiled roofs, were built early in the 19th century. They are now warehouses.

(461) House, No. 47, of three storeys with rendered brick walls and slate-covered roofs, was built *c.* 1830. The plan is of class-U. The E. front is symmetrical and of five bays; in the W. elevation the lower storey has two very large windows with hung sashes, curved on plan. Inside, the stone stairs have cast-iron balustrades and mahogany handrails.

(462) Bellevue House, of two and three storeys with rendered walls and slate-covered roofs, was built during the first quarter of the 19th century. The windows and doorway in the plain four-bay S. front were formerly

sheltered by an iron veranda, but this has now gone. The E. front has four pilasters with moulded capitals. Inside, the oak stairs have plain balustrades and are lit by a circular roof-light. Some rooms have cornices with reeded enrichment.

(463) House, No. 74, of two storeys with attics, with rendered brick walls and tiled roofs, was built early in the 18th century. The symmetrical three-bay W. front has a first-floor plat-band and the remains of a moulded eaves cornice. Inside, the close-string staircase has column-shaped balusters.

(464) House, No. 72 of two storeys with brick walls and a slate-covered roof, was built during the first half of the 18th century, probably after No. 74 (463). The windows in both storeys of the plain four-bay W. front were remodelled in the 19th century, but the doorway retains an original doorcase with a window in the entablature. Inside, the principal rooms have simple 18th-century joinery.

(465) Coach-house and Cottages, range, now three dwellings, Nos. 66–70, of two storeys with attics, with brick walls and tiled roofs, were built towards the end of the 18th century. The W. front is approximately symmetrical and of five bays, the middle bay projecting slightly, the lateral bays having plat-bands and dentil cornices. The lower storey of the middle bay was originally a carriage through-way and the elliptical brick arch is visible in the facade of No. 68.

(466) Houses, row of three, Nos. 60–4, of three storeys with brick walls and tiled roofs, have in the E. elevation a date-stone of 1835, presumably the date of erection.

(467) House, No. 56, of three storeys with brick walls and tiled roofs, was built about the middle of the 18th century. The two-bay W. front has an ashlar plinth, moulded brick plat-bands and a wooden cornice with modillions. The round-headed doorway has a panelled doorcase, a fanlight and an open pediment on scrolled brackets. A Palladian window with a gauged brick arch and a keystone occurs in each of the lower storeys; the

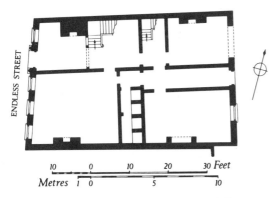

top storey has square-headed windows. Inside, the W. ground-floor room has round-headed niches flanking the fireplace. The stairs have plain balustrades. The rooms in the upper storeys have panelled dados and moulded and enriched chimneypieces. The W. first-floor room has an enriched cornice.

(468) **House**, No. 54, of three storeys and attics, with brick walls and a tiled roof, was built towards the end of the 18th century and evidently was originally an opulent town-house, but is now used as a warehouse.

ENDLESS STREET

10   0   10   20   30 Feet
Metres 1   0   5   10

(468) No. 54 Endless Street. Ground floor.

The five-bay W. front, with plain sashed windows in each storey (Plate 77), has an ashlar plinth and a wooden cornice. The doorway has an open pediment resting on Tuscan columns (Plate 98). Inside, the vestibule has fielded panelling in two heights; other rooms have moulded and fluted cornices and moulded dado rails. The open-string staircase has spandrels with acanthus scrollwork, slender mahogany balusters, column-shaped newel-posts and moulded handrails. Several rooms have original chimneypieces with moulded cornices and fluted friezes. A large E. room on the first floor was probably the drawing-room.

(469) **House**, No. 52, of three storeys with attics, with brick walls and a tile-covered roof, has a W. front

nearly identical with that of No. 54 (468) except that the doorway occupies the centre bay. At present the building is divided into several tenements. Presumably the two houses are contemporary.

BEDWIN STREET

Monuments (470–4) on the N. side of Bedwin Street appear on the maps of Gore's and Parsons Chequers, pp. 144 and 146.

(470) **Royal George Inn**, No. 17, of two storeys with timber-framed and brick walls and with a tiled roof, is of 15th-century origin, but has been extensively altered. The S. front has early 19th-century square-headed sashed windows in the lower storey and segmental-headed casement windows above. Timber framework is exposed in the N. elevation. Inside, the two middle bays of the four-bay range are original and have a roof of three tie-beam trusses with cambered collars, king-struts, lower and upper angle braces and windbraces. A first-floor doorway has a 17th-centry oak frame with chip-carving.

(471) **House**, No. 31, of two storeys with an attic, has rendered brick walls and a tiled roof and is of the late 18th or early 19th century.

(472) **House**, No. 33, of two storeys with attics, has brick walls and tiled roofs and dates from the second half of the 18th century. The five-bay S. front is approximately symmetrical, with a pedimented central doorway, square-headed sashed windows with keystones, and a moulded stringcourse. The W. bay of the lower storey contains a service through-passage. The house was extensively refitted in the 19th century and the N. wing was added.

(473) **Houses**, pair, Nos. 35–7, are two-storeyed with attics and have brick walls and tiled roofs; they were built during the second half of the 18th century. The upper storey of the S. elevation has four plain sashed windows and a parapet with a dentil cornice; the lower storey of No. 35 has a modern shop-window.

(474) **House**, No. 45, of two storeys with brick walls and a tiled roof, was built early in the 19th century. In the lower storey the two-bay S. front has a round-headed doorway and a three-light sashed window; above are a single plain sashed window and a projecting window of three sashed lights.

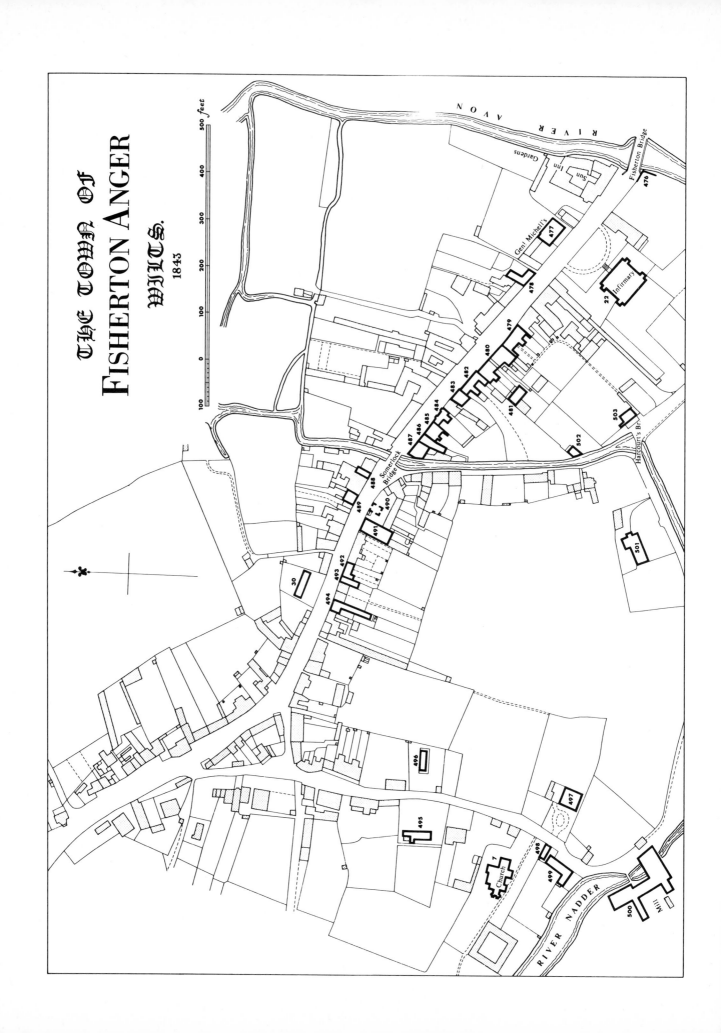

THE TOWN OF
FISHERTON ANGER
WILTS.
1843

100 0 100 200 300 400 500 feet

RIVER AVON

Gardens

Sun Inn

Fisherton Bridge

476

Genl. Michel's

477

478

Infirmary

22

479

480

482

483

484

485

486

487

481

502

503

Somerlock Bridge

Harcourt's Br.

488

489

490

491

492

493

494

30

501

496

497

495

Church

498

499

500

Mill

RIVER NADDER

(475) **School**, built in 1860, 70 yds. N. of the foregoing, incorporates part of a late 15th-century roof from the former *Maidenhead Inn* (25).[1] It has four false hammer-beam collar trusses and is largely of 1860, but moulded wall-plates, chamfered purlins and cusped windbracing are in part original.

Reset in the same building is a 15th-century carved stone fireplace with a roll-moulded elliptical head in an ogee-moulded square surround under a frieze of five quatrefoil panels enclosing plain ribbed shields; above, the moulded cornice includes a blank scroll and a deep hollow-chamfer with spaced leaf bosses. This also comes from the Maidenhead Inn.

1.   *J.B.A.A.*, xv (1859), 15.

FISHERTON AND ST. PAUL WARDS

Until brought into Salisbury by the Municipal Corporations Act of 1835 and subsequent legislation, Fisherton was an independent parish with its own church (7) and parochial administration.[1] The map on p. 156 is based on the Tithe Map of 1843.[2] Monuments not covered by this map are enumerated on the general map in the end-pocket.

1.   V.C.H., *Wilts.* vi, 180–94.
2.   Sar. Corp. MS.

FISHERTON STREET

(476) **Ashlar Walls**, part of the *Gaol* which stood from the 16th century until about 1840 on the W. bank of the R. Avon, immediately S. of Fisherton Bridge, probably date from 1783 when Quarter Sessions ordered the construction of 24 new cells.[1] The two surviving walls, of finely dressed ashlar with moulded plinths and a weathered and hollow-chamfered stringcourse, include two small iron-barred windows. Reset in the masonry is a small stone panel carved to represent gyves (Plate 20); probably it was the embellishment of a doorway. Above rises a clock-tower of 1890.

After the construction of the County Gaol (24) in 1818–22 the old gaol buildings were used for a short time as part of the Infirmary (22). The greater part had been demolished by 1843 (Tithe Map).

1.   *S.J.*, 5 May and 15 Dec., 1783.

(477) **House**, No. 32 Fisherton Street, called 'Genl. Michell's' on the Tithe Map, is of two storeys with attics and has brick walls and tiled roofs. Dating probably from the second quarter of the 18th century, it has been used as a shop and somewhat disfigured; nevertheless several original features remain. In the S.W. front the square-headed doorway with a panelled and bolection-moulded surround, and three plain sashed windows survive; above is a moulded cornice and parapet. Inside, the plan was originally of class U. The S. room on the ground floor retains a plaster ceiling with delicate rococo enrichment. The main stairs have Tuscan-column balustrades and dados with fielded panelling. On the first-floor landing is an archway with a moulded and enriched elliptical head and panelled jambs. The staircase ceiling has an acanthus cornice and a mask surrounded by a sun-burst. Several first-floor rooms have 18th-century joinery.

(478) **House**, No. 40, of two storeys with slate-hung timber-framed walls and tiled roofs, is of the early 16th century. The plan is L–shaped, with a S. range parallel to the road and a rear wing on the north. The roof of the S. range is said to have arch-braced trusses, but is inaccessible; the S. elevation is masked by a modern front. In the N. wing the upper storey was originally jettied on the E., but it has been underbuilt. The N. gable is masked by an early 19th-century extension. Inside, a ground-floor room in the S. part of the N. wing has a stone fireplace surround with a four-centred head. The next room on the N. has original moulded timber wall-plates and intersecting moulded beams forming a ceiling of four panels; the walls have oak panelling, probably of 17th-century origin, altered in the 18th century; the fireplace and a doorway are flanked by fluted pilasters. In its original form the 19th-century N. extension comprised a first-floor room supported on iron columns over an open porch, but the porch has been enclosed to make a ground-floor room.

(479) **Houses**, range of four, Nos. 21–7, on the S. side of the street, are three-storeyed with rendered brick walls and slate-covered roofs; they appear to have been built early in the 19th century. Above modern shop-windows each storey of the N. front has uniform square-headed sashed windows.

(480) **Houses**, range of five, Nos. 29–39 (No. 35 is a through-passage giving access to an adjacent building (481)), are two-storeyed with attics and have brick walls and tiled roofs. They appear to have been built early in the 19th century and originally were approximately uniform. In the N. fronts the lower storeys have modern shop-windows, but the upper storeys retain original square-headed sashed windows with keystones.

(481) **Club Room**, originally a Primitive Methodist Chapel, is of one storey and has rendered brick walls and a slate-covered roof. Built in 1826, it was extended on the S.W. after 1843 (V.C.H., *Wilts.* vi, 193). The hall is lit by round-headed windows, formerly with timber mullions and pointed casements.

(482) **Houses**, range of three, Nos. 41–5, are two-storeyed and have brick walls and tiled roofs. They were built towards the end of the 18th century, but have been extensively altered.

(483) **House**, No. 47, of two storeys with attics, has rendered and tile-hung timber-framed walls, and tiled roofs in two ranges ridged N.E.–S.W. It is of 16th-century origin, but the ground floor has been extensively altered. The upper storey and attics are derelict.

(484) **Houses**, two adjacent, Nos. 55–7, of two storeys with attics, have rendered brick walls and tiled roofs. They were built during the first half of the 18th century and have plain N. street-fronts, each with two sashed first-floor windows; the lower storeys have modern shop-windows. On the ground floor the houses are separated by a covered through-passage giving access to a yard.

(485) **House**, divided into three tenements (Nos. 59–63) during the late 18th or early 19th century, is two-storeyed with rendered brick walls and tiled roofs; it was built about the middle of the 17th century. The N. elevation has a 19th-century facade of three bays; the S. side is masked by outbuildings. Inside, the original plan has gone, but a staircase retains a short length of original balustrade with three upright planks profiled to represent balusters. The original roof has four stout collared tie-beam trusses with lower king-struts and principals with deep chamfers.

(486) **Cottage**, No. 65, of two storeys with attics, has timber-framed walls cased in brickwork and a tiled roof. It is probably of late 16th or early 17th-century origin, but little remains of the original structure. The stairs retain three profiled uprights as in monument (485). A few rough-hewn members of timber framework are exposed.

(487) **Houses**, two adjacent, Nos. 67–9, are three-storeyed with brick walls and slate-covered roofs and were built during the first half of the 19th century.

(488) **Cottage**, No. 96, on the N. of the street, is of two periods. The N.E. wing, single-storeyed with an attic, with timber-framed walls cased in brickwork and with a tiled roof, is of the 17th century. The part of the house which fronts the street is two-storeyed with brick walls

and a slated roof and dates from *c.* 1800. Inside, the N.E. room has an exposed beam.

(489) **House**, No. 102, of two storeys with brick walls and a slate-covered roof, is of the 19th century but earlier than 1843 (Tithe Map). The S. front has three plain sashed windows in the upper storey.

(490) **House**, No. 79, of three storeys with brick walls and slated roofs, was built after 1843 and has recently been demolished.

(491) **Cottage**, No. 81, of two storeys with brick-cased timber-framed walls and a tiled roof, is perhaps of *c.* 1600. The lower storey is occupied by a modern shop; the upper part of the N.E. front has two 18th-century sashed windows; The roof has chamfered purlins, but all other features are concealed. O.S., 1880 names it the Lamb Inn.

(492) **Cottages**, range of three, Nos. 89–93, originally single-storeyed with attics, but now two-storeyed, have brick-cased timber-framed walls and tile-covered roofs. The cottages were probably built in the 16th

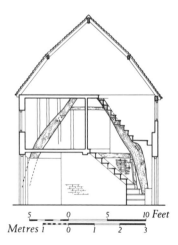

(492) No. 93 Fisherton Street. Section, looking E.

century. In the 18th century the N.E. fronts were cased in brickwork and the attics were made into upper storeys. Both blades of an open cruck truss are seen in the wall between Nos. 91 and 93. Masonry with a large socketed stone at the W. corner of No. 89 is perhaps the footing for another cruck, now gone.

(493) **House and Shop**, No. 95, of three storeys with brick walls and a slate-covered roof, were built during the first half of the 19th century.

(494) **King's Arms Inn**, of two storeys with rendered brick walls and a slate-covered roof, is of 18th-century origin, but it was extensively altered in the 19th century and later.

Hayter's Almshouses, see (30).

CHURCH STREET, MILL ROAD AND CRANE BRIDGE ROAD

(495) **Clovelly Hotel**, of two storeys with brick walls and slate-covered roofs, was built in 1830. The five-bay E. front has plain sashed windows in each storey; the doorway is modern.

(496) **Cottage**, of one storey with brick walls and a slate-covered roof, is of the first half of the 19th century.

(497) **Fisherton Rectory**, demolished in 1972, was of two storeys with attics and had brick-faced walls and tile-covered roofs. On demolition the S.W. part of the house was found to be mainly of timber-frame construction and probably of 16th-century origin. During the 17th century the building had been cased in brickwork and extended northwards, giving it a class-T plan with a symmetrical W. front of five bays. In the 18th century

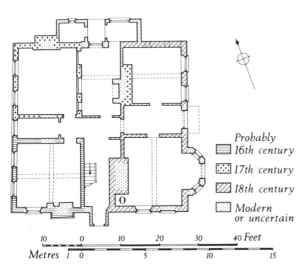

Probably
▤ *16th century*
▨ *17th century*
▨ *18th century*
▦ *Modern or uncertain*

10   0   10   20   30   40 Feet
Metres 1 0   5   10   15

(497) Fisherton Rectory. Ground floor.

the house was again enlarged, the plan becoming square and of class U. After a fire in 1834 the interior was remodelled and the entrance was transferred from the W. front to the E. (V.C.H., *Wilts.* vi, 192).

Inside, the S.W. ground-floor room had a N.–S. ceiling beam with double ogee mouldings supporting

lateral beams with run-out chamfers. The N. and E. walls in this room and in the chamber above were of timber framework. A jowl-headed post supported a large beam in the attic floor; the roof contained one blade of a cruck. A large chimneybreast and the remains of a bread-oven (o) show that the S.E. room of the 18th-century house was the kitchen. In the 17th century the kitchen had probably been on the E. of the N.W. room.

(498) **Cottage**, of two storeys with brick walls and a slate-covered roof, was built early in the 19th century.

(499) **House and Cottages**, subsequently combined as one dwelling, are two-storeyed with attics and have brick walls and tiled roofs; they were built about the middle of the 18th century. The house at the S.W. end of the range has a symmetrical S.W. front of five bays with a central doorway and plain square-headed casement windows. The three cottages in the N.E. wing are each of one bay. Inside, the house has a class-T plan; that of each cottage is class S. Some fireplaces have brick jambs and plain timber bressummers.

(500) **Mill House** (the adjoining **Mills** were demolished *c.* 1970), beside the R. Nadder, is in fact in Harnham (below, p. 169), but it is listed here for convenience of perambulation. Mills appear to have been on the site since Domesday,[1] but nothing seen today is earlier than the three-storeyed house, with brick walls and tiled roofs, which dates from about the middle of the 18th century. The three-bay S.E. front has moulded brick plat-bands and cornice, and a brick parapet divided into bays. The square-headed windows have plain sashes and the doorway has a panelled doorcase flanked by fluted pilasters which support an arched and moulded hood. Inside, the main rooms retain original fittings and have panelled dados and moulded plaster cornices.

A range of mill buildings which formerly adjoined the house to N.E. (photographs in N.M.R.) was three-storeyed with attics and had brick walls and slate-covered roofs. Although of 18th-century origin it was later than the mill house and appears to have been of two periods, the three English-bonded western bays being earlier than the two Flemish-bonded bays on the east. A similar range of mill buildings extended N.W. from the mill house, parallel with the river, and was of the 19th century, but earlier than 1843 (Tithe Map). A third demolished range, in the same alignment as that last mentioned and of similar character, is probably the 'new-erected mill for machinery' which was advertised in 1806,[2] it appeared, however, to make use of 18th-century walls.

1. V.C.H., *Wilts.* vi, 192.
2. *S.J.*, 24 March.

(501) **Harcourt House**, formerly 'Fisherton Cottage',[1] is of two storeys with attics and has brick walls and tiled roofs; it was built late in the 18th century. On the Reform Act map of 1833, land on the N. is named Harcourt's Garden. The S. front is symmetrical and of three wide bays with a round-headed central doorway under a small pedimented hood, a plain sashed window above it and wide windows of three sashed lights in the other bays. To the E. is an extension with bow windows in both storeys. Inside, the original plan was of class T, but the house has been incorporated in a large modern building and all the original fittings have gone.

1. V.C.H., *Wilts.* vi, 183.

(502) **Harcourt Cottage**, of two storeys with brick walls and a low-pitched slate-covered roof, was built early in the 19th century.

(503) **House**, No. 6 Crane Bridge Road, has characteristics similar to the foregoing. On O.S. 1880 it is 'Lavington Cottage'.

(504) **Cottage and Outbuilding**, demolished *c.* 1965, were two-storeyed with brick walls and tiled roofs and were built about the end of the 18th century. Part of the outbuilding was used for malting and part appears to have been stables.

(505) **Bowling Green House**, of two storeys with attics, has brick walls, partly rendered, and tiled roofs and appears to have been built early in the 18th century. A house is shown in this position on Naish's map of 1716. The S.E. front is symmetrical and of two bays with a central doorway. Inside, no notable features are seen.

(506) **Crane Lodge**, demolished in 1963, was of two storeys with attics and had brick walls and tiled and slated roofs. The main rooms in the N.W. part of the house were of the 18th century. Later in the same century the S.E. service wing was added or rebuilt, and *c.* 1800 the N.E. front of the main range was partly refaced and a two-storeyed porch bay was added. Other extensions were of *c.* 1900.

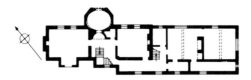

The symmetrical five-bay N.E. front was of red brick with a white brick plat-band and a moulded plaster cornice. From the use of different brick bonds and from minor changes in level it appeared that the two W. bays

were original (with later windows) while the octagonal porch and the facing of the two E. bays were of *c.* 1800. The central doorcase and fanlight were good examples of their period. The S.W. elevation was tile-hung and to a large extent masked by modern additions (not shown on plan).

Inside, the oval vestibule of *c.* 1800 had shallow round-headed recesses. The apsidal staircase hall, presumably of the same date, had a frieze of palm-leaves and sunflowers. The dining-room had a wood chimney-piece of *c.* 1800 (Plate 94) with a pastoral scene carved on the frieze. The staircase had been rebuilt *c.* 1900 and there were no other notable features.

WILTON ROAD

(507) **Evelyn House** and **College House**, Nos. 49 and 51, on the S. side of the road, demolished in 1965, were two-storeyed with brick walls and slate-covered roofs and were built between 1833 (Reform Act map) and 1854 (Kingdon & Shearm).

(508) **Pembroke Lodge**, adjacent to the foregoing and now part of the Old Manor Hospital, is two-storeyed with rendered walls and slate-covered roofs. It is not shown on the map of 1833 but appears by style to be of about that date. In the N. front, rounded on plan, the lower storey has a peripteral colonnade of Tuscan columns which support the overhanging first floor. The windows have four-centred heads. The building is named on the map of 1854.

(509) **House**, No. 20, on the N. of the road, demolished *c.* 1965, was two-storeyed with rendered brick walls and tiled roofs. It probably was of the late 17th or early 18th century. The original range had a S. front of two bays with three-light sashed windows in the lower storey and with single-light windows above. An E. extension had two plain sashed windows in each storey and was probably of the late 18th century. The N. side was masked by 19th-century additions. Inside, the house had been entirely refitted in the 19th century. The map of 1854 shows the building as divided into two houses.

(510) **The Paragon**, two nearly uniform pairs of houses in an enclosure on the N. side of the road, does not appear on the map of 1833 but was complete by 1854. The buildings are two-storeyed, with brick walls and low-pitched slate-covered roofs. Each pair of houses has a symmetrical four-bay facade with sashed windows, and square-headed doorways flanked by reeded half-columns. Inside, the principal rooms have moulded ceiling cornices and simple 19th-century joinery.

(511) **Llangarren**, house, of two storeys with cellars and attics, has brick walls and a low-pitched slate-covered roof. It occupies a central position in The Paragon (510) and is of the same date. The symmetrical S. front is of three bays and the middle window of the principal storey is accentuated by a pediment. As this window is false, it is probable that the building originated as a pair of houses with a common facade, but they are now united and the interior has been entirely remodelled.

(512) **The Old Manor**, formerly Fisherton House (V.C.H., *Wilts.* vi, 183), hospital, on the S. of Wilton Road, is of three storeys with rendered walls and lead-covered roofs. The building has been much altered, but it has as its nucleus a 19th-century house shown on the Reform Act map of 1833.

(513) **House**, adjacent to the foregoing and also adapted for hospital use, was demolished *c.* 1965. It was two-storeyed with brick walls and a tiled roof and had been built early in the 19th century. Both N. and S. elevations were symmetrical and of three bays.

(514) **House**, on the S. of the road and now part of the hospital (512), is of two storeys with brick walls and slate-covered roofs. It was built during the first quarter of the 19th century and has a class-U plan. The N. front was originally symmetrical and of three bays, with two-storeyed semicircular bow windows flanking a central doorway. About the middle of the 19th century a three-storeyed porch was added.

(515) **Elm Cottage**, on the N. of the road, directly opposite the foregoing, was demolished *c.* 1970. It was two-storeyed with brick walls and a slate-covered roof and was built after 1833 (Reform Act map). A pair of two-storeyed bow windows closely resembling those of the opposite house (514) were added after 1854 (Kingdon & Shearm).

(516) **West End Hotel**, some 100 yds. W. of the foregoing, is of three storeys with brick walls and tiled roofs. It is mainly of the early 19th century, but parts of an 18th-century cottage are incorporated in the structure.

(517) **House**, No. 161, on the S. side of the road, ¼ mile W. of the foregoing, is two-storeyed with attics and has brick walls and tiled roofs. The N. range is perhaps of 18th-century origin, but it was extensively altered in the 19th century and later and no notable features remain. The original plan was of class T.

BEMERTON VILLAGE

St. Andrew's Church, see (9).

(518) **Bridge House**, of two storeys with walls partly of cob and partly of rendered brickwork and with slate-covered roofs, originated late in the 18th century as a cottage, probably with a class-S plan. In the 19th century, probably before 1838,[1] the building was enlarged on the north-west. The S.E. front has square-headed casement windows of two lights with the glazing-bars set to form marginal panes; these occur in both storeys. Inside, a horizontal ledge in the earlier part of the S.W. wall indicates that the original cottage was of one storey with an attic.

1. Bemerton Estate sale catalogue, 1838. Copy in Devizes Museum.

(519) **Elm Tree Cottage**, now of two storeys with brick walls and an asbestos-covered roof, is of 18th-century origin, but much altered. The building was formerly single-storeyed and had a class-S plan. Inside, the main room contains an original fireplace with brick jambs and a chamfered bressummer. The ceiling has a chamfered beam and stout joists.

(520) **Bemerton House**, of two storeys with cellars, has slate-hung cob walls and a low-pitched slate-covered roof; it was built shortly before 1850. The N. and S. fronts are each approximately symmetrical and of three bays with square-headed sashed windows with glazing-bars set to form marginal panes. The S. front has a bow window in the E. bay of the lower storey and another centrally in the upper storey. A modern projection in the lower storey masks the original front doorway. Inside, the plan is of class U. The staircase has plain balustrades and a mahogany handrail with a curtail.

(521) **Manor House**, of two storeys with walls largely of brick, but with some timber framework and with tiled roofs, is mainly of the 17th century. The

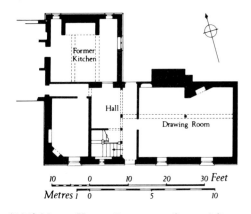

(521) Manor House, Bemerton. Ground floor.

rendered S. front was rebuilt early in the 18th century and has plain sashed windows and a square-headed doorway. The 17th-century N. elevation has a large brick chimneybreast with ashlar quoins; in the upper storey is a stone window of three square-headed lights with hollow-chamfered mullions and heads. Beside it is a chamfered timber window of two lights.

Inside, the drawing-room has been formed by the removal of a partition between two rooms; the beam in the E. part is deeply chamfered, that in the W. has narrow chamfers. Exposed in the partition on the W. of the staircase is a jowl-headed post supporting an oak beam which formerly was jettied to S.; the 18th-century S.W. front evidently supersedes a jettied timber-framed elevation. The stairs have stout turned oak balusters, plain newel-posts with ball finials, moulded strings and stout handrails. In the former kitchen, 17th-century chamfered beams support stout joists; the fireplace is masked by reset 18th-century panelling. Rooms on the first floor have panelled dados, moulded ceiling cornices and chamfered beams. Some timber framework is exposed in the W. wall. The single-storeyed W. wing (not shown), containing the present service rooms, is probably of the late 18th century and was formerly stables.

(522) **House**, of two storeys with walls mainly of brickwork, but partly of flint and rubble and with a tiled roof, is of the first half of the 18th century. Extensions N.E. and S.W. of the original range are of c. 1800. The original range has a brick plat-band on the S.E. front and casement windows of two and three square-headed lights. Inside, the partition between the two original ground-floor rooms is of plank-and-muntin construction. The S.W. room has a large fireplace with a heavy timber bressummer.

(523) **House**, of two storeys with attics and a cellar, has rendered cob walls and a slate-covered roof. The N., S. and E. elevations have windows and a doorway uniform with those of Bemerton House (520); the W. elevation is masked by an extension. Inside, the plan is of class U. A carved stone plaque depicting a female astride a horse, set in the wall of the cellar stairs, bears the inscription 'This house was built in 1848'.

(524) **Cottage**, of one storey with cob walls and a thatched roof, is probably of the 18th century. Although now a single dwelling, the plan suggests that it was originally a pair of class-S dwellings set end-to-end with a common chimneystack. The end walls are rounded on plan.

(525) **Barn**, with weatherboarded timber-framed walls set on brick plinths and with an iron-covered roof, is probably of c. 1850.

(526) **House**, now two cottages, 150 yds. E.S.E. of St. Andrew's Church (8), is of one storey with attics. The walls are mainly of 18th-century brickwork and the roofs are asbestos-covered, but the house is of 16th-century origin. Some original flint and rubble masonry remains at the base of the walls. The roof rests on four raised crucks which had dove-tailed or tenoned collars at two levels and carried two purlins on each side. The dove-tailed mortices of former wall-spurs remain. Crucks ii, iii and iv are closed in the upper part with panels of wattle and daub. The lower collar of cruck ii (no longer *in situ*, but partly preserved) has foliate decoration

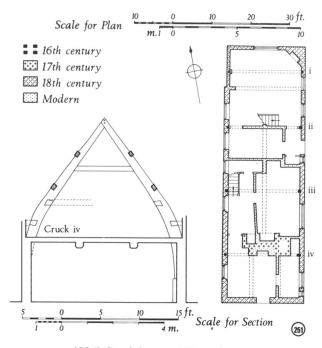

Scale for Plan

■ ■ *16th century*

▨ *17th century*

▨ *18th century*

▨ *Modern*

Cruck iv

Scale for Section

(526) Cruck house at Bemerton.

painted in grey on a white ground. Heavy smoke-blackening on the S. side of cruck iii and on the N. side of cruck iv indicates an original open hearth in the intervening bay. In the 17th century a brick chimney-stack with back-to-back fireplaces and an oven was built close to the N. side of cruck iv, and an attic floor was inserted in the bay to S.; the floor rests on two stout beams with deep chamfers ending in splayed stops. Of the beams which support the attic floors in the bays between crucks ii and iv, that to S. has narrow chamfers and that to N. has deep chamfers with stepped and concave stops.

During the 18th century the outside walls were re-built in brickwork. In c. 1800 the N. bay was remodelled.

(527) **House**, of two storeys with brick walls and low-pitched slate-covered roofs, was built during the second quarter of the 19th century. A vertical joint in the six-bay S. front suggests that the two E. bays are later than the others. A seventh bay at the W. end, with a projecting window in each storey, is later than 1850. The square-headed openings of the original range have french casements in the lower storey and sashed windows above. The main rooms have mid 19th-century joinery and moulded cornices.

(528) **The Rectory**, of two storeys with attics, has original walls of knapped flint and rubble with ashlar dressings, and tiled roofs. In style the original walls are of the early 17th century and no doubt represent the house built for the poet George Herbert (rector 1630–2). Nothing is distinguishable of the earlier house, 'fallen down or decayed by reason of his predecessor's living 16 or 20 miles from this place'.[1] Extensive additions during the second half of the 19th century have walls partly of flint and partly of brick with ashlar dressings. (W. addition demolished, 1978.)

The S. elevation of the 17th-century range retains an ogee-moulded ashlar plinth and rubble walls, but all original openings have been replaced by 18th-century sashed windows or by casement windows of later date. The attic dormer windows are modern. The gabled E. wall has masonry of chequered flint and ashlar above a chamfered plinth; the only opening is a small square-headed attic window. The N. side of the main range is hidden by 19th-century additions, but the E. and N. walls of the original N. wing are exposed (Plate 68); they are of chequered flint and ashlar and have chamfered plinths. An original N. window in the lower storey has two square-headed casement lights with ovolo-moulded surrounds under a weathered and hollow-chamfered label; the label continues E. to embrace the adjacent window, rebuilt in the 19th century. Both corresponding first-floor windows are of the 19th century, but the original label remains. In the gable there is a modern sashed window under an original label. The E. wall of the N. wing has an original casement window in the lower storey with two square-headed lights in a double-chamfered surround under a label as before; the mullion has gone. At the centre of the 19th-century N. facade a modern ashlar panel is inscribed with the verses which Herbert 'caused to be writ upon or engraved in the mantel of the chimney in his hall':

To my successor:
If thou chance to find a new house to thy mind
    And built without thy cost,
Be good to the poor as God gives thee store,
    And then my labour's not lost.[2]

Inside, the former hall has a large projecting chimney-breast upon which these verses were no doubt inscribed, but the present chimneypiece is modern. The former kitchen has a chamfered E.–W. ceiling beam with beaded and ogee stops; the E. end rests on a modern beam, similarly chamfered, no doubt replacing a former wall. The kitchen fireplace has chamfered ashlar jambs and a cambered timber bressummer; the tiled lining and inner hearth are modern. To S. there may originally have been an oven. The S. wall of the former kitchen has painted deal panelling. The parlour has a moulded plaster cornice, perhaps of the 18th century. The chamber over the parlour has a late 18th-century

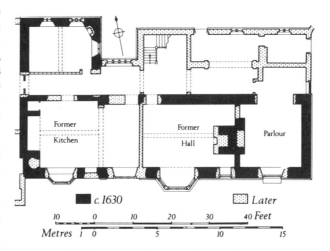

(528) Bemerton Rectory. Ground floor.

chimneypiece, moulded dados and a coved cornice; on the N. is an arched recess. Three first-floor rooms in the main range have original chamfered ceiling beams similar to that of the former kitchen; another such beam is in the first-floor room of the N. wing. In the roofs, original collared tie-beam trusses are made with plain rough-hewn timbers.

Adjoining the house on the W. is a late 18th-century stable range with brick walls and tiled roofs. Further W. is a walled garden, probably of the same date. A barn to S., with weather-boarded timber-framed walls set on brick plinths and with an iron-covered roof, is probably of the early 19th century.

1.   Izaac Walton, *Life of Mr. George Herbert*, passim.
2.   *ibid.*

(529) **Cottage**, of two storeys with brick walls and a slated roof, is of the early 19th century.

DEVIZES ROAD

(530) **House**, No. 23, now demolished, was of two storeys with rendered brick walls and slate-covered roofs. It was of the 19th century, but earlier than 1833 (Reform Act map). The S. front was approximately symmetrical and of three bays, with plain sashed windows and with a doorway with a reeded surround. Extensions to E. and W. were of c. 1850.

(531) **House**, No. 61, of two storeys with brick walls and a slate-covered roof, is of the first half of the 19th century. The symmetrical N.E. front has three bays with plain sashed windows and a square-headed doorway with a reeded surround. The plan is of class U.

(532) **Cottages**, pair, Nos. 1 and 2 Prospect Place, are two-storeyed with rendered brick walls and slate-covered roofs. Although advertised as 'new built' in 1831,[1] they are not shown on the map of 1833. The combined E. fronts originally formed a symmetrical composition of five bays. Inside, the stairs have plain balustrades and column-shaped newel posts.

1. *S.J.*, 5 Sept., 1831.

(533) **Cottages**, pair, Nos. 81–3 Devizes Road, recently demolished, were two-storeyed with cellars and attics and had rendered brick walls and slate-covered

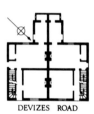

DEVIZES ROAD

roofs; they were built not long before 1833. The four-bay N.E. front had plain sashed windows and square-headed doorways with reeded surrounds. Inside, the front-room fireplaces had reeded decoration.

(534) **Cottages**, two, Nos. 85–7, recently demolished, were of two storeys with rendered brick walls and slate-covered roofs. They were built before 1833.

(535) **Barn**, with weather-boarded timber-framed walls set on a tall brick plinth and with a slated roof, is of c. 1850.

(536) **Cottage**, formerly on the N.E. side of the road, but recently demolished, was two-storeyed with rendered brick walls and a slated roof and was built between 1833 and 1854. The S.E. front was of two bays with a central doorway.

(537) **Farmhouse**, on the N.E. side of the road, ¾ mile N.W. of the junction with Wilton Road, is two-storeyed with brick walls and slate-covered roofs. It was built c. 1850 and has a symmetrical S.E. front of three bays with sashed windows and a round-headed doorway.

ST. MARK WARD

For location of monuments, see folding map in end-pocket.

STRATFORD—sub—CASTLE

(538) **Portway Cottage**, of two storeys with brick walls and a thatched roof, was built c. 1700. On the N. is a 19th-century extension with a tiled roof. The S.E. front has a plain plat-band and segmental-headed casement windows. Inside, two fireplaces have oak bressummers with ogee mouldings. A ground-floor room has a chamfered beam with ogee stops. The roof has collared tie-beam trusses.

(539) **Moreton Cottage**, of one storey with attics, has flint walls with brick dressings and a thatched roof. The middle part of the range is of the first half of the 18th century. Extensions to E. and W. were originally separate cottages, but the whole range is now united. Inside, rough-hewn beams are exposed.

(540) **Cottage**, of two storeys with brick walls and a tiled roof, was built about the middle of the 18th century. A single-storeyed extension on the N.W. is of the 19th century.

(541) **Cottage**, of two storeys with brick walls and a tiled roof, was built early in the 19th century.

(542) **Cottages**, two adjoining, perhaps originally a range of four small dwellings, are single-storeyed with attics and have walls mainly of flint and rubble with brick dressings, and thatched roofs; they date from early in the 18th century. Several rooms are spanned by chamfered beams.

(543) **Orchard Cottage**, of one storey with attics, has rendered brick, flint and rubble walls and a tiled roof. It was built early in the 18th century and until recently was thatched. Inside, chamfered beams are exposed.

(544) **Orchard House**, of two storeys with brick walls and slate-covered roofs, was built towards the end of the 18th century. The symmetrical three-bay N.E. front has a doorway with pilasters supporting a moulded cornice, and plain sashed windows in each storey. The plan, originally of class T, is modified by an extensive S.W. wing suitable for present use as a hostel.

(545) **House**, of two storeys with walls of rendered brick and flint and with slated and tiled roofs, was built early in the 19th century.

(546) **Cottage**, formerly a coach-house adjoining the foregoing, has similar characteristics.

(547) **Cottage**, of one storey with an attic, with flint and rubble walls with brick dressings and with a thatched roof, is of 17th-century origin. Inside, a chamfered beam has ogee stops; another is cambered.

(548) **Cottages**, two adjacent, formerly divided into four dwellings, are two-storeyed and have timber-framed walls set on rubble plinths, and thatched roofs; they were built late in the 16th century. Inside, chamfered beams are exposed. An open fireplace has stone jambs and a cambered timber lintel.

(549) **Parsonage Farm House**, of 16th-century origin with 18th-century and early 19th-century additions and alterations, has walls mainly of flint and rubble with ashlar dressings and tiled roofs; the E. front is of brick. The E. range, of two storeys with attics, dates from about the middle of the 16th century; the single-storeyed S. range, also with attics, was built later in the same century.[1]

The symmetrical five-bay E. front, added early in the 19th century, masks an older elevation which, to judge by the wall-thicknesses, is of stone in the lower storey and of timber framework above the first floor. The rubble and ashlar N. and S. walls of the S. range retain some original openings: The N. window in the dining-room, of stone, has four square-headed lights with chamfered and ovolo-moulded jambs, mullions and head, and a hollow-chamfered and weathered label; to the W. is a similar single-light window. Further W. is an 18th-century doorway and a four-light window. The S. elevation of the range has an original window of two lights as described, and the original labels of three more 16th-century openings, now with modern casements; that which lights the S. end of the dining-room formerly had five stone-mullioned lights. The W. end of the S. range is concealed by an extension, later than 1850 and not shown on the plan.

Presumably the E. range originally contained a hall, but it can no longer be distinguished. The vestibule has 17th-century oak panelling on the S. side. The drawing-room and study have 19th-century joinery and plaster-work. A stone doorway at the W. end of the vestibule has a chamfered four-centred head and continuous jambs. In the S. range the dining-room ceiling has a chamfered beam with shaped stops. In the W. sitting room a bread-oven and a blocked fireplace are of the early 19th century, but the chamfers on the ceiling beam indicate that there was originally a much deeper open fireplace in

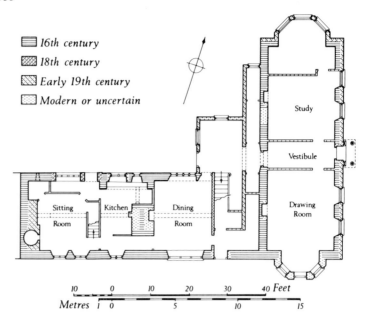

16th century
18th century
Early 19th century
Modern or uncertain

Study

Vestibule

Sitting Room

Kitchen

Dining Room

Drawing Room

10 0 10 20 30 40 Feet
Metres 1 0 5 10 15

(549) Parsonage Farm House. Ground floor.

the same position. The attic chamber over the dining-room is lined with 17th-century oak panelling and has an original barrel-vaulted plaster ceiling; the square-headed doorway has chamfered jambs with run-out stops. The roof of the E. range has collared trusses with butt purlins and curved windbraces.

1. Nothing seen today corresponds with buildings mentioned in 15th-century documents (V.C.H., *Wilts.* vi, 205).

(550) **Barns**, two, formerly associated with Parsonage Farm, have weather-boarded timber-framed walls and tiled and iron-covered roofs; they date from late in the 17th century. The walls have plinths of flint and brick.

(551) **Cottage**, of two storeys with an attic, with timber-framed and brick walls and with a thatched roof, is of the early 17th century. The N.W. and S.W. sides retain original framework; the N.E. and S.E. sides were rebuilt or cased in brickwork in 1703 (inscription). Inside, the plan is of class I. A first-floor room has a 17th-century plaster overmantel with a moulded border enclosing roundels depicting birds and flowers.

(552) **House**, of two storeys with rendered brick walls and tiled roofs, is probably of 18th-century origin, but has been altered in recent times.

(553) **House**, of two storeys with brick walls and slate-covered roofs, was formerly a water-mill, probably of the late 18th century. The upper storey is modern.

(554) **Cottage**, of two storeys with walls of banded flint and brickwork and with a tiled roof, dates from the first quarter of the 19th century. The N.E. front is symmetrical and of three bays. The plan is of class S.

(555) **House**, of two storeys with attics, was built at two periods. The S.W. range has slate-hung timber-framed walls and a tiled roof and is of the 17th century; the parallel N.E. range, with brick walls and a slated roof, is of *c*. 1850. Inside, the S.W. range has a class-J plan. The S.E. room has a large fireplace with chamfered stone jambs and a chamfered oak bressumer; a single-storeyed S.E. extension is of the later 17th century. The N.E. range has a class-T plan and a symmetrical facade of three bays with plain sashed windows and a central doorway.

(556) **Vicarage**, now called Prebendal House although its association with the former prebendal estate is uncertain (V.C.H., *Wilts*. vi, 203), is two-storeyed with attics and has walls mainly of brick, with areas of flint and rubble, and tiled roofs (Plate 70). Different wall-thicknesses, room-heights and standards of construction and decoration separate the house into two parts. By its style the N.W. bay is good quality domestic architecture of *c*. 1700; the remaining two-thirds of the building appear to be inferior work of the first half of the 19th century. The inconsistency cannot be positively explained. The N.W. bay may be the surviving wing of a substantial house, the rest of which has perished, or it may have been built as a country retreat of only two rooms for occasional use by a rich man who generally lived elsewhere.

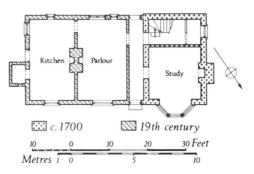

(556) Stratford Vicarage. Ground floor.

The N.E. front of the earlier bay has in each storey a bow window of Palladian form; above is a coved eaves cornice. The N.W. elevation, of flint with brick quoins, has a Palladian window on the first floor to light the staircase. The S.W. elevation is of squared rubble with flint and brick banding; above the first floor it is rendered. In the 19th-century part of the house the walls are wholly of brick.

Inside, the study has original joinery of good quality, including a chimneypiece with an eared and enriched surround and a frieze with foliate scrollwork. The door-case has an eared architrave and a pulvinated entablature. The stairs have close strings and column-shaped balustrades. The room over the study has a moulded cornice and dado, and a chimneypiece with a moulded and enriched cornice, consoles flanking a rococo frieze and an eared surround with egg-and-dart enrichment. The S.E. rooms have no notable features.

(557) **Mawarden Court**, house, partly of one and partly of two storeys with attics, has ashlar-faced walls and tiled roofs. The two-storeyed E. range is of *c*. 1600; the single-storeyed W. range was added during the second half of the 17th century, probably in 1673. The E. range was originally larger than at present and had a half-H plan, but the N. wing was demolished *c*. 1835. A drawing of 1805 by J. Buckler shows the E. front as symmetrical and of five bays with a gabled bay at the centre and with projecting N. and S. wings, also gabled.[1] After 1835 the E. wall of the N. wing was re-erected S. of its original position, maintaining the symmetry of the E. front, but reducing its length from five bays to three and suppressing the middle gable (Plate 69).

The E. front has chamfered plinths, and windows with chamfered and ovolo-moulded stone surrounds under weathered and hollow-chamfered labels. A single-storeyed porch between the two gabled bays has a square-headed doorway flanked by rusticated pilasters; these were taken from the old central porch, and a date-stone of 1673 with the inscription 'parva sed apta domino' has been reset above the opening. The oak door appears to be of the early 17th century.

The N. elevation of the E. range is composed of the S. side of the demolished N. wing, refaced in ashlar *c*. 1835. The N. end of the W. range is of brick. Reset above the modern window in the short W. wall which links the two N. elevations is a damaged cartouche-of-arms of *c*. 1600: Herbert quartering Cradock, Horton and Cantelupe with crescent for difference; above is a plain helmet without crest.

The W. front of the single-storeyed W. range (Plate 69) has five sashed windows with rebated architraves and a doorway with a similar architrave under a segmental broken pediment which rests on fluted brackets. The window sashes have stout glazing-bars and are largely original. The attic windows are modern.

The S. elevation is of ashlar chequered with flint. Two windows in the later 17th-century range have modern sashes; further E. is an original staircase window of four transomed lights with ovolo-moulded surrounds and a label. The eastern part of the elevation is masked by a 19th-century service wing.

Inside, the hall formerly had an original fireplace with a cambered and moulded head and continuous

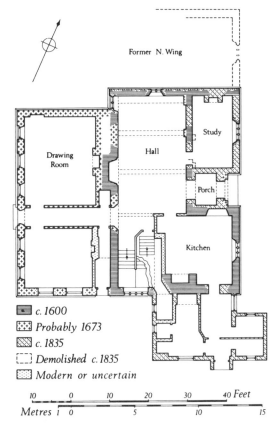

c. 1600

Probably 1673

c. 1835

Demolished c.1835

Modern or uncertain

(557) Mawarden Court. Ground floor.

stone jambs ending in shaped stops; a 16th-century carved stone chimneypiece, from elsewhere, was substituted in 1976. The transomed two-light N. window of c. 1600 is evidently reset. The cased ceiling beams have 18th-century mouldings. The present kitchen, perhaps originally the parlour (the original kitchen is likely to have been in the N. wing), has a large chimneybreast; a recess in the N. wall marks the position of a former window. The study, formed in 1835, has an early 17th-century E. window transferred from the original N. wing. The oak close-string stairs are of dog-leg form with rounded oak newel-posts; a plastered partition takes the place of a balustrade. The rooms of the W. range have late 17th-century bolection-moulded panelling in two heights. The drawing-room (Plate 97) has a bolection-moulded fireplace surround of red marble. The doorway in the W. front has panelled half-doors surmounted by glazed sashes. On the first floor, several rooms in the E. range have 17th-century panelling, cornices etc. and there is some woodwork of c. 1600. A window of three lights in the W. wall of the E. range was blocked when the W. range was added. The attic rooms in the W. range have modern fittings. The original roof of the E. range has collared tie-beam trusses with queen-struts.

1. V.C.H., *Wilts*. vi, 206.

(558) **House**, of two storeys with brick walls and tiled roofs, originated in the 18th century as a single-storeyed building, perhaps agricultural in use. In the 19th century it was converted into a row of cottages (probably four) and an upper storey was built; later it was changed to two larger cottages. The walls have recently been reused in the construction of a modern house.

(559) **Dean's Farm House**, of two storeys with walls mainly of banded brick and flint and with tiled and slated roofs, dates from late in the 18th century. The original house comprised two parallel ranges separated by an open space; the N. range had a large kitchen in

the lower storey. Early in the 19th century the W. range was added, with a symmetrical brick W. front of three bays, with plain sashed windows and a central doorway sheltered by a small columned porch. Later in the 19th century, bow windows were added to N. and S. and the space between the two original ranges was partly filled in.

(560) **Granary**, at Dean's Farm, with walls of timber framework clad in corrugated iron and with a corrugated iron roof, is of 18th-century origin. The five-bay roof has collared tie-beam trusses with lower angle struts. The floor rests on staddle-stones.

CASTLE HILL

(561) **Cottages**, pair, with cob walls on brick and flint plinths and with slated roofs, are of the first half of the 19th century. Formerly the roofs were thatched.

(562) **Old Castle Inn**, of two storeys with walls of flint, rubble and brick and with a tiled roof, has as its nucleus a flint-walled cottage with a class-S plan, probably of the second half of the 16th century. The original S.E. front is defined by a chamfered stone plinth and ashlar quoins, probably taken from the nearby castle of Old Sarum; permission to use the castle as a quarry for building materials was given in 1514 (p. 4, note 34). A single-storeyed extension to S.W. has a plinth continuous with that of the cottage. During the 18th century the S.W. extension was heightened and a brick

end-wall and a tile-hung chimneystack were built. An extension to N.E., with rendered walls, is also of the 18th century. Inside, the original ground-floor room has a stout chamfered beam and an open fireplace with ashlar jambs and an oak bressummer. The three-bay roof has tie-beam trusses to which collars have been added.

For a mediaeval cemetery and evidence of mediaeval occupation in the area 100 yds. N. of the inn, see p. 12.

Old Sarum, see (1) and (2).

MILFORD WARD

Monuments (563–4) and (567) appear on the map on p. 94. For the location of other monuments in Milford Ward, see folding map in end-pocket.

(563) **Winchester Gate Inn**, of two storeys, with original walls of timber framework set on brick plinths and nogged with brickwork, and with a tiled roof, is of the early 17th century. The E. wing with brick walls and a tiled roof was added in the 18th century. An extension to S. is of the first half of the 19th century. Timber framework is exposed in the W. front. Inside, there are several stout chamfered beams. The 17th-century roof has trusses with cambered tie-beams and lower angle struts.

(564) **Cottages**, two adjoining, Nos. 89–91 Milford Hill, are two-storeyed with brick walls and slate-covered roofs and date from about the middle of the 19th century.

(565) **Cottages**, pair, Nos. 103–5 Milford Hill, of two storeys with brick walls and tiled roofs, were built c. 1800.

(566) **Milford Hill House**, of two storeys and a cellar, has rendered walls and low-pitched slate-covered roofs; it was built between 1833 (Reform Act map) and 1840 (Waterworks survey). The S. and W. elevations have plain sashed windows. The main doorway has wooden pilasters supporting a moulded pediment. The openings of the lower storey are sheltered by a veranda with a concave metal roof supported by trellised iron stanchions.

(567) **Eva Cottages** (O.S., 1880), two adjacent, Nos. 94–6 Milford Hill, formerly a single house, are two-storeyed with attics and have brick walls and slate-covered roofs. Although greatly altered in the 19th century when it was divided into two dwellings, the range is of 17th-century origin and is clearly defined on Naish's map of 1716 (Plate 16). Inside, a ground-floor room in the E. cottage is spanned by a beam cased in 17th-century plaster with roll-mouldings and fleur-de-lis decoration. The W. cottage has 18th-century joinery. A

five-bay roof covers the whole range. Adjacent on the S., Nos. 59–67 Rampart Road (Thomas's Row in 1880) were built soon after 1850 in place of an earlier building, probably a barn. Part of the earlier roof remains *in situ*.

(568) **Cottage**, adjacent to Dairyhouse Bridge (21), of two storeys with brick walls and a slate-covered roof, was built c. 1840. The W. front is of two bays with a central doorway.

(569) **Milford Manor House** was rebuilt c. 1900, but the N. wall of the garden, extending E. from the present house for some 50 yds. beside the ancient road which formerly led to Clarendon (see (19)), is built of roughly squared blocks of Chilmark stone and other ashlar, alternating with panels of flint. The coping is tiled. The wall probably is of the 17th or early 18th century.

(570) **Summer-house**, in Milford Manor House garden, of one storey and a cellar, has brick walls with ashlar quoins and is roofed with tiles. Dating from the first half of the 18th century and restored in 1902 the building is said to have been used as a workroom by the writer Henry Fielding. It comprises a small square room with a glazed door to the N. and a sashed window in each of the other sides; a fireplace occupies the S.W. corner. Interior plasterwork includes an acanthus cornice and a domical ceiling enriched with garlands. A plaster cartouche contains a shield-of-arms of Swayne (cf. St. Martin's Church (4), wall-monument 3).

(571) **Little Manor**, of two storeys with attics, with brick walls with stone quoins and with tiled roofs, dates from late in the 17th century. The symmetrical three-bay E. front has large sashed windows, a central doorway with a flat hood on shaped wooden brackets, a plat-band and a coved eaves cornice. Inside, the house retains no original features. The stairs are of the 19th century.

(572) **Manor Farm**, house, demolished in 1973, was two-storeyed with brick walls and tiled roofs. A small part of the building was of 18th-century origin, but the main E. range was added c. 1800; further additions were of c. 1870. A barn adjacent on the E. had weather-boarded timber-framed walls and a slate-covered roof and appeared to be of the 18th century.

(573) **House**, No. 15 Tollgate Road, is two-storeyed with rendered brick walls and slate-covered roofs and was built between 1833 (Reform Act map) and 1854 (Kingdon & Shearm). The S.E. front is symmetrical and of three bays.

(574) **House**, No. 17 Tollgate Road, is two-storeyed with rendered brick walls and tiled roofs and was built c. 1850. It does not appear on the Reform Act map of 1833.

ST. THOMAS WARD (HARNHAM)

For the location of monuments (575)–(595), see folding map in end-pocket.

(575) **Cottages**, range of seven, Nos. 2–14 Harnham Road, are two-storeyed and have walls of brickwork (except in Nos. 2 and 4 where they are of brick banded with flint) and tiled roofs. The range was built during the first half of the 19th century. Nos. 6 and 8 appear to be of c. 1800, Nos. 2 and 4 are somewhat later and Nos. 10–14 are of c. 1850. No. 8 may incorporate part of an older structure, an internal timber-framed wall being possibly of the 17th century. Nos. 2, 4, 8 and 14 have class-T plans and approximately symmetrical S.E. elevations, each being of two bays with a central doorway. The other dwellings are smaller.

(576) **Rose and Crown Hotel**, of two storeys with attics, has timber-framed walls partly masked by brickwork, and tiled roofs; in the oldest part a thick external wall is probably of rubble and stone, but its composition is concealed by rendering. The N. range dates from the 14th century and has an original crown-post roof; the W. wing appears to be contemporary and retains some timbers of a former collar-rafter roof, but it was extensively altered in 1963. The S. range is of the 16th century.

In the E. elevation of the N. range the thick-walled lower storey has an original square-headed window of four narrow unglazed lights with plain oak mullions set diagonally. The projecting window is modern. Original timber framework is exposed in the jettied upper storey. The timber framework of the gabled N. elevation (masked in the lower storey by a lean-to annex) includes a blocked attic window of four plain lights; as the first-floor room was originally open to the roof the attic window is probably secondary. The barge-boards of the N. gable are moulded.

The W. wing seems originally to have been mainly of timber framework, but the walls are now of brick. A large inserted chimneystack was removed in 1963.

The S. range is linked to the N. range by a carriage through-way (now a vestibule) with a jettied upper storey. The upper storey of the S. range, with exposed timber framework on the E. side, was originally jettied, but it has been underbuilt in modern brickwork. Details of the timber framework of the W. side of the range, seen internally, suggest that the 16th-century W. elevation originally included an inn-yard gallery.

Inside, a first-floor room in the N. range retains two bays of the 14th-century crown-post rafter roof with a cambered beam, chamfered and braced. Originally the roof was probably of three bays, with two crown-posts, but an attic floor has been inserted and the N. bay has been partitioned. The W. wing has been remodelled inside and no old features remain. The S. wing has 16th-century beams.

(577) **Cottages**, range of four, Nos. 53–9 Harnham Road, are two-storeyed with cob walls and thatched roofs. They appear to have been built early in the 19th century. Each dwelling has an approximately symmetrical N.W. elevation of two bays, with a central doorway sheltered by a thatched porch. Inside the plans are of class T.

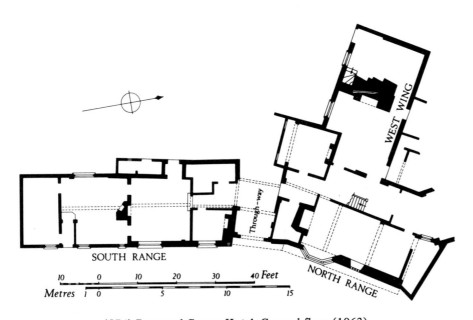

(576) Rose and Crown Hotel. Ground floor (1963).

(578) **Harnham House**, demolished *c.* 1970, was two-storeyed and had brick walls and slate-covered roofs; it was built *c.* 1830. The N. front was symmetrical and of three bays, the lateral bays having two-storeyed sashed bay windows. Inside, the plan was of class U.

(579) **Harnham Lodge**, with cob walls and thatched roofs, is of the early 19th century. The single-storeyed W. part, comprising three rooms in an L-shaped plan, with a chimneystack in the re-entrant angle serving three fireplaces, is a small *cottage orné* of *c.* 1800. The two-storeyed E. range, with a class-J plan was added during the first quarter of the 19th century.

(580) **Cliff House**, demolished in 1972, was partly of two storeys with cellars and partly three-storeyed; it had rendered brick walls and slate-covered roofs. Erected in 1825 as a substantial suburban mansion, the original building was subsequently much enlarged and in the present century was in military use; on some maps it is named Government House. The date of erection, inscribed on a board in the roof, came to light during demolition.

(581) **Old Parsonage Farm**, house, of two storeys with attics, has walls of timber framework, partly exposed and partly tile-hung, and tiled roofs. Two bays at the W. end of the range are of the 16th century; the six eastern bays are of *c.* 1600; a small N. wing was added in the 18th century.

The W. elevation is of close-studded timber framework with middle rails in each storey. Several original windows were blocked up, *c.* 1600, when a brick chimneybreast was added. The S. elevation is masked by tile-hanging and all openings are modern. The E. elevation, of brickwork, appears to be of the mid 17th century. The original N. elevation is hidden by modern additions. Inside, unmoulded beams are exposed in several rooms. The stairs are modern. A large first-floor room, now divided into two parts by an 18th-century

partition and chimneystack, has an ornate plaster ceiling of *c.* 1600 (Plate 93). In the attic, the E. gable of the 16th-century house can be seen with the western truss of the roof of *c.* 1600 set close beside it; the original gable is of close-studded timber framework and had a central window. The two easternmost bays of the roof flank a collared tie-beam truss with queen-struts and probably are contemporary with the mid 17th-century E. elevation.

(582) **Cottages**, range of five, of two storeys with brick walls and tiled roofs, are of the first half of the 19th century. Each dwelling has a class-S plan.

(583) **Manor Farm**, house, of two storeys with brick walls and a tiled roof, dates from the second half of the 18th century. Chamfered beams are exposed inside.

(584) **Cottages**, two adjacent, originally one dwelling, are single-storeyed with attics and have walls of timber framework and brick, and thatched roofs. The range is of 15th-century origin and has a cruck roof, but it was partly rebuilt in the 17th century and the E. bay (comprising one cottage) is mainly of 18th-century brickwork.

The S. front and the W. end wall are of the 17th century and have exposed timber framework with a brick plinth and brick nogging. The N. wall was partly rebuilt in brickwork in the 18th century, but some original framework remains near the middle. The E. end wall is masked by an adjacent house which has modern walls simulating timber framework.

Inside, the original plan was a straight E.—W. range of three bays. The bays are defined by two well-preserved full-cruck trusses. Smoke-blackening of the crucks indicates an original open hearth. An open fireplace with a brick chimney was built on the W. side of the E. truss in the 17th century; the chimneybreast now forms part of the W. wall of the E. cottage. The E. cottage has an open fireplace on the E. with brick jambs and a cambered and chamfered oak bressummer; a similar fireplace heats the upper room.

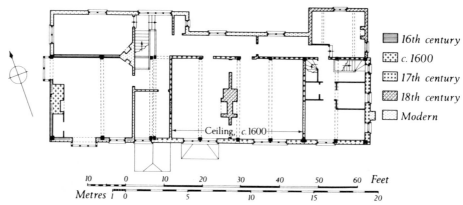

16th century
c. 1600
17th century
18th century
Modern

(581) Old Parsonage Farm House. Ground floor.

(585) **Three Crowns Inn**, of two storeys with brick and flint walls and with a tiled roof, is of the late 18th or early 19th century. Plasterwork in some ground-floor rooms appears to be earlier 18th-century material, reset.

(586) **Old Mill Cottage**, of two storeys with brick walls and tile-covered roofs, dates from *c*. 1800.

(587) **Old Mill Hotel**, of four storeys with brick walls and a tiled roof, originated during the first quarter of the 19th century as a warehouse associated with the adjacent mill (588); it did not exist *c*. 1808, but it is seen in an engraving published in 1834.[1] A late 18th-century

doorway in the S. front, with a pediment-shaped hood resting on scroll brackets with acanthus enrichment, has evidently been brought from elsewhere.

1. Cf. J. Buckler's watercolour of 1808 (Plate 11) and Hall, *Memorials*, pl. viii.

(588) **Harnham Mill**, of two storeys with attics, with walls mainly of chequered flint and ashlar and with a tile-covered roof, appears from the style of its architectural ornament to have been built *c*. 1500 (Plate 58). Although the Tithe Map of 1843 designates it a tucking mill, paper mills existed in the neighbourhood from the 16th to the 19th century,[1] and the four large fireplaces

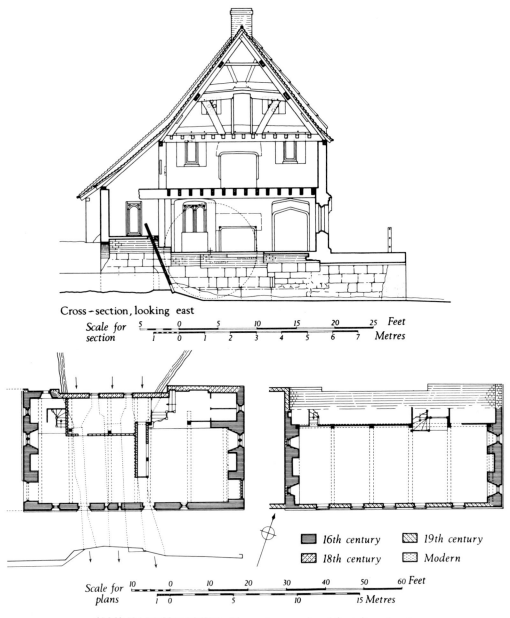

Cross-section, looking east

Scale for section — 5 0 5 10 15 20 25 Feet / 1 0 1 2 3 4 5 6 7 Metres

16th century   19th century
18th century   Modern

Scale for plans — 10 0 10 20 30 40 50 60 Feet / 1 0 5 10 15 Metres

(588) HARNHAM MILL. Plans at ground and first-floor levels.

may suggest that the building was designed primarily for paper-making.[2] According to local records a deed of 1700 states that it was then a paper mill.[3] When Buckler was there in 1808 the building appears not to have been in use as a mill; he titled his drawing 'ancient building' (Plate 11) and shows no mill-race; one of the existing races, however, was constructed in the same year.

In the S. front, the lower storey has two original doorways and two original windows, all with hollow-chamfered two-centred heads and continuous jambs in square, casement-moulded surrounds under moulded labels with returned stops. Two small loops with chamfered ashlar surrounds between the doorways are of uncertain purpose, but evidently original. The wall has a chamfered plinth; above the windows a wave-moulded hollow-chamfered and roll-moulded stringcourse is continuous with the labels. The brick-faced upper storey of the S. front replaces a louvred timber elevation depicted by Buckler and also by Hall.[4] Presumably the brickwork is of the 19th century.

The gabled E. wall is largely original. The lower storey has a blocked doorway similar to those of the S. front and windows of one and two lights as shown on the drawing. In the attic storey a shallow recess with a cinquefoil two-centred head below an abraded stone canopy, carved underneath to represent vault tracery, is set between two cross-shaped stone ventilation-loops.

The single-storeyed N. elevation was rebuilt in the 18th century and is mainly of brick. Carved on the side of a sluice in the basement is J.F.J. 1808. Until masked by the adjacent building, the W. wall was evidently exposed; the lower storey flanking a passage-way has openings uniform with those of the E. elevation.

Inside, the lower storey contains three narrow brick and stone-walled water channels, but the exact position of the former water-wheel is uncertain. The main E. and W. walls of the building have large open fireplaces with chamfered jambs and shouldered and chamfered stone bressummers. Corresponding fireplaces in the upper storey are somewhat taller and have cambered bressummers. The original first-floor windows have oak inner lintels. The roof is of five bays, with six collared tie-beam trusses with lower angle braces. The cambered collars have been cut to receive the heads of secondary attic doorways and the tie-beams are morticed for inserted floor-joists, but the attic floor has gone. There are curved wind-braces to the lower purlins.

1. V.C.H., *Wilts.* iv, 245.
2. For a closely comparable mill building, see R.C.H.M., *Dorset* V, 98.

3. *History of Harnham* (Harnham Womens' Institute, Salisbury, 1954), 9.
4. See (587), note.

(589) **Cottage**, of two storeys with brick walls and a slate-covered roof, is perhaps of late 18th-century origin, but it has been extensively altered.

(590) **Cottage**, of two storeys with brick walls, partly tile-hung, and with a tiled roof, was built *c.* 1840. The S.W. front is symmetrical and of two bays with a central doorway.

(591) **Manor Cottage**, 50 yds. N. of the church, is of two storeys and has brick walls and tiled roofs. The S.W. range is of the late 18th century and has a large original chimneybreast at the S.E. end. Inside, there are chamfered beams with run-out stops.

(592) **The Laurels**, house of two storeys with an attic, has rendered brick walls and a tiled roof and is of *c.* 1800.

(593) **Cottages**, pair, of two storeys with attics, have cob walls and tiled roofs. They were formerly in a range of four dwellings, but the two northernmost were burned in 1962. They are of the early 19th century.

(594) **House**, adjoining the foregoing on the W., is of two storeys with rendered walls and an iron-covered roof, formerly thatched; it was built *c.* 1700. The N. front appears originally to have been symmetrical and of five bays; the central doorway has a plain ashlar surround. The ground-floor casement windows are each of two square-headed lights with beaded ashlar surrounds; one retains original iron bars. The upper storey has three similar windows symmetrically disposed over the five openings of the lower storey. Inside, the two ground-floor rooms have chamfered beams with shaped stops.

(595) **Cottages**, range, probably originally three, now united as a house, have walls partly of timber framework and partly of brick, and thatched roofs. They appear to be of mid 17th-century origin, but have been altered in recent years; much of the external timber framework is reset. Inside, an original open fireplace has a chamfered oak bressummer with shaped stops.

APPENDIX

Contract dated 7 October 1366 between Henry Stourmy and Thomas Erlestoke for repairs at Salisbury Castle (P.R.O., E 101/593/31(1)):

Hec indentura facta apud Castrum Sarum septimo die Octobris anno regni Regis Edwardi tercij post conquestum quadragesimo, inter Henricum Stourmy vicecomitem Wiltes' ex parte una et Thomam Erlestoke clericum supervisorem operacionum domini Regis in Castro Sarum ex altera, testatur quod idem Henricus vicecomes posuit in reparacione et emendacione diversorum domorum turellorum et murorum infra dictum Castrum ut patet per parcellas subscriptas, videlicet:

In primis, in duobus carpentariis locatis pro carpentria camere inter capellam et coquinam in Castro Sarum cum quodam novo solario et quodam staire ligneo et quodam interclauso in eadem camera cum duobus hostiis et tribus fenestris de novo construendis in dicta camera in grosso ad thascam per visum et testimonium predicti Thome Erlestoke lxvj.s.viij.d. Et in stodes emptis et expensis pro dicto interclauso in eadem camera faciendo xxij.d.ob. Et in tabulis emptis et expensis pro dicto solario bordando et duobus hostiis et tribus fenestris in eadem camera de novo faciendis xxx.s.viij.d. Et in C. spiknaill' et D. bordnaill' emptis et expensis pro dicto solario bordando et pro dictis hostiis et fenestris faciendis vij.s. In quinque paribus vertivellorum et gumphorum cum clavibus et latches et catches emptis et expensis pro dictis hostiis et fenestris pendendis xj.s.iiij.d. In diversis operariis conductis pro dictis solario et interclauso plastrandis et tarrandis ad thascam vij.s.iij.d. In duobus tynis emptis pro aqua portanda ij.s.j.d. In quatuor cribris emptis et expensis pro diversis operibus in Castro xij.d. In duobus pailles emptis et expensis pro eodem xij.d. In tribus cyveris emptis et expensis pro eodem ix.d. In littura fodeenda et carianda usque Castrum Sarum pro solario et interclauso predictis terrandis iiij.s.vj.d. In stipendiis duorum latomorum cum eorum servientibus pro tribus fenestris et uno camino in dicta camera de novo construendis cum petra empta xliij.s.iiij.d. In ferramentis emptis pro dictis fenestris xiij.s.iiij.d. In v. quarteriis grossis calcis emptis et expensis in dicta camera x.s. cum cariagio. In duobus carectatis sabuli emptis et expensis ad idem xij.d. In quatuor carectis cum eorum equis locatis pro meremium querendo in Foresta de Savernak' et cariando usque dictum Castrum per viginti leucas pro dicta camera perficienda viij.s.

In stipendiis diversorum latomorum et laborariorum pro quodam novo hostio in aula faciendo et pro muris eiusdem aule scrutandis et emendendis et pro quodam muro in celario vini emendo et faciendo in grosso ad thascam per visum eiusdem Thome xxxvj.s.viij.d. In stipendiis eorundem pro

duabus novis fenestris in alta camera iuxta Harlewynestour cum petra pro eisdam empta in grosso per visum eiusdem Thome xl.s. In decem quarteris grossis calcis emptis et expensis pro dictis muris et fenestris faciendis xx.s. cum cariagio. In sex carectatis sabuli ad idem emptis et expensis iij.s. In xxiij. tabulis oriental' emptis et expensis pro hostio aule et dictis fenestris inde faciendis vij.s.viij.d. In duobus carpentariis conductis pro dictis hostio et fenestris et aliis necessariis in dicta aula faciendis per visum eiusdem Thome x.s.vj.d. In novem paribus vertevellorum et gumphorum emptis et expensis pro dictis hostio et fenestris pendendis, cum uno anulo ad hostium aule, et latches et katches pro eisdem, xiij.s.iiij.d. Et in quodam astro faciendo in aula cum ferramentis pro dicto astro pendendo et affirmando in areo eiusdem aule xxij.s.

Et in stipendiis diversorum latomorum et laborariorum pro camino in alto turri cum grosso muro ibidem et duabus fenestris in camera Militum in eodem turri et muris ibidem scrutandis emendis et faciendis in grosso ad thascam per visum et testimonium eiusdem Thome l.s. In xvj. quarteris grossis calcis emptis et expensis ad idem xxxij.s. cum cariagio. In octo carectatis sabuli emptis ad idem iiij.s.

Et in vj.Mill'.D. tegulis emptis et expensis pro coopertura domorum xxvj.s., precium Ml'. iiij.s. In uno coopertore locato pro domo pistrine et alia camera iuxta pistrinam et pro defectibus in coopertura stabuli et claustri emendis et cooperiendis ad thascam xx.s. In cavillis emptis ad idem xviij.d. In uno camino in dicta camera emendo et faciendo ad thascam iiij.s. In ix. quarteris grossis calcis emptis et expensis pro dicta coopertura et aliis in Castro faciendis et emendis xviij.s. cum cariagio. In quatuor carectatis sabuli emptis ad idem ij.s.

Et in meremio empto apud Clarindon' pro quodam interclauso in magna camera iuxta Harlewynestour et duabus longis scalis faciendis, cum cariagio eiusdem meremii, xij.s. Et in carpentariis conductis pro dictis interclauso et scalis faciendis ad thascam per visum eiusdem Thome x.s. In stodes emptis et expensis pro dicto interclauso faciendo vj.s.viij.d. In virgis emptis et expensis pro dicto interclauso breydando xviij.d. In laborariis conductis pro dicto interclauso plastrando pargettando et dealbando ad thascam vj.s. viij.d. In littura fodeenda et carianda usque dictum Castrum pro eodem iiij.s. In latomis conductis pro quadam fenestra in eadem camera de novo construenda ad thascam x.s. In ferramentis pro dicta fenestra cum uno pare vertevellorum et gumphorum cum j. latche et j. catche emptis pro dicta fenestra v.s. In stipendiis carpentariorum pro dicta fenestra facienda cum tabulis ad idem emptis xviij.d.

Et in uno buketto de novo faciendo cum stipendiis fabri pro eodem de ferro ligando vj.s.ij.d. In carpentariis locatis pro rota putei cum grossis spiknaill' et bordnaill' emptis emenda et facienda per diversas vices xx.s.ij.d.

In cementariis et laborariis conductis pro diversis defectibus in Scaccario emendis et pro quodam hostio in eodem Scaccario de novo faciendo xvj.s.

In uno plastratore locato pro diversis defectibus in muris · et parietibus in diversis cameris infra dictum Castrum pargettandis et dealbandis vj.s.

In CC. Shyndellis emptis et expensis pro emendacione cooperature aule dicti Castri ij.s.

viij.d., precium C. xvj.d. In CC. clavis ad idem emptis v.d. Et in uno coopertore conducto pro emendacione eiusdem cooperature vj.d.

In uno plumbatore locato ad emendum diversas defectus super turrim vocatum Harlewynestour v.s. per visum eiusdem Thome.

Unde summa coniuncta xxxj.li.xiiij.s.viij.d.ob.

In cuius rei testimonium tam presens vicecomes quam prefatus Thomas presenti indenture sigilla sua alternatim apposuere. Datum die loco et anno supradictis.

ABBREVIATIONS

and shortened titles of works and sources frequently consulted.

Ant. J.	*Antiquaries Journal.*
Arch.	*Archaeologia.*
Arch. J.	*Archaeological Journal.*
A.S.C.	*Anglo-Saxon Chronicle* (ed. D. Whitelock, 1961).
Baker, *St. Martin's*	T.H. Baker, *Notes on St. Martin's Church and Parish,* Salisbury, 1906.
Benson & Hatcher	Robert Benson and Henry Hatcher, *The History of Old and New Sarum* (constituting volume vi of R.C. Hoare, *History of Modern Wiltshire*), 1843.
B.L.	British Library.
B.M.	British Museum.
Bothams, map	J.C. Bothams, City Surveyor, *Plan of the Borough of Salisbury,* 1860.
Cal. Inq. Misc.	*Calendar of Inquisitions Miscellaneous (Chancery),* P.R.O.
Cal. Lib. Rolls	*Calendar of Liberate Rolls,* P.R.O.
Cal. Papal Letters	*Calendar of entries in the papal registers relating to Great Britain and Ireland,* P.R.O.
Cal. Pat. Rolls	*Calendar of Patent Rolls,* P.R.O.
Close Rolls	*Close rolls of the reign of Henry III,* P.R.O.
Colvin	H.M. Colvin, *Biographical Dictionary of English Architects,* London, 1954.
Cordingley	R.A. Cordingley, 'British Historical Roof Types' in *Trans. Ancient Monuments Society,* ix (1961), 73–117.
Council Mins.	Sarum Corporation MS.; Ledgers A–C, 1387–1640; Ledgers 4–8, 1641–1835; Borough Council Minutes, vols, 1–4, 1835–68.
Dodsworth, *Account*	William Dodsworth, *Historical Account of the Episcopal See and Cathedral Church of Salisbury,* 1814.
Dom. Bks.	Sarum Corporation MS., Z/217; 'Domesday Books', vols. i–iv.
Duke, *Prolusiones*	Edward Duke, *Prolusiones Historicae,* Salisbury, 1837.
E.P.N.S.	Publications of English Place-Names Society.
E.V.H.	R.C.H.M., *English Vernacular Houses,* H.M.S.O., 1976.
Frere, *Use*	W.H. Frere, *The Use of Sarum,* Cambridge, 1898.
Hall, *Memorials*	P. Hall, *Picturesque Memorials of Salisbury,* 1834.
Haskins, *Guilds*	Charles Haskins, *The Ancient Trade Guilds and Companies of Salisbury,* 1912.
Hawley MS.	Manuscript diary by Lt. Col. W. Hawley, recording excavations at Old Sarum, 1909–15, preserved in Salisbury & South Wiltshire Museum.
Hoare, *Mod. Wilts.*	Sir Richard Colt Hoare, Bt., *The History of Modern Wiltshire,* six vols., 1822–43 (see also Benson & Hatcher).
J.B.A.A.	*Journal of the British Archaeological Association.*
King's Works	H.M. Colvin (ed.), *History of the King's Works,* vols. i–ii, H.M.S.O., 1963.
Kingdon & Shearm, map	Map of Salisbury, scale 1:500, made by Kingdon and Shearm, engineers, Launceston, 1854. Unpublished MS. kept in the office of City Engineer. This map forms the basis of Bothams's map.
Leland, *Itin.*	*The Itinerary of John Leland in c. 1535–43* (ed. L. Toulmin Smith), 1906–10.
L. & P.	*Letters & papers, foreign and domestic, of the reign of Henry VIII.* P.R.O.
Liber Niger	E.R. Nevill, 'Salisbury in 1455', in *W.A.M.,* xxxvii (1911), 66–91.
Lov. Cn.	Collection of 289 photographs dating from *c.* 1850–1900, mainly of buildings near the centre of the city, assembled by J.L. Lovibond and now kept by the Town Clerk. Copies in N.M.R.
Maps	Early 17th century, see Speed; 1716–51, see Naish; 1833–5, see Reform Act; 1843, see Tithe Map; 1849, see Water Works Map; 1854, see Kingdon & Shearm; 1860, see Bothams; 1880, see O.S.

Med. Arch.	*Mediaeval Archaeology* (journal).
Naish, map	*Map of the City of Salisbury...surveyed by William Naish.* Sold by J. Senex and W. Taylor, London, 1716 (Plate 16); 2nd edition, by John Senex, undated, similar to the first; 3rd edition, by Benjamin Collins, Salisbury, 1751, with minor additions and alterations. See *W.A.M.,* lviii (1963), 453–4.
Nightingale, *Plate*	J.E. Nightingale, *Church Plate of the County of Wilts.*, 1891.
N.M.R.	The National Monuments Record.
O.S., 1880	Ordnance Survey, town plan of Salisbury, scale 1:500, surveyed 1879, published 1880;
Parl. Svy., 1649	Survey of church lands in Salisbury, ordered by Parliament and carried out 1649–50; Sar. D. & C.M.
Peniston plans	Plans of houses and other properties drawn by J. and H. Peniston, Surveyors 1822–64, now in W.R.O. (Portfolios 451/73–5 and loose rolls 451/–). MS. copies of some plans are held by Salisbury City Engineer.
Pipe R.	*Great Rolls of the Pipe, 1158–,* P.R.S., 1884–.
P.R.O.	Public Record Office, London.
P.R.S.	Pipe Roll Society.
P.S.A.	*Proceedings of the Society of Antiquaries of London.*
Reeves, *Inscriptions*	J.A. Reeves, *Abstract of Monumental Inscriptions in Salisbury Churches,* Salisbury Museum, 1975.
Reform Act maps	1. G.O. Lucas, surveyor, *Plan of the City...with boundaries as laid down by the Reform Act,* 1833. 2. Gilmour, Minster St., *Plan of the City...Reform Act,* 1835 (includes names of inns).
Reg. St. Osmund	*Register of St. Osmund* (ed. W.H. Rich-Jones), 1883–4. Rolls Series, lxxviii.
R.C.H.M.	The Royal Commission on Historical Monuments (England).
Rowe, *Coinage*	C.M. Rowe, *Salisbury's Local Coinage,* 1966.
Salzman, *Building*	L.F.Salzman, *Building in England down to 1540,* 1967.
Sar. Chart.	*Charters and Documents illustrating the history...of Salisbury in the 12th*
	and 13th centuries, ed. W.H. Rich-Jones and W. Dunn Macray, 1891. Rolls Series, xcvii.
Sar. Corp. MS.	Manuscript in the archives of Salisbury District Council (formerly Salisbury Corporation).
Sar. D. & C.M.	Muniments of the Dean and Chapter of Salisbury.
Sar. Dioc. Regy.	Salisbury Diocesan Registry.
Sar. C.L.	Salisbury Cathedral Library.
Shortt, *Salisbury*	*City of Salisbury* (ed. Hugh Shortt), Phoenix, London, 1957.
Speed, map	Bird's-eye view of Salisbury (Plate 1) from S.W.; *Theatre of the Empire of Great Britain,* 1611.
Swayne, *Accounts*	H.J.F. Swayne, *Churchwardens' Accounts of St. Edmund and St. Thomas, Sarum, 1443–1702;* Wilts. Record Society, 1896.
S.J.	*Salisbury Journal,* 1729–
Tithe map	Map of Fisherton Anger, Wilts. Pt. 2, 1843; scale 1 inch = 1 chain (Sar. Corp. MS.).
Tropenell Cart.	*The Tropenell Cartulary*, ed. J.S. Davies; Wilts Arch. & N.H. Soc., 1908.
T.H. Arch.	Trinity Hospital Archives; Sar. Corp. MS., Z/231 (uncatalogued).
V.C.H.	Victoria History of the Counties of England.
W.A.M.	*Wiltshire Archaeological and Natural History Magazine,* 1854–.
Water Works map	Plan of proposed water works, scale 1 in. = 5 chains, 1849, tracing in W.R.O.; another, 1854, with Wessex Water Authority, Salisbury (No. 335).
W.R.O.	Wiltshire County Record Office, Trowbridge, Wilts.
Wordsworth, *Processions*	C. Wordsworth, *Ceremonies and Processions of Salisbury Cathedral,* 1901.
Wordsworth, *St. Nicholas*	C. Wordsworth, *Cartulary of St. Nicholas Hospital,* 1903.
Wordsworth, *Statutes*	C. Wordsworth and D. Macleane, *Statutes and Customs of Salisbury Cathedral,* 1915.
Wilts. Rec. Soc.	Publications of the Wiltshire Arch. and N.H. Society, Records Branch; later the Wiltshire Record Society.

For a general bibliography of Salisbury, see E.H. Goddard, *Wiltshire Bibliography* (Wilts. Education Committee, 1929), 191–217.

GLOSSARY

ACHIEVEMENT – In heraldry, the shield accompanied by the appropriate external ornaments, helm, crest, mantling, supporters, etc. In the plural the term is also applied to the insignia of honour carried at the funerals and suspended over the monuments of important personages, comprising helmet and crest, shield, tabard, sword, gauntlets and spurs, banners and pennons.

AEDICULE – A small temple or shrine, or a miniature representation of the same.

AGGER – The earthen ridge carrying a Roman road.

ALTAR – The name used in the Inventory to distinguish pre-reformation stone altars from post-reformation *Communion Tables* of wood.

APRON – A plain or decorated panel below a window, or at the base of a wall-monument.

ARABESQUE – Decoration, in colour or low relief, with fanciful intertwining of leaves, scroll-work, etc.

ARCADE – A range of arches carried on piers or columns. *Blind arcade,* a series of arches, sometimes interlaced, carried on shafts or pilasters against a solid wall.

ARCH – The following are some of the most usual forms:
Equilateral – A pointed arch struck with radii equal to the span.
Flat or straight – Having the soffit horizontal.
Four-centred – A pointed arch of four arcs, the two outer and lower arcs struck from centres on the springing line and the two inner and upper arcs from centres below the springing line. For want of a better expression the term is also used of pointed door-heads, etc., in which the upper arcs are replaced by straight lines, the centres then being at infinity.
Lancet – A pointed arch, struck at the level of the springing, with radii greater than the span.
Nodding – An ogee arch curving also forward from the plane of the wall face.
Ogee – A pointed arch of four or more arcs, the two uppermost being reversed, *i.e.,* convex instead of concave to the base line.
Pointed or two-centred – Two arcs struck from centres on the springing line, and meeting at the apex with a point.
Relieving – An arch, generally of rough construction, placed in the wall above the true arch or head of an opening, to relieve it of the superincumbent weight.
Segmental – A single arc struck from a centre below the springing line.
Segmental-pointed – A pointed arch, struck from two centres below the springing line.
Skew – An arch spanning between responds not diametrically opposite one another.
Stilted – An arch with its springing line raised above the level of the imposts.
Three-centred, elliptical – Formed with three arcs, the middle or uppermost struck from a centre below the springing line.

ARCHITRAVE – The lowest member of an entablature (*q.v.*); often adopted as a moulded enrichment to the jambs and head of a doorway or window-opening.

ARRIS – The sharp edge formed by the meeting of two surfaces.

ASHLAR – Masonry wrought to an even face and with square edges.

AUMBRY – Wall-cupboard, usually for sacred vessels in a church.

BAILEY – The courtyard of a castle.

BALL-FLOWER – In architecture, a decoration peculiar to the first quarter of the 14th century, consisting of a globular flower of three petals enclosing a small ball.

BARGE-BOARD – A board, often carved, fixed to the edge of a gabled roof a short distance from the face of the wall.

BASTION – A projection from the general outline of a fortress, from which the garrison is able to see, and defend by a flanking fire, the ground before the ramparts.

BAYS – The main vertical divisions of the facade of a building; the archways of an arcade or the intercolumniations of a colonnade; also the divisions of a roof, marked by its principals (*q.v.*) which usually correspond with the bays of the facade, etc., below it.

BEAD – A small rounded moulding.

BILLET – In architecture, an ornament used in the 11th and 12th centuries, consisting of short attached cylinders or rectangles with intervening spaces. In heraldry, a small upright oblong charge.

BOLECTION-MOULDING – A bold moulding raised above the general plane of the framework of a doorway, fireplace or panelling.

BOND – *See* BRICKWORK.

BOSS – A square or round projecting ornament, often covering the intersections of the ribs in a vault, panelled ceiling, roof, etc.

BRACE – In roof construction, a subsidiary timber designed to strengthen the framing of a truss. *Wind-brace:* a subsidiary timber between the purlins and principals of a roof, designed to resist the pressure of the wind.

BRACKET – A projecting flat-topped support, usually decorated on the underside; also, in open-string stairs, the spandrel or exposed triangular end of a step.

BRATTISHING – Ornamental cresting on the top of a screen, cornice, etc.

BRESSUMMER – A beam spanning a broad opening and supporting an upper wall.

BRICKWORK – The following terms are used:
Header – A brick laid so that the end appears on the face of the wall.
Stretcher – A brick laid so that the long side appears on the face of the wall.
English Bond – A method of laying bricks so that alternate courses on the face of the wall are composed of headers and stretchers.
Flemish Bond – A method of laying bricks so that alternate headers and stretchers appear in each course on the face of the wall.

BROACH-STOP – A half-pyramidal stop against a chamfer, effecting the change from chamfer to arris.

BUTTRESS – Masonry or brickwork projecting from or built against a wall to give additional strength.
Angle-buttresses – Two meeting, or nearly meeting, at an angle of 90° at the corner of a building.
Clasping-buttress – One that clasps or encases an angle.
Diagonal-buttress – One placed against the right-angle formed by two walls, and more or less equiangular with both.
Flying-buttress – An arch or half-arch transmitting the thrust of a vault or roof from the upper part of a wall to an outer support.

CABLE-MOULDING – A moulding carved in the form of a rope or cable.

CANONS – The metal loops by which a bell is hung.

CARTON-PIERRE – A patent composition cast in moulds to form fine decorative details for application to the surfaces of joinery, thus simulating carved woodwork; the process was introduced into Britain by Robert Adam, *c.* 1780.

CARYATID – Sculptured figure used as a column or support.

CASEMENT MOULDING – A wide and deep hollow moulding on the jambs and head of a window or doorway; usually characteristic of the 15th or 16th century.

CASEMENT WINDOW – One closed with a hinged lattice.

CHALICE – The name used in the Inventory to denote the pre-reformation type of communion vessel with a small, shallow bowl, distinguishing it from the post-reformation *Cup* which has a larger and deeper bowl.

CHAMFER – The small plane formed when an arris of stone or wood is cut away, usually at an angle of 45°. When the plane is concave it is termed a *hollow chamfer*.

CHANTRY – A foundation, usually supporting a priest, for the celebration of mass for the soul of the founder and of such others as he may direct.

CHEVRON – In heraldry, a charge resembling an inverted V. In architecture, a decorative form similar to the heraldic chevron and often used in a consecutive series.

CHIP-CARVING – Simple geometrical patterns gouged on the surface of joinery; the work is characteristic of the 17th century.

CINQUEFOIL – *See* FOIL.

CLEARSTOREY – In a church that has colonnades, an upper storey with windows rising above the aisle roof. The term is applicable in secular architecture.

CLOSE – Enclosure. In earthworks, an area enclosed by banks.

CLUNCH – Hard stratum of the Lower Chalk used for building and sculpture.

COLLAR-BEAM – In a roof, a horizontal beam framed to and serving to tie together a pair of rafters, some distance above wall-plate level.

CORBEL – A projecting stone or piece of timber for the support of a superincumbent feature. *Corbel-table* – A row of corbels, usually carved.

COUNTERSCARP – The outer face or slope of the ditch of a fortification. *Counterscarp bank* – a small bank immediately beyond the counterscarp of a hill-fort or defensive work.

COVE – A concave moulding at the junction of wall and ceiling, or masking the eaves of a roof.

COVER-PATEN – A cover to a communion cup, used as a paten when inverted.

CRENELLES – The openings in an embattled parapet.

CROCKETS – Carvings projecting at regular intervals from the sloping sides of spires, canopies, hood-moulds, etc.

CROP-MARK – A trace of a buried feature revealed by differential growth of crops, best seen from the air.

CRUCK TRUSS – *See* ROOFS

CURTAIN – The connecting wall between the towers or bastions of a castle.

CUSPS – The projecting points forming the foils in Gothic windows, arches, panels, etc.; they are sometimes ornamented at the ends (*cusp-points*) with leaves, flowers, berries, etc. *Sub-cusps* – cusps within the foils formed by larger cusping.

DADO – The protective or decorative treatment applied to the lower part of a wall-surface to a height, normally, of 3 to 4 feet. *Dado-rail* – the moulding or capping at the top of the dado.

DIAPER – All-over decoration of surfaces with reticulate and other patterns.

DOG-TOOTH ORNAMENT – A typical 13th-century carved ornament consisting of a series of pyramidal flowers of four petals; used to cover hollow mouldings.

DORMER – A sleeping recess contrived as a projection from the slope of a roof and having a roof of its own; it usually is unlighted, but occasionally it has small windows in the cheeks.

DORMER-WINDOW – A vertical window projecting from the slope of a roof, and having a roof of its own, as in a dormer.

DRESSINGS – The stone or brickwork used about an angle, window, or other feature, when worked to a finished face, whether smooth, tooled or rubbed, moulded, or sculptured.

EARED (OR LUGGED) ARCHITRAVE – Enrichment of an opening whereby the horizontal mouldings of the head continue beyond the sides of the vertical mouldings of the jambs and are returned to form a π-shaped feature.

EASTER SEPULCHRE – Aedicule or recess, usually on the N. side of the chancel, in which the sacrament, chalices and reliquaries were enshrined during the three days before Easter in commemoration of Christ's entombment (cf. *W.A.M.,* II (1855), 309).

EMBATTLED – In architecture, a parapet with an indented outline comprising *merlons* and *crenelles* is said to be embattled.

ENTABLATURE – In classical architecture, the moulded horizontal capping of a wall, colonnade or opening. A full entablature consists of *architrave, frieze* and *cornice.*

FAN-VAULT – *See* VAULTING.

FASCIA – A plain or moulded facing board.

FIELDED PANEL – A panel, usually of woodwork, with recessed and bevelled margins.

FINIAL – An ornament at the top of a pinnacle, gable, canopy, etc.

FOIL (*trefoil, quatrefoil, cinquefoil, multifoil,* etc.) – A leaf-shaped space defined by the curve of the cusping in an opening or panel.

FOLIATE (Capital, corbel, etc.) – Carved with leaf ornament.

FOUR-CENTRED ARCH – *See* ARCH.

GADROON ORNAMENT – A series of convexities and/or concavities forming the edge of a prominent moulding in stone, wood or metalwork.

GARDEROBE – Wardrobe. Antiquarian usage applies the word to a latrine.

GARGOYLE – A carved projecting figure pierced or channelled to carry off rainwater from the roof of a building.

GAUGING – In brickwork, bringing every brick exactly to a certain form by cutting and rubbing.

GREENSAND – A cretaceous sandstone containing the green iron-bearing mineral glauconite.

GRISAILLE – Formal patterns painted in greyish tints on wall surfaces or on glass windows.

GROINED VAULT – *See* VAULTING.

GUILLOCHE – A geometrical ornament consisting of two or more intertwining bands forming a series of circles or other regular shapes.

HALL – The principal room of a mediaeval house, normally open to the roof.

HILL-FORT – A defensive enclosure of the Iron Age, fortified with rampart and ditch, single or multiple, usually on dominant ground.

HIPPED ROOF – A roof with sloped instead of vertical ends. *Half-hipped*: a roof in which the ends are partly vertical and partly sloped.

HOLD-WATER BASE – A column base with a deep concave moulding in the upper surface.

HOOD-MOULD – A projecting moulding on the face of a wall above an arch, doorway, or window; it may follow the form of the arch or it may be square in outline. Also called *Label*.

HORNWORK – An outwork of an earthwork enclosure, such as a hill-fort, often consisting of a single arm thrown out to protect an entrance.

IMPOST– The projection, often moulded, at the springing of an arch, upon which the arch appears to rest.

INDENT – The sinking in a tomb slab for a monumental brass.

INTERLACE – Stone decoration in relief simulating woven or entwined bands, in England usually associated with the period before the Norman Conquest.

IRON AGE – The period which in Britain is taken to date from *c.* 600 B.C. to the Roman Conquest, A.D. 43.

JAMB – The side of an archway, doorway, window or other opening.

JETTY – The projection of the upper storey of a building beyond the vertical plane of the lower storey.

JOGGLING – The method of cutting the adjoining faces of the voussoirs of an arch with rebated, zigzagged or wavy surfaces to provide a key.

KEEL MOULDING – A stone moulding, in profile resembling the cross-section through the keel of a boat.

KING-POST – The middle vertical post in a roof-truss. *See* ROOFS.

KNEELER – The stone at the foot of a gable, on which the inclined coping stones rest.

LABEL – *See* HOOD-MOULD.

LANCET – A narrow window with a pointed head, typical of the 13th century.

LIERNE-VAULT – *See* VAULTING.

LOMBARDIC LETTERING – Lettering, based on N. Italian manuscripts, often used by mediaeval bellfounders.

LOOP – A small narrow window, usually unglazed.

LOUVRE – A lantern-like structure on the roof of a hall or other building, with openings for ventilation or for the escape of smoke; it is usually crossed by sloping slats (called louvre-boards), to exclude rain. Louvre-boards are also used in belfry windows.

MATHEMATICAL TILES – Revetment for walls of timber or cob, consisting of hung tiles wherein each tile is so shaped that, when pointed with mortar, the exposed surface resembles brickwork.

MERLON – The solid part of an embattled parapet between the crenelles.

MILL-RIND – The iron fixed to the centre of a millstone. A heraldic charge.

MISERICORD – A bracket, often elaborately carved, on the underside of the hinged seat of a choir-stall. When the seat is turned up the bracket comes into position to support the occupant during long periods of standing.

MOTTE – In earthworks, a steep flat-topped mound forming the main feature of an 11th or 12th-century castle; originally often surmounted by a timber tower and usually associated with a BAILEY.

MUNTIN – In joinery or carpentry, an intermediate upright between panels, tenoned into or stopping against upper and lower rails.

NAIL-HEAD – Architectural ornament of small pyramidal form used extensively in 12th-century work.

NODDING ARCH – *See under* ARCH.

OBIT – Mass said on specified days (usually the anniversary of death) in commemoration of a defunct benefactor.

OGEE – A compound curve of two parts, one convex, the other concave; a *double-ogee moulding* has two ogee profiles side by side, the convexities adjacent to one another.

ORDERS – In an arch, the receding concentric rings of voussoirs.

ORIEL – A projecting bay-window, sometimes carried upon corbels or brackets; also a compartment or embrasure with a large window opening off one side of a mediaeval hall.

OVOLO MOULDING – A convex moulding of rounded profile.

PALLADIAN WINDOW – A three-light window with a round-headed middle light and square-headed lights on either side, the side lights having flanking pilasters, and small entablatures which form the imposts to the arch of the centre light. *See also* VENETIAN WINDOW.

PATEN – A shallow vessel for holding the Bread or Wafer at the celebration of the Holy Communion.

PATERA – A flat disc-shaped ornament applied to a frieze, moulding, or cornice; in Gothic work it commonly takes the form of a four-lobed leaf or flower.

PEDIMENT – A low-pitched gable used in classical architecture above a portico, at the end of a building, or above doors, windows, niches, etc.; sometimes the apex is omitted, forming a *broken pediment*, or the horizontal members are omitted, forming an *open pediment*.

PELICAN-IN-PIETY – A pelican shown, according to the mediaeval legend, feeding her young upon drops of blood which she pecks from her own breast.

PISCINA – A basin in a church, for washing the sacred vessels and provided with a drain; it is generally set in or against the S. wall of the chancel, but sometimes is sunk in the pavement.

PLANK-AND-MUNTIN PARTITION – A wooden division between two rooms, composed of vertical planks alternating with, and tongued into, grooved upright posts.

PLAT-BAND – A projecting horizontal band of plain masonry or brickwork, as distinct from a moulded string-course.

POPPY-HEAD – Type of finial commonly found at the heads of bench-standards or desks in churches; generally it is carved with foliage and flowers and resembles a fleur-de-lis.

PORTLAND STONE – A fine white oolitic limestone of the Upper Jurassic system.

PRESBYTERY – The part of a church, usually reserved for priests, in which is placed the communion table.

PRINCIPALS – The main as opposed to the common rafters of a roof.

PULPITUM – A screen in a monastic church, dividing the monastic choir from the nave.

PULVINATED FRIEZE – In Classical and Renaissance architecture, a frieze having a convex or bulging profile.

PURBECK MARBLE – A shelly limestone of the Upper Jurassic system, quarried in S. Dorset and capable of being polished.

PURLIN – In roof construction, a horizontal timber resting on the principal rafters of a truss and forming an intermediate support for the common rafters. For *Collar-purlins*, see *King-post* under ROOFS.

QUARRY – In windows, a small pane of glass, often lozenge-shaped. In pavements, a square tile.

QUATREFOIL – A four-petalled flower. *See* also FOIL.

QUEEN-POSTS – A pair of vertical posts in a roof-truss, equidistant from the centre line of the roof. *See also* under ROOFS.

QUOIN – The dressed stones at the angle of a building, or distinctive brickwork in this position. Normally the quoin stones are long and short in alternate courses; if they are of equal length it is called a French quoin.

RAIL – A horizontal member in the framing of a door, screen, panelling or other woodwork.

REAR-ARCH – The arch, on the inside of a wall, spanning a doorway or window-opening.

REREDOS – A screen of stone or wood at the back of an altar, usually enriched.

RESPONDS – The half-columns or piers at the ends of an arcade, or abutting a single arch.

REVEAL – The internal side surface of a recess, doorway or window opening.

RINCEAUX – Decoration composed of a sinuous stem between parallel margins, with a coiled branch in each interstice, usually with acanthus enrichment.

ROLL-MOULDING – A continuous convex moulding cut upon the edges of stone, woodwork, etc.

ROOD (*Rood-beam, Rood-screen, Rood-loft*) – A cross or crucifix. The *Great Rood* was set up at the E. end of the nave with accompanying figures of St. Mary and St. John; it was generally carved in wood, and fixed on the loft or head of the rood-screen, or on a special beam (the *Rood-beam*), reaching from wall to wall. Sometimes the rood was merely painted on the wall above the chancel-arch or on a closed wood partition or tympanum in the upper half of the arch. The *Rood-screen* is the open screen spanning the E. end of the nave, shutting off the chancel; in the 15th century a narrow gallery was often constructed above the cornice to carry the rood and other images and candles, and it was also used as a music-gallery. This loft was approached by a staircase (and occasionally by more than one), either of wood or built in the wall, wherever most convenient, and, when the loft was carried right across an aisled building, the intervening walls of the nave were often pierced with narrow archways. Many roods were destroyed at the Reformation and their removal, with the rood loft, was ordered in 1561.

ROOFS – *Collar-beam* – a principal-rafter roof with collar-beams (*q.v.*) connecting the principals.

Cruck – having a truss with principals springing from below the level of the wall-plate. The timbers are usually curved, but examples with straight timbers are recorded.

Hammer-beam – in which cantilevered beams instead of tie-beams, braced from a level below the wall-plates, form the basis of construction.

King-post and Collar-purlin – a trussed-rafter roof with king-posts standing on the tie-beams to carry a centre purlin supporting the collars.

King-post and Ridge – in which king-posts standing on tie-beams or collar-beams directly support the ridge.

Mansard – characterised in exterior appearance by two pitches, the lower steeper than the upper.

Principal Rafter – with rafters at intervals, of greater scantling than the common rafters and framed to form trusses; they are normally called by the name of the connecting member used in the truss, *tie-beam* or *collar-beam*.

Queen-post – with two vertical or nearly vertical posts standing on the tie-beam of a truss and supporting a collar-beam or the principal rafters.

Scissors-truss – as trussed-rafter, but with crossed braces instead of collars.

Tie-beam – a principal rafter roof with a simple triangulation of a horizontal beam linking the lower ends of the pairs of principals to prevent their spread.

Trussed-rafter – in which all the timbers in the slopes are common rafters of uniform size, and each pair of rafters is connected by a collar-beam, which is often braced. At intervals, pairs of rafters may be tenoned into a tie-beam.

Wagon – a trussed-rafter roof with curved braces, forming a semi-circular arch, springing from wall-plate level. The soffit is usually plastered, and the longitudinal members and transverse member at intervals are decorated with mouldings which project below the plaster to form coffers.

RUBBLE – Walling of rough unsquared stones or flints. *Coursed Rubble* – rubble walling with the stones or flints very roughly dressed and levelled up in courses.

RUSTICATION – Masonry in which only the margins of the stones are worked; the word is also used for any masonry where the joints are emphasised by mouldings, grooves, etc. Rusticated columns are those in which the shafts are interrupted by square blocks of stone, or by broad projecting bands.

SCREEN – In secular buildings, the wooden partition separating the main space of a hall from the service end. *Screens-passage*, the space at the service end of a hall between the screen and the end wall.

SEDILIA – The seats, on the S. side of the chancel, used by the ministers during the Mass.

SILL – The lower horizontal member of a window or door-frame; the stone, tile or wood base below a window or door-frame, usually with a weathered surface projecting beyond the wall-face to throw off water. In timber-framed walls, the lower horizontal member into which the studs are tenoned.

SLIP-TILES – Tiles moulded with a design in intaglio which is filled in, before burning, with clay of a different colour.

SOIL-MARK – A trace of a levelled or buried feature revealed by differences in colour or texture of the soil, usually in ploughed land.

SOLAR – In a mediaeval house, a chamber occupied by the master, usually adjoining the dais end of the hall.

SPANDREL – The space between the outside curve of an arch and the surrounding rectangular framework or moulding, or the space between the outside curves of two adjoining arches and a moulding above them. Also, in open-string staircases, the bracket or triangular exposed end of a step, often decorated with a scroll.

SPLAT – A flat board with shaped sides used in place of a turned and moulded member, often having the outline of a baluster.

SPRINGING-LINE – The level at which an arch springs from its supports.

SQUINCH – An arch thrown across the angle between two walls to support an obliquely set superstructure, such as the base of a dome or spire.

SQUINT – An aperture pierced through a wall to allow a view of an altar from places whence it could otherwise not be seen.

STAIRCASES – A *close-string* staircase is one having a raking member into which the treads and risers are morticed. An *open-string* staircase has the raking member cut to the shape of the treads and risers. A *dog-legged* staircase has adjoining flights running in opposite directions, with a common newel. A *well-staircase* has stairs rising round a central opening.

STILE – The vertical member of a timber frame, into which are tenoned the ends of the rails or horizontal pieces.

STOPS – Blocks terminating mouldings or chamfers in stone or wood; stones at the ends of labels, string-courses, etc., against which the mouldings finish, frequently carved to represent shields, foliage, human or grotesque masks; also, plain or decorative, used at the ends of a moulding or a chamfer to form the transition from the angle to the square.

STOUP – A receptacle to contain holy water. Those remaining are usually in the form of a deeply-dished stone set in a niche or on a pillar near a church doorway.

STRAPWORK – Decoration consisting of strap-like bands, often interlaced, characteristic of the late 16th and early 17th century.

STRING-COURSE – A projecting horizontal band in a wall, usually moulded.

STUDS – The common posts or uprights in timber-framed walls.

SWAG – An architectural ornament; a festoon suspended at both ends and carved to represent cloth, or flowers and fruit.

TABLE-TOMB – A chest-like funeral monument, usually with panelled sides and a flat top, sometimes with a recumbent effigy on top; occasionally without sides, the top being supported on legs.

TAS-DE-CHARGE – The lower courses of a vault or arch, laid in horizontal courses.

TESSERA – A small cube of stone, glass, marble etc., used in mosaic.

THUMB-GAUGING – An ornamental top-edge to a ridge-tile, made with the thumb before the tile is baked.

TIE-BEAM – The horizontal transverse beam in a roof, tying together the feet of opposed rafters to counteract thrust.

TIMBER-FRAMED BUILDING – A building in which the walls are built of open timbers and the interstices are filled in with brickwork or lath and plaster ('wattle and daub'); the whole often covered with plaster or boarding.

TOOLING – Dressing or finishing a masonry surface with an axe or other tool, usually in parallel lines.

TOUCH – A soft black marble quarried near Tournai.

TRACERY – The ornamental work in the head of a window, screen, panel, etc., formed by curving and interlacing of bars of stone or wood, grouped together, generally over two or more lights or bays.

TRANSOM – A horizontal bar of stone or wood across a window-light.

TREFOIL – *See* FOIL.

TRELLIS, TREILLAGE – Lattice-work of light wood or metal bars.

TRIFORIUM – In larger churches, an arcaded wall-passage at about midwall height, between the aisle arcades and the clearstorey. A large gallery the full width of the aisle below is termed a *Tribune*.

TRUSS – A number of timbers framed together to bridge a space, designed to be self-supporting and to carry other timbers. The *trusses* of a roof are generally named after a peculiar feature in their construction, such as *King-post, Queen-post, Hammer-beam, Cruck; see* ROOFS.

TYMPANUM – The triangular or segmental field in the face of a pediment or in the head of an arch.

VAULTING – An arched ceiling or roof of stone or brick, sometimes imitated in wood and plaster. *Barrel Vaulting* is a continuous vault unbroken in its length by cross-vaults. A *Groined Vault* (or *Cross-vaulting*) results from the intersection of simple vaulting surfaces. A *Ribbed Vault* is a framework of arched ribs carrying the cells that cover in the spaces between them. One bay of vaulting, divided into four quarters or compartments, is termed *quadripartite*; but often the bay is divided longitudinally into two subsidiary bays, and the vaulting bay is thus divided into six compartments and is termed *sexpartite*. Increased elaboration is given by *tiercerons*, secondary ribs springing from the wall-supports and rising to a point other than the centre, and *liernes*, tertiary ribs that do not spring from the wall-supports, but cross from main rib to main rib. In *fan-vaulting* numerous ribs rise from the springing in equal curves, diverging equally in all directions, giving fan-like effects when seen from below.

VENETIAN WINDOW – Similar to Palladian window.

VESICA PISCIS – An oval frame, pointed at top and bottom, common in mediaeval art.

VICE – A small circular stair.

VOUSSOIRS – The stone forming an arch.

WAGON-ROOF – *See* under ROOFS.

WALL-PLATE – A timber laid lengthwise on the wall to receive the ends of the rafters and other joists. In timber-framing, the studs are tenoned into it.

WAVE-MOULDING – A compound moulding formed by a convex curve between two concave curves.

WEATHERING (to sills, tops of buttresses, etc.) – A sloping surface for casting off rainwater.

MONUMENTAL HERALDRY IN SALISBURY

The following Armorial blazons all arms mentioned in the present volume. The coats etc. are described in the form seen and are not always the version generally accepted as correct. The position of each representation is given in the general index, *s.v.* **HERALDRY**.

ROYAL ARMS

EDWARD THE CONFESSOR. *Azure, a cross flory between four martlets argent.*

ENGLAND AND FRANCE (*c.*1405–1603). *Azure, three fleurs-de-lys or,* for France Modern, quartering *Gules, three lions passant gardant or,* for England.

ELIZABETH I. Supporters: *a lion gardant crowned and a dragon.*

STUART (1603–1707). Quarterly: 1 and 4, France Modern quartering England; 2, *Or, a lion within a double tressure flory counterflory gules,* for Scotland; 3, *Azure, a harp or stringed argent,* for Ireland. Supporters: *a lion and a unicorn.*

STUART (1707–1714). Quarterly: 1 and 4, England impaling Scotland; 2, France Modern; 3, Ireland.

HANOVERIAN (1714–1800). Quarterly: 1, England impaling Scotland; 2, France Modern; 3, Ireland; 4, *per pale and per chevron: Gules, two lions passant gardant in pale or;* ii *Or, semy of hearts gules, a lion azure;* iii *Gules, a horse courant argent,* for Hanover. Supporters: as Stuart.

GENERAL ARMORIAL

ABAROUGH. *Two swords in saltire between four fleurs-de-lys.*

AUDLEY. Quarterly, 1 and 4, *Gules, a fret or,* 2 and 3, *Ermine, a chevron gules.*

BAKER. *A tower between three keys erect.*

BARNES. *Azure, three leopards' heads argent.*

BATT. *Sable, a fess ermine between three dexterhands erect argent.*

BAYLYE or BAYLY. *On a fess engrailed between three horses' heads couped, three fleurs-de-lys.*

BEAUCHAMP. Quarterly, 1 and 4, *Gules, a fess between six martlets or,* 2, *Gules, two lions passant or,* 3, *Azure, three fishes in pale argent,* all within a border (ermine?) (Monument (3)).

BEAUCHAMP. *Gules, a fess between six crosses crosslet or* (Monument (185)).

BLACKALL. *Argent, a greyhound courant sable, on a chief indented sable, three bezants.*

BLAKE. *A chevron, or, between three garbs.*

BOUCHER. *A cross engrailed between four water bougets.*

BOURCHIER. Quarterly, 1 and 4, *Argent, a cross engrailed gules between four water bougets sable,* 2 and 3, *Gules, a fess argent between six billets or.*

BOWERMAN or BOWREMAN. *Ermine, on a bend cotised sable three boars' heads couped or, a mullet or for difference.*

BRERETON? *Argent, two bars sable.*

BURROUGH. *Gules, the stump of a tree eradicated argent, with two leaves vert.*

BURT. *Argent, on a chevron gules between three buglehorns sable stringed or, three crosses crosslet fitchy or.*

CALDER. *Argent, a buck's head cabossed sable, in chief a canton of Ulster.*

CAMPBELL. *Gyronny gules and ermine.*

CANTELUPE. *Three leopards' heads jessant-de-lys.*

CHESTER. 1. *Per pale a chevron engrailed between three goats' heads erased* (Monument (3)).

2. *Ermine, on a chief sable, a griffin statant or* (Monument (4)).

CLARE. *Or, three chevronels gules.*

CLARKE. 1. *Argent, on a bend gules between three torteaux, three swans argent* (Monument (7)).

2. *Three escallops in pale or, between two flaunches ermine* (Monument (3)).

CLIFFORD. 1. *Checky azure and argent, a fess gules.*

2. *Barry of six argent and sable.*

COURTENAY. Quarterly, 1 and 4, *Argent, three torteaux,* 2 and 3, *Or, a lion azure,* for REDVERS.

CRADOCK. *Three boars' heads couped between nine crosses crosslet.*

DAVIES. *A fess ermine between three cinquefoils.*

DRAPERS COMPANY. *Azure, three clouds proper, radiated in base or, each surmounted with a triple crown or, cap gules.*

DESPENSER. Quarterly *Argent and gules, in the 2nd and 3rd A fret or,* overall a bend sable.

EARLE. *Ermine, on a chief indented three crowns.*

EGERTON. *Argent, a lion gules between three pheons azure (sable).*

ESTCOURT. *Ermine, on a chief indented gules three estoiles or, a crescent for difference.*

EYRE. *Argent, on a chevron sable three quatrefoils or, a crescent for difference.* Crest: *A leg in armour, couped at the thigh sable.*

FITZ-ALAN? *Barry of eight azure and or.*

FITZHUGH. *Azure, three chevrons interlaced and a chief or.*

FITZGERALD. *Ermine, a saltire gules.*

GANTLET. *A mailed hand, and on a chief two cinquefoils.*

GODDARD. *A chevron vair between three crescents.*

GOLDWYER. *Azure, three stirrups in bend between two cotises or,* Crest: *A stag's head erased.*

GORGES. *Gules, six lozenges conjoined or.*

GOUGH. *Sable, on a fess gules between three boars' heads couped, a lion passant.*

GREENHILL. *Two bars and in chief a lion passant.*

GREVILE. *On a cross five roundels, a border engrailed.*

HALES. *A chevron between three lions.*

HALL. *Argent, a chevron sable between three columbines azure.*

HALSWELL. *Azure, three bars wavy, overall a bend gules, a crescent for difference.*

HAMBURG, Merchant Adventurers of, *Barry nebuly, a chief.* Quarterly 1 and 4, *A lion passant gardant,* 2 and 3, *Two roses in fess.*

HANCOCK. *Three cocks.* Crest: *A cockerel statant.*

HAWES. *Azure, a fess wavy between three lions passant or.*

HAWKINS. *Sable, on a base wavy vert a lion passant or, in chief three bezants. On a canton argent an escallop azure between two crosses fitchy sable.*

HAYTER. *Azure, three bulls' heads erased or.*

HEATH. *A cross engrailed between twelve billets.*

HELE. *Sable, on a bend – five lozenges –.*

HERBERT, Earl of Pembroke. *Per pale, three lions.*

HILL. *Gules, two bars ermine, in chief a lion passant or.*

HINXMAN. *Argent, a chevron gules between three bugle-horns stringed, on a chief gules three lions.* Crest: *A bugle-horn stringed.*

HORTON. *Three bends engrailed and a canton.*

HUNGERFORD. *Sable, two bars argent and in chief three plates.*

HYDE. Quarterly, 1 and 4, *A chevron between three lozenges,* 2 and 3, *Paly of six and a bend,* for LANGFORD.

KEENE. *Ermine, three crescents.*

KNIGHT. *On a fess between three bucks' heads erased, a fret between two martlets.*

LEE. *Gules, a fess checky or and azure between ten billets argents,* impaling unidentified coat.

LONG. *Sable, semy of crosses crosslet and a lion argent.*

LUCY. *Semy of crosses crosslet, three lucies haurient.*

LUDLOW. *Argent, a chevron between three foxes, heads erased sable.*

MATRAVERS or FITZ-ALAN. Quarterly 1 and 4, *Gules a lion or*, 2 and 3, *Sable, a fret or.*

MAYNE. *Argent, on a bend engrailed sable three hands couped at the wrist argent.*

MICHELL. *Per chevron sable and gules, a chevron between three swans argent.*

MINIFIE. *On a chevron between three annulets, three eagles.*

MOMPESSON? *Argent, a lion –.*

MONTACUTE. Quarterly 1 and 4, *Argent, three fusils conjoined in fess gules*, 2 and 3, *Or, an eagle vert, for* MONTHERMER.

MONTHERMER. *Or, an eagle vert.*

MOULTON. *Argent, three bars gules between eight escallops sable, 3, 2, 2 and 1.*

MUSGRAVE. *Six annulets, 3, 2 and 1.*

NEVILL. *Gules, a saltire argent* (Monument (3)). *Gules, a saltire argent, a label gobony argent and azure* (Monument (185)).

NISBET. *Argent, three boars' heads erased sable, a border invected gules.*

NORRIS. Quarterly, *Argent and gules, in the 2nd and 3rd A fret or, overall a fess azure.*

NOWES. *Vair, gules and argent,* impaling unidentified coat.

PAGE. *On a chevron between three birds, three pheons.*

PAYNE. *A fess between three leopards' faces.*

PHIPPS. *A trefoil within an orle of eight mullets.*

PITT. Quarterly 1 and 4, *A fess checky between three bezants*, 2 and 3, *A cross crosslet.*

POWELL. *Or, two chevronels between three lions – gambs erased gules.*

POWELL. *A chevron between three lions – gambs erased.*

PRIAULX. *Gules, an eagle argent.*

PRINCE. *A saltire, overall a cross engrailed ermine.*

RAY. *A fess between three battleaxes.*

ROLFE. *Three ravens.*

ST. GEORGE. *Argent, a cross gules.*

SALISBURY, City of. *Barry of eight, or and azure.*

SALISBURY, See of? *Azure, a human figure or.*

SALTERS COMPANY. *Per chevron azure and gules, three covered salts argent.*

SLATER. *A saltire.*

SMITHES. *Argent, a chevron between three oak leaves vert, each charged with an acorn or.*

SPOONER. *Sable, a boar's head erect couped argent.*

STONING. *On a chevron between three roundels, each charged with a fleur-de-lys, three …*

STOURTON. *Sable, a bend argent between six fountains.*

SWAYNE. 1. *Azure, a chevron between three pheons or* (Monument (3)).

 2. *Azure, a chevron erminois between three pheons or, a border erminois* (Monument (570)).

TALBOT? *Bendy of eight gules and argent.*

TERRY. *Ermine, on a pile a leopard's face jessant-de-lys.*

TOWNSEND. *A chevron between three escallops.*

VINER. *A bend and on a chief or three choughs.*

WALMESLEY. *Gules, on a chief ermine two harts,* impaled by unidentified coat.

WARWICK. *Checky or and azure, a chevron ermine.*

WASTFELDE or WASTFIELD. *On a fess between six billets, three Catherine wheels.* Crest: *A Pascal lamb.*

WEBBE. *A cross between four falcons.*

WILLES or WILLIS. *Argent, a chevron azure between three mullets sable.*

WILLOUGHBY? Quarterly 1 and 4, *Gules, a cross moline argent*, 2 and 3, *Azure, a cross argent.*

WINCHESTER, See of? *A sword and key in saltire.*

WINDOVER. *Sable, two bars and in chief three demi-lions or, in fess point, a mullet for difference.*

WROUGHTON. *A chevron between three boars' heads couped.*

WYLFORD or WILFORD. *A chevron engrailed between three leopards' faces.*

WYNDHAM. *Azure, a chevron between three lions' heads erased or,* Crest: *A lion's head erased within a fetterlock or.*

UNIDENTIFIED COATS

1. *Gules, a lion passant or.* (3), 26b.
2. *Argent, a fess gules.* (3), 26b.
3. *Argent, a cross gules.* (3), 27a, 28a.
4. *Gules, two keys in saltire or.* (3), 28a.
5. *Sable, a cross paty.* (3), 28a.
6. *Gules, a harp or.* (3), 28a.
7. *Gules, a cross argent.* (3), 28a.
8. *Gules, in a border azure semy of crosses paty, three lions passant or.* (3), 28a.
9. *Argent, a chevron gules.* (3), 28a, 28b, see 19 below, 28b.
10. *Argent, a chevron sable.* (3), 28a.
11. *Gules, a chevron sable.* (3), 28a.
12. *Sable, a chevron between three lilies argent, quartering ermine.* (3), 28a.
13. *Gules, a chevron between three catherine wheels or.* (3), 28a.
14. *Argent, a chevron between three roses gules.* (3), 28a.
15. *Argent, a fess between three moorhens.* (3), 28a.
16. *Sable, a chevron ermine between three hurdles argent.* (3), 28b.

17. *Argent, a bend engrailed sable.* (3), 28b.
18. *Gules, six drops argent.* (3), 28b.
19. *Gules, a pallium azure,* impaling (9) above. (3), 28b.
20. *On a chief three lions' heads erased,* impaling Eyre. (3), 30a.
21. *Azure, on a fess between three riding boots argent, the two in chief in saltire, a heart between two roses gules,* impaled by Chester. (4), 35a.
22. *Argent, a cross engrailed between four mullets sable,* impaled by Lee. (4), 35a.
23. *A lion,* impaled by Greenhill. (4), 35a.
24. *On a fess between three griffins heads erased,* impaled by Rolfe. (4), 35a.
25. *Azure, a fess ermine, a chief three fleurs-de-lys or, quartering gules, a lion or,* impaling Eyre. (5), 38b.
26. *A lion and a chief,* impaled by Earle. (6), 41a.
27. *On a cross, five buckles.* (98), 76.
28. *Ermine, a lion regardant or.* (185), 104b.
29. *Ermine, a lion or.* (185), 104b.

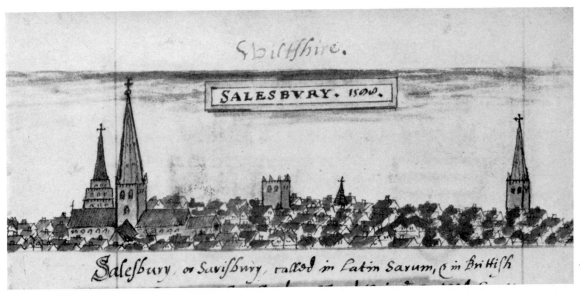

Salisbury from S. by William Smith, 1588.

B.L., Sloane MS., 2596.

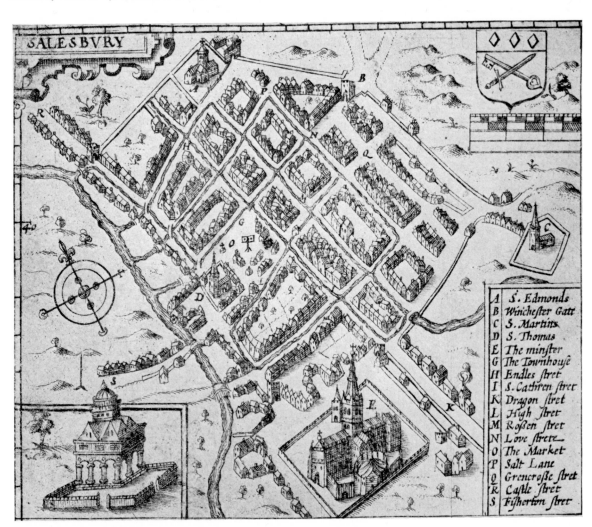

A	S. Edmonds
B	Winchester Gate
C	S. Martins
D	S. Thomas
E	The minster
G	The Townhouse
H	Endles ftret
I	S. Cathren ftret
K	Dragon ftret
L	High ftret
M	Roffen ftret
N	Love ftrete
O	The Market
P	Salt Lane
Q	Grencroffe ftret
R	Caftle ftret
S	Fifherton ftret

John Speed's plan of Salisbury, *c.* 1600.

Empire of Great Britaine, 1611.

Plate 2   OLD VIEWS ETC.

Old Council House, Guildhall, and adjacent buildings, *c.* 1780.   Benson & Hatcher, opp. p. 533.

(15) Poultry Cross, 1810. Watercolour by J. Buckler.   Devizes Museum.

Courtyard and S. front, 1690.   Salisbury Museum.

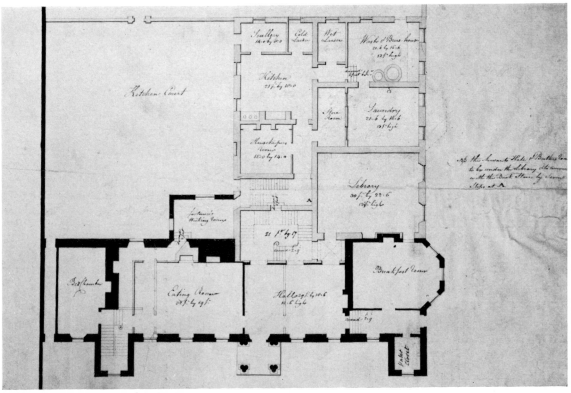

Ground plan showing extensions of 1788, by S. P. Cockerell.   Salisbury Museum.

(14) St. EDMUNDS COLLEGE, now COUNCIL HOUSE.

W. front, 1805. Watercolour by J. Buckler.   Devizes Museum.

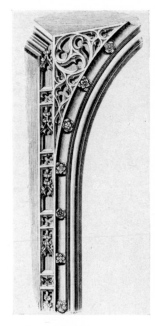 

Oak post flanking
entrance.   Parker.
    Courtyard, looking N.W., c. 1850.
    Oil painting by E. A. Goodall & J. B. Surgey.   Salisbury Museum.

(173) THE GEORGE INN.

W. front, 1833. Drawing by William Twopeny. British Museum.

(173) THE GEORGE INN.

Plate 6

OLD VIEWS ETC.

Courtyard, looking E., 1859. Watercolour by Sir H. Dryden.
Northampton Public Library.

Courtyard, looking S.W., 1813. Drawing by W. H. Charlton.
Salisbury Museum.

(173) THE GEORGE INN.

Plate 7

OLD VIEWS ETC.

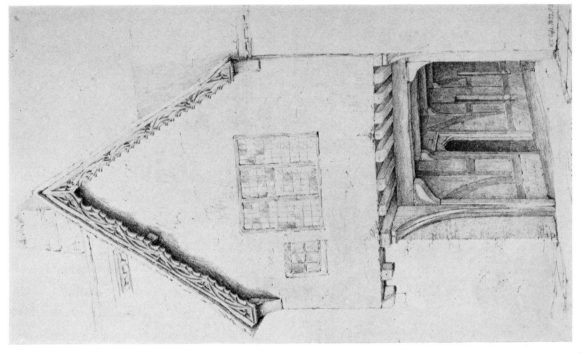

(177) No. 49 New Canal. N. front, 1833. William Twopeny.
British Museum.

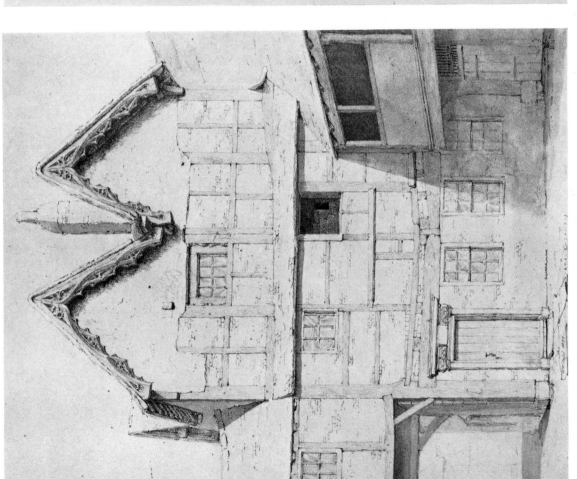

(173) The George Inn. Courtyard, 1833. William Twopeny. British Museum.

Plate 8

OLD VIEWS ETC.

Demolition of the Bishop's Guildhall, c. 1790.

Salisbury Museum.

Plate 9

OLD VIEWS ETC.

Salisbury from N.E., before 1771.

Salisbury Museum.

(97) Church House. N. front, 1833. W. Twopeny.

B.M.

(258) 'The Barracks'. E. front, 1833. W. Twopeny.

B.M.

Plate 10

OLD VIEWS ETC.

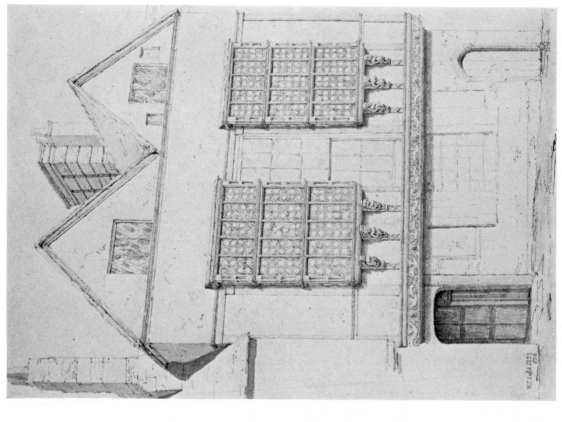

(293) Joiners' Hall.
Drawing by William Twopeny, 1833.   British Museum.

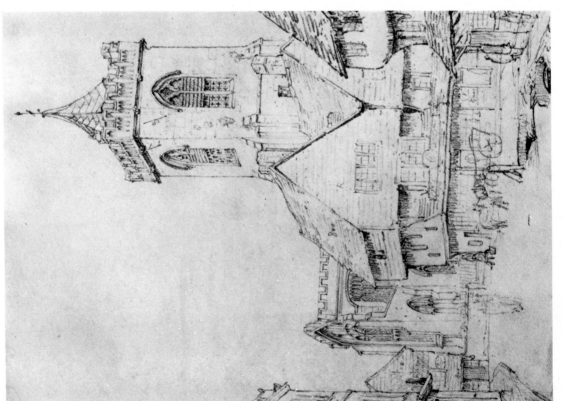

(3) St. Thomas's Church and (63) Nos. 48–52 Silver Street.
Drawing by W. H. Charlton, 1813.   Salisbury Museum.

Plate 11

OLD VIEWS ETC.

(26) St. Nicholas's Hospital from N.W., 1803.

(588) Harnham Mill from S.E., 1803.

(97) Church House. Courtyard, looking W., 1805.

(9) Harnham Church from N.E., 1803.

Watercolours by J. Buckler, Devizes Museum.

Plate 12

OLD PLANS

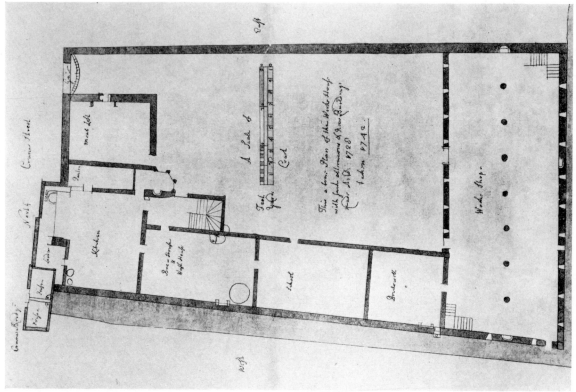

(97) Church House. Plan, 1748.   Sar. Dioc. Bd. of Finance.

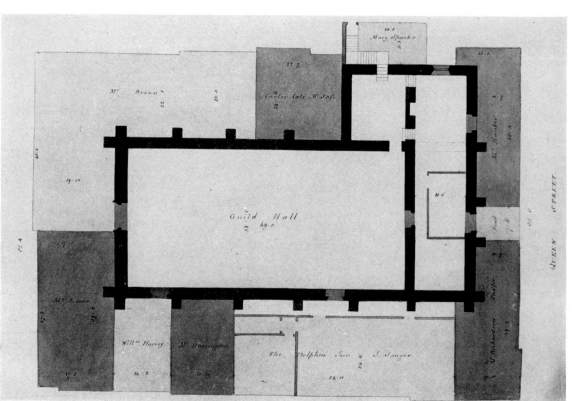

Bishop's Guildhall (demolished c. 1790). Plan by J. Buckler.
Devizes Museum.

Plate 13

OLD PLANS

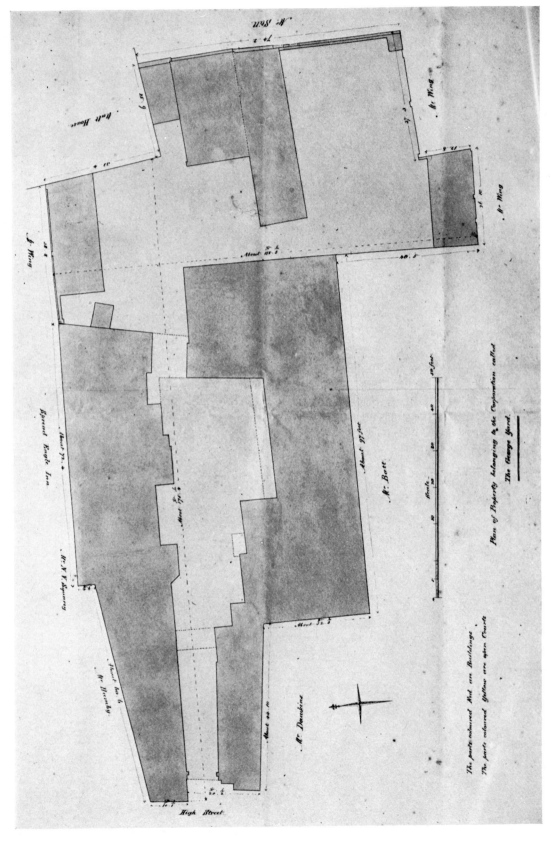

Sar. Corp. MS.

(173) The George Inn. Plan by F. R. Fisher, c. 1850.

Plate 14

EARLY PHOTOGRAPHS

Blue Boar Row.

Nos. 43–5 Castle Street.

Cheesemarket, before 1857.

Hall adjacent to Trinity Hospital.

Plate 15

EARLY PHOTOGRAPHS

(22) General Infirmary.

Winchester St. from E., showing ? remains of Wynman Gate.

354) Nos. 10–12 Rollestone Street.

N.W. corner of Mitre Chequer, from W.

Plate 16

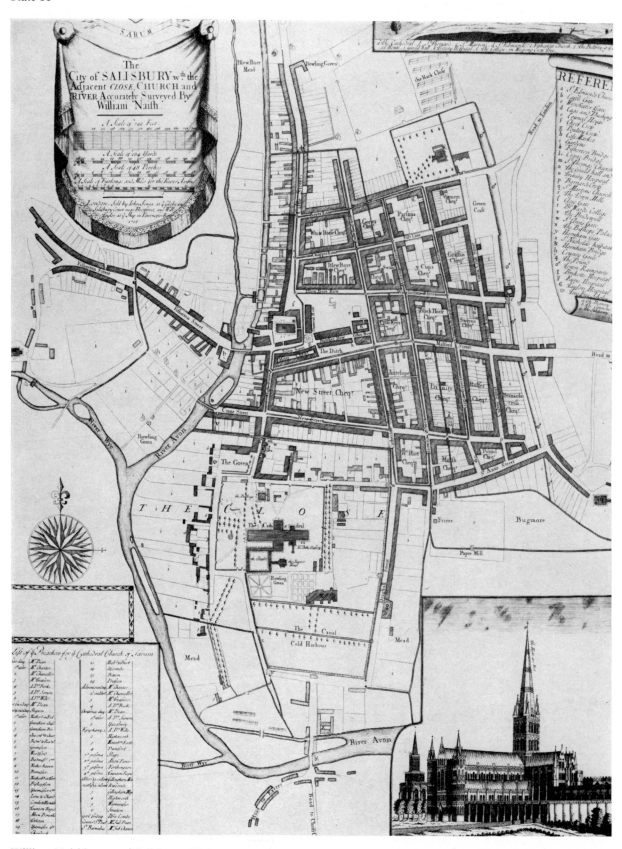

William Naish's map of Salisbury, 1716.

Plate 17

Vertical air photograph of central area.

(16) Remains of City Rampart adjoining St. Edmund's College. Looking S.

Plate 18   PUBLIC BUILDINGS

(13) The Guildhall. N. front.   1788 and 1829.

(14) St. Edmund's College, now Council House. S. front.   18th century.

(19) Milford Bridge, from S.

Late 14th or early 15th century.

(18) Crane Bridge, from N.

Mainly 17th century.

(17) Ayleswade Bridge, from S.W.

c. 1244 and 1774.

Plate 20   CIVIC INSIGNIA ETC.

Royal Arms formerly over Castle Street gate.   Probably 1638.

Carved panel from former Gaol (476).   1783.

Inscription on St. Edmund's Church.   1653.

Mayoral Chair. 1585.

Mayoral Chair. 1795.

Silver Mace. 1749.

Standard Weights. 1825.

Standard Measures 1825.

S. front.

Courtyard, looking N. Chapel doorway.

(27) TRINITY HOSPITAL.

Courtyard, looking S.W.

Rebuilt 1702.

N. elevation

S. elevation.

(33) FROWD'S ALMSHOUSES. 1750.

(22) GENERAL INFIRMARY. 1767.

Plate 24

OLD SARUM

(1) Old Sarum. Iron Age Hill-fort and Mediaeval Castle. From N.

Plate 25

OLD SARUM

Looking S. from Old to New Sarum. Foreground, East Gate of Inner Bailey.

From N.

From S.W.

Air Views.

(1) Courtyard House. Looking N.W.

(1) West Gate (outer curtain) during excavation. Looking W.

Plate 28   OLD SARUM

(1) Masonry of Great Tower.   (1) E. range of Courtyard House. ?Fireplace.

(2) Cathedral Treasury.

Plate 29

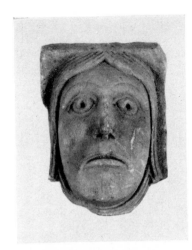

Head corbels.

Arcaded panel.

Voussoirs.

Carved stones from (2) Old Sarum Cathedral.

Salisbury Museum.

Plate 30   OLD SARUM TOMB-SLABS NOW IN SALISBURY CATHEDRAL

Bishop Osmund.

Bishop Jocelyn.

Lettering of Bishop Osmund's inscription.

Mid 12th century.

(4) St. MARTIN'S CHURCH. Chancel, from S.E.

13th century.

Plate 32 CHURCHES

(3) St. THOMAS'S CHURCH. S. aisle and S. tower, from S.E. 1400 and later.

(3) St. THOMAS'S CHURCH, from N.W.   15th century.

From N.W.   From W.

(5) St. EDMUND'S CHURCH.   Tower, 1656.

C

Plate 34　　　　　　　　　　　　　　　CHURCHES

(3) St. THOMAS'S CHURCH. Nave, looking E.　　　　　　　　　Second half of 15th century.

Last Judgement.

Late 15th century.

Capitals in chancel.

c. 1450.

(3) St. THOMAS'S CHURCH.

Plate 36

CHURCHES

Doorway, 13th century.

Interior of S. aisle and E. wall of tower.

Tower, early 14th century

W. end and tower.

(4) St. MARTIN'S CHURCH.

Plate 37

CHURCHES

12th century and later.

(9) St. GEORGE'S CHURCH. Interior, looking E.

Plate 38 CHURCHES

(6) St. LAWRENCE'S CHURCH, Stratford-sub-Castle.   Mainly 15th and 16th century. Tower, 1711.

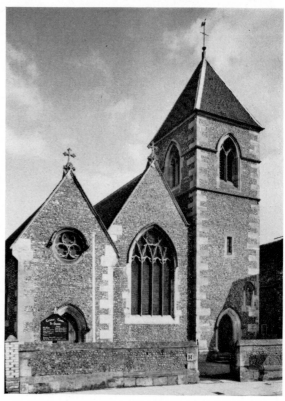

(9) St. GEORGE'S CHURCH. Doorway.   12th cent.   (10) St. OSMUND'S CHURCH.   1847.

(4) St. MARTIN'S CHURCH. Interior, looking S.E.   15th century.

Plate 40

PISCINAE

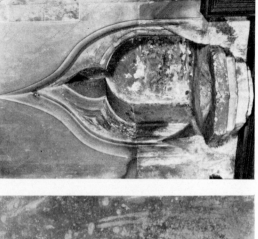

13th century. (9) St. George's Church.
14th century.

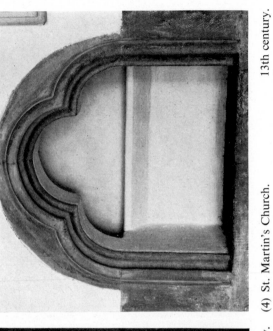

13th century. (4) St. Martin's Church.

13th century. (9) St. George's Church.

(26) St. Nicholas's Hospital.

(4) St. Martin's Church.
Late 15th century.

Plate 41

FONTS

13th century.   (7) From St. Clement's Church, now in St. Paul's.

13th century.   (4) St. Martin's Church.

Plate 42   CARVED STONEWORK IN CHURCHES

(4) St. Martin's Church. N. aisle roof-brackets and rear-arch corbel.   Late 15th century.

(3) St. Thomas's Church. Capitals in chancel.   15th century.

(5) St. Edmund's Church.   15th century.   (11) St. John's Chapel.   13th century.

(3) St. Thomas's Church. S. chapel. Adoration.   15th century.

(3) St. Thomas's Church. S. chapel. Annunciation and Visitation.   15th century.

(95) No. 86 Crane Street.   13th century.

Plate 44   CHURCH SCREENS ETC.

(6) St. Lawrence's Church.   15th and 18th centuries.

(9) St. George's Church.   Early 17th century.   (4) St. Martin's Church. Wall-post and cornice
                                                        in N. aisle.   Late 15th century.

(3) St. Thomas's Church.   1724.

(4) St. Martin's Church (formerly). Pulpit now in St. Mark's.   15th century.

(6) St. Lawrence's Church. Pulpit.

Early 17th century.

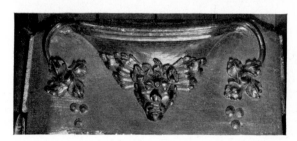

(3) St. Thomas's Church. Misericord.   15th century.   (8) St. Andrew's Church. Door.   17th century.

(3) St. Thomas's Church. Roof of S. chapel.   Mid 15th century.

(6) St. Lawrence's Church. Wall-plate bosses.   15th century.

(3) St. Thomas's Church. Beckham monument.   17th century.

Plate 48

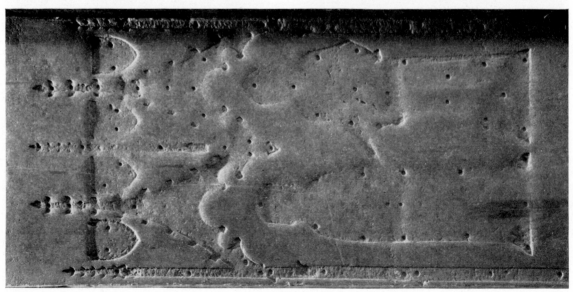

BRASSES AND INDENTS

1570.

St. Thomas's Church. Brasses and tomb-slab of John Webbe.

15th century.   (3)

(5) St. Edmund's Church.

Plate 49

WALL MONUMENTS

First erected c. 1624.

(9) Christopher and Esther (Smithes) Eyre.

(10) Thomas and Elizabeth (Rogers) Eyre.

St. THOMAS'S CHURCH. Monuments formerly in chancel, now in S. chapel.

D

St. Martin's. (1) Bennet and Thomas Swayne, 1747–8.

St. Thomas's. (8) Alexander Powell, 1748.

St. Martin's. Floorslab (1) of Catherine Egerton and
Elizabeth Grevile, 1743–5.

St. Thomas's. (1)   William Wroughton, 1770.

(2) Wm. and Anne Ludlow, 1749.

(12) Edward Baker, 1796.

(13) Thomas Snow, 1776.

(14) Mary Edgar, 1770.

(6) Mary Thomas, 1781.

(7) Joseph Willis, 1772.

Eighteenth-century monuments in St. Martin's Church.

Plate 52

EIGHTEENTH-CENTURY WALL MONUMENTS

(3) St. Thomas's. John Gough, 1709/10.

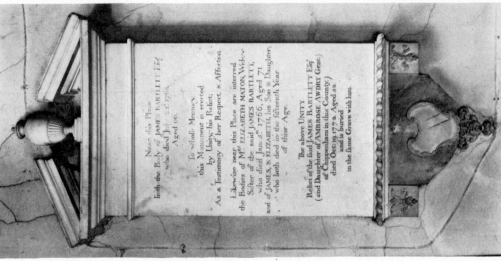

(4) St. Martin's. James Bartlett, 1768.

(5) St. Edmund's. Marshall Hill, 1707.

Plate 53

MISCELLANEOUS CHURCH FITTINGS

(3) St. Thomas's. Fifteenth-century textile, probably from a cope.

(3) St. Thomas's. Early 16th-century chest.

(4) St. Martin's. Fifteenth-century lectern.

Plate 54

Cup and cover-paten, 1595.   (Ht. 8½ ins.)   Almsdish, 1662. (Diameter 18 ins.)

(4) St. MARTIN'S CHURCH.

Plate 55

CHURCH PLATE

(5) St. EDMUND'S. Paten, 1533. (Diam. 6 ins.)

(4) St. MARTIN'S. Flagon, 1669. (Ht. 10 ins.)

(5) St. EDMUND'S. Almsdish, 1734. (Diameter 17 ins.)

Plate 56   ROYAL ARMS IN CHURCHES

(5) St. Edmund's. Arms of George III on mace-rest.

(4) St. Martin's.   Elizabeth I.   (3) St. Thomas's.   Probably 1593.

(6) St. Lawrence's.   1713.

(15) Poultry Cross, from S.E.   15th century and 1852.

Plate 58   MEDIAEVAL STONE BUILDINGS

(26) St. Nicholas's Hospital. Arcade, from N.   *c.* 1230.

(588) Harnham Mill, from S.   *c.* 1500.

Porch from cathedral reset at (14) St. Edmund's College.

(185) Hall of John Hall. Part of E. elevation.

(97) Church House. Gateway, from N.

(97) Church House. Oriel and stair tower, from S.E.

Plate 60   FOURTEENTH-CENTURY TIMBER-FRAMED HOUSES

(82) Nos. 52–4 High Street.

(305) No. 18 St. Ann Street.

(177) No. 49 New Canal (1961).

(173) The George Inn. W. front (1961).

Plate 62   TIMBER-FRAMED HOUSES

(107) New Inn.

(290–3) Nos. 58–66 St. Ann's Street.

(128) No. 8 Queen Street.

Plate 64

TIMBER-FRAMED HOUSES

(71) Wheatsheaf Inn.

(399) Pheasant Inn.

Plate 65

TIMBER-FRAMED HOUSES

(383) Toone's Court.

(250) No. 88 Milford Street.

E

Plate 66

SEVENTEENTH-CENTURY TIMBER-FRAMED HOUSES

(252) King's Arms Hotel.

(155) No. 41 Milford Street.

Plate 67

SEVENTEENTH-CENTURY TIMBER-FRAMED HOUSES

(165) Tailors' Guild Hall.

(293) Joiners' Guild Hall.

Plate 68   SEVENTEENTH-CENTURY STONE HOUSES

(528) Bemerton Rectory. N. wing.   1630.

(557) Mawarden Court. W. front.   Probably 1673.

(557) Mawarden Court. E. front.   c. 1600; remodelled, 1835.

Plate 70   SEVENTEENTH-CENTURY HOUSES

(304) House in Friary Lane.   Probably 1619.

(359) No. 47 Winchester Street.   1673.   (556) Stratford-sub-Castle.   *c.* 1700.

Plate 71

(102) No. 91 Crane Street.   14th-century house with 16th and 17th-century additions.

Plate 72   LATE SEVENTEENTH-CENTURY AND

(368) No. 24 St. Edmund's Church Street.

(273) Barnard's Cross House, from N.E.

(101) No. 93 Crane Street.

(230) Nos. 37–9 Brown Street.

Plate 74

LATE 17TH AND EARLY 18TH-CENTURY HOUSES

Late 17th century.   (247) No. 53 Payne's Hill.

c. 1701.   (99) Audley House.

Plate 75

(287) No. 82 St. Ann's Street.

EIGHTEENTH-CENTURY HOUSES

(427) No. 45 Castle Street.

Plate 76

EIGHTEENTH-CENTURY HOUSES

(199) No. 4 New Street.

(297) No. 44 St. Ann's Street.

Plate 77

EIGHTEENTH-CENTURY HOUSES

(468) No. 54 Endless Street.

(419) No. 1 Castle Street.

Plate 78   EIGHTEENTH-CENTURY STREET FRONTS

(300) Nos. 36–8 St. Ann's Street.

(289) No. 68 St. Ann's Street.

(266) Nos. 89–91 Brown Street.

(350) Old George Inn.

Plate 80 NINETEENTH-CENTURY STREET FRONTS

(219) Red Lion Hotel.

(422) Nos. 19–25 Castle Street.

Plate 81

(254) White Hart Hotel.

F

Plate 82   MEDIAEVAL ROOFS

(129) No. 9 Queen Street.   *c.* 1314.

(351) Balle's Place.   Before 1387.   (173) George Inn.   Third quarter of 14th century.

(185) Hall of John Hall.   Late 15th century.   (97) Church House.   Second half of 15th century.

(173) George Inn. Hammer-beams.

(81) No. 50 High Street.

(173) George Inn. Post flanking through-way.

(97) Church House. Corbels supporting hall roof.   Second half of 15th century.

F*

Plate 86   SEVENTEENTH-CENTURY STAIRCASES

(132) Plume of Feathers Inn (19th-century photograph).

(36) No. 29 Cheesemarket.

(173) George Inn.

(350) Old George Inn.

(307) No. 6 St. Ann's Street.

(302) Windover House.

(77) No. 32 High Street.

(133) No. 20 Queen Street.

(427) No. 45 Castle Street.

(286) No. 84 St. Ann's Street.

(273) Barnard's Cross House.

(14) The College.

(139) Cathedral Hotel.

(181) No. 33 New Canal.

(97) Church House.

(55) Nos. 3 and 5 Minster Street.

(71) Wheatsheaf Inn.

(97) Church House, solar.

(97) Church House.

(185) Hall of John Hall.

(97) Church House, hall. Formerly in Mere.

(98) Church House, S. range. Formerly in a house in St. Ann's Street.

(97) Church House. Formerly at Longford Castle.

Doorway in (102) No. 91
Crane Street.

Plate 92   SEVENTEENTH-CENTURY CHIMNEYPIECES

(174) No. 11 High Street.

(252) King's Arms Hotel.

(101) No. 93 Crane Street.

(128) No. 8 Queen Street.

(581) Old Parsonage Farm House, Harnham.

(234) No. 34 Milford Street.

(173) George Inn.

(302) Windover House. Soffit of plaster-cased beam.

(199) No. 4 New Street.

(391) Loder House.

(111) No. 31 New Street.

(506) Crane Lodge.

(111) No. 31 New Street.

(199) No. 4 New Street.

(266) No. 89 Brown Street.

(355) No. 14 Rolleston Street.

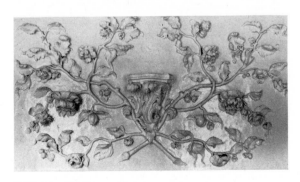

(133) No. 20 Queen Street.

(391) Loder House.

(299) Salisbury Museum.

Plate 96   INTERIORS

(87) No. 47 High Street. Hall.

(181) No. 93 Crane Street. Hall.

(307) No. 6 St. Ann's Street. Drawing room.

(87) No. 47 High Street. Drawing room.

(557) Mawarden Court. Drawing room.

Plate 98   EIGHTEENTH-CENTURY DOORCASES

(297) No. 44 St. Ann's Street.

(468) No. 54 Endless Street.

(289) No. 68 St. Ann's Street.

(442) No. 93 Castle Street.

(397) No. 24 Bedwin Street.

(381) No. 26 Castle Street.

(342) No. 13 Endless Street.

(446) No. 206 Castle Street.

Plate 100

Minster Street and Silver Street, looking N.W. (1970).

Plate 101

Queen Street. Houses of Cross Keys Chequer facing Market Place (1966).

Plate 102

High Street, looking S.E. (1966).

Plate 103

S. side of Crane Street (1976).

Plate 104

High Street, looking N.E., *c.* 1850.

ANALYTICAL INDEX

The numbers in brackets are the serial numbers of the monuments.

Abarough, arms of, *see* **Heraldry.**
Adoration, painted panel, (3) 31a.
Albion Inn (301) 125b.
Aldermen, *see* **Occupations.**
Alessaundre, William, owner of The Barracks, (258) 118a.
All Saints, *see* **Dedications of Churches.**
Allesley, Thomas, tenant at George Inn, (173) 97b.
Almshouses and Hospitals:
  13TH-CENTURY: St. Nicholas, (26) 54b.
  18TH-CENTURY: Frowd's, (33) 58b; General Infirmary, (22), 52b;
    Hayter's, (30) 58a; Trinity, (27) 56b.
  19TH-CENTURY: Blechynden's, (28) 58a; Brown's, (31) 58b; Culver
    Street, (29) 58a; Taylor's, (32) 58b.
Altars: *see also* **Communion Tables.**
  12TH-CENTURY: liv; Old Sarum, (1) 9a; (2) 22b; St. George's (9) 44a.
  MEDIAEVAL: Trinity Hospital, (27) 56b.
  19TH-CENTURY: St. Osmund's, (10) 45a.
Alward of Ramsbury, tomb-slab, Old Sarum, (2) 21a–b.
Anchor Inn (235) 113b.
Anchor and Hope Inn (374) 141a.
Andrew, St., *see* **Dedications of Churches.**
Angel Inn (77), 68a.
Anne, Queen, arms of, *see* **Heraldry**; portrait in Guildhall, (13) 47a.
Annunciation, painted panel, (3) 30b; embroidered, (3) 31a; sculptured,
  (4) 35a.
Antelope Chequer, 107.
  ,,   **Inn** (208) 108a.
Antrum, William, churchwarden of St. Martin's, (4) 35b.
Apothecaries, *see* **Occupations.**
Architects, Builders and Surveyors:
  ATKINSON, T.: (22) 52b.
  BATH, Frederick: (185) 104a.
  BUTTERFIELD, William: (9) 43b.
  CARTER, Owen: (15) 50a.
  COCKERELL, S. P.: (14) 49a.
  CRICKMAY & SON: (4), liii; (26) 56a; (97) 73b; (98) 76a.
  FIGES, Sarum: (20) 52a.
  FISHER, F. R.: (173) 98a; (185) 104a.
  HALL, H: (133) Pinkney's Bank, 89a.
  HOPPER, Thomas: (13) 46b.
  KINGDON & SHEARM: xxvi.
  NAISH: xxxvi, xxxvii, Pl. 16; (16) 51b; (27) 57a; (187) 105a; (199)
    106b; (415) 147b; (423) 148b.
  OSMUND, W.: (15) 50a.
  PENISTON, J., J. M. and H.: xxvii; (25) 54b; (55) 63b; (64) 65a; (67)
    65a; (83) 70a; (84) 70a; (110) 80a; (140) 90a; (142) 91a; (159)
    93b; (162–4) 94a; (203) 107b; (208) 108a; (287) 123a; (304), (305)
    128a; (306) 128b; (307) 129a; (330) 131b; (351) 136a; (352)
    137b; (359) 139a; (381) 142b; Vanner's Chequer, 146b; (423)
    148b.
  PILKINGTON, William: (13) 46a.
  PUGIN, A. W. N.: (10) 44b, 45a; (185) 104a.
  SCOTT, George Gilbert: (5), liii.
  SLEAT, W.: xxvii; (165) 94a; (172) 97a.
  SPEED, John: xlvii; li; Pl. 1; (5) 37a; (16) 51a.
  STRAPP, W.: (25) 54b.
  STREET, G. E.: (3), liii, 25a.
  SURMAN, Robert: (22) 52b.
  TAYLOR, Sir Robert: (13) 46a.
  WEBB, D.: (10), liii.
  WOOD, John: (22), xlix, lxiii, 52b.
  WYATT, T. H.: St. Paul's church (replacing (7)), liii.

Arney, Jane, 1650, floorslab, (6) 41a.
Ashlar, *see* **Building Construction**
Ashleigh, William, owner of land in White Hart Chequer, (259) 118b.
Askew, Robert, 1814, and Thomas, 1831, table-tomb (7) 42a.
Assembly House, former, on site of, (199) 105b.
  ,,   **Rooms,** former, (175) 100a, Pl. 104.
Athelstan, coins of, xxix.
Atkinson, T., *see* **Architects, Builders and Surveyors.**
  ,,   Thomas, 1838, and Charlotte, 1845, tablet, (7) 42a.
Aubyn, Philip, owner of Bolehall, (140) 89b.
Audeley, Sir Thomas, 1495, owner of The Leg, (172) 97a.
Audley, arms of, *see* **Heraldry.**
Audley House (99) 76b.
Aumbry, 13th-century, (26) 56b.
Avon Valley, the bishop's estates in, xxix.
Ayleswade Bridge (17), xxxiii, xxxvii, li, lxi, 51b.

Bailey, M., 1771, churchwarden of St. Thomas's, (3) 29a.
Bailiff, *see* **Occupations.**
Baker:
  Arms of, *see* **Heraldry.**
  Colonel, 18th-century resident, xlix.
  Edward, 1796, HP, 1794, Jane, 1800, hatchments, (4) 34b.
  Edward, 1796, Jane, 1800, monument, (4) 34b.
Bakers, *see* **Occupations.**
Ballard, Dorothea, 1709, brass, (3) 29a.
  ,,   Dr. John, lessee of No. 47 High Street, (87), 1698, 71a.
Balle's Place (351), xlii, xliv, xlv, lxi, 135b; *see also* (361) 140a.
Baly, William, owner of shops etc., 1396, (35) 59b.
Banks, Ann, 1785, and Benjamin, 1795, musical instrument maker,
  monument, (3) 30b.
  ,,   Richard, 1649, purchaser of part of Pynok's Inn, (77) 68a.
Barber, John, brazier, 1403, xlii.
Barbers, *see* **Occupations.**
Bargeboards:
  14TH-CENTURY: George Inn, (173) 98a; New Canal, (177) 101a; Rose
    & Crown, (576) 169b.
  19TH-CENTURY: Minster Street, (55) 64a.
Barley Mow Inn (372) 141a.
Barnaby, Mary, 1724, floorslab, (3) 30b.
Barnard's Cross Chequer, 115a.
  ,,   ,,   **House** (273), lxii, 121a.
Barnes, arms of, *see* **Heraldry.**
Barns and Outbuildings: xliv.
  BARNS: Toll Gate Inn, (279) 121b; Bemerton, (528) 163b; Devizes
    Road, (535) 164a; Stratford, (550) 165b; Milford, (572) 168b.
  COACH-HOUSES AND STABLES: Bell & Crown, (310) 129a; Five Bells,
    (369) 141a; Anchor & Hope, (374) 141b; Greencroft Street, (416)
    147b; Endless Street, (465) 154b; Fisherton, (504) 160a;
    Bemerton, (521) 162a; (528) 163b; Stratford, (546) 165a.
  GARDEN HOUSES: Castle St., (427) 151a; Milford Manor, (570) 168b.
  GRANARY: Stratford, (560) 167b.
  MALT-HOUSE: Crane Bridge Rd., (504) 160a.
Baron, Christina, owner of house in Oatmeal Row, xli.
'Barracks, The' (258), xlii, xliv, lxii, 118a. Fireplace from, (102) 78a.
Bartlett, James, 1768 monument, (4) 35a.
  ,,   , Mr., 1818, hospital benefactor, (22) 52b.
Baskerville, Ann, 1749, John, 1761, Mary, 1768, Thomas, 1781,
  monuments, (5) 38b.
Bath, Frederick, *see* **Architects, Builders and Surveyors.**
Batt:
  Arms of, *see* **Heraldry.**

Batt—*contd*
John, 1723, hatchment, (4) 34b.
William, 1794, donor of plate, (22) 52b.
Batten, John, lessee of cottages in Crane Street, (93) 72b.
Baudrey, John, 14th-century property owner, Brown Street, (259) 118b; St. Ann's Street, (305) xlvi, 128a.
Baxter, Richard, 1692, churchwardens' inscription on bell, (9) 44b.
Bayley, John, owner of Church House, 1578, (97) 73b.
Baylye:
Arms of, *see* **Heraldry**.
John and Catherine, 1600, brass, (3), lv, 29a.
Beare, J., restorer of glass, (185) 104a.
Beauchamp, arms of *see* **Heraldry**.
    ,,   , Bishop, rental of, xxvi; (102) 77b.
Becket or **Beckot**, John, will of, 1416, (233) 113a; (305) 128a.
Beckham:
Humphrey, 1671, wood carver, lvii; monument, (3) 30b; chimneypiece, (128) 82b.
Reynald, 1593, joiner, lix.
Beckingham, John, 16th-century owner of College, (14) 48a.
Beconsall, Robert, *see* **Bellfounders**.
Bedwin Street, 145a, 146, 147, 155b, 157a.
Bee, Matthew, mayor 1600, xlvii; builder of Cradock House, (304) 127a.
Bell and Crown Inn (203) 107b.
Bell-cage, 1711, (6) 40b.
Bell-cote, 18th-century, (27) 57a; *c.* 1800, (8) 42b.
Bellevue House (462) 154b.
Bellfounders: liv
BECONSALL, Robert: (7) 41b.
BOLTER, Nathanial: (5) 38a.
DANTON, John: (4) 34a.
FLOWER or FLOREY, Richard: (4) 34a.
MEARS, Thomas: (4) 34a; (5) 38a; (7) 41a.
PURDUE, William: (5) 38a.
READING FOUNDRY: (8) 43a.
RUDHALL, Abraham: (3) 29a.
TOSIEAR, Clement: (9) 44b.
WALLIS, John: (3) 29a; (4) 34a; (6) 40b; (7) 41b; (26) 56b.
WELLS, Robert: (3) 29a; (4) 38a; (6) 40b.
Bell-foundry, (248) 115a.
Bell-frame, 1656, (5) 38a.
Bells: liv
14TH-CENTURY: liv.
16TH-CENTURY: *c.* 1540, (8) 43a; Wallis, 1581, (3) 29a; 1582, (4) 34a; 1594, (6) 40b.
17TH-CENTURY: Wallis, 1609, (7) 41b; Beconsall, 1616, (7) 41b; Wallis, 1623, (26) 56b; Wallis and Danton, 1624, (4) 34a; Purdue and Bolter, 1656, (5) 38a; Florey, 1675, (4) 34a; Anon., 1683 (recast), (3) 29a; Tosiear, 1692, (9) 44b.
18TH-CENTURY: Wallis? 1702? (27) 57b; Rudhall, 1716, (3) 29a; Wells, 1767, (6) 40b; 1771, (3) 29a; 1773, (5) 38a.
19TH-CENTURY: Mears, 1832, 1842, (7), 41b; 1842–3, (4), 34a; 1846, (5) 38a.
Bemerton, development of, l.
    ,,   **House** (520) 161b.
    ,,   **Rectory** (528), lxiv, 163a.
    ,,   **Village**, 161–163.
Benefactor's Tables:
18TH-CENTURY: St. Nicholas's (26) 56b.
19TH-CENTURY: (3) 29a; (7) 41b.
Berber, James, 1762, scratching, (5) 38b.
Berecorner, (Bear Corner) mediaeval tenement, (219) 109a.
Bernasconi, Francis, *see* **Plasterers**.
Bewde, Elizabeth, 1662, floorslab, (6) 41a.
Bingham, Bishop, xxxviii, li, lxi, builder of St. John's, (11) 45a; Ayleswade Bridge, (17) 51b; St. Nicholas's Hospital, (26) 55a.
Bishop's Guildhall, demolished, (13) 46a.
Bishop's Mill, now Town Mill, (66), xxxiii, 65a.
Bishop's Palace, Old Sarum, (2) 21b.
Bishopsdown, pottery found, Old Sarum, (1) 5b; track to, (1) 12b.
Blackall, arms of, *see* **Heraldry**.
Black Horse Chequer, 89b.
    ,,   ,,   **Inn**, former, (142) 91a.
Blake:
Arms of, *see* **Heraldry**.
I., churchwarden, (6) 40b.

John, 1803, Margaret, 1812, tablet, (4) 35a.
Blakebrigge, across Town Ditch near Raie d'Or Inn, (227) 111b.
Blecher, Thomas, 1405, ironmonger, xli.
Blechynden's Almshouses (28) 58a.
Blue Boar Chequer, 132a.
    ,,   ,,   **Inn** (344), xlv, 133b.
    ,,   ,,   **Row**, xl, xlvii; (335)–(341) 132a–133a; old views, Pls. 8, 14.
Bolehall, (140), xliv, lxi, 89b.
Bolter, Nathaniel, *see* **Bellfounders**.
Borough, I., churchwarden, 1711, (6) 41a.
Borry, Henry, 14th-century owner of Bolehall, (140) 89b.
Bothelrewe, Bottle Row, xl.
Boucher:
Arms of, *see* **Heraldry**.
William, 1676, and others, monument, (7) 42a.
Bouchier, arms of, *see* **Heraldry**.
Bower, Robert, Mayor, 1584, donor of chair, (13) 47b.
Bowerman:
Arms of, *see* **Heraldry**.
Anne, 1630, monument, (6) 41a.
Anne, 1652, monument, (6) 41a.
Andrew, 1655, floorslab, (6) 41a.
Bowling Green House (505) 160a.
Bowyers, *see* **Occupations**.
Boyton, Thomas and William, owners of property in Cheesemarket, (37) 61a; and in Queen Street, (133) 88a.
Box-Pews, *see* **Seating**.
Brasses, Monumental: liv
16TH-CENTURY (figures): Webbe, (3) 29a,
17TH-CENTURY (inscriptions): Eyre, Bayle, Viner, (3) 29a; Carpenter, (4) 34a; Dove, (5) 38a.
18TH-CENTURY (inscriptions): Ballard, (3) 29a; Godwin, (4) 34a.
Brereton, arms of, *see* **Heraldry**.
Brick, *see* **Building Construction**.
Bridewell, xlvii.
Bridge House, Bemerton, (518) 161b.
    ,,   **Street**, xli, xlviii.
Bridges: xxxvii, Pl. 19.
13TH-CENTURY: Ayleswade, (17) 51b.
14TH-CENTURY: Milford, (19) 52a.
17TH-CENTURY: Crane, (18) 51b.
18TH-CENTURY: Mutton's, (21) 52a.
19TH-CENTURY: Laverstock, (20) 52a; Dairyhouse (21) 52a; Hatches, (21) 52a.
Bridport, Bishop Giles de, founder of De Vaux College, (327–8), xl, lxi.
Brown, *see* **Sculptors and Monumental Masons**.
Brown Street, xliii, 84b, 108a.
Monuments in, (140)–(142) 89b–91a; (222)–(224) 111a; (228)–(230) 112a; (256)–(259) 117b–118b; (264)–(269) 119b–120a.
Brown, Thomas, Almshouses, (31) 58b.
Buckingham, Duke of, supposed execution place, 1483, (344) 134a.
Buckler, John, *see* **Painters and Engravers**.
Bugmore, xxxii, xxxiv. Defences, (16) 50b.
Building Construction (notable): lx–lxiii
ASHLAR:
11TH-CENTURY: (1) 6–9; (2) 16b.
12TH-CENTURY: (2) 17b, 18a.
13TH-CENTURY: (3) 24a; (173) 97a.
15TH-CENTURY: (5) 37a; (15) 50a; (19) 52a; (97) 73a; (185) 104a; (258) 118a.
16TH-CENTURY: (557) 166b; (588) 171b.
17TH-CENTURY: (18) 51b; (97) 73a; (173) 98a; (557) 166b.
BRICK: xlvii–l, lxii, lxiii.
17TH-CENTURY: (3) 60a; (87) 71a; (247) 115a.
18TH-CENTURY: (22) 52b; (33) 58a; (297) 124a; (307) 128b; (354) 138a; (468) 155a.
BRICK WITH STONE DRESSINGS:
17TH-CENTURY: (22) 52b; (27) 56b; (86) 70b; (101) 77a; (234) 113a; (247) 115a; (264) 119b; (304) 127a.
18TH-CENTURY: (27) 56b; (101) 77a; (199) 105b; (230) 112a; (289) 123a; (419) 148a; (427) 150a.
CHALK INFILL: xliv, (132) 80a.
FLINT:
11TH-CENTURY: (1) 6, 7, 9b; (2) 16b.
12TH-CENTURY: (2) 17b, 18a; (9) 43a.
13TH-CENTURY: lxi; (3) 24a, 25b; (4) 32b.

Building Construction—contd
  14TH-CENTURY: (106) 78b.
  16TH-CENTURY: (165) 94a.
  FLINT AND ASHLAR: lxi.
    14TH-CENTURY: lxii; (106) 78b.
    15TH-CENTURY: (6) 39b; (97) 73a; (185) 103b.
    16TH-CENTURY: (549) 165a; (588) 171b.
    17TH-CENTURY: (528) 163a.
  MATHEMATICAL-TILING: xlviii; (85) 70b; (94) 72b; (132) 85b; (137)
    89a; (186), (187) 104b; (190), (192) 105a; (195) 105b; (203) 107a;
    (211) 108a; (320) 130a; (359) 139a; (383) 142b.
  TIMBER FRAMEWORK: xliv, lxi, lxii.
    14TH-CENTURY: (35) 59b; (71) 65a; (82) 68b; (102) 77b; (129) 82b;
      (132) 86a; (140) 90b; (173) 97a; (177) 100b; (219) 109a; (225)
      111a; (302) 125b; (305) 128a; (351) 137a; (458) 153b; (576) 169a.
    15TH-CENTURY: (55) 63b; (56) 64a; (63) 64b; (71) 65b; (107) 79;
      (128) 82a; (174) 99b; (250) 115b; (344) 133b; (399) 145a.
    16TH-CENTURY: (44) 62a; (73) 66a; (92) 72a; (95) 73a; (102) 77b;
      (165) 94a; (310) 129a; (549) 165a; (581) 170a.
    17TH-CENTURY: (155) 93a; (252) 116b; (293) 123b; (413) 147a.
  WATTLE AND DAUB INFILL: xliv; (302) 126a; (443) 152b.
Burford, Thomas, 1404, owner of Blue Boar, (344), xlvi, 133b.
Burnham, John, wax chandler 1480, tenant of house, (215) 108b.
Burrough:
  Arms of, see **Heraldry.**
  Sydenham, 1782, tablet, (5) 38b.
Burry, Henry, 1328, owner of Duynescorner, now Red Lion, (219)
  109a.
Burt, arms of, see **Heraldry.**
Butcher Row, xl, xli.
Butchers, see **Occupations.**
Buterlegh or **Byterlegh**:
  John, c. 1390, owner of property in New Canal, (177) 100b; of the
    Bolehall (140), 89b; of the Red Lion, (219) 109a.
  Alice, 1396, owner of house in Milford Street, (250) 115b.
Butterfield, William, see **Architects, Builders and Surveyors.**
Bystone, Thomas, 1417, owner of property in Milford Street, (249)
  115a.

Calder:
  Arms of, see **Heraldry.**
  Amelia, 1830, tablet, (7) 42a.
Cambrigg, Wm., 1418, owner of property in Milford Street, (151) 92a;
  and St. Ann's Street, (302) 126a.
Cammell (Camel, Camyl):
  John, 1397, owner of No. 8 Queen Street, (128) 82a; of Bolehall, (140)
    90a; of Red Lion, (219) 109a.
  John, mayor 1449, owner of No. 8 Queen Street, (128) 82a.
  Alice, 1400, and Joanna, 1455, owners of Bolehall, (140) 90a.
Campbell, arms of, see **Heraldry.**
Cantelupe, arms of, see **Heraldry.**
Capon, William, see **Painters and Engravers.**
Carpenter, John Sebastian, 1632, brass, (4), lv, 34a.
Carpenters, see **Occupations.**
Carter, Owen, see **Architects, Builders and Surveyors.**
Carved Stonework (notable): Plates 29, 30, 42.
  12TH-CENTURY: Old Sarum, (2) 16b, 19b, 20a.
  13TH-CENTURY: (11) 46a; (93) 72b.
  15TH-CENTURY: (3) chancel capitals, 26a; (4) corbels, 33a, 33b; (5)
    38a; (97) 75a.
  16TH-CENTURY: (4) 33b; (97) 75b.
Carved Woodwork (notable): Plates 10, 46–7, 67, 84.
  14TH-CENTURY: George Inn (173) hammer-beams, 99a; 50 High
    Street (81) corbel, 68b.
  15TH-CENTURY: (3) roof, 27b; (4) roof, 33b; (6) bosses, 40b; (9) bosses,
    43b.
  17TH-CENTURY: (3) Beckham monument, lvii, 30b; (6) pulpit, 41a;
    No. 8 Queen Street, (128) 82b; Joiner's Hall, (293) 123b.
Castle Hill: (561), (562) 167b.
  ,,   **Street**: (354) 132a; (381) 142b; (419)–(446) 148–153.
  ,,   ,,   **Gate** (16) 50b, 51a.
Castlehaven, Lord, 1630, purchaser of property, (97) 73b.
Castleton, Thomas, 1400, owner of Plume of Feathers, (132) 85b.
Cathedral Choristers, tenements owned by, xxvii.
  ,,   **Hotel** (139) 89b.

Catherine Street, xxxvii; (188)–(198) 105; (203)–(217) 107, 108.
  ,,   **Wheel Inn** (151) 91b.
Caundel, John, dwelling of, (225) 111a.
Cave, see **Sculptors and Monumental Masons.**
Ceilings, plaster (notable): Plates 93, 95.
  16TH-CENTURY: (14) 49b; (102) 78a; (549) 165b.
  17TH-CENTURY: (234) 113a; (581) 170b.
  18TH-CENTURY: (419) 148a.
  19TH-CENTURY: (299) 124b.
Cemeteries and Burials:
  SAXON: Old Sarum xxviii; (1) 1b.
  MEDIAEVAL: Old Sarum (1) 4a, 12b; (2) 16a, 19b, 21a.
  See also **Monuments, Funeral.**
Chafin or **Chafyn**:
  Thomas, 1679, inscriptions, (3) lvii, 30a.
  Thomas, 1523, and Scholastica, owners of property, (97), 73a.
Chairs:
  MAYORAL: (13) 47a, b.
  IN CHURCHES, see **Seating.**
Chalk infill, see **Building Construction.**
Chandlers, see **Occupations.**
Chapelyn, Thomas, will 1415, (203) 107b; (270) 120a.
Chaplain, see **Occupations.**
Charlton, W. H., see **Painters and Engravers.**
Chaundeler, Chaundiler:
  John, 1390, purchaser of Raie d'Or, (227) 111b; benefactor of Trinity
    Hospital, (236) 113b; will, 1406–7, (215) 108b.
Cheese Cross, xli.
Cheesecorner, xliii; tenement, (126) 81b; (128) 82b.
Cheesemarket, xl, xli, xlviii; (34)–(38) 59a–61b.
Chester:
  Arms of, see **Heraldry.**
  Henry, 1786, and Hetty, 1812, tablet, (4) 35a.
Chests: lv, Plate 53.
  MEDIAEVAL: (6) 40b.
  16TH-CENTURY: (4) 34b.
  17TH-CENTURY: (6) 40b; (9) 44b.
  18TH-CENTURY: (5) 38a; (6) 40b.
  19TH-CENTURY: (4) 34b; (7) 42a.
Chese (Chuse or Juvws), 14th-century owners of Cheesecorner, (126)
  81b.
Chiffinch, Thomas, churchwarden 1620, (4) 35b.
Chimneypieces, see **Fireplaces and Overmantels.**
Chipper Lane, xxxvii, xlvi.
Chough Hotel (333) 132a.
Christopher, St., glass, (3) 29b.
Chubbe, Henry, 1399, baker in Brown Street, (219) 109a.
Church House (97–8), xlv, xlvii, lxii, lxiii, 73a–76a.
  ,,   **Street**, 159a,b.
Churches and Chapels: l–liii. See also **Meeting Places, Non-
  Conformist.**
  11TH-CENTURY: (2) Old Sarum cathedral, 15; (4) St. Martin's,
    foundations, c. 1100, 31b.
  12TH-CENTURY: (1) Old Sarum, chapels of St. Margaret and St.
    Nicholas, 8b, 9, 10a; (2) Cathedral, enlargements, 15b; (9) St.
    George's, 43a.
  13TH-CENTURY: (3) St. Thomas's, 24a; (4) St. Martin's, 31b; (5) St.
    Edmund's, foundation of, 36a; (6) St. Lawrence's, 39a; (9) St.
    George's, window, 43a,b; (11) St. John's, 45a; (26) St.
    Nicholas's Hospital, 54b.
  14TH-CENTURY: (3) St. Thomas's, 24b; (4) St. Martin's, tower, 31b;
    (6) St. Lawrence's, chancel arch, 39a; (8) St. Andrew's, 42a; (9)
    St. George's, chancel arch and S. chapel, 43a.
  15TH-CENTURY: (3) St. Thomas's; (4) St. Martin's 32a; (5) St.
    Edmund's, 36a; (6) St. Lawrence's, 39a.
  16TH-CENTURY: (3) St. Thomas's, vestry, 25a; (6) St. Lawrence's,
    buttresses, 39a.
  17TH-CENTURY: (5) St. Edmund's, tower, 37a; (6) St. Lawrence's,
    repairs, 40a; (8) St. Andrew's, repairs, 42b.
  18TH-CENTURY: (5) St. Edmund's, chancel 1776, 37a; (6) St.
    Lawrence's W. tower, 39a; (22) Infirmary chapel, 52b; (27)
    Trinity Hospital chapel, 56b, 57a.
  19TH-CENTURY: (3) St. Thomas's, restoration, 25a; (4) St. Martin's,
    restorations, 32b; (5) St. Edmund's, chancel, 1865, 37a; (9) St.
    George's, restorations, 43b; (10) St. Osmund's, 44b.
Churchwardens, see **Occupations.**
City Arms Inn (47) 62b.

City Defences: xxxviii, (16) 50b. *See also* **Ditches** and **Gates**.
Clare, arms of, *see* **Heraldry**.
Clarendon, track to, 12b.
Clarendon, Lord, *see* **Hyde**.
    ,,   **Forest,** timber from, xl.
Clarke, arms of, *see* **Heraldry**.
Classification of House-plans, *see* **Dwellings with classified plans**.
Clement, St., church dedicated to, *see* **Dedications**.
Clerk, John, tanner, 1415, (203) 107b.
Clerk, *see* **Occupations**.
    ,, **-of-Works,** *see* **Occupations**.
Cliff House, Harnham, (580) 170a.
Clifford, arms of, *see* **Heraldry**.
Clock-bells: liv, lv.
    16TH-CENTURY: (3) 29a.
Clock-makers:
    HUGHES, Hugh: (26) 56b.
    PHILLIPS, James: (5) 38a.
    SHUTTLEWORTH, Francis: (3) 29b.
Clock-tower, 1890, (476) 157a.
Clocks: lv.
    18TH-CENTURY: (3) tower, vestry, 29b; (26) 56b; (27) 57b.
    19TH-CENTURY: (5) 38a.
Cloister, Old Sarum, (2) 21b.
Close Ditch, *see* **Ditches**.
Close Wall, xxxvi.
Clothiers, *see* **Occupations**.
Clovelly Hotel (495) 159a.
Club Room, former chapel, (481) 158a.
Coach and Horses Inn (360) 140a.
    ,, **House,** *see* **Barns and Outbuildings**.
Cockerell, S. P., *see* **Architects, Builders and Surveyors**.
Coffin Lids: lvi, lvii.
    12TH-CENTURY: (2) 19b.
    13TH-CENTURY: (4) 35a.
Coffin Stools: (6) 40b.
Coins, of Athelstan and Edgar, xxix.
Coke, Thomas, 1523, owner of Church House, (97) 73a.
Cole, Isabel, 1390, owner of tenement, (153) 92b.
College House (507) 160b.
Collins: William and Benjamin, offices, (187) 105a; house, (300) 125a.
Collyer, William, 1649, tenant, (87) 71a.
Combe, Walter, hosier, 1649, tenant, (63) 64b.
Communion Rails: lv, (6) 40b.
Communion Tables: lv; (3) 29b; (4) 34b; (5) 38a; (9) 44b.
Compton, Thomas, grant of 1514, Old Sarum, (1) 4a.
Conant, John, 1653, floorslab, (3) 30b.
Cook *see* **Occupations**.
Cooksey, T., inscribed stone, (294) 124a.
Cooper:
    Thomas, 1680, acquired part of Minster Street house, (55) 63b.
    Thomas, 1724, builder of house in Blue Boar Row, (338) 132b.
    Robert and others, 1778, tablet, (5) 38b.
Cordwainer Row, xli.
Corn Exchange, *see* **Market House**.
Coroner, *see* **Occupations**.
Cottage Orné, (579) 170a.
Council House, site of, (38) 61b.
County Gaol, former, (24) 54a.
Courtenay, arms of, *see* **Heraldry**.
Courtyard House, *see* **Old Sarum**.
Courtyard houses, xlvi.
Cove, Robert, 15th-century owner of Cheesecorner, (126) 81b.
Coxe, William, 1828, and Eleanor, 1830, tablet, (8) 43a.
Cradock, arms of, *see* **Heraldry**.
    ,,   **House** (304), lxii, 127a.
Craft Companies, *see* **Guilds**.
Cranborn, John, canon, rebuilding by, 1471, (63) 64b.
Crane, le, (102) lxi, 77b.
    ,,   **Bridge** (18) xxxvi, xxxvii, lxii, 51b.
    ,,   **Bridge Road** (503) 160a.
    ,,   **Lodge** (506) lxiv, 160a.
    ,,   **Street,** xlvi, lxi; (93)-(103) 72b-78b.
Crests, *see* **Heraldry**.
Crew, Philip, schoolmaster 1638, (399) 145a.
Crickmay and Son, *see* **Architects, Builders and Surveyors**.

Crise, John, tanner 1460, tenant of property, (297) 124b.
Croft House (415) 147a.
Croome, *see* **Sculptors and Monumental Masons**.
Cross, mediaeval, (4) 34b.
Cross, St., *see* **Dedications of Churches and Chapels**.
Cross Keys Chequer, (126)-(139) 81b-89b.
    ,,   ,, **Inn** (131) 84b.
Crown Inn (93) 72b.
    ,, **and Anchor Inn** (320) 129b.
Crucifixion, carving, (3) 29b.
Crystal Fountain Inn (164) 94a.
Culver Street, xxxvii.
    ,,   **Street Almshouses** (29) 58a.
Cups, *see* **Plate, Church**.
Curtain Wall, Old Sarum, (1) 7a.
Cutlers, *see* **Occupations**.

Dahl, *see* **Painters and Engravers**.
Dairyhouse Bridge (21) 52a; cottage adjacent, (568) 168b.
Danton, John, *see* **Bellfounders**.
Dates inscribed on buildings: (73) 1664, 66a; (289) beam, 1610, 123a; (294) wall, 1751, 124a; (302) chimneypiece, 1630?, 126b; (309) boundary wall, 1814, 129a; (404) 1844, 146a; (429) 1755, 151a; (466) 1835, 154b; (523) 1848, 162a; (557) 1673, 166b; (580) 1825 170a.
    See also **Rainwater Heads**.
Davies, arms of, *see* **Heraldry**.
Dayes, Edward, *see* **Painters and Engravers**.
De Vaux College (327-8), xl, lxi, lxii, 130b, 131a; cartulary of, xxv.
    ,,   **House** (327) 130b.
    ,,   **Place** (330) 131b.
Dean's Farm House (559) 167b.
Dean and Chapter, property belonging to: xxv, xxvii; (37) 61a; (63) 64b; (77) 68a; (86-92) 70-72; (129) 82b; (131) 84b; (153) 92b; (174) 99b; (203) 107b; (225) 111a; (252) 116b; (259) 118b; (326), 130b.
Deanery, Old Sarum, (2) 22b.
Dedications of Churches, Chapels and Altars:
    ALL SAINTS: (2) 18b, 22b.
    HOLY CROSS: (2) 22b.
    HOLY TRINITY: (2) 22b.
    ST. ANDREW: (8) 42a.
    ST. CLEMENT: (7) 41b.
    ST. CROSS: (1) 3b, 12a.
    ST. EDMUND: (5) 36a.
    ST. GEORGE: (9) 43a.
    ST. JOHN: (1) 4a; (5) 36b; (11) 45a.
    ST. LAWRENCE: (6) 39a.
    ST. MARGARET: (1) 8b, 9a.
    ST. MARTIN: (2) 19b; (4) 31b.
    ST. MARY: (1) 3a; (2) 16a.
    ST. MARY MAGDALEN: (1) 3b.
    ST. NICHOLAS: (1) 3b; (2) 18b, 22b.
    ST. OSMUND: (10) 44b.
    ST. STEPHEN: (2) 22b.
    ST. THOMAS: (3) 24a.
Defences, (16), xxxviii, 50b. *See also* **Ditches,** and **Gates**.
Denham, Alice, 1686, donor of almsdish, (4), lix, 35b; house of, (302) 126a.
Derby Court (250) 115b.
Development of the mediaeval city, xl.
Deverell's Inn, site of, (25) 54b.
Devizes Road (530)-(536) 164.
Digh House, tenement, xli.
Ditches, Close Ditch, xxxiv; Town Ditch, xxxiv, xli, xliii. *See also* **Water Channels** and **Sluices**.
Documentary Sources, xxv, xxvii.
Dolphin, room in Vine Inn, (37) 61a.
    ,,   **Inn** (227) 121b.
    ,,   **Street,** (276) 121b.
Dominicans, arrival in Salisbury, xl.
Dondyng, William, merchant 1415, owner of tenement, (208) 108a.
Doorways (notable):
    12TH-CENTURY: (9) 44a.
    13TH-CENTURY: (173) 97a.
    14TH-CENTURY: (102) 78a.
    15TH-CENTURY: (4) 33a; (185) 104a; (441) 152b; (588) 172a.

Doorways—*contd*
16TH-CENTURY: (205) 107b; (298) 124b; (438), (439) 152a; (549) 165a.
17TH-CENTURY: (8) 43a; (350) 135a; (398) 145a; (470) 155b; (557) 166b; (571) 168b.
18TH AND 19TH-CENTURY: (381) 142b; (397) 145a; (442) 152b; (468) 155a. Plates 98–9.
Dove, Henry, 1616, mayor, brass, (5) 38a.
Dowse, Sir Gabriel, owner of the Barracks, (258) 118a.
Drake Hall Street (Dragall Street; Exeter Street), xxxvii.
Drapers, *see* **Occupations.**
Drapers' Company, arms of, *see* **Heraldry.**
Dryden, Sir Henry, *see* **Painters and Engravers.**
Duchess of Albany Inn (50) 62b.
Duke: John, 1670, Avis, 1687, and Elizabeth, 1692, floorslabs (6) 41a.
Duynes, Agnes, 1327, owner of property, (219) xlvi, 109a.
Duynescorner (219) 109a.
Dwellings with classified plans: lxiv.
CLASS C: (290) 123a.
CLASS I: (551) 165b.
CLASS J: (555) 166a; (579) 170a.
CLASS S: (499) 159b; (518), (519) 161b; (554) 116a; (562) 167b; (582) 170b.
CLASS T: (287) 122b; (288) 123a; (409) 146b; (415) 147b; (497) 159a; (499) 155b; (501), (506) 160a; (517) 161a; (544) 164a; (555) 166a; (575) 169a; (577) 169b.
CLASS U: (268) variant, 119b; (289) 123a; (324) variant, 130a; (358) 139a; (396) 145a; (446) 153a; (461) 154a; (477) 157a; (497) 159a; (514) 161a; (520) 161b; (523) 162a; (531) 164a; (578) 170a.
Dyers, *see* **Occupations.**

Earle:
Arms of, *see* **Heraldry.**
Bridget, wife of Bishop Earle, 1696, floorslab, (6) 41a.
Earlsman, Richard, 1831, tablets, (3) 30b; (4) 34b; (12) 46b. *See also* **Sculptors and Monumental Masons.**
Earthworks, *see* **Iron Age, Old Sarum, City Defences.**
East Gate, Old Sarum, (1) 6b, 7a.
Easter Sepulchre, Old Sarum, (2) 19b.
Ecclesiastical Buildings, xxxviii, l. *See also* **Churches and Chapels.**
Edgar, coins of, xxix.
Edgar, Mary, 1770, tablet, (4) 35a.
Edmonds, Edmond, linendraper, 1649, purchaser of land, (259) 118b.
Edmund, St., *see* **Dedications.**
Edmunds, St., Church Street, xxxiv; (357) (358) 139a; (409)–(412) 146b–147a.
Edmund, St., College of, (14, xxxviii, xlii, lxii, 48a. Land owned by, (300) 125b.
  „ „ Parish of, xxxviii; *see also* **Parishes and Wards.**
Edward the Confessor, arms of, i *see* **Heraldry.**
Effigies, Monumental: lvi.
12TH-CENTURY: (2) lvi, 19b.
Egerton:
Arms of, *see* **Heraldry.**
Catherine, 1743, floorslab, (4) 35a.
Elizabeth, St., school of, (324) 130a.
Elliot, Robert, mayor, inscription on clock-bell, (3) 29a.
Elm Cottage (515) 161a.
  „ **Tree Cottage** (519) 161b.
Emily, Edward, 1795, benefactor of St. Nicholas's Hospital, (26) 56b.
Endless Street, xxxiv, xxxvi, xlvii; (343) 133b; (346) (347), 135a; (384)–(393) 143b–144; (460)–(469), 154, 155.
Enefeld, Edmund, 1400, owner of tenement, (302), xlii, xlvii.
England, arms of, *see* **Heraldry.**
Engravers, *see* **Painters and Engravers.**
Estcourt:
Arms of, *see* **Heraldry.**
Giles, 1575, owner of College, (14) 48a.
Eva Cottages, Milford, (567) 168a.
Evelyn House (507) 160b.
Excavations at Old Sarum, (1) 4a.
Exeter Street, xxxvi, xxxvii; (311)–(332) 129–131.
Eyr, Thomas and Alice, 1384, owners of land, (236) 113b.
Eyre:
Arms of, *see* **Heraldry.**
Family, xlvii; owners of tenements, (35–6) 59a, 60a; (77) 68a.
Christopher, [1624], monument, (3) 30a.
Elizabeth, 1612, brass, (3) 29a.

Elizabeth (Chester), 1705, Jane, 1695, floorslabs, (3) 30b.
Robert, 1638, brass, (3) 29a.
Sir Robert, vault, 1724, (3) 30a.
Sir Samuel, 1633–98, builder of house, (36), 60a; initials on rainwater head, 1689, (132) 87b.
Thomas, 1628, and Elizabeth (Rogers), 1612, monument, (3) 30a.

'Faucon, le', 1455, house, (97) 73a.
Fawconer, Samuel, hosier, 1741, buyer of property in Minster Street, (55) 63b.
Fayrbowe, John, carpenter, 1444, builder of property, (344) 133b.
Fayrecroys, xli.
Fielding, Henry, workroom of, (570) 168b.
Figes, Sarum, *see* **Architects, Builders and Surveyors.**
Finch's Court, range of cottages, (145), xlix, 91.
Fireplaces and Chimneypieces (notable): xliv, Pls. 90–92, 94.
12TH AND 13TH-CENTURY: (1) 9b, 10a, Pl. 28.
15TH-CENTURY: (55) 64a; (71) 66a; (97) 75a, 75b; (98) 76a; (185) 104a; (250) 116a; (302) 126b; (475) 157a.
16TH-CENTURY: (98) 76a; (478) 157b.
17TH-CENTURY: (101) 77a; (128) 82b; (174) 100a; (252) 117a.
18TH AND 19TH-CENTURY: (111) 80a; (133) 88b; (199) 106a, b; (391) 144b; (427) 150b; (506) 160b; (556) 166b.
Fish Row, xl, xli; (71)–(73) 65b, 66a.
Fisher, F. R., *see* **Architects, Builders and Surveyors.**
Fisherton, development of, l. Plan, 156.
Fisherton Church (7) 41b.
  „ **Bridge**, xxxvi, xxxvii, xli, xlviii.
  „ **Cottage** (501) 160a.
  „ **House** (512) 161a.
  „ **Rectory** (497) 159a.
  „ **Street** (476)–(494) 157–159.
  „ **Ward**, *see* **Parishes and Wards.**
Fishmonger, *see* **Occupations.**
Fitzalan, arms of, *see* **Heraldry.**
Fitzgerald, arms of, *see* **Heraldry.**
Fitzhugh, arms of, *see* **Heraldry.**
Five Bells Inn (369) 141a.
Flagons, *see* **Plate, Church.**
Fleming, Henry, 1354, (129) 82b; 1365, (177) 100b.
Flint, *see* **Building Construction.**
Floorslabs, *see* **Monuments, Funeral.**
Florent, St., of Saumur, confirmation of land, Old Sarum, (1) 2a.
Florentyn, William and Agatha, 1297, (92) 72a.
Florentyne's Corner, xxxvii, 72b.
Flower (Florey), Richard, *see* **Bellfounders.**
Fonthill Abbey, columns said to come from, (446) 153a.
Fonts: lv, Pl. 41:
12TH-CENTURY: (6) 40b.
OF *c.* 1200: (9) 44b.
13TH-CENTURY: (3) bowl, 29b; (4) 34b; (5) 38b; (7) 42a.
16TH-CENTURY: (3) shaft, 29b.
17TH-CENTURY: (6) shaft and base, 40b.
19TH-CENTURY: (3) base, 29b.
Ford Lane, buildings aligned on, (1), 12b.
Foster, Richard, 1419, buyer of tenement, (220) 109b.
Foxe's Book of Martyrs, (7) 42a.
France, arms of, *see* **Heraldry.**
Francis, St., glass (3) 29b.
Franciscans, arrival in Salisbury, xl.
Freeman, Richard, 1504, owner of land in Vanners Chequer, 146b.
Friars' Orchard (304) 128a.
Friary, the, xxxvi, xliii, xlvii; (298) 124b; (302) 125b; (304) 127b.
Frowd's Almshouses (33), xlix, 58b.
Fuller, John, 1777, hatchment (4) 34b.
Fuystour, William and Edith, 1385, lessees of Pynnok's Inn (77) 67b.
Fyschamels, *see* **Fish Row**, xl.

Gaffi, T., *see* **Sculptors and Monumental Masons.**
Gage, John and Richard, owners of house in Cheesemarket, (35) 59b.
Gandavo, Bishop, *see* **Simon of Ghent.**
Gantlet, arms of, *see* **Heraldry.**
Gaol, remains of, (476) 157a; *see also* **County Gaol**, and King's Gaol, (1) 11b.
Garlick, William, 1796, table tomb, (4) 35a.
Gates (New Sarum):
CASTLE STREET GATE (16), xxxviii, xlviii, 51a.

Gates (New Sarum)—*contd*
WYNMAN GATE (16), xxxviii, 51a.
General Infirmary (22), xlix, lxiii, 52b.
George, St., arms of, *see* **Heraldry**; church dedicated to, *see* **Dedications**; guild of, xxvi.
George Inn (173), xxvii, xlii, xliv, lxi, 97a.
  ,, **and Dragon Inn** (438) 152a.
Gigant Street, xxxiv, xxxvii, 114a.
Gigorstrete, xxxvii, 92b.
'Gillingham', *see* **Silversmiths**.
Ginaway, William, 1670, inscription on flagon, (4) 35b.
Glass (in windows): lv.
  MEDIAEVAL: (27) Trinity Hospital, 57b; (97) Church House, 75b; (185) Hall of John Hall, 103b.
  15TH-CENTURY: (3) St. Thomas's, 29b.
  17TH-CENTURY: (Swiss), (5) St. Edmund's, 38b; (27), 57b.
Glastyngburiecorner, tenement, (234), xliii, 113a.
Glastyngbury, Edward, 1366, owner of tenement, (234) 113a.
Goat Inn (232) 112b.
Goddard, arms of, *see* **Heraldry**.
Goddard, Thomas, 1791, lessee of house, (130) 84b.
Godfry, John, 1495, lessee of tenement, (172) 97a.
Godmanstone, family, owners of tenement, (220) *c.* 1400, 109b.
Godwin, 12th-century tomb-slab, (2) 97a.
Godwin, M., 1785, brass, (4) 34a.
Goldsmiths, *see* **Occupations**.
Goldwyer:
  Arms of, *see* **Heraldry**.
  Family, 1748–1812, tablet and floorslab, (4) 35a.
Goodall, E. A., *see* **Painters and Engravers**.
Gooding, Hatchment, (4) 34b.
Goodyer, Edward, 1432, and Dionisia, owner of tenement, (130) 84a.
Gore's Chequer, 144–145.
Gorges, arms of, *see* **Heraldry**.
Gough:
  Arms of, *see* **Heraldry**.
  John, 1709/10, wall monument, (3), lviii, 30a.
Government House, Harnham, (580) 170a.
Gowayn of Norrington:
  John, 1410, owner of La Hotecorner, (81) 68b.
  Lawrence, 1399, owner of Red Lion, (219) 109a.
Grafton, Richard, inscription on bell, (5) 38a.
Granary, *see* **Barns and Outbuildings**.
Grandon, John, 1409, vendor of plot in Cross Keys Chequer, (133) 89a.
Great Tower, *see* **Old Sarum**.
  ,, **Western Railway**, l.
Green:
  Maurice, 1621, mayoral chair, (13) 47b.
  Samuel, organ builder, (3) 30b.
Greencroft, 142a.
  ,, **Street**, xxxvii.
Greenhill:
  Arms of, *see* **Heraldry**.
  John, 1674, floorslab, (4) 35a.
Grevile:
  Arms of, *see* **Heraldry**.
  Elizabeth, 1745, floorslab, (4) 35a.
Greyfriars, *see* **Friary**.
Griffin Chequer, 140, 141.
Grocers, *see* **Occupations**.
Grove Place (153), xliii, 92b.
Gryme, John, 1474, lessee of George Inn, (173) 97b.
Guest, Douglas, *see* **Painters and Engravers**.
Guilder Lane, (158), xlvi, 93b.
Guildhall, *see* **Public Buildings**.
Guildhall Chequer, xl, xlix.
Guild halls: xlvii
  JOINERS': (293) 123b.
  SHOEMAKERS': (399) 145a.
  TAILORS': (165) 94a.
Guilds, *see* **George, St., Joiners, Shoemakers, Tailors, Tanners, Weavers**.

Hales:
  Arms of, *see* **Heraldry**.
  Daniel and Edward, 1645, tablet, (4) 34b.
  Tho., churchwarden, inscription on bell, (3) 29a.

Hall:
  Arms of, *see* **Heraldry**.
  John, d. 1479, also William and Christian, d. 1504, occupiers of tenement, (185) 103b.
  John, hall of (185), xlv, 103b.
Hall, H., *see* **Architects, Builders and Surveyors**.
Hall, Peter, proposals for Poultry Cross, (15) 50a; *see also* **Painters and Engravers**.
'Hall The' (199), xlix, lxiii, 105b.
Halstede:
  Walter, 1417, buyer of house, (249) 115a.
  William, 1416, will of, xli, note.
Halswell, arms of, *see* **Heraldry**.
Hamburg, Merchant Adventurers, arms of, *see* **Heraldry**.
Hampton, John, 1407, xlii.
  ,, Walter, 1314, xli.
Hamptonscorner, xli.
Hancock:
  Arms of, *see* **Heraldry**.
  Thomas, 1725, slab, (4) 35a.
Harcourt Cottage (502) 160a.
  ,, **House** (501) 160a.
Harding Family, 1398–1459, owners of property, xxvii, in Cross Keys chequer, (129) 82b, in Black Horse chequer, (153) 92b, in High Street, (174) 99b.
Hardman, glass designer, St. Osmund's, (10) 45a.
Harnhalle, William, 1420, owner of property in Queen Street, (132) 85b.
Harnham, 169–172.
  ,, **Bridge**, *see* **Ayleswade Bridge**.
  ,, **Hill**, Saxon cemetery, (1), xxviii, 1b.
  ,, **House** (578) 170a.
  ,, **Lodge** (579) 170a.
  ,, **Mill** (588), lxi, 171b.
  ,, **Road**, 169.
Harrington, Thomas, 1828, tablet (3) 30b.
Harris, Piers, *c.* 1559, owner of Church House, (97) 73a.
Harvey, Master, 1228, li.
Hatches Bridge (21) 52a.
Hatchments: lvi.
  18TH-CENTURY: (3) 29b; (4) 34b.
  19TH-CENTURY: (3) 29b; (4) 34b.
Haunch of Venison Inn (56) 64a.
Hawes:
  Arms of, *see* **Heraldry**.
  Herbert, 1837, tablet, (5) 38b.
  John, 1787, and others, tablet, (8) 43a.
  Margaret, 1820, Herbert, 1837, tablet, (8) 43a.
Hawker, Thomas, 1636, floorslab, (3) 30b.
Hawkins, arms of, *see* **Heraldry**.
Hawley, Lt. Col. William, excavations at Old Sarum, (1) 4a; (2) 18b, 23b.
Hayter:
  Arms of, *see* **Heraldry**.
  Mrs. Sarah, endowed almshouses, (30) 58b.
Headstones, *see* **Monuments, Funeral**.
Heely, George, 1660, churchwarden, inscription on plate, (7) 42a.
Hele:
  Arms of, *see* **Heraldry**.
  Margaret, 1672, floorslab, (3) 30b.
Helme, The, (77) 68a.
Heraldry: *See also* ARMORIAL, 182.
  ROYAL ARMS: lxi, Pls. 20, 56.
    EDWARD THE CONFESSOR: (3) 28a.
    ENGLAND: (3) 28a; (98) 76b; (185) 104a, b.
    FRANCE MODERN: (3) 26b, 28a; (98) 76a; (185) 104a, b.
    ELIZABETH I: (3) 31a; (4) 35b.
    JAMES I: (4) 35b.
    1603–89: (27) 57b.
    ANNE: (6) 41a; (27) 57b; after 1707, (13) 47a.
    1714–1801: (5) 38b.
    GEORGE III: (7) 42a.
  CRESTS:
    EYRE: (3) 30a.
    GOLDWYER: (4) 35a.
    HANCOCK: (4) 35a.
    HINXMAN: (4) 35a.

Heraldry—*contd*
  WASTFIELD or WASTFELDE: (4) 35a.
  SHIELDS-OF-ARMS:
    ABAROUGH: (3) 29a.
    AUDLEY: (3) 26b, 28a.
    BAKER: (4) 35a.
    BARNES: (252) 117a.
    BATT: (22) 52b.
    BAYLYE or BAYLE: (3) 29a.
    BEAUCHAMP: (3) 28a, b; (185) 104b.
    BLACKALL: (3) 29b.
    BLAKE: (4) 35a.
    BOUCHER: (7) 42a.
    BOURCHIER: (3) 26b, 28a.
    BOWERMAN or BOWREMAN: (6) 41a.
    BRERETON: (3) 28a.
    BURROUGH: (3) 29b.
    BURT: (3), 29b.
    CALDER: (7) 42a.
    CAMPBELL: (185) 104b.
    CANTELUPE: (557) 166b.
    CHESTER: (3) 30b; (4) 35a.
    CLARE: (185) 104b.
    CLARKE: (22) 52b.
    CLIFFORD: (3) 28b (bis).
    COURTENAY: (3) 27b.
    CRADOCK: (557) 166b.
    DAVIES: (6) 41a.
    DRAPERS' COMPANY: (302) 126b.
    EARLE: (6) 41a.
    EGERTON: (3) 29b; (4) 35a.
    ESTCOURT: (14) 48a.
    EYRE: (3) 30a, b.
    FITZALAN: (3) 28a.
    FITZGERALD: (3) 28a, b.
    FITZHUGH: (185) 104b.
    GANTLET: (4) 34b.
    GEORGE, SAINT: (3) 28a.
    GODDARD: (4) 35a; (8), 43a.
    GOLDWYER: (4) 35a.
    GORGES: (3) 28a.
    GOUGH: (3) 30a.
    GREENHILL: (4) 35a.
    GREVILE: (4) 35a.
    HALES: (4) 34b.
    HALL: (185) 103b, 104a, b.
    HALSWELL: (6) 41a.
    HAMBURG, MERCHANT ADVENTURES: (3), 29a; (302), 126b.
    HANCOCK: (4) 35a.
    HAWES: (3) 29b; (8) 43a.
    HAWKINS: (3) 29b; (8) 43a.
    HAYTER: (3) 29b.
    HELE: (252) 117a.
    HERBERT: (557) 166b.
    HILL: (5) 38b.
    HINXMAN: (4) 35a.
    HORTON: (557) 166b.
    HUNGERFORD: (3) 26b, 27b, 28b; (185) 103b, 104b.
    HYDE: (4) 35b.
    KEENE: (7) 42a.
    KNIGHT: (3) 30b.
    LEE: (4) 35a.
    LONG: (3) 29b, 30b; (5) 38b.
    LUCY: (3) 30a, b.
    LUDLOW: (3) 26b, 28b; (4) 34b.
    MATRAVERS: (3) 28a.
    MAYNE (OF TEFFONT): (252) 117a.
    MICHELL: (7) 42a.
    MINIFIE: (3) 30b.
    MOMPESSON: (252) 117a.
    MONTACUTE: (3) 28a; (185) 104b.
    MONTHERMER: (3) 28a; (185) 104b.
    MOULTON: (7) 42a.
    MUSGRAVE: (3) 30a.
    NEVILLE: (3) 28a; (185) 104b.
    NISBET: (6) 41a.
    NORRIS: (8) 43a.

    NOWES: (7) 41b.
    PAGE: (3) 30b.
    PAYNE: (4) 35a.
    PHIPPS: (4) 35a.
    PITT: (6) 41a.
    POWELL: (3) 29b.
    PRIAULX: (3) 29b.
    PRINCE: (4) 35a.
    RAY: (3) 30a.
    ROLFE: (4) 35a.
    SALISBURY CITY: (5) 38a; (13) 47a; (15) 50a.
    SALISBURY, SEE: (3) 28a.
    SALTERS' COMPANY: (302) 126b.
    SLATER: (4) 35a.
    SMITHIES': (3) 30a.
    SPENCER: (185) 104b.
    SPOONER: (3) 29b.
    STONING: (3) 30b.
    STOURTON: (3) 26b, 28a, b.
    SWAYNE: (3) 27a; (4) 34b; (570) 168b.
    TALBOT: (3) 28b.
    TERRY: (4) 35a.
    TOWNSEND: (6) 41a.
    VINER: (3) 29a.
    WALMSLEY: (133) 88b.
    WARWICK: (185) 104b.
    WASTFIELD or WASTFELDE: (4) 35a.
    WEBBE: (3) 29a.
    WILLES: (3) 30a.
    WILLOUGHBY: (3) 26b.
    WINCHESTER, SEE: (185), 104b.
    WINDOVER: (4) 35a; (302) 126b.
    WROUGHTON: (3) 30a.
    WYLFORD: (3) 29a.
    WYNDHAM: (14) 49a.

Herbert:
  Arms of, *see* **Heraldry.**
  George, 1630, restored St. Andrew's, (8) liii, 42b; builder of rectory, (528) lxii, 163a.
Herlewin's Tower, *see* **Old Sarum.**
Herman, Bishop, 1075, Old Sarum, (1) and (2) xxxi, 15a.
Hersent, Sara, 1741, tablet, (3) 30a.
Hewett, Henry, 1649, occupant of house, (252) 116b.
High Street, xlvi, xlviii, xlix, 66–72, 80b, 95–100, Pls. 102, 104.
Hilary, John, churchwarden, inscription on tower, (5) 38b.
Hill:
  Arms of, *see* **Heraldry.**
  Marshall, 1707, wall monument, (5) lviii, 38b.
Hinxman:
  Arms of, *see* **Heraldry.**
  Edward, 1807, and Henry, 1829, tablets, (4) 35a.
Hoare, Sir Richard Colt, xlix.
Holmes, Robert, 1611, owner of property in Minster Street, (55) 63b.
Holy Cross, *see* **Dedications.**
  ,,   **Lamb** (92) 72a.
Homyngton, John de, 14th-century owner of property in High Street, (173) 97b.
Hooper, Thomas, 1649, lessee, Blue Boar chequer, (341) 133a.
Hope, Sir William St. John, excavations at Old Sarum, (1) and (2), 4a, 23a, b.
Hopper, Thomas, *see* **Architects, Builders and Surveyors.**
Horseshoe Inn (86) 70b.
Horte, Christopher, 1620, churchwarden of St. Martin's, (4) 35b.
Horton, arms of, *see* **Heraldry.**
Hosiers, *see* **Occupations.**
Hospitals, *see* **Almshouses and Hospitals.**
Hourglasses: lvi. Iron, 1652, (6) 40b; Brass, 1721, (4) 34b.
Houses etc. (notable): lx–lxiii.
  OF THE 12TH CENTURY: (1) 8a; (2) 21b.
  OF THE 13TH CENTURY: (1) 10b; (95) 73a; (173) 97a; (328) 131a.
  OF THE 14TH CENTURY: (35) 59; (71) 65a; (82) 68b; (102) 77b; (106) 78b; (129) 82b; (131) 84b; (132) 85; (140) 89b; (173) 97a; (177) 100b; (203) 107b; (219) 109; (225) 111a; (302) 125b; (305) 128a; (341) 133a; (351) 135b; (458) 153b; (576) 169a.
  OF THE 15TH CENTURY: (37) 61a; (40) 61b; (55) 63b; (57), 64a; (63) 64b; (71) 65b; (72) 66a; (83) 69b; (84) 70a; (97) 73a; (102) 77b; (107) 78b; (128) 82a; (131) 84b; (132) 87a; (151) 91b; (153) 92b;

Houses etc—*contd*
(158) 93b; (174) 99b; (185) 103b; (250) 115b; (253) 117b; (258)
118a; (291) 123b; (327) 130b; (344) 133b; (362) 140a; (376)
141b; (399) 145a; (441) (442) 152b; (470) 155b; (584) 170b; (588)
171b.
OF THE 16TH CENTURY: (14) 48a; (44) 62a; (73) 66a; (92) 72a; (102)
77b; (165) 94a; (260) 118b; (269) 120a; (290) 123a; (300) 124b;
(302) 125b; (310) 129a; (315) (316) 129b; (350) 135a; (383) 142b;
(438) 152a; (478) 157b; (492) 158b; (497) 159a; (549) 165a; (581)
170a.
OF THE 17TH CENTURY: (36) 60a; (42) 62a; (86) 70b; (87) 71a; (101)
77a; (234) 113a; (247) 115a; (252) 116b; (264) 119b; (273) 121a;
(293) 123b; (302) 125b; (304) 127a; (307) 128b; (359) 139a; (399)
145a; (413) 147a; (497) 159a; (521) 161b; (528) 163a; (556) 166a;
(557) 166b.
OF THE 18TH CENTURY:
1ST THIRD: (27) 56b; (98) 76a; (99) 76b; (266) 119b; (354) 138a;
(368) 140b; (427) 149a; (463) (464) 154b.
2ND THIRD: (14) 48b; (33) 58b; (110) 80a; (133) 88b; (199) 105b;
(289) 123a; (307) 128b; (355) 138a; (391) 144a; (419) 148a; (429)
151a; (467) 154b; (477) 157a.
3RD THIRD: (13) 46a; (14) 49a; (22) 52b; (85) 70b; (139) 89b; (287)
122b; (297) 124a; (468–9) 155.
OF THE 19TH CENTURY: (299) 124b; (325) 130b; (330) 131b; (381)
142b; (393) 144b; (434) 151b; (446) 153a; (462) 154b; (510)
160b; (511) 161a; (566) 168a.
Hughes, Hugh, *see* Clockmakers.
Hull, William, 1397, occupier of tenement, (234) 113a.
Hungerford:
Arms of, *see* Heraldry.
Family, 1356, owner of houses, (82) 68b.
Sir Thomas, and Walter, 1483, (185) 103b.
Hunter, H., *see* Sculptors and Monumental Masons.
Hussey, William, builder of The Hall, (199) lxiii, 105b.
Hyde:
Arms of, *see* Heraldry.
Edward, Earl of Clarendon, almsdish, (4) lix.
Hyndon, Thomas, 1368, occupier of tenement, (129) 82b.
Hupewell, Roger, 1306, owner of tenements, (129–30) 82a.

Images: lvi.
LATE 14TH OR EARLY 15TH-CENTURY: Crucifixion, (3) 29b.
15TH-CENTURY: Virgin and Child, (3) 29b; Annunciation, (4) 35a.
Indents: liv.
FOR FIGURES: (3) 29a; (4) 34a; (5) 38a.
FOR INSCRIPTION PLATES: (3) 29a, b; (4) 34a.
FOR SHIELDS: (3) 29a.
Ingland, Thomas, 1709, headstone, (9) 44b.
Ingles, John, *see* Silversmiths.
Innkeepers, *see* Occupations.
Inns and Taverns: xli, xlvi, xlviii; Albion (301) 125b; Anchor (235)
113b; Anchor and Hope (374) 141a; Angel (77) 68a; Antelope
(208) 108a; Barley Mow (372) 141a; Bell and Crown (203), 107b;
Black Horse (142), 91a; Blue Boar (344) 133b; Cathedral Hotel
(139) 89b; Catherine Wheel (151) 91b; Chough (333) 132a; City
Arms (47) 62b; Coach and Horses (360) 140a; Cross Keys (131)
84b; Crown (93) 72b; Crown and Anchor (320) 129b; Crystal
Fountain (164) 94a; Dolphin (277) 121b; Duchess of Albany (50)
62b; Five Bells (369) 141a; George (173) 97a; George and
Dragon (438) 152a; Goat (232) 68a; Haunch of Venison (56) 64a;
Helme (77) 68a; Horseshoe (86) 70b; Holy Lamb (92) 72a; King's
Arms (494) 159a; King's Arms Hotel (252) 116b; La Rose or La
Hôtecorner (81) 68b; London (67) 65a; Maidenhead (25) 54a;
(475) 157a; Milford Arms (153) 92b; New (107) 78b; Oddfellows
Arms (220) 109b; Old Bell (310) 129a; Old Castle (562) 167b;
Old George (350) 135a; Pheasant (399) 145a; Plume of Feathers
(132) 85a; Pynnok's (77) 67a; Queen's Arms (225) 111a; Raie
d'Or (227) 111b; Red Lion (219) 109a; Rose and Crown (576)
169a; Royal George (470) 155b; Shoulder of Mutton (64) 65a;
Spread Eagle (176) 100a; Star (227) 111b; Sun and Lamb (92)
72a; Sun (86) 71a; Three Crowns (585) 171a; Three Cups (359)
139a; Three Lions, xlviii; Three Swans (345) 134a; Toll Gate
(279) 121b; Vine (37) 61a; West End (516) 161a; Wheatsheaf (71)
65b; White Bear (219) 109a; White Hart (254) 117b; White
Horse (86) 70b; Winchester Gate (563) 168a.
Inscriptions and Scratchings (notable): lvi.
15TH-CENTURY: (3) 27a; (4) 34b.

16TH-CENTURY: 1578 (102) 78a.
17TH-CENTURY: 1653 (5) 38b; 1673 (557) 166b.
18TH-CENTURY: 1794 (4) 34b; 1711 (6) 40a.
Invicta Terrace (248) 115a.
Iron Age:
HILL-FORT: (1) xxviii, 1a, 4b, 5a, b.
STORAGE PIT: (1), 11a.
Ironmonger Row, xli.
Ironmongers, *see* Occupations.
Isaac, William, 1396, purchaser of tenement, (250) 115b.
Isaac, sacrifice of, carved in oak, (3), lvii, 30b; (128), 82b.
Ivie, John, mayor 1627, xlvii; (259), 118b, n.
Ivy Place, xlix, 151b.
  ,,   Street, xlvi; (203) 107b; (226) 111a.

Jeffrey, H., 1797, acquired tenement, (38) 61b.
Jocelyn, Bishop, effigy of, (2), lvi, 20a.
John, St., *see* Dedications.
  ,,   ,,   with crucifixion, relief, (3) 29b.
Joiners, *see* Occupations.
  ,,   Hall (293), xlvii, lxii, 123b.
Jole, Robert, 1611, lessee of property, (55) 63b.
Joyce, John, 1649, occupier of houses, (174) 99b.
  ,,   William, 1637, purchaser of house, (37) 61a.
Judgement, Last, painting, (3) 30b.
Jukes, Frederick, *see* Painters and Engravers.
Juwys, Ralph, xlii. Family, (126) 81b.
Juwyscorner, *see* Cheesecorner.

Keene:
Arms of, *see* Heraldry.
Mary, 1841, tomb-slab, (7) 42a.
Kellow, James, stonemason, (22) 52b.
Kent:
Arms of, *see* Heraldry.
Richard, 1692, and Margaret, 1711, monument (7) 42a.
Kenton, Col. Francis, 1716, owner of tenement, (354) 138a.
King, of Bath, *see* Sculptors and Monumental Masons.
King's Arms Hotel (252) lxii, 116b.
  ,,   ,,   Inn (494) 159a.
Kingdon and Shearm, surveyors, xxvi.
Kirkman, Maria, 1791, Ann, 1799, and Maria, 1805, tablets, (9) 44a.
Kitchen Tower, *see* Old Sarum.
Knight:
Arms of, *see* Heraldry.
Anne (Minifie), 1709, floorslab, (3) 30b.

La Rose or La Hotecorner, inn, (81) 68b.
Lambert, Edmund, benefactors table, (7) 42a.
Lanfranc, Archbishop, Old Sarum, (2) 15a.
Langley, John, 1649, owner of tenement, (82) 68b.
Laverstock, track to, (1) 12b.
  ,,   Bridge (20) 52a.
Lavington Cottage (503) 160a.
Lawrence, St., *see* Dedications.
Le Breton, Francis, 1798, floorslab, (3) 30b.
Lectern, 15th-century, (4) lvi, 34b.
Lee:
Arms of, *see* Heraldry.
Laetitia, 1800, tablet, (4) 35a.
Leg, The, tenement, (172) xlii, 97a.
Leland, John, Old Sarum, (1) 4a.
Lightfoot, William, mayor 1451, (97) 73a; *see also* Merchant Marks.
Little Durnford, xxix.
  ,,   Manor, Milford, (571) 168b.
Llangarren (511) 161a.
Loder House (391) 144a.
London and South Western Railway, l; (25) 54b.
'London Inn' (67) 65a.
Long:
Arms of, *see* Heraldry.
Family, 1723–1824, tablet, (3) 30b; 1724–87, floorslabs, (5) 38b.
Henry, 1727, floorslab, (3) 30b.
Walter, 1736, lessee of house, (87) 71a.
Longford Castle, chimneypiece from, (97) 75b.
Loom-house, probably 1738, (430) 151a.
Lovell, Roger, lix.

Lowe, John, 1609, lessee of inn, (86) 70b.

Lower Bailey, see **Old Sarum.**

Lucy, arms of, see **Heraldry.**

Ludlow:
  Arms of, see **Heraldry.**
  William, c. 1455, provided roof, (3) 24b; owned land in Black Horse chequer, (151) 92a; in Blue Boar chequer, (344), 133b.
  William, of Clarendon, and Anne, 1749, tablet, (4) 34b.

Lush, Edmund, carpenter, (22) 52b.

Lyming, Zachary, 1591, tenant of Balle's Place, (351) 135b.

Lyons, John, see **Painters and Engravers.**

Lysle, John, 1455, (102) 77b.

Lythenard, Stephen, 1419, owner of land, (151) 92a.

Mace-rests, (3) 31a; (5) 38b.

Maidenhead Inn, former site of, (25) 54b; Roof from, (475) 157a.

Malmesbury, William of, xxxi.

Malthouses: (159) 93b; (420) 148b; (504) 160a.

Mannying, John, 1405, xli, n.9.

Manor Cottage (591) 172b.
  „ **Farm:** Milford, (572) 168b; Harnham, (583) 170b.
  „ **House:** Bemerton, (521) 161b; Milford, (56g) 168b.

Maps and Surveys:
  17TH-CENTURY: Speed, xlvii, li, Pl. 1.
  18TH-CENTURY: Naish, xlviii, Pl. 16.
  19TH-CENTURY: 1833, Reform Act, (23) 54a; 1854, Kingdon and Shearm's survey, xxvi; 1860, Bothams's plan, (23) 54a; 1880, O.S., 6-ins., in end-pocket.

Marchant, John, 1660, inscription on flagon, (7) 42a.

Marchy, Wm., 1479, owner of house, (250) 115b.

Margaret, St., see **Dedications.**

Markes, Thomas Chafin, 1727, (3) 30a.

Market House (25) l, 54b; (419) 148a.
  „ **Place,** xxxii, xxxvi, xl, 59a.

Marsh Chequer, xxxvi, 119, 120.

Martin, St., see **Dedications.**
  „ „ parish of, xxix, xxxiv, xxxviii; see also **Parishes and Wards.**
  „ „ **Church Street,** xxxvii; (279)–(285) 121b–122a.
  „ „ **Ward,** xxxviii; see also **Parishes and Wards.**

Martin, Nicholas, 1512, xli.

Martyn, William, c. 1475, occupier of tenement, (234) 113b.

Mary, St., see **Dedications.**

Mary Magdalen, St., see **Dedications.**

Maryabbey (St. Mary's Abbey), (131), xliii, 84b.

Mason, Richard, 1632, Henry 1680, owners of property, 63b.

Mathematical Tiles, see **Building Construction.**

Maton, Mrs., c. 1850, occupant of house on Bolehall site, (140) 90a.

Matravers, arms of, see **Heraldry.**

Mawarden Court (557) lxii, 116b.

Mayne, arms of, see **Heraldry.**

Mayor and Commonalty, tenements associated with: xxv, xxvi, xli, xlviii; (37) 61a; (38) 61b; (77) 67b; (97) 73b; (173) 97b; (233) 113a; (234) 113b; (249) 115a; (259) 118b; (305) 128a; (351) 135b; (359) 139a; (423) 148b.

Mead Ward, xxxviii.

Mears, Thomas, see **Bellfounders.**

Meeting Places, Non-Conformist: liii.
  METHODIST: (early 19th-century), (12) 46a; (234) 113b; (356), 138b; (481) 158a.
  PRESBYTERIAN: (356) 138a.
  See also **Salvation Army Citadel.**

Melemonger Street, xxxvii.

Mercer, William, 1407, bequest to St. Edmund's Church, (5) 36b.

Mercers, see **Occupations.**

Merchant Marks:
  Of John Hall, in hall of, (185) 104a.
  „ Wm. Lightfoot, St. Thomas's, (3) 26a.
  „ Wm. Swayne, St. Thomas's, (3) 27a.
  „ Wm. Windover, (302) 126b.
  „ John Wyot?, St. Thomas's, (3) 26a; Church House, (97) 75a.
  Unidentified, Minster Street, (55) 64a; King's Arms Hotel, (252) 117a.

Merchants, see **Occupations.**

Meriot, Sir George, 1410, (173) 97b; (177) 100b.

Methodist Chapel, see **Meeting Places, Non-Conformist.**

Michell:
  Arms of, see Heraldry.
  General George, 1831, benefactors' table, (7) 41b; house, (477) 157a.

Miles, Mr., house of, (140) 90a.

Milford, pp. xxix, xxiv; track to Old Sarum, (1) 12b.
  „ **Arms Inn** (153) 92b.
  „ **Bridge** (19) lxii, 52a.
  „ **Hill,** xxxiii; (564)–(567) 168a.
  „ **House** (566) 168a.

Manor House (569) 168a.
  „ **Railway Terminal,** l.
  „ **Street,** xxxvii, xliii, 89, 91–94, 108b, 112–115.
  „ **Ditch,** xxxvi, (233) 112a.
  „ **Ward,** see **Parishes and Wards.**

Milk Cross (Cheese Cross), xli.

Mill House, (500) 159b.

Mills: Fisherton, (500) 159b; Harnham, (588) 171b; Paper, (304) 127b; Town, (66) xxxiii, 65a.

Minifie:
  Arms of, see **Heraldry.**
  Anne, 1683, Richard, 1706, Anne Knight, 1709, floorslab, (3) 30b.

Minster Street, xxxvii, xli.

Mints, Old Sarum, (1) 1b.

Minty and Godwin, 1768, glaziers, (22) 52b.

Misericord, 15th-century, (3) lx, 31a.

Mitcherd, see **Sculptors and Monumental Masons.** Louisa, 1827, headstone, (7) 42a.

Mitre Chequer, (118)–(125) 80b, 81a.
  „ **House,** (92) 72a.

Mompesson:
  Arms of, see **Heraldry.**
  Sir Giles, 1649, lessee of King's Arms, (252) 116b.

Montacute, arms of, see **Heraldry.**

Montagu, William, 1371, owner of property, (173) 97b.

Montague, James, Bp. of Winchester, (185) 104b.

Montgomerie, D. H., excavations at Old Sarum, (1) 4a, (2) 21a.

Monthermer, arms of, see **Heraldry.**

Monumental Masons, see **Sculptors and Monumental Masons.**

Monuments, Funeral: lvi, Pls. 49–52. See also **Coffin Lids.**
  ALTAR TOMBS, see TABLE-TOMBS.
  FLOORSLABS (notable):
    15TH-CENTURY: (5) 38a.
    16TH-CENTURY: (3) Webb, 30b; (4) Jacob, 35a.
    17TH-CENTURY: (3) Hawker, Conant, Vyner, Hele, Eyre, 30b; (4) Windover, Greenhill, 35a; (6), Arny, Young, Bowerman, Bewde, Duke, Earle, 41a.
    18TH-CENTURY: (3) Banks, Barnaby, Powell, Long, le Breton, Eyre, 30b; (4) Egerton, Greville, Reaves, Slater, Terry, Hancock, Wastfield, Rolfe, Goldwyer, Payne, 35a; (5) Long family, 38b; (6) Tompson, 41a.
  TABLE-TOMBS:
    15TH-CENTURY: (3) 30a; (4) 34a, 35a.
    17TH-CENTURY: (5) 38b; (6) Townsend, 41a.
  WALL MONUMENTS AND TABLETS (notable):
    17TH-CENTURY: (3) Eyre, Beckham, Ray, 30a, b; (4) Hales, 34b; (6) Bowernman, 41a; (7) Kent, 42a.
    18TH-CENTURY: (3) Wroughton, Gough, Eyre, Powell, 30a; (4) Swayne, Ludlow, Bartlett, Edgar, Thomas, Willis, Baker, Snow, Lee, 34b, 35a; (5) Hill, 38b; (6) Nisbet, Webb, 41a; (7) D'Oyly, 42a; (8) Norris, Hawes, 43a; (9) Kirkman, 44a.

Moorland House (286) 122a.

More, William, 1386, owner of tenement, (130) 84a.

Moreton Cottage (539) 164b.

Mosely, Dr. John, 1630, owner of Castle St. property, (423) 148b.

Motte and Bailey, see **Old Sarum.**

Moulton:
  Arms of, see **Heraldry.**
  Martha, 1801, and William, 1803, tablet, (7) 42a.

Moundelard, Peter, 1342, occupier of High St. tenement, (173) 97b.

Munday, John, 1834, lessee of house, (130), 84b.

Musgrave, arms of, see **Heraldry.**

Musical Instrument Maker, see **Occupations.**

Musical Instruments, see **Organs.**

Mustin, George, 1649, innholder, (225) 111a.

Mutton's Bridge (21) 52a.

Myrfield House (326) 130b.

Naish, see **Architects, Builders and Surveyors.**
  „ Edith, donor of almsdish, (5) 39a.
  „ Gyles, 1671, and Thomas, lessees, Winchester Street, (359) 139a.

Naish, William, 1716, *see* **Maps and Surveys.**
,, Wm., mayor, inscription on bell, (3) 29a.
Nelle, Symon, churchwarden, inscription on clock-bell, (3) 29a.
Neville, arms of, *see* **Heraldry.**
New Canal, xxxiv; (125) 81a; (175)–(188) 100–102.
,, **Hall**, *see* **Old Sarum.**
,, **Inn** (107) 78b.
,, **Street**, xxxvi; (104)–(117) 78b–80.
,, ,, **Chequer:** (171)–(202) 95b–107a.
,, ,, **Ward**, l.
Newbridge Hospital, bell, liv.
Newman, Robert, 1456, William *c.* 1562, owners of 'le Crane', (102) 77b.
Newton Westgate, 'suburb' of Old Sarum, (1) 13a.
Nichol, John and Jhne, his wife, inscription on pillar, (3) 26a.
Nicholas, St., *see* **Dedications.**
,, ,, , Hospital of, (26), xxxviii, xl, lxi, 54b.
,, ,, , ,, , house belonging to, (111) 80a.
,, ,, , **Road**, (325)–(331) 130b, 131.
Nisbet:
Arms of, *see* **Heraldry.**
Josiah, 1781, wall-monument, (6) 41a.
Norris:
Arms of, *see* **Heraldry.**
John, 1711, tablet, (8) 43a.
Novus Vicus, ward, xxxviii.
Nowes:
Arms of, *see* **Heraldry.**
John, 1819, benefactors' table from St. Clement's, (7) 41b.
Nugge, Hugh, 1268, owner of tenement in Blue Boar Row, (341) xxxvii, xlvi, 133a.
Nuggescorner, tenement, (341), *see* **Nugge.**

Oatmeal Row, xli, lxii; (40)–(44) 61b, 62a.
Occupations, Trades and Businesses of persons mentioned in the Inventory: xl–xlii.
ALDERMEN: Pervys (151) 92a; Hussey (199) 105b.
APOTHECARIES: Younge (36) 60a; Joyce (174) 99b.
BAILIFF: Whittokesmeade (351), 135b.
BAKERS: Chubbe (219) 109a; Martyn (234) 113b; Isaac (250) 115b; Smith (260) 119a; Wood (270) 120a.
BARBERS: Wynchestre (57) xlvi; Harnhalle (132) 85b.
BOWYERS: Boyton (37) 61a; (133) 88a.
BUTCHER: Halstede (249) 115a.
CARPENTERS: Fayrhowe (344) 133b; Lush (22) 52b.
CHANDLER: Burnham (215) 108b.
CHAPLAIN: Ashleigh (259) 118b.
CHURCHWARDENS: Bailey, Ogden, Sturidg, Hales, Nelle, Yonge (3) 29a; Smith, Pope, Adams, Young, Horte, Chiffinch, Antrum, Ginaway (4) 34a, b, 35b; Percevall, Wilkins, Fort, Staples, Hilary, Percevall (5) 38a, b; Blake, Randall, Borough (6) 40b, 41a; Heely, Marchant (7) 42a; Baxter, Samells (9) 44b.
CLERKS: Caundel (225) 111a; Enefeld (302) 126a; (302) 126a.
CLERKS OF WORKS: Harding (174) 99b; Naish (359) 139a.
CLOTHIERS: (37) 61a; Hussey (199) 105b; Hinxman (430) 151a.
COOK: Homyngton (173) 97b.
CORONER: Aubyn (140) 89a.
CUTLERS: (127) 82a; Goddard (130) 84b; Snook (216) 108b.
DRAPERS: Taillour, Baly, (35) 59b; Harding (129) 82b; Taillour (132) 85b; Bover (133) 89a; Buterlegh (140) 89b; Edmonds (259) 118b.
DYERS: (25) 54b.
FISHMONGER: Pervys (151) 92a.
GOLDSMITH: (37) 61a.
GROCERS: Steward (63) 64b; Cammell (128) 82a; (140) 90a; Spencer (151) 92a; Camel (219) 109a; Bakere (233) 113a.
HOSIERS: Fawconer (55) 63b; Comb (63) 64b.
INNKEEPERS: Mustin (225) 111a; Story (344) 133b; Sanborn (359), 139a.
IRONMONGERS: xli.
JOINER: White (215) 108b.
MERCERS: Newman (102) 77b; Castleton (132) 85b.
MERCHANTS: Swayne (3) 27a; Frowd (33) 58b; Teynturer (173) 97b; Payne (185) 104a; Dondyng (208) 108a; Windover (302) 125b; Sanborne (359) 139a. See also **Woolmerchants.**
OSTLER: Allesley (173) 97b.
PARCHMENT MAKER: Snowe (297) 124b.

PRINTERS: Collins, (187) 105a; (300) 125a.
PUBLIC NOTARY: Whitmarsh (63) 64b.
SCHOOLMASTER: Crew (399) 145a.
SHOEMAKER: Mason (55) 63b.
SOLICITOR: Tinney (307) 128b.
SPICER: Shaftesbury (82) 68b.
STONEMASON: Kellow (22) 52b.
TAILORS: Pope (81) 68b; More, Goodyer, Munday (130) 84a, b; Godfrey (172) 97a; Trewman (236) 113b; Marchy (250) 115b.
TANNERS: (37) 61a; Clerk (203) 107b; Crise (297) 124b.
VINTNERS: Vyner (37) 61a; Underhill, Westbury (86) 70b, 71a. Wyse (233) 113a; (234) 130b.
WATCHMAKER: Langley (82) 68b.
WOOLMERCHANTS: Russel, Fleming, Hyndon, Harding (129) 82b; Woodford (132) 85b; Byterlegh (177) 100b; Hall (185) 103b; Balle (351) 135b.
Oddfellows Arms Inn (220) 109b.
Ogden, T., churchwarden, inscription on bell, (3) 29a.
Okebourne, Robert, 1421, owner of tenement, (37) 61a.
Old Bell Inn (310) 129a.
,, **Castle Inn** (562) 167b; excavations at, (1) 12b.
,, **Manor**, hospital, (508) 160b; (512) 161a.
,, **Mill Cottage**, Harnham, (586) 171a.
,, ,, **Hotel**, Harnham, (587) 171a.
,, **Parsonage Farm** (581) lxii, 171a.
Old Sarum : xxviii–xxxii, Pls. 24–30. See also **Iron Age** and **Roman Monument5.**
HILL-FORT AND CASTLE (1) 1–15.
Bakehouse, 10b, 11a; Bridges, 3a, 4b, 6b; Chapels, 3a, b, 8b, 9a, b, 10a; Church of St. Cross, 12a; Courtyard House, 2b, 3b, 8a–10a; Curtain walls, 3a, 5b, 7a, 11b; Excavations 5a, b, 10b, 11a, 12b; Gates, 6b, 11b; Great Tower, 2b, 3a, 6a, 7a, b; Great Chamber, 10a; Hall, 10a; Herlewin's Tower, 3b, 6a, 7a, 10b, 11a; King's Gaol, 11b; Kitchen Tower, 6a, 7a, 10a, b; Latrines, 6b, 7a, b, 9b, 10a, b; Lower Bailey, 11a; Motte, 2a, 6a, 7a; New Hall, 3a, 10b; Ovens, 11a; Palisades, 5b, 6a, b; Saw-pit, 10b; stone removed, 4a; Suburbs, 12a, 13a; Tower above the Postern, 6a, 7b, 8a; Treasury, 7a; Tunnel, 12a; Wells, 11a.
CATHEDRAL (2) 2–23:
Altars, 22b; Ambulatory, 19b; Apse, 16b; Bishop's Palace, 21b; Blocking Wall, 20b; Capitulum, 19a; Cemeteries, 16b, 21a; Chapels, 18b–20a; Cloister, 21b; Crossing, 67a, 20a; Crypt, 19a; Damage to, 15a; Deanery, 22b; Easter Sepulchre, 19b; Gravestones, 19b; Narthex, 21b; Nave, 20a; Pavements, 16b–20; Porch, 20b; Presbytery, 17b, 19b; Pulpitum, 20b; Tombs, 19b; Towers, 21a; Transepts, 17a, 20a; Treasury, 17b; Vestry, 15b, 17b; Well-house, 21b.
Old Sarum, carved stones possibly from, (4) 35b; (383) 143a; (562) 167b.
Orchard Cottage (543) and **Orchard House** (544) 164b.
Organs: lviii; of 1739 by Thomas Swarbrick, of 1792 by Samuel Green, (3) 30b.
Osmond, William, *see* **Sculptors and Monumental Masons**, *also* **Architects, Builders and Surveyors.** Atelier of, (251) 116a.
Osmund, St, *see* **Dedications.**
,, ,, charter of 1091, (1) 4a (2); 15a; tomb of, lvi, 19b.
Ostler, *see* **Occupations.**
Otemele corner, xli.
Outbuildings, *see* **Barns.**
Ovens, bread, (1) 11a; (355) 138b; (497) 159b; (528) 163b; (549) 165a.
Oword, Richard, 1417, owner of tenement, (35) 59b.
Ox Row, 62a, b.

Page, arms of, *see* **Heraldry.**
Pain's Brewery (420), (422) 148b.
Painters and Engravers: xlix.
BUCKLER, JOHN: (3) 25b; (4) 34a; (5) 37a; (6) 39a; (7) (8) 42b; (9) 43b; (11) 45a; (13) 46a; (14) 49a, b; (15) 50a; (26) 56a; (97) 73b; (173) 98a; (208) 108a; (258) 118a; (293) 123b; (557) 116b; (587) 171b, n; (588) 172a; Plates 2, 4, 11.
CAPON, WILLIAM: (258) 118a.
CHARLTON, W. H.: (63) 64b, Pl. 10; (173) 98a, Pl. 6.
DAHL: (13) 47a.
DAYES, EDWARD: (13) 46a; (132) 85a, n.
DRYDEN, SIR H.: (173) 98a, Pl. 6.
GOODALL, E. A., AND SURGEY, J. B.: (173) 98a, Pl. 4.
GUEST, Douglas: (3) 31a.

Painters and Engravers—*contd*
LYONS, JOHN: (3) 25b.
JUKES, FREDERICK: (13) 46a.
SMITH, WILLIAM: Plate 1.
SURGEY, J. B., *see* GOODALL.
TWOPENY, WILLIAM: (97) 73b, Pl. 9; (173) 98a, Pls. 5, 7; (177) 101a, Pl. 7; (258) 118a, Pl. 9; (293) 123b, Pl. 10.
WINTERHALTER: (13) 47a.
Paintings in Churches: lviii, Pl. 43.
13TH-CENTURY: (9) 44b.
15TH-CENTURY: (3) 30b.
17TH-CENTURY: (6) 41a.
19TH-CENTURY: (3) 31a.
Paintings, secular (notable):
13TH-CENTURY: (95) 73a.
C. 1550: (391) 144b.
17TH-CENTURY: (302) 126b; (399) 145b.
19TH-CENTURY: (300) 125a.
Palisades, *see* **Old Sarum.**
Panelling:
16TH-CENTURY: (77) 67a; (174) 100a.
17TH-CENTURY: (43) 62a; (101) 77a; (117) 80b; (128) 82b; (165) 94b; (174) 100a; (234) 113a; (247), 115a; (252), 117a; (253) 117b; (264) (267) 119b; (273) 121a; (294) 124a; (300) 125a; (304) 127b; (315) 129b; (329) 131b; (338) 133b; (346) 135a; (436) 151b; (478) 157b; (549) 165a; (557) 167a.
18TH-CENTURY: (86) 71a; (87) 71b; (99) 76b; (106) 78b; (107) 79a; (115) 80a; (128) 82a; (139) 89b; (156) 93b; (230) 112a; (267) 119b; (286) 122b; (296) 124a; (314) (315) 129b; (323) 130a; (340) 133a; (347) 135a; (355) 138b; (358) 139a; (359) 139b; (406) 146a; (415) 147b; (424) 149a; (427) 150b; (430) 151a; (467) (468) 155a; (477) 157b; (521) 162a.
Paper Mill (304) 127b.
Papier-mache, decoration, (419) 148a.
Parade Coffee Tavern (338) 132b.
Paragon, The, (510) 160b.
Parchment makers, *see* **Occupations.**
Parishes and Wards: xxxviii–l.
FISHERTON AND ST. PAUL: (476)–(537) 157–164.
MILFORD: (563)–(574) 168.
ST. EDMUND: (333)–(475) 132–157.
ST. MARK: (538)–(562) 164–168.
ST. MARTIN: (34)–(332) 59–131.
ST. THOMAS: (575)–(595) 169–172.
Park, John, 1429, inherited tenement, (362) 140a.
Parry, Anthony, 1595, owner of Boar Inn, (344) 133b.
Parsonage Farm House (549) lxii, 165a.
Parsonages etc.:
BEMERTON RECTORY (528) 163a.
FISHERTON RECTORY (497) 159a.
ST. OSMUND'S (315) 129b.
STRATFORD-SUB-CASTLE (556) 166a.
Parsons Chequer, 146.
Patens, *see* **Plate, Church.**
Paul's Dene, Roman finds at, xxviii.
Paul, Saint, church of, *see* St. Clement's, (7) 41b.
Pavements, *see* **Old Sarum. Cathedral.**
Payne:
Arms of, *see* **Heraldry.**
Elizabeth, 1734, slab, (4) 35a.
Sampson, 1834, owner of Hall of John Hall, (185) 104a.
Payne's Hill, (247) 115a.
Pembroke, earl of, benefactor of General Infirmary, (22) 52b.
     ,,   Lodge (508) 160b.
Peniston, *see* **Architects, Builders and Surveyors.**
Penkere, Henry, 1482, owner of house, (249) 115a.
Pennyfarthing Street, xliii.
Penruddock, Sir Henry, tenant of house, (37) xlviii, 61a.
Perceval, John, churchwarden, inscription on bell, (5) 38a; on tower, 38b.
Pervys, John, 1418, owner of tenement, (151) 92a.
Petersfinger, pagan Saxon cemetery, xxviii; (1) 1b.
Pethen, Joanna, 1350, will xl, n.6.
Pewter, *see* **Plate, Church.**
Pheasant Inn (399) 145a.
Phebis, Wm., 1416, purchaser of house, (305) 128a.
Phillips, James, *see* **Clockmakers.**

Phipps, arms of, *see* **Heraldry.**
Piggot, Anna Maria, 1851, tablet, (8) 43a.
Pilkington, William, *see* **Architects, Builders and Surveyors.**
Pinkney's Bank, 1879, adjacent to Queen Street tenement, (133) 89a.
Piscinae: lvii, lix, Pl. 40.
13TH-CENTURY: (4) 35b; (6) 41a; (9) 44b; (11) 46a; (26) 56b.
14TH-CENTURY: (6) 41a; (9) 44b.
15TH-CENTURY: (4) 35a; (5) 38b.
Pitt:
Arms of, *see* **Heraldry.**
Thomas, benefactor of St. Lawrence's, (6) liii, 40a.
Plank-and-Muntin partitions:
17TH-CENTURY: (260) 118b.
18TH-CENTURY: (295) 124a; (522) 162a.
Plasterers:
BERNASCONI, FRANCIS: The College, (14) 49b.
SCHAFFLIN, ROBERT: Infirmary, (22) 52b.
Plasterwork: Pls. 93, 95. See also **Ceilings.**
15TH OR 16TH-CENTURY: (40) 61b.
16TH-CENTURY: (82) 69a.
17TH-CENTURY: (42) 62a; (173) 99a; (174) 100a; (184) 103b; (302) 126a; (304) 127b; (567) 168a.
18TH-CENTURY: (77) 67a; (110) 80a; (180) 102b; (273) 121a; (287) (289) 123a; (297) 124a; (391) 144b; (500) 159b; (570) 168b; (585) 171a.
19TH-CENTURY: (175) 100a; (299) 124b; (549) 165a.
Plate, Church: lix, Pls. 54–5.
PEWTER:
  FLAGONS:
    17TH-CENTURY: (7) 42a.
    18TH-CENTURY: (27) 57b.
  PATENS:
    17TH-CENTURY: (7) 42a.
SILVER:
  ALMSDISHES:
    17TH-CENTURY: (4) 35b.
    18TH-CENTURY: (5) 39a; (6) 41a.
  CUPS WITH COVER-PATENS:
    16TH-CENTURY: (4) 35b; (8) 43a.
  CUPS WITHOUT COVERS:
    16TH-CENTURY: (8) 43a.
    18TH-CENTURY: (27) 57b.
  FLAGONS:
    17TH-CENTURY: (4) 35b.
    18TH-CENTURY: (6) 41a.
  PATENS:
    16TH-CENTURY: (5) 39a.
    17TH-CENTURY: (4) 35b.
    18TH-CENTURY: (6) 41a; (8) 43a.
  STAND-PATEN:
    18TH-CENTURY: (4) 35b; (27) 57b.
Plate, Civic, (13) 47b.
Plume of Feathers (132) xliv, lxi, 85a.
Polatrie, la, xli.
Police Station and Lock-up, (23) 54a.
Poore:
Bishop Herbert, xxxii.
Bishop Richard, xxxii; (2) 16a; (3) 24a; mill of, (66) 65a.
Pope, Silvester, 1649, lessee of tenement, (81) 68b.
     ,,   Walter, 1671, churchwarden's inscription on bell, (4) 34a.
Porches:
12TH-CENTURY: (2) 20b.
13TH-CENTURY: (26) 55a, 56.
15TH-CENTURY: (3) S. porch *c.* 1400, N. porch (demolished), 24b, 25a; (6) 39a; (14) from Cathedral, 49b.
17TH-CENTURY: (264) 119b; (304) gone, 127b; (557) 166b.
18TH-CENTURY: (14) 49a; (199) 105b; (427) 150a.
19TH-CENTURY: (13) 46b; (254) 117b.
Porte, John and Juliana, 1423, owners of Deverell's Inn, (25) 54b.
Portway, Old Sarum, (1) 12a.
     ,,   Cottage (538) 164b.
Post Office, 19th-century, (35) 60a.
Postern Tower, *see* **Old Sarum.**
Pot Row, xl.
Pottery: Iron Age (1) 5b; 11th–12th century (1) 12b.
Poultry Cross (15), xli, lxi, 50a.
     ,,   Street, xli.

Pound Chequer, (262)–(271) 119, 120.
Powell:
  Arms of, *see* **Heraldry.**
  Sir Alexander, 1748, and Catherine, 1772, monument, (3) lviii, 30a.
  Alexander, 1751, altered, (427) 149a.
  Catherine, 1772, floorslab, (3) 30b.
  Francis, 1746, and Anna, 1825, tablet, (5) 38b.
  John, 1737, and Catherine, 1757, floorslab, (3) 30b.
Powelscorner, xli.
Prebendal House (556) 166a.
Precey:
  Mary, 1810, and James, 1822, headstones, (9) 44a.
  Sarah, 1787, and William ..., headstone, (9) 44a.
Presbyterian Meeting House, *see* **Meeting Places, Non-Conformist.**
Presbytery, *see* **Old Sarum.**
Priaulx, arms of, *see* **Heraldry.**
Prince, arms of, *see* **Heraldry.**
Printers, *see* **Occupations.**
'Priory', the, (264), (265) 119b.
Prospect Place (292) 123b.
    ,,   ,, , **Devizes Road, (532) 164a.**
Public Buildings: xlvii, xlix, lxiii.
  COUNCIL HOUSE: (14) 48a.
  COUNTY GAOL: (24) 54a.
  GAOL, FORMER: (476) 157a.
  GENERAL INFIRMARY: (22) 52b.
  GUILDHALL: (13) xl, xlix, 46a.
  MARKET HOUSE: (25) 54b.
  PENITENTIARY, FEMALE: (285) 122a.
  POLICE STATION AND LOCK-UP: (23) 54a.
Public Notary, *see* **Occupations.**
Pugin, A. W. N., *see* **Architects, Builders and Surveyors.**
Pulpits: lix, Pl. 46.
  15TH-CENTURY: (4) 35b.
  17TH-CENTURY: (6) 41a.
  19TH-CENTURY: (12) 46b.
Pulpitum, *see* **Old Sarum** (2).
Purdue, William, *see* **Bellfounders.**
Pynkebrygge, William, 1452, owner of tenement, (236) 113b.
Pynnok, William, 1270, Richard, John and Isabella, 1386, owners of property, (77) 67a, b.
Pynnok's Inn (77) xlii, xlvi, 67a, b.

Queen's Arms Inn (225) lxi, 111a.
Queen Street, (126)–(133) 81b–89a.
Queensberry, Duchess of, benefactor of Infirmary, (22) xlix, 52b.
Quintin, Nicholas de St., *see* **St. Quintin.**

Radnor, earl of, benefactor of Guildhall, (13) xlix; of Infirmary, (22) xlix, 52b.
Raie d'or Inn (227) 111b.
Railways: their arrival, l; branch line to Market House, (25) 54b.
Rainwater heads (dated):
  1682, 1748, 1751, (3) 31a; 1773 (77) 67a; 1569 (106) 78b; 1689 (132) 85b; 1784 (297) 124a; 1788 (343) 133b; 1787 (409) 146b.
Rampart, *see* **Defences.**
  ,,   Road (16) 50b; (567) 168b.
Ramsbury and Sherborne, Bishop of, xxix; (2) 15a.
Randall, W., 1767, churchwarden, inscription on bell, (6) 40b.
Ray:
  Arms of, *see* **Heraldry.**
  Family, 17th-century owners of White Bear, (219) 109a.
  Thomas, 1670, and Margaret, 1682, wall-monument, (3) 30a.
  William, 1625, lessee of house in Catherine Street, (216) 108b.
Reading, bell from, *see* **Bellfounders.**
Reaves, Ann (Goddard), 1754, floorslab, (4) 35a.
Rectory, *see* **Parsonages.**
Red Lion Hotel (219) lxi, 109a.
Reeves of Bath, *see* **Sculptors and Monumental Masons.**
Reform Act, Old Sarum, (1) 4a.
Reredos, 18th-century, (6) 41a.
Retreat, (285), 122a.
Richeman, John, 1362, benefactor of College, (14), xliii.
Roger, Bishop, xxxi, l, li; (1) 3a, 6a, 8a; (2) 15b, 17b, 19b, 20a, b.
Rogers, *see* **Eyre.**

Rolfe:
  Arms of, *see* **Heraldry.**
  John, 1735, floorslab, (4) 35a.
Rolfe's Chequer, (237)–(246) 114, 115a.
Rolleston Place, (404) 146a.
  ,,   Street, xliii.
Rolvestone, xxxvii.
Roman Monuments: xxviii; (1) building, 11a; roads and settlement, 1a, b.
Rood-lofts: lix; (3) 26a; (4) 32a.
Roofs, mediaeval (in churches): liv.
  KING-STRUT TIE-BEAM: (3) 26a, 27b.
  PANELLED: (3) 26b, 27a.
  VAULT: (3) 28b.
  WAGON: (4) 33a, b; (6) 40b; (9) 43b.
Roofs, mediaeval and later (in secular buildings); xliv, Pls. 82–3.
  RAFTER:
    COLLARED: (131), 15th-century, 84a; (195), 14th-century, 105b.
    CROWN-POST: (71) 66a; (102) 77b; (129) 83b; (140) 90b, 91a; (173) 99a; (203) 107b, 225) 111a; (351) 136b, 137a; (458) 153b; (576) 169b. (All 14th-century).
    SCISSOR-BRACED: (219) 14th-century, 109b; (328) 13th-century, 131a.
  TRUSSES:
    ARCH-BRACED COLLAR:
      14TH-CENTURY: (132) 86b; (140) 91a.
      15TH-CENTURY: (81) 68b; (97) 75a, b; (441) 152b.
      16TH-CENTURY: (185) 104a.
    COLLARED TIE-BEAM:
      14TH-CENTURY: (132) 87a.
      15TH-CENTURY: (52) 63a; (55) (56) 64a; (63), 65a; (183) 103a; (341) 133a; (344), 134a; (399) 145b; (430) 151a.
      16TH-CENTURY: (315) 129b; (383) 143a; (422) 148b; (438) 152b; (549) 165b; (557) 167a; (581) 170b; (588) 172a.
    CRUCKS:
      15TH-CENTURY: (107) 79a; (132) 87a; (250) 116a; (306) 128b; (376) 141b; (584) 170b.
      16TH-CENTURY: (492) 158b; (497) 159b; (526) 162b.
    FALSE HAMMERBEAM:
      14TH-CENTURY: (173) 99a.
      15TH-CENTURY: (185) 104a; (236) 113b; (344) 134a; (475) 157a.
      16TH-CENTURY: (177) 102a.
    HAMMERBEAM:
      14TH-CENTURY: (132) 87b; (351) 136b.
      C. 1440: (302) 126a, b.
      15TH-CENTURY: (151) 91b.
    KING STRUT:
      14TH-CENTURY: (305) 128b.
      16TH-CENTURY: (383) 143b.
    SCISSOR-TRUSS:
      14TH-CENTURY: (82) 69a; (132) 87a.
      C. 1400: (302) 125b, 126a.
      15TH-CENTURY: (97) 75b.
    SPERE:
      14TH-CENTURY: (177) 101b; (351) 137a.
      16TH-CENTURY: (94) 73a.
Rose and Crown Hotel (576), lxi, 169a.
Rotunda (299) 124b.
Royal Arms, *see* **Heraldry.**
  ,,   George Inn (470) 155b.
Rudhall, Abraham, *see* **Bellfounders.**
Russel:
  Henry, c. 1354, property-holder in Cross Keys chequer, (129) 82b; before 1365, in New Canal, (177) xl, 100b.
  William, 1306, builder of house, (129) 82b.
Restehale, Alice, 14th-century owner of tenement, (225) 111a.
Rydedore (Raie d'or), Clement atte, tenement of, (227) 111b.

St. Ann's Gate/Street, xxxiv, xxxvii; (260), 118b: (261), (262) 119a; (274), (275), (278) 121b; (286)–(310) 122–129a.
St. Barbe, William, purchaser of College, (14) 48a.
St. John's Street, (251)–(254) 116, 117.
St. Quintin, Nicholas de, 1265, owner of property in High Street, xliii, 70b.
  Robert, 1297, owner of tenement, (92) 72a.
Saints, *see under* proper names.
Salisbury City, arms of, *see* **Heraldry.**

Salisbury, John, 1391, owner of tenement, (233) 113a.
Salisbury, Patrick, earl of, 1153, (1) 3a.
Salisbury, See, arms of, *see* **Heraldry.**
Salt Lane, (348) 135a; (357) 139a; (369)–(371) 141a; (399)–(403) 145; (417)(418) 147b.
Salters' Company, arms of, *see* **Heraldry.**
Salvation Army Citadel (356) 138b.
Samells, James, 1692, churchwarden, inscription on bell, (9) 44b.
Sanborn, Richard, wine merchant, license granted to, (359) 139a.
Sanger, Joseph, 1846, tablet, (12) 46b.
Sarjeant, Harriet, 1836, tablet, (6) 41a.
Saw-pit, Old Sarum, (1) 10b.
Saxon occupation: xxviii, xxix; (1) 1, 6a.
Schafflin, Robert, *see* **Plasterers.**
School, free, 1624, Castle Street, (423) 149a.
Schoolmaster, *see* **Occupations.**
Scot, John, 1269, house of, xxxvii.
Scot's Lane, xxxvii; (383) 142b; (459) 154a.
Scott, Gilbert, *see* **Architects, Builders and Surveyors.**
Screens: lix, lx, Pls. 44–5.
    15TH-CENTURY: (3) 31a; (6) 41a, b.
    17TH-CENTURY: (9) 44b.
    18TH-CENTURY: (3) 30a; (6) 41a.
Screens-passages: 14th-century, (177) 101b; 16th-century (290) 123a.
Scratch-dial, mediaeval, (4) 35b.
Sculptors and Monumental Masons: lxii.
    BROWN: (5) Wych, 38b.
    CAVE: (3) Earlsman, 30b; (4) Earlsman, 34b.
    CROOME: (5) Burrough, 38b.
    EARLSMAN: (3) Powell, 30a.
    GAFFI: (8) Piggot, 43a.
    HUNTER: (6) Nisbet, 41a.
    KING: (4) Baker, 35a.
    MITCHERD: (3) Powell, 30b; (7), d'Oyly, Louisa Mitcherd, 42a.
    OSMOND: (3) Harrington, Popple, Long, 30b; (4) Tinney, 34b, Hinxman, 35a; (5) Cooper, White, 38b; (6) Sarjeant, 41a; (7) Calder, Atkinson, Woodward, 42a; (8) Hawes, Coxe, 43a.
    REEVES: (4) Lee, 35a.
Sculpture, *see* **Carved Stonework.**
Searobyrg, xxviii, 1b.
Seating (in churches).
    BOX PEWS: (6), 41b.
    CHAIRS:
        17TH-CENTURY: (3) 29b; (6) 40b; (9) 44b.
        18TH-CENTURY: (4) 34b.
        19TH-CENTURY: (5) 38a.
    STALLS: (3), 31a.
Serryge, Henry, 1508, (97) 75b.
Seven Deadly Sins, tenements, (252) 116b.
Seynt Maryabbey, 1465, tenement, (131) 84b.
Shaftesbury, John de, 1314, lessor of tenement, (82) 68b.
Sherborne, removal of see to Old Sarum, (1) xxxi, 15a.
Shields-of-arms, *see* **Heraldry.**
Shirley, Walter, 1416, owner of Balle's Place, (351) 135a, and houses in Winchester Street, (361–2) 140a.
Shoemakers, *see* **Occupations.**
    ,, **Guild Hall** (399) xlvii, 145a.
Short, Walter, 1431, occupant of tenement, (233) 113a.
Shorto's Cutlery (127) 82a.
Shoulder of Mutton Inn (64) 65a.
Shoves Corner, xlv, 120b.
Shuttleworth, Francis, *see* **Clockmakers.**
Silver, *see* **Plate, Church.**
Silversmiths: lxxxv.
    DR: (4) 35b.
    G.S.: (5) 39a.
    I.F.: (8) 43a.
    INGLES, JOHN: (7) 42a.
    SLEATH, GABRIEL: (4) 35b.
    T.W.: (5) 39a.
Simon of Ghent, Bishop, xxxviii.
Slater:
    Arms of, *see* **Heraldry.**
    Sarah, 1797, floorslab, (4) 35a.
Sleat, W., *see* **Architects, Builders and Surveyors.**
Sleath, Gabriel, *see* **Silversmiths.**
Sluices: xxxiv, xli; (427) 149a. *See also* **Ditches** and **Water Channels.**

Smith, Robert, 1649, occupant of tenement, (260) 119a.
    ,, , William, *see* **Painters and Engravers.**
    ,, ,, , 1675, inscription on bell, (4) 34a.
Smithies, arms of, *see* **Heraldry.**
Smoke louvres and blackened rafters: xliv; (302) 126b; (376) 141b; (414) 147a; (526) 162b; (584) 170b.
Snook, Charles, 1649, tenant of Holy Lamb, (92) 72a.
    ,, William, 1754, occupant of tenement, (216) 108b.
Snow, Thomas, 1776, tablet, (4) 35a.
Snowe, John, parchment maker 1649, occupant of tenement, (297) 124b.
Solicitors, *see* **Occupations.**
Sorviodunum, xxviii; (1) 1.
South-East Chequer, (276)–(278) 121b.
Speed, John, *see* **Architects, Builders and Surveyors.**
Spencer:
    Arms of, *see* **Heraldry.**
    Richard, 1399, owner of property in Milford St., (151) 92a; in St. Ann's Street, (302) 126a.
    Edith, 1414, widow of Richard, (151) 92a.
Spicers, *see* **Occupations.**
Spooner, arms of, *see* **Heraldry.**
Spread Eagle Inn (176) 100a.
Stables, *see* **Barns and Outbuildings.**
Staircases (notable): Plates 86–9.
    15TH OR 16TH-CENTURY: (40) 61b.
    16TH-CENTURY: (77) 67a.
    17TH-CENTURY: (36) 60b; (87) 71b; (90) 72a; (101) 77a; (132) 88a; (173) 99a; (182) 103a; (302) 126a; (304) 127b; (307) 129a; (333) 132a; (350) 135a; (359) 139b; (485) (486) 158a; (521) 162a; (557) 167a.
    18TH-CENTURY: (14) 49a; (37) (38) 61b; (46) 62b; (58) 64b; (74) 66b; (77) 67a; (99) 76b; (110) 80a; (124) 81a; (127) 82a; (130) 84b; (133) 88b; (139) 89b; (156) 93b; (180) 102b; (181) 103a; (199) 106a; (228) 112a; (230) 112b; (252) 117a; (273) 121a; (286) 122b; (287)(289) 123a; (294) 124a; (330) 131b; (338) 132b; (340) 133a; (354) 138a; (355) 138b; (368) 141a; (384) 143b; (415) 147b; (419) 148a; (427) 150b; (435) 151b; (463) 154b; (468) 155a; (477) 157a; (556) 166b.
    19TH-CENTURY: (95) 73a; (389) 144a; (391) (393) 144b; (428) 151a; (446) 153a; (461) 154a; (462) 154b; (520) 161b; (532) 164a.
Stalls, *see* **Seating.**
Stand-paten, *see* **Plate.**
Star Inn (227) 111b.
Stephen, King, 1153, writ for demolition of Old Sarum, (1) 3a; plundering of Cathedral, (2) 15b.
    ,, **Saint**, *see* **Dedications.**
Steward, Henry, 1649, occupant of house, (63) 64b.
Steynings, plaque inscribed, (101) 77a.
Stokes, John, 1471, (63), 64b.
Stone, William, mayor 1656, inscription on bell, (5) 38a.
Stonemason, *see* **Occupations.**
Stoning, arms of, *see* **Heraldry.**
Storage Pits, *see* **Iron Age.**
Storehouse Yard (259) 118b.
Story, George, 1595, innkeeper, Boar Inn, (344) 133b.
Stoups: lx; (4) 35b.
Stourton:
    Arms of, *see* **Heraldry.**
    Sir John, 1447, granted Old Sarum, (1), 3b.
Strapp, John, *see* **Architects, Builders and Surveyors.**
Stratford-sub-Castle, xxix, li; (538)–(562) 164b–168a.
Stratfordescorner, (234) 113a.
Street, G. E., *see* **Architects, Builders and Surveyors.**
Street-names, xxxvi–vii, xl–xli.
Stricland, John, 1656, inscription on bell, (5) 38a.
Summer-houses; Castle Street (427), 151b; Milford, (570) 168b.
Sun and Lamb (92) 72a.
Sunn, sign of the, (86) 71a.
Sundials:
    MEDIAEVAL: (9) 44b.
    17TH-CENTURY: (3) 31a.
    18TH-CENTURY: (4) 35b.
Surgey, J. B., *see* **Painters and Engravers.**
Surman, Robert, *see* **Architects, Builders and Surveyors.**
Swarbrick, Thomas, 1739, organ builder, (3) 30b.

Swayne:
  Arms of, *see* **Heraldry.**
  Bennet, 1748, and Thomas, 1747, monument, (4) 34b.
  Merchant mark (3) 27a.
  William, *see* **Architects, Builders and Surveyors.**
  William, Christian his wife, James, inscriptions, (3) 27a.
Swayne's Chequer, (155)–(165) 93, 94.
Swein, King of Denmark, xxix.
Swift, John, 1416, xli.
Symonds, Willia, 1638, lessee of King's Arms, (252) 116b.

Tables: *See also* **Communion Tables.**
  17TH-CENTURY: (3) 31a; (26) 56b.
  18TH-CENTURY: (27) 57b.
Tables of the Decalogue, (6) lx, 41b.
Taillour, Nicholas le, owner of house in Cheesemarket, (35) 59b; in Queen Street, (132) 85b.
Tailors, *see* **Occupations.**
Tailors' Guild: xxv, xxvii, xlvii; (130) 84a; (165) 94a; (172) 97a; (269–70) 120b.
Tailors' Hall (165), xlvii, 94a.
Talbot, arms of, *see* **Heraldry.**
Tanner, Joseph, 1795, initials on chair, (13) 47b; house, (427), 149a.
Tanner Street, xlii; *see also* **St. Ann's Street.**
Tanners, *see* **Occupations.**
  „ **Guild Hall,** xlv, xlvii.
Tatum, Elizabeth, 1798, tablet, (4) 35a.
Tavel, Robert, 1400, lessee of tenement, (297) 124b.
Taverner, John and Alice le, 1333, lessees of Pynnok's Inn, (77) 67b.
Taylor's Alsmhouses (32) 58b.
Taylor, Sir Robert, *see* **Architects, Builders and Surveyors.**
Terry:
  Arms of, *see* **Heraldry.**
  Peter, 1727, and Mary, 1739, floorslab, (4) 35a.
Teynturer:
  William, 1363, owner of Queen St. property, (131) 84b.
  William the younger, mayor 1361, 1375, owned George Inn, (173) 97b; house in New Canal, (177) 100b; house in Milford St., (234), 113a.
  Alice, wife of William, later m. Sir George Meriot, (173) 97b; (177) 100b.
Textile, 15th-century, (3) lx, 31a.
Thomas's Row, Milford, (567) 168b.
Thomas, St.:
  Church, *see* **Dedications of Churches.**
  Parish, *see* **Parishes and Wards.**
  Porch, formerly in cathedral, now at (14), 49b.
  Schools, xlix.
Thomas, Mary, 1781, hatchment, tablet, (4) 34b.
Three Crowns Inn, Harnham, (585) 171a.
  „ **Cups Chequer** (351)–(362) 135–140.
  „ „ **Inn** (359) 139a.
  „ **Lions Inn,** adjacent to (133), 89a.
  „ **Swans Chequer** (345)–(350) 134–135
  „ „ **Hotel** (345) 134a.
Tiler, *see* **Occupations.**
Tiles, mediaeval, (1) glazed ridge, 9a; (2) 16b; (184) 103b; (250) crested ridge, 116a; (351) with serrated cresting, 137b; (362) 140a.
Timber-framing, *see* **Building Construction.**
Tinney, John, 1832, tablet, (4) 34b; owner of house, (307) 128a.
Tinney's Court, (404), 146a.
Todeworth, Richard, c. 1320, tenant of property, (177) 100b.
Toll Gate Inn (279) 121b.
Tollgate Road, (573), (574) 168b.
Tompson, Catherine and John, 1702, floorslab, (6) 41a.
Toone's Court (383) 142b.
Tosiear, Clement, *see* **Bellfounders.**
Town Ditch, *see* **Ditches** and **Water Channels.**
  „ **Mill** (66), xxxiii, 65a.
Townsend:
  Arms of, *see* **Heraldry.**
  James, 1679, table-tomb, (6) lvii, 41a.
Toyl, William, 1404, owner of Boar Inn, (344) 133b.
Trades, *see* **Occupations.**
Trade Guilds, *see* **Guilds.**
Transfiguration, painting, 1809, (3) 31a.

Treasury, Old Sarum (2) 17b.
Trewman, John, 1638, lessee of tenement adjoining (236), 113b.
Trinity, *see* **Dedications of Churches.**
  „ **Chequer,** xxxvi; (227)–(235) 111–113.
  „ **Hospital** (27), xlvi, xlix, lxiii, 56b.
  „ „ , tenements associated with: xxv, xxvii; (57) 64a; (215–6) 108b; (227) 112a; (236) 113b.
Tunnel, Old Sarum, (1) 12a.
Turner, Joseph, 1833, table-tomb, (7) 42a.
Twopeny, William, *see* **Painters and Engravers.**

Undercroft, Old Sarum, (2) 15b.
Underhill, James, 1649, tenant, (86) 70b.
Upton, Walter de, 1341, lessee of High Street tenement, (82) 68b.
Urn, probably 16th-century, (14) 49b.
Use of Sarum, Old Sarum, (2) 15a, 22b.

Vale House (297) 124a.
Vanners Chequer, (410)–(418) 146–147.
Vaults: (2) 17b, 19a, 22a; (3) 28b.
Vicarage, Stratford-sub-Castle (556) 166a.
Vicars Choral, tenements associated with: xxv, xxvii; (77) 67b; (81), (82) 68b; (219) 109a; (269–70) 120a.
Victoria, Queen, portrait of, (13) 47a.
Vine Inn (37), xlviii, xlix, 61a.
Viner:
  Arms of, *see* **Heraldry.**
  William, 1680, brass, (3) 29a.
  Mary, 1682, floorslab, (3) 30b.
Vintners, *see* **Occupations.**
Visitation, painted panel, (3) 31a.
Vyner, William, 1647, lessee of the Vine, (37), xlviii, 61a.

Walker, Richard and Alice, 1435, tenants of house, (129) 82b.
  „ Richard, 1464, vendor of house, (249) 115a.
Walls, precinct:
  CASTLE, *see* **Old Sarum** (curtain).
  FRIARY, (302) 126a; (304) 127b.
  GARDEN, (398) 145a.
  TOWN DEFENCES, xxxviii.
  WINDOVER HOUSE, (302) 126b.
Wallis, John, *see* **Bellfounders.**
Wall-monuments, *see* **Monuments, Funeral.**
Walmsley:
  Arms of, *see* **Heraldry.**
  Maude, 1591, (133) 88b.
Walton, Izaac, biographer of George Herbert, (528), liii, 163b (n).
Waltham, bishop, 1388, owner of property in Silver St., (63) 64a.
Warbilton, John, 1418, associated with tenement, (151) 92a.
Ward Taxation Lists, xxvi, xlii.
Wards, *see* **Parishes and Wards.**
Warehouses:
  16TH-CENTURY: (348) 135a; (440) 152b.
  18TH-CENTURY: (46) 62b; (170) 95b; (345) 134a.
  LATE 18TH OR EARLY 19TH-CENTURY: (224) 111a.
  19TH-CENTURY: (39) 61b; (120) 81a; (154) 92b; (194) 105b; (208) 108a; (218) 105b; (394) 145a; (460) 154a; (587) 171a.
Warwick, arms of, *see* **Heraldry.**
Wastfield:
  Arms of, *see* **Heraldry.**
  William, 1735, floorslab, (4) 35a.
Watchmakers, *see* **Occupations.**
Water-channels (in streets): xxxiii–xxxvi, xliii, xlviii. Conduit in Castle Street, (427) 149a. *See also* **Ditches.**
Water Lane, xli.
Waterman, William, mayor 1702, donor of plate, (27).
Wattle and daub, *see* **Building Construction.**
Weavers' Hall, xlvii.
Webb, Webbe:
  Arms of, *see* **Heraldry.**
  Doran, *see* **Architects, Builders and Surveyors.**
  John, 1570, brass, (3), lv, lvii, 29a.
  Sir John, 1637, vendor of tenement, (37), 61a.
  Sir John, 1767, owner of hall in Trinity St., (236) 113b.
  Joseph, 1779, wall-monument, (6), 41a.
  William, 1523, owner of tenement near Water Lane, xli.

Weekes, Anthony, *c.* 1570, owner of tenement, (102) 77b.
Wells: xlv; Old Sarum, (1) 11a; (2) 21b.
Wells, Robert, *see* **Bellfounders.**
West End Hotel (516) 161a.
Westbury, William, 1423, purchaser of tenement, (302) 126a.
   ,,   Robert, 1682, lessee of tenement, (86) 71a.
Wheatsheaf Inn (71), lxi, 65b.
Whelernrow, xli.
White:
   Ann, 1797, and John, 1815, headstones, (9) 44b.
   Elizabeth, 1833, tablet, (5) 38b.
   Isaac, 1865, occupier of Windover House, (302) 126a.
   Peter, 1455, tenant of House, (215) 108b.
   William, of Mere, 1455, owner of the Leg, (172) 97a.
White Bear Inn, now Red Lion, (219) 109a.
   ,,   **Hart Chequer,** (251)–(261) 116–119.
   ,,   ,,   **Hotel** (254) 117b.
   ,,   **Horse Chequer,** (381)–(389) 142–144.
   ,,   ,,   **Inn,** 1609, (86) 70b.
Whitmarsh, Henry, 1649, notary, occupant of house, (63) 64b.
Whittokesmeade, John, 1455, tenant of Balle's Place, (351), xlii, 135b.
Wichford, William de, 1362, purchaser of tenement, (132) 85b; 1370, rent given by, (231) 112b.
Wickham, William, Bishop of Winchester, 1595, donor of cup, (4), lix 35b.
Wilkins, Mr., churchwarden, inscription on bell, (5) 38a.
Willes, arms of, *see* **Heraldry.**
Willis, Joseph, 1772, tablet, (4) 35a.
Willoughby, arms of, *see* **Heraldry.**
Wilton: Mediaeval road to Winchester, xxxiii; Saxon settlement, xxix, 1b.
Wilton Road: (507)–(517) 160b, 161a.
Winchester, arms of see, *see* **Heraldry.**
   ,,   **Gate Inn** (563) 168a.
   ,,   **Street:** xxxiv, xxxvii, xl; 89a, 91a, 93b, 134a, 137b, 140a, 141, 142a.
Windham, John, donor of bell, (3) 29a.
Windover:
   Arms of, *see* **Heraldry.**
   Edward, 1645, floorslab, (4) 35a.
   William, 17th-century owner of house, (302), xlv, xlvii, 125b.
Windover House (302), xlii, xliv, xlv, lxi, 125b.

Windows (stone, notable):
   15TH-CENTURY: (97) 74b, oriel; (185) 104a; (258) 118a.
   16TH-CENTURY: (102) 78a; (588) 172a.
Windows (wood-framed, early):
   14TH-CENTURY: (129) 83b, 84a; (177) 102a; (341) 133a; (576) 169a.
   15TH-CENTURY: (63) 65a; (97) 75a.
   16TH-CENTURY: (92) 72a; (165) 94a.
Winterbourne Gunner, pagan Saxon cemetery, xxviii.
Winterhalter, *see* **Painters and Engravers.**
Wynman Street, xxxvii.
Wood, John, *see* **Architects, Builders and Surveyors.**
   ,,   Robert, 1794, lessee of bakehouse, (270) 120a.
Woodford Chantry, xliii.
   ,,   , Robert de, 1340, owner of Queen St. tenement, (132) 85b.
Woodward, John: benefactor's table and monument, 1828, (7) 42a.
Woolmerchants, *see* **Occupations.**
Workhouse (97–8) 73b, 76a.
Wroughton:
   Arms of, *see* **Heraldry.**
   William, 1770, and Dorothy, 1799, tablet, (3) 30a.
Wyatt, T. H., *see* **Architects, Builders and Surveyors.**
Wyche, Benjamin, 1701, builder of Audley House (99) 76b.
Wych, John: 1773, lessee of house (359) 139a; 1805, tablet, (5) 38b.
Wychebury, Gilbert and Nicholas de, 1357, 1361, owners of property, (233) 113a.
Wyle, Bishop Walter de la, li; (5) 36a.
Wylford, arms of, *see* **Heraldry.**
Wynchestre, John, 1458, donor of treatment to Trinity Hospital, (57) xlvi, 64a.
Wyndham:
   Arms of, *see* **Heraldry.**
   Family, 1668–1868, marble tablet, (5) 38b.
   Henry Penruddock, 1790, enlarged The College, (14) 49a.
   Wadham, 1839, donor of clock, (5) 38a.
   Wadham, 1660, purchaser of The College, (14) 48a.
Wynman Gate (16) xxxviii, 51a.
Wyse, John, vintner, 15th-century tenant of property, (233) (234) 113.

Yarn Market, xl.
Yonge, Willym, churchwarden, inscription on clock-bell, (3) 29a.
Young, Sara, 1652, floorslab, (6) 41a.
Younger, John, 1549, occupant of Windover House, (302) 126a.

Printed in England for her Majesty's Stationery Office
by Ebenezer Baylis & Son Ltd., Worcester and London.
Dd 587503 K12